The
EVERYDAY
Writer

With Exercises

Fourth Edition

The EVERYDAY Writer

With Exercises

Andrea A. Lunsford
STANFORD UNIVERSITY

A section for multilingual writers with

Paul Kei Matsuda
ARIZONA STATE UNIVERSITY

Christine M. Tardy
DEPAUL UNIVERSITY

BEDFORD / ST. MARTIN'S

Boston ◆ New York

For Bedford / St. Martin's

Senior Developmental Editor: Carolyn Lengel
Senior Production Editor: Harold Chester
Assistant Production Manager: Joe Ford
Senior Marketing Manager: John Swanson
Art Director: Lucy Krikorian
Text Design: Anne Carter
Copy Editor: Wendy Polhemus-Annibell
Photo Research: Martha Friedman, Connie Gardner
Cover Design: Donna Lee Dennison
Cover Art and Illustrations: Eric Larsen
Composition: Pre-Press PMG
Printing and Binding: Quebecor World Taunton

President: Joan E. Feinberg
Editorial Director: Denise B. Wydra
Editor in Chief: Karen S. Henry
Director of Development: Erica T. Appel
Director of Marketing: Karen R. Soeltz
Director of Editing, Design, and Production: Marcia Cohen
Assistant Director of Editing, Design, and Production: Elise S. Kaiser
Managing Editor: Shuli Traub

Library of Congress Control Number: 2009928112

Manufactured in the United States of America.

4 3 2 1 0 9
f e d c b a

For information, write: Bedford/St. Martin's, 75 Arlington Street, Boston, MA 02116   (617-399-4000)

ISBN-10: 0-312-59458-5; ISBN-13: 978-0-312-59458-9

Acknowledgments

Acknowledgments and copyrights appear at the back of the book on pages 624–625, which constitute an extension of the copyright page.

How to Use This Book

The Everyday Writer provides a "short and sweet" writing reference you can use easily on your own — at work, in class, even on the run. Small enough to tuck into a backpack or briefcase, this text has been designed to help you find information quickly, efficiently, and easily. I hope that this book will prove to be an everyday reference — and that the following tips will lead you to any information you need.

Ways into the book

QUICK ACCESS MENU. Inside the front cover you'll find a list of the book's contents. Once you locate a general topic on the quick access menu, flip to the tabbed section of the book that contains information on the topic, and check the menu on the tabbed divider for the exact page.

USER-FRIENDLY INDEX. The index lists everything covered in the book. You can look up a topic either by its formal name (*ellipses*, for example) or, if you're not sure what the formal name is, by a familiar word you use to describe it (such as *dots*).

BRIEF CONTENTS. Inside the back cover, a brief but detailed table of contents lists chapter titles and major headings.

GUIDE TO THE TOP TWENTY. The first tabbed section provides guidelines for recognizing, understanding, and editing the most common errors in student writing today. This section includes brief explanations, hand-edited examples, and cross-references to other places in the book where you'll find more detail.

CLEAR ADVICE ON RESEARCH AND DOCUMENTATION. Easy-to-follow source maps walk you step-by-step through the processes of selecting, evaluating, using, and citing sources. Documentation models appear in two tabbed sections — gold for MLA style and white for APA, *Chicago*, and CSE styles — with the different documentation styles color-coded in these sections.

REVISION SYMBOLS. If your instructor uses revision symbols to mark your drafts, you can consult the list of symbols at the back of the book and its cross-references to places in the book where you'll find more help.

GLOSSARY OF USAGE. Chapter 19 gives quick advice on commonly confused and misused words.

Ways to navigate the pages

❶ GUIDES AT THE TOP OF EVERY PAGE. Headers tell you what chapter or subsection you're in, the chapter number and section letter, the name of the tab, and the page number.

❷ "AT A GLANCE" BOXES. These boxes at the beginning of most chapters — and elsewhere in the book as well — help you check your drafts with a critical eye and revise or edit.

❸ BOXED TIPS THROUGHOUT THE BOOK.

- **Tips on academic language, concepts, and style.** "Talking the Talk" and "Talking about Style" boxes help you make sense of how writing works in the academic world and help you make stylistic choices for various kinds of writing — in communities, jobs, and disciplines.

- **Tips for multilingual writers.** Advice for multilingual writers appears in a separate tabbed section and in boxes throughout the book. You can also find a list of the topics covered, including language-specific tips, at the back of the book.

- **Tips for considering disabilities.** These boxes, which also appear throughout the book, help you make your work accessible to readers with disabilities. If you're a writer with a disability, these boxes also point out resources and strategies you may want to use.

- **Tips on common assignments.** Advice about dealing with the most common assignments in first-year writing — and in other disciplines — appears in boxed tips throughout the book.

❹ HAND-EDITED EXAMPLES. Many examples are hand-edited in blue, allowing you to see the error and its revision at a glance. Pointers and boldface type make examples easy to spot on the page.

❺ CROSS-REFERENCES TO THE WEB SITE. *The Everyday Writer* Web site expands the book's coverage. The cross-references to the Web site point you to practical online resources — tutorials, interactive exercises, model papers, research and documentation help, and more.

308   Grammar   **34b**   *Adjectives and adverbs* ──────────────────── **①**

── **②**

┌───┐
AT A GLANCE
Editing Adjectives and Adverbs

- Scrutinize each adjective and adverb. Consider synonyms for each word to see whether you have chosen the best word possible.

- See if a more specific noun would eliminate the need for an adjective (*mansion* rather than *enormous house,* for instance). Do the same with verbs and adverbs.

- Look for places where you might make your writing more specific or vivid by adding an adjective or adverb.

- Check that adjectives modify only nouns and pronouns and that adverbs modify only verbs, adjectives, and other adverbs. (34b) Check especially for proper use of *good* and *well, bad* and *badly, real* and *really.* (34b and c)

- Make sure all comparisons are complete. (34c)
└───┘

34b   **Adverbs to modify verbs, adjectives, and adverbs**

In everyday conversation, you will often hear (and perhaps use) adjectives in place of adverbs. For example, people often say *go quick* instead of *go quickly.* When you write in standard academic English, however, use adverbs to modify verbs, adjectives, and other adverbs.

                                          carefully.
▶ You can feel the song's meter if you listen ~~careful.~~
                                  ^

                really
▶ The audience was ~~real~~ disappointed by the show. ──────── **④**
               ^

┌───┐
FOR MULTILINGUAL WRITERS ──────────────────── **③**
Using Adjectives with Plural Nouns

In Spanish, Russian, and many other languages, adjectives agree in number with the nouns they modify. In English, adjectives do not change number this way: *the kittens are cute* (not *cutes*).
└───┘

bedfordstmartins.com/everydaywriter For exercises, go to **Exercise Central** and click on **Adjectives and Adverbs**. ── **⑤**

Preface

Today, perhaps more than ever before, *everyone* can be a writer — every day. From contributing entries to Wikipedia to blogging, texting, and posting to YouTube and Facebook, student writers are participating widely in what philosopher Kenneth Burke calls "the conversation of humankind." As access to new writing spaces grows, so too do the potential audiences: many writers, for example, are in daily contact with people around the world, and their work goes out to millions. In such a time, writers need to think more carefully than ever about how to craft effective messages and how best to represent themselves to others.

These ever-expanding opportunities for writers, as well as the challenges that inevitably come with them, have inspired this edition of *The Everyday Writer* — from the focus on thinking carefully about audience and purposes for writing and on attending to the "look" of writing, to the emphasis on the ways writing works across disciplines, to the questions that new genres and forms of writing raise about citing and documenting sources and about understanding and avoiding plagiarism. What remains constant is the focus on the "everydayness" of writing and on down-to-earth, practical advice for how to write well in a multitude of situations.

What also remains constant is the focus on rhetorical concerns. In a time of such challenging possibilities, taking a rhetorical perspective is particularly important. Why? Because a rhetorical perspective rejects either/or, right/wrong, black/white approaches to writing in favor of asking what choices will be most appropriate, effective, and ethical in a given writing situation. A rhetorical perspective also means paying careful attention to the purposes we want to achieve and the audiences we want to address. Writers today need to maintain such a rhetorical perspective every single day, and *The Everyday Writer,* Fourth Edition, provides writers with the tools for doing so.

A note about MLA style

The guidelines for MLA documentation in this update to the Fourth Edition of the *Everyday Writer with Excercises* follow the recommendations in the *MLA Handbook for Writers of Research Papers,* Seventh Edition (2009).

Highlights

ATTENTION TO GOOD WRITING, NOT JUST TO SURFACE CORRECTNESS. *The Everyday Writer* helps students understand that effective texts follow conventions that always depend on their audience, situation, and discipline.

HELP FOR THE MOST COMMON WRITING PROBLEMS. A new nationwide study that I conducted with Karen Lunsford — revisiting the original 1986 research that Bob Connors and I conducted on student writing — shows the problems U.S. college students are most likely to have in their writing today. This book's first chapter presents a quick guide to troubleshooting the Top Twenty — with examples, explanations, and information on where to turn in the handbook for more detailed information. Additional findings from the study inform advice throughout the book.

UP-TO-DATE ADVICE ON RESEARCH AND DOCUMENTATION. As best practices for research continue to evolve, so does *The Everyday Writer*. In this edition, you'll find integrated coverage of library and online research to help students find authoritative and credible information in any medium, plus advice on integrating sources, avoiding plagiarism, using social bookmarking tools for research, and citing sources in MLA, APA, *Chicago*, and CSE documentation styles. Visual source maps in all four documentation sections show students how to evaluate, use, and document print and online sources.

COMPREHENSIVE COVERAGE OF CRITICAL THINKING AND ARGUMENT. My work on *Everything's an Argument* has strengthened my belief that argument is integral to many kinds of writing, and I have expanded the coverage of critical thinking and argument in this edition and placed them in a separate tab to make the information even easier to find and use. Chapters 11–13 offer extensive advice on critical reading and analysis of both visual and verbal arguments, instruction on composing arguments, and two complete student essays.

EXPANDED HELP FOR WRITING IN THE DISCIPLINES. Along with strategies for understanding discipline-specific assignments, vocabulary, style, and use of evidence, this edition offers more student writing samples than ever before, including research projects in MLA, APA, *Chicago*, and CSE styles, business documents, and sample writing from introductory humanities, social sciences, and natural sciences courses.

UNIQUE COVERAGE OF LANGUAGE AND STYLE. Unique chapters on language help students think about language in context and about the consequences that language choices have on writers and readers. Boxed tips throughout the book help students communicate effectively across cultures — and use varieties of language both wisely and well.

INTEGRATED EXERCISES. Exercises to help students practice writing, revising, thinking critically, and editing appear throughout the book. (An answer key appears in the *Instructor's Notes.*)

AN INVITING DESIGN. *The Everyday Writer* makes information easy to find and appealing to read.

New to this edition

New advice based on Andrea Lunsford's teaching and research

- New "Talking the Talk" boxes answer real questions students ask about academic concepts.

> TALKING THE TALK
> ### Conventions
>
> "Aren't conventions really just rules with another name?" Not entirely. Conventions — agreed-on language practices of grammar, punctuation, and style — convey a kind of shorthand information from writer to reader. In college writing, you will want to follow the conventions of standard academic English unless you have a good reason to do otherwise. But unlike hard-and-fast rules, conventions are flexible; a convention appropriate for one time or situation may be inappropriate for another. You may even choose to ignore conventions to achieve a particular effect. (You might, for example, write a sentence fragment rather than a full sentence, such as the *Not entirely* at the beginning of this box.) As you become more experienced and confident in your writing, you will develop a sense of which conventions to apply in different writing situations.

- New "Common Assignments" boxes provide tips for succeeding with the kinds of writing projects and assignments that research shows students today are most likely to encounter in their classes.

> COMMON ASSIGNMENTS
> ### Rhetorical Analysis
>
> You are almost certain to get some form of analysis assignment during your first year of college. One common variety is the rhetorical analysis assignment, which essentially answers two big questions — What is the purpose of the text you are analyzing? How is that purpose achieved? — and focuses on *how* the text gets its meaning across.
>
> SPECIAL CONSIDERATIONS OF A RHETORICAL ANALYSIS ASSIGNMENT
>
> - Identify the purpose or purposes of the text. If the text has multiple purposes, point out any conflicts.
> - Identify the primary audience for the text and any secondary audiences, and explore how the text meets audience expectations or needs.
> - Examine the author's stance or attitude toward the topic: is it favorable, critical, suspicious, neutral, or mocking? Identify parts of the text where such attitudes are evident, and show how they work to appeal to the audience.
> - Explain how the text uses deliberate strategies (such as tone, word choice, sentence structure, design, special effects, choice of medium, choice of evidence, and so on) to achieve its purposes.

- A new chapter on expectations for college writing helps students grapple with academic work.

- **New and expanded coverage of reviewing and revising** clarifies the relationship between review and revision, with advice on how to offer useful comments on peers' writing and how to benefit from comments from both peers and instructors.

- **A new section on reflecting on writing** guides students in thinking back on their completed writing projects. A student reflective essay models the writing students are often asked to do for portfolio assessment.

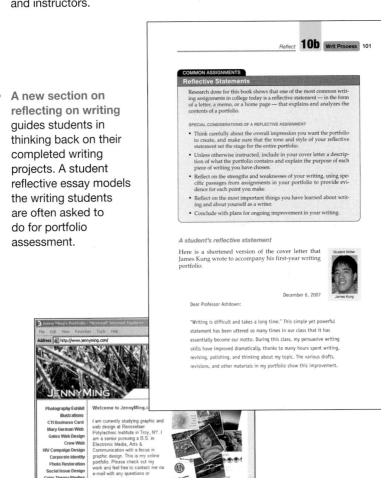

Reflect **10b** Writ Process 101

COMMON ASSIGNMENTS
Reflective Statements

Research done for this book shows that one of the most common writing assignments in college today is a reflective statement — in the form of a letter, a memo, or a home page — that explains and analyzes the contents of a portfolio.

SPECIAL CONSIDERATIONS OF A REFLECTIVE ASSIGNMENT

- Think carefully about the overall impression you want the portfolio to create, and make sure that the tone and style of your reflective statement set the stage for the entire portfolio.
- Unless otherwise instructed, include in your cover letter a description of what the portfolio contains and explain the purpose of each piece of writing you have chosen.
- Reflect on the strengths and weaknesses of your writing, using specific passages from assignments in your portfolio to provide evidence for each point you make.
- Reflect on the most important things you have learned about writing and about yourself as a writer.
- Conclude with plans for ongoing improvement in your writing.

A student's reflective statement

Here is a shortened version of the cover letter that James Kung wrote to accompany his first-year writing portfolio.

Student Writer
James Kung

December 6, 2007

Dear Professor Ashdown:

"Writing is difficult and takes a long time." This simple yet powerful statement has been uttered so many times in our class that it has essentially become our motto. During this class, my persuasive writing skills have improved dramatically, thanks to many hours spent writing, revising, polishing, and thinking about my topic. The various drafts, revisions, and other materials in my portfolio show this improvement.

- **Integrated coverage of writing and media** helps students understand that smarter rhetorical choices produce better writing, no matter what the genre or format.

- **New coverage for multilingual writers** clarifies U.S. academic writing for every student with a multilingual background.

Writing in U.S. Academic Genres **55**

Xiaoming Li, now a college English teacher, says that before she came to the United States as a graduate student, she had been a "good writer" in China — in both English and Chinese. Once in the United States, however, she struggled to grasp what her teachers expected of her college writing. While she could easily use grammar books and dictionaries, her instructors' unstated expectations seemed to call for her to write in a way that was new to her.

Of course, writing for college presents many challenges; such writing differs in many ways from high school writing as well as from personal writing like text messaging or postings to social networking sites. If you grew up speaking and writing in other languages, however, the transition to producing effective college writing can be even more complicated. Not only will you have to learn new information and new ways of thinking and arguing, but you also have to do it in a language that may not come naturally to you — especially in unfamiliar rhetorical situations.

55a U.S. academic writing

The expectations for college writing are often taken for granted by instructors. To complicate the matter further, there is no single "correct" style of communication in any country, including the United States. Effective oral styles differ from effective written styles, and what is considered good writing in one field of study is not necessarily appropriate in another. Even the variety of English often referred to as "standard" covers a wide range of styles (see Chapter 21). In spite of this wide variation, several features are often associated with U.S. academic English:

- conventional grammar, spelling, punctuation, and mechanics
- organization that links ideas explicitly

493

A new Top Twenty based on new research

- The 2006 Lunsford and Lunsford study's results show an increasing emphasis on researched and documented writing in college — a major change from the kinds of assignments given in the past. The new Top Twenty reflects this change as well as students' evolving use of technology (including spell checkers).

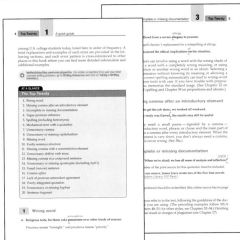

- Advice from the new research study is integrated throughout the text, giving students the benefit of the most up-to-date information available on how college writing works.

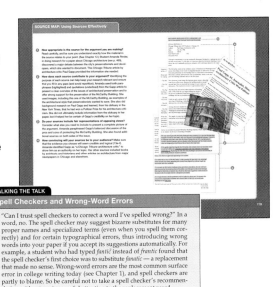

TALKING THE TALK

Spell Checkers and Wrong-Word Errors

"Can I trust spell checkers to correct a word I've spelled wrong?" In a word, no. The spell checker may suggest bizarre substitutes for many proper names and specialized terms (even when you spell them correctly) and for certain typographical errors, thus introducing wrong words into your paper if you accept its suggestions automatically. For example, a student who had typed *fantič* instead of *frantic* found that the spell checker's first choice was to substitute *fanatic* — a replacement that made no sense. Wrong-word errors are the most common surface error in college writing today (see Chapter 1), and spell checkers are partly to blame. So be careful not to take a spell checker's recommendation without paying careful attention to the replacement word.

A more visual approach to writing, research, and documentation

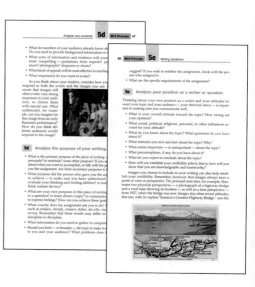

- Ample photographs and illustrations show as well as tell students how to make better choices throughout the writing process.

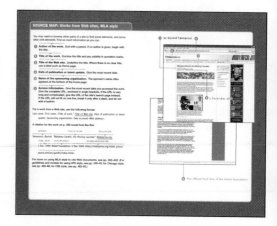

- Color-coded source maps in the Research tab, the MLA tab, and the APA, *Chicago*, and CSE tab make it easier than ever to see what's needed to evaluate, use, and document sources well.

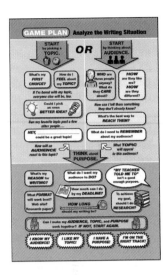

- Fresh, fun new visual "game plans" help students take a hands-on approach to planning and developing their writing. A complete list of game plan pages appears in a directory at the back of the book.

- An updated design makes the look more student-friendly than ever.

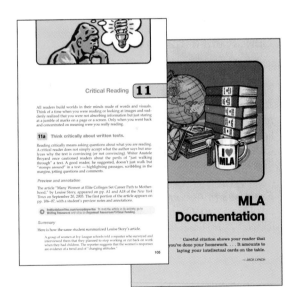

A wide array of ancillaries

NEW MEDIA RESOURCES

CompClass with *The Everyday Writer e-Book*
bedfordstmartins.com/compclass

Online Student Center for *The Everyday Writer* (free book-specific resources and premium content, including *The Everyday Writer e-Book*)
bedfordstmartins.com/everydaywriter

Exercise Central 3.0 bedfordstmartins.com/exercisecentral

Electronic Diagnostic Tests bedfordstmartins.com/lunsforddiagnostics

Just-in-Time Teaching bedfordstmartins.com/justintime

Exercise Central to Go for Handbooks by Andrea A. Lunsford CD-ROM
ISBN-10: 0-312-43114-7
ISBN-13: 978-0-312-43114-3

PRINT RESOURCES

Instructor's Notes, Andrea Lunsford, Alyssa O'Brien, and Lisa Dresdner (includes answer key for exercises in *The Everyday Writer with Exercises*)
ISBN-10: 0-312-48861-0
ISBN-13: 978-0-312-48861-1

Exercises to Accompany THE EVERYDAY WRITER, **Fourth Edition,**
Lex Runciman, Carolyn Lengel, and Kate Silverstein
ISBN-10: 0-312-38653-2
ISBN-13: 978-0-312-38653-5

Answer Key to Exercises to Accompany THE EVERYDAY WRITER,
Fourth Edition
ISBN-10: 0-312-48858-0
ISBN-13: 978-0-312-48858-1

OTHER COMPOSITION RESOURCES FROM BEDFORD/ST. MARTIN'S

ix visual exercises CD-ROM
ISBN-10: 0-312-41562-1
ISBN-13: 978-0-312-41562-4

i-cite visualizing sources CD-ROM
ISBN-10: 0-312-44179-7
ISBN-13: 978-0-312-44179-1

i-claim visualizing argument CD-ROM
ISBN-10: 0-312-44015-4
ISBN-13: 978-0-312-44015-2

COURSE MANAGEMENT CONTENT

Resources developed for *The Everyday Writer* are available for use in course management systems.

Acknowledgments

I owe an ongoing debt of gratitude to Carolyn Lengel, my editor for this and two other books as well: her patience, fortitude, and sheer hard work, her astute judgment, her wellspring of good ideas, her meticulous attention to detail, and her great good humor are gifts that just keep on giving. I am also very fortunate to have had the advice and help of Fran Weinberg, who has made invaluable and ongoing contributions to this text; to Stephanie Butler, for her outstanding work on the ancillaries to this text, including the *Instructor's Notes;* to Wendy Annibell for her meticulous copyediting; to Mara Weible for huge contributions to our online handbook tutorials; to Sarah Ferguson for her work on the book's new media components; to Anne Carter and Anna Palchik for their brilliant contributions to art and design; to Donna Dennison for cover art; to Eric Larsen for his imaginative illustrations; and to Harold Chester, project editor *par excellence.*

Many thanks, also, to the unfailingly generous and supportive members of the Bedford/St. Martin's team: Erica Appel, Kristin Bowen, Nick Carbone, Joan Feinberg, Jimmy Fleming, Joe Ford, Karen Henry, Nancy Perry, Katie Schooling, Karen Soeltz, John Swanson, Shuli Traub, Kim White, and Denise Wydra.

I am especially indebted to Paul Kei Matsuda and Christine Tardy for their extraordinarily helpful additions to the Multilingual Writer sections of this book; to Lisa Ede for her ongoing support and advice, particularly about writing across the disciplines; to Lisa Dresdner at Norwalk Community College for her fine work on updating the *Instructors' Notes;* and to Dànielle Nicole DeVoss at Michigan State University for her help in making this a more visual book. I have also benefited greatly from the excellent advice of some very special colleagues: Colin Gifford Brooke, Syracuse University; Barbara Fister, Gustavus Adolphus College; Patrick Clauss, Butler University; Arnold Zwicky, Stanford University; Beverly Moss, Ohio State University; and Marilyn Moller.

I owe special thanks to the group of student writers whose work appears in and enriches this book and its companion Web site: Michelle Abbott, Carina Abernathy, Milena Ateyea, Julie Baird, Jennifer Bernal, Valerie Bredin, Taurean Brown, Tessa Cabello, Ben Canning, Leah Clendening, David Craig, Kelly Darr, Allyson Goldberg, Tara Gupta, Joanna Hays, Dana Hornbeak, Ajani Husbands, Bory Kea, James Kung, Emily Lesk, Nastassia Lopez, Heather Mackintosh-Sims, Merlla McLaughlin, Jenny Ming, Laura Montgomery, Elva Negrete, Katie Paarlberg, Shannan Palma, Teal Pfeifer, Amrit K. Rao, Heather Ricker, Amanda Rinder, Dawn Rodney, Rudy Rubio, Melissa Schraeder, Bonnie Sillay, Jessica Thrower, and Dennis Tyler.

Once again, I have been guided by a group of hard-working and meticulous reviewers, including Thomas Amorose, Seattle Pacific

University; Heidi R. Anderson, University of Minnesota Duluth; Dominic Ashby, West Virginia University; Susan Bailor, Front Range Community College; Peggy Beck, Kent State University Stark; Judy Bennett, University of Louisiana at Monroe; Mona Diane Benton, Eastern Michigan University; Monica Bosson, City College of San Francisco; Domenic Bruni, University of Wisconsin Oshkosh; Jo Anne R. Bryant, Troy University; Jennifer Castillo, Eastern Michigan University; Christian M. Clark, Community College of Southern Nevada; Barbara Cole, The State University of New York at Buffalo; Teresa Cordova, California State University, Sacramento; Margaret Cotter-Lynch, Southeastern Oklahoma State University; Cynthia Cox, Belmont University; Charles DiDomenico, Middlesex County College; Sid Dobrin, University of Florida; Doug Downs, Utah Valley State College; Lisa Dresdner, Norwalk Community College; Anne-Marie Drew, United States Naval Academy; Violet A. Dutcher, Eastern Mennonite University; Heidi Estrem, Boise State University; Diana Fernandez, Florida International University; Patricia Rowe Geenen, Alverno College; Holly Geil, Kent State University; Nathan Gorelick, State University of New York at Buffalo; Andrew Green, University of Miami; Eric Gunnink, University of St. Francis; Kim Gunter, The University of North Carolina at Pembroke; Scot Hanson, Texas Christian University; Christopher S. Harris, University of Louisiana at Monroe; Kimberly Harrison, Florida International University–Biscayne Bay; Anneliese Homan, State Fair Community College; Cynthia Lewiecki-Wilson, Miami University of Ohio; Jon A. Leydens, Colorado School of Mines; Meredith A. Love-Steinmetz, Francis Marion University; Suzanne Blum Malley, Columbia College Chicago; Patricia Mandia, Kent State University Stark; Jessica Matthews, George Mason University; Cynthia Maxson, Rio Salado College; Kathy Mendt, Front Range Community College; Kerri Mitchell, Front Range Community College; Winifred Morgan, Edgewood College; Roxanne Munch, Joliet Junior College; Kim Murray, University of Southern Florida; Beverly A. Neiderman, Kent State University; Jerry L. Nelson, Lincoln University; Troy D. Nordman, Butler Community College; Shelley Harper Palmer, Rowan-Cabarrus Community College; Cherri Porter, American River College and Woodland Community College; Carolee Ritter, Southeast Community College; Deidre Farrington Schoolcraft, Pikes Peak Community College; Shawna Shapiro, University of Washington; Mary Beth Simmons, Villanova University; Kimberly Skeen, College of Southern Idaho; Wayne Stein, University of Central Oklahoma; Jane VanderVelde, University of Kansas; Megan Ward, Miami University of Ohio; Elizabeth Wardle, University of Dayton; Peggy Woods, University of Massachusetts, Amherst; Susan Dara Wright, William Paterson University; and Sarah L. Yoder, Texas Christian University.

For offering advice and perspectives from disciplines other than composition, I would like to extend particular thanks to the following reviewers: Carole Anderson, The Ohio State University; Robert Bulman, St. Mary's College of California; Patrick J. Castle, United States Air Force Academy; Rosemary Cunningham, Agnes Scott College; Bridget Drinka, University of Texas at San Antonio; John Hnida, Peru State College; Kareem J. Johnson, Temple University; Steve Naragon, Manchester College; Tracy Ann Robinson, Oregon State University; and Timothy J. Shannon, Gettysburg College.

Finally, and always, I continue to learn—from my students, who serve as the major inspiration for just about everything I do; from the very best sisters, nieces, and nephews anyone has ever had; and from my spectacular great-nieces, Audrey and Lila: this book is for all of you.

–Andrea A. Lunsford

About College Writing

A mind that is stretched by a new experience can
never go back to its old dimensions.

— OLIVER WENDELL HOLMES

About College Writing

The Top Twenty: A Quick Guide to Troubleshooting Your Writing

Surface errors — grammar, punctuation, word choice, and other small-scale matters — don't always disturb readers. Whether your instructor marks an error in any particular assignment will depend on personal judgments about how serious and distracting it is and about what you should be focusing on in the draft. In addition, not all surface errors are consistently viewed as errors: some of the patterns identified in the research for this book are considered errors by some instructors but as stylistic options by others. Such differing opinions don't mean that there is no such thing as correctness in writing — only that *correctness always depends on some context*, on whether the choices a writer makes seem appropriate to readers.

Research for this book reveals a number of changes that have occurred in student writing over the past twenty-plus years. First, writing assignments in first-year composition classes now focus less on personal narrative and much more on research essays and argument. As a result, students are now writing longer essays than they did twenty years ago and working much more often with sources, both print and nonprint. Thus it's no surprise that students today are struggling with the conventions for using and citing sources, a problem that did not show up in most earlier studies of student writing.

What else has changed? For starters, wrong-word errors are *by far the most common* errors among first-year student writers today. Twenty years ago, spelling errors were most common by a factor of more than three to one. The use of spell checkers has reduced the number of spelling errors in student writing — but spell checkers' suggestions may also be responsible for some (or many) of the wrong words students are using.

All writers want to be considered competent and careful. You know that your readers judge you by your control of the conventions you have agreed to use, even if the conventions change from time to time. To help you in producing writing that is conventionally correct, you should become familiar with the twenty most common error patterns among U.S. college students today, listed here in order of frequency. A brief explanation and examples of each error are provided in the following sections, and each error pattern is cross-referenced to other places in this book where you can find more detailed information and additional examples.

 bedfordstmartins.com/everydaywriter For advice on learning from your own most common writing problems, go to **Writing Resources** and click on **Taking a Writing Inventory.**

AT A GLANCE

The Top Twenty

1. Wrong word
2. Missing comma after an introductory element
3. Incomplete or missing documentation
4. Vague pronoun reference
5. Spelling (including homonyms)
6. Mechanical error with a quotation
7. Unnecessary comma
8. Unnecessary or missing capitalization
9. Missing word
10. Faulty sentence structure
11. Missing comma with a nonrestrictive element
12. Unnecessary shift in verb tense
13. Missing comma in a compound sentence
14. Unnecessary or missing apostrophe (including *its/it's*)
15. Fused (run-on) sentence
16. Comma splice
17. Lack of pronoun-antecedent agreement
18. Poorly integrated quotation
19. Unnecessary or missing hyphen
20. Sentence fragment

1 Wrong word

> *precedence*
> ▶ Religious texts, for them, take ~~prescience~~ over other kinds of sources.
>   ^

Prescience means "foresight," and *precedence* means "priority."

> *allergy*
> ► The child suffered from a severe ~~allegory~~ to peanuts.
> ^

Allegory is a spell checker's replacement for a misspelling of *allergy*.

> *of*
> ► The panel discussed the ethical implications ~~on~~ the situation.
> ^

Wrong-word errors can involve using a word with the wrong shade of meaning, using a word with a completely wrong meaning, or using a wrong preposition or another wrong word in an idiom. Selecting a word from a thesaurus without knowing its meaning or allowing a spell checker to correct spelling automatically can lead to wrong-word errors, so use these tools with care. If you have trouble with prepositions and idioms, memorize the standard usage. (See Chapter 22 on word choice and spelling and Chapter 59 on prepositions and idioms.)

2 Missing comma after an introductory element

> ► Determined to get the job done, we worked all weekend.
> ^
> ► Although the study was flawed, the results may still be useful.
> ^

Readers usually need a small pause — signaled by a comma — between an introductory word, phrase, or clause and the main part of the sentence. Use a comma after every introductory element. When the introductory element is very short, you don't always need a comma, but including it is never wrong. (See 38a.)

3 Incomplete or missing documentation

> *(263)."*
> ► Satrapi says, "When we're afraid, we lose all sense of analysis and reflection."
> ^

The page number of the print source for this quotation must be included.

> ► According to one source, James Joyce wrote two of the five best novels
> *(Modern Library 100 Best).*
> of all time.
> ^

The source mentioned should be indentified (this online source has no page numbers).

Cite each source you refer to in the text, following the guidelines of the documentation style you are using. (The preceding examples follow MLA style — see Chapters 48–51; for other styles, see Chapters 52–54.) Omitting documentation can result in charges of plagiarism (see Chapter 17).

4 Vague pronoun reference

POSSIBLE REFERENCE TO MORE THAN ONE WORD

▶ Transmitting radio signals by satellite is a way of overcoming the

the airwaves

problem of scarce airwaves and limiting how ~~they~~ are used.
^

In the original sentence, *they* could refer to the signals or to the airwaves.

REFERENCE IMPLIED BUT NOT STATED

a policy

▶ The company prohibited smoking, ~~which~~ many employees resented.
^

What does *which* refer to? The editing clarifies what employees resented.

A pronoun should refer clearly to the word or words it replaces (called the *antecedent*) elsewhere in the sentence or in a previous sentence. If more than one word could be the antecedent, or if no specific antecedent is present, edit to make the meaning clear. (See Chapter 33.)

5 Spelling (including homonyms)

Reagan

▶ Ronald ~~Regan~~ won the election in a landslide.
^

Everywhere

▶ ~~Every where~~ we went, we saw crowds of tourists.
^

The most common misspellings today are those that spell checkers cannot identify. The categories that spell checkers are most likely to miss include homonyms, compound words incorrectly spelled as separate words, and proper nouns, particularly names. After you run the spell checker, proofread carefully for errors such as these — and be sure to run the spell checker to catch other kinds of spelling mistakes. (See 22e.)

6 Mechanical error with a quotation

▶ "I grew up the victim of a disconcerting confusion~~,~~"*,* Rodriguez says (249).
^

The comma should be placed *inside* the quotation marks.

Follow conventions when using quotation marks with commas (38h), colons (43d), and other punctuation (42f). Always use quotation marks in pairs, and follow the guidelines of your documentation style for block quotations (42b). Use quotation marks for titles of short works (42c), but use italics for titles of long works (46a).

7 Unnecessary comma

BEFORE CONJUNCTIONS IN COMPOUND CONSTRUCTIONS THAT ARE NOT COMPOUND SENTENCES

▶ This conclusion applies to the United States⁄ and to the rest of the world.

No comma is needed before *and* because it is joining two phrases that modify the same verb, *applies.*

WITH RESTRICTIVE ELEMENTS

▶ Many parents⁄ of gifted children⁄ do not want them to skip a grade.

No comma is needed to set off the restrictive phrase *of gifted children,* which is necessary to indicate which parents the sentence is talking about.

Do not use commas to set off restrictive elements that are necessary to the meaning of the words they modify. Do not use a comma before a coordinating conjunction (*and, but, for, nor, or, so, yet*) when the conjunction does not join parts of a compound sentence. Do not use a comma before the first or after the last item in a series, between a subject and verb, between a verb and its object or complement, or between a preposition and its object. (See 38j.)

8 Unnecessary or missing capitalization

traditional   *medicines*   *ephedra*
▶ Some T̶r̶a̶d̶i̶t̶i̶o̶n̶a̶l̶ Chinese M̶e̶d̶i̶c̶i̶n̶e̶s̶ containing E̶p̶h̶e̶d̶r̶a̶ remain legal.
         ^   ^   ^

Capitalize proper nouns and proper adjectives, the first words of sentences, and important words in titles, along with certain words indicating directions and family relationships. Do not capitalize most other words. When in doubt, check a dictionary. (See Chapter 44.)

9 Missing word

                    against
▶ The site foreman discriminated women and promoted men with less
                          ^
experience.

Proofread carefully for omitted words, including prepositions (59a), parts of two-part verbs (58b), and correlative conjunctions (30h). Be particularly careful not to omit words from quotations.

10   Faulty sentence structure

▶ ~~The information which high~~ *High* school athletes are presented with
mainly ~~includes~~ information on what credits *they* needed to graduate,
~~and thinking about the college~~ which *colleges to try* athletes ~~are trying~~ to play for,
and *how to* apply.

A sentence that starts out with one kind of structure and then changes to another kind can confuse readers. Make sure that each sentence contains a subject and a verb (30b), that subjects and predicates make sense together (25b), and that comparisons have clear meanings (25e). When you join elements (such as subjects or verb phrases) with a coordinating conjunction, make sure that the elements have parallel structures (see Chapter 26).

11   Missing comma with a nonrestrictive element

▶ Marina**,** who was the president of the club**,** was first to speak.

The clause *who was the president of the club* does not affect the basic meaning of the sentence: Marina was first to speak.

A nonrestrictive element gives information not essential to the basic meaning of the sentence. Use commas to set off a nonrestrictive element (38c).

12   Unnecessary shift in verb tense

▶ Priya was watching the great blue heron. Then she ~~slips~~ *slipped* and ~~falls~~ *fell* into the swamp.

Verbs that shift from one tense to another with no clear reason can confuse readers (27a).

13 Missing comma in a compound sentence

▶ Meredith waited for Samir, and her sister grew impatient.
    ^

Without the comma, a reader may think at first that Meredith waited for both Samir and her sister.

A compound sentence consists of two or more parts that could each stand alone as a sentence. When the parts are joined by a coordinating conjunction, use a comma before the conjunction to indicate a pause between the two thoughts (38b).

14 Unnecessary or missing apostrophe (including *its/it's*)

child's
▶ Overambitious parents can be very harmful to a ~~childs~~ well-being.
                                                      ^

its   *It's*
▶ The car is lying on ~~it's~~ side in the ditch. ~~Its~~ a white 2004 Passat.
                        ^   ^

To make a noun possessive, add either an apostrophe and an *-s* (*Ed's book*) or an apostrophe alone (*the boys' gym*). Do *not* use an apostrophe in the possessive pronouns *ours*, *yours*, and *hers*. Use *its* to mean *belonging to it*; use *it's* only when you mean *it is* or *it has*. (See Chapter 41.)

15 Fused (run-on) sentence

but
▶ Klee's paintings seem simple, they are very sophisticated.
                              ^

Although she
▶ ~~She~~ doubted the value of meditation, she decided to try it once.
  ^   ^

A fused sentence (also called a *run-on*) joins clauses that could each stand alone as a sentence with no punctuation or words to link them. Fused sentences must either be divided into separate sentences or joined by adding words or punctuation. (See Chapter 36.)

16 Comma splice

         for
▶ I was strongly attracted to her, she was beautiful and funny.

      that
▶ We hated the meat loaf, the cafeteria served ~~it~~ every Friday.

A comma splice occurs when only a comma separates clauses that could each stand alone as a sentence. To correct a comma splice, you can insert a semicolon or period, connect the clauses with a word such as *and* or *because*, or restructure the sentence. (See Chapter 36.)

17 Lack of pronoun-antecedent agreement

All students   *uniforms.*
▶ ~~Every student~~ must provide their own ~~uniform.~~

                      its
▶ Each of the puppies thrived in ~~their~~ new home.

Pronouns must agree with their antecedents in gender (male or female) and in number (singular or plural). Many indefinite pronouns, such as *everyone* and *each*, are always singular. When a singular antecedent can refer to a man or a woman, either rewrite the sentence to make the antecedent plural or to eliminate the pronoun, or use *his or her*, *he or she*, and so on. When antecedents are joined by *or* or *nor*, the pronoun must agree with the closer antecedent. A collective noun such as *team* can be either singular or plural, depending on whether the members are seen as a group or as individuals. (See 33f.)

18 Poorly integrated quotation

                                   showed how color affects taste:
▶ A 1970s study of what makes food appetizing "Once it became apparent

  that the steak was actually blue and the fries were green, some people

  became ill" (Schlosser 565).

According to Lars Eighner,
▶ "Dumpster diving has serious drawbacks as a way of life" (~~Eighner~~ 383).

  Finding edible food is especially tricky.

Quotations should fit smoothly into the surrounding sentence structure. They should be linked clearly to the writing around them (usually with a signal phrase) rather than dropped abruptly into the writing. (See 17b.)

19 Unnecessary or missing hyphen

▶ This paper looks at fictional and real life examples.
    ^

A compound adjective modifying a noun that follows it requires a hyphen.

▶ The buyers want to fix̸up the house and resell it.

A two-word verb should not be hyphenated.

A compound adjective that appears before a noun needs a hyphen. However, be careful not to hypenate two-word verbs or word groups that serve as subject complements. (See Chapter 47.)

20 Sentence fragment

NO SUBJECT

▶ Marie Antoinette spent huge sums of money on herself and her favorites.

Her extravagance
~~And~~ helped bring on the French Revolution.
^

NO COMPLETE VERB

                was
▶ The old aluminum boat sitting on its trailer.
                ^

BEGINNING WITH A SUBORDINATING WORD

                        where
▶ We returned to the drugstore.̸ ~~Where~~ we waited for our buddies.
                        ^

A sentence fragment is part of a sentence that is written as if it were a complete sentence. Reading your draft out loud, backwards, sentence by sentence, will help you spot sentence fragments. (See Chapter 37.)

bedfordstmartins.com/everydaywriter For practice identifying and correcting these writing problems, click on **The Top Twenty**. For additional exercises, click on **Exercises**.

2 | Expectations for College Writing

A generation ago, many college students counted on holding one job throughout their careers and expected college to prepare them for that single job. Today's students, however, are likely to hold a number of positions — and each new position will call for new learning. That's why looking at your college years as simply a step you have to take on the way toward your first job is a big mistake. College must do much more than simply prepare you for that first work experience, and you may need to adjust your expectations of what college should do *for* you in order to understand what your instructors will expect *from* you.

2a Meeting expectations

Your instructors — and your future colleagues and supervisors — will expect you to demonstrate your ability to think critically, to consider ethical issues, to identify as well as solve problems, to research effectively, and to work productively with people of widely different backgrounds. In each of these endeavors, writing will be of crucial importance, since writing is closely tied to thinking, to collaboration, and to communication.

But if you are like most students, you may not have written anything much longer than five pages before coming to college. Perhaps you have done only minimal research. Your college classes will demand much more from you as a writer; meeting these demands will help prepare you for all the writing you will need to do in the future.

TALKING THE TALK

Conventions

"Aren't conventions really just rules with another name?" Not entirely. Conventions — agreed-on language practices of grammar, punctuation, and style — convey a kind of shorthand information from writer to reader. In college writing, you will want to follow the conventions of standard academic English unless you have a good reason to do otherwise. But unlike hard-and-fast rules, conventions are flexible; a convention appropriate for one time or situation may be inappropriate for another. You may even choose to ignore conventions to achieve a particular effect. (You might, for example, write a sentence fragment rather than a full sentence, such as the *Not entirely* at the beginning of this box.) As you become more experienced and confident in your writing, you will develop a sense of which conventions to apply in different writing situations.

2b Academic writing

You can begin the process of learning by considering what your instructors expect you to be able to do. Of course, expectations about academic writing vary considerably from field to field (see Chapters 60–64), but becoming familiar with widespread conventions will prepare you well for most academic situations.

Establishing authority

In the United States, most college instructors expect student writers to begin to establish their own authority — to become constructive critics who can analyze and interpret the work of others. But what does establishing authority mean in practice?

- Assume that your opinions count (as long as they are informed rather than tossed out with little thought) and that your audience expects you to present them in a well-reasoned manner.
- Show your familiarity with the ideas and works of others, both from the assigned course reading and from good points your instructor and classmates have made.

Being direct and clear

Your instructors will most often expect you to get to the point quickly and to be direct throughout an essay or other project. Research for this book confirms that readers depend on writers to organize and present their material — using sections, paragraphs, sentences, arguments, details, and source citations — in ways that aid understanding. Good academic writing prepares readers for what is coming next, provides definitions, and includes topic sentences. (See 19f for a description of the organization that instructors often prefer in student essays.) To achieve directness in your writing, try the following strategies:

- State your main point early and clearly.
- Avoid overqualifying your statements. Instead of writing *I think the facts reveal*, come right out and say *The facts reveal*.
- Avoid digressions. If you use an anecdote or example from personal experience, be sure it relates directly to the point you are making.
- Use appropriate evidence, such as examples and concrete details, to support each point.

- Make transitions from point to point obvious and clear. The first sentence of a new paragraph should reach back to the paragraph before and then look forward to what is to come (see Chapter 8).
- Follow logical organizational patterns (see Chapter 8).
- Design and format the project appropriately for the audience and purpose you have in mind (see Chapter 4).
- If your essay or project is longer than four or five pages, you may also want to use brief summary statements between sections, but avoid unnecessary repetition.

EXERCISE 2.1: THINKING CRITICALLY

How do you define good college writing? List the characteristics you come up with. Then list what you think your instructors' expectations are for good college writing, and note how they may differ from yours. What might account for the differences — and the similarities — in the two lists? Do you need to alter your ideas about good college writing to meet your instructors' expectations? Why, or why not?

AT A GLANCE

U.S. Academic Style

- Consider your purpose and audience carefully, making sure that your topic is appropriate to both. (Chapter 5)
- State your claim or thesis explicitly, and support it with examples, statistics, anecdotes, and authorities of various kinds. (Chapter 7)
- Carefully document all of your sources. (Chapters 48–54)
- Make explicit links between ideas. (Chapter 8)
- Consistently use the appropriate level of formality. (Chapter 22)
- Use conventional formats for academic genres. (Chapters 3–4 and 60–63)
- Use conventional grammar, spelling, punctuation, and mechanics. (Chapters 30–47)
- Use an easy-to-read type size and typeface, conventional margins, and double spacing. (Chapter 4)

2c Academic reading

Your instructors expect you to be an active reader — to offer informed opinions on what readings say. Stating your opinion doesn't require you to be negative or combative, just engaged with the class and the text. The following strategies will help you read actively:

- Note the name of the author and the date and place of publication; these items can give you clues to the writer's purpose and intended audience.

- Understand the overall content of a piece well enough to summarize it.

- Formulate critical questions about the text, and bring these questions up in class.

- Understand each sentence, and make direct connections between sentences and paragraphs. Keep track of repeated themes or images, and figure out how they contribute to the entire piece.

- Note the author's attitude toward and assumptions about the topic. Then you can speculate on how the attitude and assumptions may have affected the author's thinking.

- Distinguish between the author's stance and the author's reporting on the stances of others. Watch for key phrases an author uses to signal an opposing argument: *while some have argued that, in the past,* and so on.

- Go beyond content to notice organizational patterns, use of sources, and choice of words.

- Consider annotating your readings, especially if they are very important. Make notes in the margins that record your questions, challenges, or counter-examples to the text.

EXERCISE 2.2

One of the best ways to improve your writing process is to analyze it from time to time in a writing log. Answer the following questions about your writing:

- How do you typically go about preparing for a writing assignment?

- When and where do your best ideas often come to you?

- Where do you usually write? Are you usually alone and in a quiet place, or is there music, conversation, or other sound in the background?

- What materials do you use? What do you find most and least helpful about your materials?

- What audience do most assignments ask you to address? How much thought do you typically give to your audience?

- What strategies do you typically use to explore a topic?

- How do you usually write a first draft? Do you finish in one sitting, or do you prefer to work in sections?
- How do you typically revise, and what do you pay most attention to as you revise?
- If you get stuck while writing, what do you usually do to get moving again?
- What is most effective about your writing and your writing process?
- What about your writing and your writing process worries you? What specific steps can you take to address these worries?
- What is your favorite part of your writing process — and why?

You can also use the log to jot down your thoughts about a writing project while you are working on it and after you have completed it. Studying your notes on your writing process will help you identify patterns of strength and weakness in your writing and allow you to see how your writing process changes over time and for different writing assignments or situations.

2d Electronic communication in academic life

Your instructors will probably expect you to communicate both in and out of class using a variety of media. You may be asked to post your work to course management systems, lists, blogs, and wikis, and you may respond to the work of others on such sites. In addition, you will probably write email and text messages to your instructors and other students. Many people communicate electronically so quickly and so often that their writing tends to be very informal or to take shortcuts. As always, remember to consider your audience and your situation: you can write informally in a quick text message to a classmate, but when contacting your instructor, you should stick to the conventions of formal academic English unless invited to do otherwise.

Email

- Use a subject line that states your purpose accurately and clearly.
- Take care not to offend or irritate your reader. Tone is difficult to convey in online messages: what you intend as a joke may come across as an insult. Avoid writing messages in ALL CAPS.
- Be pertinent. Instructors generally expect short and to-the-point messages.

- Use a more formal tone along with a formal greeting and closing when posting a message to an instructor (*Dear Ms. Aulie* rather than *Hi*).
- Except in very informal situations, use the conventions of academic English. Proofread email messages just as you would other writing.
- Consider your email messages permanent and always findable, even if you delete them. Many people have been embarrassed (or worse, prosecuted) because of email trails.
- Conclude your message with your name and email address.
- Make sure that the username on the email account you use for contacting instructors and other authority figures does not present a poor impression. If your username is Party2Nite, consider changing it, or use your school email account for academic and professional communication.

Lists and discussion forums

Discussion forums are used in many college courses as a way for students to communicate with one another and the instructor about the course. Academic lists and forums are an extension of class discussions; remember to treat all participants with respect.

- Avoid unnecessary criticism of spelling or other errors. If a message is unclear, ask politely for a clarification. If you disagree with an assertion of fact, offer what you believe to be the correct information, but don't insult the writer.
- If you think you've been insulted (flamed), give the writer the benefit of the doubt. Replying with patience establishes your credibility and helps you seem mature and fair.
- Reply off-list to the sender of a message if the whole group does not need to read your reply.
- Keep in mind that many discussion forums and listservs are archived and that more people than you think may be reading your messages. Your postings create an impression of you, so make it a good one.

Web logs (blogs) and social networking spaces

Blogs and social networking sites such as Facebook allow users to say almost anything about themselves and to comment freely on the postings of others. Such online spaces can also be useful for academic discussion or for posting writing for others' comments.

- These sites may feel private, but most aren't — don't post anything you don't want everyone (including instructors and potential employers) to see.

- To comment, follow the same conventions you would for commenting on a discussion-list posting. It's wise to become familiar with the conversation before you add a comment of your own and to avoid commenting on entries that are several days old.

⊙ **bedfordstmartins.com/everydaywriter** For more information on effective electronic communication, go to **Writing Resources** and click on **Online Writing**.

EXERCISE 2.3

Choose several email messages you have sent recently — at least one of which is more formal than the others. Take a critical look at the messages you have chosen, noting differences and similarities and thinking about how easily readers could follow them. Bring your findings to class for discussion.

3 Oral and Multimedia Assignments

When the Gallup Poll reports on what U.S. citizens say they fear most, the findings are always the same: public speaking is apparently more frightening to us than almost anything else, even scarier than an attack from outer space. This chapter aims to allay any such fears you may have by offering guidelines that can help you prepare and deliver successful presentations.

AT A GLANCE

Preparing for Presentations

- How effectively do you contribute to class discussions? (3a)
- How does your presentation fulfill your purpose, including the goals of the assignment? (3b)
- How do the introduction and conclusion hold the audience's attention? (3b)
- Is your organizational structure crystal clear? How do you guide listeners? Are your transitions and signpost language explicit? Do you effectively repeat key words or ideas? (3b)
- Have you practiced your presentation and gotten response to it? (3b)
- Have you marked the text you are using for pauses and emphasis? (3b)
- Have you prepared all necessary visuals, including presentation slides and other multimedia? Are they large enough to be seen? Would other visuals be helpful? (3b)

3a Class discussions

The contributions you make to class discussions are mini-presentations. Make sure your contributions are effective by following these guidelines:

- Be prepared.
- Listen purposefully, following the flow of conversation and perhaps taking notes.
- Make sure your comments are relevant. Ask a key question, take the conversation in a new direction, or summarize or analyze what others have said.
- Be specific in your comments: *The passage in the middle of page 42 backs up what you're saying* is more useful than *I agree.*

FOR MULTILINGUAL WRITERS
Speaking Up in Class

Speaking up in class is viewed as inappropriate or even rude in some cultures. In the United States, however, doing so is expected and encouraged. Some instructors even assign credit for such class participation.

3b Effective presentations

More and more students report that formal presentations are becoming part of their work both in and out of class. As you begin to plan for such a presentation, you should consider a number of issues.

Considering your task, purpose, and audience

Think about how much time you have to prepare; where the presentation will take place; how long the presentation should run; whether you will use written-out text or note cards; whether visual aids, handouts, or other accompanying materials are necessary; and what equipment you will need. If you are making a group presentation, you will need time to divide duties and to practice with your classmates.

As with any writing assignment, consider the purpose of your presentation. Are you to lead a discussion? teach a lesson? give a report? engage a group in an activity? Also consider your audience. What do they know about your topic, what opinions do they already hold about it, and what do they need to know to follow your presentation and perhaps accept your point of view?

> **CONSIDERING DISABILITIES**
>
> ### Accessible Presentations
>
> Do all you can to make your presentations accessible.
>
> - Do not rely on color or visuals alone to get across information — some individuals may be unable to pick up such cues.
> - If you use video, provide captions to explain any sounds that won't be audible to some audience members.

Making your introduction and conclusion memorable

Listeners tend to remember beginnings and endings most readily, so try to make these sections memorable. Consider, for example, using a startling statement, opinion, or question; a vivid anecdote; or a powerful quotation.

Using explicit structure and signpost language

Organize your presentation clearly and carefully, and give an overview of the main points at the outset. (You may want to recall these points toward the end of the talk.) Then, throughout your presentation, call attention to a new point by pausing before it and by using signpost language as an explicit transition: *The second crisis point in the breakup of the Soviet Union occurred shortly after the first* is more explicit than *Another thing went wrong.* (For a list of transitions, see 8e.) Repeated key words and ideas work as signposts, too.

Turning writing into a script for presentation

If you will be using a full script in your presentation, double- or triple-space it, and use fairly large print so that it will be easy for you to see. Try to end each page with the end of a sentence so that you won't have to pause while you turn a page. You may prefer to work from a detailed topic outline or from note cards. In any case, be sure to mark the places where you want to pause and to highlight the words you want to emphasize. To help listeners follow you, shorten long, complicated sentences, and use action verbs and concrete nouns.

The first example that follows is from an essay that the writer expects the audience to read. The second example contains the same information, but its writer plans to deliver it orally. Note how this second version uses explicit structure, signpost language, and repetition to make it easy to follow by ear. Note also how the student writer has rewritten complex sentences, marked his text for emphasis and pauses, and asked questions to involve the audience.

TEXT FROM A WRITTEN ESSAY

The Simpson family has occasionally been described as a "nuclear" family, which obviously has a double meaning: first, the family consists of two parents and three children, and, second, Homer works at a nuclear power plant with very relaxed safety codes. The overused label dysfunctional, when applied to the Simpsons, suddenly takes on new meaning. Every episode seems to include a scene in which son Bart is being choked by his father; the baby is being neglected; or Homer, transfixed by the television screen, is sitting in a drunken stupor. The comedy in these scenes comes from the exaggeration of commonplace household events (although some talk shows and news programs would have us believe that these exaggerations are not confined to the madcap world of cartoons).

TEXT REVISED FOR ORAL PRESENTATION

What does it mean to pick an overused label and to describe the Simpsons as a nuclear family? Clearly, a double meaning is at work. First, the Simpsons fit the dictionary meaning--a family unit consisting of two parents and some children. The second meaning, however, packs more of a punch. You see, Homer works at a nuclear power plant [pause here] with VERY relaxed safety codes!

Besides nuclear, another overused family label describes the Simpsons. Did everyone guess the label is dysfunctional? And like nuclear, when it comes to the Simpsons, dysfunctional takes on a whole new meaning.

Remember the scenes when Bart is choked by his father?

How about the many times the baby is neglected?

Or the classic view--Homer, transfixed by the TV screen, sitting in a drunken stupor!

My point here is that the comedy in these scenes often comes from double meanings--and from a lot of exaggeration of everyday household events.

Speaking from notes

Here are tips for speaking from notes rather than from a full script:

- In general, use one note card for each point in your presentation.
- Number the cards in case they get scrambled.
- On each card, start with the major point you want to make, in large bold text. Include subpoints in a bulleted list below, printed large enough for you to see easily.
- Include signpost language on each note, and use it to guide your listeners.

- Use color or brackets to mark material that you can skip if you run out of time.

The following note card for an introduction reminds the speaker to emphasize her title and her three points. She has highlighted signpost language and the card's number.

NOTE CARD FOR AN ORAL PRESENTATION

---

[1] Title: The Rise of the Graphic Novel

Graphic novels are everywhere — but where do they come from?

- First, from "funnies" in early American newspapers
- Second, from comics, esp. great-adventure comic books
- Finally, from focus on images and visuals throughout society

---

Integrating visuals

Visual information displayed on PowerPoint slides, posters, or other media during an oral presentation can add interest, clarify points, keep the speaker on track, and help members of the audience who learn better by listening *and* looking. For any visual information you display, remember to follow basic design principles (see Chapter 4), avoiding clutter and making information as legible as possible. In addition, be sure that all the information you show is clear, well organized, and relevant to your presentation. The following tips will ensure that your visuals work for rather than against your presentation.

DISPLAYING WRITTEN INFORMATION

- Ensure that your audience can read any written information you display with your presentation. Choose background and type colors that contrast well for easy reading. A poster heading should be at least 2 inches high; for text on a PowerPoint slide, use 44- to 50-point type for headings, and 30- to 34-point type for subheads.

- Use bulleted lists, not paragraphs, to guide your audience through your main points. Less is more when it comes to displaying writing.

USING POWERPOINT SLIDES

- Don't put too much information on one slide. Use no more than five bullet points (or no more than fifty words) — and don't simply read the bullet points. Instead, say something that will enhance the material on the slide.

- Use light backgrounds in a darkened room, and dark backgrounds in a lighted one.
- If you include audio or video clips, make sure they are audible.

GIVING POSTER PRESENTATIONS

- Include important text and at least one striking image, table, or figure.
- Near the bottom of the poster, ask a provocative question that hints at your conclusion.
- Include your name and other identifying or contact information.

USING HANDOUTS

- Use handouts for text too extensive to be presented during your talk.
- Unless you want the audience to look at handouts while you are speaking, distribute them at the end of your presentation.

Practicing your presentation

Prepare a draft of your presentation far enough in advance to allow for several run-throughs. Some speakers record their rehearsals and then revise based on the taped performance. Others practice in front of a mirror or in front of colleagues or friends, who can comment on content and style.

Make sure you will be heard clearly. If you are soft-spoken, concentrate on projecting your voice; if your voice tends to rise when you're in the spotlight, practice lowering the pitch. If you speak rapidly, practice slowing down. It's usually best to avoid sarcasm in favor of a tone that conveys interest in your topic and listeners.

Timing your run-throughs will tell you whether you need to cut (or expand) material to make the presentation an appropriate length.

Making your presentation

To calm your nerves and get off to a good start, know your material thoroughly and use the following strategies to good advantage before, during, and after your presentation:

- Visualize your presentation with the aim of feeling comfortable during it.
- Consider doing some deep-breathing exercises before the presentation, and concentrate on relaxing; avoid too much caffeine.
- Pause before you begin, concentrating on your opening lines.
- If possible, stand up. Most speakers make a stronger impression standing rather than sitting.
- Face your audience at all times, and make eye contact as much as possible.

- Allow time for the audience to respond and ask questions.
- Thank your audience at the end of your presentation.

SLIDES AND SCRIPT FROM A STUDENT'S POWERPOINT PRESENTATION

Following is a portion of a PowerPoint presentation prepared by student Jennifer Bernal in response to an assignment to analyze a graphic novel. The excerpts from her script show highlights that cue slides or remind her what to point out. Note that she cites each source on the slides; her list of sources appears on her final slide, not shown here.

Student Writer

Jennifer Bernal

[slide 1] Hello, I'm Jennifer Bernal. And I've been thinking about the voice of the child narrator in the graphic novel *Persepolis* by Marjane Satrapi, an autobiographical narrative of a young girl's coming of age in Iran during the Islamic revolution. My research questions seemed fitting for a child: what? how? why? What is the "child's voice"? How is it achieved? Why is it effective? The child's voice in this book is characterized by internal conflict: the character sometimes sounds like a child and sometimes like an adult. She truly is a child on the threshold of adulthood. I'm going to show how Satrapi expresses the duality of this child's voice, not only through content but also through her visual style.

[slide 2] The main character, Marjane, faces a constant conflict between childhood and adulthood. But the struggle takes place not only between the child and the adults in her society but also between the child and the adult within Marjane herself. For example, Marjane is exposed to many ideas and experiences as she tries to understand the world around her. Here [first image] we see her suprising an adult by discussing Marx. But we also see her being a kid. Sometimes, like all children, she is unthinkingly cruel: here [second image] we see her upsetting another little girl with the horrifying (and, as it turns out, incorrect) "truth" about her father's absence.

The Child's Voice through Content

Fig. 1 - from Marjane Satrapi, *Persepolis* (New York: Pantheon, 2003) 59.

Fig. 2 - from Satrapi 48.

[slide 3] In her review of *Persepolis* for the *Village Voice,* Joy Press says that "Satrapi's supernaive style . . . persuasively communicates confusion and horror through the eyes of a precocious preteen." It seems to me that this simple visual style is achieved through repetition and filtering. Let's take a look at this. [point to slide] First, there's *repetition* of elements. We often see the same images being used over and over. Sometimes [point to first image] the repetition suggests the sameness imposed by the repressive government. At other times similar images are repeated throughout the book for emphasis. For example [point to examples], on several occasions we see her raising her finger and speaking directly to the reader to make an emphatic point. The repetition throughout *Persepolis* makes it look and feel more like a children's book. . . .

The Child's Voice through Visual Style: Repetition

Fig. 3 from Marjane Satrapi, *Persepolis* (New York: Pantheon, 2003) 96.

Figs. 4, 5, 6 - from Satrapi 19, 114, 117.

 bedfordstmartins.com/everydaywriter For other examples of effective presentations, click on **Student Writing Models**.

EXERCISE 3.1

Attend a lecture or presentation on your campus, and analyze its effectiveness. How does the speaker capture and hold your interest? What signpost language and other guides to listening can you detect? How well are visuals integrated into the presentation? How do the speaker's tone of voice, dress, and eye contact affect your understanding and appreciation (or lack of it)? What is most memorable about the presentation, and why? Bring your analysis to class, and report your findings.

3c   Online presentations

You may have the opportunity to make a presentation online by speaking into a camera that captures your presentation and relays it, via the Internet, to viewers anywhere in the world. Most strategies for online presentations are the same as for other multimedia presentations, but keep these special considerations in mind:

- Practice extensively, since viewers and listeners expect online presentations to be polished and accurately timed. Be especially certain that you can immediately access everything you need online.

- Speak clearly and enunciate your words carefully; it is often difficult to hear what people are saying online.
- Remember to look into the camera. This allows your audience eye contact with you, whether you can see them or not.
- Assume that your microphone is always live, so don't say anything that you don't want your audience to hear.

EXERCISE 3.2: THINKING CRITICALLY

Study the text of an oral or multimedia presentation you've prepared or given. Using the advice in this chapter, see how well your presentation appeals to your audience. Look in particular at how well you catch and hold their attention. How effective is your use of signpost language or other structures that help guide your listeners? How helpful are the visuals (PowerPoint slides, posters) in conveying your message? What would you do to improve this presentation?

Design for College Writing

Because visual and design elements such as headings, lists, fonts, images, and graphics can help us get and keep a reader's attention, they bring a whole new dimension to writing — what some refer to as *visual rhetoric*. This chapter will help you design your documents and use visual elements effectively.

4a Visual structure

Effective writers consider the visual structure of any text they create and guide readers by making design decisions that are easy on the eyes and easy to understand.

Print and electronic options

One of your first document design decisions will be choosing between print delivery and electronic delivery. In general, print documents are easily portable and relatively fast to produce. In addition, the tools for producing print texts are highly developed and stable. Electronic documents, on the other hand, can include sound, animation, and video; updates are easy to make; distribution is fast and efficient; and feedback can be swift. In many writing situations, the assignment will tell you whether to create a print or electronic text. Whether you are working to produce a document to be read in print or on a screen, however, you should rely on some basic design principles.

Design principles

Most design experts begin with several very simple principles that guide the design of all texts. These principles are illustrated in the documents shown on pp. 28–30. (For more on the design of nonprint documents, see Chapter 3.)

- *Contrast.* The contrast in a design attracts and guides readers around the document. You may achieve contrast through color, icons, boldface or large type, white space (areas without type or graphics), and so on. Begin with a focal point — the dominant visual or words on the page or screen — and structure the flow of all your other information from this point.

- *Proximity.* Whether they are text or visuals, parts of a document that are topically related should be physically close (*proximate* to one another).

- *Repetition.* Readers are guided in large part by the repetition of key words or design elements. You can take advantage of this principle by using color, type style, and other visual elements consistently throughout the document.

- *Alignment.* This principle refers to how visuals and text on a page are lined up, both horizontally and vertically. The headline, title, or banner on a document, for example, should be carefully aligned horizontally so that the reader's eye is drawn easily along one line from left to right. Vertical alignment is equally important. In general, you can choose to align things with the left side, the right side,

The Centers for Disease Control and Prevention site uses contrasting colors effectively by placing white type against a dark blue background and dark type against lighter-colored backgrounds. The site also demonstrates proximity, placing each image above its label and supporting text.

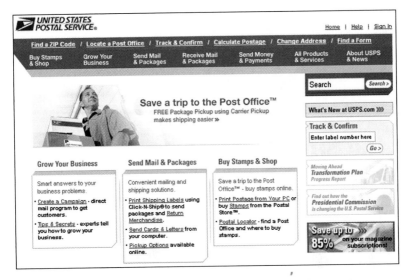

The U.S. Postal Service site repeats the red and blue horizontals from the home page, shown here, on many other screens. The site also makes the content's alignment clear by placing information in boxes under three major headings.

or the center of a page or screen. If you begin with left alignment, stick with it. The result will be a cleaner and more organized look.

- *Overall impression.* Aim for a design that creates the appropriate overall impression or mood for your document. For an academic essay, you will probably make conservative choices that strike a serious scholarly note. In a newsletter for a campus group, you might choose bright colors and arresting images.

4b Appropriate formats

Because writers have so many design possibilities to choose from, it's important to spend some time thinking about the most appropriate format for a document. Although the following basic formatting guidelines often apply, remember that print documents, Web pages, multimedia presentations, videos, and other genres all have their own formatting conventions.

Margins and white space

The margins and other areas of white space in a print or electronic document guide readers around the page. Since the eye takes in only so

A BROCHURE USING WHITE SPACE EFFECTIVELY

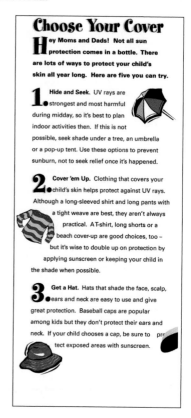

The inviting white space on the cover of this brochure sets off the title dramatically. On interior pages, white space sets off the images, marks section breaks, and frames the text for a clean, readable look.

much data in one movement, very long lines can be hard to read. Set margins so that the average line includes about twelve words (or sixty-five characters). Use white space around graphics, headings, or lists to make them stand out.

Color

Your use of color should relate to the purpose(s) of your document and its intended audience. As you design documents, keep in mind that some colors (red, for example) can evoke powerful responses, so take care that the colors you use match the message you want to send and the mood you want to create. Here are some other tips for using color:

- Use color to draw attention to elements you want to emphasize: headings and subheadings, bullets, text boxes, parts of charts or graphs, and other visuals.
- Be consistent in your use of color; use the same color for all main headings, for example.
- For most documents, keep the number of colors fairly small; too many colors can create a jumbled or confused look. In addition, avoid colors that clash or that are hard on the eyes (certain shades of yellow, for example). Check to make sure that all color visuals and text are legible.
- Remember that when colors are printed or projected, they may not look the same as they do on your computer screen.
- Look for examples of effective use of color. Find color combinations that you think look especially good — and then try them out.

Certain color combinations clash and are hard to read.

Other combinations are easier on the eyes.

CONSIDERING DISABILITIES
Color for Contrast

Remember that not everyone will see color as you do. Some individuals don't perceive color at all. When putting colors next to one another, then, try to use those that reside on opposite sides of the color spectrum, such as purple and yellow, in order to achieve high contrast. Doing so will allow readers to see the contrast between, if not the nuances of, colors.

Paper

The quality of the paper and the readability of the type affect the overall look and feel of print documents. Although inexpensive paper is fine for your earlier drafts, use $8\frac{1}{2}$" × 11" good-quality white paper for your final drafts. For résumés, you may wish to use parchment or cream-colored paper. For brochures and posters, colored paper may be most appropriate. Try to use the best-quality printer available to you for your final product.

Pagination

Your instructor may ask you to follow a particular format (see Chapters 48–54 for format preferences in well-known documentation styles); if not, beginning with the first page of text, place your last name and the page number in the upper-right-hand corner of the page.

Type

Computers allow writers to choose among a great variety of type sizes and typefaces, or fonts. For most college writing to be printed or read on a screen, 10- to 12-point type sizes are best. A serif font (as used in the main text of this book) is generally easier to read than a sans serif font. And although unusual fonts might seem attractive at first glance, readers may find such fonts distracting and hard to read over long stretches of material.

Remember that typefaces help you create the tone of a document, so consider your audience and purpose when selecting type.

Different fonts convey different feelings.
Different fonts convey different feelings.
DIFFERENT FONTS CONVEY DIFFERENT FEELINGS.
Different fonts convey different feelings.

Most important, be consistent in the size and style of type you choose. Unless you are striving for some special effect, shifting sizes and fonts can give an appearance of disorderliness.

Spacing

Final drafts for most print documents in college should be double-spaced, with the first line of paragraphs indented one-half inch or five spaces. Other documents, however, may call for different spacing. Letters, memos, lab reports, and Web texts, for example, are usually single-spaced, with no paragraph indentation; instead, single-spaced documents usually add extra space between paragraphs to make the text easier to read. Other kinds of documents, such as flyers and newsletters, may call for multiple columns of text. Consult a style guide (such as the *MLA Handbook*), or ask your instructor about appropriate spacing.

4c   Effective headings

In longer documents, headings call attention to the organization of the text and thus aid comprehension. Some kinds of reports have standard headings (like *Abstract* or *Summary*), which readers expect (and writers therefore should provide). If you use headings, you need to decide on type size and style, wording, and placement.

Type size and style

This book uses multiple levels of headings distinguished by different type sizes and fonts as well as by color. In a college paper, you will usually distinguish levels of headings using only type — for example, all capitals for the first-level headings, capitals and lowercase boldface for the second level, capitals and lowercase italics for the third level, and so on.

FIRST-LEVEL HEADING

Second-Level Heading

Third-Level Heading

On page 32, "4c Effective headings" is a first-level head; "Type size and style" above is a second-level head.

Consistent headings

Look for the most succinct and informative way to word your headings. Most often, state the topic in a single word, usually a noun (*Toxicity*); in a phrase, usually a noun phrase (*Levels of Toxicity*) or a gerund phrase (*Measuring Toxicity*); in a question that will be answered in the text (*How Can Toxicity Be Measured?*); or in an imperative that tells readers what steps to take (*Measure the Toxicity*). Whichever structure you choose, make sure you use it consistently for all headings of the same level. Remember also to position each level of heading consistently throughout your paper.

4d Effective visuals

Creating a visual design is more likely than ever before to be part of your process of planning for a completed writing project. Visuals can help make a point more vividly and succinctly than words alone. In some cases, visuals may even be your primary text.

Selecting visuals

Consider carefully what you want visuals to do for your writing before making your selections. What will your audience want or need you to show? Try to choose visuals that will enhance your credibility, allow you to make your points more emphatically, and clarify your overall text. (See the following table for advice on which visuals are best for particular situations.)

Effective visuals can come from many sources — your own drawings or photographs, charts or graphs you create on a computer, or materials created by others. If you are using a visual from another source, be sure to give appropriate credit and to get permission before using any visual that will be posted online or otherwise available to the public.

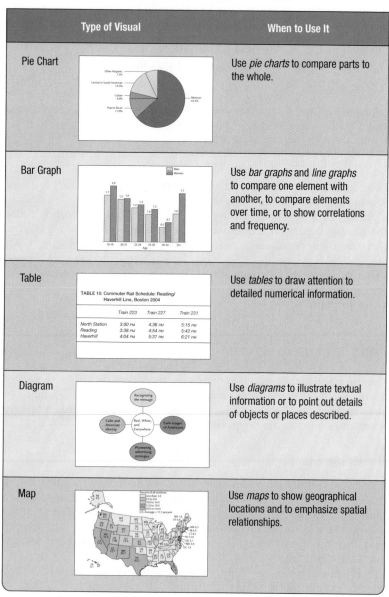

Type of Visual		When to Use It
Pie Chart		Use *pie charts* to compare parts to the whole.
Bar Graph		Use *bar graphs* and *line graphs* to compare one element with another, to compare elements over time, or to show correlations and frequency.
Table		Use *tables* to draw attention to detailed numerical information.
Diagram		Use *diagrams* to illustrate textual information or to point out details of objects or places described.
Map		Use *maps* to show geographical locations and to emphasize spatial relationships.

(continued)

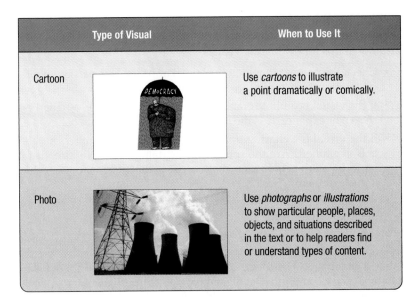

Type of Visual	When to Use It
Cartoon	Use *cartoons* to illustrate a point dramatically or comically.
Photo	Use *photographs* or *illustrations* to show particular people, places, objects, and situations described in the text or to help readers find or understand types of content.

Identifying visuals in your writing

Position visuals alongside or after the text that refers to them. Number your visuals (number tables separately from other visuals), and give them informative titles. In some instances, you may need to provide captions to give readers additional data such as source information.

Figure 1. College Enrollment for Men and Women by Age, 2007 (in millions)

Table 1. Word Choice by Race: *Seesaw* and *Teeter-totter,* Chicago, 1986

Analyzing and altering visuals

Technical tools available to writers and designers today make it relatively easy to manipulate visuals. For example, the image below on the far left was circulated widely via email as a *National Geographic* Photo of the Year. Instead, the photograph was a collage that a digital artist had made of two separate pictures — the photo in the middle, from *National Geographic,* and the photo on the right, from the U.S. Air Force Web site.

As you would with any source material, carefully assess any visuals you find for effectiveness, appropriateness, and validity. Here are additional tips for evaluating visuals:

- Check the context in which the visual appears. Is it part of an official government, school, or library site?
- If the visual is a photograph, are the date, time, place, and setting shown or explained? Is the information about the photo believable?
- If the visual is a chart, graph, or diagram, are the numbers and labels explained? Are the sources of the data given? Will the visual representation help readers make sense of the information, or could it mislead them? (See 12f.)
- Is biographical and contact information for the designer, artist, or photographer given?

At times, you may make certain changes to visuals that you use, such as cropping an image to show the most important detail or digitally brightening a dark image. Here, for example, are separate photos of a mountaintop cabin and a composite that digitally combines the originals into a single panoramic image to convey the setting more accurately. As long as the photograph is identified as a composite, the alteration is ethical.

Combining photos can sometimes be an appropriate choice.

This composite photo conveys the setting more effectively than the individual images.

To ensure that alterations to images are ethical, follow these guidelines:

- Do not attempt to mislead readers. Show things as accurately as possible.
- Tell your audience what changes you have made.
- Include all relevant information about the visual, including the source.

> **bedfordstmartins.com/everydaywriter** For more on effective design, go to **Writing Resources** and click on **Design Tutorials**.

AT A GLANCE

Using Visuals Effectively

- Use visual elements for a specific purpose in your text — to illustrate something, to help prove a point, or to guide readers, for example.
- Tell the audience explicitly what the visual demonstrates, especially if it presents complex information. Do not assume readers will "read" the visual the way you do; your commentary on it is important.
- Number and title all visuals. Number and label tables and figures separately.
- Refer to each visual *before* it appears.
- Follow established conventions for documenting visual sources, and ask permission for use if your work will become available to the public. (17c and e)
- Get responses to your visuals in an early draft. If readers can't follow them or are distracted by them, revise accordingly.
- If you crop, brighten, or otherwise alter visuals to include them in your writing, be sure to do so ethically. (4d)

EXERCISE 4.1: THINKING CRITICALLY

Examine a piece of writing you have done recently — an essay, a report, or a term project. First, look at the layout of the text: How visually appealing is it? Is the text easy to read? Do you use subheadings, color, or type size and font in ways that help convey your message? Do you include visuals in this piece of writing? Why, or why not? Consider how visuals (or additional visuals) could be helpful in presenting the information in the most memorable and readable way, and note any other changes that would enhance how your intended audience will perceive this piece of writing.

4e   Sample documents

A group of annotated documents collected from college students and others follow; these samples should help you create similar documents of your own. (For examples of academic essays, see Chapters 13 and 51–54.)

bedfordstmartins.com/everydaywriter   For more sample documents, click on **Student Writing Models.**

FIRST PAGE OF A REPORT (ON THE WEB)

Action-group sponsor clearly identified

Logo in distinctive font

Color used only in headings, visuals, and links

Structure of overall report clearly presented

Informative section heading appears in large type

Sources clearly cited in text

Visual suggests extent of problem

Double spacing between paragraphs

Pull-quote emphasizes possible solution

NEWSLETTER

Organization logo uses distinctive visual

NEWS

WEST COAST
environmental law

Sponsoring organization identified

Volume 26:01 June 12, 2000   **FROM WEST COAST ENVIRONMENTAL LAW**

Public interest environmental law for British Columbia

Question used as attention-getting title

Safe to Drink?

Italics signal overview of problem

The events in Walkerton, Ontario, provide an urgent wake-up call: BC has the highest per capita incidence of water-borne disease of any province in Canada, and the province is not adequately protecting drinking water sources from human related impacts.

The tragic events that have recently unfolded in Walkerton, Ontario, should provide a wake-up call to governments across the country because the agenda of downsizing environment ministries, privatizing government inspection and monitoring services, and abandoning environmental regulation is not unique to the Harris government. We have known for some time that there are very real human costs associated with failing to ~~protect the air we breathe and the~~ water we drink — the horrendous impacts of the E. coli contamination of drinking water in Walkerton remind us of how immediate those consequences can be.

Text wraps around appropriate visual

BC's drinking water is at risk
There is certainly no reason for BC residents to be complacent when it comes to water quality. In fact this province has an ignominious record when it comes to safe drinking water. Here are the troubling statistics:

Double spacing between sections of text

Bullets call out important statistics

* BC has the highest per capita incidence of water-borne disease of any province in Canada. A 1998 government study reported that there had been 27 outbreaks of toxoplasmosis, cryptosporidium, giardia, and other diseases in the past eighteen years.
* The CVRD's water supply frequently exceeds the minimum federal guidelines for water turbidity. It is the only unfiltered Canadian water

supply which often exceeds the standards on which Canada's safe drinking water guidelines are based.
* Contamination is a serious problem for some provincial groundwater sources. For example, drinking water guidelines for nitrate-nitrogen are not being met in certain aquifers because of contamination from manure and fertilizers.
* The government's first Water Quality Status Report of April 1996 found that of 124 water-bodies surveyed, only 60% had source waters which fell into the "good to excellent" category for drinking water purposes. Even for the 60% in that category, disinfection was still required.
* Over 200 BC communities are on permanent "boil water" advisories, i.e. they cannot safely drink the water from their tap without boiling it first.

Audit brings bad news
A disturbing indictment of the province's efforts to ensure safe drinking water for BC residents was recently offered by the Auditor General (Protecting Drinking Water Sources 1998/99). According to the Auditor: "...the province is not adequately protecting drinking water sources from human

related impacts, and this could have significant cost implications in the future for the province, for municipal governments and for citizens in general."

The Auditor pointed the finger at the lack of a coherent and integrated approach to land use management. The role of the Ministry of Forests in watershed and agricultural land management is particularly problematic because it bears so little responsibility for the impact or costs associated with poor management decisions. Unfortunately, the Auditor's mandate didn't extend to examining the adequacy of the province's legislative framework for protecting water. Had it, he would have no doubt noted the inadequate patchwork of water quality regulation in BC.

For instance, BC is the only Canadian province with no groundwater protection legislation. While safe drinking water regulations have been established under the *Health Act*, only one of hundreds of water quality guidelines is actually given the force of regulatory protection. Even where regulatory controls exist, inadequate monitoring and indifferent enforcement policies often render them ineffective.

see Safe to Drink?, continued on page 2

Visuals indicate what's coming up inside the newsletter

2 Emissions Trading: the great leap forward?
3 Is Canada Sinking Kyoto?

4 Blowing Cold over Hot Air
5 Chinese brochures
5 Fish habitat workshops

6 Environmental Dispute Resolution Fund in Action
7 In Good Company

FLYER

Light background with starkly contrasting visual gets attention

Central image draws attention and alludes to well-known film, *The Usual Suspects*

Typefaces and sizes used consistently to differentiate sections of the flyer

Related information grouped together for easy reading

Web site address featured prominently for further information

HOME PAGE

Eye-catching graphic makes attractive background

Menu shows portfolio pieces

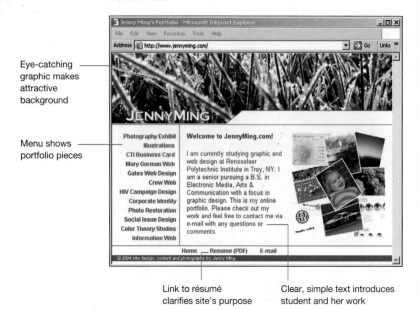

Link to résumé clarifies site's purpose

Clear, simple text introduces student and her work

The Writing Process

There may be people who like various aspects of the writing process. For some, it may be the excitement of facing a blank page. (Hate them!) For others, it could be a sense of getting a sentence just right. (Jerks!) There may be those who like the revision process, who can go over what they've produced with a cold eye and a keen ear and feel a satisfaction in making it better. (Liars!)

— RACHEL TOOR

The Writing Process

Writing Situations **5**

What do a magazine article on stem-cell research, a blog about home-schooling, an email to an Internet service provider about spam filtering, and an engineering report on a proposed dam site all have in common? To succeed, the writers of all four must analyze a complex situation and respond to it effectively.

5a Write to connect.

If it is true that "no man [or woman!] is an island," then it is equally true that no piece of writing is an island, isolated and alone. Instead, writing is connected to a web of other writings as a writer extends, responds to, or challenges what others say. This has always been the case, but now that messages can circle the globe in seconds, it's especially important to remember this principle: all writing exists within a rich and broad context in which every writer says or writes something to others for a purpose. As a writer today, you need to remember several key points:

- Writing can use a wide range of tools — from pencils to software and video — to convey messages.
- Writing is visual as well as verbal; design elements are key to the success of many documents.
- Writing is often collaborative — from planning to designing and producing the final product.
- Writing increasingly involves global communication and includes multiple languages and cultures.
- Writing has the potential to reach massive audiences in a very, very short time.
- Writing today is increasingly public; once on the Web, it can take on a life of its own. As a result, writers need to consider their own — and others' — privacy.

5b Understand rhetorical situations.

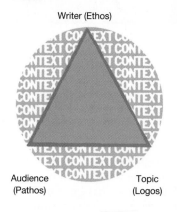

Writer (Ethos)

Audience
(Pathos)

Topic
(Logos)

A *rhetorical* situation is one that a writer analyzes, looking at it from all possible points of view and considering each element of the situation carefully. Of the many possible elements in a rhetorical situation, the most important include the topic and purpose; the audience being addressed; the speaker or writer; and the context, including time and space limitations, the medium and genre, tone and style, and level of language. Careful choices about all these elements are necessary for effective communication to take place.

It can be helpful to think of the rhetorical situation in visual terms.

Imagine this triangular representation of the rhetorical situation as dynamic, with all the angles interacting with one other and with the context. In addition to the key elements of audience, writer, and topic, we've introduced three additional terms that are very helpful in thinking through a rhetorical situation: *ethos, pathos,* and *logos*. Some 2,500 years ago, Aristotle identified these terms as basic appeals any speaker or writer could use. *Ethos* refers to the credibility of the writer or speaker; *pathos* to appeals to the heart — the emotions and values of the audience; and *logos* to appeals to reason or logic.

EXERCISE 5.1

Think back to a recent writing assignment. What helped you finally decide to write? Once you had decided to write, what exactly did you do to get going? In a paragraph or two, describe your situation, and answer these questions. Then compare your description with those of two or three classmates.

5c Consider your topic and audience.

Your topic

When the topic is left open, many writers put off getting started because they can't decide what to do. Experienced writers say that the best way to choose a topic is literally to let it choose you. Look to the topics that compel, puzzle, confuse, or pose a problem for you: these are likely to engage your interest and hence produce your best writing.

TALKING THE TALK

Assignments

"How do instructors come up with these assignments?" Assignments, like other kinds of writing, reflect particular rhetorical contexts that vary from instructor to instructor. Assignments also change over time. The assignment for an 1892 college writing contest was to write an essay "on coal." Later in the twentieth century, many college writing assignments asked students to write about their own experiences; in research conducted for this textbook in the 1980s, the most common writing assignment was a personal narrative. But assignments have kept changing in response to changes in expectations for college students and in the needs of society. Competing effectively in today's workforce calls for high-level thinking, for being able to argue convincingly, and for knowing how to do the research necessary to support a claim — so it's no surprise that college writing courses today give students assignments that allow them to develop such skills. A 2006 study of first-year college writing in the United States found that by far the most common assignment today asks students to compose a researched argument. (See Chapters 11–13.)

- What topics do you wish you knew more about?
- What topics get you really engaged and fired up?
- What about these topics is most confusing or infuriating or exciting to you?
- Who might be interested in this topic?
- What will you need to know to pursue this topic, and how will you go about finding information?

On the other hand, you may be given a topic to write about within an assignment from your instructor.

Your audience

Every writer can benefit from thinking carefully about who the audience is, what the audience already knows or thinks, and what the audience needs and expects to find out. Even if the writing can theoretically reach people all over the world (writing on the Web, for example), focus your analysis on those you most want to reach and those who are most likely to take an interest.

- In what ways are the members of your audience different from you? from one another?
- What assumptions can you legitimately make about your audience? What might they value?

START
by picking a **TOPIC.**

OR

START
by thinking about **AUDIENCE.**

What's my **FIRST CHOICE?**

How do I **FEEL** about my **TOPIC?**

If I'm bored with my topic, everyone else will be, too.

WHO are these people anyway? What do they **CARE** about?

HOW are they like me? **HOW** are they different?

Could I pick an even **BETTER IDEA?**

How can I tell them something they don't already know?

Run my favorite topic past a few other people....

HEY, _____ could be a great topic!

What's the best way to **REACH THEM?**

What do I need to **REMEMBER** about my audience?

How will an **AUDIENCE** react to this topic?

THINK about **PURPOSE.**

What **TOPIC** will appeal to this audience?

What's my **REASON** for **WRITING?**

What do I want my audience to **DO?**

"MY TEACHER TOLD ME TO" isn't a good enough purpose.

What **FORMAT** will work best? Web site? Research paper?

How much can I do by my **DEADLINE?**

To achieve my goal, should I do **RESEARCH?**

HOW LONG

should my writing be?

Can I make my **AUDIENCE, TOPIC,** and **PURPOSE** work together? *IF NOT, START AGAIN.*

I KNOW MY AUDIENCE!

I LIKE MY TOPIC!

I HAVE A PURPOSE!

I'M ON THE RIGHT TRACK!

CONSIDERING DISABILITIES

Your Whole Audience

Remember that considering your whole audience means thinking about members with varying abilities and special needs. Approximately one in five Americans was living with a disability in the year 2000. All writers need to think carefully about how their words reach out and connect with such very diverse audiences.

- What do members of your audience already know about your topic? Do you need to provide background information or to define terms?
- What sorts of information and evidence will your audience find most compelling — quotations from experts? personal experiences? photographs? diagrams or charts?
- What kinds of appeals will be most effective in reaching this audience?
- What response(s) do you want to evoke?

As you think about your readers, consider how you want them to respond to both the words and the images you use. Be particularly aware that images will often evoke very strong responses in your audience, so choose them with special care. What audience(s), for example, can you imagine for this image from an early Ramones performance? How do you think different audiences would respond to this image?

EXERCISE 5.2

The following assignment was given to an introductory business class: "Discuss in an essay the contributions of the Apple and Microsoft companies to the personal computing industry." What would you need to know about the assignment in order to respond successfully? Using the questions in 5c and 5d, analyze this assignment.

EXERCISE 5.3

Consider a writing assignment you are currently working on. What are its purposes in terms of the assignment, the instructor, and you, the writer?

EXERCISE 5.4

Describe one of your courses to three audiences: your best friend, your parents, and a group of high school students attending an open house at your college. Then describe the differences in content, organization, and wording that the differences in audience led you to make.

5d Analyze the purpose of your writing.

- What is the primary purpose of the piece of writing — to explain? to persuade? to entertain? some other purpose? If you aren't sure, think about what you want to accomplish, or talk with the person who gave you the assignment. Are there secondary purposes to keep in mind?

- What purpose did the person who gave you the assignment want to achieve — to make sure you have understood something? to evaluate your thinking and writing abilities? to test your ability to think outside the box?

- What are your own purposes in this piece of writing — to respond to a question? to learn about a topic? to communicate your ideas? to express feelings? How can you achieve these goals?

- What, exactly, does the assignment ask you to do? Look for words such as *analyze, classify, compare, define, describe, explain, prove,* and *survey.* Remember that these words may differ in meaning from discipline to discipline.

- What information do you need to gather to complete the task?

- Should you limit — or broaden — the topic to make it more compelling to you and your audience? What problems does the assignment suggest? If you wish to redefine the assignment, check with the person who assigned it.

- What are the specific requirements of the assignment?

5e Analyze your position as a writer or speaker.

Thinking about your own position as a writer and your attitudes toward your topic and your audience — your *rhetorical stance* — is important to making sure you communicate well.

- What is your overall attitude toward the topic? How strong are your opinions?

- What social, political, religious, personal, or other influences account for your attitude?

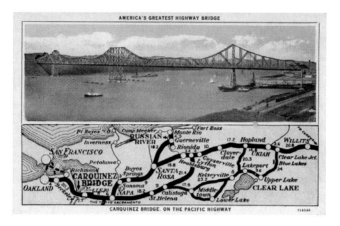

- What do you know about the topic? What questions do you have about it?
- What interests you *most* and *least* about the topic? Why?
- What seems important — or unimportant — about the topic?
- What preconceptions, if any, do you have about it?
- What do you expect to conclude about the topic?
- How will you establish your credibility (*ethos*); that is, how will you show that you are knowledgeable and trustworthy?

Images you choose to include in your writing can also help establish your credibility. Remember, however, that images always have a point of view or perspective. The postcard seen here, for example, illustrates two physical perspectives — a photograph of a highway bridge and a road map showing its location — as well as a time perspective — from 1927, when the bridge was new. Images also often reveal attitudes; this one, with its caption "America's Greatest Highway Bridge," sees the construction of the bridge as a triumph of modern technology. So when you choose an image, think hard about its perspective and about how well it fits in with your topic and purpose. Does the image have an attitude, and does that attitude serve the purpose of your writing?

5f   Consider other elements of the writing context.

As a writer, you'll want to consider a number of contextual elements that will help determine the form and scope of your project. In any writing you do, be sure to make choices that suit your topic, purpose, and audience.

Time and length

- How much time do you have to complete the writing? Do you need to schedule research? Be sure to allow time for revision and editing.
- How long is the finished draft of the writing supposed to be? How much space or bandwidth is available for your work? If you are writing a presentation, what time limits do you face for delivering it?

Medium and genre

You may be assigned — or able to choose — to work in a medium other than print, or in a genre other than a straightforward essay.

- What genre, or form, of writing does your task call for — a report? a review? an essay? a poem? a letter? a poster? a brochure? a Web site? a speech?
- Where and how will the writing appear — on the Internet? on a password-protected Web site? in a paper submitted to your instructor? in a spoken presentation? How will this affect the writing choices you make?
- Does the genre or medium require a particular format or method of organization? (See Chapter 7.)
- What design considerations should you keep in mind? Will your audience expect (or be interested in) visuals, such as illustrations, photographs, tables, or graphs? (See Chapter 4.)

Language and clarity

- Is the language as clear as it needs to be for the audience? If your readers can't understand what you mean, they're not likely to accept your points.
- If you need to produce academic writing, should you use any specialized varieties of English along with standard academic English? any occupational, professional, regional, or ethnic varieties? any words from a language other than English? any dialogue?
- Do the visuals and text make sense together?

Tone and style

- What tone do you want to achieve — humorous? serious? impassioned? ironic?
- What words, sentence structures, and visuals will help you achieve this tone?

- Is the tone of the writing appropriate to your audience and topic? Do the words or visuals you choose have the connotations you intend?

FOR MULTILINGUAL WRITERS

Bringing In Other Languages

Even when you write in English, you may want or need to include words, phrases, or whole passages in another language. If so, consider whether your readers will understand that language and whether you need to provide a translation. See 21d for more on bringing in other languages.

Remember that visual elements can have as much influence on the tone of your writing as the words you choose. Visuals create associations in viewers' minds: one reader may react much more positively than another to this Wal-Mart logo, for example, based on experiences shopping there or views about the company's business practices.

However, writers can influence how an image is perceived by carefully analyzing their audience and choosing visuals with a tone appropriate to the point they want to make. For example, in a serious academic essay about Albert Einstein, you would probably choose the first of the images below rather than the second or third — unless you were trying to make a point about Einstein's ability to poke fun at himself.

EXERCISE 5.5

Use a search engine to find a Web page you haven't visited before but that addresses a topic you know something about. Consider the following questions: What is the purpose of the Web page? Who is its intended audience? What rhetorical stance does it take? What overall impression does the page create, and how are color, visuals, and multimedia used to create that impression?

5g A sample writing situation

Let's take an example of how one writer analyzes a rhetorical situation. Emily Lesk, a student in a first-year English course, gets an assignment that asks her to "explore the ways in which one or more media have affected an aspect of American identity." (More examples of Emily's work appear in the following chapters.) Because Emily is interested in advertising, she plans first to investigate how advertising might help shape American identity. Deciding that such a broad topic is not manageable in the time she has available, however, she shifts her focus to advertising for one company that seems particularly "American," Coca-Cola.

Since Emily's primary audience includes her instructor and her classmates, she needs to find ways to connect with them on an emotional as well as a logical level. She will do so, she decides, first by telling a story about being drawn into buying Coca-Cola products (even though she didn't really like the soft drink) because of the power of the advertising. She thinks that others in her audience may have had similar experiences. Here is a portion of her story and the visual she chose to illustrate it:

> Even before setting foot in the Promised Land three years ago, I knew exactly where I could find the Coke T-shirt. The shop in the central block of Jerusalem's Ben Yehuda Street did offer other shirt designs, but the one with the bright white "Drink Coca-Cola Classic" written in Hebrew cursive across the chest was what drew in most of the dollar-carrying tourists. While waiting almost twenty minutes for my shirt (depicted in Fig. 1), I watched nearly everyone ahead of me say "the Coke shirt, *todah rabah* [thank you very much]."
>
> At the time, I never thought it strange that I wanted one, too. Yet, I *had* absorbed sixteen years of Coca-Cola propaganda.

Fig. 1. Hebrew Coca-Cola
T-shirt. Personal photograph.

Thinking about how she relates to her audience brings Emily to reflect more deeply on herself as the writer: Why has she chosen this topic? What does it say about her beliefs and values? What is her attitude toward her topic and toward her audience? What does she need to do to establish her credentials to write on this topic and to this audience?

Finally, Emily knows she will need to pay careful attention to the context in which she is writing: the assignment is due in two weeks, so she needs to work fast; the assignment calls for an essay written in academic English, though she plans to include some dialogue and a number of visuals to keep it lively; and since she knows she tends to sound like a know-it-all, she determines to work carefully on her tone and style.

EXERCISE 5.6: THINKING CRITICALLY

Reading with an Eye for Purpose and Audience

Advertisements provide good examples of writing that is tailored carefully for specific audiences. Find two ads for the same product that appeal to different audiences. You might compare ads in a men's magazine to those in a women's magazine to see what differences there are in the messages and photography. Take a look, for example, at advertisements for various kinds of drinks: Which seem designed to appeal primarily to men and which to women? What conclusions can you draw about ways of appealing to specific audiences?

Thinking about Your Own Attention to Purpose and Audience

Analyze a text you have written or are working on right now.

- Can you state its purpose(s) clearly and succinctly? If not, what can you do to clarify its purpose(s)?

- What other purposes for this piece of writing can you imagine? How would fulfilling some other purpose change the writing?

- Can you tell from reading the piece who the intended audience is? If so, what in your text clearly relates to that audience? If not, what can you add that will strengthen your appeal to this audience?

- What other audiences can you imagine? How would the writing change if you were to address a different audience? How would it change if you were writing to a largely unknown audience, such as people on the Web?

- Does your writing follow the conventions of standard academic English — and if not, how should you revise so that it will?

Note your conclusions about purpose and audience in your own writing.

6 | Exploring Ideas

The point is so simple that we often forget it: we write best about topics we know well. So among the most important parts of the entire writing process are choosing a topic that will engage your interest, exploring that topic by surveying what you know about it, and determining what you need to find out. You can explore a topic in many ways; the goal is to find strategies that work well for you.

6a Try brainstorming.

One of the best ways to begin exploring a topic is also the most familiar: talk it over with others. Consider beginning with a brainstorming session. Brainstorming means tossing out ideas — often with other people, either in person or online. You can also brainstorm by yourself.

1. Within a time limit of five or ten minutes, list every word or phrase that comes to mind about the topic. Jot down key words and phrases, not sentences. No one has to understand the list but you. Don't worry about whether or not something will be useful — just list as much as you can in this brief span of time.
2. If little occurs to you, try coming up with thoughts about the opposite side of your topic. If you are trying, for instance, to think of reasons to reduce tuition and are coming up blank, try concentrating on reasons to increase tuition. Once you start generating ideas in one direction, you'll find that you can usually move back to the other side fairly easily.
3. When the time is up, stop and read over the lists you have made. If anything else comes to mind, add it to your list. Then reread the list, looking for patterns of interesting ideas or one central idea.

6b Try freewriting or looping.

Freewriting is a method of exploring a topic by writing about it for a period of time *without stopping.*

1. Write for ten minutes or so. Think about your topic, and let your mind wander; write down whatever occurs to you. Don't worry about grammar or spelling. If you get stuck, write anything — just don't stop.
2. When the time is up, look at what you have written. You may discover some important insights and ideas.

If you like, you can continue the process by looping: find the central or most intriguing thought from your freewriting, and summarize it in a single sentence. Freewrite for five more minutes on the summary sentence, and then find and summarize the central thought from the second "loop." Keep this process going until you discover a clear angle or something about the topic that you can pursue.

CONSIDERING DISABILITIES

Freespeaking

If you are better at talking out than writing out your ideas, try freespeaking, which is basically the talking version of freewriting. Speak into a tape recorder or into a computer with voice-recognition software, and keep talking about your topic for at least seven to ten minutes. Say whatever comes to your mind — don't stop talking. You can then listen to or read the results of your freespeaking and look for an idea to pursue at greater length.

6c Try drawing or making word pictures.

If you're someone who prefers visual thinking, you might either create a drawing about the topic or use figurative language — such as similes and metaphors — to describe what the topic resembles. Working with pictures or verbal imagery can sometimes also help illuminate the topic or uncover some of your unconscious ideas or preconceptions about it.

1. If you like to draw, try sketching your topic. What images do you come up with? What details of the drawing attract you

most? What would you most like to expand on? A student planning to write an essay on her college experience began by thinking with pencils and pen in hand. Soon she found that she had drawn a vending machine several times, with different products and different ways of inserting money to extract them (one of her drawings appears here). Her sketches led her to think about what it might mean to see an education as a product. Even abstract doodling can lead you to important insights about the topic and to focus your topic productively.

2. Look for figurative language — metaphors and similes — that your topic resembles. Try jotting down three or four possibilities, beginning with "My subject is _____" or "My subject is like _____." A student working on the subject of genetically modified crops came up with this: "Genetically modified foods are like empty calories: they do more harm than good." This exercise made one thing clear to this student writer: she already had a very strong bias that she would need to watch out for while developing her topic.

FOR MULTILINGUAL WRITERS

Using Your Native Language to Explore Ideas

For generating and exploring ideas — the work of much brainstorming, freewriting, looping, and clustering — you may be most successful at coming up with good ideas quickly and spontaneously if you work in your native language. Later in the process of writing, you can choose the best of these ideas and begin working with them in English.

6d Try clustering.

Clustering is a way of generating ideas using a visual scheme or chart. It is especially helpful for understanding the relationships among the parts of a broad topic and for developing subtopics. If you have a software program for clustering, put it to use. If not, follow these steps:

1. Write down your topic in the middle of a blank piece of paper or screen and circle it.
2. In a ring around the topic circle, write what you see as the main parts of the topic. Circle each part, and then draw a line from it to the topic.
3. Think of more ideas, examples, facts, or other details relating to each main part. Write each of these near the appropriate part, circle each one, and draw a line from it to the part.
4. Repeat this process with each new circle until you can't think of any more details. Some trails may lead to dead ends, but you will still have many useful connections among ideas.

Here is an example of the clustering Emily Lesk did for her essay about Coca-Cola and American identity:

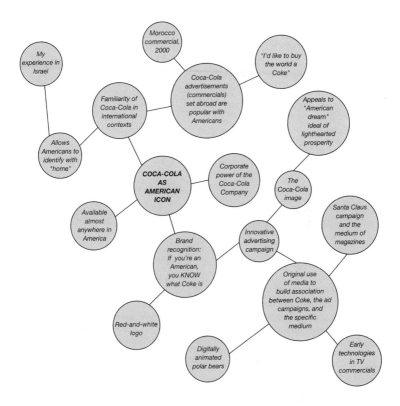

6e Ask questions.

Another basic strategy for exploring a topic and generating ideas is simply to ask and answer questions. Here are two widely used sets of questions to get you started.

Questions to describe a topic

Originally developed by Aristotle, the following questions can help you explore a topic by carefully and systematically describing it:

1. **What is it?** What are its characteristics, dimensions, features, and parts? What does it look like? What do other senses — taste, smell, touch, sound — tell you about it?

2. *What caused it?* What changes occurred to create your topic? How is it changing? How will it change?
3. *What is it like or unlike?* What features make your topic different from others? What comparisons can you make about your topic?
4. *What larger system is your topic a part of?* How does your topic fit into this system?
5. *What do people say about it?* What reactions does your topic arouse? What about the topic causes those reactions?

Questions to explain a topic

The well-known questions *who, what, when, where, why,* and *how,* widely used by news reporters, are especially helpful for explaining a topic.

1. *Who* is doing it?
2. *What* is at issue?
3. *When* does it begin and end?
4. *Where* is it taking place?
5. *Why* does it occur?
6. *How* is it done?

EXERCISE 6.1

Choose a topic that interests you, and explore it by using two of the strategies described in Chapter 6. When you have generated some material, you might try comparing your results with those of other members of the class to see how effective or helpful each strategy was. If you have trouble choosing a topic, use one of the preliminary working theses in Exercise 7.1.

6f Browse sources.

Look around in your library or on the Internet for a topic you want to learn more about. Many search engines have directories organized by topic that you can browse for ideas and sources. Some advanced searches allow you to search for only visual images, current events, and government sites and to otherwise specify your results.

 bedfordstmartins.com/everydaywriter For more on exploring topics, go to **Writing Resources** and click on **Links** to find useful directories online.

6g Collaborate.

The texts you write are shaped in part by conversations with others. You might also consider using online tools that facilitate collaborative writing, such as wikis, to gather ideas and generate drafts. Writers often work together to come up with ideas, to respond to one another's drafts, or even to coauthor something. Here are some strategies for working with others:

1. Establish a regular meeting time and exchange contact information.
2. Establish ground rules for the group. Be sure every member has an equal opportunity — and responsibility — to contribute.
3. With final deadlines in mind, set an agenda for each group meeting.
4. Listen carefully to what each person says. If disagreements arise, try paraphrasing to see if everyone is hearing the same thing.
5. Use group meetings to work together on particularly difficult problems. If an assignment is complex, have each member explain one section to all the others. If the group has trouble understanding part of the task, check with whoever made the assignment.
6. Expect disagreement, and remember that the goal is not for everyone just to "go along." The challenge is to get a really spirited debate going and to argue through all possibilities.
7. If you are preparing a group-written document, divide up the drafting duties. Set reasonable deadlines for each stage of work. Schedule at least two meetings to iron out the final draft by reading it aloud and working for consistency of tone. Have everyone proofread the final draft, with one person making the corrections.
8. If the group will be making a presentation, be sure you know exactly how much time you will have. Decide how each member will contribute to the presentation. Leave time for at least two practice sessions.
9. Make a point of assessing the group's effectiveness. What has the group accomplished? What has it done best? What has it been least successful at? What has each member contributed? How could the group function more effectively?

EXERCISE 6.2: THINKING CRITICALLY

Begin by making a list of all the ways in which you collaborate with others. Then reflect on the kinds of collaboration you find most effective. Finally, take an example of a recent collaboration you have been part of, and examine how well it worked by answering the following questions: What did I contribute to the collaboration? What worked well and did not work well? What could I have done to improve the collaboration?

Planning and Drafting

Some writers just plunge right into their work and develop it as they go along. Others find that they work more effectively by making detailed blueprints before they begin drafting. Your planning and drafting may fall anywhere along this spectrum. As you plan and draft, you narrow your topic, decide on your thesis, organize materials to support that central idea, and sketch out a plan for your writing. As one student said, this is the time in the writing process "when the rubber meets the road."

7a Narrow your topic.

After exploring ideas, you may have found a topic that interests you and would also be interesting to your readers. The topic, however, may be too large to be manageable. If that is the case, narrow your topic in order to focus on a more workable idea. Emily Lesk narrowed her original vast topic (American advertising) by asking herself questions.

TOPIC	American advertising
	Okay, what do I most want to know about this topic? How powerful is advertising? Could advertising be related to how we define "American"?
FIRST FOCUS ATTEMPT	American advertising and national identity
	Ah, I may be onto something. How about portrayals of women and how they affect U.S. identity? Better yet, how about choosing a particular company that might be linked to American identity: McDonald's? Weight Watchers? Coca-Cola? Chevrolet?
SECOND FOCUS ATTEMPT	Advertising icons that shape American identity
	Yes, but how many icons are there? LOTS — and I just named a few. Better choose one.
NARROWED TOPIC	Coca-Cola as a cultural icon that shapes American identity

7b Craft a working thesis.

Most academic or professional writing contains a thesis statement, often near the beginning. The thesis functions as a promise to readers, letting them know what the writer will discuss. You should establish a tentative working thesis early on in your writing process.

The word *working* is important here because the thesis may well change as you write — your final thesis may be very different from the working thesis you begin with. Even so, a working thesis focuses your thinking and research, and helps keep you on track.

GAME PLAN   Develop a Working Thesis

(SO FAR I've thought about my purpose, audience, and topic....)

Not sure what to say about the topic? START HERE.

Got something to say about the topic? START HERE.

THINK about my personal connection to the topic.

WHAT *INTERESTS* me about it?

WHAT *POINT* do I want to make?

WHAT is the most important thing to tell my audience?

OKAY! I CAN COMMENT ON MY TOPIC.

WHAT do I know about my topic?

WHAT do I need to find out?

Can I write a sentence that *DESCRIBES* my topic and comments on it?

Maybe I've got a **WORKING THESIS!**

If I'm just *STATING FACTS*, I don't have a thesis yet.

TEST THE SENTENCE.

Will it *GRAB* my audience's attention?

A *VAGUE* thesis is a boring thesis.

...stay focused...

An *OBVIOUS* thesis is a boring thesis, too.

Can I cover this topic in the *TIME* and *SPACE* I have, or would I have to write a book?

REWRITE until I have a sentence to work with.

I'VE MADE A COMMENT ON MY TOPIC!

IT'S INTERESTING, SPECIFIC, AND MANAGEABLE!

I HAVE A WORKING THESIS!

(and I can refine it—or change it—as I go)

A working thesis should have two parts: a topic, which indicates the subject matter the writing is about, and a comment, which makes an important point about the topic.

```
┌──────── TOPIC ────────┐  ┌──────── COMMENT ────────┐
```
▶ **The current health care crisis arises from three major causes.**

A successful working thesis has three characteristics:

1. It is potentially *interesting* to the intended audience.
2. It is as *specific* as possible.
3. It limits the topic enough to make it *manageable*.

You can evaluate a working thesis by checking it against each of these characteristics, as in the following example:

PRELIMINARY WORKING THESIS

▶ **Theories about global warming are being debated around the world.**

INTERESTING?	The topic itself holds interest, but it seems to have no real comment attached to it. The thesis merely states a bare fact, and the only place to go from here is to more bare facts.
SPECIFIC?	The thesis is not specific. Who is debating these theories? What is at issue in this debate?
MANAGEABLE?	The thesis is not manageable; it would require research on global warming in many countries.
ASSESSMENT:	This thesis can be narrowed by the addition of a stronger comment and a sharper focus.

REVISED WORKING THESIS

▶ **Working independently, scientists from several countries have now confirmed that global warming is demonstrably caused by humans.**

FOR MULTILINGUAL WRITERS

Stating a Thesis

In some cultures, it is considered rude to state an opinion outright. In the United States, however, academic and business practices require writers to make key positions explicitly clear.

EXERCISE 7.1

Choose one of the following preliminary working theses, and after specifying an audience, evaluate the thesis in terms of its interest, specificity, and manageability. Revise the working thesis as necessary to meet these criteria.

1. Homeland security presents the United States with an ongoing problem.
2. Vaccinations are dangerous.
3. Too many American parents try to micromanage their children's college education.
4. White-collar crime poses greater danger to the economy than street crime, even though the latter is more obvious.
5. An educated public is the key to a successful democracy.

EXERCISE 7.2

Using the topic you chose in Exercise 6.1, write a preliminary working thesis. Evaluate the thesis in terms of its interest, specificity, and manageability. Revise it as necessary to create a satisfactory working thesis.

7c Gather information to support your thesis.

Once you have a working thesis, consider whether you need to do research for your writing project. Your assignment may require research, or you may decide on your own to find out more about your topic or to locate visuals that will enhance your writing. You may even need to do research at more than one stage of the writing process as you define, narrow, and perhaps change your topic. Library research, online research, and field research can all help you find the information and visuals you need. (For more on conducting research and working with sources, see Chapters 15 and 16. For more on organizing your support into paragraphs, see Chapter 8.)

7d Organize information.

Remember to consider your audience, purpose, and topic as you think about how you will organize information to make it accessible and persuasive to your audience. At the simplest level, writers most often group information according to four principles — space, time, logic, and association.

Organizing according to space

The organizational principle of space refers to *where* bits of information occur within a setting. If the information you have gathered is descriptive, you may choose to organize it spatially. Using spatial organization allows the reader to "see" your information, to fix it in space.

INFORMATION ORGANIZED SPATIALLY

This photo shows the spatial arrangement described, with the darkened side areas for spectators and the brightly lighted front of the room. The photograph and writing together help readers see the scene vividly.

The scene was being filmed in a windowless building with a corrugated tin roof. We entered through the single side door and sat in folding chairs on a platform along one wall, separated from the rest of the room by beaded red curtains. Behind us was darkness. On the far wall, neon lights glowed dimly, illuminating a few unoccupied barstools on the other side of the room. But the front of the room was ablaze with light. Purple and white floodlights beamed down onto a circular dance floor, creating an almost supernatural glow. The film crew in the center of the room stood silhouetted against the light like an audience waiting for a show to begin.

Organizing according to time

The principle of time refers to *when* bits of information occur, usually chronologically. Chronological organization is the basic method used in cookbooks, lab reports, instruction manuals, and stories. Writers of these products organize information according to when it occurs in some process or sequence of events (narrative).

INFORMATION ORGANIZED CHRONOLOGICALLY

This photo series shows the rapid passage of time, with each image capturing an instant too fast to see with the eye alone. The image and text together give readers a clear idea of Muybridge's achievement.

In July of 1877, Eadweard Muybridge photographed a horse in motion with a camera fast enough to capture clearly the split second when the horse's hooves were all off the ground — a moment never before caught on film. Throughout the fall of that year, newspapers were full of the news of Muybridge's achievement. His next goal was to photograph a sequence of such rapid images. In the summer of

1878, he set up a series of cameras along a track and snapped successive photos of a horse as it galloped past. Muybridge's technical achievement helped to pave the way for the first motion pictures a decade later.

Organizing according to logic

The principle of logic refers to *how* bits of information are related logically. The most commonly used logical patterns include *illustration, definition, division and classification, comparison and contrast, cause and effect, problem and solution, use of analogies,* and *narration*. The example that follows organizes information logically, according to the principle of division. For other examples of paragraphs organized according to these logical patterns, see Chapter 8.

INFORMATION ORGANIZED LOGICALLY

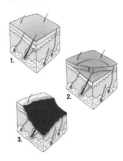

The images are logically arranged to show burns of increasing severity.

Burns can be divided into three types based on the severity of tissue damage: (1) Superficial, or first-degree, burns damage only the top layer of skin (epidermis). They are red and painful, but not serious. (2) Partial thickness, or second-degree, burns damage both the epidermis and the layer just below it (dermis). Second-degree burns, which can be very painful, are characterized by blistering, swelling, and redness. (3) Full thickness, or third-degree, burns destroy both the epidermis and the dermis and damage underlying muscle and other tissues. They appear charred and black. The burn area itself is numb, but the surrounding area can be very painful. Third-degree burns can be fatal if the percentage of affected skin is sufficiently large.

Organizing according to association

The principle of association refers to how bits of information are related in terms of visuals, motifs, personal memories, and so on. Many contemporary essays are organized through a series of associations that grow directly out of the writer's memory or experience. Thus, associational organization is often used in personal narrative, where writers can use a chain of associations to render an experience vividly for readers.

INFORMATION ORGANIZED ASSOCIATIONALLY

Flying from San Francisco to Atlanta, I looked down to see the gentle roll of the Smoky Mountains begin to appear. Almost at once, I was back on my Granny's porch, sitting next to her drinking iced tea and eating

*This image works by associ-
ation, its old-fashioned look
emphasizing the nostalgic
charm of homemade ice
cream and peaches.*

peaches. Those peaches tasted good —
picked ripe, skinned, and eaten with no
regard for the sweet juice trickling everywhere. And on special occasions, we'd
make ice cream, and Granny would
empty a bowl brimming with chopped
peaches into the creamy dish. Now — that
was the life!

In much of your writing, you will
want to use two or more principles of
organization. In addition, you may
want to include not only visuals but
sound and other multimedia effects
as well.

EXERCISE 7.3

Using the topic you chose in Exercise 6.1, identify the most effective means of organizing your information. Write a brief paragraph explaining why you chose this particular
method (or these methods) of organization.

AT A GLANCE

Organizing Visuals

- Use images and visuals to capture your readers' attention and interest
  in a vivid way, to emphasize a point you make in your text, to present
  information that is difficult to convey in words, or to communicate
  with audiences with different language skills.
- Consider how the image works as an image and in combination with
  the text, and think about how readers are likely to respond to it.
- Place each visual as near as possible to the text it illustrates.
- Introduce each visual clearly: *As the map to the right depicts.* . . .
- Comment on the significance or effect of the visual: *Figure 1 corrobo-
  rates the firefighters' statements.* . . .
- Label each visual appropriately, and cite the source.

7e   Make a plan.

At this point, you will find it helpful to create an organizational plan or
outline. To do so, simply begin with your thesis; review your exploratory
notes, research materials, and visuals; and then list all the examples and
other good reasons you have to support the thesis.

A sample organizational plan

One informal way to organize your ideas is to figure out what belongs in your introduction, body paragraphs, and conclusion. Here is how one student, who was writing about solutions to a problem, used this kind of plan:

WORKING THESIS

▶ **Increased motorcycle use demands the reorganization of campus parking lots.**

INTRODUCTION

give background and overview (motorcycle use up dramatically) and use a photograph of overcrowding in a lot

state purpose — to fulfill promise of thesis by offering solutions

BODY

describe the current situation (tell of my research at area parking lots)

describe the problem in detail (report on statistics; cars vs. cycles) and include a graph representing findings

present two possible solutions (enlarge lots or reallocate space)

CONCLUSION

recommend against first solution because of cost and space

recommend second solution, and summarize benefits of it

A formal outline

Even if you have made an informal written plan before drafting, you may also want — or be required — to prepare a formal outline, which can help you see exactly how the parts of your writing will fit together — how your ideas relate, where you need examples, and what the overall structure of your work will be. Most formal outlines follow a conventional format of numbered and lettered headings and subheadings, using roman numerals, capital letters, arabic numerals, and lowercase letters to show the levels of importance of the various ideas and their relationships. Each new level is indented to show its subordination to the preceding level.

Thesis statement
I. First main idea
   A. First subordinate idea
      1. First supporting detail or point
      2. Second supporting detail
      3. Third supporting detail

      B. Second subordinate idea
        1. First supporting detail
        2. Second supporting detail
   II. Second main idea
      A. First subordinate idea
        1. First supporting detail
        2. Second supporting detail
      B. Second subordinate idea
        1. First supporting detail
        2. Second supporting detail
          a. First supporting detail
          b. Second supporting detail

Note that each level contains at least two parts, so there is no A without a B, no 1 without a 2. Also keep in mind that headings should be stated in parallel form — either all sentences or all grammatically parallel structures.

A storyboard

The technique of storyboarding — working out a narrative or argument in visual form — can be a good way to come up with an organizational plan, especially if you are developing a Web site or other multimedia project. For such projects you can even find storyboard templates online to help you get started. For a typical college essay, however, you can create your own storyboard by using note cards or even sticky notes, taking advantage of different colors to keep track of threads of argument, subtopics, and so on. Remember that flexibility is a strong feature of storyboarding: you can move the cards and notes around, trying out different arrangements, until you find an organization that works well for your writing situation. Basic patterns for a storyboard include linear, hierarchical, and spoke-and-hub organization.

LINEAR ORGANIZATION

Use this when you want most readers to move in a particular order through your material. The Web report on p. 39 uses the following linear organization:

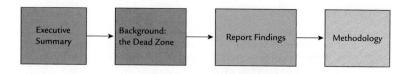

HIERARCHICAL ORGANIZATION

A hierarchy puts the most important material first, with subtopics branching out from the main idea. A multimedia presentation on dog bite prevention might be arranged like this:

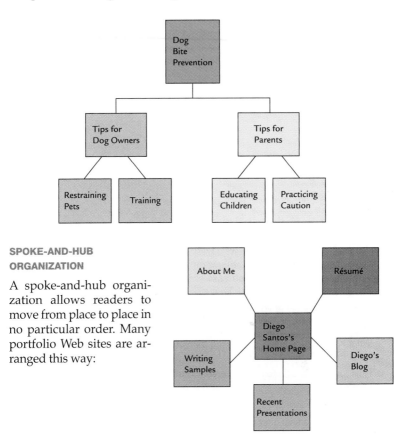

SPOKE-AND-HUB ORGANIZATION

A spoke-and-hub organization allows readers to move from place to place in no particular order. Many portfolio Web sites are arranged this way:

Whatever form your plan takes, you may want or need to change it along the way. Writing has a way of stimulating thought, and the process of drafting may generate new ideas. Or you may find that you need to reexamine some data or information or gather more material.

EXERCISE 7.4

Write out a plan for an essay supporting the working thesis you developed for Exercise 7.2.

7f Write out a draft.

No matter how good your planning, investigating, and organizing have been, chances are you will need to do more work as you draft. This fact of life leads to the first principle of successful drafting: be flexible. If you see that your plan is not working, don't hesitate to alter it. If some information now seems irrelevant, leave it out — even if you went to great lengths to obtain it. Throughout the drafting process, you may need to refer to points you have already written about. You may learn that you need to do more research, that your whole thesis must be reshaped, or that your topic is still too broad and should be narrowed further. Very often you will continue planning, investigating, and organizing throughout the writing process.

EXERCISE 7.5
Write a draft essay from the plan you produced for Exercise 7.4.

EXERCISE 7.6: THINKING CRITICALLY
Using the following guidelines, reflect on the process you went through as you prepared for and wrote your draft essay for Exercise 7.5. Make your answers an entry in your writing log if you are keeping one.

1. How did you arrive at your specific topic?
2. When did you first begin to think about the assignment?
3. What kinds of exploring or planning did you do? What kinds of research did you need to do?
4. How long did it take to complete your draft (including the time spent gathering information)?
5. Where did you write your draft? Briefly describe the setting.
6. How did awareness of your audience help shape your draft?
7. What have you learned from your draft about your own rhetorical stance on your topic?
8. What did you learn about your ideas for this topic by exploring, planning, and talking with others about it?
9. What do you see as the major strengths of your draft? What is your favorite sentence, and why?
10. What do you see as the major weaknesses of your draft? What are you most worried about, and why?
11. What would you like to change about your process of exploring, planning, and drafting?

AT A GLANCE

Drafting

- *Set up a computer folder or file for your essay.* Give the file a clear and relevant name, and save to it often. Number your drafts. If you decide to try a new direction, save the file as a new draft — you can always pick up with a previous one if the new version doesn't work out.

- *Have all your information close at hand and arranged according to your organizational plan.* Stopping to search for a piece of information can break your concentration or distract you.

- *Try to write in stretches of at least thirty minutes.* Writing can provide momentum, and once you get going, the task becomes easier.

- *Don't let small questions bog you down.* Just make a note of them in brackets — or in all caps — or make a tentative decision and move on.

- *Remember that first drafts aren't perfect.* Concentrate on getting all your ideas down, and don't worry about anything else.

- *Stop writing at a place where you know exactly what will come next.* Doing so will help you start easily when you return to the draft.

---

 bedfordstmartins.com/everydaywriter To see student drafts, click on **Student Writing Models**.

Developing Paragraphs

Paragraphs serve as signposts — pointers that help guide readers through a piece of writing. A look through a popular magazine will show paragraphs working this way: the first paragraph of an article almost always aims to get our attention and to persuade us to read on, and subsequent ones often indicate a new point or a shift in focus or tone.

Put most simply, a paragraph is a group of sentences or a single sentence set off as a unit. All the sentences in a paragraph usually revolve around one main idea.

8a Focus on a main idea.

An effective paragraph often focuses on one main idea. A good way to achieve such paragraph unity is to state the main idea clearly in one sentence and then relate all the other sentences in the paragraph to that idea. The sentence that presents the main idea is called the topic sentence.

AT A GLANCE
Editing Paragraphs

- Is there a topic sentence that makes the main idea of each paragraph clear? If not, should there be? (8a)
- Does the first sentence of each paragraph let readers know what that paragraph is about? Does the last sentence in some way conclude that paragraph's discussion? If not, does it need to?
- Within each paragraph, how does each sentence relate to the main idea? Revise or eliminate any that do not. (8a)
- How completely does each paragraph develop its main idea? What details and images are included? Are they effective? Do any paragraphs need more detail? (8b)
- What other methods of development might be used — definition? example? comparison and contrast? analogy? (8c)
- Is each paragraph organized in a way that is easy to follow? Are sentences within each paragraph clearly linked? Do any of the transitions try to create links between ideas that do not really exist? (8e)
- Are the paragraphs clearly linked? Do any links need to be added? Are any of the transitions from one paragraph to another artificial? (8e)
- How does the introductory paragraph catch readers' interest? How does the last paragraph draw the piece to a conclusion? (8f)

Announcing the main idea in a topic sentence

The following paragraph opens with a clear topic sentence, and the rest of the paragraph builds on the idea stated in that sentence:

> *Our friendship was the source of much happiness and many memories.* We grooved on every new recording from Jay-Z. We sweated together in the sweltering summer sun, trying to win the championship for our softball team. I recall the taste of pepperoni pizza as we discussed the highlights of our team's victory. Once we even became attracted to the same person, but luckily we were able to share his friendship.

FOR MULTILINGUAL WRITERS
Being Explicit

Native readers of English generally expect that paragraphs will have an explicitly stated main idea and that the connections between points in a paragraph will also be stated explicitly. Such step-by-step explicitness may strike you as unnecessary or ineffective, but it follows the traditional paragraph conventions of English.

A topic sentence does not always come at the beginning of a paragraph; it may come at the end. Occasionally a paragraph's main idea is so obvious that it need not be stated explicitly in a topic sentence.

EXERCISE 8.1

Choose an essay you have written, and identify the topic sentence of each paragraph, noting where in the paragraph the topic sentence appears or whether it is implied rather than stated. Experiment with one paragraph, positioning its topic sentence in at least two different places. What difference does the change make? If you have any implied topic sentences, try stating them explicitly. Does the paragraph become easier to read?

Relating each sentence to the main idea

Whether the main idea of a paragraph is stated in a topic sentence or is implied, make sure that all other sentences in the paragraph contribute to the main idea. In the preceding example about friendship, all of the sentences clearly relate to the point that is made in the first sentence. The result is a unified paragraph.

TALKING THE TALK

Paragraph Length

"How long should a paragraph be?" In college writing, paragraphs should address a specific topic or idea and develop that idea with examples and evidence. There is no set rule about how many sentences are required to make a complete paragraph. So write as many sentences as you need — and no more.

8b Provide details.

An effective paragraph develops its main idea by providing enough details — including visual details — to hold the reader's interest. Without such development, a paragraph may seem lifeless and abstract.

A POORLY DEVELOPED PARAGRAPH

No such thing as human nature compels people to behave, think, or react in certain ways. Rather, from our infancy to our death, we are constantly being taught, by the society that surrounds us, the customs, norms, and mores of a distinct culture. Everything in culture is learned, not genetically transmitted.

This paragraph is boring. Although its main idea is clear and its sentences hold together, it fails to gain our interest or hold our attention because it lacks any specific examples or details. Now look at the paragraph revised to include needed specifics.

THE SAME PARAGRAPH, REVISED

A child in Los Angeles decorates a Christmas tree with shiny red ornaments and sparkling tinsel. A few weeks later, a child in Beijing celebrates the Chinese New Year with feasting, firecrackers, and gift money in lucky red envelopes. It is not by instinct that one child knows how to decorate the tree while the other knows how to celebrate the New Year. No such thing as human nature compels people to behave, think, or react in certain ways. Rather, from the time of our infancy to our death, we are constantly being taught, by the society that surrounds us, the customs, norms, and mores of one or more distinct cultures. Everything in culture is learned, not genetically transmitted.

Though both paragraphs present the same point, only the second one comes to life. It does so by bringing in specific details *from* life, including images that show readers what the paragraph describes. We want to read this paragraph because it appeals to our senses (shiny red ornaments, firecrackers) and our curiosity (why are red envelopes considered lucky?).

Details are important not only in written texts but in visual ones as well. If you decide to use an image because of a particular detail, for instance, make sure that your readers will notice the detail you want them to see — crop out any unnecessary information and clarify what's important about the image with a caption.

EXERCISE 8.2

Choose one of the following topic sentences, and spend some time exploring the topic (see Chapter 6). Then write a paragraph that includes the topic sentence. Make sure that each of the other sentences relates to it. Assume that the paragraph will be part of a letter you are writing to an acquaintance.

1. I found out quickly that college life was not quite what I had expected.
2. Being part of the "in crowd" used to be essential to me.
3. My work experience has taught me several important lessons.
4. Until recently, I never appreciated my parents fully.
5. I expect my college education to do more than assure me of a job.

EXERCISE 8.3

Choose an essay you have written recently, and examine the second, third, and fourth paragraphs. Does each have a topic sentence or strongly imply one? Do all the other sentences in the paragraph focus on its main idea? Would you now revise any of these paragraphs — and, if so, how?

PHOTO CROPPED TO SHOW DETAIL

Fig.1. Venetians have worn masks like these during Carnival for centuries.

8c Use effective methods of development.

As noted in Chapter 7, there are several common methods of development. You can use them to develop paragraphs.

Narrative

A narrative paragraph uses the chronological elements of a story to develop a main idea. The following is one student's narrative paragraph that tells a personal story to support a point about the dangers of racing bicycles with flimsy alloy frames:

> People who have been exposed to the risk of dangerously designed bicycle frames have paid too high a price. I saw this danger myself in last year's Putney Race. An expensive graphite frame failed, and the rider was catapulted onto Vermont pavement at fifty miles per hour. The pack of riders behind him was so dense that other racers crashed into a tangled, sliding heap. The aftermath: four hospitalizations. I got off with some stitches, a bad road rash, and severely pulled tendons. My Italian racing bike was

pretzeled, and my racing was over for that summer. Others were not so lucky. An Olympic hopeful, Brian Stone of the Northstar team, woke up in a hospital bed to find that his cycling was over — and not just for that summer. His kneecap had been surgically removed. He couldn't even walk.

COMMON ASSIGNMENTS
Narrative Essay

Personal narratives — the most common assignment of all some twenty years ago — are assigned less often today. But variations of the genre, such as literacy narratives, are still very common. Writing about yourself can be more difficult than it sounds, requiring a major point you want to make, clear organization, vivid description, and some kind of conclusion that ties the narrative together and highlights its significance.

SPECIAL CONSIDERATIONS OF A NARRATIVE ASSIGNMENT

- Make your story engaging and meaningful to your audience.
- Brainstorm a list of memories, concentrating on capturing them as vividly as possible. Use your senses: how did things look, smell, feel, taste, and sound?
- Use specific details and concrete words to create pictures in your readers' minds. You may want to include photos or other illustrations as well.
- Consider organization: chronological order may be the most natural way to tell your story, but you might want to use flashbacks or flash-forwards, too.
- Try using dialogue to bring the voices of characters to life.
- Think carefully about the overall point you want to make. When you have a clear sense of the major point, make sure that each part of the narrative leads up to that point.
- Don't just dump memories onto paper. Craft and organize your work carefully to lead to the insights or points you want to make.

Description

A descriptive paragraph uses specific details to create a clear impression. Notice how the following paragraph includes details about an old schoolroom; they convey a strong impression of a room where "time had taken its toll." Notice as well how the writer uses spatial organization, moving from the ceiling to the floor.

The professor's voice began to fade into the background as my eyes wandered around the classroom in the old administration building. The water-stained ceiling was cracked and peeling, and the splitting wooden beams played host to a variety of lead pipes and coils. My eyes followed these pipes down the walls and around corners until I eventually saw the electric outlets. I thought it was strange that they were exposed, and not built in, until I realized that there probably had been no electricity when the building was built. Below the outlets the sunshine was falling in bright rays across the hardwood floor, and I noticed how smoothly the floor was worn. Time had taken its toll on this building.

Definition

You may often need to write an entire paragraph in order to define a word or concept, as in the following example:

> Economics is the study of how people choose among the alternatives available to them. It's the study of little choices ("Should I take the chocolate or the strawberry?") and big choices ("Should we require a reduction in energy consumption in order to protect the environment?"). It's the study of individual choices, choices by firms, and choices by governments. Life presents each of us with a wide range of alternative uses of our time and other resources; economists examine how we choose among those alternatives. — TIMOTHY TREGARTHEN, *Economics*

Example

One of the most common ways of developing a paragraph is by illustrating a point with one or more examples.

> The Indians made names for us children in their teasing way. Because our very busy mother kept my hair cut short, like my brothers', they called me Short Furred One, pointing to their hair and making the sign for short, the right hand with fingers pressed close together, held upward, back out, at the height intended. With me this was about two feet tall, the Indians laughing gently at my abashed face. I am told that I was given a pair of small moccasins that first time, to clear up my unhappiness at being picked out from the dusk behind the fire and my two unhappy shortcomings made conspicuous. — MARI SANDOZ, "The Go-Along Ones"

Division and classification

Division breaks a single item into parts. Classification groups many separate items according to their similarities. A paragraph evaluating one history course might divide the course into several segments — textbooks, lectures, assignments — and examine each one in turn. A paragraph giving an overview of many history courses might classify the courses in a number of ways — by time periods, by geographic areas, by the kinds of assignments demanded, by the number of students enrolled, or by some other principle.

DIVISION

We all listen to music according to our separate capacities. But, for the sake of analysis, the whole listening process may become clearer if we break it up into its component parts, so to speak. In a certain sense, we all listen to music on three separate planes. For lack of a better terminology, one might name these: (1) the sensuous plane, (2) the expressive plane, (3) the sheerly musical plane. The only advantage to be gained from mechanically splitting up the listening process into these hypothetical planes is the clearer view to be had of the way in which we listen.

— AARON COPLAND, *What to Listen For in Music*

CLASSIFICATION

Two types of people are seduced by fad diets. Those who have always been overweight turn to them out of despair; they have tried everything, and yet nothing seems to work. A second group of people to succumb appear perfectly healthy but are baited by slogans such as "look good, feel good." These slogans prompt self-questioning and insecurity — do I really look good and feel good? — and as a direct result, many healthy people fall prey to fad diets. With both types of people, however, the problems surrounding such diets are numerous and dangerous. In fact, these diets provide neither intelligent nor effective answers to weight control.

Comparison and contrast

When you compare two things, you look at their similarities; when you contrast two things, you focus on their differences. You can structure paragraphs that compare or contrast in two basic ways. One way is to present all the information about one item and then all the information about the other item, as in the following paragraph:

You could tell the veterans from the rookies by the way they were dressed. The knowledgeable ones had their heads covered by kerchiefs, so that if they were hired, tobacco dust wouldn't get in their hair; they had on clean dresses that by now were faded and shapeless, so that if they were hired they wouldn't get tobacco dust and grime on their best clothes. Those who were trying for the first time had their hair freshly done and wore attractive dresses; they wanted to make a good impression. But the dresses couldn't be seen at the distance that many were standing from the employment office, and they were crumpled in the crush.

— MARY MEBANE, "Summer Job"

Or you can switch back and forth between the two items, focusing on particular characteristics of each in turn.

Malcolm X emphasized the use of violence in his movement and employed the biblical principle of "an eye for an eye and a tooth for a tooth." King, on the other hand, felt that blacks should use nonviolent civil disobedience and employed the theme "turning the other cheek," which Malcolm X rejected as "beggarly" and "feeble." The philosophy of Malcolm X was one of revenge, and often it broke the unity of black Americans. More radical blacks supported him, while more conservative ones supported King. King thought that blacks should transcend their humanity. In contrast, Malcolm X thought they should embrace it and reserve their love for one another, regarding whites as  "devils" and the "enemy." The distance between Martin Luther King Jr.'s thinking and Malcolm X's was the distance between growing up in the seminary and growing up on the streets, between the American dream and the American reality.

EXERCISE 8.4

Outline the preceding paragraph on Martin Luther King Jr. and Malcolm X, noting its alternating pattern. Then rewrite the paragraph using block organization: the first part of the paragraph devoted to King, the second to Malcolm X. Finally, write a brief analysis of the two paragraphs, explaining which seems more coherent and easier to follow — and why.

Analogy

Analogies (comparisons that explain an unfamiliar thing in terms of a familiar one) can also help develop paragraphs. In the following paragraph, the writer draws an unlikely analogy — between the human genome and Thanksgiving dinner — to help readers understand what scientists know about the human genome.

Think of the human genome as the ingredients list for a massive Thanksgiving dinner. Scientists long have had a general understanding of how the feast is cooked. They knew where the ovens were. Now, they also have a list of every ingredient. Yet much remains to be discovered. In most cases, no one knows exactly which ingredients are necessary for making, for example, the pumpkin pie as opposed to the cornbread. Indeed, many, if not most, of the recipes that use the genomic ingredients are missing, and

there's little understanding why small variations in the quality of the ingredients can "cook up" diseases in one person but not in another.
– *USA TODAY*, "Cracking of Life's Genetic Code Carries Weighty Potential"

Cause and effect

You can often develop paragraphs by explaining the causes of something or the effects that something brings about. The following paragraph discusses how our desire for food that tastes good has affected history:

The human craving for flavor has been a largely unacknowledged and unexamined force in history. For millennia royal empires have been built, unexplored lands traversed, and great religions and philosophies changed by the spice trade. In 1492 Christopher Columbus set sail to find seasoning. Today the influence of flavor in the world marketplace is no less decisive. The rise and fall of corporate empires — of soft-drink companies, snack-food companies, and fast-food chains — is often determined by how their products taste.

– ERIC SCHLOSSER, *Fast Food Nation*

Process

Paragraphs that explain a process often use the principle of time or chronology to order the stages in the process.

By the late 20s, most people notice the first signs of aging in their physical appearance. Slight losses of elasticity in facial skin produce the first wrinkles, usually in those areas most involved in their characteristic facial expressions. As the skin continues to lose elasticity and fat deposits build up, the face sags a bit with age. Indeed, some people have drooping eyelids, sagging cheeks, and the hint of a double chin by age 40 (Whitbourne, 1985). Other parts of the body sag a bit as well, so as the years pass, adults need to exercise regularly if they want to maintain their muscle tone and body shape. Another harbinger of aging, the first gray hairs, is usually noticed in the 20s and can be explained by a reduction in the number of pigment-producing cells. Hair may become a bit less plentiful, too, because of hormonal changes and reduced blood supply to the skin.

– KATHLEEN STASSEN BERGER, *The Developing Person through the Life Span*

Problem and solution

Another way to develop a paragraph is to open with a topic sentence that states a problem or asks a question about a problem and then to offer a solution or answers in the sentences that follow — a technique used in this paragraph from a review of Ted Nordhaus and Michael Shellenberger's book *Break Through: From the Death of Environmentalism to the Politics of Possibility*:

Unfortunately, at the moment growth means burning more fossil fuel. . . . How can that fact be faced? How to have growth that Americans want, but without limits that they instinctively oppose, and still reduce carbon emissions? [Nordhaus and Shellenberger's] answer is: investments in new technology. Acknowledge that America "is great at imagining, experimenting, and inventing the future," and then start spending. They cite examples ranging from the nuclear weapons program to the invention of the Internet to show what government money can do, and argue that too many clean-energy advocates focus on caps instead.

– Bill McKibben, "Can Anyone Stop It?"

Reiterating

Increasingly an important method of development, reiterating calls for an early statement of the main point of a paragraph. The paragraph then goes on to restate the point, hammering home the point and often building in intensity as well.

> *We are on the move now.* The burning of our churches will not deter us. *We are on the move now.* The bombing of our homes will not dissuade us. *We are on the move now.* The beating and killing of our clergymen and young people will not divert us. *We are on the move now.* The arrest and release of known murderers will not discourage us. *We are on the move now.* Like an idea whose time has come, not even the marching of mighty armies can halt us. *We are moving* to the land of freedom.
>
> – Martin Luther King Jr., "Our God Is Marching On"

EXERCISE 8.5

Choose two of the following topics or two others that interest you, and brainstorm or freewrite about each one for ten minutes (6a and 6b). Then use the information you have produced to determine what method(s) of development would be most appropriate for each topic.

1. the pleasure a hobby has given you
2. the different images of two noted athletes
3. an average Saturday morning
4. why the game Monopoly is (or is not) an appropriate metaphor for U.S. society
5. the best course you've ever taken

EXERCISE 8.6

Take an assignment you have written recently, and study the ways you developed each paragraph. For one of the paragraphs, write a brief evaluation of its development. How would you expand or otherwise improve the development?

8d Consider paragraph length.

Paragraph length is determined by content and purpose. Paragraphs should develop an idea, create any desired effects (such as suspense or humor), and advance the larger piece of writing. Fulfilling these aims will sometimes require short paragraphs, sometimes long ones. For example, if you are writing a persuasive piece, you may put all your evidence into one long paragraph to create the impression of a solid, overwhelmingly convincing argument. In a story about an exciting event, on the other hand, you may use a series of short paragraphs to create suspense, to keep the reader rushing to each new paragraph to find out what happens next.

REASONS TO START A NEW PARAGRAPH

- to turn to a new idea
- to emphasize something (such as an idea or an example)
- to change speakers (in dialogue)
- to get readers to pause
- to take up a subtopic
- to start the conclusion

EXERCISE 8.7

Examine the paragraph breaks in something you have written recently. Explain briefly in writing why you decided on each of the breaks. Would you change any of them now? If so, how and why?

8e Make paragraphs flow.

A paragraph has coherence — or flows — if its details fit together clearly in a way that readers can easily follow. When you arrange information in a particular order (as described in 7d and 8c), you help readers move from one point to another. Regardless of your organization, however, be aware of several other ways to achieve paragraph coherence.

Repeating key words and phrases

Weaving in repeated key words and phrases — or pronouns that point to them — not only links sentences but also alerts readers to the importance of those words or phrases in the larger piece of writing. Notice in the following example how the repetition of the italicized key words and the use of pronouns that refer to those words help hold the paragraph together:

> Over the centuries, *shopping* has changed in function as well as in style. Before the Industrial Revolution, most consumer goods were sold in open-air *markets, customers* who went into an actual *shop* were expected to *buy* something, and *shoppers* were always expected to *bargain* for the best possible *price*. In the nineteenth century, however, the development of the department *store* changed the relationship between buyers and sellers. Instead of visiting several *market* stalls or small *shops, customers* could now *buy* a variety of merchandise under the same roof; instead of feeling expected to *buy,* they were welcome just to look; and instead of *bargaining* with several merchants, they paid a fixed *price* for each *item.* In addition, *they* could return an *item* to the *store* and exchange *it* for a different one or get their money back. All of these changes helped transform *shopping* from serious requirement to psychological recreation.

EXERCISE 8.8

Read the following paragraph. Then identify the places where the author uses repetition of key words and phrases, and explain how they bring coherence to the paragraph.

> In our time it is broadly true that political writing is bad writing. Where it is not true, it will generally be found that the writer is some kind of rebel, expressing his private opinions and not a "party line." Orthodoxy, of whatever color, seems to demand a lifeless, imitative style. The political dialects to be found in pamphlets, leading articles, manifestos, white papers, and the speeches of under-secretaries do, of course, vary from party to party, but they are all alike in that one almost never finds in them a fresh, vivid, homemade turn of speech. When one watches some tired hack on the platform mechanically repeating the familiar phrases — *bestial atrocities, iron heel, bloodstained tyranny, free peoples of the world, stand shoulder to shoulder* — one often has a curious feeling that one is not watching a live human being but some kind of dummy. . . . And this is not altogether fanciful. A speaker who uses that kind of phraseology has gone some distance toward turning himself into a machine. The appropriate noises are coming out of his larynx, but his brain is not involved as it would be if he were choosing his words for himself. If the speech he is making is one that he is accustomed to make over and over again, he may be almost unconscious of what he is saying, as one is when one utters the responses in church. And this reduced state of consciousness, if not indispensable, is at any rate favorable to political conformity.
>
> — GEORGE ORWELL, "Politics and the English Language"

Using parallelism

Parallel structures can help connect the sentences within a paragraph. As readers, we feel pulled along by the force of the parallel structures in the example on the following page:

William Faulkner's "Barn Burning" tells the story of a young boy trapped in a no-win situation. If he betrays his father, he loses his family. If he betrays justice, he becomes a fugitive. In trying to free himself from his trap, he does both.

Using transitions

Transitions are words such as *so, however,* and *thus* that signal relationships between sentences and paragraphs. Transitions help guide the reader from one idea to another. To understand how important transitions are in directing readers, try reading the following paragraph, from which all transitions have been removed.

A PARAGRAPH WITH NO TRANSITIONS

In "The Fly," Katherine Mansfield tries to show us the real personality of the boss beneath his exterior. The fly helps her to portray this real self. The boss goes through a range of emotions and feelings. He expresses these feelings to a small but determined fly, whom the reader realizes he unconsciously relates to his son. The author basically splits up the story into three parts, with the boss's emotions and actions changing quite measurably. With old Woodifield, with himself, and with the fly, we see the boss's manipulativeness. Our understanding of him as a hard and cruel man grows.

If we work at it, we can figure out the relationship of these sentences to one another, for this paragraph is essentially unified by one major idea. But the lack of transitions results in an abrupt, choppy rhythm; the paragraph lurches from one detail to the next, dragging the confused reader behind. See how much easier the passage is to read and understand with transitions added.

THE SAME PARAGRAPH WITH TRANSITIONS

In "The Fly," Katherine Mansfield tries to show us the real personality of the boss beneath his exterior. The fly in the story's title helps her to portray this real self. In the course of the story, the boss goes through a range of emotions. At the end, he finally expresses these feelings to a small but determined fly, whom the reader realizes he unconsciously relates to his son. To accomplish her goal, the author basically splits up the story into three parts, with the boss's emotions and actions changing measurably throughout. First with old Woodifield, then with himself, and last with the fly, we see the boss's manipulativeness. With each part, our understanding of him as a hard and cruel man grows.

Commonly used transitions

TO SIGNAL SEQUENCE

again, also, and, and then, besides, finally, first . . . second . . . third, furthermore, last, moreover, next, still, too

TO SIGNAL TIME

after a few days, after a while, afterward, as long as, as soon as, at last, at that time, before, earlier, immediately, in the meantime, in the past, lately, later, meanwhile, now, presently, simultaneously, since, so far, soon, then, thereafter, until, when

TO SIGNAL COMPARISON

again, also, in the same way, likewise, once more, similarly

TO SIGNAL CONTRAST

although, but, despite, even though, however, in contrast, in spite of, instead, nevertheless, nonetheless, on the contrary, on the one hand . . . on the other hand, regardless, still, though, yet

TO SIGNAL EXAMPLES

after all, for example, for instance, indeed, in fact, of course, specifically, such as, the following example, to illustrate

TO SIGNAL CAUSE AND EFFECT

accordingly, as a result, because, consequently, for this purpose, hence, so, then, therefore, thereupon, thus, to this end

TO SIGNAL PLACE

above, adjacent to, below, beyond, closer to, elsewhere, far, farther on, here, near, nearby, opposite to, there, to the left, to the right

TO SIGNAL CONCESSION

although it is true that, granted that, I admit that, it may appear that, naturally, of course

TO SIGNAL SUMMARY, REPETITION, OR CONCLUSION

as a result, as has been noted, as I have said, as mentioned earlier, as we have seen, in any event, in conclusion, in other words, in short, on the whole, therefore, to summarize

8f   Work on opening and closing paragraphs.

Opening paragraphs

Even a good piece of writing may remain unread if it has a weak opening paragraph. In addition to announcing your topic, an introductory paragraph must engage readers' interest and focus their attention on what is to follow. One common kind of opening paragraph follows a general-to-specific sequence, in which the writer opens with a general statement and then gets more and more specific, concluding with the thesis. The following paragraph illustrates such an opening:

> Throughout Western civilization, places such as the ancient Greek agora, the New England town hall, the local church, the coffeehouse, the village square, and even the street corner have been arenas for debate on public affairs and society. Out of thousands of such encounters, "public opinion" slowly formed and became the context in which politics was framed. Although the public sphere never included everyone, and by itself did not determine the outcome of all parliamentary actions, it contributed to the spirit of dissent found in a healthy representative democracy. Many of these public spaces remain, but they are no longer centers for political discussion and action. They have largely been replaced by television and other forms of media — forms that arguably isolate citizens from one another rather than bringing them together.
>
> – MARK POSTER, "The Net as a Public Sphere"

In this paragraph, the opening sentence introduces a general subject — sites of public debate throughout history; subsequent sentences focus more specifically on political discussion; and the last sentence presents the thesis, which the rest of the essay will develop.

OTHER EFFECTIVE WAYS OF OPENING

- with a quotation: *There is a bumper sticker that reads, "Too bad ignorance isn't painful."* – NIKKI GIOVANNI, "Racism 101"
- with an anecdote: *I first met Angela Carter at a dinner in honor of the Chilean writer José Donoso at the home of Liz Calder, who then published all of us.* – SALMAN RUSHDIE, "Angela Carter"
- with a question: *Why are Americans terrified of using nuclear power as a source of energy?*
- with a strong opinion: *Men need a men's movement about as much as women need chest hair.* – JOHN RUSZKIEWICZ, *The Presence of Others*

Concluding paragraphs

A good conclusion wraps up a piece of writing in a satisfying and memorable way. A common and effective strategy for concluding is to restate the central idea (but not word for word), perhaps specifying it in several sentences, and then ending with a much more general statement.

> Lastly, and perhaps greatest of all, there was the ability, at the end, to turn quickly from war to peace once the fighting was over. Out of the way these two men [Generals Grant and Lee] behaved at Appomattox came the possibility of a peace of reconciliation. It was a possibility not wholly realized, in the years to come, but which did, in the end, help the

two sections to become one nation again . . . after a war whose bitterness might have seemed to make such a reunion wholly impossible. No part of either man's life became him more than the part he played in this brief meeting in the McLean house at Appomattox. Their behavior there put all succeeding generations of Americans in their debt. Two great Americans, Grant and Lee — very different, yet under everything very much alike. Their encounter at Appomattox was one of the great moments of American history.

> – BRUCE CATTON, "Grant and Lee: A Study in Contrasts"

OTHER EFFECTIVE WAYS OF CONCLUDING

- with a quotation
- with a question
- with a vivid image
- with a call for action
- with a warning

 bedfordstmartins.com/everydaywriter For more help with writing, go to **Writing Resources** and click on **Links**.

EXERCISE 8.9: THINKING CRITICALLY

Reading with an Eye for Paragraphs

Read something by a writer you admire. Find one or two paragraphs that impress you in some way, and analyze them, using the guidelines on p. 74. Try to decide what makes them effective paragraphs.

Thinking about Your Own Use of Paragraphs

Examine two or three paragraphs you have written, using the guidelines on p. 74, to evaluate the unity, coherence, and development of each one. Identify the topic of each paragraph, the topic sentence (if one is explicitly stated), any patterns of development, and any means used to create coherence. Decide whether or not each paragraph successfully guides your readers, and explain your reasons. Then choose one paragraph, and revise it.

Reviewing and Revising

The ancient Roman poet Horace advised aspiring writers to get distance from their work by putting it away for *nine years*. Although impractical for most college writers, this advice still holds a nugget of truth: putting the draft away even for a day or two will clear your mind and give you more objectivity about your writing.

9a Reread.

After giving yourself and your draft a rest, review the draft by reread-ing it carefully for meaning; recalling your purpose and audience; re-considering your stance; and evaluating your organization and use of visuals.

Meaning

When you pick up the draft again, don't sweat the small stuff. Instead, concentrate on your message and on whether you have expressed it clearly. Note any places where the meaning seems unclear.

Purpose

If you responded to an assignment, make sure that you have produced what was asked for. If you set out to prove something, have you suc-ceeded? If you intended to propose a solution to a problem, have you set forth a well-supported solution rather than just an analysis of the problem?

Audience

How appropriately do you address your audience members, given their experiences and expectations? Will you catch their interest, and will they be able to follow your discussion?

Stance

Ask yourself one central question: where are you coming from in this draft? Consider whether your stance appropriately matches the stance you started out with, or whether your stance has legitimately evolved.

Organization

One way to check the organization of your draft is to outline it. After numbering the paragraphs, read through each one, jotting down its main idea. Do the main ideas clearly relate to the thesis and to one another? Can you identify any confusing leaps from point to point? Have you left out any important points?

Use of visuals

If you've used visuals, do they help make a point? Are all visuals clearly labeled and the sources appropriately credited? Are they referred to in the text? Consider whether there is information in your draft that would be better presented as a visual.

> **FOR MULTILINGUAL WRITERS**
> ## Asking an Experienced Writer to Review Your Draft
>
> One good way to make sure that your writing is easy to follow is to have someone else read it. You might find it especially helpful to ask someone who is experienced in the kind of writing you are working on to read over your draft and to point out any words or patterns that are unclear or ineffective.

EXERCISE 9.1

Take twenty to thirty minutes to look critically at the draft you prepared for Exercise 7.5. Reread it carefully, check to see how well the purpose is accomplished, and consider how appropriate the draft is for the audience. Then write a paragraph about how you would go about revising the draft.

9b Get responses from peers.

In addition to your own critical appraisal and that of an instructor, you may want to get responses to your draft from friends, classmates, or colleagues. Use the questions here to respond to someone else's draft or to analyze your own. If you ask other people to evaluate your draft, be sure that they know your assignment, intended audience, and purpose.

EXERCISE 9.2

To prepare for a peer review, write a description of your purpose, rhetorical stance, and audience for your reviewer(s) to consider. For example, Emily Lesk might write, "I want to figure out why Coca-Cola seems so American and how the company achieves this effect. My audience is primarily college students like me, learning to analyze their own cultures. I want to sound knowledgeable, and I want this essay to be fun and interesting to read." This type of summary statement can help your reviewers keep your goals in mind as they give you feedback.

GAME PLAN Work with Peer Reviewers

START to work with others on a *DRAFT.*

(1st)

WHAT SHOULD WE FOCUS ON?
Big picture, development, sentence-level questions?

IT DOESN'T MATTER *if this writer has more or less experience than I do —we can still help each other....*

REVIEWERS

1 **READ CAREFULLY.**

What should I look at *FIRST*? (ASK if I'm not sure....)

What's the draft doing? Do I get the *MAIN POINTS?*

Is the writer on the *RIGHT TRACK?*

2 **MARK UP THE WRITING.**
Compliment what's good. Criticize constructively.
BE HELPFUL, NOT HARSH!

Should I *ASK* more questions?

Are my markings *CLEAR?*

3 **SUGGEST NEXT STEPS.**
What changes could make the next draft stronger? Be specific....

WRITERS

1 **GUIDE MY READERS.**

What *PROBLEMS* do I see in this draft?

TELL readers what I want them to do first.

ASK QUESTIONS

Does this *WORK?* What's wrong here?

2 **ACCEPT HELP.**
Remember that all writing can be improved— EVEN MINE!

3 **CONFIRM SUGGESTIONS.**

Do I *UNDERSTAND* what my *REVIEWERS* think?

If the comments don't seem helpful, ask for better ones....

Have I gotten *FEEDBACK* on what to do next?

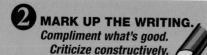

I'M ASKING GOOD QUESTIONS...

I'M HELPING OTHER WRITERS THINK...

I KNOW WHERE THIS WRITING SHOULD GO FROM HERE!

Guidelines for Peer Response

- *Initial thoughts.* What are the main strengths and weaknesses of the draft? What might confuse readers? What is the most important thing the writer says in the draft? What will readers want to know more about?
- *Assignment.* Does the draft carry out the assignment?
- *Title and introduction.* Do the title and introduction tell what the draft is about and catch readers' interest? How else might the draft begin?
- *Thesis and purpose.* Paraphrase the thesis: *In this paper, the writer will. . . .* Does the draft fulfill that promise?
- *Audience.* How does the draft interest and appeal to its audience?
- *Rhetorical stance.* Where does the writer stand? What words indicate the stance?
- *Supporting points.* List the main points, and review them one by one. How well does each point support the thesis? Do any need more explanation? Do any seem confusing or boring?
- *Visuals and design.* Do visuals, if any, add to the key points? Is the design clear and effective?
- *Organization and flow.* Is the writing easy to follow? How effective are transitions within sentences, between sentences, and between paragraphs?
- *Conclusion.* Does the draft conclude memorably? Is there another way it might end?

Tools for peer review

One of the main goals of a peer reviewer is to help the writer see his or her draft differently. When you review a draft, you want to *show* the writer what does and doesn't work about particular aspects of the draft. Visually marking the draft can help the writer absorb at a glance the revisions you suggest.

REVIEWING A PRINT DRAFT

When working with a hard copy of a draft, write compliments in the left margin and critiques, questions, and suggestions in the right margin. As long as you explain what your symbols mean, you can also use boxes, circles, single and double underlining, highlighting, or other visual annotations as shorthand for what you have to say about the draft.

REVIEWING A COMPUTER DRAFT

If the draft is an electronic file, the reviewer should save the document in a peer-review folder under an easy-to-recognize name. It's wise to

---

FOR MULTILINGUAL WRITERS

Understanding Peer Review

If you are not used to giving or receiving criticisms directly, you may be uneasy with a classmate's challenges to your work. However, constructive criticism is appropriate to peer review. Your peers will also expect you to offer your questions, suggestions, and insights.

---

include the writer's name, the assignment, the number of the draft, and the reviewer's initials. For example, the reviewer Ann G. Smith might name the file for the first draft of Javier Jabari's first essay *jabari.essay1.d1.ags.*

The reviewer can then use the word-processing program to add comments, questions, and suggestions to the text. In Microsoft Word, the REVIEWING toolbar appears as an option after the reviewer selects TOOLBARS in the VIEW menu.

THE REVIEWING TOOLBAR IN MICROSOFT WORD

INSERT COMMENT

Final Showing Markup ▾ Show ▾

TRACK CHANGES

Moving a mouse over the icons on the REVIEWING toolbar will reveal their functions. The critical functions for peer reviewers are TRACK CHANGES and the COMMENT tool. TRACK CHANGES will show a reviewer's changes to the document in a different color. The COMMENT function (which you can also find on the INSERT menu) allows you to type a note in the margin. If your word processor doesn't have a COMMENT function, you can comment in footnotes instead.

EXERCISE 9.3

Using the questions for reviewers on p. 92 as a guide, analyze the draft you wrote for Exercise 7.5, trying to imagine it through a reviewer's eyes.

Reviews of Emily Lesk's draft

On page 95 are the first three paragraphs of Emily Lesk's draft, as reviewed electronically by two students, Beatrice Kim and Nastassia Lopez. (You'll find earlier appearances of Emily's work in 5g, 6d, and 7a.) Beatrice and Nastassia decided to use highlighting for particular purposes: green for material they found effective, yellow for language that seemed unclear, blue for material that could be expanded, and gray for material that could be deleted.

As this review shows, Nastassia and Bea agree on some of the major problems — and good points — in Emily's draft. The comments on the draft, however, reveal their different responses. You, too, will find that different readers do not always agree on what is effective or ineffective. In addition, you may find that you simply do not agree with their advice.

You can often proceed efficiently by looking first for areas of agreement (*everyone was confused by this sentence — I'd better review it*) or strong disagreement (*one person said my conclusion was "perfect," and someone else said it "didn't conclude" — better look carefully at that paragraph again*).

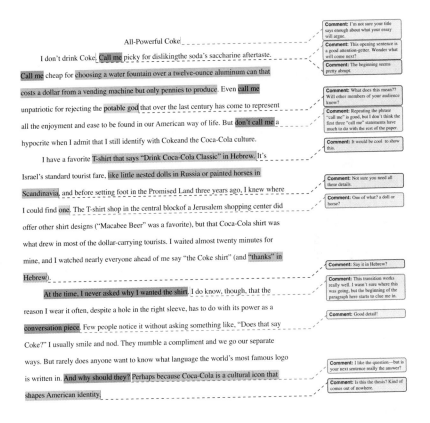

All-Powerful Coke

Comment: I'm not sure your title says enough about what your essay will argue.

I don't drink Coke. Call me picky for dislikingthe soda's saccharine aftertaste.

Comment: This opening sentence is a good attention-getter. Wonder what will come next?

Call me cheap for choosing a water fountain over a twelve-ounce aluminum can that

Comment: The beginning seems pretty abrupt.

costs a dollar from a vending machine but only pennies to produce. Even call me

Comment: What does this mean?? Will other members of your audience know?

unpatriotic for rejecting the potable god that over the last century has come to represent

Comment: Repeating the phrase "call me" is good, but I don't think the first three "call me" statements have much to do with the rest of the paper.

all the enjoyment and ease to be found in our American way of life. But don't call me a

hypocrite when I admit that I still identify with Cokeand the Coca-Cola culture.

Comment: It would be cool to show this.

I have a favorite T-shirt that says "Drink Coca-Cola Classic" in Hebrew. It's

Israel's standard tourist fare, like little nested dolls in Russia or painted horses in

Comment: Not sure you need all these details.

Scandinavia, and before setting foot in the Promised Land three years ago, I knew where

Comment: One of what? a doll or horse?

I could find one. The T-shirt shop in the central blockof a Jerusalem shopping center did

offer other shirt designs ("Macabee Beer" was a favorite), but that Coca-Cola shirt was

what drew in most of the dollar-carrying tourists. I waited almost twenty minutes for

mine, and I watched nearly everyone ahead of me say "the Coke shirt" (and "thanks" in

Comment: Say it in Hebrew?

Hebrew).

Comment: This transition works really well. I wasn't sure where this was going, but the beginning of the paragraph here starts to clue me in.

At the time, I never asked why I wanted the shirt. I do know, though, that the

reason I wear it often, despite a hole in the right sleeve, has to do with its power as a

Comment: Good detail!

conversation piece. Few people notice it without asking something like, "Does that say

Coke?" I usually smile and nod. They mumble a compliment and we go our separate

ways. But rarely does anyone want to know what language the world's most famous logo

Comment: I like the question—but is your next sentence really the answer?

is written in. And why should they? Perhaps because Coca-Cola is a cultural icon that

Comment: Is this the thesis? Kind of comes out of nowhere.

shapes American identity.

 bedfordstmartins.com/everydaywriter To explore tools for peer review, go to **Writing Resources** and click on **Working Online**. If you're using **Comment** in your course, you and your classmates can take part in peer-review activities online.

Getting the most from reviewers' comments

Consider your peer reviewers coaches, not judges. You, not the reviewers, will decide which suggestions to follow and which to disregard. After reading reviewers' comments — and, if necessary, giving yourself some distance from those comments — make a revision plan consisting of two lists: (1) areas in which reviewers agree on needed changes, and (2) areas in which they disagree. Make choices about which suggestions to take, and rank those suggestions. Concentrate first on changes having to do with purpose, audience, stance, thesis, and support. Later you can tackle changes to sentences, words, punctuation, and format.

If you received an electronically marked-up file from reviewers, you can use that file as the starting point for your next draft, titling it clearly. (For example, Javier Jabari might rename the file as *jabari.essay1.d2*.) Use the arrows in the REVIEWING toolbar to move through comments, changes, and highlighting. Decide what to do about each item by clicking the ACCEPT CHANGE or REJECT CHANGE icon. Remove comments as you deal with them by clicking the DELETE COMMENT icon.

THE REVIEWING TOOLBAR IN MICROSOFT WORD

PREVIOUS CHANGE   NEXT CHANGE

| Final Showing Markup ▾ | Show ▾ | 🖹 🖹 🗐 ▾ 🗐 ▾ | 🗐 ▾ | 🗐 | 🖻 ▾ |

ACCEPT CHANGE   REJECT CHANGE/DELETE COMMENT

Based on her own review of her work as well as on the responses she received, Emily decided to (1) make her thesis more explicit, (2) delete some extraneous information and examples, and (3) work especially hard on the tone and length of her introduction (see p. 104).

> **bedfordstmartins.com/everydaywriter** To see Emily Lesk's complete first draft, click on **Student Writing Models**.

9c   Consult instructor comments.

Instructor comments on any work that you have done can help you identify mistakes, particularly ones that you make repeatedly, and can point you toward larger issues that prevent your writing from being as effective as it could be. Whether or not you will have an opportunity to revise a particular piece of writing, you should look closely at the comments from your instructor.

In responding to student writing, however, instructors sometimes use phrases or comments that are a kind of shorthand — comments that are perfectly clear to the instructor but may be less clear to the students reading them. The instructor comments in the following chart, culled from over a thousand first-year student essays, are among those that you may find most puzzling. Alongside each comment you'll find information intended to make the comment clearer to you — and to allow you to revise as your instructor recommends. If your paper includes a puzzling comment that is not listed here, be sure to ask your instructor what the comment means and how you can fix the problem.

Instructor Comment	Possible Meaning(s)	Actions to Take in Response
"thesis not clear"	Your main point is hard to find or understand.	Make sure that you have a main point, and state it directly. (7b) The rest of the paper will need to support the main point, too — this problem cannot be corrected by adding a sentence or two.
"trying to do too much" "covers too much ground"	Your main point is too broad.	Focus your main point more narrowly so that you can say everything that you need to in a project of the assigned length. (5f) You may need to cut back on some material and then expand what remains.
"hard to follow" "not logical" "incoherent" "jumps around" "parts not connected" "transition"	The writing is not clearly or not logically organized, or the writing lacks transitions, explanations, or other signals the reader needs to understand it.	If overall organization is unclear, try mapping or outlining and rearranging your work. (7d) See if transitions and signals (8e) or additional explanation will solve the problem.
"too general" "vague"	You need to be more specific.	Use concrete language and details (22c), and make sure that you have something specific and interesting to say. (7b) If not, reconsider your topic.
"underdeveloped" "thin" "sparse"	You do not give enough information, examples, or details, or you have not considered the topic from enough angles.	Add examples and details and be as specific as possible. (22c) You may need to do more research. (Chapters 14–16)

(continued)

Instructor Comment	Possible Meaning(s)	Actions to Take in Response
"what about the opposition?" "one-sided" "condescending" "overbearing"	You misrepresent or do not include information on opposing arguments, or you imply that your opinion is the only reasonable one.	Indicate that some people disagree with you, and represent their views fairly before you refute them. Recognize that reasonable people may hold views that differ from yours. (Chapter 13)
"repetitive" "you've already said this"	You repeat arguments or reuse evidence, or you have a tendency to overuse certain words or phrases in your writing.	Revise any parts of your writing that repeat an argument, point, word, or phrase; avoid using the same evidence over and over. If your paper is too short without the repetition, develop your ideas more fully. (Chapter 8)
"awk" "awkward"	You have chosen an inappropriate word, or your sentence is confusing.	Ask a peer or your instructor for suggestions about revising awkward sentences. (Chapters 24–28)
"syntax" "awkward syntax" "convoluted"	Your sentence is too long, or the parts of the sentence are not clearly related.	Read the sentence aloud to identify the problem; revise or replace the sentence. (Chapters 24–28)
"unclear"	Your reader does not understand your point.	Find another way to explain what you mean; add any background information or examples that your audience needs to follow your reasoning.
"tone too conversational" "not an academic voice" "too informal" "colloquial" "slang"	You use slang or colloquial terms inappropriately, or you do not show enough respect for your readers.	Eliminate overly informal words and phrases. Revise material that addresses or refers to your audience too familiarly or informally. (22a)
"pompous" "stilted" "stiff"	You use inappropriately stuffy, strange, or showy language.	Check the connotations of the words you use, and revise any language or syntax that contributes to a pompous, old-fashioned, or peculiar tone. (22a–b)

(continued)

Instructor Comment	Possible Meaning(s)	Actions to Take in Response
"set up quotation" "integrate quotation"	You neglect to introduce a quotation or to explain its significance, or you use a quotation that does not fit into the words around it.	Introduce every quotation with information about the source. Explain each quotation's importance to your work. Read the sentence containing the quotation aloud; revise it if the entire sentence does not make sense. (Chapter 17)
"your words?" "source?" "cite"	You use someone else's words or ideas without citing the source.	Mark all quotations clearly. Acknowledge paraphrases and summaries of others' ideas. Give credit for help from others, and remember that you are responsible for your own work. (Chapter 17)
"doc"	You omit all or part of the source information required by the documentation style you are using, or you make punctuation or other errors in your in-text citations.	Check the citations to be sure that you include all of the required information, that you punctuate correctly, and that you omit information not required by the documentation style. (Chapters 48–54)

9d Revise.

Once you have sufficient advice on your draft from your instructor and classmates, review that advice and then read your work once more, making notes on what you want to change, add, or delete. In addition, take time to look at the "big picture" of your draft: does it get across the main points effectively? Then begin revising, making the changes you need to the following elements. And don't be afraid to make really substantial revisions: sometimes that's the only way to achieve the best results.

Thesis

Make sure that your thesis states the topic clearly and comments on what is particularly significant about the topic (7b). In addition, ask yourself whether the thesis is narrowed and focused enough to be thoroughly proven. If not, take time now to refine and/or limit your thesis further.

TALKING THE TALK

Revision

"I thought I had revised my assignment, but my instructor said I'd just corrected the typos." It's always a good idea to clarify what *revision* means with a particular instructor. Generally, though, when a writing teacher asks for a revision, minor corrections will not be enough. Plan to review your entire draft, and be prepared to make major changes if necessary. Look for sentence-level errors and typos later, during the editing stage, since these may disappear or change as you revise.

WORKING THESIS | The current health care crisis stems from several related problems.
REFINED THESIS | The current health care crisis in America is most directly the result of government reluctance to negotiate with large insurance and pharmaceutical companies.

When you revise your thesis, remember also to revise the rest of the draft accordingly.

EXERCISE 9.4

After rereading the draft you wrote for Exercise 7.5, evaluate the revised working thesis you produced for Exercise 7.2. Then evaluate its support in the draft. Identify points that need further support, and list those things you must do to provide that support.

Support

Make sure that each paragraph relates to or supports the thesis and that each paragraph has sufficient detail to support the point it is making. Eliminate unnecessary material, and identify sections that need further details or examples.

Organization

Should any sections or paragraphs be moved to clarify your point or support your thesis more logically? Are there any paragraphs or parts of paragraphs that don't fit with the essay now or that are unnecessary? Look for confusing leaps or omissions, and identify places where transitions would make the writing easier to follow.

Title, introduction, and conclusion

Does the title give information and draw readers in? Does the introduction attract their interest and present the topic in a way that makes them want

GAME PLAN Revise with Reviewer Comments

START HERE
if the comment is
CONFUSING

START HERE
if the meaning is
~CLEAR~

How does this **APPLY** to what I wrote?

What should I **ASK** the person who made the comment?

How **IMPORTANT** is this suggestion?

I'LL LOOK UP **KEYWORDS** *IN MY BOOK.*

DO OTHER READERS SAY THE SAME THING?

Did the **READER** misunderstand me?

What changes will **CLARIFY** my writing?

If I'm still **STUCK,** I can stop by the **WRITING CENTER....**

*What will happen if I **DON'T** make this change?*

How should I **RESPOND?**

OKAY!
I THINK I'VE GOT IT NOW.

REPEAT UNTIL ALL COMMENTS ARE CONSIDERED....

GET READY TO REVISE

Based on my most useful comments, **WHAT'S MY GOAL** for this revision?

HOW MUCH REVISION DO I NEED? A FEW TWEAKS, A WHOLE NEW TEXT, OR SOMETHING IN BETWEEN?

I don't want to **START AGAIN,** but sometimes that's the way it goes....

WHAT'S THE MOST IMPORTANT THING I CAN DO TO IMPROVE THIS WRITING IN THE TIME I HAVE?

I'VE REVIEWED THE COMMENTS

I'VE THOUGHT ABOUT CHANGES

I CAN MAKE THIS WRITING BETTER!

to keep reading? Does the conclusion leave readers satisfied? Because readers notice beginnings and endings more than other parts of a piece of writing, pay special attention to how you introduce and conclude your work.

Design

Take a final close look at the design of your essay or project. Do you use visuals or images effectively throughout? Is each one numbered, labeled, and commented on in the essay? Do you use font size, color, and other design elements to best advantage in terms of making your point? Do you use consistent formatting throughout? What could you do now to make your essay *look* better?

EXERCISE 9.5

Using the guidelines on p. 101, reread the draft you wrote for Exercise 7.5 with an eye for revising. Try to do this at least one day after you completed the draft. List the things you need or want to address in your revision.

EXERCISE 9.6

Revise the draft you wrote for Exercise 7.5.

EXERCISE 9.7: THINKING CRITICALLY

Answer the following questions about your reviewing and revising process.

1. How did you begin reviewing your draft?
2. What kinds of comments on or responses to your draft did you have? How helpful were they, and why?
3. How long did revising take? How many drafts did you produce?
4. What kinds of changes did you tend to make? in organization, paragraphs, sentence structure, wording, adding or deleting information? in the use of visuals?
5. What gave you the most trouble as you were revising?
6. What pleased you most? What is your very favorite sentence or passage in the draft, and why?
7. What would you most like to change about your process of revising, and how do you plan to go about doing so?

10) Editing and Reflecting

Whether you are writing a wedding invitation, an email to a client, or a history essay, make time to edit and proofread what you write. Editing involves fine-tuning the details of sentence structure, grammar, usage, punctuation, and spelling. Finally, careful proofreading aims at a perfect copy. For important writing, reflecting on how you accomplished the task can prepare you to achieve future writing goals.

10a Edit.

Once you have revised a draft for content and organization, look closely at your sentences and words. Turning a "blah" sentence into a memorable one — or finding exactly the right word to express a thought — can result in writing that is really worth reading. As with life, variety is the spice of sentences. You can add variety to your sentences by looking closely at their length, structure, and opening patterns.

Sentence length

Too many short sentences, especially one following another, can sound like a series of blasts on a car horn, whereas a steady stream of long sentences may tire or confuse readers. Most writers aim for some variety in length, breaking up a series of fairly long sentences with a very brief one.

In examining the following paragraph from her essay, Emily Lesk discovered that the sentences were all fairly long. In editing, she decided to shorten the second sentence, thereby offering a shorter sentence between two long ones.

In other words, Coca-Cola has hammered itself into our perceptions--both

conscious and subconscious--of an American cultural identity by equating

itself with media that define American culture. ~~When~~ the omnipresent ~~general~~ *As*

magazine ~~that marked the earlier part of the century fell by the wayside under~~ *gave way to*

television~~'s power,~~ Coke was there from the beginning. In its 1996 recap of

the previous fifty years in industry history, the publication *Beverage Industry*

cites Coca-Cola as a frontrunner in the very first form of television

advertising: sponsorship of entire programs such as, in the case of Coke, *The*

Bob Dixon Show and *The Adventures of Kit Carson*.

Sentence openings

Opening sentence after sentence in the same way results in a jerky, abrupt, or choppy rhythm. You can vary sentence openings by beginning with a dependent clause, a phrase, an adverb, a conjunctive adverb, or a coordinating conjunction (29b). Another paragraph in Emily Lesk's essay tells the story of how she got her Coke T-shirt in Israel. Before she revised, every sentence in the paragraph opened with the subject, so Emily decided to delete some examples and vary her sentence openings. The final version (which also appears in 5g) is a dramatic and easy-to-read paragraph.

~~I have a favorite T-shirt that says "Drink Coca-Cola Classic" in Hebrew. It's~~

~~Israel's standard tourist fare, like little nested dolls in Russia or painted horses in~~

Even   *Israel*
~~Seandinavia, and~~ before setting foot in ~~the Promised Land~~ three years ago, I

exactly   *the Coke shirt.*   *'s Ben Yehuda Street*
knew where I could find ~~it.~~ The shop in the central block of ~~a~~ Jerusalem

~~shopping center~~ did offer other shirt designs, ~~("Macabee Beer" was a favorite),~~

but ~~that Coca Cola shirt~~ was what drew in most of the dollar-carrying tourists.

While waiting   *my shirt,*
~~I waited~~ almost twenty minutes for ~~mine, and~~ I watched nearly everyone

todah rabah [thank you very much]."
ahead of me say "the Coke shirt," ~~(and "thanks" in Hebrew).~~

the one with a bright white "Drink Coca-Cola Classic"
written in Hebrew cursive across the chest

Opening with *it* and *there*

As you go over the opening sentences of your draft, look especially at those beginning with *it* or *there*. Sometimes these words can create a special emphasis, as in *It was a dark and stormy night.* But they can also appear too often. Another, more subtle problem with these openings is that they may be used to avoid taking responsibility for a statement. The following sentence can be improved by editing:

The university must
▶ ~~It is necessary to~~ raise student fees.

Tone

Tone refers to the attitude that a writer's language conveys toward the topic and the audience. In examining the tone of your draft, think about the nature of the topic, your own attitude toward it, and that of your intended audience. Does your language create the tone you want to achieve (humorous, serious, impassioned, and so on), and is that tone an appropriate one, given your audience and topic?

Word choice

Word choice — or diction — offers writers an opportunity to put their personal stamp on a piece of writing. Becoming aware of the kinds of words you use should help you get the most mileage out of each word. Check for connotations, or associations, of words and make sure you consider how any use of slang, jargon, or emotional language may affect your audience (see 22a–b).

AT A GLANCE

Word Choice

- Are the nouns primarily abstract and general or concrete and specific? Too many abstract and general nouns can result in boring prose.
- Are there too many nouns in relation to the number of verbs? This sentence is heavy and boring: *The effect of the overuse of nouns in writing is the placement of strain on the verbs.* Instead, say this: *Overusing nouns places a strain on the verbs.*
- How many verbs are forms of *be* — *be, am, is, are, was, were, being, been*? If *be* verbs account for more than about a third of your total verbs, you are probably overusing them.
- Are verbs *active* wherever possible? Passive verbs are harder to read and remember than active ones. Although the passive voice has many uses, your writing will gain strength and energy if you use active verbs.
- Are your words *appropriate*? Check to be sure they are not too fancy — or too casual.

Spell checkers

While these software tools won't catch every spelling error or identify all problems of style, they can be very useful. Most professional writers use their spell checkers religiously. Remember, however, that spell checkers are limited; they don't recognize most proper names, foreign words, or specialized language, and they do not recognize homonym errors (misspelling *there* as *their*, for example). (See 22e.)

Document design

Before you produce a copy for final proofreading, reconsider one last time the format and the "look" you want your document to have. This is one last opportunity to think carefully about the visual appearance of your final draft. (For more on document design, see Chapter 4. For more on the design conventions of different disciplines, see Chapters 60–64.)

Proofreading the final draft

Take time for one last, careful proofreading, which means reading to correct any typographical errors or other inconsistencies in spelling and punctuation. To proofread most effectively, read through the copy aloud, making sure that you've used punctuation marks correctly and consistently, that all sentences are complete (unless you've used intentional fragments or run-ons for special effects) — and that no words are missing. Then go through the copy again, this time reading backward so that you can focus on each individual word and its spelling.

EXERCISE 10.1
Find a paragraph in your own writing that lacks variety in sentence length, sentence openings, or sentence structure. Then write a revised version.

EXERCISE 10.2
Edit and proofread the draft you revised in Exercise 9.7.

EXERCISE 10.3
Using several essays you have written, establish your own editing checklist.

A student's revised draft

Following are the first three paragraphs from Emily Lesk's edited and proofread draft that she submitted to her instructor. Compare these paragraphs with those from her reviewed draft in 9b.

Student Writer

Emily Lesk

Red, White, and Everywhere

America, I have a confession to make: I don't drink Coke. But don't call me a hypocrite just because I am still the proud owner of a bright red shirt that advertises it. Just call me an American.

Fig. 1. Hebrew Coca-Cola T-shirt. Personal photograph.

Even before setting foot in Israel three years ago, I knew exactly where I could find the Coke shirt. The shop in the central block of Jerusalem's Ben Yehuda Street did offer other shirt designs, but the one with a bright white "Drink Coca-Cola Classic" written in Hebrew cursive across the chest was what drew in most of the dollar-carrying tourists. While waiting almost twenty minutes for my shirt (depicted in Fig. 1), I watched nearly everyone ahead of me say "the Coke shirt, *todah rabah* [thank you very much]."

At the time, I never thought it strange that I wanted one, too. After having absorbed sixteen years of Coca-Cola propaganda through everything from NBC's Saturday morning cartoon lineup to the concession stand at Camden Yards (the Baltimore Orioles' ballpark), I associated the shirt with singing along to the "Just for the Taste of It" jingle and with America's favorite pastime, not with a brown fizzy beverage I refused to consume. When I later realized the immensity of Coke's corporate power, I felt somewhat manipulated, but that didn't stop me from wearing the shirt. I still don it often, despite the growing hole in the right sleeve, because of its power as a conversation piece. Few Americans notice it without asking something like "Does that say Coke?" I usually smile and nod. Then they mumble a one-word compliment, and we go our separate ways. But rarely do they want to know what language the internationally recognized logo is written in. And why should they? They are interested in what they can relate to as Americans: a familiar red-and-white logo, not a foreign language. Through nearly a century of brilliant advertising strategies, the Coca-Cola Company has given Americans not only a thirst-quenching beverage but a cultural icon that we have come to claim as our own.

bedfordstmartins.com/everydaywriter To see Emily Lesk's complete final draft, click on **Student Writing Models.**

10b Reflect.

Research demonstrates a connection between careful reflection and learning: thinking back on what you've learned and assessing it help make that learning stick. As a result, first-year college writing courses are increasingly encouraging students to take time for such reflection. Whether or not your instructor asks you to write a formal reflection, whenever you finish a major piece of writing or a writing course, you should make time to think back over the experience and see what lessons you can learn from it.

Reflecting on your development as a writer

Here are some questions to get you started reflecting productively on your writing:

- What lessons have you learned from writing — from an individual piece of writing or from an entire writing course?
- From what you have learned, what can you apply to the work you will do in other classes?
- What about your writing do you feel most confident about — and why? When did you begin to develop this confidence?
- What about your writing do you find needs additional work, and what plans do you have for improving?
- What confusions did you have while writing, and what did you do to resolve them?
- What major questions do you still have about writing or about an individual piece of writing?
- How has writing helped to clarify your thinking, extend your knowledge, or deepen your understanding?
- Identify a favorite passage of your writing, and then try to articulate what about it pleases you. Can you apply what you learn from this analysis to other writing situations?
- How would you describe your development as a writer?

Portfolios

You may find it useful — or you may be required — to select samples for inclusion in a print or online portfolio of your written work. In preparing a portfolio, use these tips:

- *Consider your purpose and audience.* Do you want to fulfill course requirements for an instructor, show work to a prospective employer, keep a record of what you've done for personal reasons, or something else? Answering these questions will help you decide what to include in the portfolio and whether it should be in print or electronic form.

- *Based on the portfolio's purpose, decide on the number of entries.* You may decide to include a wide range of materials — from essays, problem sets, and photos to Web texts, multimedia presentations, a résumé, or anything else that is relevant — if readers can select only the pieces that interest them. For a portfolio that will be read from beginning to end, however, you should limit yourself to five to seven examples of your writing. You might include an academic essay that argues a claim, a personal essay, a brief report, writing based on research, significant correspondence, timed writing, or other work that you think shows your strengths as a writer.

- *Consider organization.* What arrangement — in chronological order, by genre, by topic — will make most sense to readers?

- *Think carefully about layout and design.* Will you include a table of contents or appendices? How will you use color, font and type size, and other elements of graphic design to enhance your portfolio (see Chapter 4)? Remember to label and date each piece of writing in the portfolio to help readers follow along easily. For print portfolios, number pages in consecutive order.

- *Edit and proofread* each piece in your portfolio and the reflective statement (see box below). Ask for responses from peers or an instructor.

COMMON ASSIGNMENTS
Reflective Statements

Research done for this book shows that one of the most common writing assignments in college today is a reflective statement — in the form of a letter, a memo, or a home page — that explains and analyzes the contents of a portfolio.

SPECIAL CONSIDERATIONS OF A REFLECTIVE ASSIGNMENT

- Think carefully about the overall impression you want the portfolio to create, and make sure that the tone and style of your reflective statement set the stage for the entire portfolio.

- Unless otherwise instructed, include in your cover letter a description of what the portfolio contains and explain the purpose of each piece of writing you have chosen.

- Reflect on the strengths and weaknesses of your writing, using specific passages from assignments in your portfolio to provide evidence for each point you make.

- Reflect on the most important things you have learned about writing and about yourself as a writer.

- Conclude with plans for ongoing improvement in your writing.

A student's reflective statement

Here is a shortened version of the cover letter that James Kung wrote to accompany his first-year writing portfolio.

Student Writer

James Kung

December 6, 2007

Dear Professor Ashdown:

"Writing is difficult and takes a long time." This simple yet powerful statement has been uttered so many times in our class that it has essentially become our motto. During this class, my persuasive writing skills have improved dramatically, thanks to many hours spent writing, revising, polishing, and thinking about my topic. The various drafts, revisions, and other materials in my portfolio show this improvement. I entered this first-quarter Writing and Rhetoric class with both strengths and weaknesses. I have always written fairly well-organized essays. However, despite this strength, I struggled throughout the term to narrow and define the various aspects of my research-based argument.

The first aspect of my essay that I had trouble narrowing and defining was my major claim, or my thesis statement. In my "Proposal for Research-Based Argument," I proposed to argue about the case of Wen Ho Lee, the Los Alamos scientist accused of copying restricted government documents. I stated, "The Wen Ho Lee incident deals with the persecution of not only one man, but of a whole ethnic group." You commented that the statement was a "sweeping claim" that would be "hard to support."

I spent weeks trying to rework that claim. Finally, as seen in my "Writer's Notebook 10/16/07," I realized that I had chosen the Lee case because of my belief that the political inactivity of Asian Americans contributed to the case against Lee. Therefore, I decided to focus on this issue in my thesis. Later I once again revised my claim, stating that the political inactivity did not cause but rather contributed to racial profiling in the Wen Ho Lee case.

I also had trouble defining my audience. I briefly alluded to the fact that my audience was a "typical American reader." However, I later decided to address my paper to an Asian American audience for two reasons. First, it would establish a greater ethos for myself as a Chinese American. Second, it would enable me to target the people the Wen Ho Lee case most directly affects: Asian Americans. As a result, in my final research-based argument, I was much more sensitive to the needs and concerns of my audience, and my audience trusted me more.

I hope to continue to improve my writing of research-based arguments.

Sincerely,

James Kung

James Kung

---

 bedfordstmartins.com/everydaywriter For more information on writing portfolios and reflective statements, go to **Writing Resources** and click on **Writing Portfolios**.

Critical Thinking
and Argument

To repeat what others have said requires education;
to challenge it requires brains.

— MARY PETTIBONE POOLE

Critical Thinking and Argument

Critical Reading 11

All readers build worlds in their minds made of words and visuals. Think of a time when you were reading or looking at images and suddenly realized that you were not absorbing information but just staring at a jumble of marks on a page or a screen. Only when you went back and concentrated on meaning were you really reading.

11a Think critically about written texts.

Reading critically means asking questions about what you are reading. A critical reader does not simply accept what the author says but analyzes why the text is convincing (or not convincing). Writer Anatole Broyard once cautioned readers about the perils of "just walking through" a text. A good reader, he suggested, doesn't just walk but "stomps around" in a text — highlighting passages, scribbling in the margins, jotting questions and comments.

Preview and annotation

The article "Many Women at Elite Colleges Set Career Path to Motherhood," by Louise Story, appeared on pp. A1 and A18 of the *New York Times* on September 20, 2005. The first portion of the article appears on pp. 116–17, with a student's preview notes and annotations.

 bedfordstmartins.com/everydaywriter To read the article in its entirety, go to **Writing Resources** and click on **Argument Resources/Critical Reading.**

Summary

Here is how the same student summarized Louise Story's article.

A group of women at Ivy League schools told a reporter who surveyed and interviewed them that they planned to stop working or cut back on work when they had children. The reporter suggests that the women's responses are evidence of a trend and of "changing attitudes."

Many Women at Elite Colleges Set Career Path to Motherhood

BY LOUISE STORY

Title suggests author's conclusion. A new trend? Why is it on the front page?

Who is Louise Story? See if her article generated any response.

Is Cynthia Liu a typical female student? How can I tell?

Cynthia Liu is precisely the kind of high achiever Yale wants: smart (1510 SAT), disciplined (4.0 grade point average), competitive (finalist in Texas oratory competition), musical (pianist), athletic (runner) and altruistic (hospital volunteer). And at the start of her sophomore year at Yale, Ms. Liu is full of ambition, planning to go to law school.

Main point, as expected from the title. But she's only one example — how many are like her?

So will she join the long tradition of famous Ivy League graduates? Not likely. By the time she is 30, this accomplished 19-year-old expects to be a stay-at-home mom.

"My mother's always told me you can't be the best career woman and the best mother at the same time," Ms. Liu said matter-of-factly. "You always have to choose one over the other."

Generalizations about how women are "groomed" — but no evidence.

At Yale and other top colleges, women are being groomed to take their place in an ever more diverse professional elite. It is almost taken for granted that, just as they make up half the students at these institutions, they will move into leadership roles on an equal basis with their male classmates.

How many is "many"? The same word appears in the title.

There is just one problem with this scenario: many of these women say that is not what they want.

Many women at the nation's most elite colleges say they have already decided that they will put aside their careers in favor of raising children. Though some of these students are not planning to have children and some hope to have a family and work full time, many others, like Ms. Liu, say they will happily play a traditional female role, with motherhood their main commitment.

Is "many" more than "some"? Who did the writer talk to? Whose stories did she leave out — and why?

Much attention has been focused on career women who leave the work force to rear children. What seems to be changing is that while many women in college two or three decades ago expected to have full-time careers, their daughters, while still in college, say they have already decided to suspend or end their careers when they have children.

Who says? Where are the sources for these claims?

"At the height of the women's movement and shortly thereafter, women were much more firm in their expectation that they could somehow combine full-time work with child rearing," said Cynthia E. Russett, a professor of American history who has taught at Yale since

Expert source — her quotation underscores the main point. Do other experts disagree?

Is it realistic to expect to be able to raise a family without the income from working?

1967. "The women today are, in effect, turning realistic."

Dr. Russett is among more than a dozen faculty members and administrators at the most exclusive institutions who have been on campus for decades and who said in interviews that they had noticed the changing attitude.

"Many" — that word is here a lot.

Many students say staying home is not a shocking idea among their friends.

Here's another student example, but, again, just one person.

Shannon Flynn, an 18-year-old from Guilford, Conn., who is a freshman at Harvard, says many of her girlfriends do not want to work full time.

"Most probably do feel like me, maybe even tending toward wanting to not work at all," said Ms. Flynn, who plans to work part time after having children, though she is torn because she has worked so hard in school.

Wonder why nobody is asking why expectations are different for men?

"Men really aren't put in that position," she said.

Another student says the same thing. Three so far.

Uzezi Abugo, a freshman at the University of Pennsylvania who hopes to become a lawyer, says she, too, wants to be home with her children at least until they are in school.

"I've seen the difference between kids who did have their mother stay at home and kids who didn't, and it's kind of like an obvious difference when you look at it," said Ms. Abugo, whose mother, a nurse, stayed home until Ms. Abugo was in first grade.

While the changing attitudes are difficult to quantify, the shift emerges repeatedly in interviews with Ivy League students, including 138 freshman and senior females at Yale who replied to e-mail questions sent to members of two residential colleges over the last school year.

Author conducted interviews and an email survey. The sample seems pretty small, though, and comes from a single school.

The interviews found that 85 of the students, or roughly 60 percent, said that when they had children, they planned to cut back on work or stop working entirely. About half of those women said they planned to work part time, and about half wanted to stop work for at least a few years.

Interview results. What about survey results? How many were sent out and how many completed? The author doesn't say.

Two of the women interviewed said they expected their husbands to stay home with the children while they pursued their careers. Two others said either they or their husbands would stay home, depending on whose career was furthest along.

85 + 2 + 2 = 89, and she interviewed 138. What about the others?

The women said that pursuing a rigorous college education was worth the time and money because it would help position them to work in meaningful part-time jobs when their children are young or to attain good jobs when their children leave home. . . .

I wonder if they're paying for college themselves!

 bedfordstmartins.com/everydaywriter For the rest of this article, go to **Writing Resources** and click on **Argument Resources/Critical Reading.**

Analysis

Here are some of the student's notes for an analysis of Louise Story's *New York Times* article. Because the student felt that the article — and her response to it — raised many unanswered questions, she decided to research responses to the article as well as information about how the writer came up with the data cited.

> The evidence for a trend seems pretty skimpy. The reporter interviews several students who indicate that they plan to stop working or work part-time when they have children. The reporter says "many" students feel this way. But according to the numbers the reporter provides, she talked to just 138 people out of an unknown number of responses to an email survey. The reporter doesn't provide any information about what previous generations of women at Ivy League schools felt about working or staying home with their children either, so there's no way to identify this point of view as a change in college women's attitudes — even though the reporter uses the phrase "changing attitudes" twice.

TALKING THE TALK

Critical Thinking

"It seems impolite to criticize. Why do I have to be critical?" Thinking critically does not require you to be relentlessly negative. Instead, critical thinking means, first and foremost, asking good questions — not simply accepting what you see and read at face value. By asking not only what words and images mean but also how meaning gets across, critical thinkers consider why an author makes a particular claim, what an author may be leaving out or ignoring, and how to tell whether evidence is accurate and believable. If you're asking, and answering, questions like these, then you are thinking critically.

EXERCISE 11.1

Following the guidelines in 11a, read one of the assigned essays from your course text or the student essay in Chapter 12 or 13 of this book. Summarize the reading briefly, and note any thoughts you have about your critical reading process (in your writing log, if you keep one).

EXERCISE 11.2: THINKING CRITICALLY

To think critically about your own writing, try approaching it as a reader. Choose a piece of writing that you completed for an earlier class and that you have not recently read. Using the guidelines for critical reading on p. 120, preview, read, and analyze the writing as objectively as you can. What impression does it make on you as a reader? What questions does it leave you with? Write a one-page report analyzing your piece of writing from a critical reader's point of view.

11b Think critically about visuals.

Visual images now shape our lives at least as much as words do. The images that bombard us daily influence us to think and behave in certain ways, and images profoundly affect the way we see ourselves and others. So being visually literate — being able to read an image and understand how it aims to persuade or manipulate — is crucial to becoming a critical thinker.

Visual literacy requires you to analyze images and the arguments they contain — in the same way that you think critically about words that you read. You ask questions and think about the message the visual conveys and the context in which it was presented. You consider the creator(s) of the image and think about why it was created and for whom. You also look at the design as another way of communicating with readers, considering, for example, how color, size, shape, texture, layout, sound, and other design elements influence the viewer.

TALKING THE TALK

Visual Texts

"How can a picture be a text?" In its traditional sense, a *text* involves printed words on paper. But in our media-saturated age, we spend at least as much time reading and analyzing images — including moving images — as we spend on printed words. So it makes sense to broaden the definition of *text* to refer to almost anything that sends a message. That's why images are often called *visual texts*.

QUESTIONS ABOUT DESIGN

- *Detail*. What do you notice first? Why is your attention drawn to that spot, and what effect does this have on your response?

- *Composition*. How does the composition of the image affect the message? What is in the foreground, and what is in the background? What is in the middle, at the top, and at the bottom of the image? Why might the composition be arranged as it is? What effect do the designer's choices have on how you feel about what you see?

- *Color*. Does the use of color enhance or conflict with the images and words? Are some parts of the image highlighted with brighter or lighter colors? If so, why? How do you explain the color choices? If the visual is black and white, is that choice appropriate?

- *Words*. If the visual contains both words and images, what is the relationship between the two? How well do they work together? If no words appear, is the message clear without them? Why, or why not?

- *Repetition*. Are any words or images repeated? If so, what is the effect of the repetition?

GAME PLAN Read Critically

START with a **PREVIEW**.

What does the **TITLE** tell me?

WHAT do I think about the topic?

WHAT do I know?

READ CAREFULLY.

The **MAIN** idea is....

WHO'S THIS AUTHOR, ANYWAY?

Think about context: **WHEN**, **WHERE**, and **HOW** was this first published?

Supporting **IDEAS** are....

WHERE did this information come from?

Look up anything that's **CONFUSING**

Who's the **AUDIENCE** supposed to be?

Am *I* part of it?

What purpose does this text serve?

Have I got it? **TELL A FRIEND** in my own words.

SUMMARIZE THE TEXT.

ANALYZE the text.

What do I **LIKE** most?

Do the parts **WORK** together?

What's assumed? Do the assumptions make sense?

Have I gotten what I expected out of this text?

Was the text's **PURPOSE** accomplished?

WHAT ELSE do I need to **KNOW**?

 REREAD and CHECK UNDERSTANDING.

I'VE KEPT AN OPEN MIND....

I'VE READ CAREFULLY....

I'VE ASKED QUESTIONS....

I HAVE A CRITICAL PERSPECTIVE ON THIS TEXT!

QUESTIONS ABOUT THE CREATOR

- Who created this visual text? What other work has he or she done?
- What does the creator's attitude seem to be toward the visual? What effects do you think the creator intends the image to have on viewers?

QUESTIONS ABOUT CONTENT

- What is the subject?
- How well do visuals explain the subject?

QUESTIONS ABOUT CONTEXT

- Where and in what form was the visual originally seen — in a magazine, on television, online, or somewhere else?
- What can you infer about the message from the place where the visual first appeared?

QUESTIONS ABOUT AUDIENCE

- Who is the intended audience? Are you part of the group the creator is trying to reach? If so, does the visual affect you as the creator(s) intended?

COMMON ASSIGNMENTS
Rhetorical Analysis

You are almost certain to get some form of analysis assignment during your first year of college. One common variety is the rhetorical analysis assignment, which essentially answers two big questions — What is the purpose of the text you are analyzing? How is that purpose achieved? — and focuses on *how* the text gets its meaning across.

SPECIAL CONSIDERATIONS OF A RHETORICAL ANALYSIS ASSIGNMENT

- Identify the purpose or purposes of the text. If the text has multiple purposes, point out any conflicts.
- Identify the primary audience for the text and any secondary audiences, and explore how the text meets audience expectations or needs.
- Examine the author's stance or attitude toward the topic: is it favorable, critical, suspicious, neutral, or mocking? Identify parts of the text where such attitudes are evident, and show how they work to appeal to the audience.
- Explain how the text uses deliberate strategies (such as tone, word choice, sentence structure, design, special effects, choice of medium, choice of evidence, and so on) to achieve its purposes.

- What assumptions does the visual make about the audience's values?

QUESTIONS ABOUT PURPOSE

- Why do you think the visual was created? Does it achieve its purpose?

OVERALL IMPRESSION

- What works and doesn't work about the text?
- What overall impression does the visual text create?

How an image is designed and formatted affects how others will receive it. Look at the striking image on this page, from TurnAround, an

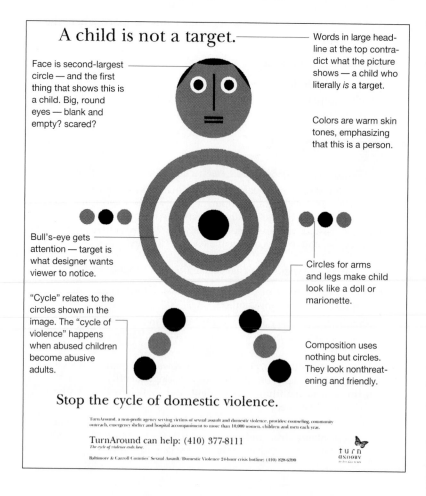

A child is not a target.

Words in large head-line at the top contra-dict what the picture shows — a child who literally *is* a target.

Face is second-largest circle — and the first thing that shows this is a child. Big, round eyes — blank and empty? scared?

Colors are warm skin tones, emphasizing that this is a person.

Bull's-eye gets attention — target is what designer wants viewer to notice.

Circles for arms and legs make child look like a doll or marionette.

"Cycle" relates to the circles shown in the image. The "cycle of violence" happens when abused children become abusive adults.

Composition uses nothing but circles. They look nonthreat-ening and friendly.

Stop the cycle of domestic violence.

TurnAround, a non-profit agency serving victims of sexual assault and domestic violence, provides counseling, community outreach, emergency shelter and hospital accompaniment to more than 10,000 women, children and men each year.

TurnAround can help: (410) 377-8111
The cycle of violence ends here.

Baltimore & Carroll Counties' Sexual Assault/Domestic Violence 24-hour crisis hotline: (410) 828-6390

turn
around

organization devoted to helping victims of domestic violence. The image builds on an analogy between a child and a target. Note that the design pulls the viewer's eye toward the bull's-eye at the center while also taking advantage of the top left-hand position (where readers of English begin) for the caption: "A child is not a target." The dramatic combination of words and image draws viewers' eyes back over the child-as-bull's-eye target and leads to the demand at the bottom: "Stop the cycle of domestic violence." According to TurnAround, the poster is "intended to strike a chord with abusers as well as their victims." The tension between the words and the image — the child is, in fact, depicted as a target — can make a close look at this poster an unsettling experience.

Analyzing Arguments 12

In one important sense, all language use has an argumentative edge. When you greet friends warmly, you wish to convince them that you are genuinely glad to see them, that you value their presence. Even

apparently objective news reporting has strong argumentative overtones. By putting a particular story on the front page, for example, a paper argues that this subject is more important than others; by using emotional language or by focusing on certain details, news writers try to persuade us to view an event in a particular way. Consider the different ways reporters might describe the image below, such as *an outpouring of support for our troops* or *a pro-war rally*.

It's possible, then, to read any message or text, verbal or visual, as an argument, even if argument is not its primary purpose. In much academic writing, however, *argument* is more narrowly defined as a text that makes a claim (usually in the form of an arguable statement) and supports it fully.

AT A GLANCE

Analyzing Arguments

- What cultural contexts inform the argument — and what do they tell you about where the writer or creator is coming from? (12b)
- What emotional, ethical, and logical appeals does the argument make? (12c)
- How does the writer or creator establish credibility? (12c)
- What sources does the argument rely on? How current and reliable are they? Are some perspectives left out? What effect does this exclusion have on the argument? (12c)
- What claim does the verbal or visual argument make? What reasons and assumptions support and underlie the claim? What additional evidence backs up the assumptions and claim? (12d)
- Does the thesis reflect the claim accurately?
- What fallacies can you identify, and what effect do they have on the argument's persuasiveness? (12f)
- What overall impression does the argument create? Are you convinced?

12a　Think critically about argument.

Critical thinking is a crucial component of argument, for it guides us in recognizing, formulating, and examining arguments. Here are some ways to think critically about argument:

- *Check understanding.* First, make sure you understand what is being argued and why. If you need to find out more about an unfamiliar subject to grasp the argument, do the research.
- *Play the believing — and the doubting — game.* Begin by playing the *believing game:* put yourself in the position of the person creating

the argument to see the topic from that person's point of view as much as possible. Once you have given the argument sympathetic attention, play the *doubting game:* look skeptically at each claim, and examine each piece of evidence to see how well (or poorly) it supports the claim. Eventually, this process of believing and doubting will become natural.

- **Ask pertinent questions.** Whether you are thinking about others' ideas or your own, you should question unstated purposes and assumptions, the writer's qualifications, the context, the goal of the argument, and the evidence presented. What objections might be made to the argument?

- **Interpret and assess information.** All information that comes to us has a perspective — a spin. Your job is to identify the perspective and assess it, examining its sources and finding out what you can about its context.

- **Assess your own arguments.** The ultimate goal of all critical thinking is to reach your own conclusions. These, too, you must question and assess.

12b Recognize cultural contexts.

To understand as fully as possible the arguments of others, pay attention to clues to cultural context and to where the writer or creator is coming from. Put yourself in the position of the person creating the argument before looking skeptically at every claim and examining every piece of evidence. Above all, watch out for your own assumptions as you analyze what you read or see. For example, just because you assume that the use of statistics as support for your argument holds more water than, say, precedent drawn from religious belief, you can't assume that all writers agree with you. Take a writer's cultural beliefs into account before you begin to analyze an argument. (See Chapter 19.)

12c Identify an argument's basic appeals.

Aristotle categorized argumentative appeals into three types: emotional appeals that speak to readers' hearts and values (known to the ancient Greeks as *pathos*), ethical appeals that support the writer's character (*ethos*), and logical appeals that use facts and evidence (*logos*).

Emotional appeals

Emotional appeals stir our emotions and remind us of deeply held values. When politicians argue that the country needs more tax relief, they almost always use an emotional appeal by including examples of one or more families they have met, stressing the concrete ways in which a tax cut would improve the quality of their lives. Although emotional appeals can sometimes manipulate or mislead an audience, they are an important part of almost every argument. Critical readers can judge the effectiveness of emotional appeals and then combat any unfair emotional appeals by analyzing them carefully.

Ethical appeals

Ethical appeals support the credibility, moral character, and goodwill of the argument's creator. These appeals are especially important for critical readers to recognize and evaluate. We may respect and admire an athlete, for example, but should we invest in the mutual funds the athlete promotes? To identify ethical appeals in arguments, ask yourself these questions: How does the creator of the argument show that he or she has really done the homework on the subject and is knowledgeable and credible about it? What sort of character does he or she build, and how? More important, is that character trustworthy? What does the creator of the argument do to show that he or she has the best interests of an audience in mind? Do those best interests match your own, and, if not, how does that alter the effectiveness of the argument?

Logical appeals

Logical appeals are viewed as especially trustworthy: "The facts don't lie," some say. Of course, facts are not the only type of logical appeals, which also include firsthand evidence drawn from observations, interviews, surveys and questionnaires, experiments, and personal experience; and secondhand evidence drawn from authorities, the testimony of others, statistics, and other print and online sources. Critical readers need to examine logical appeals just as carefully as emotional and ethical ones. What is the source of the logical appeal — and is that source trustworthy? Are all terms defined clearly? Has the logical evidence presented been taken out of context, and, if so, does that change its meaning?

12d   Analyze the elements of an argument.

According to philosopher Stephen Toulmin's framework for analyzing arguments, most arguments contain common features: a *claim* or *claims*; *reasons* for the claim; stated or unstated *assumptions* that underlie the argument (Toulmin calls these "warrants"); *evidence* such as facts, authoritative opinion, examples, and statistics; and *qualifiers* that limit the claim in some way. The figure on p. 127 shows how these elements might be applied to an argument about sex education.

ELEMENTS OF A TOULMIN ARGUMENT ON SEX-EDUCATION

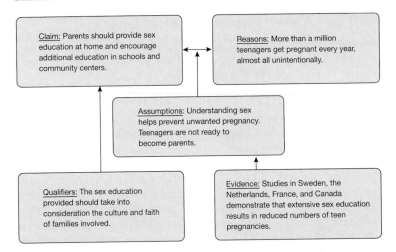

Claim: Parents should provide sex education at home and encourage additional education in schools and community centers.

Reasons: More than a million teenagers get pregnant every year, almost all unintentionally.

Assumptions: Understanding sex helps prevent unwanted pregnancy. Teenagers are not ready to become parents.

Qualifiers: The sex education provided should take into consideration the culture and faith of families involved.

Evidence: Studies in Sweden, the Netherlands, France, and Canada demonstrate that extensive sex education results in reduced numbers of teen pregnancies.

12e Analyze visual arguments.

You analyze a visual argument in much the same way that you analyze any argument. You look closely at the argument's creator, subject, audience, context, and purpose (11b) and consider cultural values (12b); emotional, ethical, and logical appeals (12c); and claims, reasons, and assumptions (12d). For visual arguments, you must also consider the effects of design and composition.

The advertising parody shown on this page contains few words, yet it makes a series of subtle arguments.

First, look at the illustration's design elements. Where is your eye first drawn — to the box, the woman, or the text? What does the box design resemble, and why? What argument do the woman's clothing and stance make, and what era of American life does the image evoke? What can you learn about the ad's creator, the nonprofit group Adbusters? What is the ad making fun of? What audience does it aim to reach? What purpose might this parody serve?

One group of students discussed this ad and came up with several possible claims that it might be making, as seen on page 128.

POSSIBLE CLAIM   Pharmaceutical companies want to convince consumers that taking drugs to cure depression is no more serious than trying a new detergent.

POSSIBLE CLAIM   Consumers should beware of drug advertisements that make hard-to-prove claims aimed at getting customers to ask for a prescription.

POSSIBLE CLAIM   Buying products will not lead to greater happiness.

All of these claims can be supported by the ad. If you were to choose the first claim, for instance, you might word a reason like this: *This parody of a Prozac ad looks like a detergent commercial from the 1960s, but the product is a chemical that promises to "wash your blues away."* With some research into the actual dangers and benefits of antidepressants, you might find evidence that ads for such drugs sometimes minimize their downside and exaggerate their promise. You might also note that the ad's design takes viewers back to a decades-old scene of domestic happiness, suggesting that Prozac could return its users to some mythically perfect, brightly colored time in the past — and you would be well on your way to an analysis of this visual argument.

AT A GLANCE
Analyzing Visual Arguments

- How does the design of the visual enhance or hinder the argument? (12e)
- What emotional appeals does the argument elicit, and how? (12c)
- What ethical appeals make the visual argument credible? Does it call on any authorities or symbols to establish character or credibility? (12c)
- How does the visual argument make logical appeals? Do words and images work together to create a logical cause-effect relationship? How are any examples used? (12c)
- What claim(s) does the visual argument make? (12d)
- What reasons are attached to the claim, and how well are they supported by evidence? (12d)
- What assumption(s) underlie the claim and the reasons? (12d)

EXERCISE 12.1: THINKING CRITICALLY

Take a look at a piece of your writing (an essay, a Web document, a report, a poster, a brochure, and so on) that uses visuals to make an argument. Using the guidelines offered in this chapter, evaluate the effectiveness of your own visual argument. If you have not created such a piece of writing, take a project that does not use visuals to advance its argument and reread it, noting ways that visuals could make the argument more effective.

12f Think critically about fallacies.

Fallacies, which are often quite convincing at first glance, can create serious flaws in an argument. But arguments are ordinarily fairly complex and occur in specific rhetorical situations, so what looks like a fallacy in one argument may not be a fallacy in another. Learn to identify fallacies, but be cautious in jumping to quick conclusions about them. Rather than thinking of them as errors you can use to discredit an arguer, you might think of them as barriers to common ground, honest debate, and understanding.

Verbal fallacies

AD HOMINEM

Ad hominem charges make a personal attack rather than focusing on the issue at hand.

▶ **Who cares what that fat loudmouth says about the health care system?**

GUILT BY ASSOCIATION

Guilt by association attacks someone's credibility by linking that person with a person or activity the audience considers bad, suspicious, or untrustworthy.

▶ **She does not deserve reelection; her husband had a gambling addiction.**

FALSE AUTHORITY

False authority is often used by advertisers who show famous actors or athletes testifying to the greatness of a product about which they may know very little.

▶ **He's today's greatest NASCAR driver — and he banks at National Mutual!**

BANDWAGON APPEAL

Bandwagon appeal suggests that a great movement is under way and the reader will be a fool or a traitor not to join it.

▶ **This new phone is everyone's must-have item. Where's yours?**

FLATTERY

Flattery tries to persuade readers by suggesting that they are thoughtful, intelligent, or perceptive enough to agree with the writer.

▶ **You have the taste to recognize the superlative artistry of Bling diamond jewelry.**

IN-CROWD APPEAL

In-crowd appeal, a special kind of flattery, invites readers to identify with an admired and select group.

▶ **Want to know a secret that more and more of Middletown's successful young professionals are finding out about? It's Mountainbrook Manor condominiums.**

VEILED THREAT

Veiled threats try to frighten readers into agreement by hinting that they will suffer adverse consequences if they don't agree.

▶ **If Public Service Electric Company does not get an immediate 15 percent rate increase, its services to you may be seriously affected.**

FALSE ANALOGY

False analogies make comparisons between two situations that are not alike in important respects.

▶ **The volleyball team's sudden descent in the rankings resembled the sinking of the *Titanic*.**

BEGGING THE QUESTION

Begging the question is a kind of circular argument that treats a debatable statement as if it had been proved true.

▶ **Television news covered that story well; I learned all I know about it by watching TV.**

POST HOC FALLACY

The post hoc fallacy (from the Latin *post hoc, ergo propter hoc,* which means "after this, therefore caused by this") assumes that just because B happened *after* A, it must have been *caused* by A.

▶ **We should not rebuild the town docks because every time we do, a big hurricane comes along and damages them.**

NON SEQUITUR

A non sequitur (Latin for "it does not follow") attempts to tie together two or more logically unrelated ideas as if they were related.

▶ **If we can send a spaceship to Mars, then we can discover a cure for cancer.**

EITHER-OR FALLACY

The either-or fallacy insists that a complex situation can have only two possible outcomes.

▶ **If we do not build the new highway, businesses downtown will be forced to close.**

HASTY GENERALIZATION

A hasty generalization bases a conclusion on too little evidence or on bad or misunderstood evidence.

▶ **I couldn't understand the lecture today, so I'm sure this course will be impossible.**

OVERSIMPLIFICATION

Oversimplification claims an overly direct relationship between a cause and an effect.

▶ **If we prohibit the sale of alcohol, we will get rid of binge drinking.**

STRAW MAN

A straw-man argument misrepresents the opposition by pretending that opponents agree with something that few reasonable people would support.

▶ **My opponent believes that we should offer therapy to the terrorists. I disagree.**

Visual fallacies

Fallacies can also take the form of misleading images. The sheer power of images can make them especially difficult to analyze — people tend to believe what they see. Nevertheless, photographs and other visuals can be manipulated to present a false impression.

MISLEADING PHOTOGRAPHS

Faked or altered photos have existed since the invention of photography. On the following page, for example, is a photograph of Joseph Stalin, the Soviet Union's leader from 1929 to 1953, with his commissar Nikolai Yezhov. Stalin and the commissar had a political disagreement that resulted in Yezhov's execution in 1940. The second image shows the same photo after Stalin had it doctored to rewrite history.

Today's technology makes such photo alterations easier than ever. But photographs need not be altered to try to fool viewers. Think of all the photos that make a politician look misleadingly bad

or good. In these cases, you should closely examine the motives of those responsible for publishing the images.

MISLEADING CHARTS AND GRAPHS

Facts and statistics, too, can be presented in ways that mislead readers. For example, the following bar graph purports to deliver an argument about how differently Democrats, on the one hand, and Republicans and Independents, on the other, felt about an issue:

DATA PRESENTED MISLEADINGLY

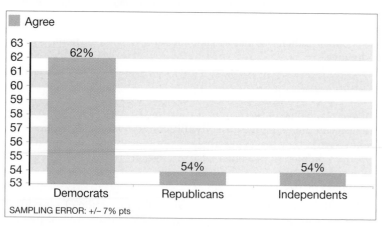

Look closely and you'll see a visual fallacy: the vertical axis starts not at zero but at 53 percent, so the apparently large difference between the groups is misleading. In fact, a majority of all respondents agree about the issue, and only eight percentage points separate Democrats from Republicans and Independents (in a poll with a margin of error of +/−

seven percentage points). Here's how the graph would look if the vertical axis began at zero:

DATA PRESENTED MORE ACCURATELY

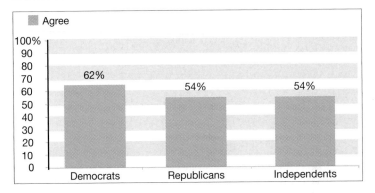

EXERCISE 12.2

Read the following brief essay by Derek Bok, which argues that college administrators should seek to educate and persuade rather than censor students who use speech or symbols that others find deeply offensive. Then carry out an analysis of the argument, beginning with identifying the audience and the author's purpose, then moving to identifying the claim, reason(s), assumption(s), evidence, and qualifiers (if any). As you work, be sure also to identify the emotional, ethical, and logical appeals as well as any fallacies put forward by Bok. You may want to compare your own analysis to the one written by Milena Ateyea in 12g.

For several years, universities have been struggling with the problem of trying to reconcile the rights of free speech with the desire to avoid racial tension. In recent weeks, such a controversy has sprung up at Harvard. Two students hung Confederate flags in public view, upsetting students who equate the Confederacy with slavery. A third student tried to protest the flags by displaying a swastika.

These incidents have provoked much discussion and disagreement. Some students have urged that Harvard require the removal of symbols that offend many members of the community. Others reply that such symbols are a form of free speech and should be protected.

Different universities have resolved similar conflicts in different ways. Some have enacted codes to protect their communities from forms of speech that are deemed to be insensitive to the feelings of other groups. Some have refused to impose such restrictions.

Rather than prohibit such communications, with all the resulting risks, it would be better to ignore them, since students would then have little reason to create such displays and would soon abandon them. If this response is not possible — and one can understand why — the wisest course is to speak with those who perform insensitive acts and try to help them understand the effects of their actions on others.

Appropriate officials and faculty members should take the lead, as the Harvard House Masters have already done in this case. In talking with students, they should seek to educate and persuade, rather than resort to ridicule or intimidation, recognizing that only persuasion is likely to produce a lasting, beneficial effect. Through such effects, I believe that we act in the manner most consistent with our ideals as an educational institution and most calculated to help us create a truly understanding, supportive community.

— DEREK BOK, "Protecting Freedom of Expression at Harvard"

12g   A student's rhetorical analysis of an argument

For a class assignment, Milena Ateyea was asked to analyze the emotional, ethical, and logical appeals in "Protecting Freedom of Expression at Harvard," an essay by Harvard president Derek Bok arguing that colleges should seek to persuade rather than to censor students who use speech or symbols that offend others.

Student Writer

Milena Ateyea

A Curse and a Blessing	Provocative title suggests Ateyea's mixed response to Bok
In 1991, when Derek Bok's essay "Protecting Freedom of Expression at Harvard" was first published in the *Boston Globe,* I had just come to America to escape the oppressive Communist regime in Bulgaria. Perhaps my background explains why I support Bok's argument that we should not put arbitrary limits on freedom of expression. Bok wrote the essay in response to a public display of Confederate flags	Connects article to her own experience to build credibility (ethical appeal)
and a swastika at Harvard, a situation that created a heated controversy among the students. As Bok notes, universities have struggled to achieve a balance between maintaining students' right of free speech and avoiding racist attacks.	Provides brief overview of Bok's argument
When choices must be made, however, Bok argues for preserving freedom of expression.	Identifies and states Bok's central claim
In order to support his claim and bridge the controversy, Bok uses a variety of rhetorical strategies. The author first immerses the reader in the controversy by	Transition sentence links Bok's claim to strategies he uses to support it

vividly describing the incident: two Harvard students had hung Confederate flags in public view, thereby "upsetting students who equate the Confederacy with slavery" (51). Another student, protesting the flags, decided to display an even more offensive symbol--the swastika. These actions provoked heated discussions among students. Some students believed that school officials should remove the offensive symbols, whereas others suggested that the symbols "are a form of free speech and should be protected" (51). Bok establishes common ground between the factions: he regrets the actions of the offenders but does not believe we should prohibit such actions just because we disagree with them.

Direct quotations show how Bok appeals to emotions through vivid description

Shows how Bok establishes common ground between two positions

The author earns the reader's respect because of his knowledge and through his logical presentation of the issue. In partial support of his position, Bok refers to U.S. Supreme Court rulings, which remind us that "the display of swastikas or Confederate flags clearly falls within the protection of the free-speech clause of the First Amendment" (52). The author also emphasizes the danger of the slippery slope of censorship when he warns the reader, "If we begin to forbid flags, it is only a short step to prohibiting offensive speakers" (52). Overall, however, Bok's work lacks the kinds of evidence that statistics, interviews with students, and other representative examples of controversial conduct could provide. Thus, his essay may not be strong enough to persuade all readers to make the leap from this specific situation to his general conclusion.

Emphasizes Bok's credibility and her respect for him (ethical appeal)

Links Bok's credibility to use of logical appeals

Reference to First Amendment serves as assumption to Bok's claim

Comments critically on kinds of evidence Bok's argument lacks

Throughout, Bok's personal feelings are implied but not stated directly. As a lawyer who was president of Harvard for twenty years, Bok knows how to present his opinions respectfully without offending the feelings of the students. However, qualifying phrases like "I suspect that" and "Under the Supreme Court's rulings, as I read them" could weaken the effectiveness of his position. Furthermore, Bok's attempt to be fair to all seems to dilute the strength of his proposed

Reiterates Bok's credibility

Identifies qualifying phrases that may weaken claim

solution. He suggests that one should either ignore the insensitive deeds in the hope that students might change their behavior, or talk to the offending students to help them comprehend how their behavior is affecting other students.

Analyzes weaknesses of Bok's proposed solution

Nevertheless, although Bok's proposed solution to the controversy does not appear at first reading to be very strong, it may ultimately be effective. There is enough flexibility in his approach to withstand various tests, and Bok's solution is general enough that it can change with the times and adapt to community standards.

Raises possibility that Bok's imperfect solution may work

Provides reasons why Bok's solution may succeed

In writing this essay, Bok faced a challenging task: to write a short response to a specific situation that represents a very broad and controversial issue. Some people may find that freedom of expression is both a curse and a blessing because of the difficulties it creates. As one who has lived under a regime that permitted very limited, censored expression, I am all too aware that I could not have written this response in 1991 in Bulgaria. As a result, I feel, like Derek Bok, that freedom of expression is a blessing, in spite of any temporary problems associated with it.

Summarizes Bok's task

Ties conclusion back to title

Concludes by returning to personal experience with censorship and oppression, which argues for accepting Bok's solution

Work Cited

Bok, Derek. "Protecting Freedom of Expression at Harvard."
    Boston Globe 25 May 1991. *Current Issues and Enduring
    Questions.* Ed. Sylvan Barnet and Hugo Bedau. 6th ed.
    Boston: Bedford, 2002. 51-52. Print.

 bedfordstmartins.com/everydaywriter To read other sample argument essays, click on **Student Writing Models**.

EXERCISE 12.3: THINKING CRITICALLY

For the following brief review for *Rolling Stone,* music critic James Hunter recaps five CDs that reissue ten Merle Haggard albums from early in the country star's career. What central claim(s) does Hunter make in this review? What emotional, ethical, and logical appeals does he present in support of his claim, and how effective are these appeals?

Outlaw Classics: The Albums That Kept Nashville Real in the Sixties and Seventies

By James Hunter

Merle Haggard — Capitol Nashville/EMI

Merle Haggard wasn't the first outsider to rebuke Nashville prissiness in the Sixties — Johnny Cash, who arrived from Sun Records in Memphis, deserves that honor — but Hag was the most down-to-earth soul that the Music City had seen for some time when he loped onto the scene in the mid- to late Sixties. An ex-con from California with Oklahoma roots, he sang eloquently about booze and prison life. His beginnings were in honky-tonk Bakersfield, where he learned first-class musical directness from guys like the great Buck Owens and Wynn Stewart.

For years, Haggard's Sixties and early-Seventies work has been represented chiefly on compilations. This bunch of reissues restores ten of those albums, all with interesting bonus tracks; four of the ten albums have never appeared before on CD. Each showcases Haggard's awesome gifts and inextricable orneriness: There is no Tennessee gothic or flashy Texas ego to this outsider; Haggard was more about subtlety and West Coast calm. A hummable, elastic honky-tonk tune can convey everything he wants to say. His melodies carry a broad range of topics, from cranky love songs ("I'm Gonna Break Every Heart I Can") to prison tunes ("Bring Me Back Home") to perfectly wrought whiskey-and-wine songs, to looks back at his parents' lives. Sometimes, as on the scarily good "I Can't Be Myself," Haggard seems to want to jump out of his own skin; other times, as on "I Threw Away the Rose," he's as centered in his own smooth, crusty tenor as any singer has ever been. In all cases, Haggard sounds like country's coolest customer.

These reissues underscore how Haggard's music far exceeds "Okie from Muskogee," the anti-hippie 1969 smash that made him internationally famous. Cash rocked country up and then went on to become his world's black-clad cultural ambassador. George Jones showed how the field needs at least one opera star, and Willie Nelson yoked local songwriting to American poetry. Haggard proved how crucial it was for a country guy to say what was on his mind — and because he was such a sublime recording artist, he was able to make it stick, right from the start.

Constructing Arguments **13**

We respond to arguments all the time. When we see a STOP sign, for example, and dutifully come to a halt, we've agreed to accept the argument that stopping at such signs is a sensible thing to do. Unfortunately, constructing an effective argument of your own is not as easy as putting up a stop sign. In fact, it's often remarkably difficult to create a thorough and convincing argument. It is especially hard to present arguments to complete strangers in cyberspace. This chapter guides you in taking up the challenges of crafting effective arguments.

AT A GLANCE

AT A GLANCE

Reviewing Your Argument

- What is the purpose of your argument — to win? to convince others? to explore an issue? (13a)
- Is the point you want to make arguable? (13a)
- Have you formulated a strong working thesis that includes a clear claim and good reasons? (13b)
- Have you considered your audience in shaping your appeals? (13d)
- How have you established your own credibility in the argument? (13e)
- How have you incorporated logical and emotional appeals into your argument? (13f and g)
- If you use visuals, do they help make your argument convincing? (13e, f, and g)
- If you use sources, how effectively are they integrated into your argument? (13h)
- How is your argument organized? (13i)
- What design elements help you make your argument? (13j)

13a Understand what counts as argument.

Although winning is an important purpose of argument, it is by no means the only purpose.

TO WIN The most traditional purpose of academic argument, arguing to win, is common in campus debating societies, in political debates, in trials, and often in business. The writer or speaker aims to present a position that will prevail over some other position.

TO CONVINCE Often, out-and-out defeat of another's position is not only unrealistic but undesirable. Instead, the goal might be to convince another person to change his or her mind. Doing so calls on a writer to provide *compelling reasons* for an audience to accept some or all of the writer's conclusions.

TO EXPLORE AN ISSUE Argument to explore an issue or reach a decision seeks a sharing of information and perspectives in order to make informed choices.

Checking whether a statement can be argued

At school, at home, or on the job, you will often need to convince someone or decide something. To do so, start with an arguable statement, which should meet the three criteria on the following page.

1. It attempts to convince readers of something, change their minds about something, to urge them to do something — or it explores a topic in order to make a wise decision.
2. It addresses a problem for which no easily acceptable solution exists or asks a question to which no absolute answer exists.
3. It presents a position that readers might realistically have varying perspectives on.

TALKING THE TALK

Arguments

"Argument seems so negative — I don't want to attack anybody or contradict what someone else says." Sometimes — in law courts, for example — argument may call for attacking an opponent's credibility, and you may have used the word *argument* to describe a conversation in which the speakers said little more than "I did not!" and "You did, too!" But in college writing, argument usually means something much broader. Instead of attacking or contradicting, you will be expected to explore ideas and to work toward convincing yourself as well as others that these ideas are valuable.

ARGUABLE   Readers should reject women's magazines with advertising that presents impossibly thin models.

This statement seeks to convince readers of a position that not all will agree with.

UNARGUABLE   Women's magazines earn millions of dollars every year from advertising that presents impossibly thin models.

This statement can easily be verified and thus does not offer a basis for argument.

EXERCISE 13.1

Using the three characteristics just listed, decide which of the following statements are arguable and which are not.

1. *The Lord of the Rings* was the best movie of the last decade.
2. The climate of the earth is gradually getting warmer.
3. The United States must further reduce social spending in order to balance the budget.
4. Shakespeare died in 1616.
5. Marlowe really wrote the plays of Shakespeare.
6. Water boils at 212 degrees Fahrenheit.
7. Van Gogh's paintings are the work of a madman.

8. The incidence of breast cancer has risen in the last ten years.

9. The Federal Emergency Management Agency's response to disasters must be radically improved.

10. A fifty-five-mile-per-hour speed limit lowers accident rates.

13b   Make a claim and formulate a working thesis.

Although the preceding arguable statement does make a kind of claim — that readers should reject certain magazines — it offers no reason for doing so. To develop a claim that can become the working thesis for an argument, you need to include at least one good reason to support the arguable statement.

REASON	Excessive dieting can cause psychological problems.
WORKING THESIS (CLAIM WITH REASON ATTACHED)	Because excessive dieting causes psychological problems, we should reject women's magazines with advertising that presents impossibly thin models.

EXERCISE 13.2

Using two arguable statements from Exercise 13.1 or two that you create, formulate two working theses, identifying the claim, reason(s), and assumption(s) for each.

13c   Examine your assumptions.

Once you have your working thesis (see also 7b), examine the assumptions that underlie it. Doing so will help test your reasoning and strengthen your argument.

WORKING THESIS	Because excessive dieting causes psychological problems, we should reject women's magazines with advertising that presents impossibly thin models.
ASSUMPTION 1	Girls and women want to look like the models in ads.
ASSUMPTION 2	Girls and women who don't look like the models in ads go on excessive diets.

Having come up with a working thesis, you may want to use qualifiers to make it more precise and thus less susceptible to criticism. The preceding thesis might be qualified this way:

▶ Because excessive dieting *can sometimes* cause psychological problems, we should reject magazines with advertising that presents impossibly thin models.

EXERCISE 13.3

Formulate an arguable statement, and create a working thesis, for two of the following general topics.

1. the Palestinian-Israeli conflict
2. mandatory HIV testing for prison inmates
3. raising the minimum wage
4. reinstatement of a U.S. military draft
5. music downloading

13d Shape your appeal to your audience.

Arguments and the claims they make are effective only if they appeal to the appropriate audience. For example, if you want to argue for increased lighting in parking garages on campus, you might appeal to students by citing examples drawn from their experiences of the safety problems in such dimly lit garages. If you are writing to university administrators, however, you might focus on the negative publicity associated with past attacks in campus garages and evoke the anger that such attacks cause in parents, alumni, and other influential groups.

13e Establish credibility through ethical appeals.

To make your argument convincing, you must first gain the respect and trust of your readers, or establish credibility with them. In general, writers can establish credibility by making ethical appeals (12c) in four ways.

Demonstrating knowledge

A writer can establish credibility first by establishing credentials. To decide whether you know enough to argue an issue credibly, consider the following questions:

- Can you provide information about your topic from sources other than your own knowledge?
- What are the sources of your information, and how reliable are they?

- If sources contradict one another, can you account for or resolve the contradictions?
- Would a personal experience relating to the issue help support your claim?

These questions may well show that you must do more research, check sources, resolve contradictions, refocus your working thesis, or even change your topic.

Establishing common ground

Many arguments between people or groups are doomed to end without resolution because the two sides seem to occupy no starting point of agreement. The following questions can help you find common ground in presenting an argument. (See also Chapter 20.)

- On this issue, how can you discover opinions that differ from your own?
- What are the differing perspectives on the issue?
- What aspects of the issue can all sides agree on?
- How can you express such common ground clearly to all sides? Can you use other languages or varieties of English to establish common ground with those you address? (See Chapter 21.)

FOR MULTILINGUAL WRITERS

Counting Your Own Experience

You may have been told that your personal experience doesn't count in making academic arguments. If so, reconsider this advice, for showing an audience that you have relevant personal experience with a topic can carry strong persuasive appeal with many English-speaking readers.

Demonstrating fairness

In arguing a position, writers must deal fairly with opposing arguments (also called counterarguments). Audiences are more inclined to listen to writers who seem to consider their opponents' views fairly than to those who ignore or distort such views.

Using visuals that make ethical appeals

Many universities, nonprofit organizations, and government agencies have followed the lead of business by creating branding images for themselves. A logo, seal, or slogan (such as the logo shown here of the

Environmental Protection Agency) may be used to give a government agency's reports, documents, and Web sites an air of strength and believability. The EPA logo suggests that the agency's publications are backed by the full authority of the federal government. It's worth remembering, however, that a logo or other visual appeal can be only as credible as the organization that the visual represents.

A VISUAL THAT MAKES AN ETHICAL APPEAL

EXERCISE 13.4

Using a working thesis you drafted for Exercise 13.2 or 13.3, write a paragraph or two describing how you would go about establishing your credibility in arguing that thesis.

13f   Use effective logical appeals.

Credibility alone cannot and should not carry the full burden of persuading readers. Indeed, many view the logic of the argument — the reasoning behind it — as equally, if not more, important.

Examples, precedents, and narratives

Just as a picture can be worth a thousand words, a well-conceived example can be valuable in arguing a point. Examples can support generalizations or bring abstractions to life. In making the general claim that video games equate violence with fun, you might include this example:

▶ **For instance, the makers of *Grand Theft Auto* present their "thou shalt kill" theme in the name of entertainment.**

Precedents are examples taken from the past. If, as part of a proposal for increased lighting in the library garage, you point out that the university has increased the lighting in four similar garages in the past year, you're arguing on the basis of precedent.

Narratives are examples that tell a story — and because storytelling is universal, they can be very persuasive in helping readers understand and accept an argument. In arguing for increased funding for the homeless, for instance, you might include a brief narrative about a day in the life of a homeless person to dramatize the issue and help readers see the need for more funding.

The following questions can help you check any example, precedent, or narrative that you use as supporting evidence:

- How representative is the example?
- Is it sufficient to lead to a generalization?
- In what ways does it support your claim?
- How well does the example relate to the claim you're making? Are the situations really similar?
- How timely is the example? (What was applicable in 1990 is not necessarily applicable today.)
- Will its significance be clear to your readers?
- Is the example one of several logical appeals, or does it have to carry the whole burden of the argument?

Authority and testimony

Another way to support an argument logically is to cite an authority. The use of authority has figured prominently in the controversy over smoking. Since the U.S. surgeon general's 1964 announcement that smoking is hazardous to health, many Americans have quit smoking, largely persuaded by the authority of the scientists offering the evidence.

Ask the following questions to be sure you are using authorities effectively:

- Is the authority *timely*? (The argument that the United States should pursue a policy just because it was supported by Thomas Jefferson will probably fail since Jefferson's time was so radically different from ours.)
- Is the authority *qualified* to judge the topic at hand? (To cite a movie star in an essay on linguistics may not help your argument.)
- Is the authority likely to be *known and respected* by readers? (To cite an unfamiliar authority without identification will reduce the impact of the evidence.)
- Are the authority's *credentials* clearly stated and verifiable? (Especially with Web-based sources, it is crucial to know whose authority guarantees the reliability of the information.)

Testimony — the evidence that an authority presents in support of a claim — is a feature of much contemporary argument. If testimony is timely, accurate, representative, and provided by a respected authority, then it, like authority itself, can add powerful support.

In research writing (see Chapters 14–18), you should cite your sources for authority and for testimony not based on your own knowledge.

Causes and effects

Showing that one event is the cause or the effect of another can help support an argument. Suppose you are trying to explain, in a petition to change your grade in a course, why you were unable to take the final examination. You would probably trace the causes of your failure to appear — your illness or the theft of your car, perhaps — so that the committee reading the petition would reconsider the effect — your not taking the examination.

Tracing causes often lays the groundwork for an argument, particularly if the effect of the causes is one we would like to change. In an environmental science class, for example, a student may argue that a national law regulating smokestack emissions from utility plants is needed because (1) acid rain on the East Coast originates from emissions at utility plants in the Midwest, (2) acid rain kills trees and other vegetation, (3) utility lobbyists have prevented midwestern states from passing strict laws controlling emissions from such plants, and (4) in the absence of such laws, acid rain will destroy most eastern forests by 2020. In this case, the fourth point ties all of the previous points together to provide an overall argument from effect: unless X, then Y.

Inductive and deductive reasoning

Traditionally, logical arguments are classified as using either inductive or deductive reasoning; in practice, the two almost always work together. Inductive reasoning is the process of making a generalization based on a number of specific instances. If you find you are ill on ten occasions after eating seafood, for example, you will likely draw the inductive generalization that seafood makes you ill. It may not be an absolute certainty that seafood is to blame, but the probability lies in that direction.

Deductive reasoning, on the other hand, reaches a conclusion by assuming a general principle (known as a major premise) and then applying that principle to a specific case (the minor premise). In practice, this general principle is usually derived from induction. The inductive generalization *Seafood makes me ill*, for instance, could serve as the major premise for the deductive argument *Since all seafood makes me ill, the shrimp on this buffet is certain to make me ill.*

Deductive arguments have traditionally been analyzed as syllogisms — reasoning that contains a major premise, a minor premise, and a conclusion.

MAJOR PREMISE	All people die.
MINOR PREMISE	I am a person.
CONCLUSION	I will die.

Syllogisms, however, are too rigid and absolute to serve in arguments about questions that have no absolute answers, and they often lack any appeal to an audience. Aristotle's simpler alternative, the enthymeme, asks the audience to supply the implied major premise. Consider the following example:

> Since violent video games can be addictive and cause psychological harm, players and their parents must carefully evaluate such games and monitor their use.

You can analyze this enthymeme by restating it in the form of two premises and a conclusion.

MAJOR PREMISE	Games that cause harm to players should be evaluated and monitored.
MINOR PREMISE	Violent video games can cause psychological harm to players.
CONCLUSION	These games should be evaluated and monitored.

Note that the major premise is one the writer can count on an audience agreeing with or supplying: safety and common sense demand that potentially harmful games be used with great care. By implicitly asking an audience to supply this premise to an argument, a writer engages the audience's participation.

Toulmin's system (12d) looks for claims, reasons, and assumptions instead of major and minor premises.

CLAIM	Violent video games should be carefully evaluated and their use monitored.
REASON	Violent video games can cause psychological harm to players.
ASSUMPTION	Games that can cause harm to players should be evaluated and monitored.

Whether it is expressed as a syllogism, an enthymeme, or a claim, a deductive conclusion is only as strong as the premise or reasons on which it is based.

EXERCISE 13.5

The following sentences contain deductive arguments based on implied major premises. Identify each of the implied premises.

1. Active euthanasia is morally acceptable when it promotes the best interests of everyone concerned and violates no one's rights.

2. Women should not serve in combat positions because doing so would expose them to a much higher risk of death.

3. Animals can't talk; therefore they can't feel pain as humans do.

Visuals that make logical appeals

Visuals that make logical appeals can be especially useful in arguments, since they present factual information that can be taken in at a glance. As shown on this page, *Business Week* used a simple bar graph to carry a big message about equality of pay for men and women. Consider how long it would take to explain all the information in this graph with words alone.

A VISUAL THAT MAKES A LOGICAL APPEAL

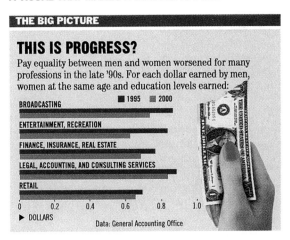

THE BIG PICTURE

THIS IS PROGRESS?

Pay equality between men and women worsened for many professions in the late '90s. For each dollar earned by men, women at the same age and education levels earned:

■ 1995 ■ 2000

BROADCASTING

ENTERTAINMENT, RECREATION

FINANCE, INSURANCE, REAL ESTATE

LEGAL, ACCOUNTING, AND CONSULTING SERVICES

RETAIL

0   0.2   0.4   0.6   0.8   1.0

▶ DOLLARS

Data: General Accounting Office

EXERCISE 13.6

Using a working thesis you drafted for Exercise 13.2 or 13.3, write a paragraph describing the logical appeals you would use to support the thesis.

13g Use appropriate emotional appeals.

Most successful arguments appeal to our hearts as well as to our minds — as is vividly demonstrated by the campaign to curb the AIDS epidemic in Africa. Facts and figures (logical appeals) convince us that the problem is real and serious. What elicits an outpouring of support, however, is the arresting emotional power of stories and images of people living with the disease. But credible writers take particular care when they use emotional appeals; audiences can easily begin to feel manipulated when an argument tries too hard to appeal to their pity, anger, or fear.

Concrete descriptive details

Like photographs, vivid words can bring a moving immediacy to any argument. A student may amass facts and figures, including diagrams and maps, to illustrate the problem of wheelchair access to the library. But only when the student asks a friend who uses a wheelchair to accompany her to the library does the student writer discover the concrete details necessary to move readers. The student can then write, "Marie inched her heavy wheelchair up the narrow, steep entrance ramp, her arms straining to pull up the last twenty feet, her face pinched with the sheer effort."

Figurative language

Figurative language, or figures of speech, paint a detailed and vivid picture by making striking comparisons between something you are writing about and something else that helps a reader visualize, identify with, or understand it (22d).

Figures of speech include metaphors, similes, and analogies. Most simply, metaphors compare two things directly: *Richard the Lion-Hearted; old age is the evening of life.* Similes make comparisons using *like* or *as: Richard is as brave as a lion; old age is like the evening of life.* Analogies are extended metaphors or similes that compare an unfamiliar concept or process to a more familiar one (see p. 81).

Visuals that make emotional appeals

Visuals that make emotional appeals can also add substance to your argument. To make sure that such visual appeals will enhance your argument, test them out with several potential readers to see how they interpret the appeal. Consider, for example, the photograph on p. 149 of coffins returning from Iraq. Some readers might see this image as making an antiwar argument — but others may well view this image as arguing instead (or also) for patriotism or for respect for sacrifices made in the line of duty.

EXERCISE 13.7

Make a list of common human emotions that might be attached to each of the following topics, and suggest appropriate ways to appeal to those emotions in a specific audience you choose to address.

1. banning drinking on campus
2. airport security
3. disarming land mines
4. attacks on places of worship
5. steroid use among athletes

A VISUAL THAT MAKES AN EMOTIONAL APPEAL

EXERCISE 13.8

Using a working thesis you formulated for Exercise 13.2 or 13.3, make a list of the emotional appeals most appropriate to your topic and audience. Then spend ten to fifteen minutes brainstorming, looking for descriptive and figurative language to carry out the appeals.

EXERCISE 13.9

Working with two or three classmates, read the following paragraph, and then write a paragraph evaluating its use of description and figurative language as well as its appeal to various audiences.

> In 1973, all women in the United States became legally entitled to have abortions performed in hospitals by licensed physicians. Earlier, abortions were frequently performed by persons who bore more resemblance to butchers than to doctors. The all-too-common result was serious complications or death for the woman. If the 1973 Supreme Court decision is completely reversed, abortion will not end. Instead, women will again resort to illegal abortions, and there will be a return to the slaughterhouse. Since abortions are going to take place no matter what the law says, why not have them done safely and legally in hospitals instead of in basements and back alleys? The decision to have an abortion is not an easy one to make, and I believe that a woman who makes it deserves to have her wish carried out in the very safest way possible. Critics of abortion stress the importance of the unborn child's life. At the very least, they should also take the woman's life and safety into consideration.

13h   Consult sources.

In constructing a written argument, it is usually necessary — and often essential — to use sources. The key to persuading people to accept your argument is good reasons; and even if your assignment doesn't specify that you must consult outside sources, they are often the most effective way of finding and establishing these reasons. Sources can help you do the following:

- provide background information on your topic
- demonstrate your knowledge of the topic to readers
- cite authority and testimony in support of your thesis
- find opinions that differ from your own, which can help you sharpen your thinking, qualify your thesis if necessary, and demonstrate fairness to opposing arguments

Argument

College writing classes concentrate on preparing you to make strong arguments, on asking you to make claims and support them well; in fact, arguments are the most common assignment in composition today. Such assignments almost always either give you a claim to support or refute or ask you to come up with a claim that has no easy solution and that might cause reasonable people to disagree. You may or may not be asked to do research to find evidence to support your argument.

SPECIAL CONSIDERATIONS OF AN ARGUMENT ASSIGNMENT

- Make sure that your introduction makes your purpose clear, shows that you are fair and credible, and introduces your claim, usually in the form of an explicit thesis statement.
- Support your claim with good reasoning, solid evidence from reliable sources (if you are using research), and effective appeals to your audience.
- Take counterarguments and alternative points of view into consideration.
- Make the organization straightforward so that readers can follow along easily.
- Conclude by summarizing the argument, elaborating on the implications of your claim or thesis, and ending with a strong appeal to your audience.

13i Organize your argument.

Once you have assembled good reasons in support of a working thesis, you must present your material convincingly. Although there is no universally favored organizational framework for an argument, you may find one of the following systems useful.

The classical system

The system of argument often followed by ancient Greek and Roman orators is now referred to as *classical*. You can adapt the ancient format to written arguments as follows:

1. Introduction

- Gain readers' attention and interest.
- Establish your qualifications to write about your topic.
- Establish common ground with readers.

- Demonstrate fairness.
- State or imply your thesis.

2. Background

- Present any necessary background information, including relevant personal narrative.

3. Lines of argument

- Present good reasons (including logical and emotional appeals) in support of your thesis.
- Present reasons in order of importance, with the most important ones generally saved for last.
- Demonstrate ways your argument may be in readers' best interest.

4. Alternative arguments

- Examine alternative points of view.
- Note advantages and disadvantages of alternative views.
- Explain why one view is better than other(s).

5. Conclusion

- Summarize the argument if you choose.
- Elaborate on the implication of your thesis.
- Make clear what you want readers to think or do.
- Reinforce your credibility.

The Toulmin system

This simplified form of the Toulmin system (12d and 13f) can help you organize an argumentative essay:

1. Make your claim (arguable statement).

▶ **The federal government should ban smoking.**

2. Qualify your claim if necessary.

▶ **The ban would be limited to public places.**

3. Present good reasons to support your claim.

▶ **Smoking causes serious diseases in smokers.**
▶ **Nonsmokers are endangered by others' smoke.**

4. Explain the assumptions that underlie your claim and your reasons. Provide additional explanations for any controversial assumptions.

ASSUMPTION	The Constitution was established to "promote the general welfare."
ASSUMPTION	Citizens are entitled to protection from harmful actions by others.
ADDITIONAL EXPLANATION	The United States is based on a political system that is supposed to serve the basic needs of its people, including their health.

5. Provide additional evidence to support your claim (facts, statistics, testimony, and other logical, ethical, or emotional appeals).

STATISTICS	Cite the incidence of deaths attributed to secondhand smoke.
FACTS	Cite lawsuits won recently against large tobacco companies, including one that awarded billions of dollars to states in reparation for smoking-related health care costs.
FACTS	Cite bans on smoking already imposed on indoor public spaces in many cities.
AUTHORITY	Cite the surgeon general.

6. Acknowledge and respond to possible counterarguments.

COUNTER-ARGUMENT	Smokers have rights, too.
RESPONSE	The suggested ban applies only to public places; smokers are free to smoke in private.

7. Finally, draw your conclusion, stated in the strongest way possible.

13j Consider design issues.

Most arguments today are carefully designed to make the best use of space, font style and type size, color, and visuals. The following tips will help you produce and design a document that will add to the ethical, logical, and emotional appeals you are making:

- Before you begin, check out any conventions that may be expected in the kind of argument you are writing. Look for examples of similar arguments, or ask your instructor for information about such conventions.

- To emphasize an important part of your argument, consider using a special design element. For example, you might put a list of essential evidence in a carefully labeled box.

- Choose colors carefully, keeping in mind that colors call up many responses: red for war, for example, or blue for purity.

For more on document design, see Chapter 4.

EXERCISE 13.10

Using the guidelines in this chapter, draft an argument in support of one of the working theses you formulated in Exercise 13.2 or 13.3.

EXERCISE 13.11: THINKING CRITICALLY

Using the guidelines in Chapter 9, analyze an argument you've recently written or the draft you wrote for Exercise 13.10. Decide what you need to do to revise your argument, and write out a brief plan for revision.

13k A student's argument essay

In this essay, Teal Pfeifer argues that images in the media affect how women see themselves, and she offers a solution to a problem. Her essay has been annotated to point out the various parts of her argument as well as her use of good reasons, evidence, and appeals to logic and emotion.

Student Writer

Teal Pfeifer

bedfordstmartins.com/everydaywriter For additional help with argumentation, go to **Writing Resources** and click on **Argument Resources**. To read other sample argument essays, click on **Student Writing Models**.

Pfeifer 1

Teal Pfeifer

Professor Rashad

English 102

April 13, 2006

Devastating Beauty

Collarbones, hipbones, cheekbones--so many bones. She looks at
the camera with sunken eyes, smiling, acting beautiful. Her dress is
Versace, or Gucci, or Dior, and it is revealing, revealing every bone and
joint in her thin, thin body. She looks fragile and beautiful, as if I could
snap her in two. I look at her and feel the soft cushion of flesh that
surrounds my own joints, my own shoulders and hips that are broad, my
own ribs surrounded by skin and muscle and fat. I am not nearly as
fragile or graceful or thin. I look away and wonder what kind of self-
discipline it takes to become beautiful like the model in my magazine.

By age seventeen a young woman has seen an average of
250,000 ads featuring a severely underweight woman whose body
type is, for the most part, unattainable by any means, including
extreme ones such as anorexia, bulimia, and drug use ("The Skinny").
The media promote clothing, cigarettes, fragrances, and even food
with images like these. In a culture that has become increasingly
visual, the images put out for public consumption feature women
that are a smaller size than ever before. In 1950, the White Rock
Mineral Water girl was 5'4" tall and weighed 140 pounds; now she is
5'10" tall and weighs only 110 pounds, signifying the growing
deviation between the weight of models and that of the normal
female population (Pipher 184).

This media phenomenon has had a major effect on the female
population as a whole, both young and old. Five to ten million women
in America today suffer from an eating disorder related to poor self-
image, and yet advertisements continue to prey on insecurities fueled
by a woman's desire to be thin. Current research shows that "80 percent

---

Title uses play on words to pique interest

Opening uses emotional appeals and tries to establish common ground with readers

Presents background information on the problem and cites sources

Introduces problem: ads encourage women's poor body image

Pfeifer 2

Good reason for thesis: stringent dieting can cause psychological problems

of American women are dissatisfied with their appearance" and that "45 percent of those are on a diet on any given day" ("Statistics"). Yet even the most stringent dieting will generally fail to create the paper-thin body so valued in the media, and continuing efforts to do so can lead to serious psychological problems such as depression.

Provides statistical evidence that problem extends across age groups

While many women express dissatisfaction with their bodies, they are not the only victims of the emaciated images so frequently presented to them. Young girls are equally affected by these images, if not more so. Eighty percent of girls under age ten have already been on a diet and expressed the desire to be thinner and more beautiful (*Slim Hopes*). Thus, from a young age, beauty is equated with a specific size. The message girls get is an insidious one: in order to be your best self, you should wear size 0 or 1. The pressure only grows more intense as girls grow up. According to results from the Kaiser Family Foundation Survey "Reflections of Girls in the Media," 16 percent of ten- to seventeen-year-old girls reported that they had dieted or exercised to look like a TV character. Yet two-thirds of teenage girls acknowledged that these thin characters were not an accurate reflection of "real life" (qtd. in Dittrich, "Children").

Uses logical appeals

Good reason for thesis: magazines feed obsession with dieting

It is tragic to see so much of the American population obsessed with weight and reaching an ideal that is, for the most part, ultimately unattainable. Equally troubling is the role magazines play in feeding this obsession. When a researcher asked female students from Stanford University to flip through several magazines containing images of glamorized, super-thin models (see Fig. 1), 68 percent of the women felt significantly worse about themselves after viewing the magazine models (qtd. in Dittrich, "Media"). Another study showed that looking at models on a long-term basis leads to stress, depression, guilt, and lowered self-worth (qtd. in Dittrich, "Media"). As Naomi Wolfe points out in *The Beauty Myth*, thinking obsessively about fat and dieting has actually been shown to change thought patterns and brain chemistry.

Backs up reasons with research and expert opinion

Pfeifer 3

Fig. 1. Young woman reading magazine. Personal photograph by author.

How do we reject images that are so harmful to the women and young girls who view them? Legislation regarding what can be printed and distributed is not an option because of First Amendment rights. Equally untenable is the idea of appealing to the industries that hire emaciated models. As long as the beauty and clothing industries are making a profit from the physically insecure girls and women who view their ads, nothing will change. *(Considers and rejects alternative solutions)*

What, however, might happen if those females stopped buying the magazines that print such destructive images? A boycott is the most effective way to rid the print medium of emaciated models and eliminate the harmful effects they cause. If women stopped buying magazines that target them with such harmful advertising, magazines would be forced to change the kinds of ads they print. Such a boycott would send a clear message: women and girls reject the victimization that takes place every time they look at a skeletally thin model and *(States working thesis: a boycott would effectively solve problem)*

Pfeifer 4

then feel worse about themselves. Consumers can ultimately control what is put on the market: if we don't buy, funding for such ads will dry up fast.

Good reason: boycotts have been effective

Presents a precedent/ example as evidence

In the past, boycotts have been effective tools for social change. Rosa Parks, often identified as the mother of the modern-day civil rights movement, played a pivotal role in the Montgomery bus boycott in December 1955. When Parks refused to give up her seat to a white bus rider, she was arrested, and this incident inspired the boycott. For more than a year, the vast majority of African Americans in Montgomery chose to walk instead of ride the buses. Many of them were terrorized or harassed, but the boycott was eventually successful: segregation on buses was declared illegal by the U.S. Supreme Court.

Presents a second precedent/ example as evidence

Between 1965 and 1973, Cesar Chavez also used boycotts successfully to change wage policies and working conditions for millions of Mexicans and Mexican Americans who were being exploited by growers of grapes and lettuce. In his boycott efforts, Chavez moved on two fronts simultaneously: he asked the workers to withhold their labor, and he asked consumers to refrain from purchasing table grapes (and later, lettuce) in order to show their support for the workers. In this situation, not only did the boycott force an industry to improve existing conditions, but it also made the public aware of pressing labor issues. Thus a bond was formed between the workers and the community their labor was benefiting.

Appeals directly to audience by using "we" in conclusion

Reinforces severity of problem and appeals to emotion

As a society, we have much to learn from boycotts of the past, and their lessons can help us confront contemporary social ills. As I have shown, body-image dissatisfaction and eating disorders are rising at an alarming rate among young girls and women in American society. This growing desire for an unrealistically thin body affects our minds and our spirits, especially when we are pummeled dozens of times a day with glamorized images of emaciated and unhealthy women. The resulting anorexia and bulimia that women suffer from

Pfeifer 5

are not only diseases that can be cured; they are also ones that can be prevented--if women will take a solid stand against such advertisements and the magazines that publish them. While we are not the publishers or advertisers who choose the pictures of starving women represented in magazines, we are the ones who decide whether or not these images will be purchased. This is where power lies--in the hands of those who hand over the dollars that support the glorification of unhealthy and unrealistic bodies. It is our choice to exert this power and to reject magazines that promote such images.

Restates thesis as a call to action

Pfeifer 6

Works Cited

Dittrich, Liz. "About-Face Facts on Children and the Media." *About-Face*. About-Face, 1996-2008. Web. 10 Mar. 2006.

---. "About-Face Facts on the Media." *About-Face*. About-Face, 1996-2008. Web. 10 Mar. 2006.

Pipher, Mary. *Reviving Ophelia: Saving the Selves of Adolescent Girls*. New York: Ballantine, 1994. Print.

"The Skinny on Media and Weight." *Common Sense Media*. Common Sense Media Inc., 27 Sept. 2005. Web. 15 Mar. 2006.

Slim Hopes. Dir. Sut Jhally. Prod. Jean Kilbourne. Media Education Foundation, 1995. Videocassette.

"Statistics." *National Eating Disorders Association*. National Eating Disorders Association, 2005. Web. 14 Mar. 2006.

Wolfe, Naomi. *The Beauty Myth*. New York: Harper, 2002. Print.

Young woman reading magazine. Personal photograph by author. 14 Mar. 2006.

Research

Research is formalized curiosity. It is poking and prying with a purpose.

— ZORA NEALE HURSTON

Research

Preparing for a Research Project **14**

Your employer asks you to recommend the best software for a particular project. You want to plan a week's vacation in Montreal. Your instructor assigns a term paper about a musician. Each of these situations calls for research, for examining various kinds of sources. Preparing to begin your research means taking a long look at what you already know, the best way to proceed, and the amount of time you have to find out what you need to know. For success in college and beyond, you need to understand how to start the process of academic research.

14a Analyze the research assignment.

In an introductory writing course, you might receive an assignment like this one:

> Choose a subject of interest to you, and use it as the basis for a research essay of approximately two thousand words that makes and substantiates a claim. You should use a minimum of five sources, including at least three print sources.

Topic

If your assignment doesn't specify a topic, consider the following questions (see also 5c):

- What subjects do you already know something about? Which of them would you like to explore more fully?
- What subjects do you care about? What might you like to become an expert on?
- What subjects evoke a strong reaction from you, whether positive or negative?

Be sure to get responses about your possible topic from your instructor, classmates, and friends. Ask them whether they would be interested in reading about the topic, whether it seems manageable, and whether they know of any good sources for information on the topic.

Situation

Be sure to consider the rhetorical situation (context) of any research project. Here are detailed questions to think about:

AUDIENCE

- Who will be the audience for your research project (5c)?
- Who will be interested in the information you gather, and why? What will they want to know? What will they already know?
- What do you know about their backgrounds? What assumptions might they hold about the topic?
- What response do you want from them?
- What kinds of evidence will you need to convince them?
- What will your instructor expect?

PURPOSE

- If you can choose the purpose, what would you like to accomplish (5d)?
- If you have been assigned a specific research project, keep in mind the key words in that assignment. Does the assignment ask that you *describe, survey, analyze, persuade, explain, classify, compare,* or *contrast*? What do such words mean in this field?

YOUR POSITION ON THE TOPIC

- What is your attitude toward your topic? Are you curious about it? critical of it? Do you like it? dislike it? find it confusing?
- What influences have shaped your position (5e)?

SCOPE

- How long is the project supposed to be? Base your research and writing schedule on the scale of the finished project (a short versus a long paper or presentation, a simple versus a complex Web site) and the amount of time you have to complete it.
- How many and what kind(s) of sources should you use (15a)? What kind(s) of visuals — charts, maps, photographs, and so on — will you need? Will you do any field research — interviewing, surveying, or observing (15e)?

Here is a sample schedule for a research project:

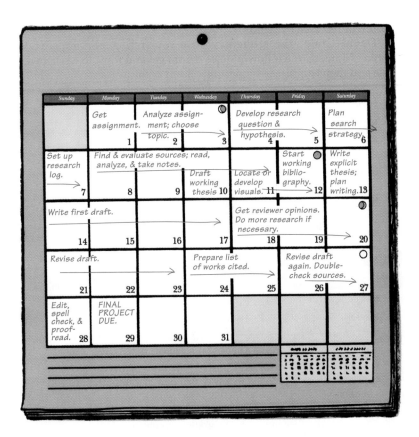

EXERCISE 14.1

Come up with at least two topics you would like to carry out research on. Then write a brief response to some key questions about each topic: How much information do you think is available on this topic? What sources on this topic do you know about or have access to? Who would know about this topic — historians, doctors, filmmakers, psychologists, others?

14b Formulate a research question and hypothesis.

Once you have analyzed your task, chosen your topic, and narrowed the topic to make it manageable (see 7a), formulate a research question that you can tentatively answer with a hypothesis. The hypothesis, a statement of what you anticipate your research will show, needs to be manageable, interesting, and specific (see 7c). In addition, it must be a debatable proposition that you can prove or disprove with a reasonable amount of research evidence.

David Craig, the student whose research paper appears in Chapter 51, made the following move from general topic to a narrowed topic and then to a research question and hypothesis:

TOPIC	Electronic messaging
NARROWED TOPIC	The language of messaging
ISSUE	The effect of messaging on youth literacy
RESEARCH QUESTION	How has the popularity of messaging affected literacy among today's youth?
HYPOTHESIS	Messaging seems to have a negative influence on the writing skills of young people.

COMMON ASSIGNMENTS

Proposal

Proposal assignments often ask you to take on a problem and find a solution for it. You may be asked to write a proposal as part of a larger project, especially a major research project.

SPECIAL CONSIDERATIONS OF A PROPOSAL ASSIGNMENT

- Think of your proposal as an answer to a problem that exists. Define or describe that problem in a way that makes it important to your audience.

- Provide ample evidence and examples from research, personal experience, or other sources to illustrate the problem.

- Introduce your proposal as a way to address the problem effectively.

- Explain your proposal thoroughly, showing how it responds to the problem and how it will solve it. Consider counter-proposals, and show that yours is a better answer.

- Show that what is being proposed is in your audience's best interest.

EXERCISE 14.2

Using the tips provided in 14b, write down as much as you can about one of the topics you identified in Exercise 14.1. Then take some time to reread your notes, and jot down the questions you still need to answer as well as the sources you need to find.

14c Plan your research.

Once you have formulated a hypothesis, determine what you already know about your topic. Tap your memory for sources by listing everything you can remember about *where* you learned about your topic: the Internet, text messages, books, magazines, courses, conversations, television. What you know comes from somewhere, and that somewhere can serve as a starting point for your research. (See Chapter 6 for more strategies for exploring ideas and getting your initial thoughts about a topic down on paper.)

Next, develop a research plan by answering the following questions:

- What kinds of sources (books, journal articles, databases, Web sites, government documents, reference works, and so on) will you need to consult (15a)? How many sources should you consult?
- How current do your sources need to be? (For topical issues, especially those related to science, current sources are usually most important. For historical subjects, older sources may offer the best information.)
- How can you determine the location and availability of the kinds of sources you need?

One goal of your research plan is to build a strong working bibliography (16b). Carrying out systematic research and keeping careful notes on your sources will make developing your works-cited list or bibliography easier.

14d Set up a research log.

Keeping a research log will make the job of writing and documenting your sources more efficient and accurate. Use your research log to jot down ideas about possible sources and to keep track of materials. When you record an online source in your log, include the URL or other information that will help you find the source again.

Here are a few guidelines for setting up a research log:

1. Create a folder, and label it with a name that will be easy to identify, such as *Research Log for Project on Instant Messaging.*
2. Within this folder, create subfolders that will help you manage your project. These subfolders might include *Notes on Hypothesis and Thesis, Background Information, Visuals, Draft 1, Working Bibliography,* and so on.

You might prefer to begin a Web log (blog) for your research project. You can use it to record your thoughts on the reading you are doing and, especially, add links from there to Web sites, documents, and articles you have found online. (For more on blogs, see 2d.)

Whatever form your research log takes, you must clearly distinguish the notes and comments you make from quoted passages you record.

14e Move from hypothesis to working thesis.

As you gather information, search catalogs and databases, and read and evaluate sources, you will probably refine your research question and change your hypothesis significantly. Only after you have explored your hypothesis, tested it, and sharpened it by reading, writing, and talking with others does it become a working thesis.

David Craig, the student whose hypothesis appears in 14b, did quite a bit of research on messaging language, youth literacy, and the possible connection between the two. The more he read, the more he felt that the hypothesis suggested by his discussion with instructors — that messaging had contributed to a decline in youth literacy — did not hold up. He shifted his attention to the positive effects of messaging on communication skills and developed the following working thesis: "Although some educators criticize messaging, it may aid literacy by encouraging young people to use words and to write — even if messaging requires a different kind of writing."

In doing your own research, you may find that your interest shifts, that a whole line of inquiry is unproductive, or that your hypothesis is simply wrong. The process of research pushes you to learn more about your hypothesis and to make it more precise.

EXERCISE 14.3: THINKING CRITICALLY

If you have done research for an essay or research project before, go back and evaluate the work you did as a researcher and as a writer in light of the principles developed in this chapter. What was the purpose of the research? Who was your audience? How did you narrow and focus your topic? What kinds of sources did you use? Did you use a research log? What about your research and your essay pleased you most? What pleased you least? What would you do differently if you were to revise the essay now?

EXERCISE 14.4: THINKING CRITICALLY

Begin to analyze the research project you are now working on by examining the ways in which you conducted your research: What use did you make of primary and secondary sources? What library, online, and field research did you carry out? What aspect of the research process was most satisfying? What was most disappointing or irritating? How could you do research more efficiently? Bring your answers to these questions to class.

Doing Research | **15**

How would you find out where to get the best coffee in town, or how to find sources for a Web project on a 1930s film star? Whether you are researching pizza or Picasso, you need to be familiar with the kinds of sources you are likely to use, the searches you can perform, and the types of research you will do most often: library, Internet, and field research.

15a Understand different kinds of sources.

Sources can include data from interviews and surveys, books and articles in print and online, Web sites, film, video, images, and more. Consider these important differences among sources.

Primary and secondary sources

Primary sources provide firsthand knowledge, while secondary sources report on or analyze the research of others. Primary sources are basic sources of raw information, including your own field research; films, works of art, or other objects you examine; literary works you read; and eyewitness accounts, photographs, news reports, and historical documents (such as letters and speeches). Secondary sources are descriptions or interpretations of primary sources, such as researchers' reports, reviews, biographies, and encyclopedia articles. Often what constitutes a primary or secondary source depends on the purpose of your research. A critic's evaluation of a film, for instance, serves as a secondary source if you are writing about the film but as a primary source if you are studying the critic's writing.

Scholarly and popular sources

While nonacademic sources like magazines can help you get started on a research project, you will usually want to depend more heavily on authorities in a field, whose work generally appears in scholarly journals in print or online. The list on the following page will help you distinguish scholarly and popular sources.

SCHOLARLY

POPULAR

SCHOLARLY	POPULAR
Title often contains the word *Journal*	*Journal* usually does not appear in title
Source available mainly through libraries and library databases	Source generally available outside of libraries (at newsstands or from a home Internet connection)
Few commercial advertisements	Many advertisements
Authors identified with academic credentials	Authors are usually journalists or reporters hired by the publication, not academics or experts
Summary or abstract appears on first page of article; articles are fairly long	No summary or abstract; articles are fairly short
Articles cite sources and provide bibliographies	Articles may include quotations but do not cite sources or provide bibliographies

Older and more current sources

Most projects can benefit from both older, historical sources and more current ones. Some older sources are classics, essential for understanding later scholarship. Others are simply dated. Whether a source appeared hundreds of years ago or this morning, evaluate it carefully to determine how useful it will be for you.

15b Use the library to get started.

Many beginning researchers are tempted to assume that all the information they could possibly need is readily available on the Internet from a home connection. However, it is a good idea to begin almost any research project with the sources available in your college library.

Reference librarians

One particularly valuable resource is your library staff — especially reference librarians. You can make an appointment to talk with a librarian about your research project and get specific recommendations about databases and other helpful places to begin your research. In addition, many libraries have online tours and chat environments where students can ask questions about their research.

Catalogs and databases

Your library's computers hold many resources not accessible to students except through the library's system. In addition to the library's own catalog of books and other holdings, most college libraries also subscribe to a large number of databases — electronic collections of information, such as indexes to journal and magazine articles, texts of news stories and legal cases, lists of sources on particular topics, and compilations of statistics — that students can access for free.

TALKING THE TALK

Wikis as Sources

"Why doesn't my instructor want me to use Wikipedia as a source?" Wikis are sites that users can add to and edit as they see fit; as a result, their contents are not always reliable. It's true that Wikipedia, a hugely popular site, has such a large and enthusiastic audience that users are likely to catch mistakes and remove deliberately false information quickly. But you can never be certain that a wiki entry has not been tampered with. Use wikis as sources for preliminary research and then make sure that you double-check any information you find there.

Reference works

Consulting general reference works is another good way to get started on a research project that is unfamiliar to you. These works are especially helpful for getting an overview of a topic, identifying subtopics, finding more specialized sources, and identifying useful keywords for electronic searches.

ENCYCLOPEDIAS

Encyclopedias offer general background on a subject and often include bibliographies that can point you to more specialized sources. Remember that encyclopedias will serve as a place to start your research — not as major sources for a research project.

BIOGRAPHICAL RESOURCES

The lives and historical settings of famous people are the topics of biographical dictionaries and indexes.

ALMANACS, YEARBOOKS, AND ATLASES

Almanacs and yearbooks contain data on current events and statistical information. Look in an atlas for maps and other geographic data.

15c   Find library resources.

The library is one of a researcher's best friends, especially in an age of electronic communication. Your college library houses a great number of print materials and gives you access to electronic catalogs, indexes, and databases.

Catalogs and databases

The most important tools your library offers are its online catalog and databases. Searching these tools will always be easier and more efficient if you use carefully chosen words to limit the scope of your research.

SUBJECT WORD SEARCHING

Catalogs and databases usually index their contents not only by author and title, but also by subject headings — standardized words and phrases used to classify the subject matter of books and articles. (For books, most U.S. academic libraries use the *Library of Congress Subject Headings*, or LCSH, for this purpose.) When you search the catalog by subject, you need to use the exact subject words.

KEYWORD SEARCHING

Searches using keywords, on the other hand, make use of the computer's ability to look for any term in any field of the electronic record. In article databases, a keyword search will look in abstracts and summaries of articles as well. Keyword searching is less restrictive, but you will need to put some thought into choosing your search terms to get the best results.

ADVANCED SEARCHING

Many library catalogs and database search engines offer advanced search options (sometimes on a separate page) to help you combine keywords, search for an exact phrase, or exclude items containing particular keywords. Often they can limit your search in other ways as well.

Many catalogs and databases offer a search option using the Boolean operators AND, OR, and NOT, and some allow you to use parentheses to refine your search or wildcards to expand it. Note that much Boolean decision making is done for you when you use an advanced search option (as on the advanced search page shown below). Note, too, that search engines vary in the exact terms and symbols they use to refine searches, so check before you search.

- AND *limits your search.* If you enter the terms *IM* AND *language* AND *literacy,* the search engine will retrieve only those items that contain *all* the terms. Some search engines use a plus sign (+) instead of AND.

- OR *expands your search.* If you enter the terms *messaging* OR *language,* the computer will retrieve every item that contains the term *messaging* and every item that contains the term *language.*

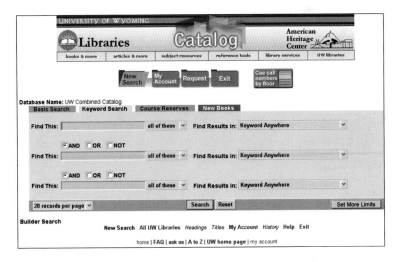

Advanced search page from a library catalog that incorporates Boolean operators

- NOT *limits your search*. If you enter the terms *messaging* NOT *language*, the search engine will retrieve every item that contains *messaging* except those that also contain the term *language*. Some search engines use a minus sign (–) or AND NOT instead of NOT.

- *Parentheses customize your search*. Entering *messaging* AND (*literacy* OR *linguistics*), for example, will locate items that mention either of those terms in connection with messaging.

- *Wildcards expand your search*. Use a wildcard, usually an asterisk (*) or a question mark (?), to find related words that begin with the same letters. Entering *messag** will locate *message, messages*, and *messaging*.

- *Quotation marks narrow your search*. Most search engines interpret words within quotation marks as a phrase that must appear with the words in that exact order.

Books

CATALOG INFORMATION

The library catalog lists all the library's holdings and offers multiple entries (usually including entries arranged by author, title, subject, ISBN, and so on) that users can search. You can also search the catalog by using a combination of subject headings and keywords. Such searches may turn up several useful titles on your topic.

Following are a search page and a page of results for noted linguist and author David Crystal:

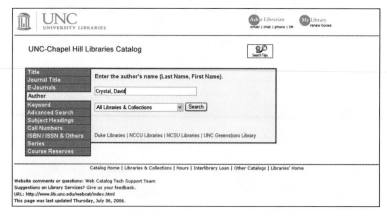

Library catalog search page

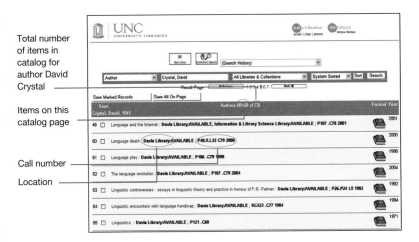

Total number of items in catalog for author David Crystal

Items on this catalog page

Call number

Location

Results for author search in library catalog database

Catalog entries for books list a call number that indicates how the book is classified and where it is shelved. Once you have the call number for a book, look for a library map or shelving plan to tell you where the book is housed. Take the time to browse through the books near the call number you are looking for. Often you will find other books related to your topic in the immediate area.

BOOK INDEXES

Indexes can help you quickly locate complete bibliographic information on a book when you know only one piece of it — the author's last name, perhaps, or the title — and can alert you to other works by a particular author or on a particular subject. If you are looking for an older book, you may find the information you need in print volumes rather than in an electronic database.

REVIEW INDEXES

A review index will help you find reviews of books you are interested in so that you can check the relevance of a source or get a thumbnail sketch of its contents before you track it down. For reviews more than ten years old, you will generally need to consult the print version of the index.

PERIODICAL ARTICLES

Titles of periodicals held by a library appear in its catalog, but the titles of individual articles do not. To find the contents of periodicals, you will need to use an index source.

PERIODICAL INDEXES

Periodical indexes are databases or print volumes that hold information about articles published in newspapers, magazines, and scholarly journals. Different indexes cover different groups of periodicals. Ask a reference librarian for guidance about the most relevant index for your topic.

Some electronic periodical indexes offer the full text of articles and some offer abstracts (short summaries) of the articles. Be sure not to confuse an abstract with a complete article. Full-text databases can be extremely convenient — you can read and print out articles directly from the computer, without the extra step of tracking down the periodical in question. However, don't limit yourself to full-text databases, which may not include the sources that would benefit your research most. Databases that offer abstracts give you an overview of the article's contents that can help you decide whether you need to spend time finding and reading the full text.

GENERAL INDEXES General indexes of periodicals list articles from general-interest magazines (such as *Time* or *Newsweek*), newspapers, or a combination of these. General indexes usually provide current sources on a topic, but you may need to look further for in-depth articles. Frequently used general indexes include InfoTrac and LexisNexis, which can both be used to access a vast collection of newspapers, magazines, and scholarly journals.

SPECIALIZED INDEXES AND ABSTRACTS Many disciplines have specialized indexes and abstracts to help researchers find detailed information. To use these resources most efficiently, ask a reference librarian to help you. Many of the most common discipline-specific online databases are listed in the following box.

AT A GLANCE

Discipline-Specific Online Databases

HUMANITIES	SOCIAL SCIENCES	NATURAL AND APPLIED SCIENCES
ABC-CLIO	ERIC	EBSCOhost
EBSCOhost	EBSCOhost	General Science Index
Humanities Index	Government Documents Catalog Services (GDCS)	JSTOR
JSTOR		
MLA Bibliography	GPO Access	**BUSINESS**
Project Muse	JSTOR	EBSCOhost
ProQuest	PAIS International	Periodical Abstracts
	ProQuest	ProQuest
	PsycInfo	

ACCESS TO INDEXED PERIODICAL ARTICLES

To locate an indexed article that seems promising for your research project, you can check the library catalog to see whether the periodical is available electronically and, if so, whether your library has access to it. Using the library computer network for access can help you avoid paying to view the text of the article that is available online only for subscribers or for a fee.

If the periodical is not available electronically (some scholarly journals, for example, are not), the library catalog also will tell you whether a print version is available in your library's periodicals room. This room probably has recent issues of hundreds or even thousands of newspapers, magazines, and scholarly journals, and it may also contain bound volumes of past issues and microfilm copies of older newspapers.

Bibliographies

Bibliographies (lists of sources) in books or articles you are using for your research can lead you to other valuable resources. In addition, check with a reference librarian to find out whether your library has more extensive bibliographies devoted to the area of your research.

Other library resources

In addition to books and periodicals, libraries give you access to many other useful materials that might be appropriate for your research.

- *Special collections and archives*. Your library may house archives (collections of valuable papers) and other special materials that are often available to student researchers.

Results of search in a specialized index

- *Audio, video, multimedia, and art collections.* Many libraries have areas devoted to media and art, where they collect films, videos, paintings, and sound recordings.
- *Government documents.* Many libraries have collections of historical documents produced by local or state government offices. You can also look at the online version of the U.S. Government Printing Office (GPO Access) for electronic versions of government publications from the past decade or so.
- *Interlibrary loans.* To borrow books, videos, copies of journal articles, or audio materials from another library, use an interlibrary loan. Some loans can take time, so be sure to plan ahead.

15d   Search the Internet.

The Internet is many college students' favorite way of accessing information, and it's true that much information — including authoritative sources identical to those your library provides — can be found online, sometimes for free. However, information in library databases comes from identifiable and professionally edited sources; because no one is responsible for regulating information on the Web, you need to take special care to find out which information online is reliable and which is not. (See Chapter 16 for more on evaluating sources.)

Internet searches

Research using a search tool such as Google usually begins with a keyword search. Because the Internet contains vastly more material than the largest library catalog or database, Internet searching requires care in the choice of keywords. For example, if you need information on legal issues regarding the Internet and enter *Internet* and *law* as keywords in a Google search, you will get over three million hits. You may find what you need on the first page of hits, but if not, you will need to choose new keywords that lead to more specific sources.

 bedfordstmartins.com/everydaywriter To find links to search engines, go to **Research Resources** and click on **Links**.

Bookmarking tools

Today's powerful bookmarking tools can help you browse, sort, and track resources online. Social bookmarking sites, such as Del.icio.us and Digg, allow users to tag information and share it with others. Once you register on a social bookmarking site, you can tag an online resource with any words you choose. Users' tags are visible to all other users. If you find a helpful site, you can check to see how others have tagged it and quickly browse similar tags to find related information. You can sort and group information according to your tags. Fellow users whose tags you like and trust can become part of your network so that you can follow their sites of interest.

Web browsers can also help you bookmark and return to online resources that you have found. However, unlike the bookmarking tools in a Web browser, which are tied to one machine, social bookmarking tools are available from any computer with an Internet connection.

A social bookmarking tool

Authoritative sources online

You can find many sources online that are authoritative and reliable. For example, the Internet enables you to enter virtual libraries that allow access to some collections in libraries other than your own. Online collections housed in government sites can also be reliable and useful sources. The Library of Congress, the National Institutes of Health, and the U.S. Census Bureau, for example, have large online collections of articles. For current national news, consult online versions of reputable newspapers such as the *Washington Post* or the *Chicago Tribune*, or electronic sites for news services such as C-SPAN. To limit your searches to scholarly works, try Google Scholar.

Some scholarly journals (such as those from Berkeley Electronic Press) and general-interest magazines (including *Slate* and *Salon*) are published only on the Web, and many other publications, like *Newsweek*, the *New Yorker*, and the *New Republic*, make at least some of their contents available online for free.

 bedfordstmartins.com/everydaywriter To find links to online governmental collections and sites for newspapers and other media, go to **Reference Resources** and click on **Links.**

15e Conduct field research.

For many research projects, particularly those in the social sciences and business, you will need to collect field data. The "field" may be many things — a classroom, a church, a laboratory, or the corner grocery store. As a field researcher, you will need to discover *where* you can find relevant information, *how* to gather it, and *who* might be your best providers of information.

Interviews

Some information is best obtained by asking direct questions of other people. If you can talk with an expert — in person, on the telephone, or via the Internet — you might get information you could not obtain through any other kind of research. In addition to getting an expert opinion, you might ask for firsthand accounts or suggestions of other places to look or other people to consult.

AT A GLANCE

Conducting an Interview

1. Determine your purpose, and be sure it relates to your research question and your hypothesis.
2. Set up the interview well in advance. Specify how long it will take, and if you wish to tape-record the session, ask permission to do so.
3. Prepare a written list of factual and open-ended questions. Brainstorming or freewriting can help you come up with questions (6a and b). Leave plenty of space for notes after each question. If the interview proceeds in a direction that seems fruitful, do not feel that you have to ask all of your prepared questions.
4. Record the subject, date, time, and place of the interview.
5. Thank those you interview, either in person or in a letter or email.

Observation

Trained observers report that making a faithful record of an observation requires intense concentration and mental agility. Moreover, an ob-

---

AT A GLANCE

Conducting an Observation

1 Determine the purpose of the observation, and be sure it relates to your research question and hypothesis.
2. Brainstorm about what you are looking for, but don't be rigidly bound to your expectations.
3. Develop an appropriate system for recording data. Consider using a split notebook or page: on one side, record your observations directly; on the other, record your thoughts and interpretations.
4. Record the date, time, and place of the observation.

server is never neutral — he or she always has an angle on what is being observed.

Opinion surveys

Surveys usually depend on questionnaires. On any questionnaire, the questions should be clear and easy to understand and designed so that you can analyze the answers easily. Questions that ask respondents to say *yes* or *no* or to rank items on a scale are particularly easy to tabulate:

The parking facilities on our campus are adequate.

| Strongly agree | Somewhat agree | Unsure | Somewhat disagree | Strongly disagree |

AT A GLANCE

Designing a Questionnaire

1. Write out your purpose, and review your research question and hypothesis to determine the kinds of questions to ask.
2. Figure out how to reach the respondents you need.
3. Draft potential questions, and make sure that each question calls for a short, specific answer.
4. Test the questions on several people, and revise questions that seem unfair, ambiguous, too hard to answer, or too time consuming.
5. For a questionnaire that is to be mailed, draft a cover letter explaining your purpose. Provide a self-addressed, stamped envelope, and be sure to state a deadline.
6. On the final version of the questionnaire, leave adequate space for answers.
7. Proofread the questionnaire carefully.

Analyzing, synthesizing, and interpreting data from field research

To make sense of your data, find a focus for your analysis, since you can't pay attention to everything. Then synthesize the data by looking for recurring words or ideas that fall into patterns. Establish a system for coding your information, labeling each pattern you identify — a plus sign for every positive response, for example. Finally, interpret your data by summing up the meaning of what you have found. What is the significance of your findings? Be careful not to make big generalizations.

16 Evaluating Sources and Taking Notes

All research builds on the careful and sometimes inspired use of sources — that is, on research done by others. Whether you are doing research to identify the most affordable laptop, to persuade your college administration to improve campus safety, or to prepare a strong academic argument for a class, you will want to make the most of your sources. In other words, you will want to use the insights you gain from your sources to help you create powerful prose of your own.

16a Understand why you should use sources.

While all research draws on sources, it is worth thinking about why writers decide to use one source rather than another. What specifically can sources provide for your research projects?

- background and contextual information that sets the scene for your project or that your audience will need to follow your argument
- explanations of concepts unfamiliar to your audience
- verbal and visual emphasis for points you are making
- authority for the claims you are making, which in turn helps you create your own authority
- evidence to support your claims
- counter-examples or counter-evidence that you need to reflect on and respond to in your own argument
- varying perspectives on your topic

16b Create a working bibliography.

A working bibliography is a list of sources that you are considering using for your project. As you find research sources — articles, books, Web sites, and so on — you should record source information for every source you think you might use. Include everything you need to find the source again and cite it correctly; the information you will need varies based on the type of source, whether you found it in a library or not, and whether you consulted it in print or online. The emphasis in a working bibliography is on *working* because the list will probably include materials that end up not being useful. For this reason, you don't absolutely need to put all entries into the documentation style you will use (see Chapters 48–54).

If you do style your entries appropriately, however, that part of your work will be done when you prepare the final draft.

Record the following information if it's available:

FOR A BOOK

Call number
Author(s) or editor(s)
Title and subtitle
Place of publication
Publisher
Year of publication
Other (translator, volume, edition)

FOR PART OF A BOOK

Call number
Author(s) of part
Title of part
Author(s) or editor(s) of book
Title of book
Place of publication
Publisher
Year of publication
Inclusive page numbers for part you are using

FOR A PERIODICAL ARTICLE

Call number of periodical
Author(s) of article
Title of article
Name of periodical
Volume number
Issue number
Date of issue
Inclusive page numbers for article

FOR AN ELECTRONIC SOURCE

Author(s)
Title of document
Title of site
Editor(s) of site
Sponsor of site
Publication information for print version of source
Name of database or online service
Date of electronic publication or last update
Date you accessed the source
URL

TALKING THE TALK

Research with an Open Mind

"What's wrong with looking for sources that back up what I want to say?" When you start researching a topic, keep an open mind: investigate every important source, even if you think you won't agree with it. If all your sources take the same position you take, you may be missing a big part of the picture. Who knows? You may change your position after learning more about the topic. And even if you don't, ignoring counterarguments and other points of view harms your credibility.

ANNOTATED BIBLIOGRAPHY

You might wish to annotate your working bibliography to include your own description and comments as well as publishing information. Annotations can help you understand and remember what the source says.

ANNOTATED BIBLIOGRAPHY ENTRY

Gere, Anne Ruggles. "Kitchen Tables and Rented Rooms: The Extracurriculum of
   Composition." *Literacy: A Critical Sourcebook*. Ed. Ellen Cushman, Eugene R.
   Kintgen, Barry M. Kroll, and Mike Rose. Boston: Bedford, 2001. 275-89.
   Print.

This history of writing instruction argues that people teach writing and learn to
write--and always have--more often in informal places like kitchens than in
traditional writing classrooms. Gere presents numerous examples and comments
on their importance to the study of writing today.

 bedfordstmartins.com/everydaywriter For additional examples of annotated
   bibliographies, click on **Student Writing Models**.

16c Evaluate a source's usefulness and credibility.

Since you want the information and ideas you glean from sources to be reliable and persuasive, you must evaluate each potential source carefully. The following guidelines can help you assess the usefulness and credibility of sources you are considering:

- *Your purpose*. What will this source add to your research project? Does it help you support a major point, demonstrate that you have thoroughly researched your topic, or help establish your own credibility?
- *Relevance*. How closely related is the source to the narrowed topic you are pursuing?
- *Level of specialization and audience*. General sources can be helpful as you begin your research, but you may then need the authority or currency of more specialized sources. On the other hand, extremely specialized works may be very hard to understand. Who was the source originally written for — the general public? experts in the field? advocates or opponents? How does this fit with your concept of your own audience?

- *Credentials of the publisher or sponsor.* What can you learn about the publisher or sponsor of the source you are using? For example, is it a newspaper known for integrity, or is it a tabloid? Is it a popular source, or is it sponsored by a professional organization or academic institution? If you're evaluating a book, is the publisher one you recognize or can find described on its own Web site?

- *Credentials of the author.* Note names that come up from one source to another, since they may indicate that the author is influential in the field. An author's credentials may also be presented in the article, book, or Web site, or you can search the Internet for information about the author.

- *Date of publication.* Recent sources are often more useful than older ones, particularly in the sciences or other fields that change rapidly. However, in some fields — such as the humanities — the most authoritative works may be older ones. The publication dates of Internet sites can often be difficult to pin down. And even for sites that include dates of posting, remember that the material posted may have been composed some time earlier.

- *Accuracy of the source.* How accurate and complete is the information in the source? How thorough is the bibliography or list of works cited that accompanies the source? Can you find other sources that corroborate what your source is saying?

- *Stance of the source.* Identify the source's point of view or rhetorical stance, and scrutinize it carefully. Does the source present facts, or does it interpret or evaluate them? If it presents facts, what is included and what is omitted, and why? If it interprets or evaluates information that is not disputed, the source's stance may be obvious, but at other times, you will need to think carefully about the source's goals (16d). What does the author or sponsoring group want — to convince you of an idea? sell you something? call you to action in some way?

- *Cross-references to the source.* Is the source cited in other works? If you see your source cited by others, notice how they cite it and what they say about it to find additional clues to its credibility.

For more on evaluating Web sources and periodical articles, see the source maps on pp. 186–87 and 188–89.

16d Read critically and interpret sources.

Reading with a critical eye can make your research process more efficient. Use the tips on p. 120 to guide your critical reading.

Determine the relevance of the source.

1 Look for an abstract, which provides a summary of the entire article. Is this source directly related to your research? Does it provide useful information and insights? Will your readers consider it persuasive support for your thesis?

Determine the credibility of the publication.

2 Consider the publication's title. Words in the title such as *Journal*, *Review*, and *Quarterly* may indicate that the periodical is a scholarly source. Most research essays rely on authorities in a particular field, whose work usually appears in scholarly journals. For more on distinguishing between scholarly and popular sources, see 15a.

3 Try to determine the publisher or sponsor. This journal is published by Johns Hopkins University Press. Academic presses such as this one generally review articles carefully before publishing them and bear the authority of their academic sponsors.

Determine the credibility of the author.

4 Evaluate the author's credentials. In this case, they are given in a note, which indicates that the author is a college professor and has written at least two books on related topics.

Determine the currency of the article.

5 Look at the publication date and think about whether your topic and your credibility depend on your use of very current sources.

Determine the accuracy of the article.

6 Look at the sources cited by the author of the article. Here, they are documented in footnotes. Ask yourself whether the works the author has cited seem credible and current. Are any of these works cited in other articles you've considered?

In addition, consider the following questions:

- What is the article's stance or point of view? What are the author's goals? What does the author want you to know or believe?

- How does this source fit in with your other sources? Does any of the information it provides contradict or challenge other sources?

Prisons and Politics in Contemporary Latin America

Mark Ungar*

ABSTRACT

Despite democratization throughout Latin America, massive human rights abuses continue in the region's prisons. Conditions have become so bad that most governments have begun to enact improvements, including new criminal codes and facility decongestion. However, once in place, these reforms are undermined by chaotic criminal justice systems, poor policy administration, and rising crime rates leading to greater detention powers for the police. After describing current prison conditions in Latin America and the principal reforms to address them, this article explains how political and administrative limitations hinder the range of agencies and officials responsible for implementing those changes.

I. INTRODUCTION

Prison conditions not only constitute some of the worst human rights violations in contemporary Latin American democracies, but also reveal fundamental weaknesses in those democracies. Unlike most other human rights problems, those in the penitentiary system cannot be easily explained with authoritarian legacies or renegade officials. The systemic killing, overcrowding, disease, torture, rape, corruption, and due process abuses all occur under the state's twenty-four hour watch. Since the mid-1990s,

* *Mark Ungar* is Associate Professor of Political Science at Brooklyn College, City University of New York. Recent publications include the books *Elusive Reform: Democracy and the Rule of Law in Latin America* (Lynne Rienner, 2002) and *Violence and Politics: Globalization's Paradox* (Routledge, 2001) as well as articles and book chapters on democratization, policing, and judicial access. He works with Amnesty International USA and local rights groups in Latin America.

Human Rights Quarterly 25 (2003) 909–934 © 2003 by The Johns Hopkins University Press

The Johns Hopkins University Press

© 2003

Determine the credibility of the sponsoring organization.

1 Consider the URL, specifically the top-level domain name. (For example, *.edu* indicates that the sponsor is an accredited college or university; *.org* indicates it's a nonprofit organization.) Might such a sponsor be biased about the topic you're researching?

2 Look for an *About* page or a link to the home page for background information on the sponsor, including a mission statement. What is the sponsoring organization's stance or point of view? Does the mission statement seem biased or balanced? Does the sponsor seem to take other points of view into account? What is the intended purpose of the site? Is this site meant to inform, or is it trying to persuade, advertise, or accomplish something?

Determine the credibility of the author.

3 Evaluate the author's credentials. On this Web page, the author appears to be a staff writer for the site. Although the author herself may not have a medical background, note that the article was reviewed by a physician and that it includes findings from a respected medical journal. If you suspect that an author may be biased, run a search on the author's name to find any affiliations with interest groups or any leaning toward one side of an issue. Ask yourself if the author seems qualified to write about the issue.

4 Look for the date that indicates when the information was posted or last updated. Here, the date is given at the beginning of the article.

5 Check to see if the sources referred to are also up-to-date. Ask yourself if, given your topic, an older source is acceptable or if only the most recent information will do.

Determine the accuracy of the information.

6 How complete is the information in the source? Examine the works cited by the author. Are sources for statistics included? Do the sources cited seem credible? Is a list of additional resources provided? Here, the author cites the *New England Journal of Medicine* and the National Center for Complementary and Alternative Medicine in addition to two of WebMD's own articles. In some cases, it may be necessary to track down additional sources and corroborate what a source is saying.

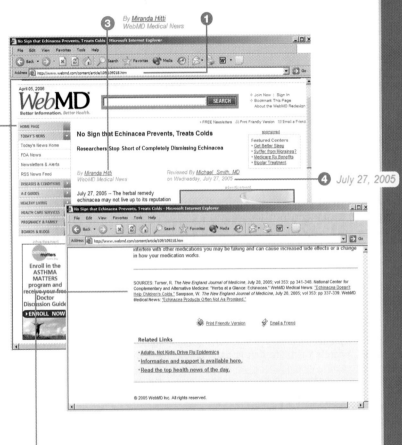

By *Miranda Hitti*
WebMD Medical News

No Sign that Echinacea Prevents, Treats Colds · Microsoft Internet Explorer

File   Edit   View   Favorites   Tools   Help

Back · Search · Favorites · Media

Address http://www.webmd.com/content/article/109/109218.htm

April 05, 2008

WebMD
Better Information. Better Health.

Join Now | Sign In
Bookmark This Page
About the WebMD Redesign

SEARCH

· FREE Newsletters   Print Friendly Version   Email a Friend

HOME PAGE
TODAY'S NEWS
Today's News Home
FDA News
Newsletters & Alerts
RSS News Feed
DISEASES & CONDITIONS
A-Z GUIDES
HEALTHY LIVING
HEALTH CARE SERVICES
PREGNANCY & FAMILY
BOARDS & BLOGS

No Sign that Echinacea Prevents, Treats Colds

Researchers Stop Short of Completely Dismissing Echinacea

By *Miranda Hitti*
WebMD Medical News

Reviewed By *Michael Smith, MD*
on Wednesday, July 27, 2005

sponsored

Featured Centers
· Get Better Sleep
· Suffer from Migraines?
· Medicare Rx Benefits
· Bipolar Treatment

July 27, 2005 -- The herbal remedy
echinacea may not live up to its reputation

July 27, 2005

advertisement

matters

Enroll in the
ASTHMA
MATTERS
program and
receive your free
Doctor
Discussion Guide

▶ ENROLL NOW

No Sign that Echinacea Prevents, Treats Colds · Microsoft Internet Explorer

File   Edit   View   Favorites   Tools   Help

Back · Search · Favorites · Media

Address http://www.webmd.com/content/article/109/109218.htm

interfere with other medications you may be taking and can cause increased side effects or a change
in how your medication works.

SOURCES: Turner, R. *The New England Journal of Medicine*, July 28, 2005; vol 353: pp 341-348. National Center for
Complementary and Alternative Medicine: "Herbs at a Glance: Echinacea." WebMD Medical News: "Echinacea Doesn't
Help Children's Colds." Sampson, W. *The New England Journal of Medicine*, July 28, 2005; vol 353: pp 337-339. WebMD
Medical News: "Echinacea Products Often Not As Promised."

Print Friendly Version   Email a Friend

Related Links

· Adults, Not Kids, Drive Flu Epidemics
· Information and support is available here.
· Read the top health news of the day.

© 2005 WebMD Inc. All rights reserved.

SOURCES: Turner, R. *The New England Journal of Medicine*, July 28, 2005; vol 353: pp 341-348. National Center for
Complementary and Alternative Medicine: "Herbs at a Glance: Echinacea." WebMD Medical News: "Echinacea Doesn't
Help Children's Colds." Sampson, W. *The New England Journal of Medicine*, July 28, 2005; vol 353: pp 337-339. WebMD
Medical News: "Echinacea Products Often Not As Promised."

YOUR RESEARCH QUESTION

As you read, keep your research question in mind, and ask questions.

- How does this material address your research question and hypothesis?
- What quotations from this source might help support your thesis?
- Does the source include counterarguments to your hypothesis that you will need to answer? If so, what answers can you provide?

THE AUTHOR'S STANCE AND TONE

Read with an eye for the author's overall rhetorical stance or perspective, for facts or explicit opinions, and for the author's tone — the way his or her attitude toward the topic and audience is conveyed.

THE AUTHOR'S ARGUMENT AND EVIDENCE

Look for the main point or the main argument the author is making. Try to identify the reasons the author gives to support his or her position. Then try to determine *why* the author takes this position.

- How persuasive is the evidence? Can you think of a way to refute it?
- Can you detect any questionable logic or fallacious thinking (12f)?

EXERCISE 16.1

You can practice learning to read texts critically by comparing several Web sites. To begin, search for a site that is fairly unregulated and unedited — a fan site, for instance, for a writer, a book, an actor, a television show, or a film. What on this site indicates credibility? Who is responsible for the site, and how can you tell?

Next, compare it to the site of a major government agency, such as the Library of Congress, or a national broadcaster, such as PBS or CNN. What kinds of connections do you see between the sponsoring organization and the Web site?

Finally, working alone or with another member of your class, analyze the sites you have looked at for trust, credibility, and authority. Bring the results of your analysis to class for discussion.

EXERCISE 16.2

Choose two sources that seem well suited to your topic, and evaluate their usefulness and credibility using the criteria presented in this chapter. If possible, analyze one print source and one electronic source. Bring the results of your analysis to class for discussion.

16e   **Synthesize sources.**

Throughout the research process, you are *synthesizing* — grouping similar pieces of data together, looking for patterns or trends, and identifying

GAME PLAN Synthesize Sources

START
by identifying **GOOD SOURCES.**

WHAT information do I **NEED?**

WHERE can I **GET IT?**

WHAT DO OTHER SOURCES SAY ABOUT THIS SOURCE?

Can I trust it? **HOW** will my readers respond to it?

A source shouldn't be too **SPECIFIC** or too **GENERAL** for my thesis....

If I'm missing important pieces, **DO MORE RESEARCH.**

What's the **MAIN IDEA?**

HOW does this relate to my **TOPIC?**

WHAT am I trying to **SAY?**

FIGURE OUT what each source **SAYS.**

What if one text says **ONE** thing, and another says **SOMETHING ELSE?**

Which source do I believe, and **WHY?**

Look for **COMMON PATTERNS.** What do they suggest about the **TOPIC?**

EXAMINE THE FIT.

HOW DO THE PARTS OF MY RESEARCH FIT WITH WHAT I WANT TO SAY?

PUT IT ALL TOGETHER.

ADD UP MY FINDINGS AND SEE WHERE I AM....

Is there a good reason to use each source? **IF NOT, DON'T!**

Does my thesis **NEED TO CHANGE?** If I need to go in a new direction, I will.

I'VE GOT SOMETHING TO SAY. (If not, rethink this project!)

My research should **BACK ME UP,** not take over.

MY SOURCES ARE SOLID!

THE PIECES ADD UP!

MY RESEARCH IS WORKING FOR ME!

I'VE SYNTHESIZED MY FINDINGS!

1 **How appropriate is the source for the argument you are making?**
Read carefully, and be sure you understand exactly how the material in the source relates to your point. (See Chapter 12.) Student Amanda Rinder, in doing research for a paper about Chicago architecture (53c), discovered a major debate between the city's preservationists and developers, which she wanted to document. This *Chicago Tribune* article by architecture critic Paul Gapp provided the information she needed.

2 **How does each source contribute to your argument?** Identifying the purpose of each source can help keep your research relevant and ensure that you fill in any gaps (and avoid repetition). Amanda used both paraphrases (highlighted) and quotations (underlined) from the Gapp article to present a clear overview of the issues of architectural preservation and to offer strong support for the preservation of the McCarthy Building. She used images, including this one of the McCarthy Building, as examples of the architectural style that preservationists wanted to save. She also did background research on Paul Gapp and learned, from his obituary in the *New York Times*, that he had won a Pulitzer Prize for his architecture criticism. She did not ultimately include information from the obituary in her paper, but it helped her be certain of Gapp's credibility on her topic.

3 **Do your sources include fair representations of opposing views?**
Consider what else you need to include to present a complete picture of the argument. Amanda paraphrased Gapp's balanced discussion of the pros and cons of protecting the McCarthy Building. She also found additional sources on both sides of the issue.

4 **How convincing will your sources be to your audience?** Make sure that the evidence you choose will seem credible and logical (13e–f). Amanda identified Gapp as "a *Chicago Tribune* architecture critic" to show him as an authority on her topic. Her other sources included books by architects and historians and other articles on architecture from major newspapers in Chicago and elsewhere.

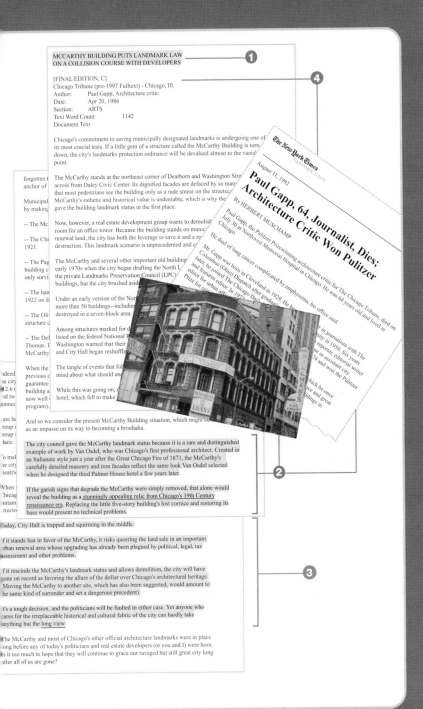

MCCARTHY BUILDING PUTS LANDMARK LAW
ON A COLLISION COURSE WITH DEVELOPERS

[FINAL EDITION, C]
Chicago Tribune (pre-1997 Fulltext) - Chicago, Ill.
Author: Paul Gapp, Architecture critic
Date: Apr 20, 1986
Section: ARTS
Text Word Count: 1142
Document Text

Chicago's commitment to saving municipally designated landmarks is undergoing one of
its most crucial tests. If a little gem of a structure called the McCarthy Building is torn
down, the city's landmarks protection ordinance will be devalued almost to the vanish
point.

forgotten t   The McCarthy stands at the northeast corner of Dearborn and Washington Stre
anchor of   across from Daley Civic Center. Its dignified facades are defaced by so many
                            that most pedestrians see the building only as a rude smear on the streetsc
Municipal   McCarthy's esthetic and historical value is undeniable, which is why th
by making   gave the building landmark status in the first place.

-- The Mc   Now, however, a real estate development group wants to demolish
                            room for an office tower. Because the building stands on munici
-- The Chi   renewal land, the city has both the leverage to save it and a re
1921.   destruction. This landmark scenario is unprecedented and c

-- The Pag   The McCarthy and several other important old building
building c   early 1970s when the city began drafting the North L
only survi   the private Landmarks Preservation Council (LPC
                            buildings, but the city brushed asid
-- The han
1922 on d   Under an early version of the Nor
                            more than 50 buildings--includin
-- The Oli   destroyed in a seven-block area.
structure o
                            Among structures marked for d
-- The Del   listed on the federal National R
Thomas. I   Washington warned that their
McCarthy   and City Hall began reshuffl

When the   The tangle of events that fol
previous c   mind about what should an
guarantee
city   and tw   While this was going on, c
building a   now well   hotel, which fell to make
connec   program).

ate la   And so we consider the present McCarthy Building situation, which might be
roup   as an impasse on its way to becoming a brouhaha.
roup
lace.   The city council gave the McCarthy landmark status because it is a rare and distinguished
              example of work by Van Osdel, who was Chicago's first professional architect. Created in
'o mak   an Italianate style just a year after the Great Chicago Fire of 1871, the McCarthy's
he city   carefully detailed masonry and iron facades reflect the same look Van Osdel selected
heatric   when he designed the third Palmer House hotel a few years later.

When   If the garish signs that degrade the McCarthy were simply removed, that alone would
Chicag   reveal the building as a stunningly appealing relic from Chicago's 19th Century
antam   renaissance era. Replacing the little five-story building's lost cornice and restoring its
irecto   base would present no technical problems.

Today, City Hall is trapped and squirming in the middle.

f it stands fast in favor of the McCarthy, it risks queering the land sale in an important
rban urban renewal area whose upgrading has already been plagued by political, legal, tax
assessment and other problems.

f it rescinds the McCarthy's landmark status and allows demolition, the city will have
gone on record as favoring the allure of the dollar over Chicago's architectural heritage.
Moving the McCarthy to another site, which has also been suggested, would amount to
he same kind of surrender and set a dangerous precedent.

t's a tough decision, and the politicians will be faulted in either case. Yet anyone who
cares for the irreplaceable historical and cultural fabric of the city can hardly take
anything but the long view:

The McCarthy and most of Chicago's other official architecture landmarks were in place
ong before any of today's politicians and real estate developers (or you and I) were born.
Is it too much to hope that they will continue to grace our ravaged but still great city long
after all of us are gone?

The New York Times

nytimes.com

August 11, 1992

Paul Gapp, 64, Journalist, Dies;
Architecture Critic Won Pulitzer

By HERBERT MUSCHAMP

Paul Gapp, the Pulitzer Prizewinning architecture critic for The Chicago Tribune, died on
July 30 at Northwest Memorial Hospital in Chicago. He was 64 years old and lived in
Chicago.

He died of lung cancer complicated by emphysema, his office said.

Mr. Gapp was born in Cleveland in 1928. He
Columbus (Ohio) Dispatch after graduat
later, he joined The Chicago Dail
and features editor. In 1972
editor for urban aff
Prize for crit

193

the main points of the data. Doing so enables you to use your sources effectively to pursue your research goals.

Using sources effectively in a research essay can pose challenges. A national study of first-year college writing conducted for this book, for example, found that student writers trying to incorporate research sometimes used sources that were not directly relevant to their point, too specific to support the larger claim being made, or otherwise ineffective for their purpose. Even after you have evaluated a source and considered the author's stance, argument, and evidence, then, it's worth taking time to look at how well the source works in your specific situation. (If you change the focus of your work after you have begun doing research, be especially careful to check whether your sources still fit.)

16f   Take notes, and annotate your sources.

While note-taking methods vary from one researcher to another, you should (1) record enough information to help you recall the major points of the source; (2) put the information in the form in which you are most likely to incorporate it into your research essay; and (3) note all the information you will need to cite the source accurately. The following example shows the major items a note should include:

ELEMENTS OF AN ACCURATE NOTE

Child labor statistics ————————————————————— **1**
Arat, *Analyzing Child Labor,* p. 180 ————————————— **2**

Accurate statistics are hard to gather
Between 200 and 500 million child laborers worldwide   **3**
95% are in the third world
2 million in the US and UK
(Summary) ———————————————————————— **4**

"[O]ne in three children in Africa works, one in four in Asia, and one in five in Latin America."
(Quotation) ————————————————————————

1 *Use a subject heading.* Label each note with a brief but descriptive subject heading so you can group similar subtopics together.

2 *Identify the source.* List the author's name and a shortened title of the source. Your working-bibliography entry (16b) for the source will contain the full bibliographic information, so you don't need to repeat it in each note.

3 *Record exact page references (if available).* For online or other sources without page numbers, record the paragraph, screen, or other section number(s), if indicated.

4 *Indicate whether the note is a summary, paraphrase, or direct quotation* (see the following). Make sure quotations are copied accurately. Put square brackets around any change you make, and use ellipses if you omit material.

Taking complete notes will help you digest the source information as you read and incorporate the material into your text without inadvertently plagiarizing the source (see Chapter 17). Be sure to reread each note carefully, and recheck it against the source to make sure quotations, statistics, and specific facts are accurate.

Quoting

Quoting involves bringing a source's exact words into your text. Use an author's exact words when the wording is so memorable or expresses a point so well that you cannot improve or shorten it without weakening it, when the author is a respected authority whose opinion supports your own ideas, or when an author challenges or disagrees profoundly with others in the field. Here is an example of a quotation note:

QUOTATION-STYLE NOTE

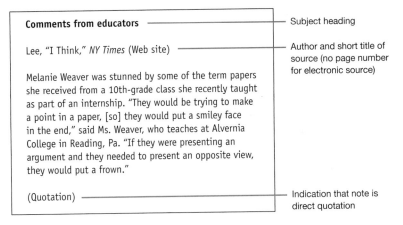

Comments from educators ———— Subject heading

Lee, "I Think," *NY Times* (Web site) ———— Author and short title of source (no page number for electronic source)

Melanie Weaver was stunned by some of the term papers she received from a 10th-grade class she recently taught as part of an internship. "They would be trying to make a point in a paper, [so] they would put a smiley face in the end," said Ms. Weaver, who teaches at Alvernia College in Reading, Pa. "If they were presenting an argument and they needed to present an opposite view, they would put a frown."

(Quotation) ———— Indication that note is direct quotation

Paraphrasing

A paraphrase accurately states all the relevant information from a passage *in your own words and sentence structures,* without any additional comments or elaborations. Use a paraphrase when the main points of a passage, their order, and some details are important but the particular wording is not. Unlike a summary, a paraphrase always restates *all* the main points of a passage in the same order and often in about the same number of words.

To paraphrase without plagiarizing inadvertently, do not simply substitute synonyms, and do not imitate an author's style. If you wish

AT A GLANCE

Quoting Accurately

- Copy quotations carefully, with punctuation, capitalization, and spelling exactly as in the original. (42a)
- Enclose the quotation in quotation marks; don't rely on your memory to distinguish your own words from those of the source. (42a)
- Use square brackets if you introduce words of your own into the quotation or make changes in it. (43b)
- Use ellipses if you omit words from the quotation. (43f)
- If you later incorporate the quotation into your research essay, copy it from the note precisely, including brackets and ellipses.
- Record the author's name, shortened title, and page number(s) on which the quotation appeared. For sources without page numbers, record the paragraph, screen, or other section number(s) if indicated.
- Make sure you have a corresponding working-bibliography entry with complete source information. (16b)
- Label the note with a subject heading, and identify it as a quotation.

to cite some of an author's words within a paraphrase, enclose them in quotation marks. The following examples of paraphrases resemble the original either too little or too much:

ORIGINAL

Language play, the arguments suggest, will help the development of pronunciation ability through its focus on the properties of sounds and sound contrasts, such as rhyming. Playing with word endings and decoding the syntax of riddles will help the acquisition of grammar. Readiness to play with words and names, to exchange puns and to engage in nonsense talk, promotes links with semantic development. The kinds of dialogue interaction illustrated above are likely to have consequences for the development of conversational skills. And language play, by its nature, also contributes greatly to what in recent years has been called *metalinguistic awareness*, which is turning out to be of critical importance in the development of language skills in general and of literacy skills in particular.

– DAVID CRYSTAL, *Language Play* (180)

UNACCEPTABLE PARAPHRASE: STRAYING FROM THE AUTHOR'S IDEAS

Crystal argues that playing with language — creating rhymes, figuring out how riddles work, making puns, playing with names, using invented words, and so on — helps children figure out a great deal about language, from the basics of pronunciation and grammar to how to carry on a conversation. Increasing their understanding of how language works in turn helps them become more interested in learning new languages and in pursuing education (180).

The previous paraphrase starts off well enough, but it moves away from paraphrasing the original to inserting the writer's ideas; Crystal says nothing about learning new languages or pursuing education.

UNACCEPTABLE PARAPHRASE: USING THE AUTHOR'S WORDS

Crystal suggests that language play, including rhyme, helps children improve pronunciation ability, that looking at word endings and decoding the syntax of riddles allows them to understand grammar, and that other kinds of dialogue interaction teach conversation. Overall, language play may be of critical importance in the development of language and literacy skills (180).

Because the underlined phrases are either borrowed from the original without quotation marks or changed only superficially, this paraphrase plagiarizes.

UNACCEPTABLE PARAPHRASE: USING THE AUTHOR'S SENTENCE STRUCTURES

Language play, Crystal suggests, will improve pronunciation by zeroing in on sounds such as rhymes. Having fun with word endings and analyzing riddle structure will help a person acquire grammar. Being prepared to play with language, to use puns and talk nonsense, improves the ability to use semantics. These playful methods of communication are likely to influence a person's ability to talk to others. And language play inherently adds enormously to what has recently been known as *metalinguistic awareness*, a concept of great magnitude in developing speech abilities generally and literacy abilities particularly (180).

Here is a paraphrase of the same passage that expresses the author's ideas accurately and acceptably:

ACCEPTABLE PARAPHRASE: IN THE STUDENT WRITER'S OWN WORDS

Crystal argues that playing with language — creating rhymes, figuring out riddles, making puns, playing with names, using invented words, and so on — helps children figure out a great deal, from the basics of pronunciation and grammar to how to carry on a conversation. This kind of play allows children to understand the overall concept of how language works, a concept that is key to learning to use — and read — language effectively (180).

Summarizing

A summary is a significantly shortened version of a passage or even of a whole chapter or work that captures main ideas *in your own words*. Unlike a paraphrase, a summary uses just enough information to record the main points you wish to emphasize. To summarize a short passage, read it carefully and, without looking at the text, write a one- or two-sentence summary. Following is David Craig's note recording a summary of the Crystal passage on p. 196. Notice that it states the author's main points selectively — and without using his words.

AT A GLANCE
Paraphrasing Accurately

- Include all main points and any important details from the original source, in the same order in which the author presents them.
- State the meaning in your own words and sentence structures. If you want to include especially memorable language from the original, enclose it in quotation marks.
- Save your comments, elaborations, or reactions on another note.
- Record the author's name, the shortened title, and the page number(s) on which the original material appears. For sources without page numbers, record the paragraph, screen, or other section number(s), if any.
- Make sure you have a corresponding working-bibliography entry with complete source information. (16b)
- Label the note with a subject heading, and identify it as a paraphrase.

SUMMARY NOTE

Language development

Crystal, *Language Play,* p. 180

Crystal argues that various kinds of language play contribute to awareness of how language works and to literacy.

(Summary)

For a long passage or an entire chapter, skim the headings and topic sentences, and make notes of each; then write your summary in a paragraph or two. For a whole book, you may want to refer to the preface and introduction as well as chapter titles, headings, and topic sentences — and your summary may take a page or more.

Annotating sources

Sometimes you may photocopy or print out a source you intend to use. In such cases, you can annotate the photocopies or printouts with your thoughts and questions and highlight interesting quotations and key terms.

> **AT A GLANCE**
> ### Summarizing Accurately
>
> - Include just enough information to recount the main points you want to cite. A summary is usually far shorter than the original.
> - Use your own words. If you include any language from the original, enclose it in quotation marks.
> - Record the author, shortened title, and page number(s) on which the original material appeared. For sources without page numbers, record the paragraph, screen, or other section number(s), if any.
> - Make sure you have a corresponding working-bibliography entry with complete source information. (16b)
> - Label the note with a subject heading, and identify it as a summary.

> **FOR MULTILINGUAL WRITERS**
> ### Identifying Sources
>
> While some language communities and cultures expect audiences to recognize the sources of important documents and texts, thereby eliminating the need to cite them directly, conventions for writing in North America call for careful attribution of any quoted, paraphrased, or summarized material. When in doubt, explicitly identify your sources.

You can copy online sources electronically, paste them into a computer file, and annotate them there. Try not to rely too heavily on copying or printing out whole pieces, however; you still need to read the material very carefully. And resist the temptation to treat copied material as notes, an action that could lead to inadvertent plagiarizing. (In a computer file, using a different color for text pasted from a source will help prevent this problem.)

EXERCISE 16.3

Choose an online source you are sure you will use in your research project. Then download and print out the source, record all essential publication information for it, and annotate it as you read it.

EXERCISE 16.4: THINKING CRITICALLY

Take a careful look at the sources you have gathered for your research project. How many make points that support your own point of view? How many provide counterarguments to your point of view? Which sources are you relying on most — and why? Which source seems most credible to you — and why? Which sources, if any, are you suspicious of or worried about? Bring the results of this investigation to class for discussion.

17 Integrating Sources and Avoiding Plagiarism

In some ways, there really is nothing new under the sun, in writing and research as well as in life. Whatever writing you do has been influenced by what you have already read and experienced. As you work on your research project, you will need to know how to use, integrate, and acknowledge the work of others. And all writers need to understand current definitions of plagiarism (which have changed over time and differ from culture to culture) as well as the concept of intellectual property — those works protected by copyright and other laws — so they can give credit where credit is due.

17a Decide whether to quote, paraphrase, or summarize.

You tentatively decided to quote, paraphrase, or summarize material when you took notes on your sources (16f). As you choose some of these sources for your research project and decide how to use them, however, you may reevaluate those decisions. The following guidelines can help you decide whether to quote, paraphrase, or summarize.

17b Integrate quotations, paraphrases, and summaries effectively.

Here are some general guidelines for integrating source materials into your writing.

Incorporating quotations

Quotations from respected authorities can help establish your credibility and show that you are considering various perspectives. However, because your essay is primarily your own work, limit your use of quotations.

BRIEF QUOTATIONS

Short quotations should run in with your text, enclosed by quotation marks (42a).

> In Miss Eckhart, Welty recognizes a character who shares with her "the love of her art and the love of giving it, the desire to give it until there is no more left" (10).

AT A GLANCE

When to Quote, Paraphrase, or Summarize

QUOTE

- wording that is so memorable or powerful, or expresses a point so perfectly, that you cannot change it without weakening its meaning
- authors' opinions you wish to emphasize
- authors' words that show you are considering varying perspectives
- respected authorities whose opinions support your ideas
- authors whose opinions challenge or vary greatly from those of others in the field

PARAPHRASE

- passages you do not wish to quote but that use details important to your point

SUMMARIZE

- long passages in which the main point is important to your point but the details are not

---

LONG QUOTATIONS

If you are following the style of the Modern Language Association (MLA), set off a prose quotation longer than four lines. If you are following the style of the American Psychological Association (APA) or the *Chicago Manual of Style*, set off a quotation of more than forty words or more than one paragraph. Begin such a quotation on a new line, and indent every line ten spaces (MLA), five to seven spaces (APA), or eight spaces (*Chicago*). This indentation sets off the quotation clearly, so quotation marks are unnecessary. Introduce long quotations by a signal phrase (see the list on this page) or a sentence followed by a colon. The following example shows MLA style:

> A good seating arrangement can prevent problems; however, *withitness*, as defined by Woolfolk, works even better:
>
>> Withitness is the ability to communicate to students that you are aware of what is happening in the classroom, that you "don't miss anything." With-it teachers seem to have "eyes in the back of their heads." They avoid becoming too absorbed with a few students, since this allows the rest of the class to wander. (359)
>
> This technique works, however, only if students actually believe that their teacher will know everything that goes on.

INTEGRATING QUOTATIONS SMOOTHLY INTO YOUR TEXT

Carefully integrate quotations into your text so that they flow smoothly and clearly into the surrounding sentences. Use a signal phrase or verb, such as those underlined in the following examples and listed below.

> As Eudora Welty notes, "learning stamps you with its moments. Childhood's learning," she continues, "is made up of moments. It isn't steady. It's a pulse" (9).

> In her essay, Haraway strongly opposes those who condemn technology outright, arguing that we must not indulge in a "demonology of technology" (181).

Notice that the examples alert readers to the quotations by using signal phrases that include the author's name. When you cite a quotation in this way, you need put only the page number in parentheses.

SIGNAL VERBS

acknowledges	concludes	emphasizes	replies
advises	concurs	expresses	reports
agrees	confirms	interprets	responds
allows	criticizes	lists	reveals
answers	declares	objects	says
asserts	describes	observes	states
believes	disagrees	offers	suggests
charges	discusses	opposes	thinks
claims	disputes	remarks	writes

BRACKETS AND ELLIPSES

In direct quotations, enclose in brackets any words you change or add, and indicate any deletions with ellipsis points (43f).

> "There is something wrong in the [Three Mile Island] area," one farmer told the Nuclear Regulatory Commission after the plant accident ("Legacy" 33).

> Economist John Kenneth Galbraith has pointed out that "large corporations cannot afford to compete with one another. . . . In a truly competitive market someone loses" (qtd. in Key 17).

Incorporating paraphrases and summaries

Introduce paraphrases and summaries clearly, usually with a signal phrase that includes the author of the source, as the underlined words in the following example indicate.

Professor of linguistics Deborah Tannen says that she offers her book *That's Not What I Meant!* to "women and men everywhere who are trying their best to talk to each other" (19). Tannen goes on to illustrate how communication between women and men breaks down and then to suggest that a full awareness of "genderlects" can improve relationships (297).

EXERCISE 17.1

Take a source-based piece of writing you have done recently or a research project you are working on now, and examine it to see how successfully you have integrated quotations. Have you used accurate signal verbs and introduced the sources of the quotations? Have you used square brackets and ellipses accurately to indicate changes in quotations?

EXERCISE 17.2: THINKING CRITICALLY

From a research project you have finished or are drafting now, choose three passages that cite sources. Then examine how well these sources are integrated into your text. Consider how you can make that integration smoother, and try your hand at revising one of them.

EXERCISE 17.3

Read the brief original passage that follows, and then look closely at the five attempts to quote or paraphrase it. Decide which attempts are acceptable and which plagiarize, prepare notes on what supports your decision in each case, and bring your notes to class for discussion.

> The strange thing about plagiarism is that it's almost always pointless. The writers who stand accused, from Laurence Sterne to Samuel Taylor Coleridge to Susan Sontag, tend to be more talented than the writers they lift from.
>
> — MALCOLM JONES, "Have You Read This Story Somewhere?"

1. According to Malcolm Jones, writers accused of plagiarism are always better writers than those they are supposed to have plagiarized.
2. According to Malcolm Jones, writers accused of plagiarism "tend to be more talented than the writers they lift from."
3. Plagiarism is usually pointless, says writer Malcolm Jones.
4. Those who stand accused of plagiarism, such as Senator Joseph Biden, tend to be better writers than those whose work they use.
5. According to Malcolm Jones, "plagiarism is . . . almost always pointless."

17c Integrate visuals effectively.

If you are using visuals (such as graphs, cartoons, maps, photographs, charts, tables, or time lines), integrate them smoothly into your text.

> **TALKING THE TALK**
>
> ## Saying Something New
>
> "What can I say about my topic that experts haven't already said?" All writers — no matter how experienced — face this problem. As you read more about your topic, you will soon see areas of disagreement among experts, who may not be as expert as they first appear. Notice what your sources say and, especially, what they don't say. Consider how your own interests and experiences give you a unique perspective on the topic. Slowly but surely you will identify a claim that you can make about the topic, one related to what others say but taking a new angle or adding something different to the discussion.

- Make sure the graphic conveys information more efficiently than words alone could do.

- Position the visual immediately after the text it illustrates or refers to — or as close to it as possible.

- Refer to the visual by number in the text *before* it appears: *As Figure 3 demonstrates.*

- Explain or comment on the relevance of the visual. This can be done *after* the visual.

- Label each visual clearly and consistently: *Fig. 1. Photograph of the New York Skyline.*

- Check the documentation system you are using to make sure you label visuals appropriately; MLA, for instance, asks that you number and title tables and figures (*Table 1: Average Amount of Rainfall by Region*).

- If you are posting your document or essay on a Web site, make sure you have permission to use any visuals that are covered by copyright.

For more on using visuals, see Chapter 4.

17d Check for excessive use of source material.

Your text needs to synthesize your research in support of your own argument; it should not be a patchwork of quotations, paraphrases, and summaries from other people. You need a rhetorical stance that represents you as the author. If you cite too many sources, your own voice will disappear, a problem the following passage demonstrates:

> The United States is one of the countries with the most rapid population growth. In fact, rapid population increase has been a "prominent feature of American life since the founding of the republic" (Day 31). In the past, the

cause of the high rate of population growth was the combination of large-scale immigration and a high birth rate. As Day notes, "Two facts stand out in the demographic history of the United States: first, the single position as a receiver of immigrants; second, our high rate of growth from natural increase" (31).

Nevertheless, American population density is not as high as in most European countries. Day points out that the Netherlands, with a density of 906 persons per square mile, is more crowded than even the most densely populated American states (33).

17e Understand why you should acknowledge your sources.

Acknowledging sources says to your reader that you have done your homework, that you have gained expertise on your topic, and that you are credible. Acknowledging sources can also demonstrate fairness — that you have considered several points of view. In addition, recognizing your sources can help provide background for your research by placing it in the context of other thinking. Most of all, you should acknowledge sources to help your readers follow your thoughts, understand how your ideas relate to the thoughts of others, and know where to go to find more information on your topic.

17f Know which sources to acknowledge.

As you carry out research, it is important to understand the distinction between materials that require acknowledgment (in in-text citations, footnotes, or endnotes; and in the works-cited list or bibliography) and those that do not.

Materials that do not require acknowledgment

- *Common knowledge.* If most readers already know a fact, you probably do not need to cite a source for it. You do not need to credit a source for the statement that George Bush was reelected in 2004, for example.
- *Facts available in a wide variety of sources.* If a number of encyclopedias, almanacs, or textbooks include a certain piece of information, you usually need not cite a specific source for it.
- *Your own findings from field research.* If you conduct observations or surveys, simply announce your findings as your own. Acknowledge people you interview as individuals rather than as part of a survey.

Materials that require acknowledgment

Some of the information you use may need to be credited to a source.

- *Quotations, paraphrases, and summaries.* Whenever you use another person's words, ideas, or opinions, credit the source. Even though the wording of a paraphrase or summary is your own, you should still acknowledge the source.

- *Facts not widely known or claims that are arguable.* If your readers would be unlikely to know a fact, or if an author presents as fact a claim that may or may not be true, cite the source. If you are not sure whether a fact will be familiar to your readers or whether a statement is arguable, cite the source.

- *Visuals from any source.* Credit all visual and statistical material not derived from your own field research, even if you yourself create a graph or table from the data provided in a source.

- *Help provided by others.* If an instructor gave you a good idea or if friends responded to your draft or helped you conduct surveys, give credit.

FOR MULTILINGUAL WRITERS

Plagiarism as a Cultural Concept

Many cultures do not recognize Western notions of plagiarism, which rest on a belief that language and ideas can be owned by writers. Indeed, in many countries other than the United States, and even within some communities in the United States, using the words and ideas of others without attribution is considered a sign of deep respect as well as an indication of knowledge. In academic writing in the United States, however, you should credit all materials except those that are common knowledge, that are available in a wide variety of sources, or that are your own creations (photographs, drawings, and so on) or your own findings from field research.

17g Uphold your academic integrity, and avoid plagiarism.

One of the cornerstones of intellectual work is academic integrity. This principle accounts for our being able to trust those sources we use and to demonstrate that our own work is equally trustworthy. While there are many ways to damage academic integrity, two that are especially important are inaccurate or incomplete acknowledgment of sources in citations — sometimes called unintentional plagiarism — and plagiarism that is deliberately intended to pass off one writer's work as another's.

Whether it is intentional or not, plagiarism can result in serious consequences. At some colleges, students who plagiarize fail the course automatically; at others, they are expelled. Instructors who plagiarize, even inadvertently, have had their degrees revoked and their books withdrawn from publication. And outside academic life, eminent political, business, and scientific leaders have been stripped of candidacies, positions, and awards because of plagiarism.

Inaccurate or incomplete citation of sources

If your paraphrase is too close to the wording or sentence structure of a source (even if you identify the source); if you do not identify the source of a quotation (even if you include the quotation marks); or if you fail to indicate clearly the source of an idea that you obviously did not come up with on your own, you may be accused of plagiarism even if your intent was not to plagiarize. Inaccurate or incomplete acknowledgment of sources often results either from carelessness or from not learning how to borrow material properly in the first place. Still, because the costs of even unintentional plagiarism can be severe, it's important to understand how it can happen and how you can guard against it.

As a writer of academic integrity, you will want to take responsibility for your research and for acknowledging all sources accurately. One easy way to keep track is to keep photocopies or printouts as you do your research; then you can identify needed quotations right on the copy.

Deliberate plagiarism

Deliberate plagiarism — handing in an essay written by a friend or purchased (or simply downloaded) from an essay-writing company; cutting and pasting passages directly from source materials without marking them with quotation marks and acknowledging your sources; failing to credit the source of an idea or concept in your text — is what most people think of when they hear the word *plagiarism*. This form of plagiarism is particularly troubling because it represents dishonesty and deception: those who intentionally plagiarize present the hard thinking and hard work of someone else as their own, and they claim knowledge they really don't have, thus deceiving their readers.

Deliberate plagiarism is also fairly simple to spot: your instructor will be well acquainted with your writing and likely to notice any sudden shifts in the style or quality of your work. In addition, by typing a few words from an essay into a search engine, your instructor can identify "matches" very easily.

Avoiding Plagiarism

- Maintain an accurate and thorough working bibliography. (16b)
- Establish a consistent note-taking system, listing sources and page numbers and clearly identifying all quotations, paraphrases, summaries, statistics, and visuals. (16f)
- Identify all quotations with quotation marks — both in your notes and in your essay. Be sure your summaries and paraphrases use your own words and sentence structures. (17b)
- Give a citation or note for each quotation, paraphrase, summary, arguable assertion or opinion, statistic, and visual that is from a source. (See Chapter 48, 52a, 53a, and 54a.)
- Prepare an accurate and complete list of sources cited according to the required documentation style. (See Chapter 50, 52c, 53a and b, and 54b.)

 bedfordstmartins.com/everydaywriter For additional help with avoiding plagiarism, click on **Research Resources**.

EXERCISE 17.4: THINKING CRITICALLY

Look at a recent piece of your writing that incorporates material from sources, and try to determine how completely and accurately you acknowledged them. Did you properly cite every quotation, paraphrase, and summary? every opinion or other idea from a source? every source you used to create visuals? Did you unintentionally plagiarize someone else's words or ideas? Make notes, and bring them to class for discussion.

18 Writing a Research Project

Everyday decisions often call for research and writing. In trying to choose between two jobs in different towns, for example, one person made a long list of questions to answer: Which job location had the lower cost of living? How did the two locations compare in terms of schools, cultural opportunities, major league sports, and so on? After conducting careful research, he was able to write a letter of acceptance to one place and a letter of regret to the other. In much the same way, when you are working on an academic project, there comes a time to draw the strands of your research together and articulate your conclusions in writing.

18a Refine your writing plans.

For almost all research writing, drafting should begin well before the deadline. There is a good reason for this: as your understanding of the subject grows and as you get responses from others, you may need to gather more information or even refine your original research question — and thus do more drafting. Before you start to write, reconsider your purpose, audience, stance, and working thesis (see Chapters 5 and 7).

- What is your central purpose? What other purposes, if any, do you have?
- What is your stance toward your topic? Are you an advocate, a critic, a reporter, an observer?
- What audience(s) are you addressing?
- How much background information does your audience need?
- What supporting information will your readers find convincing — examples? quotations from authorities? statistics? graphs, charts, or other visuals? data from your own observations or from interviews?
- Should your tone be that of a colleague, an expert, a student?
- How can you establish common ground with your readers and show them that you have considered points of view other than your own?
- What is your working thesis trying to establish? Will your audience accept it?

Developing an explicit thesis

At the drafting stage, try to develop your working thesis (see p. 63) into an explicit statement that identifies your purpose and audience as well as your topic. It might take the following form:

> **I plan to (explain/argue/demonstrate/analyze, and so on) for an audience of** _____
> **that** _____
> **because/if** _____.

For example, David Craig developed the following explicit thesis statement:

> I plan to demonstrate for an audience of classmates that instant messaging seems to be a positive force in the development of youth literacy because it promotes regular contact with words, the use of written communication, and the development of an alternative form of literacy.

Note that while David's final draft (see Chapter 51) omits the explicit reference to his audience and purpose, including this information at the drafting stage helped focus his writing.

Testing your thesis

Although writing out an explicit thesis will often confirm your research, you may find that your hypothesis is invalid, inadequately supported, or insufficiently focused. In such cases, you need to rethink your original research question and perhaps do further research. To test your thesis, consider the following questions:

1. How can you state your thesis more precisely or more clearly? Should the wording be more specific?
2. In what ways will your thesis interest your audience? What can you do to increase that interest?
3. Will your thesis be manageable, given your limits of time and knowledge? If not, what can you do to make it more manageable?
4. What evidence from your research supports each aspect of your thesis? What additional evidence do you need?

EXERCISE 18.1

Take the thesis from your current research project, and test it against the questions provided above. Make revisions if your analysis reveals weaknesses in your thesis.

Considering design

As you move toward producing a draft, take some time to think about how you want your research essay or project to look. What font size will you use? Should you use color? Do you plan to insert text boxes and visuals? Will you need headings and subheadings? (See Chapter 4.)

18b   **Organize and draft.**

To group the many pieces of information that you have collected, examine your notes for connections. Figure out what might be combined with what, which notes will be more useful and which less useful, which ideas lend support to your thesis and which should be put aside, and which visuals you will definitely use.

You can begin this process by grouping your notes and visuals into subject categories to identify main ideas; then try to order the categories in the most effective way. You may also want to develop a working outline, storyboard, or idea map from your notes, which you can revise as you go along, or you can plot out a more detailed organization in a formal outline (7e).

Begin drafting wherever you feel most confident. If you have an idea for an introduction, begin there. If you are not sure how you want to introduce the project but do know how you want to approach one point, begin with that, and return to the introduction later.

Working title and introduction

The title and introduction play special roles, for they set the stage for what is to come. Ideally, the title announces the subject of the research essay or project in an intriguing or memorable way. The introduction should draw readers in and provide any background they will need to understand your discussion. Here are some tips for drafting an introduction to a research essay:

- It is often effective to *open with a question,* especially your research question. Next, you might explain what you will do to answer the question. Then *end with your explicit thesis statement* — in essence, the answer.
- Help readers by *forecasting your main points.*
- *Establish your own credibility* by revealing how you have become knowledgeable about the topic.
- A quotation can be a good attention-getter, but you may not want to open with a quotation if doing so will give that source too much emphasis.

Conclusion

A good conclusion to a research project helps readers know what they have learned. Its job is not to persuade (the body of the essay or project should already have done that) but to contribute to the overall effectiveness of your argument. Here are some strategies that may help:

- Refer to your thesis, and then expand to a more general conclusion that reminds readers of the significance of your discussion.
- If you have covered several main points, you may want to remind readers of them. Be careful, however, to provide more than a mere summary.
- Try to end with something that will have an impact — a provocative quotation or question, a vivid image, a call for action, or a warning. But guard against sounding preachy.

18c   Incorporate source materials.

When you reach the point of drafting your research project, a new task awaits: weaving your source materials into your writing. The challenge is to use your sources yet remain the author — to quote, paraphrase, and summarize other voices while remaining the major voice in your work. (See Chapter 17 for tips on integrating sources.)

18d   Review and get responses to your draft.

Once you've completed your draft, reread it slowly. As you do so, answer the following questions, and use them as a starting point for revision:

- What do you now see as its *purpose*? How does this compare with your original purpose? Does the draft do what your assignment requires?
- What *audience* does your essay address?
- What is your *stance* toward the topic?
- What is your *thesis*? Is it clearly stated?
- What *evidence* supports your thesis? Is the evidence sufficient?

Next, ask friends, classmates, and, if possible, your instructor to read and respond to your draft. Asking specific questions of your readers will result in the most helpful advice. (See Chapter 9.)

 bedfordstmartins.com/everydaywriter To explore tools for peer review, go to **Writing Resources** and click on **Working Online**. If you're using **Comment** in your course, you and your classmates can take part in peer-reviewing activities online.

18e   Revise and edit your draft.

Once you get feedback, reread your draft very carefully, making notes for necessary changes and additions. Look closely at your support for your thesis, and gather additional verbal or visual information if necessary. Pay particular attention to how you have used both print and visual sources, and make sure you have full documentation for all of them. (For more detailed information on revising, see Chapter 9.)

Check grammar, usage, spelling, punctuation, and mechanics. Consider the advice of spell checkers (22e) and grammar checkers carefully before accepting it. (For more information on editing, see 10a.)

18f Prepare a list of sources.

Once you have your final draft and source materials in place, you are ready to prepare a list of sources. Create an entry for each source used in your essay. Then double-check your essay against your list of sources cited; be sure that you have listed every source mentioned in the in-text citations or notes and that you have not listed any sources not cited in your essay. (For guidelines on documentation styles, see Chapters 48–54.)

18g Prepare and proofread your final copy.

To make sure that the final version of your essay puts your best foot forward, proofread it carefully. Work with a hard copy, since reading on-screen often leads to inaccuracies and missed typos. Proofread once for typographical and grammatical errors and once again to make sure you haven't introduced new errors. (To locate examples of student writing in this book and on the Web site, see the Student Writing Directory at the back of this book.)

EXERCISE 18.2: THINKING CRITICALLY

Reflect on the research project you have completed. How did you go about organizing your information? What would you do to improve this process? What problems did you encounter in drafting? How did you solve these problems? How many quotations did you use, and how did you integrate them into your text? When and why did you use summaries and paraphrases? If you used any visuals, how effective were they in supporting your points? What did you learn from revising?

Language

There is nothing wrong, really, with any word—
all are good, but some are better than others.

— WILLIAM STRUNK JR. AND E. B. WHITE

Language

Writing to the World **19**

People today often communicate instantaneously across cultures and distances. Workers conduct multinational transactions, students take online classes from distant universities, and grandparents check in with family members across multiple time zones.

In this era of global communication, you might find yourself writing to (or with) students throughout the country or even across the globe, and you may be in classes with people from other language groups and countries. In business, government, and education, writers increasingly operate on an international stage and must become *world writers*, able to communicate across cultures.

AT A GLANCE

Communicating across Cultures

- Recognize what you consider normal. Examine your own customary behaviors and assumptions, and think about how they may affect what you think and say (and write). (19a)
- When writing to someone from another culture, define your terms. (19b)
- Think about your audience's expectations. How much authority are you expected to have? (19c) How explicit does your writing need to be? (19d)
- What kind of evidence will count most with your audience? (19e)
- Organize your writing with your audience's expectations in mind. (19f)
- If in doubt, use formal style. (19g)

19a What you consider "normal"

How do you decide what is "normal" in a given situation? More than likely, your judgment is based on assumptions that you are not even aware of. Remember that behavior that is considered out of place in one community may appear perfectly normal in another. If you want to communicate with people across cultures, try to learn something about the norms in those cultures and, even more important, be aware of the norms that guide your own behavior.

- Remember that most of us tend to see our own way as the "normal" or right way to do things. How do your own values and assumptions guide your thinking and behavior? If your ways seem inherently right, then you may assume — even without thinking about it — that other ways are somehow less than right.
- Know that most ways of communicating are influenced by cultural contexts and differ widely from one culture to the next.
- Pay close attention to the ways that people from cultures other than your own communicate, and be flexible.
- Pay attention to and respect the differences among individual people *within* a given culture. Don't assume that all members of a community behave in the same way or value the same things.

19b   Defining your terms

When an instructor called for "originality" in his students' essays, what did he mean? A Filipina student thought *originality* meant going to an original source and explaining it; a student from Massachusetts took *originality* to mean an idea entirely her own. The professor, however, expected students to read sources and develop a critical point of their own about the sources. This professor realized he must define *originality* in class and give examples of student work that he judged original.

This brief example points to the challenges all writers face in trying to communicate across space, across languages, across cultures. While there are no foolproof rules, here are some tips for writing to people from cultures other than your own:

- Don't hesitate to ask people to explain a point if you're not absolutely sure you understand.
- Take care to be explicit about the meanings of the words you use.
- Invite response — ask whether you're making yourself clear. This kind of back-and-forth is particularly easy (and necessary) in email.

19c   Your own authority as a writer

In the United States, students are often asked to establish authority in their writing — by drawing on certain kinds of personal experience, by reporting on research they or others have conducted, or by taking a position for which they can offer strong evidence and support (2b). But this expectation about a writer's authority is by no means universal.

Indeed, some cultures position student writers as novices whose job is to reflect what they learn from their teachers. One Japanese student, for example, said he was taught that it's rude to challenge a teacher: "Are you ever so smart that you should challenge the wisdom of the ages?"

As this student's comment reveals, a writer's tone also depends on his or her relationship with listeners and readers. As a world writer, you need to remember that those you're addressing may hold very different attitudes about authority.

- What is your relationship to those you are addressing?
- What knowledge are you expected to have? Is it appropriate for or expected of you to demonstrate that knowledge — and if so, how?
- What is your goal — to answer a question? to make a point? to agree? something else?
- What tone is appropriate? If in doubt, show respect: politeness is never inappropriate.

19d Your responsibility to your audience

In the United States and Great Britain, many audiences (and especially those in the academic and business worlds) expect a writer to "get to the point" as directly as possible and to take on the major responsibility of articulating that point efficiently and unambiguously. But not all audiences have such expectations. Thus, world writers must think carefully about whether audience members expect the writer to make the meaning of a text explicitly clear or, rather, expect to do some of the work themselves, supplying some of the information necessary to the meaning.

A typical news report on British radio or television, for example, puts the overwhelming responsibility on the writer to present an unambiguous message. Such a report begins with a clear overview of all the major points to be covered, follows with an orderly discussion of each point, and ends with a brief summary. In many other cultures, however, writers organize information differently because they expect the audience to take more responsibility for figuring out what is being said. In fact, readers or listeners from some cultures may be insulted if they think they are being led by the hand through a report. Here are tips for thinking about reader and writer responsibility:

- What general knowledge do members of your audience have about your topic? What information do they expect — or need — you to provide?
- Do members of your audience tend to be very direct, saying explicitly what they mean? Or are they more subtle — less likely to call a spade a spade? Look for cues to determine how much responsibility you have as the writer.

19e What counts as evidence

How do you decide what evidence will best support your ideas? The answer depends, in large part, on how you define *evidence.* Americans generally give great weight to factual evidence.

Every writer must think carefully about how he or she uses evidence in writing and pay attention to what counts as evidence to members of other cultures.

- Should you rely on facts? concrete examples? firsthand experience?
- Should you include the testimony of experts? Which experts are valued most, and why?
- Should you cite religious or philosophical texts? proverbs or every-day wisdom? other sources?
- Should you use analogies as support? How much do they count?
- Once you determine what counts as evidence in your own thinking and writing, think about where you learned to use and value this kind of evidence. You can ask these same questions about the use of evidence by members of other cultures.

19f Organization

As you make choices about how to organize your writing, remember that cultural influences are at work here as well: the patterns that you find pleasing are likely to be those deeply embedded in your own culture. Many U.S. instructors prefer the following structure: introduction and thesis, necessary background, overview of the parts to follow, systematic presentation of evidence, consideration of other viewpoints, and conclusion. If a piece of writing follows this pattern, Anglo-American readers ordinarily find it well organized and coherent.

However, in cultures that value indirection and subtlety, writers tend to organize materials differently. One common pattern in Korean writing, for example, includes an introduction; a topic with development; a tangential topic, again with development; and then a conclusion — with the thesis appearing only at the end. Other cultures value repetition: Arabic listeners, for example, expect a speaker to reiterate a major point from several different perspectives as a way of making that point.

When writing for world audiences, then, think about how you can organize material to get your message across effectively. One expert in international business communication recommends, for example, that businesspeople writing to others in Japan should state their requests indirectly — and only after a formal and respectful opening. There are no hard-and-fast rules to help you organize your writing for effectiveness across cultures, but here are a couple of things for you to consider:

- Determine when to state your thesis — at the beginning? at the end? somewhere else? not at all?
- Consider whether digressions are a good idea, a requirement, or a mistake with your intended audience.

19g Style

As with beauty, good style is most definitely in the eye of the beholder — and thus is always affected by language, culture, and rhetorical tradition. In fact, what constitutes effective style varies broadly across cultures and depends on the rhetorical situation — purpose, audience, and so on (see Chapter 5). Even so, there is one important style question to consider when writing across cultures: what level of formality is most appropriate? In the United States, a fairly informal tone is often acceptable in both writing and speech. Many cultures, however, tend to value a more formal approach. When in doubt, it may be wise to err on the side of formality in writing to people from other cultures, especially to elders or to those in authority.

- Be careful to use proper titles:

  Dr. Beverly Moss   Professor Jaime Mejía

- Avoid slang (22a) and informal structures such as fragments (see Chapter 37).
- Do not address readers by first names in correspondence (even in email) unless invited to do so. Note, however, that an invitation to use a first name may come indirectly; if someone signs an email message or letter to you with his or her first name, you are implicitly invited to use that name.
- For international business email, avoid contractions. Open with the salutation "Dear Mr./Ms. _____." Write dates by listing the day before the month and spelling out the name of the month rather than using a numeral (7 *June 2004*).

Beyond formality, other stylistic preferences vary widely. World writers take nothing about language for granted. To be an effective world writer, you will want to work to recognize and respect those differences as you interact with members of other cultures.

EXERCISE 19.1: THINKING CRITICALLY

Choose one or two recent essays or other pieces of your writing, and examine them carefully, noting what you assume about what counts as persuasive evidence, good organization, and effective style. How do you represent yourself in relation to your audience? What other unstated assumptions about good writing can you identify?

20 Language That Builds Common Ground

The golden rule of language use might be "Speak to others the way you want them to speak to you." The words we select have power: they can praise, delight, inspire — and also hurt, offend, or even destroy. Words that offend prevent others from identifying with you and thus damage your credibility. Few absolute guidelines exist for using words that respect differences and build common ground. Two rules, however, can help: consider carefully the sensitivities and preferences of others, and watch for words that betray your assumptions, even when you have not directly stated them.

AT A GLANCE

Using Language That Builds Common Ground

- Check for stereotypes and other assumptions that might come between you and your readers. Look, for instance, for language implying approval or disapproval and for the ways you use *we, you,* and *they.* (20a)
- Avoid potentially sexist language. (20b)
- Make sure your references to race, religion, sexual orientation, and so on are relevant or necessary to your discussion. If they are not, leave them out. (20c and d)
- Check that the terms you use to refer to groups are accurate and acceptable. (20c and d)

20a Unstated assumptions and stereotypes

Unstated assumptions that enter into thinking and writing can destroy common ground by ignoring important differences between others and ourselves. For example, a student in a religion seminar who uses *we* to refer to Christians and *they* to refer to members of other religions had better be sure that everyone in the class is Christian, or some may feel left out of the discussion.

At the same time, don't overgeneralize about or stereotype a group of people. Because stereotypes are often based on half-truths, misunderstandings, and hand-me-down prejudices, they can lead to intolerance, bias, and bigotry.

Sometimes stereotypes and assumptions lead writers to call special attention to a group affiliation when it is not relevant to the point, as in *a woman plumber* or *a white basketball player*. Even positive stereotypes — for example, *Jewish doctors are the best* — or neutral ones — *all college students like pizza* — can hurt, for they inevitably ignore the uniqueness of an individual. Careful writers make sure that their language doesn't stereotype any group *or* individual.

20b Assumptions about gender

Powerful gender-related words can subtly affect our thinking and our behavior. For instance, at one time many young women were discouraged from pursuing careers in medicine or engineering at least partially because speakers commonly referred to hypothetical doctors or engineers as *he* (and then labeled a woman who worked as a doctor *a woman doctor*, as if to say, "She's an exception; doctors are normally men"). Similarly, a label like *male nurse* may offend by reflecting stereotyped assumptions about proper roles for men. Equally problematic is the traditional use of *man* and *mankind* to refer to people of both sexes and the use of *he* and *him* to refer generally to any human being. Because such usage ignores half of the people on earth, it hardly helps a writer build common ground.

Sexist language, those words and phrases that stereotype or ignore members of either sex or that unnecessarily call attention to gender, can usually be revised fairly easily. There are several alternatives to using masculine pronouns to refer to persons whose gender is unknown to the writer. One option is to recast the sentence using plural forms.

> *Lawyers*   *they*
> ▶ ~~A lawyer~~ must pass the bar exam before ~~he~~ can begin to practice.

Another option is to substitute pairs of pronouns such as *he or she, him or her,* and so on.

>   *or she*
> ▶ A lawyer must pass the bar exam before he can begin to practice.

Yet another way to revise the sentence is to eliminate the pronouns.

>   *beginning*
> ▶ A lawyer must pass the bar exam before ~~he can begin~~ to practice.

Beyond the pronoun issue, try to eliminate sexist nouns from your writing.

INSTEAD OF	TRY USING
anchorman, anchorwoman	anchor
businessman	businessperson, business executive
chairman, chairwoman	chair, chairperson
congressman	member of Congress, representative
fireman	firefighter
mailman	mail carrier
male nurse	nurse
man, mankind	humans, human beings, humanity, the human race, humankind
manpower	workers, personnel
mothering	parenting
policeman, policewoman	police officer
salesman	salesperson, sales associate
woman engineer	engineer

EXERCISE 20.1

The following excerpt is taken from the 1968 edition of Dr. Benjamin Spock's *Baby and Child Care*. Read it carefully, noting any language we might now consider sexist. Then try bringing it up-to-date by revising the passage, substituting nonsexist language as necessary.

When you suggest something that doesn't appeal to your baby, he feels he *must* assert himself. His nature tells him to. He just says No in words or actions, even about things that he likes to do. The psychologists call it "negativism"; mothers call it "that terrible No stage." But stop and think what would happen to him if he never felt like saying No. He'd become a robot, a mechanical man. You wouldn't be able to resist the temptation to boss him all the time, and he'd stop learning and developing. When he was old enough to go out into the world, to school and later to work, everybody else would take advantage of him, too. He'd never be good for anything.

20c   Assumptions about race and ethnicity

In building common ground, writers must watch for any words that ignore differences not only among individual members of a race or ethnic group but also among subgroups. Writers must be aware, for instance, of the many nations to which American Indians belong and of the diverse places from which Americans of Spanish-speaking ancestry have emigrated.

Preferred terms

Identifying preferred terms is sometimes not an easy task, for they can change often and vary widely.

The word *colored,* for example, was once widely used in the United States to refer to Americans of African ancestry. By the 1950s, the preferred term had become *Negro.* This changed in the 1960s, however, as *black* came to be preferred by most, though certainly not all, members of that community. Then, in the late 1980s, some leaders of the American black community urged that *black* be replaced by *African American.*

The word *Oriental,* once used to refer to people of East Asian descent, is now often considered offensive. At the University of California at Berkeley, the Oriental Languages Department is now known as the East Asian Languages Department. One advocate of the change explained that *Oriental* is appropriate for objects—like rugs—but not for people.

Once widely preferred, the term *Native American* is being challenged by those who argue that the most appropriate way to refer to indigenous people is by the specific name of the tribe or pueblo, such as *Chippewa* or *Tesuque.* In Alaska and parts of Canada, many indigenous peoples once referred to as *Eskimos* now prefer *Inuit* or a specific term such as *Tlinget.* It has also become fairly common for tribal groups to refer to themselves as *Indians* or *Indian tribes.*

Among Americans of Spanish-speaking descent, the preferred terms of reference are many: *Chicano/Chicana, Hispanic, Latin American, Latino/Latina, Mexican American, Dominican,* and *Puerto Rican,* to name but a few.

Clearly, then, ethnic terminology changes often enough to challenge even the most careful writers — including writers who belong to the groups they are writing about. The best advice may be to consider your words carefully, to *listen* for the way members of groups refer to themselves (or *ask* about preferences), and to check any term you're unsure of in a current dictionary.

20d Other kinds of difference

Age

Mention age if it is relevant, but be aware that age-related terms (*matronly, well-preserved,* and so on) can carry derogatory connotations. Describing Mr. Fry as *elderly but still active* may sound polite to you, but chances are Mr. Fry would prefer being called *an active seventy-eight-year-old* — or just *a seventy-eight-year-old,* which eliminates the unstated assumption of surprise that he is active at his age.

Class

Take special care to examine your words for assumptions about class. As a writer, you should not assume that all your readers share your background or values — that your classmates all own cars, for instance. And avoid using any words — *redneck, blueblood,* and the like — that might alienate members of an audience.

Geographic area

You should not assume that geography determines personality or lifestyle. New Englanders are not all thrifty and tight-lipped; people in "red states" may hold liberal views; midwesterners are not always polite. Be careful not to make simplistic assumptions.

Check also that you use geographical terms accurately.

AMERICA, AMERICAN Although many people use these words to refer to the United States alone, such usage will not necessarily be acceptable to people from Canada, Mexico, and Central or South America.

BRITISH, ENGLISH Use *British* to refer to the island of Great Britain, which includes England, Scotland, and Wales, or to the United Kingdom of Great Britain and Northern Ireland. In general, do not use *English* for these broader senses.

ARAB This term refers only to people of Arabic-speaking descent. Note that Iran is not an Arab nation; its people speak Farsi, not Arabic. Note also that *Arab* is not synonymous with *Muslim* or *Moslem* (a believer in Islam). Most (but not all) Arabs are Muslim, but many Muslims (those in Pakistan, for example) are not Arab.

Physical ability or health

When writing about a person with a serious illness or physical disability, ask yourself whether mentioning the disability is relevant to your discussion and whether the words you use carry negative connotations. You might choose, for example, to say someone *uses* a wheelchair rather than to say he or she is *confined to* one. Similarly, you might note a subtle but meaningful difference in calling someone a *person with AIDS* rather than an *AIDS victim.* Mentioning the person first and the disability second, such as referring to a *child with diabetes* rather than a *diabetic child* or a *diabetic,* is always a good idea.

> ### CONSIDERING DISABILITIES
> #### Knowing Your Readers
>
> Nearly 10 percent of first-year college students — about 155,000 — identify themselves as having one or more disabilities. That's no small number. Effective writers consider their own and their readers' disabilities so that they can find ways to build common ground.

Religion

Assumptions about religious groups are very often inaccurate and unfair. For example, Roman Catholics hold a wide spectrum of views on abortion, Muslim women do not all wear veils, and many Baptists are not fundamentalists. In fact, many people do not believe in or practice a religion at all, so be careful of such assumptions. As in other cases, do not use religious labels without considering their relevance to your point.

Sexual orientation

If you wish to build common ground, do not assume that readers all share one sexual orientation. As with any label, reference to sexual orientation should be governed by context. Someone writing about Representative Barney Frank's economic views would probably have little if any reason to refer to his sexual orientation. On the other hand, someone writing about diversity in U.S. government might find it important to note that Frank has long made his homosexuality public.

> **bedfordstmartins.com/everydaywriter** For exercises, go to **Exercise Central** and click on **Language That Builds Common Ground.**

Language Variety **21**

Comedian Dave Chappelle has said, "Every black American is bilingual. We speak street vernacular, and we speak job interview." As Chappelle understands, English comes in many varieties that differ from one another in pronunciation, vocabulary, usage, and grammar. You probably already adjust the variety of language you use depending on how well — and how formally — you know the audience you are addressing. Adding language variety to your writing can improve your communication with your audience if you think carefully about the effect you want to achieve.

AT A GLANCE

Language Variety

You can use different varieties of language to good effect for the following purposes:

- to repeat someone's exact words
- to evoke a person, place, or activity
- to establish your credibility and build common ground
- to make a strong point
- to connect with an audience

21a Standard varieties of English

How do writers decide when to use another language or switch from one variety of English to another? Even writers who are perfectly fluent in several languages must think for a moment before switching linguistic gears. The key to shifting among varieties of English and among languages is appropriateness: you need to consider when such shifts will help your audience appreciate your message and when shifts may be a mistake. Used appropriately and wisely, *any* variety of English can serve a good purpose.

One variety of English, often referred to as the "standard" or "standard academic," is that taught prescriptively in schools, represented in this and most other textbooks, used in the national media, and written and spoken widely by those wielding social and economic power. As the language used in business and most public institutions, standard English is a variety you will want to be completely familiar with. Standard English, however, is only one of many effective varieties of English and itself varies according to purpose and audience, from the more formal style used in academic writing to the informal style characteristic of casual conversation.

21b Ethnic varieties of English

Whether you are an American Indian or trace your ancestry to Europe, Asia, Africa, Latin America, or elsewhere, you have an ethnic heritage that probably lives on in the English language. See how one Hawaiian writer uses an ethnic variety of English to paint a picture of young teens hearing a scary "chicken skin" story about sharks from their grandmother.

"— So, rather dan being rid of da shark, da people were stuck with many little ones, for dere mistake."

Then Grandma Wong wen' pause, for dramatic effect, I guess, and she wen' add, "Dis is one of dose times. . . . Da time of da sharks."

Those words ended another of Grandma's chicken skin stories. The stories she told us had been passed on to her by her grandmother, who had heard them from her grandmother. Always skipping a generation.

– RODNEY MORALES, "When the Shark Bites"

The narrator uses both standard and ethnic varieties of English — presenting information necessary to the story line mostly in standard English and using a local, ethnic variety to represent spoken language, which helps readers hear the characters talk. Another important reason for the shift from standard English is to demonstrate that the writer is a member of the community whose language he is representing and thus to build his credibility with others in the community. Take care, however, in using the language of communities other than your own. When used inappropriately, such language can have an opposite effect, perhaps destroying credibility and alienating your audience.

 bedfordstmartins.com/everydaywriter For more on using varieties of English, go to **Links** and click on **Language.**

21c   Regional varieties of English

Using regional language is an effective way to evoke a character or place. See how a linguistic anthropologist weaves together regional and standard academic English in writing about one Carolina community when she lets a resident of Roadville speak her mind — and in her own words.

For Roadville, schooling is something most folks have not gotten enough of, but everybody believes will do something toward helping an individual "get on." In the words of one oldtime resident, "Folks that ain't got no schooling don't get to be nobody nowadays."

– SHIRLEY BRICE HEATH, *Ways with Words*

EXERCISE 21.1

Identify the purpose and audience for one of this chapter's examples of ethnic or regional English. Then rewrite the passage to remove all evidence of any variety of English other than the so-called standard. Compare your revised version with the original and with those produced by some of your classmates. What differences do you notice in tone (is it more formal? more distant? something else?) and in overall impression? Which version seems most appropriate for the intended audience and purpose? Which do you prefer — and why?

21d Other languages

You might use a language other than English for the same reasons you might use different varieties of English: to represent the actual words of a speaker, to make a point, to connect with your audience, or to get their attention. See how Gerald Haslam uses Spanish to capture his great-grandmother's words and to make a point about his relationship to her.

> *"Expectoran su sangre!"* exclaimed Great-grandma when I showed her the small horned toad I had removed from my breast pocket. I turned toward my mother, who translated: "They spit blood."
>
> *"De los ojos,"* Grandma added. "From their eyes," mother explained, herself uncomfortable in the presence of the small beast.
>
> I grinned, "Awwwwwww."
>
> But my Great-grandmother did not smile. *"Son muy tóxicos,"* she nodded with finality. Mother moved back an involuntary step, her hands suddenly busy at her breast. "Put that thing down," she ordered.
>
> "His name's John," I said. — GERALD HASLAM, *California Childhood*

FOR MULTILINGUAL WRITERS

Recognizing Global English

English is used in many countries around the world, resulting in many global varieties. For example, British English differs from U.S. English in certain vocabulary (*bonnet* for *hood* of a car), syntax (*to hospital* rather than *to the hospital*), spelling (*centre* rather than *center*), and, of course, pronunciation. If you have learned a British variety of English, you will want to recognize the ways in which it differs from the U.S. standard.

EXERCISE 21.2: THINKING CRITICALLY

The following description of a meal features English that is characteristic of the Florida backwoods in the 1930s. Using this passage as an example, write a description of a memorable event from your daily life. Try to include some informal dialogue. Then look at the language you used — do you use more than one variety of English? What effect does your use of language have on your description?

> Jody heard nothing; saw nothing but his plate. He had never been so hungry in his life, and after a lean winter and a slow spring . . . his mother had cooked a supper good enough for the preacher. There were poke-greens with bits of white bacon buried in them; sandbuggers made of potato and onion and the cooter he had found crawling yesterday; sour orange biscuits and at his mother's elbow the sweet potato pone. He was torn between his desire for more biscuits and another sandbugger and the knowledge, born of painful experience, that if he ate them, he would suddenly have no room for pone. The choice was plain.
>
> — MARJORIE KINNAN RAWLINGS, *The Yearling*

Word Choice and Spelling **22**

Deciding which word is the right word can be a challenge. It's not unusual to find many words that have similar but subtly different meanings, and each makes a different impression on your audience. For instance, the "pasta with marinara sauce" presented in a restaurant may look and taste much like the "macaroni and gravy" served at an Italian family dinner, but the choice of one label rather than the other tells us not only about the food but also about the people serving it and the people they expect to serve it to.

Ensuring that you choose the correct spelling for the word you want to use is also important. Spell checkers can help you avoid some errors, but they can also make other mistakes more likely, including word choice errors, so use them with care.

AT A GLANCE

Editing for Appropriate Language and Spelling

- Check to see that your language reflects the appropriate level of formality for your audience, purpose, and topic. (22a)

- Unless you are writing for a specialized audience that will understand jargon, either define technical terms or replace them with words that are easy to understand. (22a)

- Consider the connotations of words carefully. If you say someone is *pushy,* be sure you mean to be critical; otherwise, use a word like *assertive.* (22b)

- Use both general and specific words. If you are writing about the general category *beds,* for example, do you give enough concrete detail (*an antique four-poster bed*)? (22c)

- Look for clichés, and replace them with fresher language. (22d)

- Use spell checkers with care. (22e)

22a Appropriate formality

Choose a level of formality that matches your audience, purpose, and topic. In an email or letter to a friend or close associate, informal language is often appropriate. For most academic and professional writing, however, more formal language is appropriate because you are addressing people you do not know well. Compare the following responses to a request for information about a job candidate:

EMAIL TO SOMEONE YOU KNOW WELL

Maisha is great — hire her if you can!

LETTER OF RECOMMENDATION TO SOMEONE YOU DO NOT KNOW

I am pleased to recommend Maisha Fisher. She will bring good ideas and extraordinary energy to your organization.

Slang and colloquial language

Slang, or extremely informal language, is often confined to a relatively small group and usually becomes obsolete rather quickly, though some slang gains wide use (*yuppie, duh*). Colloquial language, such as *a lot, in a bind,* or *snooze,* is less informal, more widely used, and longer lasting than most slang.

Writers who use slang and colloquial language run the risk of not being understood or of not being taken seriously. If you are writing for a general audience about gun-control legislation, for example, and you use the term *gat* to refer to a weapon, some readers may not know what you mean, and others may be irritated by what they see as a frivolous reference to a deadly serious subject.

EXERCISE 22.1

Choose something or someone to describe — a favorite cousin, a stranger on the bus, an automobile, a musical instrument, whatever strikes your fancy. Describe your subject using colloquial language and slang. Then rewrite the description, this time using neither of these. Read the two passages aloud, and note what different effects each creates.

TALKING THE TALK

Messaging Shortcuts

"Can I use messaging shortcuts when I contact my teacher?" Messaging slang, such as *u* for *you,* may be second nature for many students, but using such shortcuts when communicating with an instructor can be a mistake. On an IM thread or in a text message, shortcuts can indeed be conventional usage. But at least some of your instructors are likely to view them as disrespectful, unprofessional, or simply sloppy writing. Unless you are working to create a special effect for a special purpose and audience, keep to the conventions of standard English for college writing—and for contacting your instructor.

Jargon

Jargon is the special vocabulary of a trade or profession. Reserve technical language as much as possible for an audience that understands your terms, and replace or define such terms for audiences that may not share the vocabulary.

JARGON

The VDTs in composition were down last week, so we had to lay out on dummies and crop and size the art with a wheel.

REVISED FOR A GENERAL AUDIENCE

The video display terminals were not working last week in the composing room, where models of the newspaper pages are made up for printing, so we had to arrange the contents of each page on a large sheet and use a wheel, a kind of circular slide rule, to figure out the size and shape of the illustrations.

Pompous language, euphemisms, and doublespeak

Stuffy or pompous language is unnecessarily formal for the purpose, audience, or topic. It often gives writing an insincere or unintentionally humorous tone, making a writer's ideas seem insignificant or even unbelievable.

POMPOUS

Pursuant to the August 9 memorandum regarding the increased unit-cost of automotive fuels, it is incumbent upon us to endeavor to make maximal utilization of electronic or telephonic communication in lieu of personal visitation.

REVISED

As noted in the August 9 memo, higher gasoline prices require us to email or telephone whenever possible rather than make personal visits.

As these examples illustrate, some writers use words in an attempt to sound expert, and these puffed-up words can easily backfire.

INSTEAD OF	TRY USING	INSTEAD OF	TRY USING
ascertain	find out	optimal	best
commence	begin	parameters	boundaries
finalize	finish, complete	peruse	look at
impact (as verb)	affect	ramp up	increase
methodology	method	utilize	use

Euphemisms are words and phrases that make unpleasant ideas seem less harsh. *Your position is being eliminated* seeks to soften the blow of being fired or laid off. Other euphemisms include *pass on* or *pass away* for *die* and *sanitation engineer* for *garbage collector*. Although euphemisms can sometimes appeal to an audience by showing that you are considerate of people's feelings, they can also sound insincere or evasive.

Doublespeak is language used to hide or distort the truth. During massive layoffs and cutbacks in the business world, companies speak of firings as *work reengineering, employee repositioning, proactive downsizing, deverticalization, smartsizing,* and *special reprogramming.* The public — and particularly those who lose their jobs — recognize these terms for what they are.

EXERCISE 22.2

Revise each of these sentences to use formal language consistently. Example:

> *Although   be enthusiastic   as soon as*
> I can ~~get all enthused~~ about writing, ~~but~~ I sit down to write, ~~and~~ my
>
>   *blank.*
> mind goes ~~right to sleep.~~

1. Desdemona is a wimp; she just lies down and dies, accepting her death as inevitable.

2. Some people feel that "The Star-Spangled Banner," which is kind of obsessed with war, should be dumped as our national anthem in favor of "America the Beautiful."

3. Finding all that loot in King Tut's tomb was one of the biggest archeological scores of the twentieth century.

4. The more she freaked out about his actions, the more he rebelled and continued doing what he pleased.

5. My family lived in Trinidad for the first ten years of my life, and we went through a lot, but when we came to the United States, we thought we had it made.

FOR MULTILINGUAL WRITERS

Avoiding Fancy Language

In writing standard academic English, which is fairly formal, students are often tempted to use many "big words" instead of simple language. Although learning impressive words can be a good way to expand your vocabulary, it is usually best to avoid flowery or fancy language in college writing. Academic writing at U.S. universities tends to value clear, concise prose.

22b   Denotation and connotation

Thinking of a stone tossed into a pool and ripples spreading out from it can help you understand the distinction between denotation and connotation. Denotation refers to the general, or dictionary, meaning of a word, whereas connotation refers to the associations that accompany the word. The words *enthusiasm, passion,* and *obsession,* for instance, all carry roughly the same denotation. But the connotations are quite different: an *enthusiasm* is a pleasurable and absorbing interest; a *passion* has a strong emotional component and may affect someone positively or negatively; an *obsession* is an unhealthy attachment that excludes other interests.

Note the differences in connotation among the following three statements:

▶ Students Against Racism (SAR) erected a temporary barrier on the campus oval. They say it symbolizes "the many barriers to those discriminated against by university policies."

▶ Left-wing agitators threw up an eyesore on the oval to stampede the university into giving in to their demands.

▶ Supporters of human rights for all students challenged the university's investment in racism by erecting a protest barrier on campus.

The first statement is the most neutral, merely stating facts; the second, using words with negative connotations (*agitators, eyesore, stampede*), is strongly critical; the third, using a phrase with positive connotations (*supporters of human rights*) and presenting assertions as facts (*the university's investment in racism*), gives a favorable slant to the story.

EXERCISE 22.3

From the parentheses, choose the word with the denotation that makes most sense in the context of the sentence. Use a dictionary if necessary.

1. She listened (*apprehensively/attentively*) to the lecture and took notes.

2. The telemarketers were told to (*empathize/emphasize*) more expensive items.

3. The interns were (*conscientious/conscious*) workers who listened carefully and learned fast.

4. Franklin advised his readers to be (*feudal/frugal*) and industrious.

EXERCISE 22.4

Study the italicized words in each of the following passages, and decide what each word's connotations contribute to your understanding of the passage. Think of a synonym for each word, and see if you can decide what difference the new word would make on the effect of the passage.

1. If boxing is a sport, it is the most *tragic* of all sports because, more than any human activity, it consumes the very excellence it *displays*: Its very *drama* is this consumption. — JOYCE CAROL OATES, "On Boxing"

2. Then one evening Miss Glory told me to serve the ladies on the porch. After I set the tray down and turned toward the kitchen, one of the women asked, "What's your name, *girl*?" — MAYA ANGELOU, *I Know Why the Caged Bird Sings*

3. The Kiowas are a summer people; they *abide* the cold and keep to themselves; but when the season *turns* and the land becomes warm and *vital*, they cannot *hold still*. — N. SCOTT MOMADAY, "The Way to Rainy Mountain"

22c　General and specific language

Effective writers balance general words, which name or describe groups or classes, with specific words, which identify individual and particular things. Some general words are abstract; they refer to things we cannot perceive through our five senses. Specific words are often concrete; they name things we can see, hear, touch, taste, or smell. We can seldom draw a clear-cut line between general or abstract words on the one hand and specific or concrete words on the other. Instead, most words fall somewhere in between.

GENERAL	LESS GENERAL	SPECIFIC	MORE SPECIFIC
book	dictionary	abridged dictionary	my 2004 edition of *The American Heritage College Dictionary*

ABSTRACT	LESS ABSTRACT	CONCRETE	MORE CONCRETE
culture	visual art	painting	van Gogh's *Starry Night*

Strong writing usually provides readers with both an overall picture and specific examples or concrete details to fill in that picture. In the following passage, the author might have simply made a general statement — *their breakfast was always liberal and good* — or simply given the details of the breakfast. Instead, he is both general and specific.

> There would be a brisk fire crackling in the hearth, the old smoke-gold of morning and the smell of fog, the crisp cheerful voices of the people and their ruddy competent morning look, and the cheerful smells of breakfast, which was always liberal and good, the best meal that they had: kidneys and ham and eggs and sausages and toast and marmalade and tea.
>
> –THOMAS WOLFE, *Of Time and the River*

EXERCISE 22.5

Rewrite each of the following sentences to be more specific and concrete.

1. The entryway of the building was dirty.
2. The sounds at dawn are memorable.
3. Our holiday dinner tasted good.
4. The attendant came toward the car.
5. I woke up.

22d Figurative language

Figurative language, or figures of speech, can paint pictures in a reader's mind, allowing one to "see" a point readily and clearly. Far from being merely decorative, such language can be crucial to understanding.

Similes, metaphors, and analogies

Similes use *like, as, as if,* or *as though* to make explicit the similarity between two seemingly different things.

▶ **You can tell the graphic-novels section in a bookstore from afar, by the young bodies sprawled around it like casualties of a localized disaster.**
— PETER SCHJELDAHL

▶ **The comb felt as if it was raking my skin off.**
— MALCOM X, "My First Conk"

Metaphors are implicit comparisons, omitting the *like, as, as if,* or *as though* of similes.

▶ **The Internet is the new town square.**   — REP. JEB HENSARLING

Mixed metaphors make comparisons that are inconsistent.

▶ **The lectures were like brilliant comets streaking through the night sky,**

                dazzling   *flashes*
▶ ~~**showering**~~ **listeners with a** ~~**torrential rain**~~ **of insights.**
       ^   ^

The images of streaking light and heavy precipitation are inconsistent; in the revised sentence, all of the images relate to light.

Analogies compare similar features of two dissimilar things; they explain something unfamiliar by relating it to something familiar.

▶ **Raised from childhood with a love for the wilderness, 63-year-old Doug Seus is distinctly bearlike himself, with a voice that growls and a penchant for grabbing visitors in an affectionate hug.**
— ROGER TOLL, "The Claws in His Contract"

▶ **One Hundred and Twenty-fifth Street was to Harlem what the Mississippi was to the South, a long traveling river always going somewhere, carrying something.**   — MAYA ANGELOU, *The Heart of a Woman*

FOR MULTILINGUAL WRITERS
Learning Idioms

Why do you wear a diamond *on* your finger but *in* your ear? See 59a.

Clichés

A cliché is a frequently used expression such as *busy as a bee*. By definition, we use clichés all the time, especially in speech, and many serve usefully as shorthand for familiar ideas or as a way of connecting to an audience. But if you use too many clichés in your writing, readers may conclude that what you are saying is not very new or interesting — or true. To check for clichés, use this rule of thumb: if you can predict exactly what the next word in a phrase will be, the phrase stands a good chance of being a cliché.

EXERCISE 22.6

Return to the description you wrote in Exercise 22.1. Note any words that carry strong connotations, and identify the concrete and abstract language as well as any use of figurative language. Revise any inappropriate language you find.

EXERCISE 22.7: THINKING CRITICALLY

Read the following brief poem. What dominant feeling or impression does the poem produce in you? Identify the specific words and phrases that help create that impression.

> What happens to a dream deferred?
>
> Does it dry up
> Like a raisin in the sun?
> Or fester like a sore —
> And then run?
> Does it stink like rotten meat?
> Or crust and sugar over —
> Like a syrupy sweet?
>
> Maybe it just sags
> Like a heavy load.
>
> Or does it explode?
> — LANGSTON HUGHES, "Harlem (A Dream Deferred)"

EXERCISE 22.8

Choose the appropriate word in parentheses to fill each blank.

If _____ (*your/you're*) looking for summer fun, _____ (*accept/except*) the friendly _____ (*advice/advise*) of thousands of happy adventurers: spend three _____ (*weaks/weeks*) kayaking _____ (*thorough/threw/through*) the Inside Passage _____ (*to/too/two*) Alaska. For ten years, Outings, Inc., has _____ (*lead/led*) groups of novice kayakers _____ (*passed/past*) some of the most breathtaking scenery in North America. The group's goal is simple: to give participants the time of _____ (*their/there/they're*) lives and show them things they don't see _____ (*every day/everyday*). As one of last year's adventurers said, "_____ (*Its/It's*) a trip that is _____ (*already/all ready*) one of my favorite memories. It _____ (*affected/effected*) me powerfully."

bedfordstmartins.com/everydaywriter For exercises, go to **Exercise Central** and click on **Appropriate Language.**

22e Spell checkers

Research conducted for this textbook shows that spelling errors have changed dramatically in the past twenty years — and the reason is spell checkers. Although these programs have weeded out many once-common misspellings, they are not foolproof. Spell checkers still allow typical kinds of errors that you should look out for.

- *Homonyms.* Spell checkers cannot distinguish between words such as *affect* and *effect* that sound alike but are spelled differently.
- *Proper nouns.* A spell checker cannot tell you when you have misspelled a proper name. Proofread names with special care.
- *Compound words written as two words.* Spell checkers will not see a problem if *nowhere* is incorrectly written as *no where.* When in doubt, check a dictionary.
- *Typos.* The spell checker will not flag *heat* even if you meant to type *heart.*

To make spell checkers work best for you, you need to learn to adapt them to your own needs.

- Always proofread carefully, even after you have used the spell checker. The more important the message or document, the more careful you should be about its accuracy and clarity.
- Keep a dictionary near your computer or bookmark a good online dictionary, and look up any word the spell checker highlights that you are not sure of.
- If your spell checker's dictionary allows you to add new words, enter proper names, non-English words, or specialized language you use regularly and have trouble spelling. Be careful to enter the correct spelling!
- If you know that you mix up certain homonyms, such as *there* and *their*, check for them after running your spell checker.
- Remember that spell checkers are not sensitive to capitalization. If you write "the united states," the spell checker won't question it.

TALKING THE TALK

Spell Checkers and Wrong-Word Errors

"Can I trust spell checkers to correct a word I've spelled wrong?" In a word, no. The spell checker may suggest bizarre substitutes for many proper names and specialized terms (even when you spell them correctly) and for certain typographical errors, thus introducing wrong words into your paper if you accept its suggestions automatically. For example, a student who had typed *fantic* instead of *frantic* found that the spell checker's first choice was to substitute *fanatic* — a replacement that made no sense. Wrong-word errors are the most common surface error in college writing today (see Chapter 1), and spell checkers are partly to blame. So be careful not to take a spell checker's recommendation without paying careful attention to the replacement word.

Homonyms

A relatively small number of homonyms — just eight groups — cause writers the most frequent trouble.

accept (to take or receive)
except (to leave out)

affect (an emotion; to have an influence)
effect (a result; to cause to happen)

its (possessive of *it*)
it's (contraction of *it is* or *it has*)

their (possessive of *they*)
there (in that place)
they're (contraction of *they are*)

to (in the direction of)
too (in addition; excessive)
two (number between *one* and *three*)

weather (climatic conditions)
whether (if)

who's (contraction of *who is* or *who has*)
whose (possessive of *who*)

your (possessive of *you*)
you're (contraction of *you are*)

If you tend to confuse particular homonyms, try creating a special memory device to help you remember the differences. For example, "*We* all complain about the *weather*" will remind you that *weather* (the climate) starts with *we*.

In addition, pay close attention to homonyms that may be spelled as one word or two, depending on the meaning.

▶ Of course, they did not wear *everyday* clothes *every day*.

▶ Before the six lawyers were *all ready* to negotiate, it was *already* May.

▶ The director *may be* on time. But *maybe* she'll be late.

For additional advice on commonly confused words, see the glossary of usage in Chapter 23.

Recognizing American Spellings

Different varieties of English often use different spelling conventions. If you have learned British or Indian English, for example, you will want to be aware of some of the more common spelling differences in American English. For example, words ending in *–yse* or *–ise* in British/Indian English (*analyse, criticise*) usually end in *–yze* or *ize* in American English (*analyze, criticize*); words ending in *–our* in British/Indian English (*labour, colour*) usually end in *–or* in American English (*labor, color*); and words ending in *–re* in British/Indian English (*theatre, centre*) usually end in *–er* in American English (*theater, center*).

22f Spelling rules

General spelling rules can help writers enormously, but many rules have exceptions. When in doubt, consult a dictionary.

i *before* e *except after* c

Here is a slightly expanded version of the "*i* before *e*" rule:

I BEFORE *E*	achieve, brief, field, friend
EXCEPT AFTER *C*	ceiling, receipt, perceive
OR WHEN PRONOUNCED *AY*	eighth, neighbor, reign, weigh
OR IN WEIRD EXCEPTIONS	either, foreign, height, leisure, neither, seize

Word endings (suffixes)

FINAL SILENT *E*

Drop the final silent *e* when you add an ending that starts with a vowel.

imagine + -able = imaginable   exercise + -ing = exercising

Generally, keep the final *e* if the ending starts with a consonant. Common exceptions include *argument, judgment, noticeable,* and *truly.*

force + -ful = forceful   state + -ly = stately

FINAL *Y*

When adding an ending to a word that ends in a consonant plus *y,* change the *y* to an *i* in most cases.

try, tried   busy, busily

Keep the *y* if it is part of a proper name or if the ending begins with *i*.

>   Kennedy, Kennedyesque   dry, drying

FINAL CONSONANTS

When adding an ending beginning with a vowel to a word that ends with a vowel and a consonant, double the final consonant if the original word is one syllable or if the accent is on the same syllable in both the original and the new word.

>   stop, stopped   begin, beginner   refer, referral

Otherwise, do not double the final consonant.

>   bait, baiting   start, started   refer, reference

Plurals

ADDING –S OR -ES

For most nouns, add -*s*. For words ending in *s, ch, sh, x,* or *z*, add -*es*.

>   pencil, pencils   church, churches   bus, buses

In general, add -*s* to nouns ending in *o* if the *o* is preceded by a vowel. Add -*es* if the *o* is preceded by a consonant.

>   rodeo, rodeos   patio, patios   potato, potatoes   hero, heroes

For some nouns ending in *f* or *fe*, change *f* to *v*, and add -*s* or -*es*.

>   calf, calves   life, lives   hoof, hooves

For compound nouns written as separate or hyphenated words, make the most important part plural, whether or not it is the last part of the compound.

>   lieutenant governors   brothers-in-law

For plurals of numbers and words used as terms, see 41c.

CONSIDERING DISABILITIES

Spelling

Spelling is especially difficult for people who have trouble processing letters and sounds in sequence. Technology can help: "talking pens" can scan words and read them aloud, and voice-recognition programs can transcribe dictated text.

---

 bedfordstmartins.com/everydaywriter For exercises, go to **Exercise Central** and click on **Spelling**.

Conventions of usage might be called the "good manners" of discourse. And just as manners vary from culture to culture and time to time, so do conventions of usage. Matters of usage, like other language choices you must make, depend on what your purpose is and on what is appropriate for a particular audience at a particular time.

a, an Use *a* with a word that begins with a consonant (*a book*), a consonant sound such as "y" or "w" (*a euphoric moment, a one-sided match*), or a sounded *h* (*a hemisphere*). Use *an* with a word that begins with a vowel (*an umbrella*), a vowel sound (*an X-ray*), or a silent *h* (*an honor*).

accept, except The verb *accept* means "receive" or "agree to." *Except* is usually a preposition that means "aside from" or "excluding." *All the plaintiffs except Mr. Kim decided to accept the settlement.*

advice, advise The noun *advice* means "opinion" or "suggestion"; the verb *advise* means "offer advice." *Doctors advise everyone not to smoke, but many people ignore the advice.*

affect, effect As a verb, *affect* means "influence" or "move the emotions of"; as a noun, it means "emotions" or "feelings." *Effect* is a noun meaning "result"; less commonly, it is a verb meaning "bring about." *The storm affected a large area. Its effects included widespread power failures. The drug effected a major change in the patient's affect.*

aggravate The formal meaning is "make worse." *Having another mouth to feed aggravated their poverty.* In academic and professional writing, avoid using *aggravate* to mean "irritate" or "annoy."

all ready, already *All ready* means "fully prepared." *Already* means "previously." *We were all ready for Lucy's party when we learned that she had already left.*

all right, alright Avoid the spelling *alright*.

all together, altogether *All together* means "all in a group" or "gathered in one place." *Altogether* means "completely" or "everything considered." *When the board members were all together, their mutual distrust was altogether obvious.*

allude, elude *Allude* means "refer indirectly." *Elude* means "avoid" or "escape from." *The candidate did not even allude to her opponent. The suspect eluded the police for several days.*

allusion, illusion An *allusion* is an indirect reference. An *illusion* is a false or misleading appearance. *The speaker's allusion to the Bible created an illusion of piety.*

a lot Avoid the spelling *alot*.

already See *all ready, already*.

alright See *all right, alright*.

altogether See *all together, altogether*.

among, between In referring to two things or people, use *between*. In referring to three or more, use *among*. *The relationship between the twins is different from that among the other three children.*

amount, number Use *amount* with quantities you cannot count; use *number* for quantities you can count. *A small number of volunteers cleared a large amount of brush.*

an See *a, an.*

and/or Avoid this term except in business or legal writing. Instead of *fat and/or protein*, write *fat, protein, or both.*

any body, anybody, any one, anyone *Anybody* and *anyone* are pronouns meaning "any person." *Anyone* [or *anybody*] *would enjoy this film. Any body* is an adjective modifying a noun. *Any body of water has its own ecology. Any one* is two adjectives or a pronoun modified by an adjective. *Customers could buy only two sale items at any one time. The winner could choose any one of the prizes.*

anyplace In academic and professional discourse, use *anywhere* instead.

anyway, anyways In writing, use *anyway*, not *anyways.*

apt, liable, likely *Likely to* means "probably will," and *apt to* means "inclines or tends to." In many instances, they are interchangeable. *Liable* often carries a more negative sense and is also a legal term meaning "obligated" or "responsible."

as Avoid sentences in which it is not clear if *as* means "when" or "because." For example, does *Carl left town as his father was arriving* mean "at the same time as his father was arriving" or "because his father was arriving"?

as, as if, like In academic and professional writing, use *as* or *as if* instead of *like* to introduce a clause. *The dog howled as if* [not *like*] *it were in pain. She did as* [not *like*] *I suggested.*

assure, ensure, insure *Assure* means "convince" or "promise"; its direct object is usually a person or persons. *She assured voters she would not raise taxes. Ensure* and *insure* both mean "make certain," but *insure* usually refers specifically to protection against financial loss. *When the city rationed water to ensure that the supply would last, the Browns could no longer afford to insure their car-wash business.*

as to Do not use *as to* as a substitute for *about. Karen was unsure about* [not *as to*] *Bruce's intentions.*

at, where See *where.*

awhile, a while Always use *a while* after a preposition such as *for, in,* or *after. We drove awhile and then stopped for a while.*

bad, badly Use *bad* after a linking verb such as *be, feel,* or *seem*. Use *badly* to modify an action verb, an adjective, or another verb. *The hostess felt bad because the dinner was badly prepared.*

bare, bear Use *bare* to mean "uncovered" and *bear* to refer to the animal or to mean "carry" or "endure": *The walls were bare. The emptiness was hard to bear.*

because of, due to Use *due to* when the effect, stated as a noun, appears before the verb *be*. *His illness was due to malnutrition.* (*Illness*, a noun, is the effect.) Use *because of* when the effect is stated as a clause. *He was sick because of malnutrition.* (*He was sick,* a clause, is the effect.)

being as, being that In academic or professional writing, use *because* or *since* instead of these expressions. *Because* [not *being as*] *Romeo killed Tybalt, he was banished to Padua.*

beside, besides *Beside* is a preposition meaning "next to." *Besides* can be a preposition meaning "other than" or an adverb meaning "in addition." *No one besides Francesca would sit beside him.*

between See *among, between.*

brake, break *Brake* means "to stop" and also refers to a stopping mechanism: *Check the brakes.* *Break* means "fracture" or an interruption: *The coffee break was too short.*

breath, breathe *Breath* is a noun; *breathe,* a verb. *"Breathe," said the nurse, so June took a deep breath.*

bring, take Use *bring* when an object is moved from a farther to a nearer place; use *take* when the opposite is true. *Take the box to the post office; bring back my mail.*

but, yet Do not use these words together. *He is strong but* [not *but yet*] *gentle.*

but that, but what Avoid using these as substitutes for *that* in expressions of doubt. *Hercule Poirot never doubted that* [not *but that*] *he would solve the case.*

can, may *Can* refers to ability and *may* to possibility or permission. *Since I can ski the slalom well, I may win the race.*

can't hardly *Hardly* has a negative meaning; therefore, *can't hardly* is a double negative. This expression is commonly used in some varieties of English but is not used in academic English. *Tim can* [not *can't*] *hardly wait.*

can't help but This expression is redundant. Use *I can't help going* rather than *I can't help but go.*

censor, censure *Censor* means "remove that which is considered offensive." *Censure* means "formally reprimand." *The newspaper censored stories that offended advertisers. The legislature censured the official for misconduct.*

compare to, compare with *Compare to* means "regard as similar." *Jamie compared the loss to a kick in the head. Compare with* means "examine to find differences or similarities." *Compare Tim Burton's films with David Lynch's.*

complement, compliment *Complement* means "go well with." *Compliment* means "praise." *Guests complimented her on how her earrings complemented her gown.*

comprise, compose *Comprise* means "contain." *Compose* means "make up." *The class comprises twenty students. Twenty students compose the class.*

conscience, conscious *Conscience* means "a sense of right and wrong." *Conscious* means "awake" or "aware." *Lisa was conscious of a guilty conscience.*

consensus of opinion Use *consensus* instead of this redundant phrase. *The family consensus was to sell the old house.*

consequently, subsequently *Consequently* means "as a result"; *subsequently* means "then." *He quit, and subsequently his wife lost her job; consequently, they had to sell their house.*

continual, continuous *Continual* means "repeated at regular or frequent intervals." *Continuous* means "continuing or connected without a break." *The damage done by continuous erosion was increased by the continual storms.*

could of *Have*, not *of*, should follow *could, would, should,* or *might. We could have* [not *of*] *invited them.*

criteria, criterion *Criterion* means "standard of judgment" or "necessary qualification." *Criteria* is the plural form. *Image is the wrong criterion for choosing a president.*

data *Data* is the plural form of the Latin word *datum,* meaning "fact." Although *data* is used informally as either singular or plural, in academic or professional writing, treat *data* as plural. *These data indicate that fewer people are smoking.*

different from, different than *Different from* is generally preferred in academic and professional writing, although both phrases are widely used. *Her lab results were no different from* [not *than*] *his.*

discreet, discrete *Discreet* means "tactful" or "prudent." *Discrete* means "separate" or "distinct." *The leader's discreet efforts kept all the discrete factions unified.*

disinterested, uninterested *Disinterested* means "unbiased." *Uninterested* means "indifferent." *Finding disinterested jurors was difficult. She was uninterested in the verdict.*

distinct, distinctive *Distinct* means "separate" or "well defined." *Distinctive* means "characteristic." *Germany includes many distinct regions, each with a distinctive accent.*

doesn't, don't *Doesn't* is the contraction for *does not.* Use it with *he, she, it,* and singular nouns. *Don't* stands for *do not;* use it with *I, you, we, they,* and plural nouns.

due to See *because of, due to.*

each other, one another Use *each other* in sentences involving two subjects and *one another* in sentences involving more than two.

effect See *affect, effect.*

elicit, illicit The verb *elicit* means "draw out." The adjective *illicit* means "illegal." *The police elicited from the criminal the names of others involved in illicit activities.*

elude See *allude, elude.*

emigrate from, immigrate to *Emigrate from* means "move away from one's country." *Immigrate to* means "move to another country." *We emigrated from Norway in 1999. We immigrated to the United States.*

ensure See *assure, ensure, insure.*

enthused, enthusiastic Use *enthusiastic* rather than *enthused* in academic and professional writing.

equally as good Replace this redundant phrase with *equally good* or *as good.*

every day, everyday *Everyday* is an adjective meaning "ordinary." *Every day* is an adjective and a noun, meaning "each day." *I wore everyday clothes almost every day.*

every one, everyone   *Everyone* is a pronoun. *Every one* is an adjective and a pro-noun, referring to each member of a group. *Because he began after everyone else, David could not finish every one of the problems.*

except   See *accept, except.*

explicit, implicit   *Explicit* means "directly or openly expressed." *Implicit* means "indirectly expressed or implied." *The explicit message of the ad urged consumers to buy the product, while the implicit message promised popularity if they did so.*

farther, further   *Farther* refers to physical distance. *How much farther is it to Munich? Further* refers to time or degree. *I want to avoid further delays.*

fewer, less   Use *fewer* with nouns that can be counted. Use *less* with general amounts that you cannot count. *The world needs fewer bombs and less hostility.*

finalize   *Finalize* is a pretentious way of saying "end" or "make final." *We closed* [not *finalized*] *the deal.*

firstly, secondly, etc.   *First, second,* etc., are more common in U.S. English.

flaunt, flout   *Flaunt* means to "show off." *Flout* means to "mock" or "scorn." *The drug dealers flouted authority by flaunting their wealth.*

former, latter   *Former* refers to the first and *latter* to the second of two things previously mentioned. *Kathy and Anna are athletes; the former plays tennis, and the latter runs.*

further   See *farther, further.*

good, well   *Good* is an adjective and should not be used as a substitute for the adverb *well. Gabriel is a good host who cooks well.*

good and   *Good and* is colloquial for "very"; avoid it in academic and profes-sional writing.

hanged, hung   *Hanged* refers to executions; *hung* is used for all other meanings.

hardly   See *can't hardly.*

herself, himself, myself, yourself   Do not use these reflexive pronouns as sub-jects or as objects unless they are necessary. *Jane and I* [not *myself*] *agree. They in-vited John and me* [not *myself*].

he/she, his/her   Better solutions for avoiding sexist language are to write out *he or she,* to eliminate pronouns entirely, or to make the subject plural. Instead of writing *Everyone should carry his/her driver's license,* try *Drivers should carry their licenses* or *People should carry their driver's licenses.*

himself   See *herself, himself, myself, yourself.*

hisself   Use *himself* instead in academic or professional writing.

hopefully   *Hopefully* is often misused to mean "it is hoped," but its correct meaning is "with hope." *Sam watched the roulette wheel hopefully* [not *Hopefully, Sam will win*].

hung   See *hanged, hung.*

illicit   See *elicit, illicit.*

illusion   See *allusion, illusion.*

immigrate to   See *emigrate from, immigrate to.*

impact Avoid the colloquial use of *impact* or *impact on* as a verb meaning "affect." *Population control may reduce* [not *impact*] *world hunger.*

implicit See *explicit, implicit.*

imply, infer To *imply* is to suggest indirectly. To *infer* is to guess or conclude on the basis of an indirect suggestion. *The note implied they were planning a small wedding; we inferred we would not be invited.*

inside of, outside of Use *inside* and *outside* instead. *The class regularly met outside* [not *outside of*] *the building.*

insure See *assure, ensure, insure.*

interact, interface *Interact* is a vague word meaning "do something that somehow involves another person." *Interface* is computer jargon; when used as a verb, it means "discuss" or "communicate." Avoid both verbs in academic and professional writing.

irregardless, regardless *Irregardless* is a double negative. Use *regardless.*

is when, is where These vague expressions are often incorrectly used in definitions. *Schizophrenia is a psychotic condition in which* [not *is when* or *is where*] *a person withdraws from reality.*

its, it's *Its* is the possessive form of *it. It's* is a contraction for *it is* or *it has. It's important to observe the rat before it eats its meal.*

kind, sort, type These singular nouns should be modified with *this* or *that*, not *these* or *those*, and followed by other singular nouns, not plural nouns. *Wear this kind of dress* [not *those kind of dresses*].

kind of, sort of Avoid these colloquialisms. *Amy was somewhat* [not *kind of*] *tired.*

know, no Use *know* to mean "understand." *No* is the opposite of *yes.*

later, latter *Later* means "after some time." *Latter* refers to the second of two items named. *Juan and Chad won all their early matches, but the latter was injured later in the season.*

latter See *former, latter* and *later, latter.*

lay, lie *Lay* means "place" or "put." Its main forms are *lay, laid, laid.* It generally has a direct object, specifying what has been placed. *She laid her books on the desk. Lie* means "recline" or "be positioned" and does not take a direct object. Its main forms are *lie, lay, lain. She lay awake until two.*

leave, let *Leave* means "go away." *Let* means "allow." *Leave alone* and *let alone* are interchangeable. *Let me leave now, and leave* [or *let*] *me alone from now on!*

lend, loan In academic and professional writing, do not use *loan* as a verb; use *lend* instead. *Please lend me your pen so that I may fill out this application for a loan.*

less See *fewer, less.*

let See *leave, let.*

liable See *apt, liable, likely.*

lie See *lay, lie.*

like See *as, as if, like.*

likely See *apt, liable, likely.*

literally   *Literally* means "actually" or "exactly as stated." Use it to stress the truth of a statement that might otherwise be understood as figurative. Do not use *literally* as an intensifier in a figurative statement. *Mirna was literally at the edge of her seat* may be accurate, but *Mirna is so hungry that she could literally eat a horse* is not.

loan   See *lend, loan.*

loose, lose   *Lose* is a verb meaning "misplace." *Loose* is an adjective that means "not securely attached." *Sew on that loose button before you lose it.*

lots, lots of   Avoid these informal expressions meaning "much" or "many" in academic or professional discourse.

man, mankind   Replace these terms with *people, humans, humankind, men and women,* or similar wording.

may   See *can, may.*

may be, maybe   *May be* is a verb phrase. *Maybe* is an adverb that means "perhaps." *He may be the head of the organization, but maybe someone else would handle a crisis better.*

media   *Media* is the plural form of the noun *medium* and takes a plural verb. *The media are* [not *is*] *obsessed with scandals.*

might of   See *could of.*

moral, morale   A *moral* is a succinct lesson. *The moral of the story is that generosity is rewarded. Morale* means "spirit" or "mood." *Office morale was low.*

myself   See *herself, himself, myself, yourself.*

no   See *know, no.*

nor, or   Use *either* with *or* and *neither* with *nor.*

number   See *amount, number.*

off, of   Use *off* without *of. The spaghetti slipped off* [not *off of*] *the plate.*

OK, O.K., okay   All are acceptable spellings, but avoid the term in academic and professional discourse.

on account of   Use this substitute for *because of* sparingly or not at all.

one another   See *each other, one another.*

or   See *nor, or.*

outside of   See *inside of, outside of.*

owing to the fact that   Avoid this and other wordy expressions for *because.*

passed, past   Use *passed* to mean "went by" or "received a passing grade": *The marching band passed the reviewing stand.* Use *past* to refer to a time before the present: *Historians study the past.*

per   Use the Latin *per* only in standard technical phrases such as *miles per hour.* Otherwise, find English equivalents. *As mentioned in* [not *As per*] *the latest report, the country's average food consumption each day* [not *per day*] *is only 2,000 calories.*

percent, percentage   Use *percent* with a specific number; use *percentage* with an adjective such as *large* or *small. Last year, 80 percent of the members were female. A large percentage of the members are women.*

plenty   *Plenty* means "enough" or "a great abundance." *They told us America was a land of plenty.* Colloquially, it is used to mean "very," a usage you should avoid in academic and professional writing. *He was very* [not *plenty*] *tired.*

plus   *Plus* means "in addition to." *Your salary plus mine will cover our expenses.* Do not use *plus* to mean "besides" or "moreover." *That dress does not fit me. Besides* [not *Plus*], *it is the wrong color.*

precede, proceed   *Precede* means "come before"; *proceed* means "go forward." *Despite the storm that preceded the ceremony, the wedding proceeded on schedule.*

pretty   Avoid using *pretty* as a substitute for "rather," "somewhat," or "quite." *Bill was quite* [not *pretty*] *disagreeable.*

principal, principle   When used as a noun, *principal* refers to a head official or an amount of money; when used as an adjective, it means "most significant." *Principle* means "fundamental law or belief." *Albert went to the principal and defended himself with the principle of free speech.*

proceed   See *precede, proceed.*

quotation, quote   *Quote* is a verb, and *quotation* is a noun. *He quoted the president, and the quotation* [not *quote*] *was preserved in history books.*

raise, rise   *Raise* means "lift" or "move upward." (Referring to children, it means "bring up.") It takes a direct object; someone raises something. *The guests raised their glasses to toast.* *Rise* means "go upward." It does not take a direct object; something rises by itself. *She saw the steam rise from the pan.*

rarely ever   Use *rarely* by itself, or use *hardly ever.* *When we were poor, we rarely went to the movies.*

real, really   *Real* is an adjective, and *really* is an adverb. Do not substitute *real* for *really.* In academic and professional writing, do not use *real* or *really* to mean "very." *The old man walked very* [not *real* or *really*] *slowly.*

reason is because   Use either *the reason is that* or *because* — not both. *The reason the copier stopped is that* [not *is because*] *the paper jammed.*

reason why   This expression is redundant. *The reason* [not *reason why*] *this book is short is market demand.*

regardless   See *irregardless, regardless.*

respectfully, respectively   *Respectfully* means "with respect." *Respectively* means "in the order given." *Karen and David are, respectively, a juggler and an acrobat. The children treated their grandparents respectfully.*

rise   See *raise, rise.*

set, sit   *Set* usually means "put" or "place" and takes a direct object. *Sit* refers to taking a seat and does not take an object. *Set your cup on the table, and sit down.*

should of   See *could of.*

since   Be careful not to use *since* ambiguously. In *Since I broke my leg, I've stayed home,* the word *since* might be understood to mean either "because" or "ever since."

sit   See *set, sit.*

so   In academic and professional writing, avoid using *so* alone to mean "very." Instead, follow *so* with *that* to show how the intensified condition leads to a result. *Aaron was so tired that he fell asleep at the wheel.*

someplace   Use *somewhere* instead in academic and professional writing.

some time, sometime, sometimes   *Some time* refers to a length of time. *Please leave me some time to dress. Sometime* means "at some indefinite later time." *Sometime I will take you to London. Sometimes* means "occasionally." *Sometimes I eat sushi.*

sort   See *kind, sort, type.*

sort of   See *kind of, sort of.*

stationary, stationery   *Stationary* means "standing still"; *stationery* means "writing paper." *When the bus was stationary, Pat took out stationery and wrote a note.*

subsequently   See *consequently, subsequently.*

supposed to, used to   Be careful to include the final *-d* in these expressions. *He is supposed to attend.*

sure, surely   Avoid using *sure* as an intensifier. Instead, use *surely* (or *certainly* or *without a doubt*). *I was surely glad to see you.*

take   See *bring, take.*

than, then   Use *than* in comparative statements. *The cat was bigger than the dog.* Use *then* when referring to a sequence of events. *I won, and then I cried.*

that, which   A clause beginning with *that* singles out the item being described. *The book that is on the table is a good one* specifies the book on the table as opposed to some other book. A clause beginning with *which* may or may not single out the item, although some writers use *which* clauses only to add more information about an item being described. *The book, which is on the table, is a good one* contains a *which* clause between the commas. The clause simply adds extra, nonessential information about the book; it does not specify which book.

theirselves   Use *themselves* instead in academic and professional writing.

then   See *than, then.*

thorough, threw, through   *Thorough* means "complete": *After a thorough inspection, the restaurant reopened. Threw* is the past tense of *throw,* and *through* means "in one side and out the other": *He threw the ball through a window.*

to, too, two   *To* generally shows direction. *Too* means "also." *Two* is the number. *We, too, are going to the meeting in two hours.* Avoid using *to* after *where. Where are you flying* [not *flying to*]?

two   See *to, too, two.*

type   See *kind, sort, type.*

uninterested   See *disinterested, uninterested.*

unique   *Unique* means "the one and only." Do not use it with adverbs that suggest degree, such as *very* or *most. Adora's paintings are unique* [not *very unique*].

used to   See *supposed to, used to.*

very   Avoid using *very* to intensify a weak adjective or adverb; instead, replace the adjective or adverb with a stronger, more precise, or more colorful word. Instead of *very nice,* for example, use *kind, warm, sensitive, endearing,* or *friendly.*

way, ways When referring to distance, use *way*. *Graduation was a long way* [not *ways*] *off.*

well See *good, well.*

where Use *where* alone, not with words such as *at* and *to*. *Where are you going* [not *going to*]?

which See *that, which.*

who, whom Use *who* if the word is the subject of the clause and *whom* if the word is the object of the clause. *Monica, who smokes incessantly, is my godmother.* (*Who* is the subject of the clause; the verb is *smokes*.) *Monica, whom I saw last winter, lives in Tucson.* (*Whom* is the object of the verb *saw*.)

who's, whose *Who's* is a contraction for *who is* or *who has*. *Who's on the patio? Whose* is a possessive form. *Whose sculpture is in the garden? Whose is on the patio?*

would of See *could of.*

yet See *but, yet.*

your, you're *Your* shows possession. *Bring your sleeping bag along. You're* is the contraction for *you are. You're in the wrong sleeping bag.*

yourself See *herself, himself, myself, yourself.*

Sentence Style

Look: wear your black some days, and wear your purple others. There is no other rule besides pulling it off.

— ZADIE SMITH

Sentence Style

Coordination, Subordination, and Emphasis

24

Coordination and subordination are ways of joining ideas in sentences that show relationships between ideas and emphasize more important ideas. In speech, people tend to use *and* and *so* as all-purpose connectors.

> He enjoys psychology, and he has to study hard.

The meaning of this sentence may be perfectly clear in speech, which provides clues with voice, facial expressions, and gestures. But in writing, the sentence could have multiple meanings, including these:

> Although he enjoys psychology, he has to study hard.
>
> He enjoys psychology, although he has to study hard.

A coordinating conjunction such as *and* gives ideas equal emphasis, and a subordinating conjunction such as *although* emphasizes one idea more

---

AT A GLANCE

Editing for Coordination, Subordination, and Emphasis

How do your ideas flow from one sentence to another? Do they connect smoothly and clearly? Are the more important ideas given more emphasis than less important ones?

- Look for strings of short sentences that might be combined to join related ideas. (24a)

  > The report was short. It was persuasive. It changed my mind.
  >
  > *but it*   *it*

- If you use *and* excessively, decide whether all the ideas are equally important. If they are not equal, edit to subordinate the less important ones. (24b)
- Make sure that the most important ideas appear in independent clauses that can stand alone as complete sentences. (24b)

(continued)

▶ *Even though the*
~~The~~ report was short, ~~even though~~ it changed my mind.
^

- Identify the word or words you want to receive special emphasis. If those words are buried in the middle of a sentence, edit the sentence to change their position. The end and the beginning are generally the most emphatic. (24c)
- If a sentence includes a series of three or more words, phrases, or clauses, try to arrange the items in the series in climactic order, with the most important item last. (24c)

than another. Choosing appropriate conjunctions also allows a writer to specify how the ideas are related.

24a Use coordination to relate equal ideas.

When you want to give equal emphasis to different ideas in a sentence, link them with a coordinating conjunction (*and, but, for, nor, or, so, yet*) or a semicolon.

▶ They acquired horses, *and* their ancient nomadic spirit was suddenly free of the ground.

▶ There is perfect freedom in the mountains, *but* it belongs to the eagle and the elk, the badger and the bear.

▶ No longer were they slaves to the simple necessity of survival; they were a lordly and dangerous society of fighters and thieves, hunters and priests of the sun.

— N. Scott Momaday, *The Way to Rainy Mountain*

Coordination can help make explicit the relationship between two separate ideas.

forced
▶ My son watches *The Simpsons* religiously~~,~~; ~~Forced~~ to choose, he
^
would probably pick Homer Simpson over his sister.

Connecting these two sentences with a semicolon strengthens the connection between two closely related ideas.

When you connect ideas in a sentence, make sure that the relationship between the ideas is clear.

but
▶ Watching television is a common way to spend leisure time, ~~and~~ it
^
makes viewers apathetic.

The relationship between the two ideas in the original sentence is unclear: what does being a common form of leisure have to do with making viewers apathetic? Changing *and* to *but* better relates the two ideas.

EXERCISE 24.1

Using coordination to signal equal importance or to create special effects, combine and revise the following twelve short sentences into several longer and more effective ones. Add or delete words as necessary.

The bull-riding arena was fairly crowded. The crowd made no impression on me. I had made a decision. It was now time to prove myself. I was scared. I walked to the entry window. I laid my money on the counter. The clerk held up a Stetson hat filled with slips of paper. I reached in. I picked one. The slip held the number of the bull I was to ride. I headed toward the stock corral.

24b Use subordination to distinguish main ideas.

Subordination allows you to distinguish major points from minor points or to bring in supporting details. If, for instance, you put your main idea in an independent clause — words that could stand alone as a sentence (30m) — you might then put any less significant ideas in dependent clauses, phrases, or even single words. The following sentence shows the subordinated point in italics:

▶ **Mrs. Viola Cullinan was a plump woman** *who lived in a three-bedroom house somewhere behind the post office.*
— MAYA ANGELOU, "My Name Is Margaret"

The dependent clause adds important information about Mrs. Cullinan, but it is subordinate to the independent clause.

Notice that the choice of what to subordinate rests with the writer and depends on the intended meaning. Angelou might have given the same basic information differently.

▶ **Mrs. Viola Cullinan,** *a plump woman,* **lived in a three-bedroom house somewhere behind the post office.**

Subordinating the information about Mrs. Cullinan's size to that about her house would suggest a slightly different meaning, of course. When you write, think carefully about what you want to emphasize and subordinate information accordingly.

Subordination also establishes logical relationships among ideas. These relationships are often specified by relative pronouns — such as *which, who,* and *that* — and by subordinating conjunctions.

COMMON SUBORDINATING CONJUNCTIONS

after	if	though
although	in order that	unless
as	once	until
as if	since	when
because	so that	where
before	than	while
even though		

The following sentence shows the subordinate clause in italics and the subordinating word underlined:

▶ **She usually rested her smile until late afternoon** <u>*when*</u> *her women friends dropped in and Miss Glory, the cook, served them cold drinks on the closed-in porch.* — MAYA ANGELOU, "My Name Is Margaret"

Using too many coordinate structures can be monotonous and can make it hard for readers to recognize the most important ideas. Subordinating lesser ideas can help highlight the main ideas.

▶ **Many people come home tired in the evening, so they turn on the TV to**
Though they
relat. ~~They~~ may intend to watch just the news, ~~but then~~ a game show
which   *Eventually,*
comes on next, ^and they decide to watch ~~it~~ for just a short while/. and

they get too comfortable to get up, and they end up spending the

whole evening in front of the TV.

Determining what to subordinate

Although our
▶ **~~Our~~ new boss can be difficult, ~~although~~ she has revived and maybe**

even saved the division.

The editing puts the more important information — that she has saved part of the company — in an independent clause and subordinates the rest.

Avoiding excessive subordination

When too many subordinate clauses are strung together, readers may have trouble keeping track of the main idea.

TOO MUCH SUBORDINATION

▶ Philip II sent the Spanish Armada to conquer England, which was ruled by Elizabeth, who had executed Mary because she was plotting to overthrow Elizabeth, who was a Protestant, whereas Mary and Philip were Roman Catholics.

REVISED

▶ Philip II sent the Spanish Armada to conquer England, which was ruled by Elizabeth, a Protestant. She had executed Mary, a Roman Catholic like Philip, because Mary was plotting to overthrow her.

Putting the facts about Elizabeth executing Mary into an independent clause makes key information easier to recognize.

TALKING ABOUT STYLE
Subordination

Carefully used subordination can create powerful effects. Some particularly fine examples come from Martin Luther King Jr.

> Perhaps it is easy for those who have never felt the stinging darts of segregation to say, "Wait." But *when* you have seen vicious mobs lynch your mothers and fathers at will and drown your sisters and brothers at whim; *when* you have seen hate-filled policemen curse, kick, and even kill your black brothers and sisters; . . . *when* you have to concoct an answer for a five-year-old son who is asking: "Daddy, why do white people treat colored people so mean?"; *when* you take a cross-country drive and find it necessary to sleep night after night in the uncomfortable corners of your automobile because no motel will accept you; . . . *when* your first name becomes "nigger," your middle name becomes "boy" (however old you are) and your last name becomes "John," and your wife and mother are never given the respected title "Mrs."; . . . *when* you are forever fighting a degenerating sense of "nobodiness" — then you will understand why we find it difficult to wait.
> — MARTIN LUTHER KING JR., "Letter From Birmingham Jail"

EXERCISE 24.2

Combine each of the following sets of sentences into one sentence that uses subordination to signal the relationships among ideas. Example:

I was looking through the refrigerator.

I noticed the Swiss cheese was missing.

This snack is a favorite of my roommate.

While I was looking through the refrigerator, I noticed that the Swiss cheese, one of my roommate's favorite snacks, was missing.

1. The *Hindenburg* was gigantic.

   It was an airship.

   It was destroyed in an explosion.

2. Athena was the goddess of wisdom.

   Ancient Greeks relied on Athena to protect the city of Athens.

   Athens was named in Athena's honor.

3. Stephen King was arrested in 1970.

   He had stolen traffic cones.

   His fine was one hundred dollars.

4. Flappers seemed rebellious to their parents' generation.

   They broke with 1920s social conventions.

   They cut their hair short and smoked in public.

5. Skateboarding originated in Venice, California.

   The time was the mid-seventies.

   There was a drought.

   The swimming pools were empty.

 bedfordstmartins.com/everydaywriter For exercises, go to **Exercise Central** and click on **Coordination and Subordination.**

24c Use closing and opening positions for emphasis.

When you read a sentence, the part you are most likely to remember is the ending. This part of the sentence should move the writing forward by providing new information, as it does in the following example:

▶ To protect her skin, she took along *plenty of sunblock lotion.*

▶ We hear language through a powerful filter of *social values and stereotypes.*

A less emphatic but still important position in a sentence is the opening, which often associates the new sentence with the meaning of what has come before.

▶ When Rosita went to the beach, she was anxious not to get a sunburn. *So plenty of sunblock lotion* went with her.

If you place relatively unimportant information in the memorable closing position of a sentence, you may undercut what you want to emphasize or give more emphasis to the closing words than you intend.

> *Last month, she* $500,000.
> ▶ ~~She~~ gave $500,000 to the school capital campaign ~~last month.~~

Moving *$500,000* to the end of the sentence emphasizes the amount.

Using climactic order to emphasize important ideas

When you arrange ideas in order of increasing importance, power, or drama, your writing builds to a climax. By saving its most dramatic item for last, the following sentence makes its point forcefully and memorably:

> ▶ **After they've finished with the pantry, the medicine cabinet, and the attic, [neat people] will throw out the red geranium (too many leaves), sell the dog (too many fleas), and send the children off to boarding school (too many scuffmarks on the hardwood floors).**
> – SUSANNE BRITT, "Neat People vs. Sloppy People"

The original version of the next sentence fails to achieve strong emphasis because its verbs are not sequenced in order of increasing power; the editing provides climactic order.

> *offend our ears, and*
> ▶ **Soap operas assault our eyes, damage our brains/. ~~and offend our ears.~~**

TALKING ABOUT STYLE

Anticlimax and Humor

Sometimes it's fun to turn the principle of climactic order upside down, opening with grand or exaggerated language only to end anticlimactically, with everyday words.

He is a writer for the ages — the ages of four to eight.
                                                    – DOROTHY PARKER

Parker builds up high expectations at the beginning of the sentence — only to undercut them unexpectedly by shifting the meaning of *ages*. Having led readers to expect something dramatic, she makes us laugh, or at least smile, with words that are decidedly undramatic.

EXERCISE 24.3

Revise each of the following sentences to highlight what you take to be the main or most important ideas. Example:

> *hybrids of cold-blooded capabilities,*
> Theories about dinosaurs have run the gamut — simple lizards, fully adapted warm-blooded creatures/ . ~~hybrids of cold-blooded capabilities.~~

1. The president persuaded the American people, his staff, and Congress.

2. We can expect a decade of record-breaking tropical storms and hurricanes, if meteorologists are correct in their predictions.

3. From the sightseeing boat, we saw a whale dive toward us and then, before crashing its tail on the waves, lift itself out of the water.

4. The presence of the Indian in these movies always conjures up destructive stereotypes of scalping, horse theft, and drunkenness.

5. Victorian women were warned that if they smoked, they would become sterile, grow a mustache, die young, or contract tuberculosis.

 bedfordstmartins.com/everydaywriter For exercises, go to **Exercise Central** and click on **Emphasis.**

EXERCISE 24.4: THINKING CRITICALLY

Reading with an Eye for Sentence Style

Look for strong, emphatic sentences in a piece by one of your favorite writers. Bring in one or two sentences to compare with those chosen by your classmates.

Thinking about Your Own Sentences

Find two or three paragraphs you have written recently, and study them with an eye for coordination, subordination, and emphasis. Do your sentences help readers identify the most important ideas in your writing? Revise any sentences that do not use coordination and subordination effectively.

25 Consistency and Completeness

In conversation, you will hear inconsistent and incomplete structures all the time. For instance, during an interview with journalist Bill Moyers, Jon Stewart discussed the supposed objectivity of news reporting.

> But news has never been objective. It's always . . . what does every newscast start with? "Our top stories tonight." That's a list. That's a subjective . . . some editor made a decision: "Here's our top stories. Number one: There's a fire in the Bronx."

Because Stewart is talking casually, some of his sentences begin one way but then move in another direction. The mixed structures pose no problem for the viewer — they sound like conversations we hear every day — but sentences such as these can be confusing in writing.

25a Revise faulty sentence structure.

One inconsistency that poses problems for writers and readers is a mixed structure, which results from beginning a sentence with one grammatical pattern and then switching to another one.

MIXED | The fact that I get up at 5:00 AM, a wake-up time that explains why I'm always tired in the evening.

The sentence starts out with a subject (*The fact*) followed by a dependent clause (*that I get up at 5:00 AM*). The sentence needs a predicate to complete the independent clause, but instead it moves to another phrase followed by a dependent clause (*a wake-up time that explains why I'm always tired in the evening*), and what results is a fragment.

REVISED | The fact that I get up at 5:00 AM explains why I'm always tired in the evening.

Deleting *a wake-up time that* changes the rest of the sentence into a predicate.

REVISED | I get up at 5:00 AM, a wake-up time that explains why I'm always tired in the evening.

Deleting *The fact that* turns the beginning of the sentence into an independent clause.
(For information about subjects and predicates, see 30j and k; for information about independent and dependent clauses, see 30m.)

25b Match up subjects and predicates.

Another kind of mixed structure, called faulty predication, occurs when a subject and predicate do not fit together grammatically or simply do not make sense together. Many cases of faulty predication result from using forms of *be* when another verb would be stronger.

generosity.
▶ A characteristic that I admire is ~~a person who is generous.~~
         ^

A person is not a characteristic.

require
▶ The rules of the corporation ~~expect~~ employees to be on time.
         ^

Rules cannot expect anything.

AT A GLANCE

Editing for Consistency and Completeness

- If you find an especially confusing sentence, check to see whether it has a subject and a predicate. If not, revise as necessary. (25a) If you find both a subject and a predicate, and you are still confused, see whether the subject and verb make sense together. (25b)

- Revise any *is when*, *is where*, and *reason . . . is because* constructions. (25b)

  the practice of sending
  ► Spamming is ~~where companies send~~ electronic junk mail.

- Check all comparisons for completeness. (25e)

  we like
  ► We like Lisa better than ~~Margaret.~~

Is when, is where, *and* reason . . . is because

Although you will often hear expressions such as *home is where the heart is* in everyday use, these constructions are inappropriate in academic or professional writing.

an unfair characterization of
► A stereotype is ~~when someone characterizes~~ a group~~. unfairly.~~

a place
► A confluence is ~~where~~ two rivers join to form one.

► ~~The reason~~ I like to play soccer ~~is~~ because it provides aerobic exercise.

EXERCISE 25.1

Revise each of the following sentences in two ways to make its structures consistent in grammar and meaning. Example:

Because
~~The fact that~~ our room was cold, we put a heater between our beds.

led us to
The fact that our room was cold, we put a heater between our beds.

1. To enjoy my job, my dream in life, which has kept me in school and working hard.

2. The reason air-pollution standards should not be relaxed is because many people would suffer.

3. By not prosecuting white-collar crime as vigorously as violent crime encourages white-collar criminals to think they can ignore the law.

4. Irony is when you expect one thing and get something else.
5. The best meal I've ever eaten was sitting by a river eating bread and cheese from a farmers' market.

25c Use elliptical structures carefully.

Sometimes writers omit a word in a compound structure. This type of structure, known as an elliptical structure, is appropriate when the word omitted later in the compound is exactly the same as the word earlier in the compound.

> ► **That bell belonged to the figure of Miss Duling as though it grew directly out of her right arm, as wings grew out of an angel or a tail [grew] out of the devil.** — EUDORA WELTY, *One Writer's Beginnings*

If the omitted word does not match a word in the other part of the compound, readers might be confused, so the omission is inappropriate.

> ► **His skills are weak, and his performance** *is* **only average.**

The verb *is* does not match the verb in the other part of the compound (*are*), so the writer needs to include it.

25d Check for missing words.

The best way to catch inadvertent omissions is to proofread carefully.

> ► **The new Web site makes it easier to look** *at* **and choose from the company's inventory.**

25e Make comparisons complete, consistent, and clear.

When you compare two or more things, the comparison must be complete, logically consistent, and clear.

> ► **I was embarrassed because my parents were so different** *from my friends' parents.*

Different from what? Adding *from my friends' parents* tells readers with what the comparison is being made.

the one by
▶ **Woodberry's biography is better than Fields.**
⌃

This sentence illogically compares a book with a person. The editing makes the comparison logical.

UNCLEAR	Aneil always felt more affection for his brother than his sister.
CLEAR	Aneil always felt more affection for his brother *than his sister did.*
CLEAR	Aneil always felt more affection for his brother *than he did for his sister.*

EXERCISE 25.2

Revise each of the following sentences to eliminate any inappropriate elliptical constructions; to make comparisons complete, logically consistent, and clear; and to supply any other omitted words that are necessary for meaning. Example:

is
Most of the candidates are bright, and one⌃brilliant.

1. Convection ovens cook more quickly and with less power.
2. Argentina and Peru were colonized by Spain, and Brazil by Portugal.
3. She argued that children are even more important for men than women.
4. Were the traffic jams in Texas any worse than many other states?
5. The equipment in our new warehouse is guaranteed to last longer than our current facility.

 bedfordstmartins.com/everydaywriter For exercises, go to **Exercise Central** and click on **Consistency and Completeness.**

EXERCISE 25.3: THINKING CRITICALLY

Read over three or four paragraphs from a draft or completed essay you have written recently. Check for mixed sentences and incomplete or missing structures. Revise the paragraphs to correct any problems you find. If you find any, do you recognize any patterns? If so, make a note of them for future reference.

26 Parallelism

Parallel grammatical structures show up in many familiar phrases: *sink or swim, rise and shine, shape up or ship out.* If you look and listen for these structures, you will see parallelism in everyday use. Bumper stickers often use parallel grammatical structures to make their messages memorable (*Minds are like parachutes; both work best when open*), but the pleasing effects of parallel structures can benefit any kind of writing.

AT A GLANCE

Editing for Parallelism

- Look for any series of three or more items, and make all of the items parallel in structure. (26a)
- Be sure items in lists and in related headings are parallel. (26a)
- Check for places where two ideas are paired in the same sentence. Often these ideas will appear on either side of *and, but, or, nor, for, so,* or *yet,* or after each part of *both . . . and, either . . . or, neither . . . nor, not only . . . but also, whether . . . or,* or *just as . . . so.* Edit to make the two ideas parallel in structure. (26b)
- Check parallel structures to be sure that you have included all necessary words — prepositions, the *to* of the infinitive, and so on. (26c)

26a Make items in a series parallel.

Parallelism makes a series both graceful and easy to follow.

▶ In the eighteenth century, armed forces could fight *in open fields* and *on the high seas.* Today, they can clash *on the ground anywhere, on the sea, under the sea,* and *in the air.*
— DONALD SNOW AND EUGENE BROWN, *The Contours of Power*

The parallel phrases, as well as the parallel structure of the sentences themselves, highlight the contrast between warfare in the eighteenth century and warfare today.

In the following sentences, note how the revisions make all items in the series parallel:

▶ The quarter horse skipped, pranced, and ~~was sashaying.~~ *sashayed.*

▶ The children ran down the hill, skipped over the lawn, and *jumped* into the swimming pool.

▶ The duties of the job include babysitting, housecleaning, and *preparing* ~~preparation of~~ meals.

Items in a list, on a formal outline (p. 69), and in headings in a paper (p. 33) should be parallel.

▶ Kitchen rules: (1) Coffee to be made only by library staff. (2) Coffee

service to be closed at 4:00 PM. (3) Doughnuts to be kept in cabinet.
Coffee materials not to be handled by faculty.
(4) ~~No faculty members should handle coffee materials.~~
^

26b   Make paired ideas parallel.

Parallel structures can help you pair two ideas effectively. The more nearly parallel the two structures are, the stronger the connection between the ideas will be.

▶ History became popular, and historians became alarmed.

– WILL DURANT

▶ I type in one place, but I write all over the house.

– TONI MORRISON

the flesh.
▶ Writers are often more interesting on the page than they are in ~~person.~~
^

In these examples, the parallel structures help readers see an important contrast between two ideas or acts.

With coordinating conjunctions

When you link ideas with a coordinating conjunction — *and, but, or, nor, for, so,* or *yet* — try to make the ideas parallel in structure.

who is
▶ Consult a friend in your class or who is good at math.
^

accepts
▶ The wise politician promises the possible and ~~should accept~~ the
inevitable.   ^

In both sentences, the editing links the two ideas by making them parallel.

With correlative conjunctions

Use the same structure after both parts of a correlative conjunction: *either . . . or, both . . . and, neither . . . nor, not . . . but, not only . . . but also, just as . . . so,* and *whether . . . or.*

live in
▶ I wanted not only to go away to school but also to New England.
^

Balancing *to go* with *to live* links the two ideas and makes the sentence easier to read.

EXERCISE 26.1

Complete the following sentences, using parallel words or phrases in each case. Example:

The wise politician *promises the possible*, *faces the unavoidable*, and *accepts the inevitable*.

1. Before buying a used car, you should _____ , _____ , and _____ .
2. My favorite pastimes include _____ , _____ , and _____ .
3. Working in a restaurant taught me not only _____ but also _____ .
4. We must either _____ or _____ .
5. Graduates find that the job market _____ , _____ , and _____ .

EXERCISE 26.2

Revise the following sentences as necessary to eliminate any errors in parallel structure. Example:

texting

I enjoy skiing, playing the guitar, and ~~I send text~~ to my friends.

1. I remember watching it the first time, realizing I'd never seen anything like it, and immediately vowed never to miss an episode of *The Daily Show*.
2. A crowd stood outside the school and were watching as the graduates paraded by.
3. An effective Web site is well designed, provides useful information, and links are given to other relevant sites.
4. It is impossible to watch *The Simpsons* and not seeing a little of yourself in one of the characters.
5. TV networks now face the question of either coming up with new situations, or they'll have to acknowledge the death of the sitcom.

26c Include all necessary words.

In addition to making parallel elements grammatically similar, be sure to include any words — prepositions, articles, verb forms, and so on — that are necessary for clarity, grammar, or idiom.

in

▶ We'll move to a town in the Southwest or Mexico.

To a town in Mexico or to Mexico in general? The editing makes the meaning clear.

 bedfordstmartins.com/everydaywriter For exercises, go to **Exercise Central** and click on **Parallelism**.

EXERCISE 26.3: THINKING CRITICALLY

Reading with an Eye for Parallelism

Read the following paragraph about a bareback rider practicing her circus act, and identify all the parallel structures. Consider what effect they create on you as a reader, and try to decide why the author chose to put his ideas in such overtly parallel form. Try imitating the next-to-last sentence, the one beginning *In a week or two.*

> The richness of the scene was in its plainness, its natural condition — of horse, of ring, of girl, even to the girl's bare feet that gripped the bare back of her proud and ridiculous mount. The enchantment grew not out of anything that happened or was performed but out of something that seemed to go round and around and around with the girl, attending her, a steady gleam in the shape of a circle — a ring of ambition, of happiness, of youth. (And the positive pleasures of equilibrium under difficulties.) In a week or two, all would be changed, all (or almost all) lost: the girl would wear makeup, the horse would wear gold, the ring would be painted, the bark would be clean for the feet of the horse, the girl's feet would be clean for the slippers that she'd wear. All, all would be lost.
>
> — E. B. WHITE, "The Ring of Time"

Thinking about Your Own Use of Parallelism

Read carefully several paragraphs from a draft you have recently written, noting any series of words, phrases, or clauses. Using the guidelines in this chapter, determine whether the series are parallel, and if not, revise them for parallelism. Then reread the paragraphs, looking for places where parallel structures would add emphasis or clarity, and revise accordingly. Can you draw any conclusions about your use of parallelism?

27   Shifts

A shift in writing is an abrupt change that results in inconsistency. Sometimes a writer will shift deliberately, as Dave Barry does in noting he "would have to say that the greatest single achievement of the American medical establishment is nasal spray." Barry's shift in tone from the serious (the American medical establishment) to the banal (nasal spray) makes us laugh. Although writers sometimes make shifts for good reasons, unintentional shifts in verb tenses, pronouns, and tone can be jolting and confusing to readers.

27a   Revise unnecessary shifts in tense.

If the verbs in a passage refer to actions occurring at different times, they may require different tenses. Be careful, however, not to change tenses for no reason.

▶ **A few countries produce almost all of the world's illegal drugs, but**
  affects
  addiction ~~affected~~ many countries.
  ^

27b Revise unnecessary shifts in mood.

Be careful not to shift from one mood to another without good reason. The mood of a verb can be indicative (he *closes* the door), imperative (*close* the door), or subjunctive (if the door *were closed*) (31h).

▶ **Keep your eye on the ball, and ~~you should~~ bend your knees.**

The sentence shifts from the imperative to the indicative; the editing makes both verbs imperative since the writer's purpose is to give orders.

27c Revise unnecessary shifts in voice.

Do not shift without reason between the active voice (she *sold* it) and the passive voice (it *was sold*). Sometimes a shift in voice is justified, but often it only confuses readers (31g).

                                                        me
▶ **Two youths approached me, and ~~I was~~ asked for my wallet.**
                                        ^

AT A GLANCE

Confusing Shifts

- Make sure you have a reason for shifting from one verb tense to another. (27a)
- Revise any shifts in mood — perhaps from an indicative statement to an imperative — that are not necessary. (27b)
- Check for shifts from active (*She asks questions*) to passive voice (*Questions are asked*). Are they intentional? (27c)
- Make sure you have good reasons for any shifts in person or number — from *we* to *you*, for example. (27d)
- Check your writing for consistency in tone and word choice. (27f)

The original sentence shifts from the active (*youths approached*) to the passive (*I was asked*), so it is unclear who asked for the wallet. Making both verbs active clears up the confusion.

27d Revise unnecessary shifts in person and number.

Unnecessary shifts between first-person point of view (*I, we*), second-person (*you*), and third-person (*he, she, it, one,* or *they*), or between singular and plural subjects can be very confusing to readers.

You
▶ ~~One~~ can do well on this job if you budget your time.

It was not clear whether the writer was making a general statement or giving advice to someone. Eliminating the shift eliminates this confusion.

nurses have
▶ Nurses receive much less pay than doctors, even though ~~a nurse has~~

the primary responsibility for daily patient care.

The writer had no reason to shift from third-person plural (*nurses*) to third-person singular (*a nurse*).

27e Revise shifts between direct and indirect discourse.

When you quote someone's exact words, you are using direct discourse: *She said, "I'm an editor."* When you report what someone says without repeating the exact words, you are using indirect discourse: *She says she is an editor.* Shifting between direct and indirect discourse in the same sentence can cause problems, especially with questions.

FOR MULTILINGUAL WRITERS

Shifting Tenses in Reported Speech

If Al said to Maria, "I will marry you," why did she then correctly tell her mom, "He said that he *would* marry me"? For guidelines on reporting speech, see 58b.

---

he
▶ Viet asked what could ~~he~~ do to help~~?~~.

The editing eliminates an awkward shift by reporting Viet's question indirectly. It could also be edited to quote Viet directly: *Viet asked, "What can I do to help?"*

EXERCISE 27.1

Revise the following sentences to eliminate unnecessary shifts in tense, mood, voice, or person and number and between direct and indirect discourse. Most of the items can be revised in more than one way. Examples:

> When a person goes to college, you face many new situations.
>
> When a <u>person</u> goes to college, <u>he or she</u> faces many new situations.
>
> When <u>people</u> go to college, <u>they</u> face many new situations.

1. The greed of the 1980s gave way to the occupational insecurity of the 1990s, which in turn gives way to reinforced family ties in the early 2000s.

2. The building inspector suggested that we apply for a construction permit and that we should check with his office again when the plans are complete.

3. She studied the package, wondered what could it be, and tore off the wrapping.

4. Suddenly, we heard an explosion of wings off to our right, and you could see a hundred or more ducks lifting off from the water.

5. In my previous job, I sold the most advertising spots and was given a sales excellence award.

6. A cloud of snow powder rose as skis and poles fly in every direction.

7. The flight attendant said, "Please turn off all electronic devices," but that we could use them again after takeoff.

8. Workers with computer skills were in great demand, and a programmer could almost name their salary.

9. When in Florence, be sure to see the city's famed cathedral, and many tourists also visit Michelangelo's statue *David*.

10. The aroma, which wafts through the house, lured the adults from their beds.

27f Revise shifts in tone and word choice.

Tone, a writer's attitude toward a topic or audience, is related to word choice, and to overall formality or informality. Watch out for tone or diction shifts that can confuse readers and leave them wondering what your real attitude is (5f).

INCONSISTENT TONE

> The question of child care forces a society to make profound decisions about its economic values. Can most families with young children actually live adequately on only one salary? If some conservatives had their way, June Cleaver would still be stuck in the kitchen baking cookies for Wally and the Beaver and waiting for Ward to bring home the bacon, except that, with only one income, the Cleavers would be lucky to afford hot dogs.

In this version, the first two sentences set a serious, formal tone by discussing child care in fairly general, abstract terms. But in the third sentence, the writer shifts suddenly to sarcasm, to references to television characters of an earlier era, and to informal language like *stuck* and *bring home the bacon*. Readers cannot tell whether the writer is presenting a serious analysis or preparing for a humorous satire. The revision makes the tone consistently formal.

> **REVISED**
>
> The question of child care forces a society to make profound decisions about its economic values. Can most families with young children actually live adequately on only one salary? Some conservatives believe that women with young children should not work outside the home, but many mothers are forced to do so for financial reasons.

 bedfordstmartins.com/everydaywriter For exercises, go to **Exercise Central** and click on **Shifts**.

EXERCISE 27.2: THINKING CRITICALLY

Reading with an Eye for Shifts

The following paragraph includes several necessary shifts in person and number. Read the paragraph carefully, marking all such shifts. Notice how careful the author must be as he shifts back and forth among pronouns.

> It has been one of the great errors of our time to think that by thinking about thinking, and then talking about it, we could possibly straighten out and tidy up our minds. There is no delusion more damaging than to get the idea in your head that you understand the functioning of your own brain. Once you acquire such a notion, you run the danger of moving in to take charge, guiding your thoughts, shepherding your mind from place to place, controlling it, making lists of regulations. The human mind is not meant to be governed, certainly not by any book of rules yet written; it is supposed to run itself, and we are obliged to follow it along, trying to keep up with it as best we can. It is all very well to be aware of your awareness, even proud of it, but never try to operate it. You are not up to the job.   — LEWIS THOMAS, "The Attic of the Brain"

Thinking about Any Shifts in Your Own Writing

Find an article about a well-known person you admire. Then write a paragraph or two about him or her, making a point of using both direct and indirect discourse. Check your writing for any inappropriate shifts between direct and indirect discourse, and revise as necessary.

Conciseness **28**

You can see the importance of conciseness in directions, particularly those on medicines.

> Take one tablet daily. Some nonprescription drugs may aggravate your condition, so read all labels carefully. If any include a warning, check with your doctor.

Squeezing words onto a three-inch label is probably not your ordinary writing situation, but you will want to write as concisely as you can.

AT A GLANCE

Editing for Conciseness

- Look for redundant words. If you are unsure about a word, read the sentence without it; if meaning is not affected, leave the word out. (28a and b)
- Take out empty words — words like *aspect* or *factor, definitely* or *very*. (28c)
- Replace wordy phrases with a single word. Instead of *because of the fact that,* try *because.* (28d)
- Reconsider any sentences that begin with *it is* or *there is/are.* Unless they create special emphasis, try recasting the sentences without these words. (28e)

28a Eliminate unnecessary words.

Usually you'll want to make your point in the fewest possible words.

▶ One thing that her constant and continual use of vulgar expressions or four-letter words indicated to the day-care workers was that she might really have a great deal of trouble in terms of her ability to get along in a successful manner with other four-year-olds in her age group.

Why write that sentence when you could instead write the following?

▶ Her constant use of four-letter words told the day-care workers she might have trouble getting along with other four-year-olds.

28b Eliminate redundant words.

Sometimes writers say that something is large *in size* or red *in color* or that two ingredients should be *combined together.* Such words are redundant, or unnecessary for meaning, as are the deleted words in these examples:

Attendance
▶ ~~Compulsory attendance~~ at assemblies is required.
  ^

▶ Many different forms of hazing occur, such as physical abuse and mental abuse.

28c Eliminate empty words.

Empty words are so general or overused that they contribute no real meaning to a sentence.

EMPTY WORDS

angle, area, aspect, case, character, element, factor, field, kind, nature, scope, situation, thing, type

Many modifiers are so common that they have become empty words.

MEANINGLESS MODIFIERS

absolutely, awesome, awfully, central, definitely, fine, great, literally, major, quite, really, very

When you cannot simply delete empty words, think of a more specific way to say what you mean.

Housing   *strongly influence*
▶ ~~The housing situation~~ can ~~have a really significant impact on the~~
  ^   ^
                                   social
  ~~social aspect of~~ a student's life.
                     ^

28d Replace wordy phrases.

Wordy phrases can be reduced to a word or two with no loss in meaning.

WORDY	CONCISE
at all times	always
at the present time	now/today

at that point in time	then
due to the fact that	because
for the purpose of	for
in order to	to
in spite of the fact that	although
in the event that	if

EXERCISE 28.1

Revise the following paragraph to eliminate weak verbs, unnecessary nominalizations and expletives, and inappropriate use of the passive voice.

As dogs became domesticated by humans over many thousands of years, the canine species evolved into hundreds of breeds designed to perform specific tasks such as pulling sleds and guarding sheep. Over time, the need for many breeds decreased. For example, as humans evolved from hunter-gatherers into farmers, it was no longer necessary for them to own hunting dogs. Later, as farming societies became industrialized, shepherds were rarely needed. But by this time humans had grown accustomed to dogs' companionship, and breeding continued. Today, most dogs are kept by their owners simply as companions, but some dogs still do the work they were intentionally bred for, such as following a scent, guarding a home, or leading the blind.

28e Simplify sentence structure.

Using the simplest grammatical structures possible can tighten and strengthen your sentences considerably.

▶ Hurricane Katrina, ~~which was certainly~~ one of the most powerful storms
    widespread
ever to hit the Gulf Coast, caused damage ˆ ~~to a very wide area.~~

Reducing a clause to an appositive, deleting unnecessary words, and replacing five words with one tighten the sentence and make it easier to read.

Using strong verbs

Be verbs (*is, are, was, were, been*) often result in wordiness.

                          harms
▶ A high-fat, high-cholesterol diet ~~is bad for~~ your heart.
                              ˆ

Avoiding there is, there are, *and* it is

Sometimes expletive constructions — *there is, there are,* and *it is* — are an effective way to introduce a topic; often, however, your writing will be better without them.

> Many
> ▶ ~~There are many~~ people ~~who~~ fear success because they believe they do not deserve it.

> Presidential   need
> ▶ ~~It is necessary for presidential~~ candidates to perform well on television.
>   ^   ^

Using active voice

Some writing situations call for the passive voice (31g), but it is always wordier than the active — and often makes for dull or even difficult reading.

> Gower
> ▶ ~~In Gower's research, it was~~ found that pythons often dwell in trees.
>   ^

> **bedfordstmartins.com/everydaywriter** For exercises, go to **Exercise Central** and click on **Conciseness**.

EXERCISE 28.2: THINKING CRITICALLY

Find two or three paragraphs you have written recently, and study them with an eye for empty words. Eliminate meaningless words such as *aspect, factor, quite,* and *very*. Compare notes with one or two classmates to see what empty words, if any, you all tend to use. Finally, make a note of empty words you use, and try to avoid them in the future.

29) Sentence Variety

Row upon row of trees identical in size and shape may appeal to our sense of orderliness, but in spite of that appeal, the rows soon become boring. Constant uniformity in anything, in fact, soon gets tiresome. Variety is important in sentence structures because too much uniformity results in dull, listless prose. This chapter examines ways to revise sentences by creating variety in length and in openings.

AT A GLANCE

Editing for Sentence Variety

- Count the words in each of your sentences. If the difference between the longest and shortest sentences is fairly small — say, five words or fewer — try revising your sentences to create greater variety. (29a)
- If many sentences have fewer than ten words, consider whether any of them need more detail or should be combined with other sentences.
- How do your sentences open? If all or most of them open with a subject, try recasting some sentences to begin with a transition, a phrase, or a dependent clause. (29b)

29a Vary sentence length.

Is there a "just right" length for a particular sentence or idea? The answer depends partly on your purpose, intended audience, and topic. But note that after one or more long sentences with complex ideas or images, the punch of a short sentence can be refreshing.

TALKING ABOUT STYLE

Technical Writing

For some types of writing, varying sentence structure and length is not always appropriate. Many technical writers, particularly those who write manuals that will be translated into other languages, must follow stringent rules for sentence structure and length. One computer company, for example, requires writers to adhere to a strict subject-verb-object order and limit all sentences to no more than fifteen words. Learn the style conventions of your field as fully as possible, and bring them to bear on your own sentence revisions.

▶ To become a doctor, you spend so much time in the tunnels of preparation—head down, trying not to screw up, just going from one day to the next—that it is a shock to find yourself at the other end, with someone offering you a job. But the day comes.　　— ATUL GAWANDE, *Better*

EXERCISE 29.1

The following paragraph can be improved by varying sentence length. Read it aloud to get a sense of how it sounds. Then revise it, creating some short, emphatic sentences and combining other sentences to create more effective long sentences. Add words or change punctuation as you need to.

Before planting a tree, a gardener needs to choose a good location and dig a deep enough hole. The location should have the right kind of soil, sufficient drainage, and enough light for the type of tree chosen. The hole should be slightly deeper than the root-ball and about twice as wide. The gardener must unwrap the root-ball, for even burlap, which is biodegradable, may be treated with chemicals that will eventually damage the roots. The roots may have grown into a compact ball if the tree has been in a pot for some time, and they should be separated or cut apart in this case. The gardener should set the root-ball into the hole and then begin to fill the hole with loose dirt. After filling the hole completely, he or she should make sure to water the tree thoroughly. New plantings require extra water and extra care for about three years before they are well rooted.

29b Vary sentence openings.

If sentence after sentence begins with a subject, a passage may become monotonous or hard to read.

▶ The way football and basketball are played is as interesting as the

players. ~~Football~~ *Because football* is a game of precision~~.~~/, ~~Each~~ *each* play is diagrammed to

accomplish a certain goal. Basketball, *however,* is a game of endurance.

In fact, a ~~A~~ basketball game looks like a track meet; the team that drops of

exhaustion first, loses. Basketball players are often compared to artists~~.~~/;

their ~~The players'~~ moves and slam dunks are their masterpieces.

The editing adds variety by using a subordinating word (*Because*) and a prepositional phrase (*In fact*) and by linking sentences. Varying sentence openings prevents the passage from seeming to jerk or lurch along.

You can add variety to your sentence openings by using transitions, various kinds of phrases, and dependent clauses.

TRANSITIONAL EXPRESSIONS

▶ *In contrast,* our approach will save time and money.

▶ *Nevertheless,* the show must go on.

PHRASES

▶ *Before dawn*, tired commuters drink their first cups of coffee.

▶ *Frustrated by the delays*, the drivers started honking their horns.

▶ *To qualify for flight training*, one must be in good physical condition.

▶ *Our hopes for victory dashed*, we started home.

DEPENDENT CLAUSES

▶ *What they want* is a place to call home.

▶ *Because the hills were dry*, the fire spread rapidly.

bedfordstmartins.com/everydaywriter For exercises, go to **Exercise Central** and click on **Sentence Variety**.

EXERCISE 29.2: THINKING CRITICALLY

Reading with an Eye for Sentence Variety

Read something by an author you admire. Analyze two paragraphs for sentence length, opening, and type. Compare the sentence variety in these paragraphs with that in one of your paragraphs. What similarities or differences do you recognize, and what conclusions can you draw about sentence variety?

Thinking about Your Own Sentence Variety

Choose a piece of writing you have recently completed, and analyze two or three pages for sentence variety. Note sentence length, opening, and type (grammatical, functional, and rhetorical). Choose a passage you think can be improved for variety, and make those revisions.

Sentence Grammar

Most of us don't know a gerund from a gerbil
and don't care, but we'd like to speak
and write as though we did.

— PATRICIA T. O'CONNER

Sentence Grammar

30 Basic Grammar

The grammar of our first language comes to us almost automatically, without our thinking much about it or even being aware of it. Listen in, for instance, on a conversation between a six-year-old and her sister.

AUDREY: My new bike that Daddy got me has a pink basket and a loud horn, and I love it.

LILA: Can I ride it?

AUDREY: Sure, as soon as you get big enough.

This simple conversation features sophisticated grammar — the subordination of one clause to another, a compound object, and a number of adjectives — used effortlessly. Though native speakers know the basic grammatical rules, these rules can produce a broad range of sentences, some more effective and artful than others. Understanding the grammatical structures presented in this chapter can help you produce sentences that are grammatical — and appropriate and effective as well.

30a The basic grammar of sentences

A sentence is a grammatically complete group of words that expresses a thought. To be grammatically complete, a group of words must contain a subject, which identifies what the sentence is about, and a predicate, which says or asks something about the subject or tells the subject to do something.

SUBJECT	PREDICATE
I	have a dream.
The rain in Spain	stays mainly in the plain.
Stephen Colbert, who hosts a cable TV show,	pretends to be a conservative.

Some sentences have only a one-word predicate with an implied, or understood, subject (for example, *Stop!*). Most sentences, however, contain additional words that expand the basic subject and predicate. In the preceding example, for instance, the subject might have been simply *Stephen Colbert;* the words *who hosts a cable TV show* tell us more about the subject. Similarly, the predicate of that sentence could grammatically be *pretends;* the words *to be a conservative* expand the predicate by telling us what Colbert pretends.

EXERCISE 30.1

Identify the subject and the predicate in each of the following sentences, underlining the subject once and the predicate twice. Example:

The roaring lion at the beginning of old MGM films is part of movie history.

1. My foot got tangled in the computer cord.
2. Her first afternoon as a kindergarten teacher had left her exhausted.
3. The Croatian news media is almost entirely owned by the state.
4. Our office manager, a stern taskmaster with a fondness for Chanel suits, has been terrifying interns since 1992.
5. Making bread on a dreary winter day always cheers me up.

Parts of Speech

All English words belong to one or more of eight grammatical categories called parts of speech: verbs, nouns, pronouns, adjectives, adverbs, prepositions, conjunctions, and interjections. Many English words regularly function as more than one part of speech. Take the word *book,* for example: when you *book a flight,* it is a verb; when you *take a good book to the beach,* it is a noun; and when you *have book knowledge,* it is an adjective.

TALKING THE TALK

Grammatical Terms

"I never learned any grammar." You may lack *conscious* knowledge of grammar and grammatical terms (and if so, you are not alone — American students today rarely study English grammar). But you probably understand the ideas that grammatical terms such as *auxiliary verb* and *direct object* represent, even if the terms themselves are unfamiliar. Brushing up on the terms commonly used to talk about grammar will make it easier for you and your instructor — as well as other readers and reviewers — to share a common language when you want to discuss the best ways to get your ideas across clearly and with few distractions.

30b   Verbs

Verbs are among the most important words because they move the meanings of sentences along. Verbs show actions of body or mind (*skip, speculate*), occurrences (*become, happen*), or states of being (*be, seem*). They can also change form to show *time, person, number, voice,* and *mood.*

TIME	we *work,* we *worked*
PERSON	I *work,* she *works*
NUMBER	one person *works,* two people *work*
VOICE	she *asks,* she *is asked*
MOOD	we *see,* if we *saw*

Auxiliary verbs (also called helping verbs) combine with other verbs (often called main verbs) to create verb phrases. Auxiliaries include the various forms of *be, do,* and *have* (which can also function as main verbs) and the words *can, could, may, might, must, shall, should, will,* and *would.*

▶ You *do need* some sleep tonight!

▶ I *could have danced* all night.

▶ She *would prefer* to learn Italian rather than Spanish.

See Chapters 31 and 32 for a complete discussion of verbs.

EXERCISE 30.2

Underline each verb or verb phrase in the following sentences. Example:

Terence should sing well in Sunday's performance.

1. After the holidays, I will ask for a pay raise.
2. The faucet had been leaking all day.
3. I agree; the office does need a new copy machine.
4. Ideally, you should drink eight cups of water each day.
5. A job at an animal hospital would be great.

30c   Nouns

Nouns name persons (*aviator, child*), places (*lake, library*), things (*truck, suitcase*), and concepts (*happiness, balance*). Proper nouns name specific persons, places, things, and concepts: *Bill, Iowa, Supreme Court, Buddhism.* Collective nouns name groups: *team, flock, jury* (32d).

You can change most nouns from singular (one) to plural (more than one) by adding *-s* or *-es: horse, horses; kiss, kisses.* Some nouns, however, have irregular plural forms: *woman, women; alumnus, alumni; mouse, mice; deer, deer.* Noncount nouns — such as *dust, peace,* and *prosperity* — do not have a plural form because they name something that cannot easily be counted (22c and 57a).

To show ownership, nouns take the possessive form by adding an apostrophe plus -*s* to a singular noun or just an apostrophe to a plural noun: *the horse's owner, the boys' dilemma* (41a).

Often the article *a, an,* or *the* precedes a noun: *a rocket, an astronaut, the launch* (57e). Articles, a kind of adjective, are also known as noun markers or determiners.

FOR MULTILINGUAL WRITERS

Using Count and Noncount Nouns

Do people conduct *research* or *researches*? See 57a for a discussion of count and noncount nouns.

EXERCISE 30.3

Identify the nouns and the articles in each of the following sentences. Underline the nouns once and the articles twice. Example:

The Puritans hoped for a different king, but Charles II regained his father's throne.

1. After Halloween, the children got sick from eating too much candy.
2. Although June is technically the driest month, severe flooding has occurred in the late spring.
3. Manuel, an avid gardener, has a vegetable garden with tomatoes, lettuce, and sweet corn.
4. A sudden frost turned the ground into a field of ice.
5. In the front row sat two people, a man with slightly graying hair and a young woman in jeans.

30d Pronouns

Pronouns often take the place of nouns, other pronouns, or other words functioning as a noun. Pronouns serve as short forms so that you do not have to repeat a word or group of words you have already mentioned. A word or group of words that a pronoun replaces or refers to is called the antecedent of the pronoun. (See Chapter 33.)

ANTECEDENT   PRONOUN
▶ *Caitlin* refused the invitation even though *she* wanted to go.

Here are the categories of pronouns:

PERSONAL PRONOUNS

Personal pronouns refer to specific persons or things.

I, me, you, he, she, him, her, it, we, us, they, them

▶ **When Keisha saw the dogs,** *she* **called** *them,* **and** *they* **ran to** *her.*

POSSESSIVE PRONOUNS

Possessive pronouns are personal pronouns that indicate ownership.

my, mine, your, yours, her, hers, his, its, our, ours, their, theirs

▶ **My roommate lost** *her* **keys.**

REFLEXIVE PRONOUNS

Reflexive pronouns refer to the subject of the sentence or clause in which they appear. They end in *-self* or *-selves.*

myself, yourself, himself, herself, itself, oneself, ourselves, yourselves, themselves

▶ **The seals sunned** *themselves* **on the warm rocks.**

INTENSIVE PRONOUNS

Intensive pronouns have the same form as reflexive pronouns. They emphasize a noun or another pronoun.

▶ **He decided to paint the apartment** *himself.*

INDEFINITE PRONOUNS

Indefinite pronouns do not refer to specific nouns, although they may refer to identifiable persons or things. The following is a partial list:

all, another, anybody, both, each, either, everything, few, many, most, neither, none, no one, nothing, one, some, something

▶ *Everybody* **screamed, and** *someone* **fainted, when the lights went out.**

DEMONSTRATIVE PRONOUNS

Demonstrative pronouns identify or point to specific nouns.

this, that, these, those

▶ *These* **are Peter's books.**

INTERROGATIVE PRONOUNS

Interrogative pronouns are used to ask questions.

who, which, what

▶ **Who can help set up the chairs for the meeting?**

RELATIVE PRONOUNS

Relative pronouns introduce dependent clauses and relate the dependent clause to the rest of the sentence (30m). The interrogative pronoun *who* and the relative pronouns *who* and *whoever* have different forms depending on how they are used in a sentence (33b).

who, which, that, what, whoever, whichever, whatever

▶ **Maya, *who* hires interns, is the manager *whom* you should contact.**

RECIPROCAL PRONOUNS

Reciprocal pronouns refer to individual parts of a plural antecedent.

each other, one another

▶ **The business failed because the partners distrusted *each other*.**

EXERCISE 30.4

Identify the pronouns and any antecedents in each of the following sentences, underlining the pronouns once and any antecedents twice. Example:

As identical twins, they really do understand each other.

1. He told the volunteers to help themselves to the leftovers.
2. Kiah is the only one who understands the telephone system, and she is on vacation.
3. Who is going to buy the jeans and wear them if the designer himself finds them uncomfortable?
4. They have only themselves to blame.
5. Those people who claim they don't have to study for exams aren't fooling anyone.

30e Adjectives

Adjectives modify (limit the meaning of) nouns and pronouns, usually by describing, identifying, or quantifying those words. Some people refer to the identifying or quantifying adjectives as *determiners* (57d).

▶ **The *red* Corvette ran off the road.** [describes]
▶ ***That* Corvette needs to be repaired.** [identifies]
▶ **We saw *several* Corvettes race by.** [quantifies]

In addition to their basic forms, most descriptive adjectives have other forms that allow you to make comparisons: *small, smaller, smallest; foolish, more foolish, most foolish, less foolish, least foolish* (34c). Many of the words that function in some sentences as pronouns (30d) can function as identifying adjectives (or determiners) when they are followed by a noun.

▶ *That* is a dangerous intersection. [pronoun]

▶ *That* intersection is dangerous. [identifying adjective]

Adjectives usually precede the words they modify, though they may follow linking verbs: *The car was defective.*

Other kinds of identifying or quantifying adjectives are articles (*a, an, the*) and numbers (*three, sixty-fifth*).

Proper adjectives are adjectives formed from or related to proper nouns (*British, Emersonian*). Proper adjectives are capitalized (44b).

FOR MULTILINGUAL WRITERS

Deciding When Articles Are Necessary

Do you say "I'm working on *a* paper" or "I'm working on *the* paper"? Deciding when to use the articles *a, an,* and *the* can be challenging for multilingual writers since many languages have nothing directly comparable to them. For help using articles, see 57e.

30f Adverbs

Adverbs modify verbs, adjectives, other adverbs, or entire clauses. Many adverbs have an -ly ending, though some do not (always, never, very, well), and some words that end in -ly are not adverbs but adjectives (scholarly, lovely). One of the most common adverbs is not.

▶ Jabari *recently* visited his roommate's family in Maine. [modifies the verb *visited*]

▶ It was an *unexpectedly* exciting trip. [modifies the adjective *exciting*]

▶ He *very* soon discovered lobster. [modifies the adverb *soon*]

▶ *Frankly,* he would have liked to stay another month. [modifies the independent clause that makes up the rest of the sentence]

Many adverbs, like many adjectives, take other forms when making comparisons: *forcefully, more forcefully, most forcefully, less forcefully, least forcefully* (34c).

Conjunctive adverbs modify an entire clause and help connect the meaning between that clause and the preceding clause (or sentence). Examples of conjunctive adverbs include *however, furthermore, therefore,* and *likewise* (30h).

EXERCISE 30.5

Identify the adjectives and adverbs in each of the following sentences, underlining the adjectives once and the adverbs twice. Remember that articles and some pronouns are used as adjectives. Example:

Inadvertently, the two agents misquoted their major client.

1. An empty subject line and a somewhat familiar sender's name tricked me into opening the seemingly innocent email.

2. Nevertheless, her teenage son eventually overcame his poor study habits.

3. Koalas are generally quiet creatures that make loud grunting noises during mating season.

4. The huge red tomatoes looked lovely, but they tasted disappointingly like cardboard.

5. The youngest dancer in the troupe performed a brilliant solo.

30g Prepositions

Prepositions are important structural words that express relationships — in time, space, or other senses — between nouns or pronouns and other words in a sentence.

▶ We did not want to leave *during* the game.

▶ The contestants waited nervously *for* the announcement.

▶ Drive *across* the bridge, and go *down* the avenue *past* three stoplights.

SOME COMMON PREPOSITIONS

about	at	down	near	since
above	before	during	of	through
across	behind	except	off	toward
after	below	for	on	under
against	beneath	from	onto	until
along	beside	in	out	up
among	between	inside	over	upon
around	beyond	into	past	with
as	by	like	regarding	without

SOME COMPOUND PREPOSITIONS

according to	except for	instead of
as well as	in addition to	next to
because of	in front of	out of
by way of	in place of	with regard to
due to	in spite of	

Research for this book shows that many writers today—including native speakers of English—have trouble using prepositions correctly. For more information on choosing prepositions, see p. 4 and Chapter 59.

EXERCISE 30.6

Identify and underline the prepositions in the following sentences. Example:

<u>In</u> the dim interior <u>of</u> the hut crouched an old man.

1. The transportation board of the county is planning to add limited bus service from midnight until 5:00 AM.
2. He ran swiftly through the brush, across the beach, and into the sea.
3. Instead of creating a peaceful new beginning, the tribunal factions are constantly fighting among themselves.
4. After some hard thinking on a weeklong camping trip, I decided to quit my job and join the Peace Corps for two years.
5. The nuclear power plant about ten miles from the city has the worst safety record of any plant in the country.

30h Conjunctions

Conjunctions connect words or groups of words to each other and tell something about the relationship between these words.

Coordinating conjunctions

Coordinating conjunctions (24a) join equivalent structures — two or more nouns, pronouns, verbs, adjectives, adverbs, prepositions, conjunctions, phrases, or clauses.

▶ A strong *but* warm breeze blew across the desert.

▶ Please print *or* type the information on the application form.

▶ Taiwo worked two shifts today, *so* she is tired tonight.

COORDINATING CONJUNCTIONS

and	for	or	yet
but	nor	so	

Correlative conjunctions

Correlative conjunctions join equal elements, and they come in pairs.

▶ *Both* Bechtel *and* Kaiser submitted bids on the project.

▶ Jeff *not only* sent a card *but also* visited me in the hospital.

CORRELATIVE CONJUNCTIONS

both . . . and	just as . . . so	not only . . . but also
either . . . or	neither . . . nor	whether . . . or

Subordinating conjunctions

Subordinating conjunctions introduce adverb clauses and signal the relationship between an adverb clause and another clause, usually an independent clause (24b and 30m). For instance, in the following sentence, the subordinating conjunction *while* signals a time relationship, letting us know that the two events in the sentence happened simultaneously:

▶ Sweat ran down my face *while* I frantically searched for my child.

SOME SUBORDINATING CONJUNCTIONS

after	if	unless
although	in order that	until
as	once	when
as if	since	where
because	so that	whether
before	than	while
even though	though	

Conjunctive adverbs

Conjunctive adverbs signal a logical relationship between parts of a sentence and, when used with a semicolon, can link independent clauses (30m).

▶ The cider tasted bitter; *however,* each of us drank a tall glass of it.

▶ The cider tasted bitter; each of us, *however,* drank a tall glass of it.

SOME CONJUNCTIVE ADVERBS

also	certainly	however	instead
anyway	finally	incidentally	likewise
besides	furthermore	indeed	meanwhile

moreover	next	similarly	therefore
namely	now	still	thus
nevertheless	otherwise	then	undoubtedly

EXERCISE 30.7

Underline the coordinating, correlative, and subordinating conjunctions as well as the conjunctive adverbs in each of the following sentences. Example:

We used sleeping bags, <u>even though</u> the cabin had sheets <u>and</u> blankets.

1. After waiting for an hour and a half, both Jenny and I were disgruntled, so we went home.

2. The facilities were not only uncomfortable but also dangerous.

3. We were going to have a yard sale because we had so much junk in our garage and needed more space; however, we decided to donate everything to charity.

4. Although I live in a big city, my neighborhood has enough trees and raccoons to make me feel as if I live in the suburbs.

5. Enrique was not qualified for the job because he knew one of the programming languages but not the other; still, the interview encouraged him.

30i Interjections

Interjections express surprise or emotion: *oh, ouch, ah, hey.* Interjections often stand alone, as fragments. Even when interjections are part of a sentence, they do not relate grammatically to the rest of the sentence.

▶ *Hey*, **no one suggested that we would find an easy solution.**

Parts of Sentences

Knowing a word's part of speech helps you understand how to use that word. But you also need to look at the part the word plays in a particular sentence. Consider, for instance, the word *description*.

SUBJECT
▶ **This *description* conveys the ecology of the Everglades.**
DIRECT OBJECT
▶ **I read a *description* of the ecology of the Everglades.**

Description is a noun in both sentences, yet in the first it serves as the subject of the verb *conveys*, while in the second it serves as the direct object of the verb *read*.

AT A GLANCE
Basic Sentence Patterns

1. SUBJECT/VERB

    S   V
▶ **Babies drool.**

2. SUBJECT/VERB/SUBJECT COMPLEMENT

    S   V   SC
▶ **Babies smell sweet.**

3. SUBJECT/VERB/DIRECT OBJECT

    S   V   DO
▶ **Babies drink milk.**

4. SUBJECT/VERB/INDIRECT OBJECT/DIRECT OBJECT

    S   V   IO   DO
▶ **Babies give grandparents pleasure.**

5. SUBJECT/VERB/DIRECT OBJECT/OBJECT COMPLEMENT

    S   V   DO   OC
▶ **Babies keep parents awake.**

30j Subjects

The subject of a sentence identifies what the sentence is about. The simple subject consists of one or more nouns or pronouns; the complete subject consists of the simple subject (SS) with all its modifiers.

    SS
▶ *Baseball* **is a summer game.**

   ⌈⸺ COMPLETE SUBJECT ⸺⌉
                SS
▶ *Sailing over the fence, the ball* **crashed through Mr. Wilson's window.**

   ⌈⸺ COMPLETE SUBJECT ⸺⌉
 SS
▶ *Those who sit in the bleachers* **have the most fun.**

A compound subject contains two or more simple subjects joined with a coordinating conjunction (*and, but, or*) or a correlative conjunction (*both . . . and, either . . . or, neither . . . nor*). (See 30h.)

▶ *Baseball and softball* **developed from cricket.**

▶ *Both baseball and softball* **developed from cricket.**

The subject usually comes before the predicate, or verb, but sometimes writers reverse this order to achieve a particular effect.

▶ **Up to the plate stepped** *Casey.*

In imperative sentences, which express requests or commands, the subject *you* is usually implied but not stated.

▶ **(***You***) Keep your eye on the ball.**

In questions and certain other constructions, the subject usually appears between the auxiliary verb (30b) and the main verb.

▶ **Did** *Casey* **save the game?**

In sentences beginning with *there* or *here* followed by a form of *be,* the subject always follows the verb. *There* and *here* are never the subject.

▶ **There was no** *joy* **in Mudville.**

EXERCISE 30.8

Identify the complete subject and the simple subject in each sentence. Underline the complete subject once and the simple subject twice. Example:

<u>The tall, powerful <u>woman</u></u> defiantly blocked the doorway.

1. That container of fried rice has spent six weeks in the back of the refrigerator.
2. Did the new tour guide remember to stop in the ancient Greek gallery?
3. There goes my favorite car.
4. Japanese animation, with its cutting-edge graphics and futuristic plots, has earned many American admirers.
5. Some women worried about osteoporosis take calcium supplements.

30k Predicates

In addition to a subject, every sentence has a predicate, which asserts or asks something about the subject or tells the subject to do something. The hinge, or key word, of a predicate is the verb. The simple predicate (SP) of a sentence consists of the main verb and any auxiliaries (30b); the complete predicate includes the simple predicate plus any modifiers of the verb and any objects or complements and their modifiers.

▶ **Both of us** *are planning to major in history.*

A compound predicate contains two or more verbs that have the same subject, usually joined by a coordinating or a correlative conjunction.

S ┌──────────── COMPOUND PREDICATE ────────────┐
▶ **Omar** *shut the book, put it back on the shelf, and sighed.*

┌── S ──┐ ┌──────── COMPOUND PREDICATE ────────┐
▶ **The Amish** *neither drive cars nor use electricity.*

On the basis of how they function in predicates, verbs can be divided into three categories: linking, transitive, and intransitive.

Linking verbs

A linking verb links, or joins, a subject with a subject complement (SC), a word or group of words that identifies or describes the subject.

S   V ┌──── SC ────┐
▶ **Nastassia is a single mother.**

S   V ┌─ SC ─┐
▶ **She is patient.**

If it identifies the subject, the complement is a noun or pronoun (*a single mother*). If it describes the subject, the complement is an adjective (*patient*).
   The forms of *be,* when used as main verbs rather than as auxiliary verbs, are linking verbs (like *are* in this sentence). Other verbs — such as *appear, become, feel, grow, look, make, seem, smell,* and *sound* — can also function as linking verbs, depending on the sense of the sentence.

Transitive verbs

A transitive verb expresses action that is directed toward a noun or pronoun, called the direct object of the verb.

S ┌─V─┐ ┌──── DO ────┐
▶ **He peeled all the rutabagas.**

In the preceding example, the subject and verb do not express a complete thought. The direct object completes the thought by saying *what* he peeled.
   A direct object may be followed by an object complement, a word or word group that describes or identifies the direct object. Object complements may be adjectives, as in the next example, or nouns, as in the second example.

S V ┌────────── DO ──────────┐ ┌──── OC ────┐
▶ **I find cell-phone conversations in restaurants very annoying.**

S   V   DO   ┌──── OC ────┐
▶ **Alana considers Keyshawn her best friend.**

A transitive verb may also be followed by an indirect object, which tells to whom or what, or for whom or what, the verb's action is done. You might say the indirect object is the recipient of the direct object.

```
         ┌──────────── S ────────────┐   V    IO  ┌──────── DO ────────┐
```
► **The sound of the traffic gave me a splitting headache.**

Intransitive verbs

An intransitive verb expresses action that is not directed toward an object. Therefore, an intransitive verb does not have a direct object.

```
    ┌──── S ────┐      V
```
► **The Red Sox persevered.**
```
    ┌── S ──┐   V
```
► **Their fans watched anxiously.**

The verb *persevered* has no object (it makes no sense to ask, *persevered what?* or *persevered whom?*), and the verb *watched* has an object that is implied but not expressed.

Some verbs that express action can be only transitive or only intransitive, but most can be used either way, with or without a direct object.

```
    ┌──────────── S ────────────┐   V    ┌── DO ──┐
```
► **A maid wearing a uniform opened the door.**

The verb *opened* is transitive here.

```
    ┌── S ──┐   V
```
► **The door opened silently.**

The verb *opened* is intransitive here.

EXERCISE 30.9

Underline the predicate in each of the following sentences. Then label each verb as linking (LV), transitive (TV), or intransitive (IV). Finally, label all subject and object complements (SC, OC) and all direct and indirect objects (DO, IO). Example:

```
        TV        ┌─ DO ─┐     OC
We considered city life unbearable.
```

1. He is proud of his heritage.
2. The horrifying news story made me angry.
3. A hung jury seems likely in this case.
4. Rock and roll will never die.
5. Advertisers promise consumers the world.

30l Phrases

A phrase is a group of words that lacks either a subject or a predicate or both.

Noun phrases

A noun phrase consists of a noun and all its modifiers. In a sentence, a noun phrase can play the role of a subject, object, or complement.

▶ *Delicious, gooey peanut butter* is surprisingly healthful.
      ⌐————— SUBJECT —————¬

▶ Dieters prefer *green salad.*
         ⌐— OBJECT —¬

▶ A tuna sandwich is *a popular lunch.*
           ⌐— COMPLEMENT —¬

Verb phrases

A main verb and its auxiliary verbs make up a verb phrase, which can function only one way in a sentence: as a predicate.

▶ I *can swim* for a long time.

▶ His headaches *might have been caused* by tension.

Prepositional phrases

A prepositional phrase includes a preposition, a noun or pronoun (called the object of the preposition), and any modifiers of the object. Prepositional phrases usually serve as adjectives or adverbs.

ADJECTIVE	Our house *in Maine* is a cabin.
ADVERB	*From Cadillac Mountain,* you can see the Northern Lights.

Verbal phrases

Verbals are verb forms that do not function as verbs. Instead, they stand in for nouns, adjectives, or adverbs. A verbal phrase is made up of a verbal and any modifiers, objects, or complements. There are three kinds of verbals: participles, gerunds, and infinitives.

PARTICIPIAL PHRASES

A participial phrase always functions as an adjective and can include either a present participle (the *crying* child) or a past participle (the *spoken* word).

▶ A dog *howling at the moon* kept me awake.

▶ *Irritated by the delay*, Louise complained.

GERUND PHRASES

A gerund has the same form as a present participle, ending in *-ing*. But gerunds and gerund phrases always function as nouns.

⌐SUBJECT¬
▶ *Recycling* is not always easy.

⌐————— DIRECT OBJECT —————¬
▶ He ignored *the loud wailing from the sandbox.*

INFINITIVE PHRASES

An infinitive phrase can function as a noun, adjective, or adverb. The infinitive is the *to* form of a verb: *to be, to write.*

⌐—ADJECTIVE——¬
▶ A vote would be a good way *to end the meeting.*

⌐——ADVERB——¬
▶ *To perfect a draft*, always proofread carefully.

⌐————— NOUN —————¬
▶ My goal is *to be a biology teacher.*

Absolute phrases

An absolute phrase usually includes a noun or pronoun and a participle. It modifies an entire sentence rather than a particular word and is usually set off from the rest of the sentence with commas (38a).

▶ I stood on the deck, *the wind whipping my hair.*
▶ *My fears laid to rest*, I climbed into the plane for my first solo flight.

Appositive phrases

A noun phrase that renames the noun or pronoun immediately preceding it is called an appositive phrase.

▶ The report, *a hefty three-volume work*, included sixty recommendations.
▶ A single desire, *to change the corporation's policies*, guided our actions.

EXERCISE 30.10

Read the following sentences, and identify and label all of the prepositional, verbal, absolute, and appositive phrases. Notice that one kind of phrase may appear within another kind. Example:

```
        ┌──────ABSOLUTE ──────┐              ┌──PREP ──┐
        His voice breaking with emotion, Ed thanked us for the award.
                 └──PREP ──┘
```

1. Chantelle, the motel clerk, hopes to be certified as a river guide.
2. Countertops made of granite will last the longest.
3. My stomach doing flips, I answered the door.
4. Floating on my back, I ignored my practice requirements.
5. Learning to drive a car with a manual transmission takes time and patience.

30m Clauses

A clause is a group of words containing a subject and a predicate. There are two kinds of clauses: independent and dependent.

Independent clauses (also known as main clauses) can stand alone as complete sentences: *The window is open.* Pairs of independent clauses may be joined with a comma and a coordinating conjunction (*and, but, for, or, nor, so,* or *yet*).

▶ **The window is open,** *so* **we'd better be quiet.**

Like independent clauses, dependent clauses (also known as subordinate clauses) contain a subject and a predicate. They cannot stand alone as complete sentences, however, for they begin with a subordinating word (24b). Dependent clauses function as nouns, adjectives, or adverbs.

▶ *Because the window is open,* **the room feels cool.**

In this combination, the subordinating conjunction *because* transforms the independent clause *the window is open* into a dependent clause. In doing so, it indicates a causal relationship between the two clauses.

Noun clauses

Noun clauses can function as subjects, direct objects, subject complements, or objects of prepositions. Thus a noun clause does not stand alone but is always contained within another clause. Noun clauses usually begin with a relative pronoun (*that, which, what, who, whom, whose, whatever, whoever, whomever, whichever*) or with *when, where, whether, why,* or *how.*

▸ *That she had a good job* was important to him.
    └─────── S ───────┘

▸ He asked *where she went to college.*
         └───── DO ─────┘

▸ The real question was *why he wanted to know.*
            └───── SC ─────┘

▸ He was looking for *whatever information was available.*
             └────── OBJ OF PREP ──────┘

Notice that in each of these sentences the noun clause is an integral part of the independent clause that makes up the sentence. For example, in the second sentence, the independent clause is not just *he asked* but *he asked where she went to college.*

Adjective clauses

Adjective clauses modify nouns and pronouns in other clauses. Usually adjective clauses immediately follow the words they modify. Most of these clauses begin with the relative pronoun *who, whom, whose, that,* or *which.* Some begin with *when, where,* or *why.*

▸ The surgery, *which took three hours,* was a complete success.

▸ It was performed by the surgeon *who had developed the procedure.*

▸ The hospital was the one *where I was born.*

Sometimes the relative pronoun introducing an adjective clause may be omitted.

▸ That is one book *[that] I intend to read.*

Adverb clauses

Adverb clauses modify verbs, adjectives, or other adverbs. They begin with a subordinating conjunction (30h) and, like adverbs, they usually tell when, where, why, how, or to what extent.

▸ We hiked *where there were few other hikers.*

▸ My backpack felt heavier *than it ever had.*

▸ I climbed as swiftly *as I could under the weight of my backpack.*

EXERCISE 30.11

Identify the independent and dependent clauses and any subordinating conjunctions and relative pronouns in each of the following sentences. Example:

```
┌──────DEPENDENT CLAUSE──────┐  ┌──────INDEPENDENT CLAUSE──────┐
```
If I were going on a really long hike, I would carry a lightweight stove.
If is a subordinating conjunction.

1. The hockey game was postponed because one of the players collapsed on the bench.

2. She immediately recognized the officer who walked into the coffee shop.

3. After completing three advanced drawing classes, Jason was admitted into the fine arts program, and he immediately rented a small studio space.

4. The trip was longer than I had remembered.

5. I could see that he was very tired, but I had to ask him a few questions.

EXERCISE 30.12

Expand each of the following sentences by adding at least one dependent clause to it. Be prepared to explain how your addition improves the sentence. Example:

> *As the earth continued to shake, the*
> ~~The~~ books tumbled from the shelves.
>   ^

1. News of the virus was beginning to frighten the public.

2. Simone waited nervously by the phone.

3. The new computer made a strange noise.

4. Rob always borrowed money from friends.

5. The crowd grew louder and more disorderly.

Types of Sentences

Like words, sentences can be classified in different ways: grammatically and functionally.

30n Grammatical classifications

Grammatically, sentences may be classified as simple, compound, complex, and compound-complex.

Simple sentences

A simple sentence consists of one independent clause and no dependent clause.

```
┌───────────INDEPENDENT CLAUSE───────────┐
```
▶ **The trailer is surrounded by a wooden deck.**
```
┌───────────INDEPENDENT CLAUSE───────────┐
```
▶ **Both my roommate and I left our keys in the room.**

Compound sentences

A compound sentence consists of two or more independent clauses and no dependent clause. The clauses may be joined by a comma and a coordinating conjunction (*and, but, or, nor, for, so, yet*) or by a semicolon.

```
┌────────────IND CLAUSE────────────┐      ┌──────IND CLAUSE──────┐
```
▶ Occasionally, a car goes up the dirt trail, and dust flies everywhere.
```
┌──────────IND CLAUSE──────────┐   ┌────────────IND CLAUSE────────────┐
```
▶ Angelo is obsessed with soccer; he eats, breathes, and lives the game.

Complex sentences

A complex sentence consists of one independent clause and at least one dependent clause.

```
┌──────────IND CLAUSE──────────┐ ┌──────DEP CLAUSE──────┐
```
▶ Many people believe that anyone can earn a living.

Compound-complex sentences

A compound-complex sentence consists of two or more independent clauses and at least one dependent clause.

```
┌──────IND CLAUSE──────┐ ┌──────DEP CLAUSE──────┐   ┌──────IND CLAUSE──────┐
```
▶ I complimented Luis when he finished the job, and he seemed pleased.
```
┌────────────IND CLAUSE────────────┐     ┌──────IND CLAUSE──────
```
▶ Sister Lucy tried her best to help Martin, but he was an undisciplined
```
─┐ ┌────────────DEP CLAUSE────────────┐
```
boy who drove many teachers to despair.

30o Functional classifications

In terms of function, sentences can be classified as declarative (making a statement), interrogative (asking a question), imperative (giving a command), or exclamatory (expressing strong feeling).

DECLARATIVE	He sings with the Grace Church Boys' Choir.
INTERROGATIVE	How long has he sung with them?
IMPERATIVE	Comb his hair before the performance starts.
EXCLAMATORY	What voices those boys have!

EXERCISE 30.13

Classify each of the following sentences as simple, compound, complex, or compound-complex. In addition, note any sentence that may be classified as interrogative, imperative, or exclamatory.

1. The boat rocked and lurched over the rough surf as the passengers groaned in agony.

2. How long would he have to wait for help, or should he try to change the tire himself?

3. Hoping for an end to the rain, we huddled together in the shop doorway, unwilling to get drenched.

4. Keeping in mind the terrain, the weather, and the length of the hike, decide what you need to take.

5. The former prisoner, who was cleared by DNA evidence, has lost six years of his life, and he needs a job right away.

> **bedfordstmartins.com/everydaywriter** For exercises, go to **Exercise Central** and click on **Basic Grammar**.

EXERCISE 30.14: THINKING CRITICALLY

The following sentences come from the openings of well-known works. Identify the independent and dependent clauses in each sentence. Then choose one sentence, and write a sentence of your own imitating its structure, clause for clause and phrase for phrase. Example:

Ten days after the war ended, my sister Laura drove a car off a bridge.
— MARGARET ATWOOD, *The Blind Assassin*

A few minutes before the detectives arrived, our friend Nastassia found a passageway behind the wall.

1. We observe today not a victory of party but a celebration of freedom, symbolizing an end as well as a beginning, signifying renewal as well as change.
— JOHN F. KENNEDY, Inaugural Address

2. Once in a long while, four times so far for me, my mother brings out the metal tube that holds her medical diploma.
— MAXINE HONG KINGSTON, "Photographs of My Parents"

Verts **31**

Restaurant menus often spotlight verbs in action. One famous place in Boston, for instance, offers to bake, broil, pan-fry, deep-fry, poach, sauté, fricassée, blacken, or scallop any of the fish entrées on its menu. To someone ordering — or cooking — at this restaurant, the important distinctions lie entirely in the verbs.

When used skillfully, verbs can be the heartbeat of prose, moving it along, enlivening it, carrying its action. (See Chapter 32 for advice on subject-verb agreement and Chapter 58 for more about verbs for multilingual writers.)

AT A GLANCE

Editing the Verbs in Your Own Writing

- Check verb endings that cause you trouble. (31a and c)
- Double-check forms of *lie* and *lay*, *sit* and *set*, *rise* and *raise*. See that the words you use are appropriate for your meaning. (31d)
- If you are writing about a literary work, remember to refer to the action in the work in the present tense. (31e)
- If you have problems with verb tenses, use the guidelines on p. 288 to check your verbs.
- Check all uses of the passive voice for appropriateness. (31g)
- Check all verbs used to introduce quotations, paraphrases, and summaries. If you rely on *say*, *write*, and other very general verbs, try substituting more vivid, specific verbs (*claim*, *insist*, and *wonder*, for instance).

31a The five forms of verbs

Except for *be*, all English verbs have five forms.

BASE FORM	PAST TENSE	PAST PARTICIPLE	PRESENT PARTICIPLE	-S FORM
talk	talked	talked	talking	talks
adore	adored	adored	adoring	adores

BASE FORM	We often *go* to Legal Sea Foods.
PAST TENSE	Grandpa always *ordered* bluefish.
PAST PARTICIPLE	Grandma *has tried* the oyster stew.
PRESENT PARTICIPLE	Juanita *is getting* the shrimp platter.
-S FORM	The chowder *needs* salt and pepper.

-s and -es endings

Except with *be* and *have*, the *-s* form consists of the base form plus *-s* or *-es*. In standard English, this form indicates action in the present for third-person singular subjects. All singular nouns; the personal pronouns *he*, *she*, and *it*; and many other pronouns (such as *this*, *anyone*, *everything*, and *someone*) are third-person singular.

	SINGULAR	PLURAL
FIRST PERSON	I *wish*	we *wish*
SECOND PERSON	you *wish*	you *wish*

THIRD PERSON	he/she/it *wishes*	they *wish*
	Joe *wishes*	children *wish*
	someone *wishes*	many *wish*

Forms of be

Be has three forms in the present tense and two in the past tense.

BASE FORM	be
PAST PARTICIPLE	been
PRESENT PARTICIPLE	being
PRESENT TENSE	I *am*, he/she/it *is*, we/you/they *are*
PAST TENSE	I/he/she/it *was*, we/you/they *were*

TALKING ABOUT STYLE

Everyday Use of *Be*

The rules for the use of *be* in spoken varieties of English may differ from the rules in standard English. For instance, you may have heard speakers say sentences like "She ain't here now" (instead of the standard English *She isn't here now*) or "He be at work every Saturday" (instead of the standard English *He is at work every Saturday*). You may sometimes want to quote dialogue featuring such spoken usages of *be* when you write. In most academic and professional writing, however, you will want to follow the conventions of standard English. (For help on using varieties of English appropriately, see Chapter 21.)

31b Auxiliary verbs

Use auxiliary verbs with a base form, present participle, or past participle to form verb tenses, questions, and negatives. The most common auxiliaries are forms of *be, do,* and *have.*

▶ We *have considered* all viewpoints.

▶ The problem *is ranking* them fairly.

▶ Do you *know* the answer? No, I *do* not *know* it.

Modal auxiliaries — *can, could, might, may, must, ought to, shall, will, should, would* — indicate future actions, possibility, necessity, obligation, and so on.

▶ You *can see* three states from the top of the mountain.

▶ She *should visit* this spot more often.

> **FOR MULTILINGUAL WRITERS**
>
> ### Using Modal Auxiliaries
>
> Why do we not say "Alice can to read Latin"? For a discussion of *can* and other modal auxiliaries, see 58a.

31c   Regular and irregular verb forms

A verb is regular when its past tense and past participle are formed by adding *-ed* or *-d* to the base form.

BASE FORM	PAST TENSE	PAST PARTICIPLE
love	loved	loved
honor	honored	honored
obey	obeyed	obeyed

A verb is irregular when it does not follow the *-ed* or *-d* pattern. If you are not sure whether a verb form is regular or irregular, or what the correct form is, consult the following list or a dictionary. Dictionaries list any irregular forms under the entry for the base form.

Some common irregular verbs

BASE FORM	PAST TENSE	PAST PARTICIPLE
arise	arose	arisen
be	was/were	been
beat	beat	beaten
become	became	become
begin	began	begun
bite	bit	bitten, bit
blow	blew	blown
break	broke	broken
bring	brought	brought
broadcast	broadcast	broadcast
build	built	built

BASE FORM	PAST TENSE	PAST PARTICIPLE
burn	burned, burnt	burned, burnt
burst	burst	burst
buy	bought	bought
catch	caught	caught
choose	chose	chosen
come	came	come
cost	cost	cost
dig	dug	dug
dive	dived, dove	dived
do	did	done
draw	drew	drawn
dream	dreamed, dreamt	dreamed, dreamt
drink	drank	drunk
drive	drove	driven
eat	ate	eaten
fall	fell	fallen
feel	felt	felt
fight	fought	fought
find	found	found
fly	flew	flown
forget	forgot	forgotten, forgot
freeze	froze	frozen
get	got	gotten, got
give	gave	given
go	went	gone
grow	grew	grown
hang (suspend)[1]	hung	hung
have	had	had
hear	heard	heard
hide	hid	hidden

---

[1]*Hang* meaning "execute by hanging" is regular: *hang, hanged, hanged.*

BASE FORM	PAST TENSE	PAST PARTICIPLE
hit	hit	hit
keep	kept	kept
know	knew	known
lay	laid	laid
lead	led	led
leave	left	left
lend	lent	lent
let	let	let
lie (recline)[2]	lay	lain
lose	lost	lost
make	made	made
mean	meant	meant
meet	met	met
prove	proved	proved, proven
put	put	put
read	read	read
ride	rode	ridden
ring	rang	rung
rise	rose	risen
run	ran	run
say	said	said
see	saw	seen
send	sent	sent
set	set	set
shake	shook	shaken
shoot	shot	shot
show	showed	showed, shown
shrink	shrank	shrunk
sing	sang	sung
sink	sank	sunk

---

[2]*Lie* meaning "tell a falsehood" is regular: *lie, lied, lied.*

BASE FORM	PAST TENSE	PAST PARTICIPLE
sit	sat	sat
sleep	slept	slept
speak	spoke	spoken
spend	spent	spent
spring	sprang, sprung	sprung
stand	stood	stood
steal	stole	stolen
strike	struck	struck, stricken
swim	swam	swum
swing	swung	swung
take	took	taken
tear	tore	torn
throw	threw	thrown
wake	woke, waked	waked, woken
wear	wore	worn
write	wrote	written

EXERCISE 31.1

Complete each of the following sentences by filling in each blank with the past tense or past participle of the verb listed in parentheses. Example:

They had already __eaten__ (eat) the entrée; later they __ate__ (eat) the dessert.

1. The babysitter _____ (let) the children play with my schoolbooks, and before I _____ (come) home, they had _____ (tear) out several pages.

2. After she had _____ (make) her decision, she _____ (find) that her constant anxiety was gone.

3. The process of hazing _____ (begin) soon after fraternities were formed.

4. My parents _____ (plant) a tree for me in the town where I was born, but I have never _____ (go) back to see it.

5. Some residents _____ (know) that the levee was leaking long before the storms, but public officials _____ (ignore) the complaints.

6. I _____ (wake) up with a start because I was convinced that something had _____ (fly) through the window.

7. When the buzzer sounded, the racers _____ (spring) into the water and _____ (swim) toward the far end of the pool.

8. We had _____ (assume) for some time that surgery was a possibility, and we had _____ (find) an excellent facility.

9. Once the storm had _____ (pass), we could see that the old oak tree had _____ (fall).

10. Some high-level employees _____ (decide) to speak publicly about the cover-up before the company's official story had _____ (be) released to the media.

31d *Lie* and *lay*, *sit* and *set*, *rise* and *raise*

These pairs of verbs cause confusion because both verbs in each pair have similar-sounding forms and somewhat related meanings. In each pair, one of the verbs is transitive, meaning that it is followed by a direct object (*I laid the cloth on the table*). The other is intransitive, meaning that it does not have an object (*He lay on the floor when his back ached*). The best way to avoid confusing these verbs is to memorize their forms and meanings.

BASE FORM	PAST TENSE	PAST PARTICIPLE	PRESENT PARTICIPLE	-S FORM
lie (recline)	lay	lain	lying	lies
lay (put)	laid	laid	laying	lays
sit (be seated)	sat	sat	sitting	sits
set (put)	set	set	setting	sets
rise (get up)	rose	risen	rising	rises
raise (lift)	raised	raised	raising	raises

▶ The doctor asked the patient to ~~lay~~ *lie* on his side.

▶ She ~~sat~~ *set* the vase on the table.

▶ He ~~raised~~ *rose* up in bed and glared at us.

EXERCISE 31.2

Underline the appropriate verb form in each of the following sentences. Example:

The guests (*raised*/*rose*) their glasses to the happy couple.

1. Sometimes she just (*lies*/*lays*) and stares at the ceiling.

2. The chef (*lay*/*laid*) his knives carefully on the counter.

3. The two-year-old walked carefully across the room and (*set*/*sat*) the glass vase on the table.

4. Grandpa used to love (*sitting*/*setting*) on the front porch and telling stories of his childhood.

5. The submarine began to (*raise*/*rise*) to the surface.

31e Verb tenses

Tenses show when the action expressed by a verb takes place. The three simple tenses are the present tense, the past tense, and the future tense.

PRESENT TENSE	I *ask, write*
PAST TENSE	I *asked, wrote*
FUTURE TENSE	I *will ask, will write*

More complex aspects of time are expressed through progressive, perfect, and perfect progressive forms of the simple tenses.

PRESENT PROGRESSIVE	she *is asking, is writing*
PAST PROGRESSIVE	she *was asking, was writing*
FUTURE PROGRESSIVE	she *will be asking, will be writing*
PRESENT PERFECT	she *has asked, has written*
PAST PERFECT	she *had asked, had written*
FUTURE PERFECT	she *will have asked, will have written*
PRESENT PERFECT PROGRESSIVE	she *has been asking, has been writing*
PAST PERFECT PROGRESSIVE	she *had been asking, had been writing*
FUTURE PERFECT PROGRESSIVE	she *will have been asking, will have been writing*

The simple tenses locate an action only within the three basic time frames of present, past, and future. Progressive forms express continuing actions; perfect forms express actions completed before another action or time in the present, past, or future; perfect progressive forms express actions that continue up to some point in the present, past, or future.

Present tense

SIMPLE PRESENT

Use the simple present to indicate actions occurring now and those occurring habitually.

▶ I *eat* breakfast every day at 8:00 AM.

▶ Love *conquers* all.

Use the simple present when writing about action in literary works.

▶ Ishmael slowly ~~realized~~ *realizes* all that ~~was~~ *is* at stake in the search for the white whale.

General truths or scientific facts should be in the simple present, even when the predicate of the sentence is in the past tense.

> *makes*
> ▶ **Pasteur demonstrated that his boiling process ~~made~~ milk safe.**
>   ^

When you are quoting, summarizing, or paraphrasing a work, in general use the present tense.

> *writes*
> ▶ **Keith Walters ~~wrote~~ that the "reputed consequences and promised**
>   ^
> **blessings of literacy are legion."**

But in an essay using APA (American Psychological Association) style, the reporting of your experiments or another researcher's work should be in the past tense (*wrote, noted*) or the present perfect (*has reported*). (See Chapter 52.)

> *noted*
> ▶ **Comer (1995) ~~notes~~ that protesters who deprive themselves of food**
>   ^
> **(for example, Gandhi) are seen not as dysfunctional but rather as**
> **"caring, sacrificing, even heroic" (p. 5).**

PRESENT PROGRESSIVE

Use the present progressive to indicate actions that are ongoing in the present: *You <u>are driving</u> too fast.*

PRESENT PERFECT

Use the present perfect to indicate actions begun in the past and either completed at some unspecified time in the past or continuing into the present: *Uncontrolled logging <u>has destroyed</u> many forests.*

PRESENT PERFECT PROGRESSIVE

Use the present perfect progressive to indicate an ongoing action begun in the past and continuing into the present: *The two sides <u>have been trying</u> to settle the case out of court.*

Past tense

SIMPLE PAST

Use the simple past to indicate actions that occurred at a specific time and do not extend into the present: *Germany <u>invaded</u> Poland on September 1, 1939.*

PAST PROGRESSIVE

Use the past progressive to indicate continuing actions in the past: *Lenin was living in exile in Zurich when the tsar was overthrown.*

PAST PERFECT

Use the past perfect to indicate actions that were completed by a specific time in the past or before some other past action occurred: *By the fourth century, Christianity had become the state religion.*

PAST PERFECT PROGRESSIVE

Use the past perfect progressive to indicate continuing actions in the past that began before a specific time or before some other past action began: *Carter had been planning a naval career until his father died.*

Future tense

SIMPLE FUTURE

Use the simple future to indicate actions that have yet to begin: *The Vermeer show will come to Washington in September.*

FUTURE PROGRESSIVE

Use the future progressive to indicate continuing actions in the future: *The loans will be coming due over the next two years.*

FUTURE PERFECT

Use the future perfect to indicate actions that will be completed by a specified time in the future: *In ten years, your investment will have doubled.*

FUTURE PERFECT PROGRESSIVE

Use the future perfect progressive to indicate continuing actions that will be completed by some specified time in the future: *In May, I will have been working at IBM for five years.*

EXERCISE 31.3

Complete each of the following sentences by filling in the blank with an appropriate form of the verb listed in parentheses. Since more than one form will sometimes be possible, be prepared to explain the reasons for your choices. Example:

The supply of a product ___*rises*___ (rise) when the demand is great.

1. History _____ (show) that physical torture does not make prisoners tell the truth.
2. Ever since the first nuclear power plants were built, opponents _____ (fear) disaster.

3. Thousands of Irish peasants _____ (emigrate) to America after the potato famine of the 1840s.

4. *The Da Vinci Code* _____ (be) on the bestseller list for 138 weeks.

5. Olivia _____ (direct) the play next year.

6. While they _____ (eat) in a neighborhood restaurant, they witnessed a minor accident.

7. By this time next week, each of your clients _____ (receive) an invitation to the opening.

8. By the time a child born today enters first grade, he or she _____ (watch) thousands of television commercials.

9. In one of the novel's most famous scenes, Huck _____ (express) his willingness to go to hell rather than report Jim as an escaped slave.

10. Traffic jams usually _____ (last) longer in August, when many tourists come to the area.

AT A GLANCE

Editing Verb Tenses

If you have trouble with verb tenses, make a point of checking for these common errors as you proofread.

- Errors of verb form: writing *seen* for *saw,* for example, which confuses the past-participle and past-tense forms. (31c)

- Errors in tense: using the simple past (*Uncle Charlie arrived*) when meaning requires the present perfect (*Uncle Charlie has arrived*). (31e)

- Other errors result from using a regional or ethnic variety of English (*she nervous*) in situations calling for standard academic English (*she is nervous*). (See Chapter 21.)

31f Sequence of verb tenses

Careful and accurate use of tenses is important for clear writing. Even the simplest narrative describes actions that take place at different times; when you use the appropriate tense for each action, readers can follow such time changes easily.

▶ **By the time he *lent* her the money, she *had declared* bankruptcy.**

Use an infinitive (*to* plus a base form: *to go*) to indicate actions occurring at the same time as or later than the action of the predicate verb.

▶ Each couple *hopes to win* the dance contest.

The hoping is in the present; the winning is in the future.

Use a present participle (base form plus -*ing*) to indicate actions occurring at the same time as that of the predicate verb.

▶ **Seeking to relieve unemployment, Roosevelt established several public works programs.**

A past participle or a present-perfect participle (*having* plus a past participle) indicates actions occurring before that of the predicate verb.

Flown
▶ **~~Flying~~ to the front, the troops joined their hard-pressed comrades.**
 ^

The past participle *flown* shows that the flying occurred before the joining.

Having crushed
▶ **~~Crushing~~ all opposition at home, he launched a war of conquest.**
 ^

He launched the war after he crushed the opposition.

One common error is to use *would* in both clauses of a sentence with an *if* clause. Use *would* only in one clause.

 had
▶ **If I ~~would have~~ played harder, I would have won.**
 ^

EXERCISE 31.4

Edit each of the following sentences to create the appropriate sequence of tenses. Example:

 have sent
 He needs to ~~send~~ in his application before today.
 ^

1. When she saw *Chicago*, it had made her want to become an actress even more.
2. Leaving England in December, the settlers arrived in Virginia in May.
3. I hoped to finish reading the book before today.
4. Working with great dedication as a summer intern at the magazine, Mohan called his former supervisor in the fall to ask about a permanent position.
5. When we walked home from school, we would often stop for ice cream.

31g Active voice and passive voice

Voice tells whether a subject is acting (*He questions us*) or being acted upon (*He is questioned*). When the subject is acting, the verb is in the active voice; when the subject is being acted upon, the verb is in the passive voice. Most contemporary writers use the active voice as much as possible because it livens up their writing.

> PASSIVE   Huge pine trees *were uprooted* by the storm.
>
> ACTIVE   The storm *uprooted* huge pine trees.

The passive voice can work to good advantage in some situations. Newspaper reporters often use the passive voice to protect the confidentiality of their sources, as in the familiar expression *it is reported that.* You can also use the passive voice when you want to emphasize the recipient of an action rather than the performer of the action.

> DALLAS, NOV. 22 — President John Fitzgerald Kennedy was shot and killed by an assassin today.   – TOM WICKER, *New York Times*

Wicker uses the passive voice with good reason: to focus on Kennedy, not on who killed him.

To shift a sentence from passive to active voice, make the performer of the action the subject of the sentence.

▶ His ~~acting career was destroyed by his~~ unprofessional behavior on the set. *destroyed his acting career.*

EXERCISE 31.5

Convert each sentence from active to passive voice or from passive to active, and note the differences in emphasis these changes make. Example:

The   *is advised by Machiavelli*
~~Machiavelli advises the~~ prince to gain the friendship of the people.

1. The surfers were informed by the lifeguard of a shark sighting.

2. The comic-book artist drew a superhero with amazing crime-fighting powers.

3. For months, the baby kangaroo is protected, fed, and taught how to survive by its mother.

4. The lawns and rooftops were covered with the first snow of winter.

5. A new advertising company was chosen by the board members.

TALKING ABOUT STYLE

Technical and Scientific Writing

Much technical and scientific writing uses the passive voice effectively to highlight what is being studied rather than who is doing the studying.

The Earth's plates are created where they separate and are recycled where they collide, in a continuous process of creation and destruction.

— Frank Press and Raymond Siever, *Understanding Earth*

31h **Mood**

The mood of a verb indicates the attitude of the writer. The *indicative* mood states facts or opinions and asks questions: *I did the right thing.* The *imperative* mood gives commands and instructions: *Do the right thing.* The *subjunctive* mood (used primarily in dependent clauses beginning with *that* or *if*) expresses wishes and conditions that are contrary to fact: *If I were doing the right thing, I'd know it.*

Forming and using the subjunctive

The present subjunctive uses the base form of the verb with all subjects.

▶ It is important that children *be* psychologically ready for a new sibling.

The past subjunctive is the same as the simple past except for the verb *be,* which uses *were* for all subjects.

▶ He spent money as if he *had* infinite credit.
▶ If the store *were* better located, it would attract more customers.

Because the subjunctive creates a rather formal tone, many people today tend to substitute the indicative mood in informal conversation.

▶ If the store *was* better located, it would attract more customers.

For academic or professional writing, use the subjunctive in the following contexts:

CLAUSES EXPRESSING A WISH

were
▶ He wished that his mother ~~was~~ still living nearby.
  ^

THAT CLAUSES EXPRESSING A REQUEST OR DEMAND

be

▶ The job demands that employees ~~are~~ in good physical condition.
                                      ^

IF CLAUSES EXPRESSING A CONDITION THAT DOES NOT EXIST

were

▶ If the federal government ~~was~~ to ban the sale of tobacco, tobacco
                             ^

companies and distributors would suffer a great loss.

EXERCISE 31.6

Revise any of the following sentences that do not use the appropriate subjunctive verb forms required in formal writing. Example:

were

I saw how carefully he moved, as if he ~~was~~ holding an infant.
                                         ^

1. Her stepsisters treated Cinderella as though she was a servant.
2. Marvina wished that she was able to take her daughter along on the business trip.
3. Protesters demanded that the senator resign from her post.
4. If more money was available, we would be able to offer more scholarships.
5. It is critical that the liquid remains at room temperature for at least seven hours.

FOR MULTILINGUAL WRITERS

Using the Subjunctive

"If you were to practice writing every day, it would eventually seem much easier to you." For a discussion of this and other uses of the subjunctive, see 58g.

---

 bedfordstmartins.com/everydaywriter For exercises, go to **Exercise Central** and click on **Verbs.**

EXERCISE 31.7: THINKING CRITICALLY

Reading with an Eye for Verbs

Some years ago a newspaper in San Francisco ran the headline "Giants Crush Cardinals, 3–1," provoking the following friendly advice from John Updike about the art of sports-headline verbs:

The correct verb, San Francisco, is *whip*. Notice the vigor, force, and scorn obtained. . . . [These examples] may prove helpful: 3–1 — *whip*; 3–2 — *shade*; 2–1 — *edge*. 4–1 gets the coveted verb *vanquish*. Rule: Any three-run margin, *provided the winning total does not exceed ten*, may be described as a vanquishing.

Take the time to study a newspaper with an eye for its verbs. Copy down several examples of strong verbs as well as a few examples of weak or overused verbs. For the weak ones, try to come up with better choices.

Thinking about Your Own Use of Verbs

Writing that relies too heavily on the verbs *be*, *do*, and *have* almost always bores readers. Look at something you've written recently to see whether you rely too heavily on these verbs, and revise accordingly.

Subject-Verb Agreement

In everyday terms, the word *agreement* refers to an accord of some sort: you reach an agreement with your boss about salary; friends agree to go to a movie; the members of a family agree to share household chores. This meaning covers grammatical agreement as well. In the present tense, verbs agree with their subjects in number (singular or plural) and in person (first, second, or third).

32a Third-person singular subjects

To make a verb in the present tense agree with a third-person singular subject, add *-s* or *-es* to the base form.

▶ **A vegetarian diet *lowers* the risk of heart disease.**

▶ **What you eat *affects* your health.**

In the preceding example, the subject is the noun clause *what you eat*. The clause is singular, so the base form of the verb *affect* takes an *-s*.

To make a verb in the present tense agree with any other subject, use the base form of the verb.

▶ **I *miss* my family.**

▶ **They *live* in another state.**

AT A GLANCE

Editing for Subject-Verb Agreement

- Identify the subject that goes with each verb. Cover up any words between the subject and the verb to identify agreement problems more easily. (32b)

- Check compound subjects. Those joined by *and* usually take a plural verb. With those subjects joined by *or* or *nor*, however, the verb agrees with the part of the subject closer or closest to the verb. (32c)

- Check collective-noun subjects. These nouns take a singular verb when they refer to a group as a single unit, but they take a plural verb when they refer to the multiple members of a group. (32d)

- Check indefinite-pronoun subjects. Most take a singular verb. *Both, few, many, others,* and *several* take a plural verb, and *all, any, enough, more, most, none,* and *some* can be either singular or plural. (32e)

Have and *be* do not follow the *-s* or *-es* pattern with third-person singular subjects. *Have* changes to *has; be* has irregular forms in both the present and past tenses (31a).

▶ **War *is* hell.**

▶ **The soldier *was* brave beyond the call of duty.**

32b   Subjects and verbs separated by other words

Make sure the verb agrees with the subject and not with another noun that falls in between.

▶ **A vase of flowers *makes* a room attractive.**

 have
▶ **Many books on the best-seller list ~~has~~ little literary value.**
 ^

The simple subject is *books*, not *list*.

Be careful when you use phrases beginning with *as well as, along with, in addition to, together with,* and similar prepositions. They do not make a singular subject plural.

 was
▶ **A passenger, as well as the driver, ~~were~~ injured in the accident.**
 ^

Though this sentence has a grammatically singular subject, it suggests a plural subject. The sentence makes better sense with a compound subject: *The driver and a passenger were injured in the accident.*

EXERCISE 32.1

Underline the appropriate verb form in each of the following sentences. Example:

The benefits of family planning (*is*/*are*) not apparent to many peasants.

1. Soldiers who are injured while fighting for their country (*deserves*/*deserve*) complete medical coverage.

2. The dog, followed by his owner, (*races*/*race*) wildly down the street every afternoon.

3. Just when I think I can go home, another pile of invoices (*appears*/*appear*) on my desk.

4. The system of sororities and fraternities (*supplies*/*supply*) much of the social life on some college campuses.

5. The buck (*stops*/*stop*) here.

6. The police officer, in addition to a couple of pedestrians, (*was*/*were*) pinned to the wall as the crowd rushed by.

7. Garlic's therapeutic value as well as its flavor (*comes*/*come*) from sulfur compounds.

8. The fiber content of cereal (*contributes*/*contribute*) to its nutritional value.

9. The graphics on this computer game often (*causes*/*cause*) my system to crash.

10. Current research on AIDS, in spite of the best efforts of hundreds of scientists, (*leaves*/*leave*) serious questions unanswered.

32c Compound subjects

Subjects joined by *and* generally require a plural verb form.

▶ A backpack, a canteen, and a rifle ~~was~~ issued to each recruit.
  ^*were*

When subjects joined by *and* are considered a single unit or refer to the same person or thing, they take a singular verb form.

▶ George W. Bush's older brother and political ally *was* the governor of Florida.

▶ Drinking and driving ~~remain~~ a major cause of highway accidents
  ^*remains*

and fatalities.

In this sentence, *drinking and driving* is considered a single activity, and a singular verb is used.

If the word *each* or *every* precedes subjects joined by *and,* the verb form is singular.

▶ **Each boy and girl** *chooses* **one gift to take home.**

With subjects joined by *or* or *nor,* the verb agrees with the part closer or closest to the verb.

▶ **Either the witnesses or the defendant** *is* **lying.**

If you find this sentence awkward, put the plural noun closer to the verb: *Either the defendant or the witnesses are lying.*

32d Collective-noun subjects

Collective nouns — such as *family, team, audience, group, jury, crowd, band, class,* and *committee* — refer to a group. Collective nouns can take either singular or plural verbs, depending on whether they refer to the group as a single unit or to the multiple members of the group. The meaning of a sentence as a whole is your guide to whether a collective noun refers to a unit or to the multiple parts of a unit.

▶ **After deliberating, the jury** *reports* **its verdict.**

The jury acts as a single unit.

▶ **The jury still** *disagree* **on a number of counts.**

The members of the jury act as multiple individuals.

scatter
▶ **The family of ducklings** ~~scatters~~ **when the cat approaches.**

Family here refers to the many ducks; they cannot scatter as one.

Treat fractions that refer to singular nouns as singular and those that refer to plural nouns as plural.

▶ **Two-thirds of the park** *has* **burned.**

Two-thirds refers to the single portion of the park that burned.

▶ **Two-thirds of the students** *were* **commuters.**

Two-thirds here refers to the students who commuted as many individuals.

Even though *eyeglasses, scissors, pants,* and other such words refer to single items, they take plural verbs because they are made up of pairs.

▶ **Where *are* my reading glasses?**

Treat phrases starting with *the number of* as singular and with *a number of* as plural.

SINGULAR   The number of applicants for the internship *was* amazing.

PLURAL   A number of applicants *were* put on the waiting list.

32e Indefinite-pronoun subjects

Indefinite pronouns do not refer to specific persons or things. Most take singular verb forms.

SOME COMMON INDEFINITE PRONOUNS

another	each	much	one
any	either	neither	other
anybody	everybody	nobody	somebody
anyone	everyone	no one	someone
anything	everything	nothing	something

▶ **Of the two jobs, neither *holds* much appeal.**

depicts
▶ **Each of the plays ~~depict~~ a hero undone by a tragic flaw.**

Both, few, many, others, and *several* are plural.

▶ **Though many *apply,* few *are* chosen.**

All, any, enough, more, most, none, and *some* can be singular or plural, depending on the noun they refer to.

▶ **All of the cake *was* eaten.**

▶ **All of the candidates *promise* to improve the schools.**

32f   Antecedents of *who, which,* and *that*

When the relative pronouns *who, which,* and *that* are used as a subject, the verb agrees with the antecedent of the pronoun (see 30d and 33f).

▶ Fear is an ingredient that *goes* into creating stereotypes.

▶ Guilt and fear are ingredients that *go* into creating stereotypes.

Problems often occur with the words *one of the.* In general, *one of the* takes a plural verb, while *the only one of the* takes a singular verb.

work

▶ Carla is one of the employees who always ~~works~~ overtime.

> Some employees always work overtime. Carla is among them. Thus *who* refers to *employees,* and the verb is plural.

works

▶ Ming is the only one of the employees who always ~~work~~ overtime.

> Only one employee always works overtime, and that employee is Ming. Thus *one,* not *employees,* is the antecedent of *who,* and the verb form is singular.

32g   Linking verbs

A linking verb (30k) should agree with its subject, which usually precedes the verb, not with the subject complement, that follows it.

are

▶ The three key treaties ~~is~~ the topic of my talk.

> The subject is *treaties,* not *topic.*

was

▶ Nero Wolfe's passion ~~were~~ orchids.

> The subject is *passion,* not *orchids.*

32h   Subjects that are plural in form but singular in meaning

Some words that end in *-s* appear plural but are singular in meaning and thus take singular verb forms.

strikes

▶ Measles still ~~strike~~ many Americans.

Some nouns of this kind (such as *statistics* and *politics*) may be either singular or plural, depending on context.

SINGULAR   Statistics *is* a course I really dread.

PLURAL   The statistics in that study *are* highly questionable.

32i   Subjects that follow verbs

In English, verbs usually follow subjects. When this order is reversed, make the verb agree with the subject, not with a noun that happens to precede it.

►   *stand*
  Beside the barn s̶t̶a̶n̶d̶s̶ silos filled with grain.
                    ^

  The subject is *silos*; it is plural, so the verb must be *stand*.

In sentences beginning with *there is* or *there are* (or *there was* or *were*), *there* serves only as an introductory word; the subject follows the verb.

► **There *are* five basic positions in classical ballet.**

  The subject, *positions*, is plural, so the verb must also be plural.

32j   Titles and words used as words

►   *describes*
  One Writer's Beginnings **d̶e̶s̶c̶r̶i̶b̶e̶ Eudora Welty's childhood.**
                             ^

►   *is*
  Steroids **a̶r̶e̶ a little word that packs a big punch in the world of sports.**
            ^

EXERCISE 32.2

Revise any of the following sentences as necessary to establish subject-verb agreement. (Some of the sentences do not require any change.) Example:

                darts
Into the shadows d̶a̶r̶t̶ the frightened raccoon.
                 ^

1. If rhythm and blues is your kind of music, try Mary Lou's.

2. *Green Eggs and Ham* are one of Dr. Suess's best-loved children's books.

3. At the intersection is four gas stations.

4. Most of the students oppose the shortened dining hall hours.

5. Each of the security workers are considered trained after viewing a twenty-minute videotape.

6. Neither his charm nor his expensive wardrobe were enough to get him the job.

7. A jury rarely make a decision based on evidence alone.

8. My grandmother is the only one of my relatives who still goes to church.

9. Sweden was one of the few European countries that was neutral in 1943.

10. Economics involve the study of the distribution of goods and services.

 bedfordstmartins.com/everydaywriter For exercises, go to **Exercise Central** and click on **Subject-Verb Agreement.**

EXERCISE 32.3: THINKING CRITICALLY

Reading with an Eye for Subject-Verb Agreement

The following passage, from a 1990 essay questioning a "traditional" view of marriage, includes several instances of complicated subject-verb agreement. Note the rules governing subject-verb agreement in each case.

> Marriage seems to me more conflict-ridden than ever, and the divorce rate — with or without new babies in the house — remains constant. The fabric of men-and-women-as-they-once-were is so thin in places no amount of patching can weave that cloth together again. The longing for connection may be strong, but even stronger is the growing perception that only people who are real to themselves can connect. Two shall be as one is over, no matter how lonely we get.
> — VIVIAN GORNICK, "Who Says We Haven't Made a Revolution?"

Thinking about Your Own Use of Subject-Verb Agreement

Visiting relatives is/are treacherous. Either verb makes a grammatically acceptable sentence, yet the verbs result in two very different statements. Write a brief explanation of the two possible meanings. Then write a paragraph or two about visiting relatives. Using the information in this chapter, examine each subject and its verb. Do you maintain subject-verb agreement throughout? Revise to correct any errors you find. If you find any patterns, make a note to yourself of things to look for routinely as you revise your writing.

33 Pronouns

As words that stand in for nouns, pronouns carry a lot of weight in everyday language. These directions show one of the reasons why it's important to use pronouns clearly:

When you see a dirt road turning left off Winston Lane, follow it for two more miles.

The word *it* could mean either the dirt road or Winston Lane. Pronouns can improve understanding, but only when they're used carefully and accurately.

33a Pronoun case

Most speakers of English know intuitively when to use *I, me,* and *my.* Our choices reflect differences in case, the form a pronoun takes to indicate how it acts in a sentence. Pronouns acting as subjects are in the subjective case (*I*); those acting as objects are in the objective case (*me*); those acting as possessives are in the possessive case (*my*).

AT A GLANCE

Editing Pronouns

- Are all pronouns after forms of the verb *be* in the subjective case? *It's me* is common in spoken English, but in writing use *It is I.* (33a)

- To check for correct use of *who* and *whom* (and *whoever* and *whomever*), try substituting *he* or *him.* If *he* is correct, use *who* (or *whoever*); if *him*, use *whom* or *whomever.* (33b)

- In compound structures, make sure any pronouns are in the same case they would be in if used alone (*She and Jake were living in Spain*). (33c)

- When a pronoun follows *than* or *as*, complete the sentence mentally. If the pronoun is the subject of an unstated verb, it should be subjective (*I like her better than he [likes her]*). If it is the object of an unstated verb, make it objective (*I like her better than [I like] him*). (33d)

- If you have used *he, his,* or *him* to refer to *everyone* or another singular indefinite pronoun that includes both males and females, revise the sentence. If you have used *they* to refer to a singular indefinite pronoun, rewrite the sentence. (33f)

- For each pronoun, identify a specific word that it refers to. If you cannot find one specific word, supply one. If the pronoun refers to more than one word, revise the sentence. (33g)

- Check each use of *it, this, that,* and *which* to be sure the pronoun refers to a specific word. (33g)

- Be sure that any use of *you* refers to your specific reader or readers. (33g)

SUBJECTIVE PRONOUNS	OBJECTIVE PRONOUNS	POSSESSIVE PRONOUNS
I	me	my/mine
we	us	our/ours
you	you	your/yours
he/she/it	him/her/it	his/her/hers/its
they	them	their/theirs
who/whoever	whom/whomever	whose

Subjective case

A pronoun should be in the subjective case (*I, we, you, he/she/it, they, who, whoever*) when it is a subject, a subject complement, or an appositive renaming a subject or subject complement.

SUBJECT

She was passionate about recycling.

SUBJECT COMPLEMENT

The main supporter of the recycling program was *she*.

APPOSITIVE RENAMING A SUBJECT OR SUBJECT COMPLEMENT

Three colleagues—Peter, John, and *she*—worked on the program.

Americans routinely use the objective case for subject complements, especially in conversation: *Who's there? It's me.* If the subjective case for a subject complement sounds stilted or awkward (*It's I*), try rewriting the sentence using the pronoun as the subject (*I'm here*).

> ▸ ~~The~~ first person to see Kishore after the awards~~. was she.~~
>   *She was the*

Objective case

Use the objective case (*me, us, you, him/her/it, them*) when a pronoun functions as a direct or indirect object, an object of a preposition, an appositive renaming an object, or a subject of an infinitive.

DIRECT OBJECT

The boss surprised *her* with a big raise.

INDIRECT OBJECT

The owner gave *him* a reward.

OBJECT OF A PREPOSITION

Several friends went with *me.*

APPOSITIVE RENAMING AN OBJECT

The students elected two representatives, Joan and *me.*

SUBJECT OF AN INFINITIVE

The students convinced *him* to vote for the school bond.

Possessive case

Use the possessive case when a pronoun shows possession or ownership. The adjective forms of possessive pronouns (*my, our, your, his/her/its, their, whose*) are used before nouns or gerunds, and noun forms (*mine, ours, yours, his/hers/its, theirs, whose*) take the place of a possessive noun. Possessive pronouns do not include apostrophes (41a).

BEFORE A NOUN

The sound of *her* voice came right through the walls.

IN PLACE OF A POSSESSIVE NOUN

The responsibility is *hers.*

Pronouns before a gerund should be in the possessive case.

> his
> ► I remember ~~him~~ singing.
>   ^

His modifies the gerund *singing.*

33b Who, whoever, whom, and whomever

A common problem with pronoun case is deciding whether to use *who* or *whom.* Use *who* and *whoever,* which act as subjects, for subjects or subject complements. Use *whom* and *whomever,* to act as objects. The most common confusion with *who* and *whom* occurs when they begin a question and when they introduce a dependent clause.

In questions

You can determine whether to use *who* or *whom* at the beginning of a question by answering the question using a personal pronoun. If the answer is *he, she,* or *they,* use *who;* if it is *him, her,* or *them,* use *whom.*

TALKING THE TALK

Correctness or Stuffiness?

"Everyone has their opinion sounds a lot better than *Everyone has his or her opinion.* And I've never said *whom* in my life. Why should I write that way?"* Over time, the conventions governing certain usages — such as *who* versus *whom,* or *their* versus *his or her* to refer to an indefinite pronoun like *everyone* — have become much more relaxed. To many people, *Whom did you talk to?* and *No one finished his or her test* — both of which are technically "correct"— sound unpleasantly fussy. However, others object to less formal constructions such as *Who did you talk to?* and *No one finished their test.* How can you please everyone? Unfortunately, you can't. Make comfortable choices in informal speaking and writing, but be more careful in formal situations. If you don't know whether your audience will prefer more or less formality, try recasting your sentence to avoid such constructions.

Whom
▶ ~~Who~~ did you visit?
  ^

I visited *them. Them* is objective; thus *whom* is correct.

Who
▶ ~~Whom~~ do you think wrote the story?
  ^

I think *she* wrote the story. *She* is subjective; thus *who* is correct.

In dependent clauses

The case of a pronoun in a dependent clause is determined by its purpose in the clause, no matter how that clause functions in the sentence. If the pronoun acts as a subject or subject complement in the clause, use *who* or *whoever.* If the pronoun acts as an object in the clause, use *whom* or *whomever.*

                                        who
▶ Anyone can hypnotize someone ~~whom~~ wants to be hypnotized.
                                    ^

The verb of the clause is *wants,* and its subject is *who.*

Whomever
▶ ~~Whoever~~ the party suspected of disloyalty was executed.
  ^

Whomever is the object of *suspected* in the clause *whomever the party suspected of disloyalty.*

If you are not sure, try separating the dependent clause from the rest of the sentence and looking at it in isolation. Then rewrite the clause as a new sentence, and substitute a personal pronoun for *who(ever)* or *whom(ever).* If you substitute *he, she,* or *they,* use *who* or *whoever;* if *him, her,* or *them* is correct, use *whom* or *whomever.*

▶ **The minister grimaced at (*whoever/whomever*) made any noise.**

Isolate the clause *whoever/whomever made any noise.* Substituting a personal pronoun gives you *they made any noise. They* acts as the subject; therefore, *The minister grimaced at whoever made any noise.*

▶ **The minister smiled at (*whoever/whomever*) she greeted.**

Isolate and rearrange the clause to get *she greeted whoever/whomever.* Substituting a personal pronoun gives you *she greeted them. Them* acts as an object; therefore, *The minister smiled at whomever she greeted.*

▶ **The minister grimaced at *whoever* she thought made the noise.**

Ignore such expressions as *he thinks* and *she says* when you isolate the clause.

EXERCISE 33.1

Insert *who, whoever, whom,* or *whomever* appropriately in the blank in each of the following sentences. Example:

She is someone ___*who*___ will go far.

1. _____ did you say was our most likely suspect?
2. _____ the committee recommends is likely to receive a job offer.
3. The manager promised to reward _____ sold the most cars.
4. Professor Quiñones asked _____ we wanted to collaborate with.
5. _____ received the highest score?

33c Case in compound structures

When a pronoun is part of a compound subject, complement, object, or appositive, put it in the same case you would use if the pronoun were alone.

▶ When ~~him~~ *he* and Zelda were first married, they lived in New York.

▶ The boss invited ~~she~~ *her* and her family to dinner.

▶ This morning saw yet another conflict between my sister and ~~I.~~ *me.*

▶ Both panelists — Javonne and ~~me,~~ *I* —were stumped.

To decide whether to use the subjective or objective case in a compound structure, mentally delete the rest of the compound and try the pronoun alone.

> *me.*
> ► Come to the park with Anh and ~~I.~~
> ^

  Mentally deleting *Anh and* results in *Come to the park with I.* Rewrite as *Come to the park with Anh and me.*

33d Case in elliptical constructions

In elliptical constructions, some words are understood but left out. When an elliptical construction ends in a pronoun, put the pronoun in the case it would be in if the construction were complete.

> ► His sister has always been more athletic than *he* [is].

In some elliptical constructions, the case of the pronoun depends on the meaning intended.

> ► Willie likes Lily more than *she* [likes Lily].

  She is the subject of the omitted verb *likes.*

> ► Willie likes Lily more than [he likes] *her.*

  Her is the object of the omitted verb *likes.*

33e *We* and *us* before a noun

If you are unsure about whether to use *we* or *us* before a noun, recast the sentence without the noun. Use whichever pronoun would be correct if the noun were omitted.

> *We*
> ► ~~Us~~ fans never give up hope.
> ^

  Without *fans, we* would be the subject.

> *us*
> ► The Rangers depend on ~~we~~ fans.
> ^

  Without *fans, us* would be the object of a preposition.

EXERCISE 33.2

Underline the appropriate pronoun from the pair in parentheses in each of the following sentences. Example:

  The possibility of (*their*/*them*) succeeding never occurred to me.

1. Max has had more car accidents than Ruby, but he still insists he is a better driver than (*she*/*her*).

2. Going to the ballpark with Uncle Henry and (*they/them*) made everyone feel ten years younger.

3. The coach gave honorable-mention ribbons to the two who didn't win any races — Aiden and (*I/me*).

4. We tried to think of an explanation for (*them/their*) winning the game against all odds.

5. Tomorrow (*we/us*) recruits will have our first on-the-job test.

33f Pronoun-antecedent agreement

The antecedent of a pronoun is the word the pronoun refers to. The antecedent usually appears before the pronoun — earlier in the sentence or in the prior sentence. Pronouns and antecedents are said to agree when they match up in person, number, and gender.

SINGULAR   The *choirmaster* raised *his* baton.

PLURAL   The *boys* picked up *their* music.

Compound antecedents

Compound antecedents joined by *and* require plural pronouns.

▶ **My parents and I tried to resolve *our* disagreement.**

When *each* or *every* precedes a compound antecedent, however, it takes a singular pronoun.

Every *plant* and *animal* has *its* own ecological niche.

With a compound antecedent joined by *or* or *nor,* the pronoun agrees with the nearer or nearest antecedent. If the parts of the antecedent are of different genders, however, this kind of sentence can be awkward or ambiguous and may need to be revised.

AWKWARD   Neither Annie nor Barry got *his* work done.

REVISED   Annie didn't get *her* work done, and neither did Barry.

When a compound antecedent contains both singular and plural parts, the sentence may sound awkward unless the plural part comes last.

▶ **Neither the newspaper nor the radio stations would reveal *their* sources.**

Collective-noun antecedents

A collective noun that refers to a single unit (*herd, team, audience*) requires a singular pronoun.

▶ The *audience* fixed *its* attention on center stage.

When such an antecedent refers to the multiple parts of a unit, however, it requires a plural pronoun.

▶ The director chose this *cast* for the play because *they* had experience in the roles.

Indefinite-pronoun antecedents

Indefinite pronouns are those that do not refer to specific persons or things. Most indefinite pronouns are always singular; a few are always plural. Some can be singular or plural depending on the context.

▶ *One* of the ballerinas lost *her* balance.

▶ *Many* in the audience jumped to *their* feet.

SINGULAR   *Some* of the furniture was showing *its* age.

PLURAL   *Some* of the farmers abandoned *their* land.

Sexist pronouns

Indefinite pronouns often serve as antecedents that may be either male or female. Writers used to use a masculine pronoun, known as the generic *he*, to refer to such indefinite pronouns. However, such wording ignores or even excludes females.

When the antecedent is *anybody, each,* or *everyone,* some people avoid the generic *he* by using a plural pronoun.

▶ *Everyone* should know *their* legal rights.

You will hear such sentences in conversation and even see them in writing, but many people in academic contexts still consider *anybody, each,* and *everyone* singular, and they think using *their* with singular antecedents is too informal. They prefer one of the solutions in the box.

Editing Out Sexist Pronouns

Everyone should know his *legal rights.*

Here are three ways to express the same idea without *his*:

1. Revise to make the antecedent a plural noun.
   All citizens should know their *legal rights.*

2. Revise the sentence altogether.
   Everyone should have some knowledge of basic legal rights.

3. Use both masculine and feminine pronouns.
   Everyone should know his *or* her *legal rights.*

   This third option, using both masculine and feminine pronouns, can be awkward, especially when repeated several times in a passage.

EXERCISE 33.3

Revise the following sentences as needed to create pronoun-antecedent agreement and to eliminate the generic *he* and any awkward pronoun references. Some can be revised in more than one way. Example:

or her

Every graduate submitted his diploma card.

All graduates *their* *cards.*

~~Every graduate~~ submitted ~~his~~ diploma ~~card.~~

1. With tuition on the rise, a student has to save money wherever they can.

2. Congress usually resists a president's attempt to encroach on what they consider their authority.

3. Marco and Ellen were each given a chance to voice their opinion.

4. Although a firefighter spends most of his days reading and watching television, he is ready to answer an urgent call at a moment's notice.

5. Every dog and cat has their own personality.

33g Clear pronoun reference

The antecedent of a pronoun is the word the pronoun substitutes for. If a pronoun is too far from its antecedent, readers will have trouble making the connection between the two.

Ambiguous antecedents

Readers have trouble when a pronoun can refer to more than one antecedent.

▶ The car went over the bridge just before ~~it~~ fell into the water.
the bridge

What fell into the water—the car or the bridge? The revision makes the meaning clear.

▶ Kerry told Ellen**,** ~~she~~ should be ready soon.**"**
"I

Reporting Kerry's words directly, in quotation marks, eliminates the ambiguity.

Vague use of it, this, that, *and* which

The words *it, this, that,* and *which* often function as a shortcut for referring to something mentioned earlier. But such shortcuts can cause confusion. Like other pronouns, each must refer to a specific antecedent.

▶ When the senators realized the bill would be defeated, they tried to postpone the vote but failed. ~~It~~ was a fiasco.
The entire effort

▶ Nancy just found out that she won the lottery, ~~which~~ explains her sudden resignation from her job.
and that news

Indefinite use of you, it, *and* they

In conversation, we frequently use *you, it,* and *they* in an indefinite sense in such expressions as *you never know; in the paper, it said;* and *they say.* In academic and professional writing, however, use *you* only to mean "you, the reader," and *they* or *it* only to refer to a clear antecedent.

▶ Commercials try to make ~~you~~ buy without thinking.
people

▶ ~~On the~~ Weather Channel**/** ~~it~~ reported that an earthquake devastated parts of Pakistan.
The

▶ ~~In France, they~~ allow dogs**.** ~~in many restaurants.~~
Many restaurants in France

Possessive antecedents

A possessive may *suggest* a noun antecedent but does not serve as a clear antecedent.

> ► In Alexa's formal complaint, she showed why the test question was wrong.

her ... *Alexa*

EXERCISE 33.4

Revise each of the following items to clarify pronoun reference. Most of the items can be revised in more than one way. If a pronoun refers ambiguously to more than one possible antecedent, revise the sentence to reflect each possible meaning. Example:

> *Miranda found Jane's keys after*
> After Jane left. Miranda found her keys.
>
> *Miranda found her own keys after*
> After Jane left. Miranda found her keys.

1. All scholarship applicants must fill out a financial aid form, meet with the dean, and write a letter to the committee members. The deadline is October 24, so they should start the process as soon as possible.

2. Patients on medication may relate better to their therapists, be less vulnerable to what disturbs them, and be more responsive to them.

3. Sasha hurried to call her sister before she flew to Brazil.

4. In Texas, you often hear about the influence of big oil corporations.

5. The parents ignored the child's tantrum, which annoyed many other people in the restaurant.

EXERCISE 33.5

Revise the following paragraph to establish a clear antecedent for every pronoun that needs one.

> In the summer of 2005, the NCAA banned the use of mascots that could be considered offensive to American Indians at any of their championship games. In order to understand this, it is important to consider that movies and television programs for years portrayed them as savage warriors that were feared and misunderstood. That is why some schools have chosen to use Indians as their mascot, a role typically played by wild animals or fictional beasts. You would not tolerate derogatory terms for other ethnic groups being used for school mascots. In the NCAA's new ruling, they ask schools to eliminate mascots that may be hurtful or offensive to America's Indian population.

 bedfordstmartins.com/everydaywriter For exercises, go to **Exercise Central** and click on **Pronouns.**

EXERCISE 33.6: THINKING CRITICALLY

Reading with an Eye for Pronouns

Read the following passage, paying special attention to every pronoun: What antecedent does it refer to, and is the reference clear and direct? Does the use of any one pronoun case seem overused? Then go through and replace every pronoun with what it refers to, and read the two versions side by side to see the efficiency of good pronoun use.

> Sexual attraction has entered the Harry Potter universe. Harry (Daniel Radcliffe) is now 14, and he's one of four contestants competing in the dangerous Tri-Wizard Tournament. The first event requires him to capture a golden egg that's guarded by a ferocious Hungarian flying dragon. Terrifying as this is, it pales in comparison with having to ask the beguiling Cho Chang (Katie Leung) to Hogwarts's Yule Ball. Now, *that* takes courage. . . .
>
> The uncontestable triumph of "Goblet of Fire," however, is Brendan Gleeson's Alastor (Mad-Eye) Moody, the grizzled new Defense Against the Dark Arts professor. With a face like cracked pottery and a manner both menacing and mentoring, he becomes Harry's protector as he faces life-threatening tests. Gleeson, one of the screen's greatest character actors, steals every scene he's in — no small feat when you're up against Maggie Smith and Alan Rickman.
>
> — DAVID ANSEN

Thinking about Your Own Use of Pronouns

Turn to a recent piece of your writing (something at least four pages long), and analyze your use of pronouns. Look carefully at the pronoun case you tend to use most; if it is first person, ask whether *I* is used too much. And if you find that you rely heavily on any one case (*you*, for example), decide whether your writing seems monotonous as a result. Take a look as well at whether you tend to use masculine pronouns exclusively to refer to people generally; if so, ask whether you would be more inclusive if you used both masculine and feminine pronouns or if you should revise to use plural pronouns that are not marked as either masculine or feminine (such as *we* or *they*). Finally, check to make sure that your pronouns and their antecedents agree and that the pronouns refer clearly and directly to antecedents

Adjectives and Adverbs | **34**

Adjectives and adverbs often bring indispensable differences in meaning to the words they modify. In basketball, for example, there is an important difference between a *flagrant* foul and a *technical* foul, a *layup* and a *reverse* layup, and an *angry* coach and an *abusively angry* coach. In each instance, the modifiers are crucial to accurate communication.

Adjectives modify nouns and pronouns; they answer the questions *which? how many?* and *what kind?* Adverbs modify verbs, adjectives, and other adverbs; they answer the questions *how? when? where?* and *to what extent?* Many adverbs are formed by adding *-ly* to adjectives (*slight, slightly*), but many adverbs are formed in other ways (*outdoors*) or have forms of their own (*very*).

AT A GLANCE

Editing Adjectives and Adverbs

- Scrutinize each adjective and adverb. Consider synonyms for each word to see whether you have chosen the best word possible.

- See if a more specific noun would eliminate the need for an adjective (*mansion* rather than *enormous house*, for instance). Do the same with verbs and adverbs.

- Look for places where you might make your writing more specific or vivid by adding an adjective or adverb.

- Check that adjectives modify only nouns and pronouns and that adverbs modify only verbs, adjectives, and other adverbs. (34b) Check especially for proper use of *good* and *well*, *bad* and *badly*, *real* and *really*. (34b and c)

- Make sure all comparisons are complete. (34c)

- If English is not your first language, check that adjectives are in the right order. (57f)

34a Adjectives after linking verbs

When adjectives come after linking verbs, they usually serve as a subject complement, to describe the subject: *I am patient.* Note that in specific sentences, some verbs may or may not be linking verbs — *appear, become, feel, grow, look, make, prove, seem, smell, sound,* and *taste,* for instance. When a word following one of these verbs modifies the subject, use an adjective; when it modifies the verb, use an adverb.

ADJECTIVE   Fluffy looked *angry.*

ADVERB   Fluffy looked *angrily* at the poodle.

Linking verbs suggest a state of being, not an action. In the preceding examples, *looked angry* suggests the state of being angry; *looked angrily* suggests an angry action.

FOR MULTILINGUAL WRITERS

Using Adjectives with Plural Nouns

In Spanish, Russian, and many other languages, adjectives agree in number with the nouns they modify. In English, adjectives do not change number this way: *the kittens are cute* (not *cutes*).

34b **Adverbs to modify verbs, adjectives, and adverbs**

In everyday conversation, you will often hear (and perhaps use) adjectives in place of adverbs. For example, people often say *go quick* instead of *go quickly.* When you write in standard academic English, however, use adverbs to modify verbs, adjectives, and other adverbs.

▶ You can feel the song's meter if you listen ~~careful.~~ *carefully.*

▶ The audience was ~~real~~ *really* disappointed by the show.

Good, well, bad, *and* badly

The modifiers *good, well, bad,* and *badly* cause problems for many writers because the distinctions between *good* and *well* and between *bad* and *badly* are often not observed in conversation. Problems also arise because *well* can function as either an adjective or an adverb. *Good* and *bad* are always adjectives, and both can be used after a linking verb.

▶ The weather looks *good* today.

▶ He plays the trumpet ~~good~~ *well* and the trombone not ~~bad.~~ *badly.*

Badly is an adverb and can modify a verb, an adjective, or another adverb. After a linking verb, use *bad* instead.

>   *bad*
> ▶ **I feel ~~badly~~ for the Toronto fans.**
>   ^

The linking verb *feel* requires the adjective *bad.*

As an adjective, *well* means "in good health"; as an adverb, it means "in a good way" or "thoroughly."

ADJECTIVE	After a week of rest, Julio felt *well* again.
ADVERB	She plays *well* enough to make the team.

EXERCISE 34.1

Revise each of the following sentences to correct adverb and adjective use. Then identify each adjective or adverb that you have revised, and point out the word each modifies. Example:

>   *superbly*
> The attorney delivered a ~~superb~~ conceived summation.
>   ^

1. Getting tickets at this late date is near impossible.
2. Derek apologized for behaving so immature on the football field.
3. Nora felt badly that the package would arrive one week later than promised.
4. The summers are real hot and humid here.
5. He talked loud about volunteering, but he was not really interested.
6. Paramedics rushed to help the victim, who was bleeding bad from the head.
7. The skater performed good despite the intense competition.
8. Arjun felt terrifically about his discussion with Professor Greene.
9. After we added cinnamon, the stew tasted really well.
10. Scientists measured the crater as accurate as possible.

FOR MULTILINGUAL WRITERS

Determining Adjective Sequence

Should you write *these beautiful blue kitchen tiles* or *these blue beautiful kitchen tiles*? See 57f for guidelines on adjective sequence.

34c   Comparatives and superlatives

Most adjectives and adverbs have three forms: positive, comparative, and superlative.

POSITIVE	COMPARATIVE	SUPERLATIVE
large	larger	largest
early	earlier	earliest
careful	more careful	most careful
happily	more happily	most happily

► Canada is *larger* than the United States.

► My son needs to be *more careful* with his money.

► They are the *most happily* married couple I know.

Form the comparative and superlative of most one- or two-syllable adjectives by adding *-er* and *-est*. With some two-syllable adjectives, longer adjectives, and most adverbs, use *more* and *most: scientific, more scientific, most scientific; elegantly, more elegantly, most elegantly.* If you are not sure, consult the dictionary entry for the simple form.

Irregular adjectives and adverbs

Some short adjectives and adverbs have irregular comparative and superlative forms.

POSITIVE	COMPARATIVE	SUPERLATIVE
good, well	better	best
bad, badly	worse	worst
little (quantity)	less	least
many, much, some	more	most

Comparatives vs. superlatives

Use the comparative to compare two things; use the superlative to compare three or more.

► Rome is a much *older* city than New York.

► Damascus is one of the ~~older~~ cities in the world.
     oldest
     ^

Double comparatives and superlatives

Double comparatives and superlatives are those that unnecessarily use both the *-er* or *-est* ending and *more* or *most*. Occasionally, these forms can act to build a special emphasis, as in the title of Spike Lee's movie *Mo' Better Blues*. In academic and professional writing, however, do not use *more* or *most* before adjectives or adverbs ending in *-er* or *-est.*

▶ Paris is the ~~most~~ loveliest city in the world.

Incomplete comparisons

In speaking, we sometimes state only part of a comparison because the context makes the meaning clear. For example, you might tell a friend "Your car is better," but the context makes it clear that you mean "Your car is better *than mine.*" In writing, take the time to check for incomplete comparisons — and to complete them if they are unclear.

than those receiving a placebo.

▶ The patients taking the drug appeared healthier/
⌃

Absolute concepts

Some adjectives and adverbs — such as *perfect, final,* and *unique* — are absolute concepts, so it is illogical to form comparatives or superlatives of these words.

a

▶ Anne has ~~the most~~ unique sense of humor.
⌃

EXERCISE 34.2

Revise each of the following sentences to use modifiers correctly, clearly, and effectively. Many of the sentences can be revised in more than one way. Example:

bill to approve a financial plan for the
He is sponsoring a housing project. ~~finance plan approval bill.~~
⌃   ⌃

1. Alicia speaks both Russian and German, but she speaks Russian best.
2. People in Rome are more friendlier to children than people in Paris are.
3. The crown is set with some of the preciousest gemstones in the world.
4. Most of the elderly are women because women tend to live longer.
5. Minneapolis is the largest of the Twin Cities.

6. She came up with the most perfect plan for revenge.
7. We think you will be pleased with our very unique design proposal.
8. The student cafeteria is operated by a college food service system chain.
9. It is safer to jog in daylight.
10. Evan argued that subtitled films are boringer to watch than films dubbed in English.

TALKING ABOUT STYLE

Multiple Negation

Speakers of English sometimes use more than one negative at a time (*I can't hardly see you*). Multiple negatives, in fact, have a long history in English and can be found in the works of Chaucer and Shakespeare. It was only in the eighteenth century, in an effort to make English more uniform, that double negatives came to be seen as incorrect. Emphatic double negatives — and triple, quadruple, and more — are used in many varieties of spoken English (*Don't none of you know nothing at all*).

Even though multiple negatives occur in many varieties of English (and in many other languages), in academic or professional writing you will play it safe if you avoid them — unless you are quoting dialogue or creating a special effect.

---

 bedfordstmartins.com/everydaywriter For exercises, go to **Exercise Central** and click on **Adjectives and Adverbs**.

EXERCISE 34.3: THINKING CRITICALLY

Reading with an Eye for Adjectives and Adverbs

They came back to camp wonderfully refreshed, glad-hearted, and ravenous; and they soon had the camp-fire blazing up again. Huck found a spring of clear cold water close by, and the boys made cups of broad oak or hickory leaves, and felt that water, sweetened with such a wildwood charm as that, would be a good enough substitute for coffee.   — MARK TWAIN, *Tom Sawyer*

Identify the adjectives and adverbs in the preceding passage, and comment on what they add to the writing. What would be lost if they were removed?

Thinking about Your Own Use of Adjectives and Adverbs

Take a few minutes to study something you can observe or examine closely. In a paragraph or two, describe your subject for someone who has never seen it. Using the guidelines in this chapter, check your use of adjectives and adverbs, and revise your paragraphs. How would you characterize your use of adjectives and adverbs?

Modifier Placement 35

Modifiers enrich writing by making it more concrete or vivid, often adding important or even essential details. To be effective, modifiers should refer clearly to the words they modify and be positioned close to those words. Consider, for example, a sign seen recently in a hotel:

> DO NOT USE THE ELEVATORS IN CASE OF FIRE.

Should we really avoid the elevators altogether for fear of causing a fire? Repositioning the modifier *in case of fire* eliminates such confusion — and makes clear that we are to avoid the elevators only if there is a fire: IN CASE OF FIRE, DO NOT USE THE ELEVATORS. This chapter reviews the conventions of accurate modifier placement.

AT A GLANCE

Editing Misplaced or Dangling Modifiers

1. Identify all the modifiers in each sentence, and draw an arrow from each modifier to the word it modifies.

2. If a modifier is far from the word it modifies, try to move the two closer together. (35a)

3. Does any modifier seem to refer to a word other than the one it is intended to modify? If so, move the modifier so that it refers clearly to only the intended word. (35a)

4. If you cannot find the word to which a modifier refers, revise the sentence: supply such a word, or revise the modifier itself so that it clearly refers to a word already in the sentence. (35c)

35a Misplaced modifiers

Modifiers can cause confusion or ambiguity if they are not close enough to the words they modify or if they seem to modify more than one word in the sentence.

▶ She teaches a seminar this term ~~on voodoo~~ *on voodoo* at Skyline College.

The voodoo was not at the college; the seminar is.

▶ ~~Billowing from every window,~~ *He* ~~he~~ saw clouds of smoke, *billowing from every window.*

People cannot billow from windows.

> *After he lost the 1962 gubernatorial race,*
> ▶ Nixon told reporters that he planned to get out of politics . ~~after he lost~~
>   ^   ^
>   ~~the 1962 gubernatorial race.~~

The unedited sentence implies that Nixon planned to lose the race.

EXERCISE 35.1

Revise each of the following sentences by moving any misplaced modifiers so that they clearly modify the words they should. Example:

When they propose sensible plans, politicians
~~Politicians~~ earn support from the people. ~~when they propose sensible plans.~~
^   ^

1. The comedian had the audience doubled over with laughter relating her stories in a deadpan voice.

2. News reports can increase a listener's irrational fears that emphasize random crime or rare diseases.

3. Studying legal documents and court records from hundreds of years ago, ordinary people in the Middle Ages teach us about everyday life at that time.

4. Risking their lives in war zones, civilians learn about the conflict from the first-hand accounts of journalists abroad.

5. We recorded a wolf pack at play with our new digital camera while we were camping last summer.

6. Doctors recommend a new test for cancer, which is painless.

7. Every afternoon I find flyers for free pizza on my windshield.

8. I knew that the investment would pay off in a dramatic way before I decided to buy the stock.

9. The bank offered flood insurance to the homeowners underwritten by the federal government.

10. Revolving out of control, the maintenance worker shut down the turbine.

Limiting modifiers

Be especially careful with the placement of limiting modifiers such as *almost, even, just, merely,* and *only.* In general, these modifiers should be placed right before or after the words they modify. Putting them in other positions may produce not just ambiguity but a completely different meaning.

AMBIGUOUS	The court *only* hears civil cases on Tuesdays.
CLEAR	The court hears *only* civil cases on Tuesdays.
CLEAR	The court hears civil cases on Tuesdays *only.*

In the first sentence, placing *only* before *hears* makes the meaning ambiguous. Does the writer mean that civil cases are the only cases heard on Tuesdays or that those are the only days when civil cases are heard?

▶ The city ~~almost~~ spent $20 million on the new stadium.

almost ^

The original sentence suggests the money was almost spent; moving *almost* makes clear that the amount spent was almost $20 million.

Squinting modifiers

If a modifier can refer to either the word before it or the word after it, it is a squinting modifier. Put the modifier where it clearly relates to only a single word.

SQUINTING	Students who practice writing *often* will benefit.
REVISED	Students who *often* practice writing will benefit.
REVISED	Students who practice writing will *often* benefit.

EXERCISE 35.2

Revise each of the following sentences in at least two ways. Move the limiting or squinting modifier so that it unambiguously modifies one word or phrase in the sentence. Example:

completely
The course we hoped would engross us ~~completely~~ bored us.
^

completely.
The course we hoped would engross us ~~completely~~ bored us ⁄
^

1. The administrator promised quickly to reduce class size.
2. The soldier was apparently injured by friendly fire.
3. The collector who owned the painting originally planned to leave it to a museum.
4. Doctors can now restore limbs that have been severed partially to a functioning condition.
5. Ever since I was a child, I have only liked green peas with ham.

35b Disruptive modifiers

Disruptive modifiers interrupt the connections between parts of a grammatical structure or a sentence, making it hard for readers to follow the progress of the thought.

▶ *If they are cooked too long, vegetables will*
~~Vegetables will, if they are cooked too long,~~ lose most of their
  ^
nutritional value.

In general, do not place a modifier between the *to* and the verb of an infinitive (*to often complain*). Doing so makes it hard for readers to recognize that the two go together.

surrender
▶ Hitler expected the British to fairly quickly . ~~surrender.~~
                                  ^   ^

In some sentences, however, a modifier sounds awkward if it does not split the infinitive. In such cases, it may be best to reword the sentence to eliminate the infinitive altogether.

SPLIT   I hope *to* almost *equal* my last year's income.

REVISED I hope that I will earn almost as much as I did last year.

EXERCISE 35.3

Revise each of the following sentences by moving the disruptive modifier so that the sentence reads smoothly. Example:

During the recent economic depression, many
~~Many~~ unemployed college graduates ~~during the recent economic depression~~
                                       ^
attended graduate school.

1. Strong economic times have, statistics tell us, led to increases in the college dropout rate.

2. Sometimes in negotiations a radical proposal, due to its shock value, stimulates creative thinking by labor and management.

3. The court's ruling allows cities to lawfully seize private property and sell it to the highest bidder.

4. Michael Jordan earned, at the pinnacle of his career, roughly $40 million a year in endorsements.

5. The stock exchange became, because of the sudden trading, a chaotic circus.

35c Dangling modifiers

Dangling modifiers modify nothing in particular in the rest of a sentence. They often *seem* to modify something that is implied but not actually present in the sentence. Dangling modifiers frequently appear at the beginnings or ends of sentences.

DANGLING   Driving nonstop, Salishan Lodge is located two hours from
            Portland.

REVISED   Driving nonstop from Portland, you can reach Salishan
            Lodge in two hours.

To revise a dangling modifier, often you need to add a subject that the
modifier clearly refers to. In some cases, however, you have to revise
the modifier itself, turning it into a phrase or a clause.

> Reluctantly, the hound ~~was given away~~ to a neighbor.

our family gave away

In the original sentence, was the dog reluctant, or was someone else who is
not mentioned reluctant?

> ~~As~~ a young boy, his grandmother told stories of her years as a country
schoolteacher.

When he was

His grandmother was never a young boy.

> ~~Thumbing through the magazine, my~~ eyes automatically noticed the
perfume ads.

My

as I was thumbing through the magazine.

Eyes cannot thumb through a magazine.

EXERCISE 35.4

Revise each of the following sentences to correct the dangling phrase. Example:

a viewer gets

Watching television news, an impression ~~is given~~ of constant disaster.

1. Determined to increase its audience share, news may become entertainment.

2. Trying to attract younger viewers, news is blended with comedy on late-night
talk shows.

3. Highlighting local events, important international news stories may get overlooked.

4. Chosen for their looks, the journalistic credentials of newscasters may be weak.

5. As a visual medium, complex issues are hard to present on television.

bedfordstmartins.com/everydaywriter For exercises, go to **Exercise Central** and
click on **Modifier Placement**.

EXERCISE 35.5 THINKING CRITICALLY

Reading with an Eye for Modifiers

Look at the limiting modifier italicized in the following passage. Identify which word or words it modifies. Then try moving the modifier to some other spot in the sentence, and consider how the meaning of the sentence changes as a result.

> It was, among other things, the sort of railroad you would occasionally ride *just* for the hell of it, a higher existence into which you would escape unconsciously and without hesitation. — E. B. WHITE, "Progress and Change"

Thinking about Your Own Use of Modifiers

As you examine two pages of a draft, check for clear and effective modifiers. Can you identify any misplaced, disruptive, or dangling modifiers? Using the guidelines in this chapter, revise as need be. Then look for patterns — in the kinds of modifiers you use and in any problems you have placing them. Make a note of what you find.

36 Comma Splices and Fused Sentences

A comma splice results from placing only a comma between clauses. We often see comma splices in advertising and other slogans, where they can provide a catchy rhythm.

> Dogs have owners, cats have staff.
>   – BUMPER STICKER

Another related construction is a fused, or run-on, sentence, which results from joining two independent clauses with no punctuation or connecting word between them. The bumper sticker as a fused sentence would be "Dogs have owners cats have staff."

You will seldom profit from using comma splices or fused sentences in academic or professional writing. In fact, doing so will almost always draw an instructor's criticism.

36a Separate the clauses into two sentences.

The simplest way to revise comma splices or fused sentences is to separate them into two sentences.

COMMA
SPLICE

My mother spends long hours every spring tilling the

soil and moving manure/. ~~this~~ *This* part of gardening is

nauseating.

FUSED
SENTENCE

My mother spends long hours every spring tilling the

This

soil and moving manure. ~~this~~ part of gardening is
                    ^

nauseating.

If the two clauses are very short, making them two sentences may sound abrupt and terse, so some other method of revision is probably preferable.

AT A GLANCE

Editing for Comma Splices and Fused Sentences

If you find no punctuation between two independent clauses — groups of words that can stand alone as sentences — you have identified a fused sentence. If you find two such clauses joined only by a comma, you have identified a comma splice. Here are six methods of editing comma splices and fused sentences. As you edit, look at the sentences before and after the ones you are revising. Doing so will help you determine how a particular method will affect the rhythm of the passage.

1. Separate the clauses into two sentences. (36a)

   It

   ▶ *Education* is an elusive word/. ~~it~~ often means different
                         ^
   things to different people.

2. Link the clauses with a comma and a coordinating conjunction (*and, but, or, nor, for, so,* or *yet*). (36b)

   for

   ▶ *Education* is an elusive word, it often means different things
                       ^
   to different people.

3. Link the clauses with a semicolon. (36c)

   ▶ *Education* is an elusive word/; it often means different
                         ^
   things to different people.

   If the clauses are linked with only a comma and a conjunctive adverb — a word like *however, then, therefore* — add a semicolon.

   ▶ *Education* is an elusive word/; indeed, it often means
                         ^
   different things to different people.

(continued)

4. Recast the two clauses as one independent clause. (36d)

An elusive word, education
▶ ~~Education is an elusive word~~/it often means different
things to different people.

5. Recast one independent clause as a dependent clause. (36e)

because
▶ *Education* is an elusive word/it often means different
things to different people.

6. In informal writing, link the clauses with a dash. (36f)

—
▶ *Education* is an elusive word/its meaning varies.

36b Link the clauses with a comma and a coordinating conjunction.

If the two clauses are closely related and equally important, join them with a comma and a coordinating conjunction (*and, but, or, nor, for, so,* or *yet*). (See 24a.)

and
COMMA   I got up feeling bad, I feel even worse now.
SPLICE

but
FUSED   I should pay my tuition, I need a new car.
SENTENCE

36c Link the clauses with a semicolon.

If the ideas in the two clauses are closely related and you want to give them equal emphasis, link them with a semicolon.

COMMA   This photograph is not at all realistic/ it even uses
SPLICE   dreamlike images to convey its message.

FUSED   The practice of journalism is changing dramatically/
SENTENCE   advances in technology have sped up news cycles.

Be careful when you link clauses with a conjunctive adverb or a transitional phrase. You must precede such words and phrases with a semicolon (see Chapter 39), with a period, or with a comma combined with a coordinating conjunction (24a).

COMMA
SPLICE

Many Third World countries have very high birthrates/; therefore, most of their citizens are young.

FUSED
SENTENCE

Many Third World countries have very high birthrates . T therefore, most of their citizens are young.

FUSED
SENTENCE

Many Third World countries have very high birthrates, *and,* therefore, most of their citizens are young.

SOME CONJUNCTIVE ADVERBS AND TRANSITIONAL PHRASES

also	in contrast	next
anyway	indeed	now
besides	in fact	otherwise
certainly	instead	similarly
finally	likewise	still
furthermore	meanwhile	then
however	moreover	therefore
in addition	namely	thus
incidentally	nevertheless	undoubtedly

FOR MULTILINGUAL WRITERS

Judging Sentence Length

In U.S. academic contexts, readers sometimes find a series of short sentences "choppy" and undesirable. If you want to connect two independent clauses into one sentence, be sure to join them using one of the methods discussed in this chapter so that you avoid creating a comma splice or fused sentence. Another useful tip for writing in American English is to avoid writing several very long sentences in a row. If you find this pattern in your writing, try breaking it up by including a shorter sentence occasionally. (See Chapter 29.)

36d   Rewrite the clauses as one independent clause.

Sometimes you can reduce two spliced or fused independent clauses to a single independent clause.

> COMMA SPLICE   ~~A large part~~ *Most* of my mail is advertisements/~~most of the~~ ~~rest is~~ *and* bills.

TALKING ABOUT STYLE

Comma Splices in Context

Spliced and fused sentences appear frequently in literary and journalistic writing, where they can create momentum with a rush of details:

> Bald eagles are common, ospreys abound, we have herons and mergansers and kingfishers, we have logging with Percherons and Belgians, we have park land and nature trails, we have enough oddballs, weirdos, and loons to satisfy anybody.
>
> – ANNE CAMERON

Context is critical. Depending on the audience, purpose, and situation, many structures commonly considered errors can be appropriate and effective.

36e   Rewrite one independent clause as a dependent clause.

When one independent clause is more important than the other, try converting the less important one to a dependent clause (24b).

> COMMA SPLICE   The arts and crafts movement, *which reacted against mass production,* called for handmade objects/. ~~it reacted against mass production.~~

In the revision, the writer chooses to emphasize the first clause, the one describing what the movement advocated, and to make the second clause, the one describing what it reacted against, into a dependent clause.

> FUSED SENTENCE   *Although* Zora Neale Hurston is regarded as one of America's major novelists, she died in obscurity.

In the revision, the writer chooses to emphasize the second clause and to make the first one into a dependent clause by adding the subordinating conjunction *although*.

36f Link the two clauses with a dash.

In informal writing, you can use a dash to join the two clauses, especially when the second clause elaborates on the first clause.

COMMA
SPLICE
Exercise trends come and go/ this year yoga is hot.

EXERCISE 36.1

Using two of the methods in this chapter, revise each item to correct its comma splice or fused sentence. Use each of the methods at least once. Example:

so
I had misgivings about the marriage, I did not attend the ceremony.

Because
I had misgivings about the marriage, I did not attend the ceremony.

1. Listeners prefer talk shows to classical music, the radio station is changing its programming.
2. The tallest human on record was Robert Wadlow he reached an amazing height of eight feet, eleven inches.
3. Some students read more online than in print, some do the opposite.
4. The number of vaccine manufacturers has plummeted the industry has been hit with a flood of lawsuits.
5. Most crustaceans live in the ocean, some also live on land or in freshwater habitats.
6. She inherited some tribal customs from her grandmother, she knows the sewing technique called Seminole patchwork.
7. Don't throw your soda cans in the trash recycle them.
8. My West Indian neighbor has lived in New England for years, nevertheless, she always feels betrayed by winter.
9. The Hope diamond in the Smithsonian Institution is impressive in fact, it looks even larger in person than online.
10. You adopted the puppy now you'll have to train him.

EXERCISE 36.2

Revise the following paragraph, eliminating all comma splices by using a period or a semicolon. Then revise the paragraph again, this time using any of the other methods in this chapter. Comment on the two revisions. What differences in rhythm do you detect? Which version do you prefer, and why?

> My sister Maria decided to paint her house last summer, thus, she had to buy some paint. She wanted inexpensive paint, at the same time, it had to go on easily and cover well, that combination was unrealistic to start with. She was a complete beginner, on the other hand, she was a hard worker and willing to learn. Maria went out and bought "dark green" paint for $6.99 a gallon, it must have been mostly water, in fact, you could almost see through it. She put one coat of this paint on the house, as a result, her white house turned a streaky light green. Maria was forced to buy all new paint, the job ended up costing more than it would have if she had bought good paint at the start.

 bedfordstmartins.com/everydaywriter For exercises, go to **Exercise Central** and click on **Comma Splices and Fused Sentences.**

EXERCISE 36.3: THINKING CRITICALLY

Reading with an Eye for Special Effects

Roger Angell is known as a careful and correct stylist, yet he often deviates from the "correct" to create special effects, as in this passage about pitcher David Cone:

> And then he won. Next time out, on August 10th, handed a seven-run lead against the A's, he gave up two runs over six innings, with eight strike-outs. He had tempo, he had poise.   — ROGER ANGELL, "Before the Fall"

Angell uses a comma splice in the last sentence to emphasize parallel ideas; any conjunction, even *and*, would change the causal relationship he wishes to show. Because the splice is unexpected, it attracts just the attention that Angell wants for his statement.

Look through some stories or essays to find comma splices and fused sentences. Copy down one or two and enough of the surrounding text to show context, and comment in writing on the effects they create.

Thinking about Any Comma Splices and Fused Sentences in Your Own Writing

Go through some essays you have written, checking for comma splices and fused sentences. Revise any you find, using one of the methods in this chapter. Comment on your chosen methods.

Sentence Fragments **37**

In advertisements you will find sentence fragments in frequent use.

> Our Lifetime Guarantee may come as a shock. *Or a strut. Or a muffler.* Because once you pay to replace them, Toyota's Lifetime Guarantee covers parts and labor on any dealer-installed muffler, shock, or strut for as long as you own your Toyota! So if anything should ever go wrong, your Toyota dealer will fix it. *Absolutely free.* — TOYOTA ADVERTISEMENT

The three fragments (italicized here) grab our attention, the first two by creating a play on words and the third by emphasizing that something is free.

As this ad illustrates, sentence fragments are groups of words that are punctuated as sentences but lack either a subject or a verb or form only a dependent clause. Although you will often see and hear fragments, you will seldom want to use them in academic or professional writing, where some readers might regard them as errors.

37a Phrase fragments

Phrases are groups of words that lack a subject, a verb, or both (301). When verbal phrases, prepositional phrases, noun phrases, and appositive phrases are punctuated like sentences, they become fragments. To revise these fragments, attach them to an independent clause, or make them a separate sentence.

▶ NBC is broadcasting the debates./ ~~With~~ *with* discussions afterward.

With discussions afterward is a prepositional phrase, not a sentence. The editing combines the phrase with an independent clause.

▶ The town's growth is controlled by zoning laws., *a* A strict set of regulations for builders and corporations.

A strict set of regulations for builders and corporations is an appositive phrase renaming the noun *zoning laws*. The editing attaches the fragment to the sentence containing that noun.

AT A GLANCE

Editing for Sentence Fragments

A group of words must meet three criteria to form a complete sentence. If it does not meet all three, it is a fragment. Revise a fragment by combining it with a nearby sentence or by rewriting it as a complete sentence.

1. A sentence must have a subject. (30j)

2. A sentence must have a verb, not just a verbal. A verbal cannot function as a sentence's verb without an auxiliary verb. (30k and l)

   VERB   The terrier *is barking.*

   VERBAL   The terrier *barking.*

3. Unless it is a question, a sentence must have at least one clause that does not begin with a subordinating word. (30h) Following are some common subordinating words:

although	if	when
as	since	where
because	that	whether
before	though	which
how	unless	who

▶ **Kamika stayed out of school for three months after Linda was born.**

She did so to
~~To~~ recuperate and to take care of the baby.
   ^

To recuperate and to take care of the baby includes verbals, not verbs. The revision — adding a subject (*she*) and a verb (*did*) — turns the fragment into a separate sentence.

Fragments beginning with transitions

If you introduce an example or explanation with one of the following transitions, be certain you write a sentence, not a fragment.

also	for example	like
as a result	for instance	such as
besides	instead	that is

such
▶ **Joan Didion has written on many subjects/, ~~Such~~ as the Hoover Dam**
  and migraine headaches.
  ^

The second word group is a phrase, not a sentence. The editing combines it
with an independent clause.

37b Compound-predicate fragments

A compound predicate consists of two or more verbs, along with their
modifiers and objects, that have the same subject. Fragments occur
when one part of a compound predicate lacks a subject but is punctuated as a separate sentence. These fragments usually begin with *and*,
but, or *or*. You can revise them by attaching them to the independent
clause that contains the rest of the predicate.

and
▶ **They sold their house/ ~~And~~ moved into an apartment.**
  ^

EXERCISE 37.1

Revise each of the following items to eliminate any sentence fragments, either by
combining fragments with independent clauses or by rewriting them as separate
sentences. Example:

Zoe looked close to tears.
~~Zoe looked close to tears.~~ Standing with her head bowed/,
  She was standing ^
Zoe looked close to tears. ~~Standing~~ with her head bowed.

1. Long stretches of white beaches and shady palm trees. Give tourists the
   impression of an island paradise.
2. Being a celebrity. That is what many Americans yearn for.
3. Much of New Orleans is below sea level. Which makes it susceptible to flooding.
4. Uncle Ron forgot to bring his clarinet to the party. Fortunately for us.
5. Oscar night is an occasion for celebrating the film industry. And criticizing the
   fashion industry.
6. Diners in Creole restaurants might try shrimp gumbo. Or order turtle soup.
7. Tupperware parties go back to the late 1940s. Parties where the hosts are sales-
   persons.
8. Attempting to lose ten pounds in less than a week. I ate only cottage cheese
   and grapefruit.
9. None of the adults realized that we were hiding there. Under the porch.
10. Thomas Edison was famous for his inventions. As well as for his entrepreneurial
    skills.

37c Dependent-clause fragments

Dependent clauses contain both a subject and a verb, but they cannot stand alone as sentences; they depend on an independent clause to complete their meaning. Dependent clauses usually begin with words such as *after, because, before, if, since, though, unless, until, when, where, while, who, which,* and *that.* You can usually combine dependent-clause fragments with a nearby independent clause.

▶ When I decided to work part-time.** I gave up a lot of my earning potential.

If you cannot smoothly attach a clause to a nearby independent clause, try deleting the opening subordinating word and turning the dependent clause into a sentence.

▶ The majority of injuries in automobile accidents occur in two ways.
    An
~~When an~~ occupant either is hurt by something inside the car or is
thrown from the car.

EXERCISE 37.2

Identify all the sentence fragments in the following items, and explain why each is grammatically incomplete. Then revise each one in at least two ways. Example:

Controlling my temper/ ~~That~~ has been one of my goals this year.

One of my goals this year has been controlling
~~Controlling~~ my temper. ~~That has been one of my goals this year.~~

1. As soon as the seventy-five-year-old cellist walked onstage. The audience burst into applause.
2. The patient has only one intention. To smoke behind the doctor's back.
3. Fishing for Alaskan king crab, one of the most dangerous professions there is.
4. After writing and rewriting for almost three years. She finally felt that her novel was complete.
5. In the wake of the earthquake. Relief workers tried to provide food and shelter to victims.
6. Forster stopped writing novels after *A Passage to India.* Which is one of the greatest novels of the twentieth century.
7. Because the speaker's fee was astronomical. The student organization invited someone else.
8. The jury found the defendant guilty. And recommended the maximum sentence.

9. Production began in late September. Four months ahead of schedule.

10. Her parents simply could not understand. Why she hated her childhood nickname.

> **bedfordstmartins.com/everydaywriter** For exercises, go to **Exercise Central** and click on **Sentence Fragments.**

EXERCISE 37.3: THINKING CRITICALLY

Reading with an Eye for Fragments

Identify the fragments in the following passage. What effect does the writer achieve by using fragments rather than complete sentences?

> On Sundays, for religion, we went up on the hill. Skipping along the hexagon-shaped tile in Colonial Park. Darting up the steps to Edgecomb Avenue. Stopping in the candy store on St. Nicholas to load up. Leaning forward for leverage to finish the climb up to the church. I was always impressed by this particular house of the Lord.
> — KEITH GILYARD, *Voices of the Self*

Thinking about Any Fragments in Your Own Writing

Read through some essays you have written. Using the guidelines in this chapter, see whether you find any sentence fragments. If so, do you recognize any patterns? Do you write fragments when you're attempting to add emphasis? Are they all dependent clauses? phrases? Note any patterns you discover, and make a point of routinely checking your writing for fragments. Finally, revise any fragments to form complete sentences.

Punctuation and Mechanics

You can show a lot with
a look. . . . It's punctuation.

— CLINT EASTWOOD

Punctuation and Mechanics

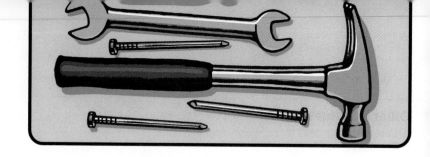

38   Commas

Commas often play a crucial role in meaning. See how important the comma is in the following directions for making hot cereal:

> Add Cream of Wheat slowly, stirring constantly.

That sentence tells the cook to *add the cereal slowly.* If the comma came before the word *slowly,* however, the cook might add all of the cereal at once and *stir slowly.* Using commas correctly can help you communicate more effectively.

38a   Use commas to set off introductory words, phrases, and clauses.

► Slowly, she became conscious of her predicament.

► In fact, health care costs keep rising.

► In Fitzgerald's novel, the color green takes on great symbolic qualities.

► Wearing new running shoes, Brendan prepared for the race.

► To win the game, Connor needed skill and luck.

► Pen poised in anticipation, Logan waited for the test to be distributed.

► While the storm was raging, we read by candlelight.

Note that some writers omit the comma after an introductory element if it is short and does not seem to require a pause after it. However, you will seldom be wrong if you use a comma. (See also 38i.)

EXERCISE 38.1

In the following sentences, add any commas that are needed after the introductory element. Example:

To find a good day-care provider, parents usually need both time and money.

1. At the worst possible moment a computer crash made me lose my document.

2. To our surprise the charity auction raised enough money to build a new technology center.

3. Unaware that the microphone was on the candidate made an offensive comment.

4. Whenever someone rings the doorbell her dog goes berserk.

5. Therefore answering the seemingly simple question is very difficult.

6. With the fifth century came the fall of the Roman Empire.

7. A tray of shrimp in one hand and a pile of napkins in the other the waiter avoided me.

8. Toward the rapids floated an empty rubber raft.

9. When they woke up the exhausted campers no longer wanted to hike.

10. Covered in glitter the children proudly displayed their art project.

AT A GLANCE

Editing for Commas

Research for this book shows that five of the most common errors in college writing involve commas. Check your writing for these errors:

1. Check every sentence that doesn't begin with the subject to see whether it opens with an introductory element (a word, phrase, or clause that describes the subject or tells when, where, how, or why the main action of the sentence occurs). Use a comma to separate the introductory material from the main part of the sentence. (38a)

2. Look at every sentence that contains one of the conjunctions *and, but, or, nor, for, so,* or *yet.* If the groups of words before and after the conjunction both function as complete sentences, you have a compound sentence. Make sure to use a comma before the conjunction. (38b)

3. Look at each adjective clause beginning with *which, who, whom, whose, when,* or *where,* and at each phrase and appositive. (28m) Decide whether the element is essential to the meaning of the sentence. If the rest of the sentence would be unclear without it, you should not set off the element with commas. (38c)

4. Make sure that adjective clauses beginning with *that* are not set off with commas. (38c and j) Do not use commas between subjects and verbs, verbs and objects or complements, or prepositions and objects; to separate parts of compound constructions other than compound sentences; to set off restrictive clauses; or before the first or after the last item in a series. (38j)

5. Do not use a comma alone to separate sentences (see Chapter 36).

38b Use commas to separate clauses in compound sentences.

A comma usually precedes a coordinating conjunction (*and, but, or, nor, for, so,* or *yet*) that joins two independent clauses in a compound sentence (30m).

▶ The title sounds impressive, but *administrative clerk* is just another word for *photocopier.*

▶ The show started at last, and the crowd grew quiet.

With very short clauses, you can sometimes omit the comma.

▶ She saw her chance and she took it.

Always use the comma if there is any chance the sentence will be misread without it.

▶ I opened the junk drawer, and the cabinet door jammed.

Use a semicolon rather than a comma when the clauses are long and complex or contain their own commas.

▶ When these early migrations took place, the ice was still confined to the lands in the far north; but eight hundred thousand years ago, when man was already established in the temperate latitudes, the ice moved southward until it covered large parts of Europe and Asia.

— ROBERT JASTROW, *Until the Sun Dies*

EXERCISE 38.2

Use a comma and a coordinating conjunction (*and, but, for, nor, or, so,* or *yet*) to combine each of the following pairs of sentences into one sentence. Delete or rearrange words if necessary. Example:

                       so

I had finished studying for the test, I went to bed.

1. The chef did not want to serve a heavy dessert. She was planning to have a rich stew for the main course.
2. My mother rarely allowed us to eat sweets. Halloween was a special exception.
3. Scientists have mapped the human genome. They learn more every day about how genes affect an individual's health.
4. The playwright disliked arguing with directors. She avoided rehearsals.
5. Tropical fish do not bark. They are not cuddly pets.

38c Use commas to set off nonrestrictive elements.

Nonrestrictive elements are clauses, phrases, and words that do not limit, or restrict, the meaning of the words they modify. Since such elements are not essential to the meaning of a sentence, they should be set off with commas. Restrictive elements, on the other hand, *are* essential to meaning and should *not* be set off with commas.

RESTRICTIVE   Drivers *who have been convicted of drunken driving* should lose their licenses.

In the preceding sentence, the clause *who have been convicted of drunken driving* is essential because it explains that only drivers who have been convicted of drunken driving should lose their licenses. Therefore, it is *not* set off with commas.

NONRESTRICTIVE   The two drivers involved in the accident, *who have been convicted of drunken driving,* should lose their licenses.

In the second sentence, however, the clause *who have been convicted of drunken driving* is not essential to the meaning because it merely provides more information about what it modifies, *The two drivers involved in the accident.* Therefore, the clause is set off with commas.

To decide whether an element is restrictive or nonrestrictive, read the sentence without the element, and see if the deletion changes the meaning of the rest of the sentence. If the deletion does change the meaning, the element is probably restrictive, and you should not set it off with commas. If it does not change the meaning, the element is probably nonrestrictive and requires commas.

Adjective and adverb clauses

An adjective clause that begins with *that* is always restrictive; do not set it off with commas. An adjective clause beginning with *which* may be either restrictive or nonrestrictive; however, some writers prefer to use *which* only for nonrestrictive clauses, which they set off with commas.

NONRESTRICTIVE CLAUSES

▶ **I borrowed books from the rental library of Shakespeare and Company,** *which was the library and bookstore of Sylvia Beach at 12 rue de l'Odeon.*
    – Ernest Hemingway, *A Moveable Feast*

The adjective clause describing Shakespeare and Company is not necessary to the meaning of the independent clause and therefore is set off with a comma.

In general, set off an adverb clause that follows a main clause only if it begins with *although, even though, while,* or another subordinating conjunction expressing contrast.

▶ He uses semicolons frequently, while she prefers periods and short sentences.

The adverb clause *while she prefers periods and short sentences* expresses the idea of contrast; therefore, it is set off with a comma.

RESTRICTIVE CLAUSES

▶ The claim *that men like seriously to battle one another to some sort of finish* is a myth. — JOHN MCMURTRY, "Kill 'Em! Crush 'Em! Eat 'Em Raw!"

The adjective clause is necessary to the meaning because it explains which claim is a myth; therefore, the clause is not set off with commas.

▶ The man/who rescued Jana's puppy/won her eternal gratitude.

The adjective clause *who rescued Jana's puppy* is necessary to the meaning because only the man who rescued the puppy won the gratitude; the clause is restrictive and so takes no commas.

With the exceptions noted, do *not* set off an adverb clause that follows a main clause.

▶ Remember to check your calculations/before you submit the form.

Phrases

Participial phrases may be restrictive or nonrestrictive. Prepositional phrases are usually restrictive, but sometimes they are not essential to the meaning of a sentence and are set off with commas (30l).

NONRESTRICTIVE PHRASES

▶ Frédéric Chopin, in spite of poor health, composed prolifically.

The phrase *in spite of poor health* does not limit the meaning of *Frédéric Chopin* and so is set off with commas.

▶ The bus drivers, rejecting the management's offer, remained on strike.

Using commas around the participial phrase makes it nonrestrictive, telling us that all of the drivers remained on strike.

RESTRICTIVE PHRASES

▶ The bus drivers/rejecting the management's offer/remained on strike.

Deleting the commas around *rejecting the management's offer* limits the meaning of *The bus drivers.* The revised sentence says that only the bus drivers who rejected the offer remained on strike, implying that the other drivers went back to work.

Appositives

An appositive is a noun or noun phrase that renames a nearby noun. When an appositive is not essential to identify what it renames, it is set off with commas.

NONRESTRICTIVE APPOSITIVES

▶ **Jon Stewart, the comic and news commentator, often pokes fun at political leaders.**

Jon Stewart's name identifies him; the appositive *the comic and news commentator* provides extra information.

RESTRICTIVE APPOSITIVES

▶ **Mozart's opera/*The Marriage of Figaro*/was considered revolutionary.**

The appositive is restrictive because Mozart wrote more than one opera.

EXERCISE 38.3

Use commas to set off nonrestrictive clauses, phrases, and appositives in any of the following sentences that contain such elements.

1. Anyone who lived through the Vietnam War remembers it as stressful and heartbreaking.
2. Embalming is a technique that preserves a cadaver.
3. I would feel right at home in the city dump which bears a striking resemblance to my bedroom.
4. The rescue workers exhausted and discouraged stared ahead without speaking.
5. The latest strip mall in our town offers the same useless junk as all the others.
6. Viruses unlike bacteria can reproduce only by infecting live cells.
7. Napoléon was forced into exile after his defeat by the British at Waterloo.
8. Hammurabi an ancient Babylonian king created laws that were carved on a stone for public display.
9. Birds' hearts have four chambers whereas reptiles' have three.
10. My grandfather always picked up pennies if he saw them lying on the sidewalk.

38d Use commas to separate items in a series.

▶ **He has plundered our seas, ravaged our coasts, burnt our towns, and destroyed the lives of our people.**   – Declaration of Independence

You may see a series with no comma after the next-to-last item, particularly in newspaper writing. Occasionally, however, omitting the comma can cause confusion.

▶ **All the cafeteria's vegetables — broccoli, green beans, peas, and carrots — were cooked to a gray mush.**

Without the comma after *peas,* you wouldn't know if there were three choices (the third being a *mixture* of peas and carrots) or four.

When the items in a series contain commas of their own or other punctuation, separate them with semicolons rather than commas.

▶ **Should I serve kidney beans, which are red; cranberry beans, which are white and red; or chickpeas, which are tan?**

Coordinate adjectives, those that relate equally to the noun they modify, should be separated by commas.

▶ **The long, twisting, muddy road led to a shack in the woods.**

In a sentence like *The cracked bathroom mirror reflected his face,* however, *cracked* and *bathroom* are not coordinate because *bathroom mirror* is the equivalent of a single word, which is modified by *cracked.* Hence, they are *not* separated by commas.

You can usually determine whether adjectives are coordinate by inserting *and* between them. If the sentence makes sense with the *and,* the adjectives are coordinate and should be separated by commas.

▶ **They are sincere *and* talented *and* inquisitive researchers.**

The sentence makes sense with the *and*s, so the adjectives should be separated by commas: *They are sincere, talented, inquisitive researchers.*

▶ **Byron carried an elegant *and* pocket watch.**

The sentence does not make sense with *and,* so the adjectives *elegant* and *pocket* should not be separated by commas: *Byron carried an elegant pocket watch.*

EXERCISE 38.4

Revise any of the following sentences that require commas to set off words, phrases, or clauses in a series.

1. The students donated clothing school supplies and nonperishable food.

2. The tiny brown-eyed Lafayette twins were the only children in the kindergarten class who could already read.

3. Landscape architects need to consider many aspects of a plant: how often it blooms how much sunlight it needs and how tall it will grow.

4. Several art historians inspected the Chinese terra-cotta figures.
5. The young athletes' parents insist on calling every play judging every move and telling everyone within earshot exactly what is wrong with the team.

38e Use commas to set off parenthetical and transitional expressions.

Parenthetical expressions add comments or information. Because they often interrupt the flow of a sentence or digress, they are usually set off with commas.

▶ Some studies, incidentally, have shown that chocolate, of all things, helps to prevent tooth decay.

▶ Roald Dahl's stories, it turns out, were often inspired by his own childhood.

Transitional expressions, conjunctive adverbs (words such as *however* and *furthermore*), and other words and phrases used to connect parts of sentences are usually set off with commas (8e).

▶ Ozone is a by-product of dry cleaning, for example.

▶ Ceiling fans are, moreover, less expensive than air conditioners.

38f Use commas to set off contrasting elements, interjections, direct address, and tag questions.

CONTRASTING ELEMENTS

▶ On official business it was she, *not my father,* one would usually hear on the phone or in stores.

        – RICHARD RODRIGUEZ, "Aria: A Memoir of a Bilingual Childhood"

INTERJECTIONS

▶ *My God,* who wouldn't want a wife?   – JUDY BRADY, "I Want a Wife"

DIRECT ADDRESS

▶ Remember, *sir,* that you are under oath.

TAG QUESTIONS

▶ The governor did not veto the unemployment bill, *did she?*

EXERCISE 38.5

Revise each of the following sentences, using commas to set off parenthetical and transitional expressions, contrasting elements, interjections, words used in direct address, and tag questions.

1. One must consider the society as a whole not just its parts.
2. Many of the parents and students did in fact support the position of the teacher who resigned.
3. You don't expect me to read this speech do you?
4. Coming in ahead of schedule and under budget it appears is the only way to keep this client happy.
5. Ladies and gentlemen I bid you farewell.

38g Use commas with dates, addresses, titles, and numbers.

Dates

Use a comma between the day of the week and the month, between the day of the month and the year, and between the year and the rest of the sentence, if any.

▶ The attacks on the morning of Tuesday, September 11, 2001, took the United States by surprise.

Do not use commas with dates in inverted order or with dates consisting of only the month and the year.

▶ She dated the letter *26 August 2008.*
▶ Thousands of Germans swarmed over the wall in *November 1989.*

Addresses and place-names

Use a comma after each part of an address or place-name, including the state if there is no ZIP code. Do not precede a ZIP code with a comma.

▶ Forward my mail to the Department of English, The Ohio State University, Columbus, Ohio 43210.
▶ Portland, Oregon, is much larger than Portland, Maine.

Titles

Use commas to set off a title such as *MD* and *PhD* from the name preceding it and from the rest of the sentence. The titles *Jr.* and *Sr.,* however, often appear without commas.

▶ Oliver Sacks, MD, has written about the way the mind works.

▶ Martin Luther King Jr. was one of the twentieth century's greatest orators.

Numbers

In numerals of five digits or more, use a comma between each group of three, starting from the right.

▶ The city's population rose to *158,000* in the 2000 census.

The comma is optional within numerals of four digits but never occurs in four-digit dates, street addresses, or page numbers.

▶ The college had an enrollment of *1,789* [or *1789*] in the fall of 2008.
▶ My grandparents live at *2428* Loring Place.
▶ Turn to page *1566.*

EXERCISE 38.6

Revise each of the following sentences, using commas appropriately with dates, addresses, place-names, titles, and numbers.

1. The abridged version of the assigned novel is 1200 pages long.
2. More than 350000 people gathered for the protest on the Washington Mall.
3. New Delhi India and Islamabad Pakistan became the capitals of two independent nations at midnight on August 15 1947.
4. MLA headquarters are at 26 Broadway New York New York 10004.
5. I was convinced that the nameplate I. M. Well MD was one of my sister's pranks.

38h Use commas to set off most quotations.

Commas set off a quotation from words used to introduce or identify the source of the quotation. A comma following a quotation goes inside the closing quotation mark. (See 43d for advice about using colons instead of commas to introduce quotations.)

▶ A German proverb warns, "Go to law for a sheep, and lose your cow."

▶ "All I know about grammar," said Joan Didion, "is its infinite power."

Do not use a comma after a question mark or exclamation point.

▶ "What's a thousand dollars?," asks Groucho Marx in *Cocoanuts.* "Mere chicken feed. A poultry matter."

▶ "Out, damned spot!," cries Lady Macbeth.

Do not use a comma when you introduce a quotation with *that.*

▶ The writer of Ecclesiastes concludes that, "all is vanity."

Do not use a comma before an indirect quotation — one that does not use the speaker's exact words.

▶ Patrick Henry declared, that he wanted either liberty or death.

EXERCISE 38.7

Insert a comma in any of the following sentences that require one.

1. "The public be damned!" William Henry Vanderbilt was reported to have said. "I'm working for my stockholders."
2. My professor insisted "The cutting edge gets dull very quickly."
3. Who remarked that "youth is wasted on the young"?
4. "Learning without thought is labor lost; thought without learning is perilous" Confucius argued.
5. "Do you have any idea who I am?" the well-dressed man asked belligerently.

38i Use commas to prevent confusion.

Sometimes commas are necessary to make sentences easier to read or understand.

▶ The members of the dance troupe strutted in, in matching costumes.

▶ Before, I had planned to major in biology.

38j Revise unnecessary commas.

Excessive use of commas can spoil an otherwise fine sentence.

Around restrictive elements

Do not use commas to set off restrictive elements — elements that limit, or define, the meaning of the words they modify or refer to (38c).

▶ I don't let my children watch films/that are violent.

▶ A law/reforming campaign financing/was passed in 2002.

▶ My only defense/against my allergies/is to stay indoors.

▶ The actor/Philip Seymour Hoffman/might win the award.

Between subjects and verbs, verbs and objects or complements, and prepositions and objects

Do not use a comma between a subject and its verb, a verb and its object or complement, or a preposition and its object. This rule holds true even if the subject, object, or complement is a long phrase or clause.

▶ Watching movies late at night/is a way for me to relax.

▶ Parents must decide/how much television their children may watch.

▶ The winner of/the community-service award stepped forward.

In compound constructions

In compound constructions (other than compound sentences — see 38b), do not use a comma before or after a coordinating conjunction that joins the two parts.

▶ Improved health care/and more free trade were two of the administration's goals.

The *and* here joins parts of a compound subject, which should not be separated by a comma.

▶ Donald Trump was born rich/and used his money to make money.

The *and* here joins parts of a compound predicate, which should not be separated by a comma.

Before the first or after the last item in a series

▶ The auction included/furniture, paintings, and china.

▶ The swimmer took slow, elegant, powerful/strokes.

bedfordstmartins.com/everydaywriter For exercises, go to **Exercise Central** and click on **Commas**.

EXERCISE 38.8: THINKING CRITICALLY

Reading with an Eye for Commas

The following poem uses commas to create rhythm and guide readers. Read the poem aloud, listening especially to the effect of the commas at the end of the first and fifth lines. Then read it again as if those commas were omitted, noting the difference. What is the effect of the poet's decision not to use a comma at the end of the third line?

> Some say the world will end in fire,
> Some say in ice.
> From what I've tasted of desire
> I hold with those who favor fire.
> But if it had to perish twice,
> I think I know enough of hate
> To say that for destruction ice
> Is also great
> And would suffice.
> — ROBERT FROST, "Fire and Ice"

Thinking about Your Own Use of Commas

Choose a paragraph that you have written. Remove all of the commas, and read it aloud. What is the effect of leaving out the commas? Now, punctuate the passage with commas, consulting this chapter. Did you replace all of your original commas? Did you add any new ones? Explain why you added the commas you did.

39 Semicolons

The following public-service announcement, posted in New York City subway cars, reminded commuters what to do with a used newspaper at the end of the ride:

> Please put it in a trash can; that's good news for everyone.

The semicolon in the subway announcement separates two clauses that could have been written as separate sentences. Semicolons, which create a pause stronger than that of a comma but not as strong as the full pause of a period, show close connections between related ideas.

> **AT A GLANCE**
>
> ## Editing for Semicolons
>
> - If you use semicolons, be sure they appear only between independent clauses — groups of words that can stand alone as sentences (39a and b) — or between items in a series. (39b)
> - If you find few or no semicolons in your writing, ask yourself whether you should add some. Would any closely related ideas in two sentences be better expressed in one sentence with a semicolon? (39a)

39a Use semicolons to link independent clauses.

Though a comma and a coordinating conjunction often join independent clauses, semicolons provide writers with subtler ways of signaling closely related clauses. The clause following a semicolon often restates an idea expressed in the first clause; it sometimes expands on or presents a contrast to the first.

▶ **Immigration acts were passed; newcomers had to prove, besides moral correctness and financial solvency, their ability to read.**
— MARY GORDON, "More than Just a Shrine"

Gordon uses a semicolon to join the two clauses, giving the sentence an abrupt rhythm that suits the topic: laws that imposed strict requirements.

A semicolon should link independent clauses joined by conjunctive adverbs such as *therefore, however,* and *indeed* or transitional expressions such as *in fact, in addition,* and *for example* (30h).

▶ **The circus comes as close to being the world in microcosm as anything I know; in a way, it puts all the rest of show business in the shade.**
— E. B. WHITE, "The Ring of Time"

If two independent clauses joined by a coordinating conjunction contain commas, you may use a semicolon instead of a comma before the conjunction to make the sentence easier to read.

▶ **Every year, whether the Republican or the Democratic party is in office, more and more power drains away from the individual to feed vast reservoirs in far-off places; and we have less and less say about the shape of events which shape our future.**
— WILLIAM F. BUCKLEY JR., "Why Don't We Complain?"

EXERCISE 39.1

Combine each of the following pairs of sentences into one sentence by using a semicolon. Example:

> *meet*
> Take the bus to Henderson Street,; Meet me under the clock.

1. Joining the chorus was a great experience for Will. It helped him express his musical talent and gave him a social life.
2. City life offers many advantages. In many ways, however, life in a small town is much more pleasant.
3. The door contains an inflatable slide to be used in an emergency. In addition, each seat can become a flotation device.
4. Most car accidents occur within twenty-five miles of the home. Therefore, you should wear a seat belt on every trip.
5. The debate over political correctness affects more than the curriculum. It also affects students' social relationships.

39b Use semicolons to separate items in a series containing other punctuation.

Ordinarily, commas separate items in a series (38d). But when the items themselves contain commas or other marks of punctuation, using semicolons to separate the items will make the sentence clearer and easier to read.

> ▶ **Anthropology encompasses archaeology, the study of ancient civilizations through artifacts; linguistics, the study of the structure and development of language; and cultural anthropology, the study of language, customs, and behavior.**

39c Revise misused semicolons.

A comma, not a semicolon, should separate an independent clause from a dependent clause or phrase.

> ▶ **The police found fingerprints;, which they used to identify the thief.**

> ▶ **The new system would encourage students to register for courses online;, thus streamlining registration.**

A colon, not a semicolon, should introduce a series or list.

▶ The tour includes visits to the following art museums; : the Prado, in
Madrid; the Louvre, in Paris; and the Van Gogh, in Amsterdam.
                                                              ^

EXERCISE 39.2

Revise the following passage, eliminating any misused or overused semicolons and,
if necessary, replacing them with other punctuation.

> Hosting your first dinner party can be very stressful; but careful planning and
> preparation can make it a success. The guest list must contain the right mix of
> people; everyone should feel comfortable; good talkers and good listeners are
> both important; while they don't need to agree on everything, you don't want
> them to have fistfights, either. Then you need to plan the menu; which should
> steer clear of problem areas; for vegans; no pork chops; for guests with shellfish
> allergies, no lobster; for teetotallers; no tequila. In addition; make sure your home
> is clean and neat, and check that you have enough chairs; dishes; glasses; nap-
> kins; and silverware. Leave enough time to socialize with your guests; and save a
> little energy to clean up when it's over!

 bedfordstmartins.com/everydaywriter For exercises, go to **Exercise Central** and
click on **Semicolons**.

EXERCISE 39.3: THINKING CRITICALLY

Reading with an Eye for Semicolons

Read the following paragraph, which describes a solar eclipse, with attention to the
use of semicolons. What different effect would the paragraph have if the author had
used periods instead of semicolons? What if she had used commas and coordinating conjunctions? What is the effect of all the semicolons?

> You see the wide world swaddled in darkness; you see a vast breadth of hilly
> land, and an enormous, distant, blackened valley; you see towns' lights, a river's
> path, and blurred portions of your hat and scarf; you see your husband's face
> looking like an early black-and-white film; and you see a sprawl of black sky and
> blue sky together, with unfamiliar stars in it, some barely visible bands of cloud,
> and over there, a small white ring. The ring is as small as one goose in a flock of
> migrating geese — if you happen to notice a flock of migrating geese. It is one
> 360th part of the visible sky. The sun we see is less than half the diameter of a
> dime held at arms' length.   — ANNIE DILLARD, "Solar Eclipse"

Thinking about Your Own Use of Semicolons

Think of something you might take five or ten minutes to observe — a football game,
a brewing storm, an argument between friends — and write a paragraph describing
your observations point by point and using semicolons to separate each point, as
Annie Dillard does in the preceding paragraph. Then, look at the way you used semicolons. Are there places where a period or a comma and a coordinating conjunction
would better serve your meaning? Revise appropriately. What can you conclude
about effective ways of using semicolons?

40 End Punctuation

Periods, question marks, and exclamation points often appear in advertising to create special effects or draw readers along from line to line.

> You have a choice to make.
> Where can you turn for advice?
> Ask our experts today!

End punctuation tells us how to read each sentence — as a matter-of-fact statement, a query, or an emphatic request. Making appropriate choices with end punctuation allows readers to understand exactly what you mean.

AT A GLANCE

Editing for End Punctuation

- If all or almost all of your sentences end with periods, see if some of them might be phrased more effectively as questions or exclamations. (40a, b, and c)
- Check to be sure you use question marks appropriately. (40b)
- If you use exclamation points, consider whether each is justified. Does the sentence call for extra emphasis? If in doubt, use a period instead. (40c)

40a Periods

Use a period to close sentences that make statements or give mild commands.

▶ **All books are either dreams or swords.**   – AMY LOWELL

▶ **Don't use a fancy word if a simpler word will do.**
                    – GEORGE ORWELL, "Politics and the English Language"

▶ **Please close the door.**

A period also closes indirect questions, which report rather than ask questions.

▶ **I asked how old the child was.**

▶ **We all wonder who will win the election.**

Until recently, periods have been used with most abbreviations in American English (see Chapter 45). However, more and more abbreviations are appearing without periods.

Mr.	MD	BC *or* B.C.
Ms.	PhD	BCE *or* B.C.E.
Mrs.	MBA	AD *or* A.D.
Jr.	RN	AM *or* a.m.
Dr.	Sen.	PM *or* p.m.

Some abbreviations rarely if ever appear with periods. These include the postal abbreviations of state names, such as *FL* and *TN* (though the traditional abbreviations, such as *Fla.* and *Tenn.*, do call for periods), and most groups of initials (*GE, CIA, AIDS, UNICEF*). If you are not sure whether a particular abbreviation should include periods, check a dictionary, or follow the style guidelines (such as those of the Modern Language Association) you are using in a research paper.

40b Question marks

Use question marks to close sentences that ask direct questions (42a).

▶ **How is the human mind like a computer, and how is it different?**
— KATHLEEN STASSEN BERGER AND ROSS A. THOMPSON,
The Developing Person through Childhood and Adolescence

Question marks do not close *indirect* questions, which report rather than ask questions.

▶ **She asked whether I opposed his nomination.**

Do not use a comma or a period immediately after a question mark that ends a direct quotation.

▶ **"Am I my brother's keeper?/" Cain asked.**

▶ **Cain asked, "Am I my brother's keeper?/"**

Questions in a series may have question marks even when they are not separate sentences.

▶ **I often confront a difficult choice: should I go to practice? finish my homework? spend time with my friends?**

A question mark in parentheses indicates that a writer is unsure of a date, a figure, or a word.

▶ **Quintilian died in AD 96 (?).**

40c Exclamation points

Use an exclamation point to show surprise or strong emotion.

▶ **In those few moments of geologic time will be the story of all that has happened since we became a nation. And what a story it will be!**
— JAMES RETTIE, "But a Watch in the Night"

Use exclamation points very sparingly because they can distract your readers or suggest that you are exaggerating.

▶ **This university is so large, so varied, that attempting to tell someone**

everything about it would take three years!.
^

Do not use a comma or a period immediately after an exclamation point that ends a direct quotation.

▶ **On my last visit, I looked out the sliding glass doors and ran breathlessly to Connor in the kitchen: "There's a *huge* black pig in the backyard!"/**
— ELLEN ASHDOWN, "Living by the Dead"

EXERCISE 40.1

Revise each of the following sentences, adding appropriate punctuation and deleting any unnecessary punctuation you find. Example:

She asked the travel agent, "What is the airfare to Greece⁄?"

1. Social scientists face difficult questions: should they use their knowledge to shape society, merely describe human behavior, or try to do both.

2. The court denied a New Jersey woman's petition to continue raising tigers in her backyard!

3. I screamed at Jamie, "You rat. You tricked me."

4. The reporter wondered whether anything more could have been done to save lives?

5. Trish asked the receptionist if Dr Margolies had office hours that afternoon

6. "Have you seen the new Spielberg film?," Mia asked casually.

bedfordstmartins.com/everydaywriter For exercises, go to **Exercise Central** and click on **End Punctuation.**

EXERCISE 40.2: THINKING CRITICALLY

Reading with an Eye for End Punctuation

Consider the use of end punctuation in the following paragraph. Then experiment with the end punctuation. What would be the effect of deleting the exclamation point from the quotation by Cicero or of changing it to a question mark? What would be the effect of changing Cicero's question to a statement?

> To be admired and praised, especially by the young, is an autumnal plea-sure enjoyed by the lucky ones (who are not always the most deserving). "What is more charming," Cicero observes in his famous essay *De Senectute*, "than an old age surrounded by the enthusiasm of youth! . . . Attentions which seem trivial and conventional are marks of honor — the morning call, being sought after, precedence, having people rise for you, being escorted to and from the forum. . . . What pleasures of the body can be compared to the prerogatives of influence?" But there are also pleasures of the body, or the mind, that are enjoyed by a greater number of older persons.   — MALCOLM COWLEY, *The View from 80*

Thinking about Your Own Use of End Punctuation

Look through something you have written recently, noting its end punctuation. Using the guidelines in this chapter, see if your use of end punctuation follows any pat-terns. Try revising the end punctuation in a paragraph or two to emphasize (or de-emphasize) some point. What conclusions can you draw about ways of using end punctuation to draw attention to (or away from) a sentence?

Apostrophes **41**

The little apostrophe can make a big difference in meaning. The follow-ing sign at a neighborhood swimming pool, for instance, says some-thing different from what the writer probably intended:

> Please deposit your garbage (and your guests) in the trash receptacles be-fore leaving the pool area.

The sign indicates that guests should be deposited in trash receptacles. Adding a single apostrophe would offer a more neighborly statement: *Please deposit your garbage (and your guests') in the trash receptacles before leaving the pool area* asks that the guests' garbage, not the guests them-selves, be thrown away.

Editing for Apostrophes

- Check each noun that ends in *-s* and shows possession. Is the apostrophe in the right place, either before or after the *-s*? (41a)
- Check the possessive form of each indefinite pronoun, such as *someone's*. Be sure the apostrophe comes before the *-s*. (41a)
- Check each personal pronoun that ends with *-s* (*yours, his, hers, its, ours, theirs*) to make sure it does not include an apostrophe. (41a)
- Check each *it's*. Does it mean *it is* or *it has*? If not, remove the apostrophe. (41b)
- Check other contractions to make sure the apostrophe is used correctly. (41b)

41a   Apostrophes and the possessive case

The possessive case denotes ownership or possession of one thing by another.

Singular nouns and indefinite pronouns

Add an apostrophe and *-s* to form the possessive of most singular nouns, including those that end in *-s*, and of indefinite pronouns (30d). The possessive forms of personal pronouns do not take apostrophes: *yours, his, hers, its, ours, theirs.*

- ▶ The *bus's* **fumes overpowered her.**
- ▶ *Star Wars* **made George** *Lucas's* **fortune.**
- ▶ *Anyone's* **guess is as good as mine.**

Plural nouns

To form the possessive case of plural nouns not ending in *-s*, add an apostrophe and *-s*.

- ▶ The *men's* **department sells business attire.**

For plural nouns ending in *-s*, add only the apostrophe.

- ▶ The three *clowns'* **costumes were bright green and orange.**

Compound nouns

For compound nouns, make the last word in the group possessive.

- ▶ The *secretary of state's* speech was televised.
- ▶ Both her *daughters-in-law's* birthdays fall in July.
- ▶ My *in-laws'* disapproval dampened our enthusiasm for the new house.

Two or more nouns

To signal individual possession by two or more owners, make each noun possessive.

- ▶ Great differences exist between *Jerry Bruckheimer's* and *Ridley Scott's* films.

  Bruckheimer and Scott have produced different films.

To signal joint possession, make only the last noun possessive.

- ▶ *Wallace and Gromit's* creator is Nick Park.

  Wallace and Gromit have the same creator.

EXERCISE 41.1

Complete each of the following sentences by inserting *'s* or an apostrophe alone to form the possessive case of the italicized words. Example:

A.J.'s older *brother's* name is Griffin.

1. Grammar is *everybody* favorite subject.
2. An *ibis* wingspan is about half as long as a *flamingo*.
3. *Charles and Camilla* first visit to the United States as a married couple included a stop at the White House.
4. The owners couldn't fulfill all the *general manager* wishes.
5. *Stephen King and Nicholas Sparks* writing styles couldn't be more different.

41b Apostrophes for contractions

Contractions are two-word combinations formed by leaving out certain letters, which are indicated by an apostrophe.

it is, it has/it's	I would, I had/I'd	will not/won't
was not/wasn't	he would, he had/he'd	let us/let's
I am/I'm	would not/wouldn't	who is, who has/who's
he is, he has/he's	do not/don't	cannot/can't
you will/you'll	does not/doesn't	

Contractions are common in conversation and informal writing. Academic and professional work, however, often calls for greater formality.

Distinguishing it's *and* its

Its is the possessive form of *it*. *It's* is a contraction for *it is* or *it has*.

▶ This disease is unusual; *its* symptoms vary from person to person.

▶ *It's* a difficult disease to diagnose.

41c Apostrophes and plurals

Many style guides now advise against using apostrophes for any plurals.

▶ The gymnasts need marks of *8s* and *9s* to qualify for the finals.

Others use an apostrophe and *–s* to form the plural of numbers, letters, and words referred to as terms.

▶ The five *Shakespeare*'s in the essay were spelled five different ways.

Check your instructor's preference.

EXERCISE 41.2

The following sentences, from which all apostrophes have been deleted, appear in Langston Hughes's "Salvation." Insert apostrophes where appropriate. Example:

> "Sister Reed, what is this child's name?"

1. There was a big revival at my Auntie Reeds church.
2. I heard the songs and the minister saying: "Why dont you come?"
3. Finally Westley said to me in a whisper: . . . "Im tired o sitting here. Lets get up and be saved."
4. So I decided that maybe to save further trouble, Id better lie. . . .
5. That night . . . I cried, in bed alone, and couldnt stop.

> **bedfordstmartins.com/everydaywriter** For exercises, go to **Exercise Central** and click on **Apostrophes.**

EXERCISE 41.3: THINKING CRITICALLY

Write a brief paragraph, beginning "I've always been amused by my neighbor's (or roommate's) _____." Then note every use of an apostrophe. Use the guidelines in this chapter to check that you have used apostrophes correctly.

Quotation Marks 42

As a way of bringing other people's words into your own, quotations can be a powerful writing tool.

> Mrs. Macken encourages parents to get books for their children, to read to them when they are "li'l," and when they start school to make certain they attend regularly. She holds herself up as an example of "a millhand's daughter who wanted to be a schoolteacher and did it through sheer hard work."
> – SHIRLEY BRICE HEATH, *Ways with Words*

The writer lets her subject speak for herself — and lets readers hear Mrs. Macken's voice.

42a Direct quotation

▶ President Bush referred to an "axis of evil" in his speech.

▶ She smiled and said, "Son, this is one incident that I will never forget."

Use quotation marks to enclose the words of each speaker within running dialogue. Mark each shift in speaker with a new paragraph.

AT A GLANCE
Editing for Quotation Marks

- Use quotation marks around direct quotations and titles of short works. (42a and c)
- Do not use quotation marks around set-off quotations of more than four lines of prose or more than three lines of poetry, or around titles of long works. Consult a style guide, such as that of the Modern Language Association (MLA), for guidelines. (42b and c)
- Use quotation marks to signal irony and coinages, but do so sparingly. (42e)
- Check other punctuation used with closing quotation marks. (42f)

  Periods and commas should be *inside* the quotation marks.

  Colons, semicolons, and footnote numbers should be *outside.*

  Question marks, exclamation points, and dashes should be *inside* if they are part of the quoted material, *outside* if they are not.

- Never use quotation marks around indirect quotations. (42g)
- Do not use quotation marks just to add emphasis to words. (42g)

"I want no proof of their affection," said Elinor; "but of their engagement I do."

"I am perfectly satisfied of both."

"Yet not a syllable has been said to you on the subject, by either of them."
                                        –JANE AUSTEN, *Sense and Sensibility*

Single quotation marks

Single quotation marks enclose a quotation within a quotation. Open and close the quoted passage with double quotation marks, and change any quotation marks that appear *within* the quotation to single quotation marks.

▶ **Baldwin says, "The title 'The Uses of the Blues' does not refer to music; I don't know anything about music."**

42b Lines of prose or poetry

If the prose passage you wish to quote is more than four typed lines, set the quotation off by starting it on a new line and indenting it one inch (or ten spaces) from the left margin. This format, known as block quotation, does not require quotation marks.

In "Suspended," Joy Harjo tells of her first awareness of jazz as a child:

> My rite of passage into the world of humanity occurred then, via jazz. The music made a startling bridge between the familiar and strange lands, an appropriate vehicle, for . . . we were there when jazz was born. I recognized it, that humid afternoon in my formative years, as a way to speak beyond the confines of ordinary language. I still hear it. (84)

This block quotation, including the ellipsis dots and the page number in parentheses at the end, follows the style of the Modern Language Association (MLA). The American Psychological Association (APA) has different guidelines for setting off block quotations. (See Chapters 48 and 52.)

When quoting poetry, if the quotation is brief (fewer than four lines), include it within your text. Separate the lines of the poem with slashes, each preceded and followed by a space, in order to tell the reader where one line of the poem ends and the next begins.

In one of his best-known poems, Robert Frost remarks, "Two roads diverged in a yellow wood, and I — / I took the one less traveled by / And that has made all the difference."

To quote more than three lines of poetry, indent the block one inch (or ten spaces) from the left margin. Do not use quotation marks. Take care to follow the spacing, capitalization, punctuation, and other features of the original poem.

> The duke in Robert Browning's poem "My Last Duchess" is clearly a jealous, vain person, whose arrogance is illustrated through this statement:
>> She thanked men — good! but thanked
>> Somehow — I know not how — as if she ranked
>> My gift of a nine-hundred-years-old name
>> With anybody's gift.

42c Titles of short works

Quotation marks are used to enclose the titles of short poems, short stories, articles, essays, songs, sections of books, and episodes of television and radio programs.

▶ **"Dover Beach" moves from calmness to sadness.** [poem]

▶ **Alice Walker's "Everyday Use" is about more than just quilts.** [short story]

▶ **The *Atlantic* published an article entitled "Illiberal Education."** [article]

▶ **In "Photography," Susan Sontag considers the role of photography in our society.** [essay]

▶ **The *Nature* episode "Echo of the Elephants" portrays ivory hunters unfavorably.** [television series episode]

Use italics rather than quotation marks for the titles of television series, magazines, movies, and other long works (see 46a).

42d Definitions

▶ **In social science, the term *sample size* means "the number of individuals being studied in a research project."**
> – KATHLEEN STASSEN BERGER AND ROSS A. THOMPSON,
> *The Developing Person through Childhood and Adolescence*

Use italics for words used as a term, like *sample size* above (see 46b).

42e Irony and coinages

To show readers that you are using a word or phrase ironically or that you made it up, enclose it in quotation marks.

▶ The "banquet" consisted of dried-out chicken and canned vegetables.

The quotation marks suggest that the meal was anything but a banquet.

▶ Your whole first paragraph or first page may have to be guillotined in any case after your piece is finished: it is a kind of "forebirth."
— JACQUES BARZUN, "A Writer's Discipline"

The writer made up the term *forebirth*.

EXERCISE 42.1

Revise each of the following sentences, using quotation marks appropriately to signal titles, definitions, irony, or invented terms.

1. Stephen Colbert introduced Americans to the concept he calls truthiness on the first episode of *The Colbert Report*.

2. In his article Race against Time, Anthony S. Fauci warns of the critical threat posed by the potent avian flu virus.

3. "The little that is known about gorillas certainly makes you want to know more," writes Alan Moorehead in his essay A Most Forgiving Ape.

4. The fun of surgery begins before the operation ever takes place.

5. Should America the Beautiful replace The Star-Spangled Banner as the national anthem?

6. In the chapter called The Last to See Them Alive, Truman Capote shows the utterly ordinary life of the Kansas family.

7. A special *Simpsons* episode called The Treehouse of Horror airs each Halloween.

8. A remix of Elvis Presley's A Little Less Conversation reached number one on the charts twenty-five years after the superstar had died.

9. My dictionary defines *isolation* as the quality or state of being alone.

10. In his poem The Shield of Achilles, W. H. Auden depicts the horror of modern warfare.

42f Other punctuation with quotation marks

Periods and commas go *inside* closing quotation marks.

▶ "Don't compromise yourself," said Janis Joplin. "You are all you've got."

EXCEPTION When you follow MLA style for documenting a short quotation, place the period *after* the parentheses with source information (see 48).

▶ In places, de Beauvoir "sees Marxists as believing in subjectivity" (Whitmarsh 63).

For more information on using a comma before or after a quotation, see 38h.

Colons, semicolons, and footnote numbers go *outside* closing quotation marks.

▶ I felt one emotion after finishing "Eveline": sorrow.

▶ Everything is dark, and "a visionary light settles in her eyes"; this vision, this light, is her salvation.

▶ Tragedy is defined by Aristotle as "an imitation of an action that is serious and of a certain magnitude."[1]

Question marks, exclamation points, and dashes go *inside* if they are part of the quoted material, *outside* if they are not.

PART OF THE QUOTATION

▶ The cashier asked, "Would you like to super-size that?"

▶ "Jump!" one of the firefighters shouted.

NOT PART OF THE QUOTATION

▶ What is the theme of "The Birth-Mark"?

▶ "Break a leg" — that phrase is supposed to bring good luck.

42g Misused quotation marks

Do not use quotation marks for indirect quotations — those that do not use someone's exact words.

▶ Mother said that ̶"̶she was sure she would never forget the incident.̶"̶

Do not use quotation marks just to add emphasis to particular words or phrases.

▶ Michael said that his views might not be ̶"̶politically correct̶"̶ but that he wasn't going to change them for anything.

▶ Much time was spent speculating about their ̶"̶relationship.̶"̶

Do not use quotation marks around slang or colloquial language; they create the impression that you are apologizing for using those words. If you have a good reason to use slang or a colloquial term, use it without quotation marks.

▶ After our twenty-mile hike, we were ready to ̶"̶turn in.̶"̶

FOR MULTILINGUAL WRITERS

Quoting in American English

Remember that the way you mark quotations in American English (" ") may not be the same as in other languages. In French, for example, quotations are marked with *guillemets* (« »), while in German, quotations take split-level marks („"). Writers of British English use single quotation marks first and, when necessary, double quotation marks for quotations within quotations. If you are writing for an American audience, be careful to follow the U.S. conventions governing quotation marks.

 bedfordstmartins.com/everydaywriter For exercises, go to **Exercise Central** and click on **Quotation Marks**.

EXERCISE 42.2: THINKING CRITICALLY

Reading with an Eye for Quotation Marks

Read the following passage about the painter Georgia O'Keeffe, and pay particular attention to the use of quotation marks. What effect is created by the author's use of quotation marks with *hardness*, *crustiness*, and *crusty*? How do the quotations by O'Keeffe help support the author's description of her?

"Hardness" has not been in our century a quality much admired in women, nor in the past twenty years has it even been in official favor for men. When hardness surfaces in the very old we tend to transform it into "crustiness" or eccentricity, some tonic pepperiness to be indulged at a distance. On the evidence of her work and what she has said about it, Georgia O'Keeffe is neither "crusty" nor eccentric. She is simply hard, a straight shooter, a woman clean of received wisdom and open to what she sees. This is a woman who could early on dismiss most of her contemporaries as "dreamy," and would later single out one she liked as "a very poor painter." (And then add, apparently by way of softening the judgment: "I guess he wasn't a painter at all. He had no courage and I believe that to create one's own world in any of the arts takes courage.") This is a woman who in 1939 could advise her admirers that they were missing her point, that their appreciation of her famous flowers was merely sentimental. "When I paint a red hill," she observed coolly in the catalogue for an exhibition that year, "you say it is too bad that I don't always paint flowers. A flower touches almost everyone's heart. A red hill doesn't touch everyone's heart."

— JOAN DIDION, "Georgia O'Keeffe"

Thinking about Your Own Use of Quotation Marks

Choose a topic that is of interest on your campus, and interview one of your friends about it. On the basis of your notes from the interview, write two or three paragraphs about your friend's views, using several direct quotations that support the points you are making. Then see how closely you followed the conventions for quotation marks explained in this chapter. Note any usages that caused you problems.

Parentheses, brackets, dashes, colons, slashes, and ellipses are all around. Pick up the television listings, for instance, and you will find these punctuation marks in abundance, helping viewers preview programs in a clear and efficient way.

⬤⑧ **College Football** *3:30* 501019/592361 — Northwestern Wildcats at Ohio State Buckeyes. The Buckeyes are looking for their 20th straight win over Northwestern. (Live) [Time approximate.]

You can use these marks of punctuation to signal relationships among sentence parts, to create particular rhythms, and to help readers follow your thoughts.

AT A GLANCE

Editing for Effective Use of Punctuation

- Be sure that any material enclosed in parentheses or set off with dashes requires special treatment — and that the parentheses or dashes don't make the sentence difficult to follow. Use parentheses to de-emphasize material they enclose and dashes to add emphasis. (43a and c)

- Use brackets to enclose parenthetical elements in material that is already within parentheses and to enclose words or comments inserted into a quotation. (43b)

- Use colons to introduce explanations, series, lists, and some quotations. Do not put a colon between a verb and its object or complement, between a preposition and its object, or after expressions like *such as*. (43d)

- Use slashes to mark line divisions in poetry quoted within your own text. (43e)

- Use ellipses (three equally spaced dots) to indicate omissions from quoted passages. (43f)

43a   Parentheses

Use parentheses to enclose material that is of minor or secondary importance in a sentence — material that supplements, clarifies, comments on, or illustrates what precedes or follows it.

▶ Inventors and men of genius have almost always been regarded as fools at the beginning (and very often at the end) of their careers.
　　　　　　　　　　　　　　　　　　　　　　　　– FYODOR DOSTOYEVSKY

▶ During my research, I found problems with the flat-rate income tax (a single-rate tax with no deductions).

Enclosing textual citations

▶ Freud and his followers have had a most significant impact on the ways abnormal functioning is understood and treated (Joseph, 1991).
　　　　　　　　　　　　　　　　　　– RONALD J. COMER, *Abnormal Psychology*

▶ Zamora notes that Kahlo referred to her first self-portrait, given to a close friend, as "your Botticelli" (110).

The first in-text citation shows the style of the American Psychological Association (APA); the second, the style of the Modern Language Association (MLA).

Enclosing numbers or letters in a list

▶ Five distinct styles can be distinguished: (1) Old New England, (2) Deep South, (3) Middle American, (4) Wild West, and (5) Far West or Californian.　　　　　　　　　　　　– ALISON LURIE, *The Language of Clothes*

With other marks of punctuation

A period may be placed either inside or outside a closing parenthesis, depending on whether the parenthetical text is part of a larger sentence. A comma, if needed, is always placed *outside* a closing parenthesis (and never before an opening one).

▶ Gene Tunney's single defeat in an eleven-year career was to a flamboyant and dangerous fighter named Harry Greb ("The Human Windmill"), who seems to have been, judging from boxing literature, the dirtiest fighter in history.　　　　　　　　　　– JOYCE CAROL OATES, "On Boxing"

Choosing among parentheses, commas, and dashes

In general, use commas when the material to be set off is least interruptive (38c, e, and f), parentheses when it is more interruptive, and dashes when it is the most interruptive (43c).

43b Brackets

Use brackets to enclose parenthetical elements in material that is itself within parentheses and to enclose explanatory words or comments that you are inserting into a quotation.

Setting off material within parentheses

▶ Eventually the investigation had to examine the major agencies (including the previously sacrosanct National Security Agency [NSA]) that were conducting covert operations.

Inserting material within quotations

▶ Massing notes that "on average, it [Fox News] attracts more than eight million people daily — more than double the number who watch CNN."

The bracketed words clarify *it* in the original quotation.

In the quotation in the following sentence, the artist Gauguin's name is misspelled. The bracketed word *sic,* which means "so," tells readers that the person being quoted — not the writer who has picked up the quotation — made the mistake.

▶ One admirer wrote, "She was the most striking woman I'd ever seen — a sort of wonderful combination of Mia Farrow and one of Gaugin's [*sic*] Polynesian nymphs."

EXERCISE 43.1

Revise the following sentences, using parentheses and brackets correctly. Example:

She was in fourth grade (or was it third?) when she became blind.

1. The committee was presented with three options to pay for the new park: 1 increase vehicle registration fees, 2 install parking meters downtown, or 3 borrow money from the reserve fund.

2. The FISA statute authorizes government wiretapping only under certain circumstances for instance, the government has to obtain a warrant.

3. The health care expert informed readers that "as we progress through middle age, we experience intimations of our own morality *sic*."

4. Some hospitals train nurses in a pseudoscientific technique called therapeutic touch TT that has been discredited by many rigorous studies.

5. The obnoxious actions of one marcher who, as it turned out, was an undercover police officer marred the otherwise peaceful protest.

43c Dashes

Dashes give more emphasis than parentheses to the material they enclose. With most word-processing software, a dash is made with two hyphens (--) with no spaces before, between, or after. Many word-processing programs automatically convert two typed hyphens into a solid dash.

▶ The pleasures of reading itself — who doesn't remember? — were like those of Christmas cake, a sweet devouring.
– EUDORA WELTY, "A Sweet Devouring"

Emphasizing explanatory material

▶ Indeed, several of modern India's greatest scholars — such as the Mughal historian Muzaffar Alam of the University of Chicago — are madrasa graduates. – WILLIAM DALRYMPLE

Emphasizing material at the end of a sentence

▶ In the twentieth century it has become almost impossible to moralize about epidemics — except those which are transmitted sexually.
– SUSAN SONTAG, *AIDS and Its Metaphors*

Marking a sudden change in tone

▶ New York is a catastrophe — but a magnificent catastrophe.
– LE CORBUSIER

Indicating hesitation in speech

▶ As the officer approached his car, the driver stammered, "What — what have I done?"

Introducing a summary or explanation

▶ In walking, the average adult person employs a motor mechanism that weighs about eighty pounds — sixty pounds of muscle and twenty pounds of bone. – EDWIN WAY TEALE

EXERCISE 43.2

Punctuate the following sentences with dashes where appropriate. Example:

He is quick, violent, and mean — they don't call him Dirty Harry for nothing — but appealing nonetheless.

1. Many people would have ignored the children's taunts but not Ace.

2. Even if marijuana is dangerous an assertion disputed by many studies it is certainly no more harmful to human health than alcohol and cigarettes, which remain legal.

3. If too much exposure to negative news stories makes you feel depressed or anxious and why wouldn't it? try going on a media fast.

4. Union Carbide's plant in Bhopal, India, sprang a leak that killed more than 2,000 people and injured an additional 200,000.

5. Hybrid vehicles especially those that require no external electric power continue to grow more popular.

43d Colons

Use a colon to introduce explanations or examples and to separate some elements from one another.

Introducing an explanation, an example, or an appositive

▶ The men may also wear the getup known as Sun Belt Cool: a pale beige suit, open-collared shirt (often in a darker shade than the suit), cream-colored loafers and aviator sunglasses.

— ALISON LURIE, *The Language of Clothes*

Introducing a series, a list, or a quotation

▶ At the baby's one-month birthday party, Ah Po gave him the Four Valuable Things: ink, inkslab, paper, and brush.

— MAXINE HONG KINGSTON, *China Men*

▶ The teachers wondered: "Do boys and girls really learn differently?"

The preceding example could have taken a comma instead of a colon (see 38h). Use a colon rather than a comma to introduce a quotation when the lead-in is a complete sentence on its own.

▶ The State of the Union address contained one surprising statement: "America is addicted to oil."

Separating elements

SALUTATIONS IN FORMAL LETTERS

▶ Dear Dr. Chapman:

HOURS, MINUTES, AND SECONDS

▶ 4:59 PM

▶ 2:15:06

RATIOS

▶ a ratio of 5:1

BIBLICAL CHAPTERS AND VERSES

▶ I Corinthians 3:3–5

TITLES AND SUBTITLES

▶ *The Joy of Insight:*
Passions of a Physicist

CITIES AND PUBLISHERS IN BIBLIOGRAPHIC ENTRIES

▶ Boston: Bedford, 2008

Editing for colons

Do not put a colon between a verb and its object or complement — unless the object is a quotation.

▶ Some natural fibers are: cotton, wool, silk, and linen.

Do not put a colon between a preposition and its object or after such expressions as *such as, especially,* and *including.*

▶ **In poetry, additional power may come from devices such as̷ simile,**
   metaphor, and alliteration.

EXERCISE 43.3

In the following items, insert a colon in any sentence that needs one and delete any unnecessary colons. Some sentences may be correct as written. Example:

> *Images: My Life in Film* includes revealing material written by Ingmar Bergman.
>   ^

1. The article made one point forcefully and repeatedly the United States must end its dependence on foreign oil.

2. Another example is taken from Psalm 139 16.

3. Roberto tried to make healthier choices, such as: eating organic food, walking to work, and getting plenty of rest.

4. A number of quotable movie lines come from *Casablanca*, including "Round up the usual suspects."

5. Sofi rushed to catch the 5 45 express but had to wait for the 6 19.

43e Slashes

Use slashes to mark line divisions between two or three lines of poetry quoted within running text. When using a slash to separate lines of poetry, precede and follow it with a space (42b).

▶ **In Sonnet 29, the persona states, "For thy sweet love rememb'red such**
   wealth brings / That then I scorn to change my state with kings."

Use a slash to separate alternatives.

▶ **Then there was Daryl, the cabdriver/bartender.**
                                        — JOHN L'HEUREUX, *The Handmaid of Desire*

Use slashes to separate parts of fractions and Internet addresses.

▶ **138¹/₂**

▶ **bedfordstmartins.com/everydaywriter**

43f Ellipses

Ellipses, or ellipsis points, are three equally spaced dots. Ellipses usually indicate that something has been omitted from a quoted passage, but they can also signal a pause or hesitation in speech in the same way that a dash can.

Indicating omissions

Just as you should carefully use quotation marks around any material that you quote directly from a source, so you should carefully use ellipses to indicate that you have left out part of a quotation that otherwise appears to be a complete sentence.

The ellipses in the following example indicate two omissions — one in the middle of the sentence and one at the end. When you omit the last part of a quoted sentence, add a period after the ellipses, for a total of four dots. Be sure a complete sentence comes before and after the four points. If you are adding your own ellipses to a quotation that already has other ellipses, enclose yours in brackets.

ORIGINAL TEXT

▶ **The quasi-official division of the population into three economic classes called high-, middle-, and low-income groups rather misses the point, because as a class indicator the amount of money is not as important as the source.** — PAUL FUSSELL, "Notes on Class"

WITH ELLIPSES

▶ **As Paul Fussell argues, "The quasi-official division of the population into three economic classes . . . rather misses the point. . . ."**

If your shortened quotation ends with a source (such as a page number, a name, or a title), follow these steps:

1. Use three ellipsis points but no period after the quotation.
2. Add the closing quotation mark, closed up to the third ellipsis point.
3. Add the source documentation in parentheses.
4. Use a period to indicate the end of the sentence.

▶ **Packer argues, "The Administration is right to reconsider its strategy . . ." (34).**

Indicating hesitation

▶ **Then the voice, husky and familiar, came to wash over us — "The winnah, and still heavyweight champeen of the world . . . Joe Louis."**
— MAYA ANGELOU, *I Know Why the Caged Bird Sings*

EXERCISE 43.4

The following sentences use the punctuation marks presented in this chapter very effectively. Read the sentences carefully; then choose one, and use it as a model for writing a sentence of your own, making sure to use the punctuation marks in the same way in your sentence.

1. The dad was — how can you put this gracefully? — a real blimp, a wide load, and the white polyester stretch-pants only emphasized the cargo.
   — GARRISON KEILLOR, "Happy to Be Here"

2. Not only are the distinctions we draw between male nature and female nature largely arbitrary and often pure superstition: they are completely beside the point.　— BRIGID BROPHY, "Women"

3. If no one, including you, liked the soup the first time round (and that's why you've got so much left over), there is no point in freezing it for some hopeful future date when, miraculously, it will taste delicious. But bagging leftovers — say, stews — in single portions can be useful for those evenings when you're eating alone.　— NIGELLA LAWSON, *How to Eat*

 bedfordstmartins.com/everydaywriter For exercises, go to **Exercise Central** and click on **Other Punctuation**.

EXERCISE 43.5: THINKING CRITICALLY

Reading with an Eye for Punctuation

In the following passage, Tom Wolfe uses dashes, parentheses, ellipses, and a colon to create rhythm and build momentum in a very long (178-word) sentence. The editorial comment inserted in brackets calls attention to the fact that the "right stuff" was, in the world Wolfe describes here, always male. Look carefully at how Wolfe and the editors use these punctuation marks, and then try writing a description of something that effectively uses as many of them as possible. Your description should be about the same length as Wolfe's passage, but it need not be all one sentence.

Likewise, "hassling" — mock dogfighting — was strictly forbidden, and so naturally young fighter jocks could hardly wait to go up in, say, a pair of F-100s and start the duel by making a pass at each other at 800 miles an hour, the winner being the pilot who could slip in behind the other one and get locked in on his [never *her* or *his or her!*] tail ("wax his tail"), and it was not uncommon for some eager jock to try too tight an outside turn and have his engine flame out, whereupon, unable to restart it, he has to eject . . . and he shakes his fist at the victor as he floats down by parachute and his million-dollar aircraft goes *kaboom!* on the palmetto grass or the desert floor, and he starts thinking about how he can get together with the other guy back at the base in time for the two of them to get their stories straight before the investigation: "I don't know what happened, sir. I was pulling up after a target run, and it just flamed out on me."　— TOM WOLFE, *The Right Stuff*

Thinking about Your Own Use of Punctuation

Look through a draft you have recently written or are working on, and check your use of parentheses, brackets, dashes, colons, slashes, and ellipses. Do you follow the conventions presented in this chapter? If not, revise accordingly. Check the material in parentheses to see if it could use more emphasis and thus be set off instead with dashes. Then check any material in dashes to see if it could do with less emphasis and thus be punctuated with commas or parentheses.

Capital Letters 44

Capital letters are a key signal in everyday life. Look around any store to see their importance: you can shop for Levi's or *any* blue jeans, for Coca-Cola or *any* cola, for Kleenex or *any* tissue. In each of these instances, the capital letter indicates a particular brand. This chapter will help you use capitals appropriately.

AT A GLANCE

Editing for Capitalization

- Capitalize the first word of each sentence. If you quote a poem, follow its original capitalization. (44a)
- Check to make sure you have appropriately capitalized proper nouns and proper adjectives. (44b)
- Review where you have used titles of people or of works to be sure you have capitalized them correctly. (44b and c)
- Double-check the capitalization of geographical directions (*north* or *North*?), family relationships (*dad* or *Dad*?), and seasons of the year (*winter,* not *Winter*). (44d)
- In email, check to see that you have not capitalized whole words or phrases. (44d)

44a Capitalize the first word of a sentence or line of poetry.

Capitalize the first word of a sentence. If you are quoting a full sentence, capitalize its first word.

▶ **Kennedy said, "Let us never negotiate out of fear."**

Capitalization of a sentence following a colon is optional.

▶ **Gould cites the work of Darwin: The [*or* the] theory of natural selection incorporates the principle of evolutionary ties among all animals.**

Capitalize a sentence within parentheses unless the parenthetical sentence is inserted into another sentence.

▶ **Gould cites the work of Darwin. (Other researchers cite more recent evolutionary theorists.)**

▶ **Gould cites the work of Darwin (see page 150).**

When citing poetry, follow the capitalization of the original poem. Though most poets capitalize the first word of each line in a poem, some poets do not.

▶ **Morning sun heats up the young beech tree leaves and almost lights them into fireflies**

— JUNE JORDAN, "Aftermath"

44b Capitalize proper nouns and proper adjectives.

Capitalize proper nouns (those naming specific persons, places, and things) and most proper adjectives (those formed from proper nouns). All other nouns are common nouns and are not capitalized unless they begin a sentence or are used as part of a proper noun: *a street* or *the street where you live,* but *Elm Street.* The following list shows proper nouns and adjectives on the left and related common nouns and adjectives on the right.

PEOPLE

Ang Lee	the film's director
Nixonian	political

NATIONS, NATIONALITIES, ETHNIC GROUPS, AND LANGUAGES

Brazil, Brazilian	their native country, his citizenship
Italian American	an ethnic group

PLACES

Pacific Ocean	an ocean
Hawaiian Islands	tropical islands

STRUCTURES AND MONUMENTS

the Lincoln Memorial	a monument
the Eiffel Tower	a landmark

SHIPS, TRAINS, AIRCRAFT, AND SPACECRAFT

the *Queen Mary*	a cruise ship
the *City of New Orleans*	the 6:00 train

ORGANIZATIONS, BUSINESSES, AND GOVERNMENT INSTITUTIONS

United Auto Workers	a trade union
Library of Congress	certain federal agencies

ACADEMIC INSTITUTIONS AND COURSES

University of Maryland	a state university
Political Science 102	my political science course

HISTORICAL EVENTS AND ERAS

the Easter Uprising	a rebellion
the Renaissance	the fifteenth century

RELIGIONS AND RELIGIOUS TERMS

God	a deity
the Qur'an	a holy book
Catholicism, Catholic	a religion, their religious affiliation

TRADE NAMES

Nike	running shoes
Cheerios	cereal

Some contemporary companies use capitals called *InterCaps* in the middle of their own or their product's names. Follow the style you see in company advertising or on the product itself — *eBay, FedEx, iTunes.*

Titles of individuals

Capitalize titles used before a proper name. When used alone or following a proper name, most titles are not capitalized. One common exception is the word *president*, which many writers capitalize whenever it refers to the president of the United States.

Chief Justice Roberts	John Roberts, the chief justice
Professor Lisa Ede	my English professor
Dr. Edward A. Davies	Edward A. Davies, our doctor

44c Capitalize titles of works.

Capitalize most words in titles of books, articles, stories, speeches, essays, plays, poems, documents, films, paintings, and musical compositions. Do not capitalize an article (*a, an, the*), a preposition, a conjunction, or the *to* in an infinitive unless it is the first or last word in a title or subtitle.

Walt Whitman: A Life	Declaration of Independence
"As Time Goes By"	*Charlie and the Chocolate Factory*
"Shooting an Elephant"	*Rebel without a Cause*

44d Revise unnecessary capitalization.

Do not capitalize a compass direction unless the word designates a specific geographic region.

▶ **Voters in the South and much of the West tend to favor socially conservative candidates.**

▶ **John Muir headed ~~West~~, motivated by the need to explore.**
   west,

Do not capitalize a word indicating a family relationship unless the word is used as part of the name or as a substitute for the name.

▶ **I could always tell when Mother was annoyed with Aunt Rose.**

▶ **When she was a child, my ~~Mother~~ shared a room with my ~~Aunt~~.**
   mother   *aunt.*

Do not capitalize seasons of the year and parts of the academic or financial year.

spring	fall semester
winter	winter term
autumn	third-quarter earnings

FOR MULTILINGUAL WRITERS

Learning English Capitalization

Capitalization systems vary considerably among languages, and some languages (Arabic, Chinese, Hindi, and Hebrew, for example) do not use capital letters at all. English may be the only language to capitalize the first-person singular pronoun (*I*), but Dutch and German capitalize some forms of the second-person pronoun (*you*). German capitalizes all nouns; English used to capitalize more nouns that it does now (see, for instance, the Declaration of Independence).

Do not capitalize whole words or phrases for emphasis in email, which comes across to readers as SHOUTING. Use italics, underlining, or asterisks to add emphasis.

▶ **Sorry for the abrupt response, but I am *very* busy.**

EXERCISE 44.1

Capitalize words as needed in the following sentences. Example:

> *T. S. Eliot,*   *The Waste Land,*   *Faber*   *Faber.*
> t.s. eliot, who wrote *the waste land,* was an editor at faber and faber.
>   ^   ^   ^   ^

1. the town in the south where i was raised had a statue of a civil war soldier in the center of main street.

2. reporters speculated about the secret location where vice president cheney had remained for several weeks.

3. the corporation for public broadcasting relies on donations as well as on grants from the national endowment for the arts.

4. every artist on a major label seems to want a lexus or a lincoln navigator and a chauffeur to drive it.

5. many americans remember where they were when they heard about the *columbia* disaster.

6. accepting an award for his score for the john wayne film *the high and the mighty,* dmitri tiomkin thanked beethoven, brahms, wagner, and strauss.

bedfordstmartins.com/everydaywriter For exercises on using capitalization, go to **Exercise Central** and click on **Capitalization**.

EXERCISE 44.2: THINKING CRITICALLY

The following poem uses unconventional capitalization. Read it over a few times, at least once aloud. What effect does the capitalization have? Why do you think the poet chose to use capitals as she did?

A little Madness in the Spring
Is wholesome even for the King,
But God be with the Clown —
Who ponders this tremendous scene —
This whole Experiment of Green —
As if it were his own!
— EMILY DICKINSON

45 Abbreviations and Numbers

Any time you open up a telephone book, you see an abundance of abbreviations and numbers, as in the following movie theater listing from the Berkeley, California, telephone book:

Oaks Theater   1875 Solano Av   Brk

AT A GLANCE

Editing Abbreviations and Numbers

- Use abbreviations and numbers according to the conventions of a specific field (see p. 415): for example, *57%* might be acceptable in a math paper, but *57 percent* may be more appropriate in a sociology essay. (45f)
- If you use an abbreviation readers might not understand, spell out the term the first time you use it, and give the abbreviation in parentheses. (45c)

Abbreviations and numbers allow writers to present detailed information in a small amount of space. This chapter explains the conventions for using abbreviations and figures in academic and professional writing.

45a Abbreviate some titles used before and all titles used after proper names.

Ms. Susanna Moller	Henry Louis Gates Jr.
Mr. Aaron Oforlea	Karen Lancry, MD
Dr. Cheryl Gold	Samuel Cohen, PhD

Other titles — including religious, academic, and government titles — should be spelled out in academic writing. In other writing, they can be abbreviated before a full name but should be written out when used with only a last name.

Rev. Fleming Rutledge	Reverend Rutledge
Prof. Jaime Mejía	Professor Mejía
Gen. Colin Powell	General Powell

Do not use both a title and an academic degree with a person's name. Use one or the other. Instead of *Dr. Beverly Moss, PhD,* write *Dr. Beverly Moss* or *Beverly Moss, PhD.* (Note that academic degrees such as *RN* and *PhD* often appear without periods; see 40a.)

45b Use abbreviations with years and hours.

You can use the following abbreviations with numerals. Notice that AD precedes the numeral; all other abbreviations follow the numeral. To-day, BCE and CE are generally preferred over BC and AD, and periods in all four of these abbreviations are optional.

399 BCE ("before the common era") or 399 BC ("before Christ")

49 CE ("common era") or AD 49 (*anno Domini,* Latin for "year of our Lord")

11:15 AM (*or* a.m.)

9:00 PM (*or* p.m.)

For abbreviations, you may use full-size capital letters or small caps, a typographical option in word-processing programs.

45c Use abbreviations for familiar business, government, and science terms.

As long as you can be sure your readers will understand them, use common abbreviations such as *PBS, NASA, DNA,* and *CIA.* If an abbreviation may be unfamiliar, however, spell out the full term the first time you use it, and give the abbreviation in parentheses. After that, you can use the abbreviation by itself.

▶ The Comprehensive Test Ban (CTB) Treaty was first proposed in the 1950s. For those nations signing it, the CTB would bring to a halt all nuclear weapons testing.

45d   Use abbreviations in official company names.

Use such abbreviations as *Co., Inc., Corp.,* and *&* if they are part of a company's official name. Do not, however, use these abbreviations in most other contexts.

> corporation
> ► Sears, Roebuck & Co. was the only large ~~corp.~~ in town.
>   ^

> Bros.
> ► Paola has a part-time job at the Warner ~~Brothers~~ store in the mall.
>   ^

45e   Use abbreviations in notes and source citations.

In general, avoid these Latin abbreviations except when citing sources:

cf.	compare (*confer*)
e.g.	for example (*exempli gratia*)
et al.	and others (*et alia*)
etc.	and so forth (*et cetera*)
i.e.	that is (*id est*)
N.B.	note well (*nota bene*)
P.S.	postscript (*postscriptum*)

> for example,
> ► Many firms have policies to help working parents — **e.g.,** flexible hours,
>   ^
> parental leave, and day care.

> ► Before the conference began, Haivan unpacked the name tags, programs,
>   and so forth.
> pens, ~~etc.~~
>   ^

45f   Abbreviate units of measurement, and use symbols in charts and graphs.

Symbols such as %, +, $, and = are acceptable in charts and graphs. Dollar signs are acceptable with figures: *$11* (but not with words: *eleven dollars*). Units of measurement can be abbreviated in charts and graphs (*4 in.*) but not in the body of a paper (*four inches*).

TALKING ABOUT STYLE

Abbreviations and Numbers in Different Fields

Use of abbreviations and numbers varies in different fields. See a typical example from a biochemistry textbook:

> The energy of a green photon . . . is 57 kilocalories per mole (kcal/mol). An alternative unit of energy is the joule (J), which is equal to 0.239 calorie; 1 kcal/mol is equal to 4.184 kJ/mol.
> — LUBERT STRYER, *Biochemistry*

These two sentences demonstrate how useful figures and abbreviations can be; reading the same sentences would be very difficult if the numbers and units of measurement were all written out.

Become familiar with the conventions governing abbreviations and numbers in your field. The following reference books provide guidelines:

MLA Handbook for Writers of Research Papers for literature and the humanities

Publication Manual of the American Psychological Association for the social sciences

Scientific Style and Format: The CSE Manual for Authors, Editors, and Publishers for the natural sciences

The Chicago Manual of Style for the humanities

AIP Style Manual for physics and the applied sciences

45g Use other abbreviations according to convention.

Some abbreviations required in notes and in source citations are not appropriate in the body of a paper.

CHAPTER AND PAGES	chapter, page, pages (*not* ch., p., pp.)
MONTHS	January, February (*not* Jan., Feb.)
STATES AND NATIONS	California, Mexico (*not* Calif., Mex.)
	Two exceptions are Washington, D.C., and U.S.

EXERCISE 45.1

Revise each of the following sentences to eliminate any abbreviations that would be inappropriate in most academic writing. Example:

United States

The population of the ~~U.S.~~ grew considerably in the 1980s.

1. Every Fri., my grandmother would walk a mi. to the P.O. and send a care package to her brother in Tenn.
2. An MX missile, which is 71 ft. long and 92 in. around, weighs 190,000 lbs.
3. Enron officials met with the V.P. of the U.S. to discuss the admin.'s energy policy, but soon afterward the Tex. co. declared bankruptcy.
4. A large corp. like AT&T may help finance an employee's M.B.A.
5. Rosie always began by saying, "If you want my two ¢," but she never waited to see if I wanted it or not.

45h Spell out numbers expressed in one or two words.

If you can write out a number in one or two words, do so. Use figures for longer numbers.

> Her screams were heard by ~~38~~ *thirty-eight* people, none of whom called the police.

> A baseball is held together by ~~two hundred sixteen~~ *216* red stitches.

If one of several numbers *of the same kind* in the same sentence requires a figure, you should use figures for all the numbers in that sentence.

> An audio system can range in cost from ~~one hundred dollars~~ *$100* to $2,599.

45i Spell out numbers that begin sentences.

When a sentence begins with a number, either spell out the number or rewrite the sentence.

> *One hundred nineteen*
> ~~119~~ years of CIA labor cost taxpayers sixteen million dollars.

Most readers find it easier to read figures than three-word numbers; thus the best solution may be to rewrite this sentence: *Taxpayers spent sixteen million dollars for 119 years of CIA labor.*

45j Use figures according to convention.

ADDRESSES
23 Main Street; 175 Fifth Avenue

DATES
September 17, 1951; 6 June 1983; 4 BCE; the 1860s

DECIMALS AND FRACTIONS	65.34; $8^{1}/_{2}$
PERCENTAGES	77 percent (*or* 77%)
EXACT AMOUNTS OF MONEY	$7,348; $1.46 trillion; $2.50; thirty-five (*or* 35) cents
SCORES AND STATISTICS	an 8–3 Red Sox victory; a verbal score of 600; an average age of 22; a mean of 53
TIME OF DAY	6:00 AM (*or* a.m.)

FOR MULTILINGUAL WRITERS

Using the Term *Hundred*

The term *hundred* is used idiomatically in English. When it is linked with numbers like two, eight, and so on, the word *hundred* remains singular: *Eight hundred years have passed and still old animosities run deep.* Add the plural *-s* to *hundred* only when no number precedes the term: *Hundreds of priceless books were lost in the fire.*

EXERCISE 45.2

Revise the numbers in the following sentences as necessary for correctness and consistency. Some sentences may be correct as written. Example:

> *twenty-first*
> Did the ~~21st~~ century begin in 2000 or 2001?
> ^

1. Al Gore won the popular vote with 50,996,116 votes, but he was still short by 5 electoral votes.
2. 2500 people wanted tickets, but the arena held only 1800.
3. The senator who voted against the measure received 6817 angry emails and only twelve in support of her decision.
4. Walker signed a three-year, $4.5-million contract.
5. In that age group, the risk is estimated to be about one in 2,500.

 bedfordstmartins.com/everydaywriter For exercises, go to **Exercise Central** and click on **Abbreviations and Numbers**.

EXERCISE 45.3: THINKING CRITICALLY

Reading with an Eye for Abbreviations and Numbers

The paragraph by Roger Angell in Exercise 47.2, at the end of Chapter 47, follows the style of the *New Yorker* magazine, which often spells out numbers in situations where this chapter recommends using figures. Read the paragraph carefully, and then consider whether it would have been easier to read if figures had been used for some of the numbers. If so, which ones? Then consider how the paragraph would have been different if Angell had used *semi-professional* instead of *semi-pro*. What effect does the abbreviated form create?

Thinking about Your Own Use of Abbreviations and Numbers

Look over an essay that you have written, noting all abbreviations and numbers. Check your usage for correctness, consistency, and appropriateness. If you discover a problem with abbreviations or numbers, make a note of it so that you can avoid the error in the future.

46 Italics

The slanted type known as *italics* is more than just a pretty typeface. Indeed, italics give words special meaning or emphasis. In the sentence "Many people read *People* on the subway every day," the italics (and the capital letter) tell us that *People* is a publication. You may use your computer to produce italic type; if not, underline words that you would otherwise italicize.

AT A GLANCE

Editing for Italics

- Check that all titles of long works are italicized. (46a)
- If you use any words, letters, or numbers as terms, make sure they are in italics. (46b)
- Italicize any non-English words or phrases that are not in an English dictionary. (46c)

46a   Italicize titles of long works.

In general, use italics for titles of long works; use quotation marks for shorter works (42c).

BOOKS	*Fun Home: A Family Tragicomic*
CHOREOGRAPHIC WORKS	Agnes de Mille's *Rodeo*
FILMS AND VIDEOS	*Juno*
LONG MUSICAL WORKS	*Brandenburg Concertos*

LONG POEMS	*Bhagavad Gita*
MAGAZINES AND JOURNALS	*Ebony,* the *New England Journal of Medicine*
NEWSPAPERS	the *Cleveland Plain Dealer*
PAINTINGS AND SCULPTURE	Georgia O'Keeffe's *Black Iris*
PAMPHLETS	Thomas Paine's *Common Sense*
PLAYS	*Sweeney Todd*
RADIO SERIES	*All Things Considered*
RECORDINGS	*Slade Alive!*
SOFTWARE	*Dreamweaver*
TELEVISION SERIES	*The Wire*
WEB SITES	*Voice of the Shuttle*

46b Italicize words, letters, and numbers used as terms.

▶ On the back of his jersey was the famous *24.*

▶ One characteristic of some New York speech is the absence of postvocalic *r* — for example, pronouncing the word *four* as "fouh."

46c Italicize non-English words and phrases.

Italicize words from other languages unless they have become part of English — like the French "bourgeois" or the Italian "pasta," for example. If a word is in an English dictionary, it does not need italics.

▶ At last one of the phantom sleighs gliding along the street would come to a stop, and with gawky haste Mr. Burness in his fox-furred *shapka* would make for our door.   — VLADIMIR NABOKOV, *Speak, Memory*

EXERCISE 46.1

In each of the following sentences, underline any words that should be italicized, and circle any italicized words that should not be. Example:

The film <u>Good Night, and Good Luck</u> tells the story of a CBS newsman

who helped to end the career of Senator Joseph McCarthy.

1. One critic claimed that few people listened to *The Velvet Underground and Nico* when the record was issued but that everyone who did formed a band.

2. Homemade *sushi* can be dangerous, but so can deviled eggs kept too long in a picnic basket.

3. The Web site Poisonous Plants and Animals lists tobacco (Nicotiana tobacum) as one of the most popular poisons in the world.

4. The monster in the Old English epic Beowulf got to tell his own side of the story in John Gardner's novel Grendel.

5. In Ray, Jamie Foxx looks as if he is actually singing Ray Charles's songs.

EXERCISE 46.2: THINKING CRITICALLY

Reading with an Eye for Italics

Read the following passage about a graduate English seminar carefully, particularly noting the effects created by the italics. How would it differ without any italic emphasis? What other words or phrases might the author have italicized?

> There were four big tables arranged in a square, with everyone's feet sticking out into the open middle of the square. You could tell who was nervous, and how much, by watching the pairs of feet twist around each other. The Great Man presided awesomely from the high bar of the square. His head was a majestic granite-gray, like a centurion in command; he *looked* famous. His clean shoes twitched only slightly, and only when he was angry.
>
> It turned out he was angry at me a lot of the time. He was angry because he thought me a disrupter, a rioter, a provocateur, and a fool; also crazy. And this was twenty years ago, before these things were *de rigueur* in the universities. Everything was very quiet in those days: there were only the Cold War and Korea and Joe McCarthy and the Old Old Nixon, and the only revolutionaries around were in Henry James's *The Princess Casamassima*.
>
> — CYNTHIA OZICK, "We Are the Crazy Lady"

Thinking about Your Own Use of Italics

Write a paragraph or two describing the most eccentric person you know, italicizing some words for special emphasis. Read your passage aloud to hear the effect of the italics. Now explain each use of italics. If you find yourself unable to give a reason, ask yourself whether the word should be italicized at all.

Then revise the passage to eliminate *all but one* use of italics. Try revising sentences and choosing more precise words to convey emphasis. Decide which version is more effective. Can you reach any conclusions about using italics for emphasis?

47 Hyphens

Hyphens are undoubtedly confusing to many people — hyphen problems are now one of the twenty most common surface errors in student writing. The confusion is understandable. Over time, the conventions for hyphen use in a given word can change (*tomorrow* was once spelled *to-morrow*).

New words, even compounds such as *firewall,* generally don't use hyphens, but controversy continues to rage over whether to hyphenate *email* (or is it *e-mail?*) And some words are hyphenated when they serve one kind of purpose in a sentence and not when they serve another.

47a **Use hyphens with compound words.**

Some compounds are one word (*rowboat*), some are separate words (*hard drive*), and some require hyphens (*sister-in-law*). You should consult a dictionary to be sure. However, the following conventions can help you decide when to use hyphens with compound words.

Compound adjectives

Hyphenate most compound adjectives that precede a noun but not those that follow a noun.

a *well-liked* boss My boss is *well liked.*
a *six-foot* plank The plank is *six feet long.*

In general, the reason for hyphenating compound adjectives is to facilitate reading.

▶ **Designers often use potted plants as living-room dividers.**

Without the hyphen *living* may seem to modify *room dividers.*

Never hyphenate an *-ly* adverb and an adjective.

▶ **They used a widely-distributed mailing list.**

AT A GLANCE

Editing for Hyphens

- Double-check compound words to be sure they are properly closed up, separated, or hyphenated. If in doubt, consult a dictionary. (47a)
- Check all terms that have prefixes or suffixes to see whether you need hyphens. (47b)
- If you break words at the end of a line, make sure they are divided at an appropriate point (47c)
- Do not hyphenate two-word verbs or word groups that serve as subject complements. (47d)

Fractions and compound numbers

Use a hyphen to write out fractions and to spell out compound numbers from twenty-one to ninety-nine.

one-seventh	thirty-seven
two and seven-sixteenths	three hundred fifty-four thousand

47b Use hyphens with prefixes and suffixes.

Most words containing prefixes or suffixes are written without hyphens: *antiwar, gorillalike*. Here are some exceptions:

BEFORE CAPITALIZED BASE WORDS	un-American, non-Catholic
WITH FIGURES	pre-1960, post-1945
WITH CERTAIN PREFIXES AND SUFFIXES	all-state, ex-partner, self-possessed, quasi-legislative, mayor-elect, fifty-odd
WITH COMPOUND BASE WORDS	pre-high school, post-cold war
FOR CLARITY OR EASE OF READING	re-cover, anti-inflation, troll-like

Re-cover means "cover again"; the hyphen distinguishes it from *recover*, meaning "get well." In *anti-inflation* and *troll-like*, the hyphens separate confusing clusters of vowels and consonants.

47c Use hyphens to divide words at the end of a line.

Word-processing programs generally wrap a word to the next line instead of breaking it with a hyphen. If you wish to divide a word at the end of a line, however, follow certain conventions.

- Break words between syllables only. All dictionaries show syllable breaks, so to divide words correctly, simply look them up.
- Never divide one-syllable words or abbreviations, contractions, or figures.
- Leave at least two letters on each line when dividing a word. Do not divide words such as *acorn* (*a-corn*) and *scratchy* (*scratch-y*) at all, and break a word such as *Americana* (*A-mer-i-can-a*) only after the *r* or the *i*.

- Divide compound words, such as *anklebone* and *mother-in-law*, only between their parts (*ankle-bone*) or after their hyphens.
- Divide words with prefixes or suffixes after the prefix (*dis-appearance*) or before the suffix (*disappear-ance*). Divide prefixed words that include a hyphen, such as *self-righteous*, after the hyphen.

47d Avoid unnecessary hyphens.

Unnecessary hyphens are at least as common a problem as omitted ones. Do not hyphenate the parts of a two-word verb such as *depend on, turn off,* or *tune out* (59b).

▶ **Player must pick⁄up a medical form before football tryouts.**

The words *pick up* act as a verb and should not be hyphenated.

However, be careful to check that two words do indeed function as a verb in the sentence; if they function as an adjective, a hyphen may be needed (30b).

▶ **Let's sign up for the early class.**

The verb *sign up* should not have a hyphen.

▶ **Where is the sign-up sheet?**

The compound adjective *sign-up*, which modifies the noun *sheet,* needs a hyphen.

Do not hyphenate a subject complement—a word group that follows a linking verb (such as a form of *be* or *seem*) and describes the subject (30k).

▶ **Audrey is almost three⁄years⁄old.**

EXERCISE 47.1

Insert or delete hyphens as necessary in the following sentences. Use your dictionary if you are not sure whether or where to hyphenate a word. Example:

The governor- elect joked about the polls.
  ^

1. She insisted that the line workers pick-up the pace.
2. Line-up quietly and wait for my signal.
3. Her ability to convey her ideas clearly has made her well-respected in the office.
4. After he spent four weeks in an alcohol re-habilitation program, he apologized to his wife for twenty two years of heavy drinking.

5. Having an ignore the customer attitude may actually make a service-industry job less pleasant.

6. Both pro and antiState Department groups registered complaints.

7. At a yard sale, I found a 1964 pre CBS Fender Stratocaster in mint condition.

8. Applicants who are over fifty-years-old may face age discrimination.

9. Neil Armstrong, a selfproclaimed "nerdy engineer," was the first person to set foot on the moon.

10. Carefully-marketed children's safety products suggest to new parents that the more they spend, the safer their kids will be.

 bedfordstmartins.com/everdaywriter For exercises, go to **Exercise Central** and click on **Hyphens**.

EXERCISE 47.2: THINKING CRITICALLY

The following paragraph uses many hyphens. Read it carefully, and note how the hyphens make the paragraph easier to read. Why do you think *semi-pro* is hyphenated? Why is *junior-college* hyphenated in the last sentence?

All semi-pro leagues, it should be understood, are self-sustaining, and have no farm affiliation or other connection with the twenty-six major-league clubs, or with the seventeen leagues and hundred and fifty-two teams . . . that make up the National Association — the minors, that is. There is no central body of semi-pro teams, and semi-pro players are not included among the six hundred and fifty major-leaguers, the twenty-five-hundred-odd minor-leaguers, plus all the managers, coaches, presidents, commissioners, front-office people, and scouts, who, taken together, constitute the great tent called organized ball. (A much diminished tent, at that; back in 1949, the minors included fifty-nine leagues, about four hundred and forty-eight teams, and perhaps ten thousand players.) Also outside the tent, but perhaps within its shade, are five college leagues, ranging across the country from Cape Cod to Alaska, where the most promising freshman, sophomore, and junior-college ballplayers . . . compete against each other. . . .   — ROGER ANGELL, "In the Country"

MLA
Documentation

Careful citation shows your reader that
you've done your homework. . . . It amounts to
laying your intellectual cards on the table.

— JACK LYNCH

MLA Documentation

This part of *The Everyday Writer* discusses the basic format for the Modern Language Association (MLA) style and provides examples of various kinds of sources. MLA style is widely used to document sources in writing that deals with literature, languages, and other fields in the humanities. For further reference, consult the *MLA Handbook for Writers of Research Papers,* Seventh Edition (2009).

 bedfordstmartins.com/everydaywriter To access this advice online, click on **Documenting Sources.**

DIRECTORY TO MLA STYLE

48 MLA Style for In-Text Citations

MLA style requires documentation in the text of an essay for every quotation, paraphrase, summary, or other material requiring documentation (see 17f). In-text citations document material from other sources with both signal phrases and parenthetical references. Parenthetical references should include the information your readers need to locate the full reference in the list of works cited at the end of the text. (See Chapter 50.) An in-text citation in MLA style gives the reader two kinds of information: (1) it indicates *which source* on the works-cited page the writer is referring to, and (2) it explains *where in the source* the material quoted, paraphrased, or summarized can be found.

The basic MLA in-text citation includes the author's last name either in a signal phrase introducing the source material (see 17b) or in parentheses at the end of the sentence. It also includes the page number in parentheses at the end of the sentence.

1. CITATION USING A SIGNAL PHRASE

In his discussion of Monty Python routines, Crystal notes that the group relished "breaking the normal rules" of language (107).

2. PARENTHETICAL CITATION

A noted linguist explains that Monty Python humor often relied on "bizarre linguistic interactions" (Crystal 108).

Note in the following examples where punctuation is placed in relation to the parentheses.

3. AUTHOR NAMED IN A SIGNAL PHRASE

The MLA recommends using the author's name in a signal phrase to introduce the material and citing the page number(s) in parentheses.

Lee claims that his comic-book creation, Thor, was "the first regularly published superhero to speak in a consistently archaic manner" (199).

4. AUTHOR NAMED IN A PARENTHETICAL REFERENCE

When you do not mention the author in a signal phrase, include the author's last name before the page number(s) in the parentheses. Use no punctuation between the author's name and the page number(s).

> The word *Bollywood* is sometimes considered an insult because it implies that Indian movies are merely "a derivative of the American film industry" (Chopra 9).

5. TWO OR THREE AUTHORS

Use all the authors' last names in a signal phrase or in parentheses.

> Gortner, Hebrun, and Nicolson maintain that "opinion leaders" influence other people in an organization because they are respected, not because they hold high positions (175).

6. FOUR OR MORE AUTHORS

Use the first author's name and *et al.* ("and others"), or name all the authors in a signal phrase or in parentheses.

> Similarly, as Belenky et al. assert, examining the lives of women expands our understanding of human development (7).

> Similarly, as Belenky, Clinchy, Tarule, and Goldberger assert, examining the lives of women expands our understanding of human development (7).

7. ORGANIZATION AS AUTHOR

Give the group's full name or a shortened form of it in a signal phrase or in parentheses.

> Any study of social welfare involves a close analysis of "the impacts, the benefits, and the costs" of its policies (Social Research Corporation iii).

8. UNKNOWN AUTHOR

Use the full title, if it is brief, in your text — or a shortened version of the title in parentheses.

> One analysis defines *hype* as "an artificially engendered atmosphere of hysteria" ("Today's Marketplace" 51).

9. AUTHOR OF TWO OR MORE WORKS CITED IN THE SAME PROJECT

If your list of works cited has more than one work by the same author, include a shortened version of the title of the work you are citing in a signal phrase or in parentheses to prevent reader confusion.

Gardner shows readers their own silliness in his description of a "pointless, ridiculous monster, crouched in the shadows, stinking of dead men, murdered children, and martyred cows" (*Grendel* 2).

10. TWO OR MORE AUTHORS WITH THE SAME LAST NAME

Include the author's first *and* last names in a signal phrase or first initial and last name in a parenthetical reference.

Children will learn to write if they are allowed to choose their own subjects, James Britton asserts, citing the Schools Council study of the 1960s (37-42).

11. INDIRECT SOURCE (AUTHOR QUOTING SOMEONE ELSE)

Use the abbreviation *qtd. in* to indicate that you are quoting from someone else's report of a source.

As Arthur Miller says, "When somebody is destroyed everybody finally contributes to it, but in Willy's case, the end product would be virtually the same" (qtd. in Martin and Meyer 375).

12. MULTIVOLUME WORK

In a parenthetical reference, note the volume number first and then the page number(s), with a colon and one space between them.

Modernist writers prized experimentation and gradually even sought to blur the line between poetry and prose, according to Forster (3: 150).

If you name only one volume of the work in your list of works cited, include only the page number in the parentheses.

13. LITERARY WORK

Because literary works are often available in many different editions, cite the page number(s) from the edition you used followed by a semicolon, and then give other identifying information that will lead readers to the passage in any edition. Indicate the act and/or scene in a play (*37; sc. 1*). For a novel, indicate the part or chapter (*175; ch. 4*).

In utter despair, Dostoyevsky's character Mitya wonders aloud about the "terrible tragedies realism inflicts on people" (376; bk. 8, ch. 2).

For a poem, cite the part (if there is one) and line(s), separated by a period. If you are citing only line numbers, use the word *line(s)* in the first reference (*lines 33–34*).

Whitman speculates, "All goes onward and outward, nothing collapses, / And to die is different from what anyone supposed, and luckier" (6.129-30).

For a verse play, give only the act, scene, and line numbers, separated by periods.

The witches greet Banquo as "Lesser than Macbeth, and greater" (1.3.65).

14. WORK IN AN ANTHOLOGY OR COLLECTION

For an essay, short story, or other piece of prose reprinted in an anthology, use the name of the author of the work, not the editor of the anthology, but use the page number(s) from the anthology.

Narratives of captivity play a major role in early writing by women in the United States, as demonstrated by Silko (219).

15. SACRED TEXT

To cite a sacred text such as the Qur'an or the Bible, give the title of the edition you used, the book, and the chapter and verse (or their equivalent) separated by a period. In your text, spell out the names of books. In parenthetical references, use abbreviations for books with names of five or more letters (*Gen.* for *Genesis*).

He ignored the admonition "Pride goes before destruction, and a haughty spirit before a fall" (*New Oxford Annotated Bible,* Prov. 16.18).

16. ENCYCLOPEDIA OR DICTIONARY ENTRY

An entry from a reference work — such as an encyclopedia or dictionary — without an author will appear on the works-cited list under the entry's title. Enclose the title in quotation marks and place it in parentheses. Omit the page number for reference works that arrange entries alphabetically.

The term *prion* was coined by Stanley B. Prusiner from the words *proteinaceous* and *infectious* and a suffix meaning *particle* ("Prion").

17. ELECTRONIC OR NONPRINT SOURCE

Give enough information in a signal phrase or in parentheses for readers to locate the source in your list of works cited. Many works found online or in electronic databases lack stable page numbers; you can omit the page number in such cases. However, if you are citing a work with stable pagination, such as an article in PDF format, include the page number in parentheses.

> As a *Slate* analysis has noted, "Prominent sports psychologists get praised for
> their successes and don't get grief for their failures" (Engber).

The source, an article on a Web site, does not have stable pagination.

> According to Whitmarsh, the British military had experimented with using
> balloons for observation as far back as 1879 (328).

The source, an online PDF of a print article, includes stable page numbers.

If the source includes numbered sections, paragraphs, or screens, include the abbreviation (*sec.*), paragraph (*par.*), or screen (*scr.*) number in parentheses.

> Sherman notes that the "immediate, interactive, and on-the-spot" nature of
> Internet information can make nondigital media seem outdated (sec. 32).

18. ENTIRE WORK

Include the reference in the text, without any page numbers.

> Jon Krakauer's *Into the Wild* both criticizes and admires the solitary impulses of
> its young hero, which end up killing him.

19. TWO OR MORE SOURCES IN ONE PARENTHETICAL REFERENCE

Separate the information with semicolons.

> Economists recommend that *employment* be redefined to include unpaid domestic
> labor (Clark 148; Nevins 39).

20. VISUALS INCLUDED IN THE TEXT

When you include an image in your text, number it and include a parenthetical reference in your text *(see Fig. 2)*. Number figures (photos, drawings, cartoons, maps, graphs, and charts) and tables separately. Each visual should include a caption with the figure or table number and information about the source. (See 4d.)

> This trend is illustrated in a chart distributed by the College Board as part of its
> 2002 analysis of aggregate SAT data (see Fig. 1).

Soon after the preceding sentence, readers find the following figure and caption (see Chapter 51 to read the student's entire research paper):

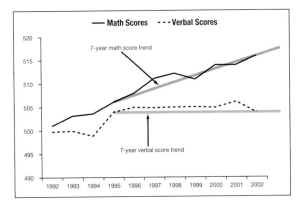

Fig. 1. Comparison of SAT math and verbal scores (1992-2002). Trend lines added. Source: Kristin Carnahan and Chiara Coletti, *Ten-Year Trend in SAT Scores Indicates Increased Emphasis on Math Is Yielding Results; Reading and Writing Are Causes for Concern*. New York: College Board, 2002; print; 9.

An image that you create might appear with a caption like this:

Fig. 4. Young woman reading a magazine. Personal photograph by author.

MLA Style for Explanatory and Bibliographic Notes

49

MLA style recommends explanatory notes for information or commentary that does not readily fit into your text but is needed for clarification or further explanation. In addition, MLA style permits bibliographic notes for citing several sources for one point and for offering thanks to, information about, or evaluation of a source. Use superscript numbers in the text to refer readers to the notes, which may appear as endnotes (typed under the heading *Notes* on a separate page after the text but before the list of works cited) or as footnotes at the bottom of the page.

1. SUPERSCRIPT NUMBER IN TEXT

Stewart emphasizes the existence of social contacts in Hawthorne's life so that the audience will accept a different Hawthorne, one more attuned to modern times than the figure in Woodberry.[3]

2. NOTE

[3] Woodberry does, however, show that Hawthorne was often an unsociable individual. He emphasizes the seclusion of Hawthorne's mother, who separated herself from her family after the death of her husband, often even taking meals alone (28). Woodberry seems to imply that Mrs. Hawthorne's isolation rubbed off onto her son.

50 MLA Style for a List of Works Cited

A list of works cited is an alphabetical list of the sources you have referred to in your essay. (If your instructor asks you to list everything you have read as background, call the list *Works Consulted*.)

Guidelines for author listings

The list of works cited is arranged alphabetically. The in-text citations in your writing point readers toward particular sources on the list (see Chapter 48).

NAME CITED IN SIGNAL PHRASE IN TEXT

Crystal explains. . . .

NAME IN PARENTHETICAL CITATION IN TEXT

. . . (Crystal 107).

BEGINNING OF ENTRY ON LIST OF WORKS CITED

Crystal, David.

AT A GLANCE

Formatting a List of Works Cited

- Start your list on a separate page after the text of your essay and any notes.
- Continue the consecutive numbering of pages.
- Center the heading *Works Cited* (not italicized or in quotation marks) one inch from the top of the page.
- Start each entry flush with the left margin; indent subsequent lines for the entry one-half inch or five spaces. Double-space the entire list.
- List sources alphabetically by the first word. Start with the author's name, if available; if not, use the editor's name, if available. If no author or editor is given, start with the title.
- List the author's last name first, followed by a comma and the first name. If a source has multiple authors, subsequent authors' names appear first name first (see model 2).
- Italicize titles of books and long works, but put titles of articles and other short works in quotation marks.
- In general, use a period and a space after each element of the entry; look at the models in this chapter for information on punctuating particular kinds of entries.
- List the city of publication without a state or country. Follow it with a colon and a shortened form of the publisher's name—omit *Co.* or *Inc.*, shorten names such as *HarperCollins* to *Harper* or *Simon & Schuster* to *Simon*, and abbreviate *University Press* to *UP*.
- List inclusive page numbers for a part of a larger work. For numbers 1–99, give all digits in the second number. For numbers larger than 99, give the last two digits of the second number (*115–18, 1378–79*) and any other digits that change in the second number (*296–301*).

Models 1–5 below explain how to arrange author names. The information that follows the name of the author depends on the type of work you are citing — a book (models 6–26); a print periodical (models 27–34); a written text from an electronic source, such as an article from a Web site or database (models 35–55); sources from art, film, radio, or other media, including online versions (models 56–68); and other kinds of sources (models 69–77). Consult the model that most closely resembles the kind of source you are using.

1. ONE AUTHOR

Put the last name first, followed by a comma, the first name (and initial, if any), and a period.

Crystal, David.

2. MULTIPLE AUTHORS

List the first author with the last name first (see model 1). Give the names of any other authors with the first name first. Separate authors' names with commas, and include the word *and* before the last person's name.

> Martineau, Jane, Desmond Shawe-Taylor, and Jonathan Bate.

For four or more authors, either list all the names, or list the first author followed by a comma and *et al.* ("and others").

> Lupton, Ellen, Jennifer Tobias, Alicia Imperiale, Grace Jeffers, and Randi Mates.

> Lupton, Ellen, et al.

3. ORGANIZATION OR GROUP AUTHOR

Give the name of the group, government agency, corporation, or other organization listed as the author.

> Getty Trust.

> United States. Government Accountability Office.

4. UNKNOWN AUTHOR

When the author is not identified, begin the entry with the title, and alphabetize by the first important word. Italicize titles of books and long works, but put titles of articles and other short works in quotation marks.

> "California Sues EPA over Emissions."

> *New Concise World Atlas.*

5. TWO OR MORE WORKS BY THE SAME AUTHOR

Arrange the entries alphabetically by title. Include the author's name in the first entry, but in subsequent entries, use three hyphens followed by a period. (For the basic format for citing a book, see model 6. For the basic format for citing an article from an online newspaper, see model 39.)

> Chopra, Anupama. "Bollywood Princess, Hollywood Hopeful." *New York Times.*
> New York Times, 10 Feb. 2008. Web. 13 Feb. 2008.

> ---. *King of Bollywood: Shah Rukh Khan and the Seductive World of Indian Cinema.*
> New York: Warner, 2007. Print.

Note: Use three hyphens only when the work is by *exactly* the same author(s) as the previous entry.

Books

6. BASIC FORMAT FOR A BOOK

Begin with the author name(s). (See models 1–5.) Then include the title and subtitle, the city of publication, the publisher, and the publication date. The source map on pp. 440–41 shows where to find this information in a typical book.

> Crystal, David. *Language Play*. Chicago: U of Chicago P, 1998. Print.

Note: Place a period and a space after the name, title, and date. Place a colon after the city and a comma after the publisher, and shorten the publisher's name — omit *Co.* or *Inc.*, and abbreviate *University Press* to *UP*.

7. AUTHOR AND EDITOR BOTH NAMED

> Bangs, Lester. *Psychotic Reactions and Carburetor Dung*. Ed. Greil Marcus.
>   New York: Knopf, 1988. Print.

Note: To cite the editor's contribution instead, begin the entry with the editor's name.

> Marcus, Greil, ed. *Psychotic Reactions and Carburetor Dung*. By Lester Bangs.
>   New York: Knopf, 1988. Print.

8. EDITOR, NO AUTHOR NAMED

> Wall, Cheryl A., ed. *Changing Our Own Words: Essays on Criticism, Theory, and*
>   *Writing by Black Women*. New Brunswick: Rutgers UP, 1989. Print.

9. ANTHOLOGY

Cite an entire anthology the same way you would cite a book with an editor and no named author (see model 8).

> Walker, Dale L., ed. *Westward: A Fictional History of the American West*.
>   New York: Forge, 2003. Print.

10. WORK IN AN ANTHOLOGY OR CHAPTER IN A BOOK WITH AN EDITOR

List the author(s) of the selection or chapter; its title, in quotation marks; the title of the book, italicized; *Ed.* and the name(s) of the editor(s); publication information; and the selection's page numbers.

> Komunyakaa, Yusef. "Facing It." *The Seagull Reader*. Ed. Joseph Kelly. New York:
>   Norton, 2000. 126-27. Print.

SOURCE MAP: Books, MLA style

Take information from the book's title page and copyright page (on the reverse side of the title page), not from the book's cover or a library catalog.

1 **Author.** List the last name first, followed by a comma, the first name, and the middle initial (if given). End with a period. For multiple authors, see model 2.

2 **Title.** Italicize the title and any subtitle; capitalize all major words. End with a period. (See 44c for more on capitalizing titles.)

3 **City of publication.** If more than one city is given, use the first one listed. For foreign cities that may be unfamiliar to your readers, add an abbreviation of the country or province (*Cork, Ire.*). Follow it with a colon.

4 **Publisher.** Give a shortened version of the publisher's name (*Harper* for *HarperCollins Publishers; Harcourt* for *Harcourt Brace; Oxford UP* for *Oxford University Press*). Follow it with a comma.

5 **Year of publication.** Consult the copyright page. If more than one copyright date is given, use the most recent one. End with a period.

6 **Medium of publication.** End with the medium (*Print*) followed by a period.

For a book by one author, use the following format:

Last name, First name. *Title of book.* City: Publisher, Year.

A citation for the book on p. 441 would look like this:

AUTHOR   TITLE AND SUBTITLE   CITY

Twitchell, James B. *Living It Up: America's Love Affair with Luxury.* New York:

PUBL.   YEAR MEDIUM

Simon, 2002. Print.

For more on using MLA style to cite books, see pp. 436–44. (For guidelines and models for using APA style, see pp. 486–90; for *Chicago* style, see pp. 514–15; for CSE style, see pp. 532–34.)

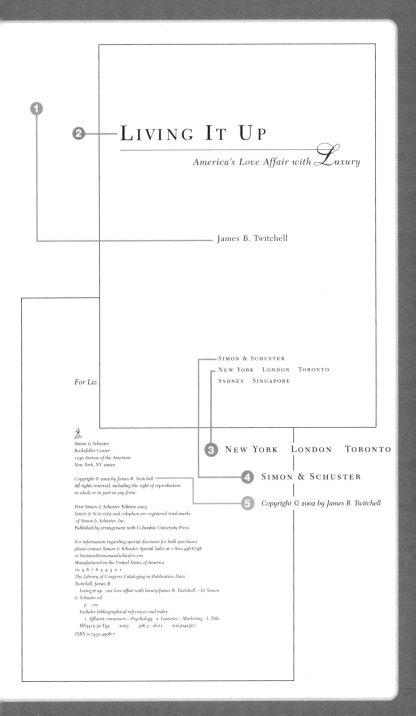

LIVING IT UP

America's Love Affair with $\mathscr{L}$*uxury*

James B. Twitchell

SIMON & SCHUSTER
NEW YORK   LONDON   TORONTO
SYDNEY   SINGAPORE

For Liz

Simon & Schuster
Rockefeller Center
1230 Avenue of the Americas
New York, NY 10020

First Simon & Schuster Edition 2003
SIMON & SCHUSTER and colophon are registered trademarks
of Simon & Schuster, Inc.
Published by arrangement with Columbia University Press

For information regarding special discounts for bulk purchases,
please contact Simon & Schuster Special Sales at 1-800-456-6798
or business@simonandschuster.com
Manufactured in the United States of America
10 9 8 7 6 5 4 3 2 1
The Library of Congress Cataloging-in-Publication Data
Twitchell, James B.
   Living it up : our love affair with luxury/James B. Twitchell. —1st Simon
& Schuster ed.
      p.   cm.
   Includes bibliographical references and index.
      1. Affluent consumers—Psychology. 2. Luxuries—Marketing. I. Title.
   HF5415.32.T95   2003   306.3—dc21   2003041507
ISBN 0-7432-4506-7

NEW YORK   LONDON   TORONTO

SIMON & SCHUSTER

Note: Use the following format to provide original publication information for a reprinted selection:

> Byatt, A. S. "The Thing in the Forest." *New Yorker* 3 June 2002: 80-89. Rpt. in *The O.*
> *Henry Prize Stories 2003*. Ed. Laura Furman. New York: Anchor, 2003. 3-22. Print.

11. TWO OR MORE ITEMS FROM THE SAME ANTHOLOGY

List the anthology as one entry (see model 9). Also list each selection
separately with a cross-reference to the anthology.

> Estleman, Loren D. "Big Tim Magoon and the Wild West." Walker 391-404. Print.
>
> Salzer, Susan K. "Miss Libbie Tells All." Walker 199-212. Print.

12. TRANSLATION

> Boethius, Anicius M. S. *The Consolation of Philosophy*. Trans. V. E. Watts. London:
> Penguin, 1969. Print.

13. BOOK WITH BOTH TRANSLATOR AND EDITOR

List the editor's and translator's names after the title, in the order they
appear on the title page.

> Kant, Immanuel. *"Toward Perpetual Peace" and Other Writings on Politics, Peace,*
> *and History*. Ed. Pauline Kleingeld. Trans. David L. Colclasure. New Haven:
> Yale UP, 2006. Print.

14. TRANSLATION OF A SECTION OF A BOOK

If different translators have worked on various parts of the book, identify the translator of the part you are citing.

> García Lorca, Federico. "The Little Mad Boy." Trans. W. S. Merwin. *The Selected*
> *Poems of Federico García Lorca*. Ed. Francisco García Lorca and Donald M.
> Allen. London: Penguin, 1969. Print.

15. TRANSLATION OF A BOOK BY AN UNKNOWN AUTHOR

> *Grettir's Saga*. Trans. Denton Fox and Hermann Palsson. Toronto: U of Toronto P, 1974. Print.

16. BOOK IN A LANGUAGE OTHER THAN ENGLISH

Include a translation of the title in brackets, if necessary.

> Benedetti, Mario. *La borra del café [The Coffee Grind]*. Buenos Aires:
> Sudamericana, 2000. Print.

17. EDITION OTHER THAN THE FIRST

> Walker, John A. *Art in the Age of Mass Media*. 3rd ed. London: Pluto, 2001. Print.

18. ONE VOLUME OF A MULTIVOLUME WORK

Give the number of the volume cited after the title. Including the total number of volumes after the publication date is optional.

> Ch'oe, Yong-Ho, Peter Lee, and William Theodore De Barry, eds. *Sources of Korean Tradition*. Vol. 2. New York: Columbia UP, 2000. Print. 2 vols.

19. TWO OR MORE VOLUMES OF A MULTIVOLUME WORK

> Ch'oe, Yong-Ho, Peter Lee, and William Theodore De Barry, eds. *Sources of Korean Tradition*. 2 vols. New York: Columbia UP, 2000. Print.

20. PREFACE, FOREWORD, INTRODUCTION, OR AFTERWORD

After the writer's name, describe the contribution. After the title, indicate the book's author (with *By*) or editor (with *Ed.*).

> Atwan, Robert. Foreword. *The Best American Essays 2002*. Ed. Stephen Jay Gould. Boston: Houghton, 2002. viii-xii. Print.

> Moore, Thurston. Introduction. *Confusion Is Next: The Sonic Youth Story*. By Alec Foege. New York: St. Martin's, 1994. xi. Print.

21. ENTRY IN A REFERENCE BOOK

For a well-known encyclopedia, note the edition (if identified) and year of publication. If the entries are alphabetized, omit publication information and page number.

> Kettering, Alison McNeil. "Art Nouveau." *World Book Encyclopedia*. 2002 ed. Print.

22. BOOK THAT IS PART OF A SERIES

Cite the series name (and number, if any) from the title page.

> Nichanian, Marc, and Vartan Matiossian, eds. *Yeghishe Charents: Poet of the Revolution*. Costa Mesa: Mazda, 2003. Print. Armenian Studies Ser. 5.

23. REPUBLICATION (MODERN EDITION OF AN OLDER BOOK)

Indicate the original publication date after the title.

> Austen, Jane. *Sense and Sensibility*. 1813. New York: Dover, 1996. Print.

24. PUBLISHER'S IMPRINT

If the title page gives a publisher's imprint, hyphenate the imprint and the publisher's name.

> Hornby, Nick. *About a Boy*. New York: Riverhead-Penguin Putnam, 1998. Print.

25. BOOK WITH A TITLE WITHIN THE TITLE

Do not italicize a book title within a title. For an article title within a title, italicize as usual and place the article title in quotation marks.

> Mullaney, Julie. *Arundhati Roy's* The God of Small Things*: A Reader's Guide.*
>
> New York: Continuum, 2002. Print.

> Rhynes, Martha. *"I, Too, Sing America": The Story of Langston Hughes.*
>
> Greensboro: Morgan, 2002. Print.

26. SACRED TEXT

To cite individual published editions of sacred books, begin the entry with the title.

> *Qur'an: The Final Testament (Authorized English Version) with Arabic Text.* Trans.
>
> Rashad Khalifa. Fremont: Universal Unity, 2000. Print.

Print periodicals

Begin with the author name(s). (See models 1–5.) Then include the article title, the title of the periodical, the date or volume information, and the page numbers. The source map on pp. 446–47 shows where to find this information in a sample periodical.

AT A GLANCE

Formatting Periodical Entries

- Put titles of articles from periodicals in quotation marks. Place the period inside the closing quotation mark.

- Give the title of the periodical as it appears on the magazine's or journal's cover or newspaper's front page; omit any initial *A, An,* or *The.* Italicize the title.

- For journals, include the volume number, a period, the issue number, if given, and the year in parentheses.

- For magazines and newspapers, give the date in this order: day (if given), month, year. Abbreviate months except for May, June, and July.

- List inclusive page numbers if the article appears on consecutive pages. If it skips pages, give only the first page number and a plus sign.

- If you accessed the article electronically, add electronic publication information—the title of the site or database, italicized; the date of publication or latest update; the name of any sponsoring institution or organization—and access information, including the most recent date you accessed the source (in day, month, year order). Include a URL only if readers will have difficulty finding your source without one. (See models 35–39 and the box on p. 448.) End with a period.

27. ARTICLE IN A JOURNAL

Follow the journal title with the volume number, a period, the issue number (if given), and the year (in parentheses).

> Gigante, Denise. "The Monster in the Rainbow: Keats and the Science of Life."
>> *PMLA* 117.3 (2002): 433-48. Print.

28. ARTICLE THAT SKIPS PAGES

When an article skips pages, give only the first page number and a plus sign.

> Tyrnauer, Matthew. "Empire by Martha." *Vanity Fair* Sept. 2002: 364+. Print.

29. ARTICLE IN A MAGAZINE

Provide the date from the magazine cover instead of volume or issue numbers.

> Surowiecki, James. "The Stimulus Strategy." *New Yorker* 25 Feb. 2008: 29. Print.

> Taubin, Amy. "All Talk?" *Film Comment* Nov.-Dec. 2007: 45-47. Print.

30. ARTICLE IN A NEWSPAPER

Include the edition (if listed) and the section number or letter (if listed).

> Bernstein, Nina. "On Lucille Avenue, the Immigration Debate." *New York Times*
>> 26 June 2006, late ed.: A1+. Print.

Note: For locally published newspapers, add the city in brackets after the name if it is not part of the name: *Globe and Mail [Toronto]*.

31. ARTICLE IN A COLLECTION OF REPRINTED ARTICLES

First give the citation for the original publication. Then give the citation for the collection in which the article is reprinted (see model 10). Indicate a compiler with *Comp.*

> Quindlen, Anna. "Playing God on No Sleep." *Newsweek* 2 July 2001: 64. Rpt. in
>> *The Best American Magazine Writing 2002*. Comp. Amer. Soc. of Magazine
>> Eds. New York: Perennial, 2002. 458-62. Print.

32. EDITORIAL OR LETTER TO THE EDITOR

Include the writer's name, if given, and the title, if any, followed by a label for the work.

> "California Dreaming." Editorial. *Nation* 25 Feb. 2008: 4. Print.

> Galbraith, James K. "JFK's Plans to Withdraw." Letter. *New York Review of Books*
>> 6 Dec. 2007: 77-78. Print.

SOURCE MAP: Articles from periodicals, MLA style

1 **Author.** List the last name first, followed by a comma, the first name, and the middle initial (if given). End with a period.

2 **Article title.** Enclose the title and any subtitle in quotation marks, and capitalize all major words. The closing period goes inside the closing quotation mark. (See 44c for more on capitalizing titles.)

3 **Periodical title.** Italicize the periodical title (omit initial *A, An,* or *The*), and capitalize major words. For journals, give the volume number and issue number (if any), separated by a period.

4 **Date of publication.** For journals, list the year in parentheses and a colon. For magazines and newspapers, list the day (if given), month, and year.

5 **Page numbers.** List inclusive page numbers unless the article skips pages; then use the first page number and a plus sign. For numbers up to 99, note all digits. For numbers above 99, note the last two digits and any other digits that change in the second number (115–18, 296–301). Include section letters for newspapers. End with a period.

6 **Medium of publication.** End with the medium of publication (*Print*) followed by a period.

For a journal article, use the following format:

Last name, First name. "Title of article." *Journal* Volume number.Issue number (year):
    Page number(s). Medium.

For a newspaper article, use the following format:

Last name, First name. "Title." *Newspaper* Date, Edition (if any): Page number(s) (includ-
    ing section letter, if any). Medium.

For a magazine article, use the following format:

Last name, First name. "Title of article." *Magazine* Date: Page number(s). Medium.

A citation for the magazine article on p. 447 would look like this:

AUTHOR ———— ARTICLE TITLE AND SUBTITLE

Conniff, Richard. "Counting Carbons: How Much Greenhouse Gas Does Your Family

    Produce?" *Discover* Aug. 2005: 54-61. Print.

    PERIODICAL   DATE   PAGE   MEDIUM
                        NOS.

For more on using MLA style to cite periodical articles, see pp. 444–48. (For guidelines and models for using APA style, see pp. 490–93, for *Chicago* style, see p. 516; for CSE style, see pp. 534–37.)

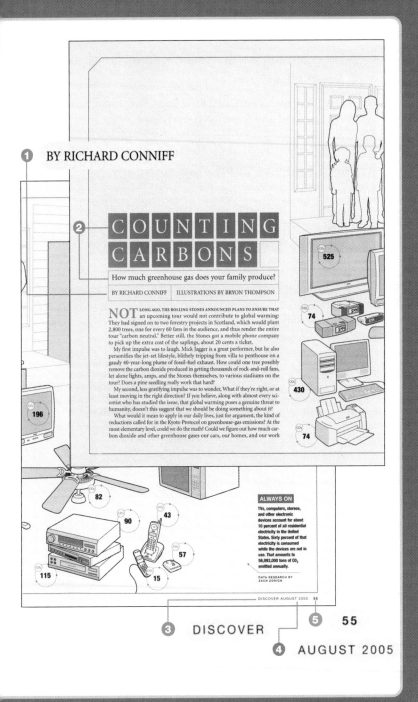

BY RICHARD CONNIFF

COUNTING CARBONS

How much greenhouse gas does your family produce?

BY RICHARD CONNIFF | ILLUSTRATIONS BY BRYON THOMPSON

NOT LONG AGO, THE ROLLING STONES ANNOUNCED PLANS TO ENSURE THAT an upcoming tour would not contribute to global warming: They had signed on to two forestry projects in Scotland, which would plant 2,800 trees, one for every 60 fans in the audience, and thus render the entire tour "carbon neutral." Better still, the Stones got a mobile phone company to pick up the extra cost of the saplings, about 20 cents a ticket.

My first impulse was to laugh. Mick Jagger is a great performer, but he also personifies the jet-set lifestyle, blithely tripping from villa to penthouse on a gaudy 40-year-long plume of fossil-fuel exhaust. How could one tree possibly remove the carbon dioxide produced in getting thousands of rock-and-roll fans, let alone lights, amps, and the Stones themselves, to various stadiums on the tour? Does a pine seedling really work that hard?

My second, less gratifying impulse was to wonder, What if they're right, or at least moving in the right direction? If you believe, along with almost every scientist who has studied the issue, that global warming poses a genuine threat to humanity, doesn't this suggest that we should be doing something about it?

What would it mean to apply in our daily lives, just for argument, the kind of reductions called for in the Kyoto Protocol on greenhouse-gas emissions? At the most elementary level, could we do the math? Could we figure out how much carbon dioxide and other greenhouse gases our cars, our homes, and our work

ALWAYS ON

TVs, computers, stereos, and other electronic devices account for about 10 percent of all residential electricity in the United States. Sixty percent of that electricity is consumed while the devices are not in use. That amounts to 56,093,000 tons of CO_2 emitted annually.

DATA RESEARCH BY
ZACH ZORICH

33. REVIEW

> Franklin, Nancy. "Dead On." Rev. of *Deadwood,* by David Milch. *New Yorker*
> 12 June 2006: 158-59. Print.

> Schwarz, Benjamin. Rev. of *The Second World War: A Short History,* by R. A. C.
> Parker. *Atlantic Monthly* May 2002: 110-11. Print.

34. UNSIGNED ARTICLE

> "Performance of the Week." *Time* 6 Oct. 2003: 18. Print.

Electronic sources

Electronic sources such as Web sites differ from print sources in the ease with which they can be — and frequently are — changed, updated, or

---

AT A GLANCE

Citing Electronic Sources

Look for the following six basic elements for an entry for an electronic source:

- *Author*. (For variations on author, see models 1–5.)
- *Title*. Italicize titles of books or entire sites; put titles of shorter works in quotation marks.
- *Print publication information.* For an online book or journal article from a database that provides information about the work's publication in print, include the volume and issue number with the year in parentheses, then a colon and the inclusive page numbers, or *n. pag.* if no page numbers are listed. (For articles taken from online newspapers and magazines, however, omit the print publication information.)
- *Electronic publication information.* List all of the following items that you can find, with a period after each one: the title of the site; the editor(s) of the site, preceded by *Ed.*; the version number of the site, preceded by *Vers.*; and the name of any sponsoring institution or organization. Then add the date of electronic publication or of the latest update, with the month, if any, abbreviated except for May, June, and July, and end with the medium consulted (*Web*).
- *Date of access.* Give the most recent date you accessed the source.
- *URLs.* Include a URL only if you think your readers will have difficulty finding your source without one. If you do include a URL, put it after the period following the date of access, enclose it in angle brackets, and put a period after the closing bracket.

Note: In your entry, you may omit author, title, and print publication information if it is unavailable, but you must include information about electronic publication and access.

even eliminated. In addition, the various electronic media do not organize their works the same way. The most commonly cited electronic sources are documents from Web sites and databases.

35. WORK FROM AN ONLINE DATABASE

The basic format for citing a work from a database appears on pp. 450-51.

For a work from an online database, provide all of the following elements that are available: the author's name (if given); the title of the work, in quotation marks; publication information from print or another medium; the name of the online database, italicized; the medium consulted (*Web*); and the date of access.

> Goldman, William. "*The Princess Bride* Shooting Draft." 1987. *Internet Movie*
> *Script Database*. Web. 12 June 2008.

36. ARTICLE FROM A DATABASE ACCESSED THROUGH A SUBSCRIPTION SERVICE

For a work from a subscription service, such as InfoTrac or LexisNexis, include the same information as for an online database: after the information about the work, give the name of the database, italicized; the medium consulted (*Web*); and the date of access.

> Collins, Ross F. "Cattle Barons and Ink Slingers: How Cow Country Journalists
> Created a Great American Myth." *American Journalism* 24.3 (2007): 7-29.
> *Communication and Mass Media Complete*. Web. 7 Feb. 2008.

37. ARTICLE IN AN ONLINE JOURNAL

Cite an online journal article as you would a print journal article (see models 27–28). If an online article does not have page numbers, use *n. pag.* End with the medium consulted (*Web*) and the date of access.

> Gallagher, Brian. "Greta Garbo Is Sad: Some Historical Reflections on the
> Paradoxes of Stardom in the American Film Industry, 1910-1960." *Images: A*
> *Journal of Film and Popular Culture* 3 (1997): n. pag. Web. 7 Aug. 2002.

38. ARTICLE IN AN ONLINE MAGAZINE

See model 29 for print publication information if the article appears in print. After the name of the magazine, give the sponsor of the Web site, the date of publication, the medium (*Web*), and the date of access.

> Shapiro, Walter. "The Quest for Universal Healthcare." *Salon*. Salon Media Group,
> Inc., 21 Feb. 2008. Web. 2 Mar. 2008.

Library subscriptions — such as InfoTrac, EBSCOhost, ProQuest, and LexisNexis — provide access to huge databases of articles.

1 **Author.** List the last name first.

2 **Article title.** Enclose the title and any subtitle in quotation marks.

3 **Periodical title.** Italicize it. Exclude any initial *A, An,* or *The.*

4 **Print publication information.** List the volume and issue number, if any; the date of publication, including the day (if given), month, and year, in that order; and the inclusive page numbers. If an article has no page numbers, write *n. pag.*

5 **Name of database.** Italicize the name of the database.

6 **Medium.** For an online database, use *Web*.

7 **Date of access.** Give the day, month, and year, then a period.

For an article from a database, use the following format:

[Citation format for journal, magazine, or newspaper article — see pp. 444–48].
    Name of database. Medium. Date accessed.

A citation for the article on p. 451 would look like this:

AUTHOR   ARTICLE TITLE   PERIODICAL TITLE

Wallace, Maurice. "Richard Wright's Black Medusa." *Journal of African American History*

88.1 (2003): 71+. *Expanded Academic ASAP*. Web. 28 July 2005.

PRINT   DATABASE   MEDIUM   ACCESS
PUBLICATION   NAME   DATE
INFORMATION

For more on using MLA style to cite articles from databases, see pages 448–49. (For guidelines and models for using APA style, see pp. 494–95; for *Chicago* style, see p. 516; for CSE style, see pp. 538–39.)

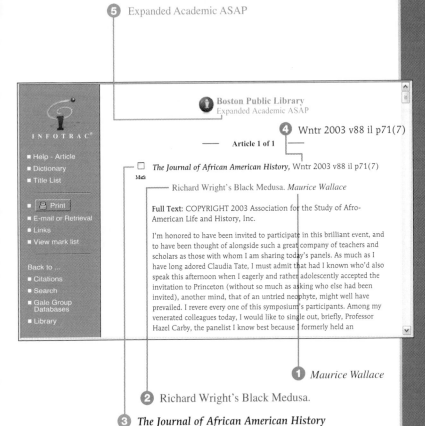

① *Maurice Wallace*

② Richard Wright's Black Medusa.

③ *The Journal of African American History*

39. ARTICLE IN AN ONLINE NEWSPAPER

After the name of the newspaper, give the publisher, publication date, medium (*Web*), and access date.

> Bustillo, Miguel, and Carol J. Williams. "Old Guard in Cuba Keeps Reins." *Los*
> *Angeles Times*. Los Angeles Times, 25 Feb. 2008. Web. 26 Feb. 2008.

40. ONLINE BOOK

Provide information as for a print book (see models 6–26); then give the electronic publication information, the medium, and the date of access.

> Euripides. *The Trojan Women*. Trans. Gilbert Murray. New York: Oxford UP,
> 1915. *Internet Sacred Text Archive*. Web. 12 Oct. 2003.

Note: Cite a part of an online book as you would a part of a print book (see models 10 and 20). Give the print (if any) and electronic publication information, the medium (*Web*), and the date of access.

> Riis, Jacob. "The Genesis of the Gang." *The Battle with the Slum*. New York:
> Macmillan, 1902. *Bartleby.com: Great Books Online*. 2000. Web. 31 Mar.
> 2005.

41. ONLINE POEM

Include the poet's name, the title of the poem, and the print publication information (if any). End with the electronic publication information, the medium (*Web*), and the date of access.

> Dickinson, Emily. "The Grass." *Poems: Emily Dickinson*. Boston, 1891. *Humanities*
> *Text Initiative American Verse Project*. Ed. Nancy Kushigian. U of Michigan.
> Web. 6 Jan. 2006.

42. ONLINE EDITORIAL OR LETTER

Include the word *Editorial* or *Letter* after the author (if given) and title (if any). End with the periodical name, the sponsor of the Web site, the date of electronic publication, the medium, and the access date.

> "The Funding Gap." Editorial. *Washington Post*. Washington Post, 5 Nov. 2003.
> Web. 19 Oct. 2006.
>
> Moore, Paula. "Go Vegetarian." Letter. *New York Times*. New York Times, 25 Feb.
> 2008. Web. 25 Feb. 2008.

43. ONLINE REVIEW

Cite an online review as you would a print review (see model 33). End with the name of the Web site, the sponsor, the date of electronic publication, the medium, and the date of access.

O'Hehir, Andrew. "The Nightmare in Iraq." Rev. of *Gunner Palace*, dir. Michael Tucker

and Petra Epperlein. *Salon*. Salon Media Group, 4 Mar. 2005. Web. 24 May 2008.

44. ENTRY IN AN ONLINE REFERENCE WORK

Cite the entry as you would an entry from a print reference work (see model 21). Follow with the name of the Web site, the sponsor, date of publication, medium, and date of access.

"Tour de France." *Encyclopaedia Britannica Online*. Encyclopaedia Britannica,

2006. Web. 21 May 2006.

45. WORK FROM A WEB SITE

For basic information on citing a work from a Web site, see pp. 454–55. Include all of the following elements that are available: the author; the title of the document in quotation marks; the name of the Web site, italicized; the name of the publisher or sponsor (if none is available, use *N.p.*); the date of publication (if not available, use *n.d.*); the medium consulted (*Web*); and the date of access.

"Hands Off Public Broadcasting." *Media Matters for America*. Media Matters for

America, 24 May 2005. Web. 31 May 2005.

Stauder, Ellen Keck. "Darkness Audible: Negative Capability and Mark Doty's

'Nocturne in Black and Gold.'" *Romantic Circles Praxis Series*. Ed. Orrin Wang.

2003. Web. 28 Sept. 2003.

46. ENTIRE WEB SITE

Follow the guidelines for a specific work from the Web, beginning with the name of the author, editor, compiler, director, narrator, or translator, followed by the title of the Web site, italicized; the name of the sponsor or publisher (if none, use *N.p.*); the date of publication or last update; the medium of publication (*Web*); and the date of access.

Bernstein, Charles, Kenneth Goldsmith, Martin Spinelli, and Patrick Durgin, eds.

Electronic Poetry Corner. SUNY Buffalo, 2003. Web. 26 Sept. 2006.

Weather.com. Weather Channel Interactive, 2006. Web. 13 Mar. 2006.

You may need to browse other parts of a site to find some of the following elements, and some sites may omit elements. Uncover as much information as you can.

1 Author of the work. List the last name first, followed by a comma, the first name, and the middle initial (if given). End with a period. If no author is given, begin with the title.

2 Title of the work. Enclose the title and any subtitle of the work in quotation marks.

3 Title of the Web site. Give the title of the entire Web site, italicized. Where there is no clear title, use *Home page* without italicizing it.

4 Name of publisher or sponsoring organization. Look for the sponsor's name at the bottom of the home page. If no information is available, write *N.p.* and follow it with a comma.

5 Date of publication or latest update. Give the most recent date, followed by a period. If no date is available, use *n.d.*

6 Medium consulted. Use *Web* and follow it with a period.

7 Date of access. Give the date you accessed the work. End with a period.

For a work from a Web site, use the following format:

Last name, First name. "Title of work." *Title of Web site*. Publisher or sponsoring organization, date. Medium. Access date.

A citation for the work on p. 455 would look like this:

AUTHOR   TITLE OF WORK   TITLE OF WEB SITE

Tønnesson, Øyvind. "Mahatma Gandhi, the Missing Laureate." *Nobelprize.org*. Nobel Foundation, 1 Dec. 1999. Web. 4 May 2005.

SITE SPONSOR   PUBL.   MEDIUM   ACCESS
             DATE   DATE

For more on using MLA style to cite Web documents, see pp. 448–58. (For guidelines and models for using APA style, see pp. 491–501; for *Chicago* style, see pp. 516–21; for CSE style, see pp. 538–41.)

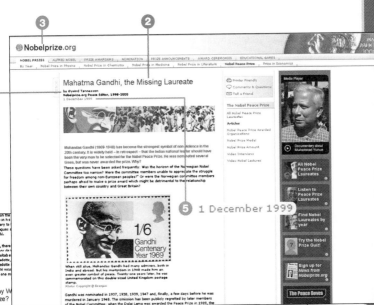

1 by Øyvind Tønnesson

3 **2**

Nobelprize.org

NOBEL PRIZES   ALFRED NOBEL   PRIZE AWARDERS   NOMINATION   PRIZE ANNOUNCEMENTS   AWARD CEREMONIES   EDUCATIONAL GAMES
By Year | Nobel Prize in Physics | Nobel Prize in Chemistry | Nobel Prize in Medicine | Nobel Prize in Literature | **Nobel Peace Prize** | Prize in Economics

Mahatma Gandhi, the Missing Laureate

by Øyvind Tønnesson
Nobelprize.org Peace Editor, 1998-2000
1 December 1999

🖨 Printer Friendly
💬 Comments & Questions
✉ Tell a Friend

The Nobel Peace Prize

All Nobel Peace Prize Laureates

Articles

Nobel Peace Prize Awarded Organizations
Nobel Prize Medal
Nobel Prize Amount
Video Interviews
Video Nobel Lectures

Mohandas Gandhi (1869-1948) has become the strongest symbol of non-violence in the 20th century. It is widely held – in retrospect – that the Indian national leader should have been the very man to be selected for the Nobel Peace Prize. He was nominated several times, but was never awarded the prize. Why?

These questions have been asked frequently: Was the horizon of the Norwegian Nobel Committee too narrow? Were the committee members unable to appreciate the struggle for freedom among non-European peoples?" Or were the Norwegian committee members perhaps afraid to make a prize award which might be detrimental to the relationship between their own country and Great Britain?

5 1 December 1999

When still alive, Mohandas Gandhi had many admirers, both in India and abroad. But his martyrdom in 1948 made him an even greater symbol of peace. Twenty-one years later, he was commemorated on this double-sized United Kingdom postage stamp.
Photo Copyright © Scanpix

1/6
Gandhi
Centenary
Year 1969

Gandhi was nominated in 1937, 1938, 1939, 1947 and, finally, a few days before he was murdered in January 1948. The omission has been publicly regretted by later members of the Nobel Committee; when the Dalai Lama was awarded the Peace Prize in 1989, the

Media Player

Documentary about Muhammad Yunus

All Nobel Peace Prize Laureates

Listen to Peace Prize Laureates

Find Nobel Laureates by year

Try the Nobel Prize Quiz!

Sign up for News from Nobelprize.org

The Peace Doves

year on the
wrote in h
contrary to
colleagues o
Gandhi.

Later, there
another de
'no suitabl
Bernadotte,
Bernadotte
Gandhi wou
alive one mo

Why W
Prize?

Up to 1960,
Americans. In retrospect, the horizon of the Norwegian Nobel Committee may seem too narrow. Gandhi was very different from earlier Laureates. He was not one politician or proponent of international law, not primarily a humanitarian relief worker and not an organiser of international peace congresses. He would have belonged to a new breed of Laureates

There is no hint in the archives that the Norwegian Nobel Committee ever took into consideration the possibility of an adverse British reaction to an award to Gandhi. Thus it seems that the hypothesis that the Committee's omission of Gandhi was due to its members' not wanting to provoke British authorities, may be rejected.

In 1947 the conflict between India and Pakistan and Gandhi's prayer-meeting statement, which made people wonder whether he was about to abandon his consistent pacifism, seem to have been the primary reasons why he was not selected by the committee's majority. Unlike the situation today, there was no tradition for the Norwegian Nobel Committee to try to use the Peace Prize as a stimulus for peaceful settlement of regional conflicts.

During the last months of his life, Gandhi worked hard to end the violence between Hindus and Muslims which followed the partition of India. We know little about the Norwegian Nobel Committee's discussions on Gandhi's candidature in 1948 other than the above quoted entry of November 18 in Gunnar Jahn's diary – but it seems clear that they seriously considered a posthumous award. When the committee, for formal reasons, ended up not making such an award, they decided to reserve the prize, and then, one year later, not to spend the prize money for 1948 at all. What many thought should have been Mahatma Gandhi's place on the list of Laureates was silently but respectfully, left open.

nobelprize.org   Privacy Policy   Terms of Use   Technical Support   RSS   The Official Web Site of the Nobel Foundation   Copyright © Nobel Web AB 2006

4 The Official Web Site of the Nobel Foundation

For a personal Web site, include the name of the person who created the site; the title, italicized, or (if there is no title) a description such as *Home page,* not italicized; the publisher or sponsor of the site (if none, use *N.p.*); the date of the last update; the medium of publication (*Web*); and the date of access.

> Lunsford, Andrea A. Home page. Stanford U, 27 Mar. 2003. Web. 17 May 2006.

47. ACADEMIC COURSE OR DEPARTMENT WEB SITE

For a course site, include the name of the instructor, the title of the course in quotation marks, a description such as *Course home page,* the dates of the course, the department name, the institution, the medium consulted (*Web*), and the access information.

> Creekmur, Corey K., and Philip Lutgendorf. "Topics in Asian Cinema: Popular Hindi
>
> Cinema." Course home page. Fall 2004. Depts. of English, Cinema, and
>
> Comparative Literature, U of Iowa. Web. 13 Mar. 2007.

For a department Web site, give the department name, a description such as *Home page,* the institution, the medium (*Web*), and the access information.

> Dept. of English. Home page. Amherst Coll., n.d. Web. 5 Apr. 2006.

48. WEB LOG (BLOG)

For an entire Web log, give the author's name; the title of the Web log, italicized; the sponsor or publisher of the Web log (if there is none, use *N.p.*); the date of the most recent update; the medium (*Web*); and the date of access.

> Atrios. *Eschaton*. N.p., 27 June 2006. Web. 27 June 2006.

49. POST OR COMMENT ON A WEB LOG

Give the author's name; the title of the post or comment, in quotation marks (if there is no title, use the description *Web log post* or *Web log comment,* not italicized); the title of the Web log, italicized; the sponsor of the Web log (if there is none, use *N.p.*); the date of the most recent update; the medium (*Web*); and the date of access.

> Parker, Randall. "Growth Rate for Electric Hybrid Vehicle Market Debated."
>
> *FuturePundit*. N.p., 20 May 2005. Web. 24 May 2005.

50. ENTRY IN A WIKI

Because wiki content is collectively edited, do not include an author. Treat a wiki as you would a work from a Web site (see model 45). Include the title of the entry; the name of the wiki, italicized; the sponsor or publisher of the wiki (use *N.p.* if there is no sponsor); the date of the latest update; the medium (*Web*); and the date of access. Check with your instructor before using a wiki as a source.

> "Fédération Internationale de Football Association." *Wikipedia*. Wikimedia
>
> Foundation, 27 June 2006. Web. 27 June 2006.

51. POSTING TO A DISCUSSION GROUP OR NEWSGROUP

Begin with the author's name and the title of the posting in quotation marks (or the words *Online posting*). Follow with the name of the Web site, the sponsor or publisher of the site (use *N.p.* if there is no sponsor), the date of publication, the medium (*Web*), and the date of access.

> Daly, Catherine. "Poetry Slams." *Poetics Discussion List*. SUNY Buffalo,
>
> 29 Aug. 2003. Web. 1 Oct. 2003.

52. POSTING TO A SOCIAL NETWORKING SITE

To cite a message on Facebook or another social networking site, include the writer's name, a description of the posting that mentions the recipient, the date of the message, and the medium of delivery. (The MLA does not provide guidelines for citing postings on such sites; this model is based on the MLA's guidelines for citing email.)

> Ferguson, Sarah. Message to the author. 6 Mar. 2008. Facebook posting.
>
> 8 Mar. 2000.

53. EMAIL

Include the writer's name; the subject line, in quotation marks; *Message to* (not italicized or in quotation marks) followed by the recipient's name; the date of the message; and the medium of delivery (*E-mail*). (MLA style hyphenates *e-mail*.)

> Harris, Jay. "Thoughts on Impromptu Stage Productions." Message to the
>
> author. 16 July 2006. E-mail.

54. COMPUTER SOFTWARE OR GAME

Include the title, italicized, version number (if given), and publication information. If you are citing downloaded software, replace the publication information with the medium and the date of access.

> *The Sims 2*. Redwood City: Electronic Arts, 2004. CD-ROM.

> *Web Cache Illuminator*. Vers. 4.02. NorthStar Solutions, n.d. Web. 12 Nov.
>
> 2003.

55. CD-ROM OR DVD-ROM

Include the medium.

> *Cambridge Advanced Learner's Dictionary*. 3rd ed. Cambridge: Cambridge UP, 2008.
>   CD-ROM.

> *Grand Theft Auto: San Andreas*. New York: Rockstar Games, 2004. DVD-ROM.

Multimedia sources (including online versions)

56. FILM, VIDEO, OR DVD

If you cite a particular person's work, start with that name. If not, start with the title; then name the director, distributor, and year of release. Other contributors, such as writers or performers, may follow the director. If you cite a DVD or video instead of a theatrical release, include the original film release date and the label *DVD* or *Videocassette*. For material found on a Web site, give the name of the site or database, the medium (*Web*), and access date.

> Jenkins, Tamara, dir. *The Savages*. Perf. Laura Linney and Philip Seymour Hoffman.
>   Fox Searchlight, 2007. *Fox Searchlight*. Web. 4 Mar. 2008.

> *Spirited Away*. Dir. Hiyao Miyazaki. 2001. Walt Disney Video, 2003. DVD.

> *There Will Be Blood*. Dir. Paul Thomas Anderson. Perf. Daniel Day-Lewis.
>   Paramount Vantage/Miramax, 2007. Film.

AT A GLANCE

Citing Sources without Models in MLA Style

To cite a source for which you cannot find a model, collect as much information as you can find — about the creator, title, sponsor, date of posting or latest update, the date you accessed the site and its location — with the goal of helping your readers find the source for themselves, if possible. Then look at the models in this section to see which one most closely matches the type of source you are using.

In an academic writing project, before citing an electronic source for which you have no model, also be sure to ask your instructor for help.

57. TELEVISION OR RADIO PROGRAM

In general, begin with the title of the program, italicized. Then list important contributors (narrator, writer, director, actors); the network; the local station and city, if any; the broadcast date; and the medium. To cite a particular person's work, begin with that name. To cite a particular episode from a series, begin with the episode title, in quotation marks.

> *The American Experience: Buffalo Bill.* Writ., dir., prod. Rob Rapley. PBS. WNET,
>
> New York, 25 Feb. 2008. Television.

> "The Fleshy Part of the Thigh." *The Sopranos.* Writ. Diane Frolov and Andrew
>
> Schneider. Dir. Alan Taylor. HBO, 2 Apr. 2006. Television.

Note: For an online version, give the name of the Web site, italicized. Then give the publisher or sponsor, a comma, and the date posted. End with the medium (*Web*) and the access date.

> Komando, Kim. "E-mail Hacking and the Law." *CBSRadio.com.* CBS Radio, Inc.,
>
> 28 Oct. 2003. Web. 11 Nov. 2003.

58. BROADCAST INTERVIEW

List the person interviewed and then the title, if any. If the interview has no title, use the label *Interview* and name the interviewer, if relevant. Then identify the source. To cite a broadcast interview, end with information about the program, the date(s) the interview took place, and the medium.

> Revkin, Andrew. Interview with Terry Gross. *Fresh Air.* Natl. Public Radio. WNYC,
>
> New York, 14 June 2006. Radio.

Note: If you listened to an archived version online, provide the site's sponsor (if known), the date of the interview, the medium (*Web*), and the access date. For a podcast interview, see model 64.

> Revkin, Andrew. Interview by Terry Gross. *Fresh Air.* NPR.org. NPR, 14 June 2006.
>
> Web. 12 Jan. 2009.

59. UNPUBLISHED OR PERSONAL INTERVIEW

List the person interviewed; the label *Telephone interview, Personal interview,* or *E-mail interview*; and the date the interview took place.

> Freedman, Sasha. Personal interview. 10 Nov. 2006.

60. SOUND RECORDING

List the name of the person or group you wish to emphasize (such as the composer, conductor, or band); the title of the recording or composition; the artist, if appropriate; the manufacturer; and the year of issue. Give the medium (such as *CD, MP3 file,* or *LP*). If you are citing a particular song or selection, include its title, in quotation marks, before the title of the recording.

> Bach, Johann Sebastian. *Bach: Violin Concertos.* Perf. Itzhak Perlman and Pinchas
>
> Zukerman. English Chamber Orch. EMI, 2002. CD.
>
> Sonic Youth. "Incinerate." *Rather Ripped.* Geffen, 2006. MP3 file.

Note: If you are citing instrumental music that is identified only by form, number, and key, do not underline, italicize, or enclose it in quotation marks.

> Grieg, Edvard. Concerto in A minor, op. 16. Cond. Eugene Ormandy. Philadelphia
>
> Orch. RCA, 1989. LP.

61. MUSICAL COMPOSITION

When you are not citing a specific published version, first give the composer's name, followed by the title.

> Mozart, Wolfgang Amadeus. *Don Giovanni,* K527.
>
> Mozart, Wolfgang Amadeus. Symphony no. 41 in C major, K551.

Note: Cite a published score as you would a book. If you include the date the composition was written, do so immediately after the title.

> Schoenberg, Arnold. *Chamber Symphony No. 1 for 15 Solo Instruments, Op. 9.*
>
> 1906. New York: Dover, 2002. Print.

62. LECTURE OR SPEECH

List the speaker; title, in quotation marks; sponsoring institution or group; place; and date. If the speech is untitled, use a label such as *Lecture.*

> Colbert, Stephen. Speech. White House Correspondents' Association Dinner.
>
> *YouTube.* YouTube, LLC, 29 Apr. 2006. Web. 20 May 2006.

Eugenides, Jeffrey. Portland Arts and Lectures. Arlene Schnitzer Concert Hall,

Portland, OR. 30 Sept. 2003. Lecture.

63. LIVE PERFORMANCE

List the title, appropriate names (such as writer or performer), the place, and the date. To cite a particular person's work, begin the entry with that name.

Anything Goes. By Cole Porter. Perf. Klea Blackhurst. Shubert Theater,

New Haven. 7 Oct. 2003. Performance.

64. PODCAST

Include all of the following that are relevant and available: the speaker, the title of the podcast, the title of the program, the host or performers, the title of the site, the site's sponsor, the date of posting, the medium (such as *MP3 file* or *Web*), and the access date. (This model is based on MLA guidelines for a short work from a Web site.)

"Seven Arrested in U.S. Terror Raid." *Morning Report.* Host Krishnan Guru-Murthy.

4 Radio. Channel 4 News, 23 June 2006. MP3 file. 27 June 2006.

65. WORK OF ART OR PHOTOGRAPH

List the artist or photographer; the work's title, italicized; the date of composition (if unknown, use *n.d.*); and the medium of composition (*Oil on canvas, Bronze*). Then cite the name of the museum or other location and the city. To cite a reproduction in a book, add the publication information. To cite artwork found online, omit the medium of composition, and after the location, add the title of the database or Web site, italicized; the medium consulted (*Web*); and the date of access.

Chagall, Marc. *The Poet with the Birds.* 1911. Minneapolis Inst. of Arts.

artsmia.org. Web. 6 Oct. 2003.

General William Palmer in Old Age. 1810. Oil on canvas. National Army Museum,

London. *White Mughals: Love and Betrayal in Eighteenth-Century India.*

William Dalrymple. New York: Penguin, 2002. 270. Print.

Kahlo, Frida. *Self-Portrait with Cropped Hair.* 1940. Oil on canvas. Museum of Mod.

Art, New York.

AT A GLANCE

Citing Visuals That Appear in Your Text

If you choose to include images in your text, you need to cite and caption them correctly in the text (see p. 434). If you include images that you created, or if you reproduce a visual from another source, include information about the visual in your list of works cited.

- For a work that you have created, the works-cited entry should begin with the descriptive phrase from the image's caption and include the label and the date. (For an example, see p. 160.)
- For a visual reproduced from another source, the works-cited entry should list the source as it is identified in the caption. (For an example, see p. 475.)

---

66. MAP OR CHART

Cite a map or chart as you would a book or a short work within a longer work and include the word *Map* or *Chart* after the title. Add the medium of publication. For an online source, end with the date of access.

> *Australia*. Map. *Perry-Castaneda Library Map Collection*. U of Texas, 1999. Web.
>
>   4 Nov. 2003.
>
> *California*. Map. Chicago: Rand, 2002. Print.

67. CARTOON OR COMIC STRIP

List the artist's name; the title (if any) of the cartoon or comic strip, in quotation marks; the label *Cartoon* or *Comic strip*; and the usual publication information for a print periodical (see models 27–30) or a work from a Web site (model 45).

> Johnston, Lynn. "For Better or Worse." Comic strip. *FBorFW.com*. Lynn Johnston
>
>   Publications, 30 June 2006. Web. 20 July 2006.
>
> Lewis, Eric. "The Unpublished Freud." Cartoon. *New Yorker* 11 Mar. 2002: 80. Print.

68. ADVERTISEMENT

Include the label *Advertisement* after the name of the item or organization being advertised.

> Microsoft. Advertisement. *Harper's* Oct. 2003: 2-3. Print.
>
> Microsoft. Advertisement. *New York Times*. New York Times, 11 Nov. 2003. Web.
>
>   11 Nov. 2003.

Other sources (including online versions)

If an online version is not shown here, use the appropriate model for the source and then end with the medium and date of access.

69. REPORT OR PAMPHLET

Follow the guidelines for a print book (models 6–26) or an online book (model 40).

> Allen, Katherine, and Lee Rainie. *Parents Online*. Washington: Pew Internet and
>
> Amer. Life Project, 2002. Print.
>
> Environmental Working Group. *Dead in the Water*. Washington: Environmental
>
> Working Group, 2006. Web. 24 Apr. 2006.

70. GOVERNMENT PUBLICATION

Begin with the author, if identified. Otherwise, start with the name of the government, followed by the agency. For congressional documents, cite the number, session, and house of Congress (*S* for Senate, *H* for House of Representatives); the type (*Report, Resolution, Document*) in abbreviated form; and the number. End with the publication information. The print publisher is often the Government Printing Office (GPO). For online versions, follow the models for a work from a Web site (model 45) or an entire Web site (model 46).

> Gregg, Judd. *Report to Accompany the Genetic Information Act of 2003*. US
>
> 108th Cong., 1st sess. S. Rept. 108-22. Washington: GPO, 2003. Print.
>
> Kinsella, Kevin, and Victoria Velkoff. *An Aging World: 2001*. US Bureau of the
>
> Census. Washington: GPO, 2001. Print.
>
> United States. Environmental Protection Agency. Office of Emergency and
>
> Remedial Response. *This Is Superfund*. Jan. 2000. *Environmental Protection*
>
> *Agency*. Web. 16 Aug. 2002.

71. PUBLISHED PROCEEDINGS OF A CONFERENCE

Cite proceedings as you would a book.

> Cleary, John, and Gary Gurtler, eds. *Proceedings of the Boston Area Colloquium in*
>
> *Ancient Philosophy 2002*. Boston: Brill Academic, 2003. Print.

72. DISSERTATION

Enclose the title in quotation marks. Add the label *Diss.*, the school, and the year the work was accepted.

> Paris, Django. "Our Culture: Difference, Division, and Unity in Multicultural Youth
> Space." Diss. Stanford U, 2008. Print.

Note: Cite a published dissertation as a book, adding the identification *Diss.* and the university after the title.

73. DISSERTATION ABSTRACT

Cite as you would an unpublished dissertation (see model 72). For the abstract of a dissertation using *Dissertation Abstracts International* (*DAI*), include the *DAI* volume, year, and page number.

> Huang-Tiller, Gillian C. "The Power of the Meta-Genre: Cultural, Sexual, and Racial
> Politics of the American Modernist Sonnet." Diss. U of Notre Dame, 2000.
> *DAI* 61 (2000): 1401. Print.

74. PUBLISHED INTERVIEW

List the person interviewed; the title of the interview (if any) or the label *Interview* and the interviewer's name, if relevant. Then identify the source.

> Paretsky, Sarah. Interview. *Progressive*. Progressive Magazine, 14 Jan. 2008. Web.
> 12 Feb. 2008.

> Taylor, Max. "Max Taylor on Winning." *Time* 13 Nov. 2000: 66. Print.

75. UNPUBLISHED LETTER

Cite a published letter as a work in an anthology (see model 10). If the letter is unpublished, follow this form:

> Anzaldúa, Gloria. Letter to the author. 10 Sept. 2002. MS.

76. MANUSCRIPT OR OTHER UNPUBLISHED WORK

List the author's name; the title (if any) or a description of the material; the form of the material (such as *MS.* for manuscript) and any identifying numbers; and the name and location of the library or research institution housing the material, if applicable.

> Woolf, Virginia. "The Searchlight." N.d. TS. Ser. III, Box 4, Item 184. Papers of
> Virginia Woolf, 1902-1956. Smith Coll., Northampton.

77. LEGAL SOURCE

To cite a court case, give the names of the first plaintiff and defendant, the case number, the name of the court, and the date of the decision. To cite an act, give the name of the act followed by its Public Law (*Pub. L.*) number, the date the act was enacted, and its Statutes at Large (*Stat.*) cataloging number.

> Eldred v. Ashcroft. No. 01-618. Supreme Ct. of the US. 15 Jan. 2003. Print.
>
> Museum and Library Services Act of 2003. Pub. L. 108-81. 25 Sept. 2003. Stat. 117.991. Print.

Note: You do not need an entry on the list of works cited when you cite articles of the U.S. Constitution and laws in the U.S. Code.

A Student Research Essay, MLA Style 51

A brief research essay by David Craig appears on the following pages. David followed the MLA guidelines described in the preceding chapters. Note that this essay has been reproduced in a narrow format to allow for annotation.

Student Writer

David Craig

 bedfordstmartins.com/everydaywriter To read the unabridged essay, click on **Student Writing**.

Name,
instructor,
course, and
date aligned
at left margin
and double-
spaced

David Craig

Professor Turkman

English 219

8 December 2003

Title
centered;
engages
readers'
interest

Instant Messaging: The Language of Youth Literacy

Opens with
attention-
getting
statement

The English language is under attack. At least, that is what
many people seem to believe. From concerned parents to local
librarians, everybody seems to have a negative comment on the state
of youth literacy today, and many pin the blame on new technology.

Background
on the prob-
lem of youth
literacy

They say that the current generation of grade school students will
graduate with an extremely low level of literacy and that although
language education hasn't changed much, kids are having more
trouble reading and writing. Slang is more pervasive than ever, and
teachers often must struggle with students who refuse to learn the
conventionally correct way to use language.

In the *Chronicle of Higher Education,* for instance, Wendy
Leibowitz quotes Sven Birkerts of Mount Holyoke College as saying

Quotation
used as
evidence

"[Students] read more casually. They strip-mine what they read" on
the Internet. Those casual reading habits, in turn, produce "quickly
generated, casual prose" (A67). When asked about the causes of this
situation, many point to instant messaging (IMing), which coincides
with new computer technology.

Definition
and example
of IMing

Instant messaging allows two individuals who are separated by
any distance to engage in real-time, written communication.
Although IMing relies on the written word, many messagers disregard
standard writing conventions. For example, here is a snippet from an
IM conversation between two teenage girls:[1]

Explanatory
note; see
Chapter 49

[1]This transcript of an IM conversation was collected on 20 Nov.
2003. The teenagers' names are concealed to protect privacy.

Annotations indicate effective choices or MLA-style formatting.

Teen One: sorry im talkinto like 10 ppl at a time

Teen Two: u izzyful person

Teen Two: kwel

Teen One: hey i g2g

As this brief conversation shows, participants must use words to communicate via IMing, but their words do not have to be in standard English.

Instant messaging, according to many, threatens youth literacy because it creates and compounds undesirable reading and writing habits and discourages students from learning standard literacy skills. Passionate or not, however, the critics' arguments don't hold up. In fact, IMing seems to be a beneficial force in the development of youth literacy because it promotes regular contact with words, the use of a written medium for communication, and the development of an alternative form of literacy. Perhaps most important, IMing can actually help students learn conventional English. Before turning to the pros and cons of IMing, however, I wish to look more closely at two background issues: the current state of literacy and the prevalence of IMing.

Regardless of one's views on IMing, the issue of youth literacy does demand attention because standardized test scores for language assessments, such as the verbal section of the College Board's SAT, have declined in recent years. This trend is illustrated in a chart distributed by the College Board as part of its 2002 analysis of aggregate SAT data (see Fig. 1).

The trend lines, which I added to the original chart, illustrate a significant pattern that may lead to the conclusion that youth literacy is on the decline. These lines display the seven-year paths (from 1995 to 2002) of math and verbal scores, respectively. Within this time period, the average SAT math score jumped more than ten points. The average verbal score, however, actually dropped a few points--and appears to be headed toward a further decline in the future. Corroborating this

---

Annotations (right margin):

- Last name and page number in upper right-hand corner
- Overview of criticism of IMing
- Explicit thesis
- Transition to discussion of background information
- Writer considers argument that youth literacy is in decline
- Figure explained in text and cited in parenthetical reference
- Discussion of Fig. 1

Craig 3

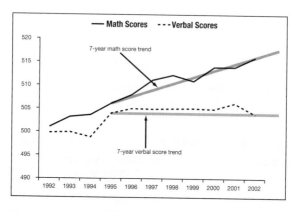

Fig. 1. Comparison of SAT math and verbal scores (1992-2002).
Trend lines added. Source: Kristin Carnahan and Chiara Coletti,
*Ten-Year Trend in SAT Scores Indicates Increased Emphasis on Math
Is Yielding Results; Reading and Writing Are Causes for Concern.*
New York: College Board, 2002; print; 9.

[Margin note: Figure labeled (as Fig. 1), titled, and credited to source; inserted at appropriate point in text]

evidence is a report from the United States Department of Education's
National Center for Education Statistics. According to this agency's study,
the percentage of twelfth graders whose writing ability was "at or above
the basic level" of performance dropped from 78 to 74 percent between
1998 and 2002 (Persky, Daane, and Jin 21).

[Margin note: Government source cited for statistical evidence]

Based on the preceding statistics, parents and educators appear
to be right about the decline in youth literacy. And this trend is
occurring while IM usage is on the rise. According to the Pew Internet
and American Life Project, 54 percent of American youths aged twelve
to seventeen have used IMing (qtd. in Lenhart and Lewis 20). This
figure translates to a pool of some thirteen million young instant
messagers. Of this group, Pew reports, half send instant messages
every time they go online, with 46 percent spending between thirty
and sixty minutes messaging and another 21 percent spending more

[Margin note: Writer acknowledges part of critics' argument; transition to next point]

[Margin note: Statistical evidence cited]

Craig 4

than an hour. The most conservative estimate indicates that American youths spend, at a minimum, nearly three million hours per day on IMing. What's more, they seem to be using a new vocabulary, and this is one of the things that bothers critics. In order to have an effect on youth literacy, however, this new vocabulary must actually exist, so I set out to determine if it did.

In the interest of establishing the existence of an IM language, I analyzed 11,341 lines of text from IM conversations between youths in my target demographic: US residents aged twelve to seventeen. Young messengers voluntarily sent me chat logs, but they were unaware of the exact nature of my research. Once all of the logs had been gathered, I went through them, recording the number of times IM language was used in place of conventional words and phrases. Then I generated graphs to display how often these replacements were used.

Writer's field research introduced

During the course of my study, I identified four types of IM language: phonetic replacements, acronyms, abbreviations, and inanities. An example of phonetic replacement is using *ur* for *you are*. Another popular type of IM language is the acronym; for a majority of the people in my study, the most common acronym was *lol*, a construction that means *laughing out loud*. Abbreviations are also common in IMing, but I discovered that typical IM abbreviations, such as *etc.*, are not new to the English language. Finally, I found a class of words that I call "inanities." These words include completely new words or expressions, combinations of several slang categories, or simply nonsensical variations of other words. My favorite from this category is *lolz*, an inanity that translates directly to *lol* yet includes a terminating *z* for no obvious reason.

Findings of field research presented

In the chat transcripts that I analyzed, the best display of typical IM lingo came from the conversations between two thirteen-year-old Texan girls, who are avid IM users. Figure 2 is a graph showing how often they used certain phonetic replacements and abbreviations. On the *y*-axis, frequency of replacement is plotted, a

Craig 5

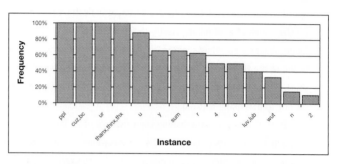

Fig. 2. Usage of phonetic replacements and abbreviations in IMing.

Figure labeled and titled

Figure introduced and explained

calculation that compares the number of times a word or phrase is used in IM language with the total number of times that it is communicated in any form. On the *x*-axis, specific IM words and phrases are listed.

Discussion of findings presented in Fig. 2

My research shows that the Texan girls use the first ten phonetic replacements or abbreviations at least 50 percent of the time in their normal IM writing. For example, every time one of them writes *see,* there is a parallel time when *c* is used in its place. In light of this finding, it appears that the popular IM culture contains at least some elements of its own language. It also seems that much of this language is new: no formal dictionary yet identifies the most common IM words and phrases. Only in the heyday of the telegraph or on the rolls of a stenographer would you find a similar situation, but these "languages" were never a popular medium of youth communication. Instant messaging, however, is very popular among young people and continues to generate attention and debate in academic circles.

Writer returns to opposition argument

My research shows that messaging is certainly widespread, and it does seem to have its own particular vocabulary, yet these two factors alone do not mean it has a damaging influence on youth literacy. As noted earlier, however, some people claim that the new

Craig 6

technology is a threat to the English language, as revealed in the following passage:

> Abbreviations commonly used in online instant messages are creeping into formal essays that students write for credit, said Debbie Frost, who teaches language arts and social studies to sixth-graders. . . . "You would be shocked at the writing I see. It's pretty scary. I don't get cohesive thoughts, I don't get sentences, they don't capitalize, and they have a lot of misspellings and bad grammar," she said. "With all those glaring mistakes, it's hard to see the content." ("Young Messagers")

Echoing Frost's concerns is Melanie Weaver, a professor at Alvernia College, who taught a tenth-grade English class as part of an internship. In an interview with the *New York Times,* she said, "[When] they would be trying to make a point in a paper, they would put a smiley face in the end [:)]. . . . If they were presenting an argument and they needed to present an opposite view, they would put a frown [:(]" (qtd. in Lee).

The critics of instant messaging are numerous. But if we look to the field of linguistics, a central concept--metalinguistics--challenges these criticisms and leads to a more reasonable conclusion--that IMing has no negative impact on a student's development of or proficiency with traditional literacy.

Scholars of metalinguistics offer support for the claim that IMing is not damaging to those who use it. As noted earlier, one of the most prominent components of IM language is phonetic replacement, in which a word such as *everyone* becomes *every1*. This type of wordplay has a special importance in the development of an advanced literacy, and for good reason. According to David Crystal, an internationally recognized scholar of linguistics at the University of Wales, as young children develop and learn how words string together to express ideas, they go through many phases of

Signal verb introduces quotation

Block quotation for a quotation more than four lines long

Parenthetical reference uses brief title, author unknown

Transition to support of thesis and refutation of critics

Linguistic authority cited in support of thesis

Craig 7

language play. The singsong rhymes and nonsensical chants of preschoolers are vital to their learning language, and a healthy appetite for such wordplay leads to a better command of language later in life (182).

As justification for his view of the connection between language play and advanced literacy, Crystal presents an argument for metalinguistic awareness. According to Crystal, *metalinguistics* refers to the ability to "step back" and use words to analyze how language works. "If we are good at stepping back," he says, "at thinking in a more abstract way about what we hear and what we say, then we are more likely to be good at acquiring those skills which depend on just such a stepping back in order to be successful--and this means, chiefly, reading and writing. . . . [T]he greater our ability to play with language, . . . the more advanced will be our command of language as a whole" (181).

If we accept the findings of linguists such as Crystal that metalinguistic awareness leads to increased literacy, then it seems reasonable to argue that the phonetic language of IMing can also lead to increased metalinguistic awareness and, therefore, increases in overall literacy. As instant messagers develop proficiency with a variety of phonetic replacements and other types of IM words, they should increase their subconscious knowledge of metalinguistics.

Metalinguistics also involves our ability to write in a variety of distinct styles and tones. Yet in the debate over instant messaging and literacy, many critics assume that either IMing or academic literacy will eventually win out in a person and that the two modes cannot exist side by side. This assumption is, however, false. Human beings ordinarily develop a large range of language abilities, from the formal to the relaxed and from the mainstream to the subcultural. Mark Twain, for example, had an understanding of local speech that he employed when writing dialogue for *Huckleberry Finn*. Yet few

---

Margin annotations:

Ellipses indicate omissions in quotation

Writer links Crystal's views to thesis

Another refutation of critics' assumptions

Example from well-known work of literature used as support

Craig 8

people would argue that Twain's knowledge of this form of English had a negative impact on his ability to write in standard English.

However, just as Mark Twain used dialects carefully in dialogue, writers must pay careful attention to the kind of language they use in any setting. The owner of the language Web site *The Discouraging Word,* who is an anonymous English literature graduate student at the University of Chicago, backs up this idea in an e-mail to me:

> What is necessary, we feel, is that students learn how to
> shift between different styles of writing--that, in other
> words, the abbreviations and shortcuts of IM should be
> used online . . . but that they should not be used in an
> essay submitted to a teacher. . . . IM might even be
> considered . . . a different way of reading and writing, one
> that requires specific and unique skills shared by certain
> communities.

The analytical ability that is necessary for writers to choose an appropriate tone and style in their writing is, of course, metalinguistic in nature because it involves the comparison of two or more language systems. Thus, youths who grasp multiple languages will have a greater natural understanding of metalinguistics. More specifically, young people who possess both IM and traditional skills stand to be better off than their peers who have been trained only in traditional or conventional systems. Far from being hurt by their online pastime, instant messengers can be aided in standard writing by their experience with IM language.

The fact remains, however, that youth literacy seems to be declining. What, if not IMing, is the main cause of this phenomenon? According to the College Board, which collects data on several questions from its test takers, enrollment in English composition and grammar classes has decreased in the last decade by 14 percent (Carnahan and Coletti 11). The possibility of instant messaging

Email correspondence cited in support of claim

Writer synthesizes evidence for claim

Transition to final point

Alternate explanation for decline in literacy

causing a decline in literacy seems inadequate when statistics on English education for US youths provide other evidence of the possible causes. Simply put, schools in the United States are not teaching English as much as they used to. Rather than blaming IMing alone for the decline in literacy and test scores, we must also look toward our schools' lack of focus on the teaching of standard English skills.

Transition to conclusion

I found that the use of instant messaging poses virtually no threat to the development or maintenance of formal language skills among American youths aged twelve to seventeen. Diverse language skills tend to increase a person's metalinguistic awareness and, thereby, his or her ability to use language effectively to achieve a desired purpose in a particular situation. The current decline in youth literacy is not due to the rise of instant messaging. Rather, fewer young students seem to be receiving an adequate education in the use of conventional English. Unfortunately, it may always be fashionable to blame new tools for old problems, but in the case of instant messaging, that blame is not warranted. Although IMing may expose literacy problems, it does not create them.

Concluding paragraph sums up argument and reiterates thesis

Craig 10

Works Cited

Carnahan, Kristin, and Chiara Coletti. *Ten-Year Trend in SAT Scores Indicates Increased Emphasis on Math Is Yielding Results: Reading and Writing Are Causes for Concern*. New York: College Board, 2002. Print.

Crystal, David. *Language Play*. Chicago: U of Chicago P, 1998. Print.

The Discouraging Word. "Re: Instant Messaging and Literacy." E-mail to the author. 13 Nov. 2003. E-mail.

Lee, Jennifer 8. "I Think, Therefore IM." *New York Times*. New York Times, 19 Sept. 2002. Web. 14 Nov. 2003.

Leibowitz, Wendy R. "Technology Transforms Writing and the Teaching of Writing." *Chronicle of Higher Education* 26 Nov. 1999: A67-68. Print.

Lenhart, Amanda, and Oliver Lewis. *Teenage Life Online: The Rise of the Instant-Message Generation and the Internet's Impact on Friendships and Family Relationships*. Washington: Pew Internet and Amer. Life Project, 2001. Print.

Persky, Hilary R., Mary C. Daane, and Ying Jin. *The Nation's Report Card: Writing 2002*. NCES 2003-529. Washington: GPO, 2003. Print.

"Young Messagers Ask: Why Spell It Out?" *Columbus Dispatch* 10 Nov. 2002: C1. *LexisNexis Academic*. Web. 14 Nov. 2003.

Heading centered

Report

Book

Email

Online newspaper article

Article in a newspaper

Works-cited entries double-spaced

Government document

Article from an online database

First line of each entry flush with left margin; subsequent lines indented

APA, *Chicago*, and CSE Documentation

Documentation styles in different disciplines vary according to what information is valued most highly. Thus in the sciences and social sciences, where timeliness of publication is crucial, the date of publication comes up front, right after the author's name.

— ANDREA A. LUNSFORD

APA, *Chicago*, and CSE Documentation

APA Style 52

Chapter 52 discusses the basic formats prescribed by the American Psychological Association (APA), guidelines that are widely used in the social sciences. For further reference, consult the *Publication Manual of the American Psychological Association*, Fifth Edition (2001), and the *APA Style Guide to Electronic References* (2007).

 bedfordstmartins.com/everydaywriter To access this advice online, click on **Documenting Sources**.

DIRECTORY TO APA STYLE

52a APA style for in-text citations

APA style requires parenthetical references in the text to document quotations, paraphrases, summaries, and other material from a source. These citations correspond to full bibliographic entries in a list of references at the end of the text.

Note that APA style generally calls for using the past tense or present perfect tense for signal verbs: *Baker (2003) showed* or *Baker (2003) has shown*. Use the present tense only to discuss results (*the experiment demonstrates*) or widely accepted information (*researchers agree*).

An in-text citation in APA style always indicates *which source* on the references page the writer is referring to, and it explains *in what year* the material was published; for quoted material, the in-text citation also indicates *where* in the source the quotation can be found.

1. BASIC FORMAT FOR A QUOTATION

Generally, use the author's name in a signal phrase to introduce the cited material, and place the date, in parentheses, immediately after the author's name. The page number, preceded by *p.,* appears in parentheses after the quotation.

> Gitlin (2001) pointed out that "political critics, convinced that the media are rigged against them, are often blind to other substantial reasons why their causes are unpersuasive" (p. 141).

If the author is not named in a signal phrase, place the author's name, the year, and the page number in parentheses after the quotation: (Gitlin, 2001, p. 141).

For electronic texts or other works without page numbers, you may use paragraph numbers, preceded by the ¶ symbol or the abbreviation *para.*

> Driver (2007) has noticed "an increasing focus on the role of land" in policy debates over the past decade (para. 1).

2. BASIC FORMAT FOR A PARAPHRASE OR SUMMARY

Include the author's last name and the year as in model 1, but omit the page or paragraph number unless the reader will need it to find the material in a long work.

> Gitlin (2001) has argued that critics sometimes overestimate the influence of the media on modern life.

3. TWO AUTHORS

Use both names in all citations. Use *and* in a signal phrase, but use an ampersand (&) in parentheses.

> Babcock and Laschever (2003) have suggested that many women do not negotiate their salaries and pay raises as vigorously as their male counterparts do.

> A recent study has suggested that many women do not negotiate their salaries and pay raises as vigorously as their male counterparts do (Babcock & Laschever, 2003).

4. THREE TO FIVE AUTHORS

List all the authors' names for the first reference.

> Safer, Voccola, Hurd, and Goodwin (2003) reached somewhat different conclusions by designing a study that was less dependent on subjective judgment than were previous studies.

In subsequent references, use just the first author's name plus *et al.*

> Based on the results, Safer et al. (2003) determined that the apes took significant steps toward self-expression.

5. SIX OR MORE AUTHORS

Use only the first author's name and *et al.* in every citation.

> As Soleim et al. (2002) demonstrated, advertising holds the potential for distorting and manipulating "free-willed" consumers.

6. CORPORATE OR GROUP AUTHOR

If the name of the organization or corporation is long, spell it out the first time you use it, followed by an abbreviation in brackets. In later references, use the abbreviation only.

FIRST CITATION (Centers for Disease Control and Prevention [CDC], 2006)

LATER CITATIONS (CDC, 2006)

7. UNKNOWN AUTHOR

Use the title or its first few words in a signal phrase or in parentheses. A book's title is italicized, as in the following example; an article's title is placed in quotation marks.

The employment profiles for this time period substantiated this trend (*Federal Employment*, 2001).

8. TWO OR MORE AUTHORS WITH THE SAME LAST NAME

If your list of references includes works by different authors with the same last name, include the authors' initials in each citation.

S. Bartolomeo (2000) conducted the groundbreaking study on teenage childbearing.

9. TWO OR MORE WORKS BY AN AUTHOR IN A SINGLE YEAR

Assign lowercase letters (*a, b*, and so on) alphabetically by title, and include the letters after the year.

Gordon (2004b) examined this trend in more detail.

10. TWO OR MORE SOURCES IN ONE PARENTHETICAL REFERENCE

List sources by different authors in alphabetical order by authors' last names, separated by semicolons: (Cardone, 1998; Lai, 2002). List works by the same author in chronological order, separated by commas: (Lai, 2000, 2002).

11. INDIRECT SOURCE

Use the phrase *as cited in* to indicate that you are reporting information from a secondary source. Name the original source in a signal phrase, but list the secondary source in your list of references.

Amartya Sen developed the influential concept that land reform was necessary for "promoting opportunity" among the poor (as cited in Driver, 2007, para. 2).

12. PERSONAL COMMUNICATION

Cite any personal letters, email messages, electronic postings, telephone conversations, or interviews as shown. Do not include personal communications in the reference list.

> R. Tobin (personal communication, November 4, 2006) supported his claims about music therapy with new evidence.

13. ELECTRONIC DOCUMENT

Cite a Web or electronic document as you would a print source, using the author's name and date.

> Link and Phelan (2005) argued for broader interventions in public health that would be accessible to anyone, regardless of individual wealth.

The APA recommends the following for electronic sources without names, dates, or page numbers:

AUTHOR UNKNOWN

Use a shortened form of the title in a signal phrase or in parentheses (see model 7). If an organization is the author, see model 6.

DATE UNKNOWN

Use the abbreviation *n.d.* (for "no date") in place of the year: (*Hopkins, n.d.*).

NO PAGE NUMBERS

Many works found online or in electronic databases lack stable page numbers. (Use the page numbers for an electronic work in a format, such as PDF, that has stable pagination.) If paragraph numbers are included in such a source, use the symbol ¶ or the abbreviation *para*: (*Giambetti, 2006, para. 7*). If no paragraph numbers are included but the source includes headings, give the heading and identify the paragraph in the section:

> Jacobs and Johnson (2007) have argued that "the South African media is still highly concentrated and not very diverse in terms of race and class" (South African Media after Apartheid, para. 3).

52b   APA style for content notes

APA style allows you to use content notes to expand or supplement your text. Indicate such notes in your text by superscript numerals. Type the notes themselves on a separate page after the last page of the text, under the heading *Footnotes,* centered at the top of the page. Double-space all entries. Indent the first line of each note five spaces, but begin subsequent lines at the left margin.

SUPERSCRIPT NUMERAL IN TEXT

The age of the children involved was an important factor in the selection of items for the questionnaire.[1]

FOOTNOTE

[1]Marjorie Youngston Forman and William Cole of the Child Study Team provided great assistance in identifying appropriate items for the questionnaire.

52c APA style for a list of references

The alphabetical list of the sources cited in your document is called *References.* If your instructor asks that you list everything you have read — not just the sources you cite — call the list *Bibliography.*

All the entries in this section of the book use hanging indent format, in which the first line aligns on the left and the subsequent lines indent one-half inch or five spaces. This is the customary APA format both for final copy and for manuscripts.

AT A GLANCE

Formatting a List of References

- Start your list on a separate page after the text of your document but before appendices or notes. Continue to number pages consecutively.
- Center the heading *References* one inch from the top of the page.
- Begin each entry flush with the left margin, but indent subsequent lines one-half inch or five spaces. Double-space the entire list.
- List sources alphabetically by authors' (or editors') last names. If no author is given, alphabetize the source by the first word of the title other than *A, An,* or *The.* If the list includes two or more works by the same author, alphabetize them by title. (For two or more works by the same author in the same year, see model 5 in 52c.)
- Italicize titles and subtitles of books and periodicals. Do not italicize titles of articles, and do not enclose them in quotation marks.
- For titles of books and articles, capitalize only the first word of the title and the subtitle and any proper nouns or proper adjectives.
- For titles of periodicals, capitalize all major words.
- Follow guidelines in 52c for punctuating an entry.

Guidelines for author listings

List authors' last names first, and use only initials for first and middle names. The in-text citations in your text point readers toward particular sources in your list of references (see 52a).

NAME CITED IN SIGNAL PHRASE IN TEXT

Driver (2007) has noted. . . .

NAME IN PARENTHETICAL CITATION IN TEXT

. . . (Driver, 2007).

BEGINNING OF ENTRY IN LIST OF REFERENCES

Driver, T. (2007).

Models 1–5 below explain how to arrange author names. The information that follows the name of the author depends on the type of work you are citing — a book (models 6–13); a print periodical (models 14–21); an electronic source (models 22–30); or another kind of source (models 31–42). Consult the model that most closely resembles the kind of source you are using.

1. ONE AUTHOR

Give the last name, a comma, the initial(s), and the date in parentheses.

Lightman, A. P. (2002).

2. MULTIPLE AUTHORS

List up to six authors, last name first, with commas separating authors' names and an ampersand (&) before the last author's name.

Walsh, M. E., & Murphy, J. A. (2003).

Note: For a work with more than six authors, list the first six and then write *et al.*

3. CORPORATE OR GROUP AUTHOR

Resources for Rehabilitation. (2003).

4. UNKNOWN AUTHOR

Begin with the work's title. Italicize book titles, but do not italicize article titles or enclose them in quotation marks. Capitalize only the first word of the title and subtitle (if any) and proper nouns and proper adjectives.

National Geographic atlas of the Middle East. (2003).

5. TWO OR MORE WORKS BY THE SAME AUTHOR

List two or more works by the same author in chronological order. Repeat the author's name in each entry.

Goodall, J. (1999).

Goodall, J. (2002).

If the works appeared in the same year, list them alphabetically by title, and assign lowercase letters (*a*, *b*, etc.) after the dates.

Shermer, M. (2002a). On estimating the lifetime of civilizations. *Scientific American, 287*(2), 33.

Shermer, M. (2002b). Readers who question evolution. *Scientific American, 287*(1), 37.

Books

6. BASIC FORMAT FOR A BOOK

Begin with the author name(s). (See models 1–5.) Then include the publication year, the title and subtitle, the city of publication (and state or country, if the city is unfamiliar), and the publisher. The source map on pp. 488–89 shows where to find this information in a typical book.

Levick, S. E. (2003). *Clone being: Exploring the psychological and social dimensions.* Lanham, MD: Rowman & Littlefield.

7. EDITOR

For a book with an editor but no author, list the source under the editor's name.

Dickens, J. (Ed.). (1995). *Family outing: A guide for parents of gays, lesbians and bisexuals.* London: Peter Owen.

To cite a book with an author and an editor, place the editor's name, followed by a comma and the abbreviation *Ed.*, in parentheses after the title.

Austin, J. (1995). *The province of jurisprudence determined* (W. E. Rumble, Ed.). Cambridge: Cambridge University Press.

8. SELECTION IN A BOOK WITH AN EDITOR

Burke, W. W., & Nourmair, D. A. (2001). The role of personality assessment in organization development. In J. Waclawski & A. H. Church (Eds.), *Organization development: A data-driven approach to organizational change* (pp. 55–77). San Francisco: Jossey-Bass.

Take information from the book's title page and copyright page (on the reverse side of the title page), not from the book's cover or a library catalog.

1 **Author.** List all authors' last names first, and use only initials for first and middle names. Separate the names of multiple authors with commas, and use an ampersand (&) before the last author's name.

2 **Publication year.** Enclose the year of publication in parentheses.

3 **Title.** Italicize the title and subtitle. Capitalize only the first word of the title and the subtitle and any proper nouns or proper adjectives.

4 **City of publication.** List the city of publication (and the country or state abbreviation if the city is unfamiliar) followed by a colon.

5 **Publisher.** Give the publisher's name, dropping any *Inc.*, *Co.*, or *Publishers*.

For a book by one author, use the following format:

Last name, initial(s). (Year). *Title of book: Subtitle*. City: Publisher.

A citation for the book on p. 489 would look like this:

AUTHOR   YEAR   TITLE AND SUBTITLE

Tsutsui, W. (2004). *Godzilla on my mind: Fifty years of the king of monsters.*

  CITY   PUBLISHER

New York: Palgrave Macmillan.

For more on using APA style to cite books, see pp. 487–90. (For guidelines and models for using MLA style, see pp. 438–44; for *Chicago* style, see pp. 514–15; for CSE style, see pp. 532–34.)

GODZILLA ON MY MIND
Copyright © William Tsutsui, 2004.
All rights reserved. No part of this book may be used or
reproduced in any manner whatsoever without written permission
except in the case of brief quotations embodied in critical articles
or reviews.

First published 2004 by
PALGRAVE MACMILLAN™
175 Fifth Avenue, New York, N.Y. 10010 and
Houndmills, Basingstoke, Hampshire, England RG21 6XS.
Companies and representatives throughout the world.

2004

New York

PALG
the Pa
Palgra
the Ur
is a re
countr

ISBN

Librar
Tsutsu
Godzil
Tsutsu
    p.
    Incl
    ISB
    1. C

PN199
791.43

A cata
Librar

Desig

10 9

Printe

GODZILLA®
ON MY MIND

*Fifty Years of the
King of Monsters*

 WILLIAM TSUTSUI

 palgrave
macmillan

9. TRANSLATION

> Al-Farabi, A. N. (1998). *On the perfect state* (R. Walzer, Trans.). Chicago: Kazi.

10. EDITION OTHER THAN THE FIRST

> Moore, G. S. (2002). *Living with the earth: Concepts in environmental health science* (2nd ed.). New York: Lewis.

11. MULTIVOLUME WORK

> Barnes, J. (Ed.). (1995). *Complete works of Aristotle* (Vols. 1-2). Princeton, NJ: Princeton University Press.

Note: If you cite just one volume of a multivolume work, list the volume used, instead of the complete span of volumes, in parentheses after the title.

12. ARTICLE IN A REFERENCE WORK

> Dean, C. (1994). Jaws and teeth. In *The Cambridge encyclopedia of human evolution* (pp. 56–59). Cambridge, England: Cambridge University Press.

If no author is listed, begin with the title.

13. REPUBLISHED BOOK

> Piaget, J. (1952). *The language and thought of the child*. London: Routledge & Kegan Paul. (Original work published 1932)

Print periodicals

Begin with the author name(s). (See models 1–5.) Then include the publication date (year only for journals, and year, month, and day for other periodicals); the article title; the periodical title; the volume and issue numbers, if any; and the page numbers. The source map on pp. 492–93 shows where to find this information in a sample periodical.

14. ARTICLE IN A JOURNAL PAGINATED BY VOLUME

> O'Connell, D. C., & Kowal, S. (2003). Psycholinguistics: A half century of monologism. *The American Journal of Psychology, 116*, 191–212.

15. ARTICLE IN A JOURNAL PAGINATED BY ISSUE

If each issue begins with page 1, include the issue number after the volume number.

Hall, R. E. (2000). Marriage as vehicle of racism among women of color. *Psychology: A Journal of Human Behavior, 37*(2), 29–40.

16. ARTICLE IN A MAGAZINE

Ricciardi, S. (2003, August 5). Enabling the mobile work force. *PC Magazine, 22,* 46.

17. ARTICLE IN A NEWSPAPER

Faler, B. (2003, August 29). Primary colors: Race and fundraising. *The Washington Post,* p. A5.

18. EDITORIAL OR LETTER TO THE EDITOR

Zelneck, B. (2003, July 18). Serving the public at public universities [Letter to the editor]. *The Chronicle Review,* p. B18.

19. UNSIGNED ARTICLE

Annual meeting announcement. (2003, March). *Cognitive Psychology, 46,* 227.

20. REVIEW

Ringel, S. (2003). [Review of the book *Multiculturalism and the therapeutic process*]. *Clinical Social Work Journal, 31,* 212–213.

21. PUBLISHED INTERVIEW

Smith, H. (2002, October). [Interview with A. Thompson]. *The Sun,* pp. 4–7.

Electronic sources

The *APA Style Guide to Electronic References* (2007) includes guidelines for citing various kinds of electronic resources. Updated guidelines are maintained at the APA's Web site (www.apa.org).

22. ARTICLE FROM AN ONLINE PERIODICAL

Give the author, date, title, and publication information as you would for a print document. Include both the volume and issue numbers for all journal articles. If the article has a digital object identifier (DOI), include it. If there is no DOI, include the URL for the article or for the periodical's home page (if the URL is long or if the article is available by subscription only). For newspaper articles accessible from a searchable Web site, give the site URL only.

1 Author. List all authors' last names first, and use only initials for first and middle names. Separate the names of multiple authors with commas, and use an ampersand (&) before the last author's name.

2 Publication date. Enclose the date in parentheses. For journals, use only the year. For magazines and newspapers, use the year, a comma, the month (spelled out), and the day, if given.

3 Article title. Do not italicize or enclose article titles in quotation marks. Capitalize only the first word of the article title and subtitle and any proper nouns or proper adjectives.

4 Periodical title. Italicize the periodical title (and subtitle, if any), and capitalize all major words.

5 Publication information. Follow the periodical title with a comma, and then give the volume number (italicized) and, without a space in between, the issue number (if given) in parentheses.

6 Page numbers. Give the inclusive page numbers of the article. For newspapers only, include the abbreviation p. ("page") or pp. ("pages") before the page numbers. End the citation with a period.

For a basic periodical article, use the following format:

Last name, First initial. (Year, month day, or year alone for journal). Title of article. *Title of Periodical, Volume number*(Issue number), Page number(s).

A citation for the periodical article on p. 493 would look like this:

AUTHORS   PUBLICATION DATE   ARTICLE TITLE

Luers, W., Pickering, T., & Walsh, J. (2008, March 20). A solution for the US-

                 PERIODICAL TITLE   PUB. INFO.   PAGE NOS.

Iran nuclear standoff. *The New York Review of Books, 55*(4), 19–22.

For more on using APA style to cite periodicals, see pp. 490–91. (For guidelines and models for using MLA style, see pp. 444–48; for *Chicago* style, see p. 516; for CSE style, see pp. 534–37.)

Volume LV, Number 4

A Solution for the
US–Iran Nuclear Impasse
by William Luers, Thomas Pickering & Jim Walsh

Volume LV, Number 4   March 20, 2008 $5.50

The New York Review
of Books

CAN$6.95

Nicholson Baker:
Why WIKIPEDIA Wins

LA's Bro

Cathl

Jennifer

Micha
A Sup
for D

A Solution for the US–Iran
Nuclear Standoff

William Luers, Thomas Pickering, and Jim Walsh

The recent National Intelligence Estimate's conclusion that Tehran stopped its efforts to develop nuclear weapons in 2003, together with the significant drop in Iranian activity in Iraq, has created favorable conditions for the US to nail direct talks with Iran on its nuclear program. The Bush administration should act on this opportunity. If for no other reason than that its current position is growing weaker, and without such an initiative, Iran will continue its efforts to produce nuclear fuel that might, in the future, be used to build nuclear weapons.

Mahmoud Ahmadinejad announcing the expansion of Iran's nuclear program at a nuclear enrichment facility in Natanz, April 9, 2007

19

493

Citing Electronic Sources

When citing sources accessed online or from an electronic database, include as many of the following elements as you can find:

- *Author.* Give the author's name, if available.
- *Publication date.* Include the date of electronic publication or of the latest update, if available. When no publication date is available, use *n.d.* ("no date"). You will need to include the date you accessed the source in your retrieval information.
- *Title.* List the document title, neither italicized nor in quotation marks.
- *Print publication information.* For articles from online journals, newspapers, or reference databases, give the publication title and other publishing information as you would for a print periodical. (See models 14–17.)
- *Retrieval information.* For a work from a database, do the following: if the article has a DOI (digital object identifier), include that number after the publication information; do not include the name of the database. If there is no DOI, write *Retrieved from* followed either by the database name and the document number assigned by the database, if any, or by the database URL. For a work found on a Web site, write *Retrieved from* and include the URL. If the work seems likely to be updated or has no date of publication, include the retrieval date. If the URL is longer than one line, break it only before a punctuation mark; do not break *http://*.

Barringer, F. (2008, February 7). In many communities, it's not easy going green. *The New York Times.* Retrieved from http://www.nytimes.com

Cleary, J. M., & Crafti, N. (2007). Basic need satisfaction, emotional eating, and dietary restraint as risk factors for recurrent overeating in a community sample. *E-Journal of Applied Psychology, 2*(3), 27–39. Retrieved from http://ojs.lib.swin.edu.au/index.php/ejap/article/view/90/116

23. ARTICLE FROM A DATABASE

Give the author, date, title, and publication information as you would for a print document. Include both the volume and issue numbers for all journal articles. If the article has a DOI, include it at the end, and omit the name of the database. If there is no DOI, include the name of the database and the document number, if any. The source map on pp. 496–97 shows where to find this information for a typical article from a database.

Hazleden, R. (2003, December). Love yourself: The relationship of the self with itself in popular self-help texts. *Journal of Sociology, 39*(4), 413–428. Retrieved from Academic Search Premier. (11798597)

Morley, N. J., Ball, L. J., & Ormerod, T. C. (2006). How the detection of insurance fraud succeeds and fails. *Psychology, Crime, & Law, 12*(2), 163–180. doi:10.1080/10683160512331316325

24. DOCUMENT FROM A WEB SITE

The APA refers to works that are not peer reviewed, such as reports, press releases, brochures, and presentation slides, as "gray literature." Include all of the following information that you can find: the author's name; the publication date (or *n.d.* if no date is available); the title of the document; the title of the site or larger work, if any; any publication information available in addition to the date; *Retrieved from* and the URL. Provide your date of access only if no publication date is given. The source map on pp. 498–99 shows where to find this information for an article from a Web site.

Behnke, P. C. (2006, February 22). The homeless are everyone's problem. *Authors' Den*. Retrieved from http://www.authorsden.com/visit/viewArticle.asp?id=21017

Hacker, J. S. (2006). The privatization of risk and the growing economic insecurity of Americans. *Items and Issues, 5*(4), 16–23. Retrieved from http://publications.ssrc.org/items/items5.4/Hacker.pdf

What parents should know about treatment of behavioral and emotional disorders in preschool children. (2006). *APA Online*. Retrieved from http://www.apa.org/releases/kidsmed.html

25. CHAPTER OR SECTION OF A WEB DOCUMENT

Follow model 24. After the chapter or section title, type *In* and give the document title, with identifying information, if any, in parentheses. End with the date of access and the URL.

Salamon, Andrew. (n.d.). War in Europe. In *Childhood in times of war* (chap. 2). Retrieved April 11, 2008, from http://remember.org/jean

26. EMAIL MESSAGE OR REAL-TIME COMMUNICATION

Because the APA stresses that any sources cited in your list of references be retrievable by your readers, you should not include entries for email messages, real-time communications (such as IMs), or any other postings that are not archived. Instead, cite these sources in your text as forms of personal communication (see p. 484).

1 Author. Include the author's name as you would for a print source. List all authors' last names first, and use initials for first and middle names.

2 Publication date. Enclose the date in parentheses. For journals, use only the year. For magazines and newspapers, use the year, a comma, the month, and the day if given.

3 Article title. Capitalize only the first word of the article title and the subtitle and any proper nouns or proper adjectives.

4 Periodical title. Italicize the periodical title.

5 Print publication information. Give the volume number (italicized), the issue number (in parentheses), and the inclusive page numbers. For newspapers, include the abbreviation *p.* or *pp.* before the page numbers.

6 Retrieval information. If the article has a DOI (digital object identifier), include that number after the publication information; do not include the name of the database. If there is no DOI, write *Retrieved from* followed either by the database name and the document number assigned by the database or by the database URL.

For a journal article retrieved from a database, use the following format:

Last name, First initial. (Year). Title of article. *Title of Journal, Volume number*(Issue number), Page number(s). doi:number OR Retrieved from Database Name. (Document number) OR database URL

A citation for the article on p. 497 would look like this:

AUTHORS   PUB. DATE   ARTICLE TITLE

Chory-Assad, R. M., & Tamborini, R. (2004). Television sitcom exposure and aggressive

PERIODICAL TITLE

communication: A priming perspective. *North American Journal of Psychology,*

PRINT PUB. INFO.   RETRIEVAL INFO.

6(3), 415–422. Retrieved from Academic Search Premier. (15630823)

For more on using APA style to cite articles retrieved from databases, see pp. 494–95. (For guidelines and models for using MLA style, see pp. 449–51; for *Chicago* style, see p. 516; for CSE style, see pp. 538–41.)

1 Chory-Assad, Rebecca M.,
Tamborini, Ron

2 2004

3 *Television Sitcom Exposure* and Aggressive Communication: A Priming Perspective

‹ 1 of 1 › Result List | Refine Search | Print | E-mail | Save | Export | Add to folder
View: Citation | HTML Full Text | PDF Full Text (390K)

Title:	Television Sitcom Exposure and Aggressive Communication: A Priming Perspective.

Find More Like This

Authors: Chory-Assad, Rebecca M.[1]
Tamborini, Ron[2]

Source: North American Journal of Psychology, 2004, Vol. 6 Issue 3, p415-422, 8p

Document Type: Article

Subject Terms: *TELEVISION comedies
*AGGRESSIVENESS
*ATTITUDE (Psychology)
*TELEVISION programs

Abstract: This study examined the relationship between exposure to verbally aggressive television sitcoms and aggressive communication, from a priming and cognitive neo-associationistic perspective. Participants reported their own verbal aggressiveness and exposure to sitcoms approximately one month prior to their participation in the lab portion of the study. Once in the lab participants evaluated four sitcoms and engaged in a question-response session that was observed and coded for aggression. Results indicated that increased exposure to television sitcoms was associated with lower levels of aggressive communication. Implications of these results for theory and research concerning the effects of exposure to aggression in a humorous context are discussed. [ABSTRACT FROM AUTHOR]

Author Affiliations: [1]West Virginia University
[2]Michigan State University

Full Text Word Count: 2880

ISSN: 1527-7143

Accession Number: 15630823

Persistent link to this record: http://search.ebscohost.com/login.aspx?direct=true&db=aph&AN=15630823&site=ehost-live

Database: Academic Search Premier

Choose Language | Translate

4 North American Journal of Psychology

5 Vol. 6 Issue 3, p415-422, 8p

6 **Accession Number:** 15630823
Database: Academic Search Premier

1 Author. If available, include the author's name as you would for a print source. List authors' last names first, and use initials for first names. The site's sponsor may be the author. If no author is identified, begin the citation with the title of the document.

2 Publication date. Include the date of publication or latest update. Use *n.d.* ("no date") when no publication date is available.

3 Title. Capitalize only the first word of the title and subtitle and any proper nouns or proper adjectives.

4 Title of Web site. Italicize the title. Capitalize all major words.

5 Retrieval information. Write *Retrieved from* and include the URL. If the work seems likely to be updated or has no date of publication, include the retrieval date.

For a document found on a Web site with one author, use the following format:

Last name, First initial. (Publication date). Title of document. *Title of Web Site*. Retrieved from URL

A citation for the Web document on p. 499 would look like this:

AUTHOR PUBL. DATE   TITLE OF WORK

Alexander, M. (2001, August 22). Thirty years later, Stanford Prison Experiment

    TITLE OF WEB SITE   RETRIEVAL INFO.

lives on. *Stanford Report*. Retrieved from http://news-service.stanford.edu/news/

2001/august22/prison2-822.html

For more on using APA style to cite works from Web sites, see p. 495. (For guidelines and models for using MLA style, see pp. 453–55; for *Chicago* style, see p. 517; for CSE style, see p. 539.)

① MEREDITH ALEXANDER

④ Stanford Report

⑤

② August 22, 2001

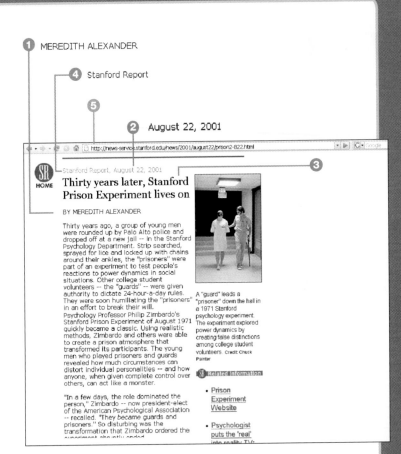

⬅ ➡ ⟳ ⊙ ⌂ 🔖 http://news-service.stanford.edu/news/2001/august22/prison2-822.html ▾ ▶ ⊙ ▾ Google

③

Stanford Report, August 22, 2001

Thirty years later, Stanford Prison Experiment lives on

BY MEREDITH ALEXANDER

Thirty years ago, a group of young men were rounded up by Palo Alto police and dropped off at a new jail -- in the Stanford Psychology Department. Strip searched, sprayed for lice and locked up with chains around their ankles, the "prisoners" were part of an experiment to test people's reactions to power dynamics in social situations. Other college student volunteers -- the "guards" -- were given authority to dictate 24-hour-a-day rules. They were soon humiliating the "prisoners" in an effort to break their will.

Psychology Professor Philip Zimbardo's Stanford Prison Experiment of August 1971 quickly became a classic. Using realistic methods, Zimbardo and others were able to create a prison atmosphere that transformed its participants. The young men who played prisoners and guards revealed how much circumstances can distort individual personalities -- and how anyone, when given complete control over others, can act like a monster.

"In a few days, the role dominated the person," Zimbardo -- now president-elect of the American Psychological Association -- recalled. "They *became* guards and prisoners." So disturbing was the transformation that Zimbardo ordered the experiment abruptly ended.

A "guard" leads a "prisoner" down the hall in a 1971 Stanford psychology experiment. The experiment explored power dynamics by creating false distinctions among college student volunteers. Credit: Chuck Painter

🆂🆁 **Related Information**

- Prison Experiment Website

- Psychologist puts the 'real' into reality TV:

Citing Sources without Models in APA style

You may sometimes need to cite a source for which you cannot find a model in APA style. To do so, collect as much information you can find — about the creator, title, sponsor, date of creation or update — with the goal of helping your readers find the source for themselves, if possible. Then look at the models in this section to see which one most closely matches the type of source you are using. For example, you might consider whether the source is most like an article (look for the appropriate print or electronic model), a work taken from a Web site (model 24), an online posting (model 27), a video (models 37 and 41), a podcast (models 39–40), or some other kind of source.

In an academic writing project, before citing an electronic source for which you have no model, also be sure to ask your instructor's advice.

27. ONLINE POSTING

List an online posting in the references list only if you are able to retrieve the message from an archive. Provide the author's name, the date of posting, and the subject line. Include other identifying information in square brackets. End with the retrieval statement, including the name of the newsgroup, online forum, or discussion group, if any, and the URL of the archived message.

> Troike, R. C. (2001, June 21). Buttercups and primroses [Msg 8]. Message posted
>
> to the American Dialect Society's electronic mailing list, archived at
>
> http://listserv.linguistlist.org/archives/ads-l.html

For a newsgroup posting, end with the name of the newsgroup.

> Wittenberg, E. (2001, July 11). Gender and the Internet [Msg 4]. Message posted
>
> to news://comp.edu.composition

28. WEB LOG (BLOG) POST

> Spaulding, P. (2008, April 16). I did laundry rather than watch tonight's debate.
>
> Message posted to http://pandagon.blogsome.com/

29. WIKI ENTRY

Use the date of posting, if there is one, or "n.d." for "no date" if there is none. Include the retrieval date because wiki content can change frequently.

Happiness. (2007, June 14). Retrieved March 24, 2008, from PsychWiki:

  http://www.psychwiki.com/wiki/Happiness

30. SOFTWARE

PsychMate [Software]. (2003). Available from Psychology Software Tools:

  http://pstnet.com/products/psychmate

Other sources (including online versions)

31. GOVERNMENT PUBLICATION

Office of the Federal Register. (2003). *The United States government manual*

  2003/2004. Washington, DC: U.S. Government Printing Office.

Cite an online government document as you would a printed government work, adding the date of access and the URL. If there is no date, use *n.d.*

U.S. Public Health Service. (1999). *The surgeon general's call to action to prevent*

  suicide. Retrieved November 5, 2003, from http://www.mentalhealth.org/

  suicideprevention/calltoaction.asp

32. DISSERTATION

If you retrieved the dissertation from a database, give the database name and the accession number, if one is assigned.

Lengel, L. L. (1968). *The righteous cause: Some religious aspects of Kansas*

  populism. Retrieved from ProQuest Digital Dissertations. (6900033)

If you retrieve a dissertation from a Web site, give the type of dissertation, the institution, and year after the title, and provide a retrieval statement.

Meeks, M. G. (2006). *Between abolition and reform: First-year writing programs,*

  e-literacies, and institutional change (doctoral dissertation, University of

  North Carolina, 2006). Retrieved from http://dc.lib.unc.edu/cgi-bin/

  showfile.exe?CISOROOT=/etd&CISOPTR=212

33. TECHNICAL OR RESEARCH REPORT

Give the report number, if available, in parentheses after the title.

McCool, R., Fikes, R., & McGuinness, D. (2003). *Semantic Web tools for enhanced*

  authoring (Report No. KSL-03–07). Stanford, CA: Knowledge Systems Laboratory.

34. CONFERENCE PROCEEDINGS

Mama, A. (2001). Challenging subjects: Gender and power in African contexts. In *Proceedings of Nordic African Institute Conference: Rethinking power in Africa.* Uppsala, Sweden, 9–18.

35. PAPER PRESENTED AT A MEETING OR SYMPOSIUM, UNPUBLISHED

Cite the month of the meeting if it is available.

Jones, J. G. (1999, February). *Mental health intervention in mass casualty disasters.* Paper presented at the Rocky Mountain Region Disaster Mental Health Conference, Laramie, WY.

36. POSTER SESSION

Barnes Young, L. L. (2003, August). *Cognition, aging, and dementia.* Poster session presented at the 2003 Division 40 APA Convention, Toronto, Ontario, Canada.

37. FILM, VIDEO, OR DVD

Mottola, G. (Director). (2007). *Superbad* [Motion picture]. United States: Sony.

38. TELEVISION PROGRAM, SINGLE EPISODE

Imperioli, M. (Writer), & Buscemi, S. (Director). (2002). Everybody hurts [Television series episode]. In D. Chase (Executive Producer), *The Sopranos.* New York: Home Box Office.

39. TELEVISION FEATURE, PODCAST

Include as much of the following information as you can find: the writer or producer; the date produced or posted; the title of the podcast; identifying information, if necessary, in brackets; the title of the series, if any; and the retrieval information.

Allen, D. (Producer). (2005). Deep jungle: New frontiers [Television series episode]. In F. Kaufman (Executive Producer), *Nature.* Podcast retrieved from WNET: http://www.pbs.org/wnet/nature/podcasts.html

40. AUDIO PODCAST

Include as much information as you can find, as for a video podcast (see model 39).

> O'Brien, K. (Writer). (2008, January 31). Developing countries. *KUSP's life in the fast lane.* Podcast retrieved from http://www.kusp.org/shows/fast.html

41. VIDEO WEB POST

> Klusman, P. (2008, February 13). An engineer's guide to cats [Video file]. Video posted to http://www.youtube.com/watch?v=mHXBL6bzAR4

42. RECORDING

> The Avalanches. (2001). Frontier psychiatrist. On *Since I left you* [CD]. Los Angles: Elektra/Asylum Records.

52d An abridged student research essay, APA style

An abridged version of an essay by Merlla McLaughlin appears on the following pages. It conforms to the APA guidelines described in this chapter. Note that this essay has been reproduced in a narrow format to allow for annotation.

Student Writer

Merlla McLaughlin

 bedfordstmartins.com/everydaywriter To read this essay in its entirety, click on **Student Writing**.

Shortened title and page number, separated by five spaces, appear on every page

Leadership Roles   1

Title, name, and affiliation centered and double-spaced

Leadership Roles in a Small-Group Project

Merlla McLaughlin

Oregon State University

Annotations indicate effective choices or APA-style formatting.

Abstract

Using the interpersonal communications research of J. K. Brilhart and G. J. Galanes as well as that of W. Wilmot and J. Hocker, along with T. Hartman's Personality Assessment, I observed and analyzed the leadership roles and group dynamics of my project collaborators in a communications course. Based on results of the Hartman Personality Assessment, I predicted that a single leader would emerge. However, complementary individual strengths and gender differences encouraged a distributed leadership style, in which the group experienced little confrontation. Conflict, because it was handled positively, was crucial to the group's progress.

Heading centered

No indentation

Study described

Key points of report discussed

Double spacing used

Leadership Roles in a Small-Group Project

Although classroom lectures provide students with volumes of information, many experiences can be understood only by living them. So it is with the workings of a small, task-focused group. What observations can I make after working with a group of peers on a class project? And what have I learned as a result?

Leadership Expectations and Emergence

The six members of this group were selected by the instructor; half were male and half were female. By performing the Hartman Personality Assessment (Hartman, 1998) in class, we learned that Hartman has associated key personality traits with the colors red, blue, white, and yellow (see Table 1). The assessment identified most of us as "Blues," concerned with intimacy and caring. Because of the bold qualities associated with "Reds," I expected that Nate, our only "Red" member, might become our leader. (Kaari, the only "White," seemed poised to become the peacekeeper.) However, after Nate missed the first two meetings, it seemed that Pat, who contributed often during our first three meetings, might emerge as leader. Pat has strong communications skills, a commanding presence, and displays

Table 1

Hartman's Key Personality Traits

Trait category	Color			
	Red	Blue	White	Yellow
Motive	Power	Intimacy	Peace	Fun
Strengths	Loyal to tasks	Loyal to people	Tolerant	Positive
Limitations	Arrogant	Self-righteous	Timid	Uncommitted

Note. Table is adapted from information found at The Hartman Personality Profile, by N. Hayden. Retrieved February 15, 2004, from http://students.cs.byu.edu/~nhayden/Code/index.php

---

Margin annotations:

Full title, centered

Paragraphs indented

Questions indicate the focus of the essay

Headings help organize the report

APA-style parenthetical reference

Background information about team members' personality types

Chart displays information concisely

Chart referred to in preceding text

Source of table listed

Leadership Roles   4

sensitivity to others. I was surprised, then, when our group

developed a *distributed style* of leadership (Brilhart & Galanes, 1998).

The longer we worked together, however, the more I was convinced

that this approach to leadership was best for our group.

As Brilhart and Galanes have noted, "distributed leadership

explicitly acknowledges that the leadership of a group is spread

among members, with each member expected to move the group

toward its goal" (p. 175). These researchers divide positive

communicative actions into two types: *task functions* that affect a

group's productivity and *maintenance functions* that influence the

interactions of group members. One of our group's most immediate

task-function needs was decision making, and as we made our first

major decision — what topic to pursue — our group's distributed-

leadership style began to emerge.

Decision-Making Methods

Our choice of topic — the parking services at Oregon State

University (OSU) — was the result not of a majority vote but of

negotiated consensus. During this decision-making meeting, several

of us argued that a presentation on parking services at OSU would

interest most students, and after considerable discussion, the other

group members agreed. Once we had a topic, other decisions came

naturally.

Roles Played

Thanks in part to the distributed leadership that our group

developed, the strengths of individual group members became

increasingly apparent. Although early in our project Pat was the key

initiator and Nate was largely an information seeker, all group

members eventually took on these functions in addition to serving as

recorders, gathering information, and working on our questionnaire.

Side annotations:

First observations about leadership roles

Source cited to define key term for this study

Minimum of one-inch margin on all sides

Discussion of the group's decision making supports claim of distributed leadership style

Another example of distributed leadership style

Leadership Roles   5

Every member coordinated the group's work at some point; several made sure that everyone could speak and be heard, and one member was especially good at catching important details the rest of us were apt to miss. Joe, McKenzie, Kaari, and I frequently clarified or elaborated on information, whereas Pat, Kaari, and Nate were good at contributing ideas during brainstorming sessions. Nate, Joe, and McKenzie brought tension-relieving humor to the group.

Transition to gender influences

Just as each member brought individual strengths to the group, gender differences also made us effective. For example, the women took a holistic approach to the project, looking at the big picture and making intuitive leaps in ways that the men generally did not. The men preferred a more systematic process. Brilhart and Galanes have suggested that men working in groups dominated by women may display "subtle forms of resistance to a dominant presence of women" (p. 98). Although the men in our group did not attend all the meetings and the women did, I did not find that the men's nonattendance implied male resistance any more than the women's attendance implied female dominance. Rather, our differing qualities complemented each other and enabled us to work together effectively.

Essay double-spaced throughout

Social Environment

Writer returns to categories defined earlier

As previously noted, most of our group members were Blues on the Hartman scale, valuing altruism, intimacy, appreciation, and having a moral conscience (Hayden). At least three of the four Blues had White as their secondary color, signifying the importance of peace, kindness, independence, and sacrifice (Hayden). The presence of these traits may explain why our group experienced little confrontation and conflict. Nate (a Red) was most likely to speak bluntly. The one time that Nate seemed put off, it was not his words but his body language that expressed his discomfort. This was an awkward moment, but a rare one given our group's generally positive handling of conflict.

Conclusion

Perhaps most important is the lesson I learned about conflict. Prior to participating in this group, I always avoided conflict because, as Wilmot and Hocker (1998) have suggested, most people think "harmony is normal and conflict is abnormal" (p. 9). Now I recognize that some kinds of conflict are essential for increasing understanding between group members and creating an effective collaborative result. It was essential, for instance, that our group explore different members' ideas about possible topics for our project, and this process inevitably required some conflict. The end result, however, was a positive one.

Constructive conflict requires an open and engaging attitude among group members, encourages personal growth, and ends when the issue at hand is resolved. Most important for our group, such conflict encouraged cooperation (pp. 47–48) and increased the group's cohesiveness. All the members of our group felt, for instance, that their ideas about possible topics were seriously considered. Once we decided on a topic, everyone fully committed to it. Thus our group effectiveness was enhanced by constructive conflict.

As a result of this project, I have a better sense of when conflict is — and isn't — productive. My group used conflict productively when we hashed out our ideas, and we avoided the kind of conflict that creates morale problems and wastes time. Although all groups operate somewhat differently, I now feel more prepared to understand and participate in future small-group projects.

In concluding section, writer answers question posed in introduction

Conclusion looks toward future

References

Brilhart, J. K., & Galanes, G. J. (1998). *Effective group discussion* (9th ed.). Boston: McGraw-Hill.

Hartman, T. (1998). *The color code: A new way to see yourself, your relationships, and your life.* New York: Scribner.

Hayden, N. (n.d.). *The Hartman Personality Profile.* Retrieved February 15, 2004, from http://students.cs.byu.edu/~nhayden/Code/index.php

Wilmot, W., & Hocker, J. (1998). *Interpersonal conflict* (5th ed.). Boston: McGraw-Hill.

List starts on new page

Book

Web site

Entries alphabetized

First line of entry flush left; subsequent lines indent

Chicago Style 53

The style guide of the University of Chicago Press has long been used in history as well as in other areas of the arts and humanities. The fifteenth edition of *The Chicago Manual of Style* (2003) provides a complete guide to *Chicago* style, including two systems for citing sources. This chapter presents the notes and bibliography system. For easy reference, examples of how to format *Chicago*-style notes and bibliographic entries are shown together in 53b.

 bedfordstmartins.com/everydaywriter To access the advice in this chapter online, click on **Documenting Sources.**

DIRECTORY TO *CHICAGO* STYLE

53a *Chicago* style for in-text citations, notes, and bibliography

In *Chicago* style, use superscript numbers (^{1}) to mark citations in the text. Place the superscript number for each note just after the relevant quotation, sentence, clause, or phrase. Type the number after any punctuation mark except the dash; do not leave space before the superscript. Number citations sequentially throughout the text. When you use signal phrases to introduce quotations or other source material, note that *Chicago* style requires you to use the present tense (*citing Bebout's studies, Meier points out.* . .).

Notes

The notes themselves can be footnotes (each typed at the bottom of the page on which the superscript for it appears) or endnotes (all typed on a separate page at the end under the heading *Notes*); check your instructor's preference. The first line of each note is indented five spaces or one-half inch and begins with a number followed by a period and one space. All remaining lines of the entry are flush with the left margin. Footnotes and endnotes should be double-spaced.

IN THE TEXT

Sweig argues that Castro and Che Guevara were not the only key players in the Cuban Revolution of the late 1950s.[19]

IN THE FIRST NOTE REFERRING TO THE SOURCE

> 19. Julia Sweig, *Inside the Cuban Revolution* (Cambridge, MA: Harvard
> University Press, 2002), 9.

IN SUBSEQUENT NOTES

After giving complete information the first time you cite a work, shorten any additional references to that work: list only the author's name, a comma, a shortened version of the title, a comma, and the page number. If the reference is to the same source cited in the previous note, you can use the Latin abbreviation *Ibid.* (for "in the same place") instead of the name and title.

> 19. Julia Sweig, *Inside the Cuban Revolution* (Cambridge, MA: Harvard University
> versity Press, 2002), 9.
>
> 20. Ibid., 13.
>
> 21. Foner and Lewis, *Black Worker*, 138–39.
>
> 22. Ferguson, "Comfort of Being Sad," 63.
>
> 23. Sweig, *Cuban Revolution*, 21.

Bibliography

The alphabetical list of the sources used is usually titled *Bibliography* in *Chicago* style. If *Sources Consulted, Works Cited,* or *Selected Bibliography* better describes your list, however, any of these titles is acceptable.

In the bibliographic entry for a source, include the same information as in the first note for that source, but omit the specific page reference. However, give the first author's name last name first, followed by a comma and the first name; separate the main elements of the entry with periods rather than commas; and do not enclose the publication information for books in parentheses. List sources alphabetically by authors' last names (or by the first major word in the title if the author is unknown).

IN THE BIBLIOGRAPHY

> Sweig, Julia. *Inside the Cuban Revolution*. Cambridge, MA: Harvard University
> Press, 2002.

Start the bibliography on a separate page after the main text and any endnotes. Continue the consecutive numbering of pages. Center the title *Bibliography* (without italics or quotation marks). Begin each entry at the left margin. Indent subsequent lines of each entry five spaces or one-half inch. Double-space the entire list.

53b *Chicago* style for notes and bibliographic entries

For easy reference, the following examples demonstrate how to format both notes and bibliographic entries according to *Chicago* style.

Books

1. ONE AUTHOR

1. James S. Hirsch, *Riot and Remembrance: The Tulsa Race War and Its Legacy* (Boston: Houghton Mifflin, 2002), 119.

Hirsch, James S. *Riot and Remembrance: The Tulsa Race War and Its Legacy.* Boston: Houghton Mifflin, 2002.

2. MULTIPLE AUTHORS

2. Margaret Macmillan and Richard Holbrooke, *Paris 1919: Six Months That Changed the World* (New York: Random House, 2003), 384.

Macmillan, Margaret, and Richard Holbrooke. *Paris 1919: Six Months That Changed the World.* New York: Random House, 2003.

When there are more than three authors, you may list the first author followed by *et al.* or *and others* in the note. In the bibliography, however, list all the authors' names.

2. Stephen J. Blank and others, *Conflict, Culture, and History: Regional Dimensions* (Miami: University Press of the Pacific, 2002), 276.

Blank, Stephen J., Lawrence E. Grinter, Karl P. Magyar, Lewis B. Ware, and Bynum E. Weathers. *Conflict, Culture, and History: Regional Dimensions.* Miami: University Press of the Pacific, 2002.

3. CORPORATE OR GROUP AUTHOR

3. World Intellectual Property Organization, *Intellectual Property Profile of the Least Developed Countries* (Geneva: World Intellectual Property Organization, 2002), 43.

World Intellectual Property Organization. *Intellectual Property Profile of the Least Developed Countries*. Geneva: World Intellectual Property Organization, 2002.

4. UNKNOWN AUTHOR

4. *Broad Stripes and Bright Stars* (Kansas City, MO: Andrews McMeel, 2002), 10.

Broad Stripes and Bright Stars. Kansas City, MO: Andrews McMeel, 2002.

5. EDITOR

5. James H. Fetzer, ed., *The Great Zapruder Film Hoax: Deceit and Deception in the Death of JFK* (Chicago: Open Court, 2003), 56.

Fetzer, James H., ed. *The Great Zapruder Film Hoax: Deceit and Deception in the Death of JFK*. Chicago: Open Court, 2003.

6. SELECTION IN AN ANTHOLOGY OR CHAPTER IN A BOOK WITH AN EDITOR

6. Denise Little, "Born in Blood," in *Alternate Gettysburgs*, ed. Brian Thomsen and Martin H. Greenberg (New York: Berkley Publishing Group, 2002), 245.

Little, Denise. "Born in Blood." In *Alternate Gettysburgs*, edited by Brian Thomsen and Martin H. Greenberg, 242–55. New York: Berkley Publishing Group, 2002.

7. EDITION OTHER THAN THE FIRST

7. Charles G. Beaudette, *Excess Heat: Why Cold Fusion Research Prevailed*, 2nd ed. (South Bristol, ME: Oak Grove Press, 2002), 313.

Beaudette, Charles G. *Excess Heat: Why Cold Fusion Research Prevailed*. 2nd ed. South Bristol, ME: Oak Grove Press, 2002.

8. MULTIVOLUME WORK

8. John Watson, *Annals of Philadelphia and Pennsylvania in the Olden Time*, vol. 2 (Washington, DC: Ross & Perry, 2003), 514.

Watson, John. *Annals of Philadelphia and Pennsylvania in the Olden Time*. Vol. 2. Washington, DC: Ross & Perry, 2003.

9. REFERENCE WORK

Cite well-known reference works in your notes, but do not list them in your bibliography. Use *s.v.*, the abbreviation for the Latin *sub verbo* ("under the word") to help your reader find the entry.

9. *Encarta World Dictionary*, s.v. "carpetbagger."

Periodicals

10. ARTICLE IN A JOURNAL

10. Karin Lützen, "The Female World: Viewed from Denmark," *Journal of Women's History* 12, no. 3 (2000): 36.

Lützen, Karin. "The Female World: Viewed from Denmark." *Journal of Women's History* 12, no. 3 (2000): 34–38.

11. ARTICLE IN A MAGAZINE

11. Douglas Brinkley and Anne Brinkley, "Lawyers and Lizard-Heads," *Atlantic Monthly*, May 2002, 56.

Brinkley, Douglas, and Anne Brinkley. "Lawyers and Lizard-Heads." *Atlantic Monthly,* May 2002, 55–61.

12. ARTICLE IN A NEWSPAPER

12. Caroline E. Mayer, "Wireless Industry to Adopt Voluntary Standards," *Washington Post,* September 9, 2003, sec. E.

Mayer, Caroline E. "Wireless Industry to Adopt Voluntary Standards." *Washington Post,* September 9, 2003, sec. E.

Electronic sources

13. ARTICLE FROM A DATABASE

The source map on pp. 518–19 indicates where to find necessary information for citing an article from a database.

13. Peter DeMarco, "Holocaust Survivors Lend Voice to History," *Boston Globe,* November 2, 2003, http://www.lexisnexis.com (accessed November 19, 2003).

DeMarco, Peter. "Holocaust Survivors Lend Voice to History." *Boston Globe,* November 2, 2003. http://www.lexisnexis.com (accessed November 19, 2003).

14. ARTICLE IN AN ELECTRONIC JOURNAL

14. Damian Bracken, "Rationalism and the Bible in Seventh-Century Ireland," *Chronicon* 2 (1998), http://www.ucc.ie/chronicon/bracfra.htm (accessed November 1, 2005).

Bracken, Damian. "Rationalism and the Bible in Seventh-Century Ireland." *Chronicon* 2 (1998). http://www.ucc.ie/chronicon/bracfra.htm (accessed November 1, 2005).

15. ARTICLE IN AN ONLINE MAGAZINE

> 15. Kim Iskyan, "Putin's Next Power Play," *Slate,* November 4, 2003, http://slate.msn.com/id/2090745 (accessed November 7, 2005).

> Iskyan, Kim. "Putin's Next Power Play." *Slate,* November 4, 2003.
>> http://slate.msn.com/id/2090745 (accessed November 7, 2005).

AT A GLANCE

Citing Sources without Models in *Chicago* Style

Chicago currently provides no guidelines or models for citing newer kinds of electronic sources, such as MP3 files, YouTube videos, and the like. To cite a source for which you cannot find a model, collect as much information you can find — about the creator, title, sponsor, date of creation or update — with the goal of helping your readers find the source for themselves, if possible. Then look at the models in this section to see which one most closely matches the type of source you are using. For example, a YouTube video might resemble an entry in a Web log (model 17), a broadcast interview (model 20), a podcast (model 21), or a video (model 22).

In an academic writing project, before citing an electronic source for which you have no model, also be sure to ask your instructor's advice.

---

16. WORK FROM A WEB SITE

The source map on pp. 520–21 shows where to find important information for a typical work from a Web site.

> 16. Rutgers University, "Picture Gallery," *The Rutgers Oral History Archives of World War II,* http://fas-history.rutgers.edu/oralhistory/orlhom.htm (accessed November 7, 2007).

> Rutgers University. "Picture Gallery." *The Rutgers Oral History Archives of World War II.* http://fas-history.rutgers.edu/oralhistory/orlhom.htm (accessed November 7, 2007).

17. ENTRY IN A WEB LOG (BLOG)

> 17. Josh Marshall, "Neologism Watch," *Talking Points Memo,* http://talkingpointsmemo.com/archives/182621.php.

> Marshall, Josh. "Neologism Watch." *Talking Points Memo.*
>> http://talkingpointsmemo.com/archives/182621.php.

1. **Author.** In a note, list author first name first. In the bibliographic entry, list the first author last name first; list other authors first name first.

2. **Article title.** Enclose title and subtitle (if any) in quotation marks, and capitalize major words. In the notes section, put a comma before and after the title. In the bibliography, put a period before and after.

3. **Periodical title.** Italicize the title and subtitle, and capitalize all major words. Follow with a comma, unless it is a journal.

4. **Publication information.** For journals, follow the title with the volume number, a comma, the abbreviation *no.*, and the issue number. For journals, enclose the publication year in parentheses and follow with a comma (in a note) or with a period (in a bibliography). For other periodicals, give the month and year or month, day, and year, followed by a comma.

5. **Retrieval information.** Give the brief URL for the database, followed, in parentheses, by the word *accessed* and the access date. End with a period.

For a journal article from a database, use the following formats:

Endnote

1. First name Last name, "Title of Article," *Periodical Title* Volume no., Issue (Year), Database URL (access date).

Bibliographic entry

Last name, First name. "Title of Article." *Periodical Title* Volume no., Issue (Year). Database URL (access date).

Citations for the article on p. 519 would look like this:

Endnote

NOTE NO.	AUTHORS	ARTICLE TITLE

1. Howard Schuman, Barry Schwartz, and Hannah D'Arcy, "Elite Revisionists and

PERIODICAL TITLE

Popular Beliefs: Christopher Columbus, Hero or Villain?" *Public Opinion Quarterly*

PUB. INFO.	RETRIEVAL INFO.

69, no. 1 (2005), http://elibrary.bigchalk.com (accessed October 15, 2007).

Bibliographic entry

Schuman, Howard, Barry Schwartz, and Hannah D'Arcy. "Elite Revisionists and
  Popular Beliefs: Christopher Columbus, Hero or Villain?" *Public Opinion Quarterly*
  69, no. 1 (2005). http://elibrary.bigchalk.com (accessed October 15, 2007).

For more on using *Chicago* style to cite articles from databases, see p. 516. (For
guidelines and models for using MLA style, see pp. 449–51; for APA style, see
pp. 494–95; for CSE style, see pp. 538–39.)

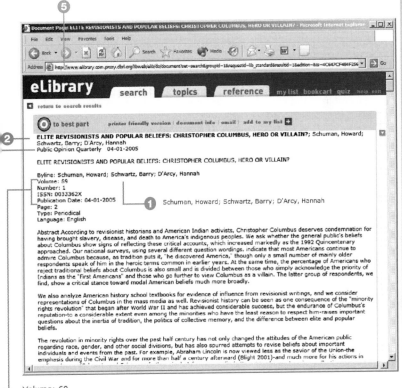

1 **Author.** In a note, list author first name first. In a bibliographic entry, list the first author last name first and additional authors first name first. Note that the host may serve as the author.

2 **Document title.** Enclose the title in quotation marks, and capitalize all major words. In a note, put a comma before and after the title. In the bibliography, put a period before and after.

3 **Title of Web site.** Italicize the title, and capitalize all major words. In the notes section, put a comma after the title. In the bibliography, put a period after the title.

4 **Retrieval information.** Give the URL for the Web site, followed, in parentheses, by the word *accessed* and the access date. End with a period.

When citing works from Web sites, use the following formats:

Endnote

1. First name Last name, "Title of Document," *Title of Web Site,* URL (access date).

Bibliographic entry

Last name, First name. "Title of Document." *Title of Web Site.* URL (access date).

Citations for the Web site on p. 521 would look like this:

Endnote

NOTE
NO.   AUTHOR   DOCUMENT TITLE   TITLE OF
                                            WEB SITE

1. Douglas Linder, "The Scopes Trial: An Introduction," *Famous Trials,*
                              RETRIEVAL INFO.

http://www.law.umkc.edu/faculty/projects/FTrials/scopes/scopes.htm (accessed

September 24, 2006).

Bibliographic entry

Linder, Douglas. "The Scopes Trial: An Introduction." *Famous Trials.* http://www.law.umkc.edu/
faculty/projects/FTrials/scopes/scopes.htm (accessed September 24, 2006).

For more on using *Chicago* style to cite works from Web sites, see p. 517. (For guidelines and models for using MLA style, see pp. 453–55; for APA style, see p. 495; for CSE style, see p. 539.)

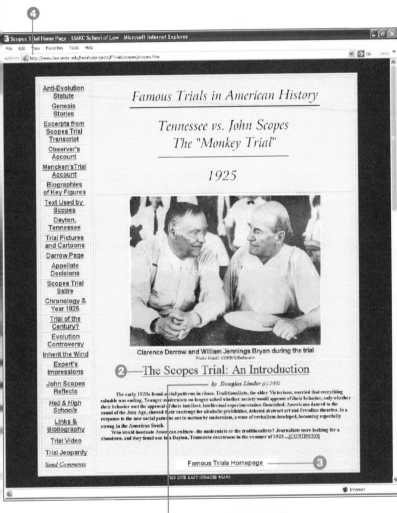

4
Scopes Trial Home Page - UMKC School of Law - Microsoft Internet Explorer
File Edit View Favorites Tools Help
Address http://www.law.umkc.edu/faculty/projects/FTrials/scopes/scopes.htm
Go Links
Anti-Evolution Statute
Genesis Stories
Excerpts from Scopes Trial Transcript
Observer's Account
Mencken'sTrial Account
Biographies of Key Figures
Text Used by Scopes
Dayton, Tennessee
Trial Pictures and Cartoons
Darrow Page
Appellate Decisions
Scopes Trial Satire
Chronology & Year 1925
Trial of the Century?
Evolution Controversy
Inherit the Wind
Expert's Impressions
John Scopes Reflects
Hell & High Schools
Links & Bibliography
Trial Video
Trial Jeopardy
Send Comments
Famous Trials in American History
Tennessee vs. John Scopes
The "Monkey Trial"
1925
Clarence Darrow and William Jennings Bryan during the trial
Photo Credit: CORBIS/Bettmann
2
The Scopes Trial: An Introduction
by Douglas Linder (c) 2002
The early 1920s found social patterns in chaos. Traditionalists, the older Victorians, worried that everything valuable was ending. Younger modernists no longer asked whether society would approve of their behavior, only whether their behavior met the approval of their intellect. Intellectual experimentation flourished. Americans danced to the sound of the Jazz Age, showed their contempt for alcoholic prohibition, debated abstract art and Freudian theories. In a response to the new social patterns set in motion by modernism, a wave of revivalism developed, becoming especially strong in the American South.
Who would dominate American culture--the modernists or the traditionalists? Journalists were looking for a showdown, and they found one in a Dayton, Tennessee courtroom in the summer of 1925....[CONTINUED]
Famous Trials Homepage
3
THIS SITE LAST UPDATED 4/25/05
Internet
1
by Douglas Linder

18. ONLINE BOOK

18. Janja Bec, *The Shattering of the Soul* (Los Angeles: Simon Wiesenthal Center, 1997), http://motlc.wiesenthal.com/resources/books/shatteringsoul/index.html (accessed December 2, 2007).

Bec, Janja. *The Shattering of the Soul.* Los Angeles: Simon Wiesenthal Center, 1997. http://motlc.wiesenthal.com/resources/books/shatteringsoul/index.html (accessed December 2, 2007).

19. EMAIL AND OTHER PERSONAL COMMUNICATION

Cite email messages and other personal communications (letters, text messages, postings on social networking sites such as Facebook, telephone calls, and so on) in the text or in a note. Do not cite personal communications in the bibliography.

19. Kareem Adas, e-mail message to author, February 11, 2008.

Other sources

20. PUBLISHED OR BROADCAST INTERVIEW

20. Warren Buffett, interview by Charlie Rose, *The Charlie Rose Show*, PBS, June 26, 2006.

Buffett, Warren. Interview by Charlie Rose. *The Charlie Rose Show*. PBS, June 26, 2006.

Interviews you conduct are personal communications (see model 19).

21. PODCAST

Treat a podcast like a work from a Web site, and include as much of the following information as you can find: the author (or speaker); the title of the podcast; the title of the site on which it appears; the site sponsor; and the URL.

21. Kelly O'Brien, "Developing Countries," *KUSP's Life in the Fast Lane*, Central Coast Public Radio, http://www.kusp.org/shows/fast.html.

O'Brien, Kelly. "Developing Countries." *KUSP's Life in the Fast Lane*. Central Coast Public Radio. http://www.kusp.org/shows/fast.html.

22. VIDEO OR DVD

22. Denzel Washington and Forest Whitaker, *The Great Debaters*, DVD, directed by Denzel Washington (2007; Los Angeles: MGM, 2008).

Washington, Denzel, and Forest Whitaker. *The Great Debaters*. DVD. Directed by
Denzel Washington, 2007. Los Angeles: MGM, 2008.

23. CD-ROM

23. *The Civil War*, CD-ROM (Fogware, 2000).

The Civil War. CD-ROM. Fogware, 2000.

24. PAMPHLET, REPORT, OR BROCHURE

Information about the author or publisher may not be readily available,
but give enough information to identify your source.

24. Jamie McCarthy, *Who Is David Irving?* (San Antonio, TX: Holocaust
History Project, 1998).

McCarthy, Jamie. *Who Is David Irving?* San Antonio, TX: Holocaust History Project,
1998.

25. GOVERNMENT PUBLICATION

25. U.S. House Committee on Ways and Means, *Report on Trade Mission to
Sub-Saharan Africa*, 108th Cong., 1st sess. (Washington, DC: U.S. Government
Printing Office, 2003), 28.

U.S. House Committee on Ways and Means. *Report on Trade Mission to
Sub-Saharan Africa*. 108th Cong., 1st sess. Washington, DC: U.S.
Government Printing Office, 2003.

53c An excerpt from a student research essay, *Chicago* style

On the following pages are portions of an essay by
Amanda Rinder, conforms to the *Chicago* guidelines described in this chapter. Note that this essay has been reproduced in a narrow format to allow for annotation.

Student Writer

Amanda Rinder

 bedfordstmartins.com/everydaywriter To read the entire paper, click on **Student Writing.**

Title page
not num-
bered

Title and
writer's
name cen-
tered about
halfway
down title
page

Title an-
nounces
topic clearly

Sweet Home Chicago: Preserving the Past,
Protecting the Future of the Windy City
Amanda Rinder

Course title,
instructor's
name, and
date cen-
tered at bot-
tom of
title page

Twentieth-Century U.S. History
Professor Goldberg
November 27, 2006

Annotations indicate effective choices or *Chicago*-style formatting.

Rinder 1

Only one city has the "Big Shoulders" described by Carl Sandburg: Chicago (fig. 1). So renowned are its skyscrapers and celebrated building style that an entire school of architecture is named for Chicago. Presently, however, the place that Frank Sinatra called "my kind of town" is beginning to lose sight of exactly what kind of town it is. Many of the buildings that give Chicago its distinctive character are being torn down in order to make room for new growth. Both preserving the classics and encouraging new creation are important; the combination of these elements gives Chicago architecture its unique flavor. Witold Rybczynski, a professor of urbanism, told Tracie Rozhon of the *New York Times,* "Of all the cities we can think of . . . we associate Chicago with new things, with building new. Combining that with preservation is a difficult task, a tricky thing. It's hard to find the middle ground in Chicago."[1] Yet finding a middle ground is essential if the city is to

Fig. 1. Chicago skyline, circa 1940s. (Postcard courtesy of Minnie Dangburg.)

Paper refers to each figure by number

Thesis introduced

Double-spaced text

Source cited using superscript numeral

Figure caption includes number, short title, source

Rinder 2

retain the original character that sets it apart from the rest. In order to maintain Chicago's distinctive identity and its delicate balance between the old and the new, the city government must provide a comprehensive urban plan that not only directs growth, but calls for the preservation of landmarks and historic districts as well.

Chicago is a city for the working man. Nowhere is this more evident than in its architecture. David Garrard Lowe, author of *Lost Chicago,* notes that early Chicagoans "sought reality, not fantasy, and the reality of America as seen from the heartland did not include the pavilions of princes or the castles of kings."[2] The inclination toward unadorned, sturdy buildings began in the late nineteenth century with the aptly named Chicago School, a movement led by Louis Sullivan, John Wellborn Root, and Daniel Burnham and based on Sullivan's adage, "Form follows function."[3] Burnham and Root's Reliance Building (fig. 2) epitomizes this vision: simple, yet possessing a unique angular beauty.[4] The early skyscraper, the very symbol of the Chicago style, represents the triumph of function and utility over sentiment, America over Europe, and perhaps even the frontier over the civilization of the East Coast.[5] These ideals of the original Chicago School were expanded upon by architects of the Second Chicago School. Frank Lloyd Wright's legendary organic style and the famed glass and steel constructions of Mies van der Rohe are often the first images that spring to mind when one thinks of Chicago.

Yet the architecture that is the city's defining attribute is being threatened by the increasing tendency toward development. The root of Chicago's preservation problem lies in the enormous drive toward economic expansion and the potential in Chicago for such growth. The highly competitive market for land in the city means that properties sell for the highest price if the buildings on them can be obliterated

Rinder 3

Fig. 2. The Reliance Building. (Photo
courtesy of The Art Institute of Chicago.)

to make room for newer, larger developments. Because of this
preference on the part of potential buyers, the label "landmark" has
become a stigma for property owners. "In other cities, landmark
status is sought after — in Chicago, it's avoided at all costs," notes
Alan J. Shannon of the *Chicago Tribune*.[6] Even if owners wish to keep
their property's original structure, designation as a landmark is still
undesirable as it limits the renovations that can be made to a. . . .

Signal verb
"notes"
introduces
quotation

Rinder 12

Notes

1. Tracie Rozhon, "Chicago Girds for Big Battle over Its Skyline," *New York Times,* November 12, 2000, http://www.lexisnexis.com (accessed November 7, 2006).

2. David Garrard Lowe, *Lost Chicago* (New York: Watson-Guptill Publications, 2000), 112.

3. *Microsoft Encarta Encyclopedia 2000,* s.v. "Sullivan, Louis Henri," CD-ROM (Microsoft, 2000).

4. Lowe, *Lost Chicago,* 123.

5. Daniel Bluestone, *Constructing Chicago* (New Haven: Yale University Press, 1991), 105.

6. Alan J. Shannon, "When Will It End?" *Chicago Tribune,* September 11, 1987, quoted in Karen J. Dilibert, *From Landmark to Landfill* (Chicago: Chicago Architectural Foundation, 2000), 11.

7. Steve Kerch, "Landmark Decisions," *Chicago Tribune,* March 18, 1990, sec. 16.

8. Patrick T. Reardon, "'No' Vote Makes It a Landmark Day for the Berghoff," *Chicago Tribune,* April 5, 1991, sec 1.

9. Ibid.

10. John W. Stamper, *Chicago's North Michigan Avenue* (Chicago: University of Chicago Press, 1991), 215.

11. Nancy Stuenkel, "Success Spoiling the Magnificent Mile?" *Chicago Sun-Times,* April 9, 1995, http://www.lexisnexis.com (accessed November 8, 2006).

12. Stamper, *North Michigan Avenue,* 215.

Margin annotations:

Encyclopedia entry appears in notes but not in bibliography

Second reference to source

Reference to preceding source

Note number indented; subsequent lines flush left

Rinder 14

Bibliography

Bluestone, Daniel. *Constructing Chicago*. New Haven: Yale University Press, 1991.

Bruegmann, Robert. *The Architects and the City*. Chicago: University of Chicago Press, 1997.

Dilibert, Karen J. *From Landmark to Landfill*. Chicago: Chicago Architectural Foundation, 2000.

Hein, Rich. "Preservationists Rally behind 'Mies and Moe's.'" *Chicago Sun-Times*, November 4, 1994. http://www.lexisnexis.com (accessed November 10, 2006).

Kerch, Steve. "Landmark Decisions." *Chicago Tribune*, March 18, 1990, sec. 16.

Lowe, David Garrard. *Lost Chicago*. New York: Watson-Guptill Publications, 2000.

Mendell, David, and Gary Washburn. "Daley Acts to Protect Michigan Ave. Skyline." *Chicago Tribune*, March 8, 2001.

Reardon, Patrick T. "'No' Vote Makes It a Landmark Day for the Berghoff." *Chicago Tribune*, April 5, 1991, sec. 1.

Rozhon, Tracie. "Chicago Girds for Big Battle over Its Skyline." *New York Times*, November 12, 2000. http://www.lexisnexis.com (accessed November 7, 2006).

Stamper, John W. *Chicago's North Michigan Avenue*. Chicago: University of Chicago Press, 1991.

Stuenkel, Nancy. "Success Spoiling the Magnificent Mile?" *Chicago Sun-Times*, April 9, 1995. http://www.lexisnexis.com (accessed November 8, 2006).

Bibliography starts on new page

Book

Pamphlet

Article from database

Newspaper article

Bibliography entries use hanging indent and are not numbered

54 CSE Style

Writers in the physical sciences, the life sciences, and mathematics use the documentation and format style of the Council of Science Editors (CSE). Guidelines for citing print and electronic sources can be found in *Scientific Style and Format: The CSE Manual for Authors, Editors, and Publishers*, Seventh Edition (2006).

 bedfordstmartins.com/everydaywriter To access the advice in this chapter online, click on **Documenting Sources.**

DIRECTORY TO CSE STYLE

54a CSE style for in-text citations

In CSE style, citations within an essay follow one of three formats.

- The *citation-sequence format* calls for a superscript number or a number in parentheses after any mention of a source. The sources are numbered in the order they appear. Each number refers to the same source every time it is used. The first source mentioned in the paper is numbered 1, the second source is numbered 2, and so on.

- The *citation-name format* also calls for a superscript number or a number in parentheses after any mention of a source. The numbers are added after the list of references is completed and alphabetized, so that the source numbered 1 is alphabetically first in the list of references, 2 is alphabetically second, and so on.

- The *name-year format* calls for the last name of the author and the year of publication in parentheses after any mention of a source. If the last name appears in a signal phrase, the name-year format allows for giving only the year of publication in parentheses.

Before deciding which system to use, ask your instructor's preference.

1. CITATION-SEQUENCE OR CITATION-NAME FORMAT

VonBergen[12] provides the most complete discussion of this phenomenon.

For the citation-sequence and citation-name formats, you would use the same superscript ([12]) for each subsequent citation of this work by VonBergen.

2. NAME-YEAR FORMAT

VonBergen (2003) provides the most complete discussion of this phenomenon. Hussar's two earlier studies of juvenile obesity (1995, 1999) examined only children with diabetes.

The classic examples of such investigations (Morrow 1968; Bridger et al. 1971; Franklin and Wayson 1972) still shape the assumptions of current studies.

54b   **CSE style for a list of references**

The citations in the text of an essay correspond to items on a list titled *References*, which starts on a new page at the end of the essay. Continue to number the pages consecutively, center the title *References* one inch from the top of the page, and double-space before beginning the first entry.

The order of the entries depends on which format you follow:

- *Citation-sequence format*: number and list the references in the order the references are first cited in the text.

- *Citation-name format*: list and number the references in alphabetical order.

- *Name-year format*: list the references, unnumbered, in alphabetical order.

In the following examples, you will see that the citation-sequence and citation-name formats call for listing the date after the publisher's name in references for books and after the periodical name in references for articles. The name-year format calls for listing the date immediately after the author's name in any kind of reference.

CSE style also specifies the treatment and placement of the following basic elements in the list of references:

- *Author.* List all authors last name first, and use only initials for first and middle names. Do not place a comma after the author's last name, and do not place periods after or spaces between the initials. Use a period after the last initial of the last author listed.

- *Title.* Do not italicize or underline titles and subtitles of books and titles of periodicals. Do not enclose titles of articles in quotation marks. For books and articles, capitalize only the first word of the title and any proper nouns or proper adjectives. Abbreviate and capitalize all major words in a periodical title.

As you refer to these examples, pay attention to how publication information (publishers for books, details about periodicals for articles) and other specific elements are styled and punctuated.

Books

1. ONE AUTHOR

CITATION-SEQUENCE AND CITATION-NAME

1. Buchanan M. Nexus: small worlds and the groundbreaking theory of networks. New York: Norton; 2003.

NAME-YEAR

Buchanan M. 2003. Nexus: small worlds and the groundbreaking theory of networks. New York: Norton.

2. TWO OR MORE AUTHORS

CITATION-SEQUENCE AND CITATION-NAME

2. Wojciechowski BW, Rice NM. Experimental methods in kinetic studies. 2nd ed. St. Louis (MO): Elsevier Science; 2003.

NAME-YEAR

Wojciechowski BW, Rice NM. 2003. Experimental methods in kinetic studies. 2nd ed. St. Louis (MO): Elsevier Science.

3. CORPORATE OR GROUP AUTHOR

CITATION-SEQUENCE AND CITATION-NAME

3. World Health Organization. The world health report 2002: reducing risks, promoting healthy life. Geneva (Switzerland): The Organization; 2002.

Place the organization's abbreviation at the beginning of the name-year entry, and use the abbreviation in the corresponding in-text citation. Alphabetize the entry by the first word of the full name, not by the abbreviation.

NAME-YEAR

[WHO] World Health Organization. 2002. The world health report 2002: reducing risks, promoting healthy life. Geneva (Switzerland): The Organization.

4. BOOK PREPARED BY EDITOR(S)

CITATION-SEQUENCE AND CITATION-NAME

4. Torrence ME, Issacson RE, editors. Microbial food safety in animal agriculture: current topics. Ames: Iowa State University Press; 2003.

NAME-YEAR

Torrence ME, Isaacson RE, editors. 2003. Microbial safety in animal agriculture: current topics. Ames: Iowa State University Press.

5. SECTION OF A BOOK WITH AN EDITOR

CITATION-SEQUENCE AND CITATION-NAME

5. Kawamura A. Plankton. In: Perrin MF, Wursig B, Thewissen JGM, editors. Encyclopedia of marine mammals. San Diego: Academic Press; 2002. p. 939–942.

NAME-YEAR

Kawamura A. 2002. Plankton. In: Perrin MF, Wursig B, Thewissen JGM, editors. Encyclopedia of marine mammals. San Diego: Academic Press. p. 939–942.

6. CHAPTER OF A BOOK

CITATION-SEQUENCE AND CITATION-NAME

6. Honigsbaum M. The fever trail: in search of the cure for malaria. New York: Picador; 2003. Chapter 2, The cure; p. 19–38.

NAME-YEAR

Honigsbaum M. 2003. The fever trail: in search of the cure for malaria. New York: Picador. Chapter 2, The cure; p. 19–38.

7. PAPER OR ABSTRACT IN CONFERENCE PROCEEDINGS

CITATION-SEQUENCE AND CITATION-NAME

7. Gutierrez AP. Integrating biological and environmental factors in crop system models [abstract]. In: Integrated Biological Systems Conference; 2003 Apr 14–16; San Antonio, TX. Beaumont (TX): Agroeconomics Research Group; 2003. p. 14–15.

NAME-YEAR

Gutierrez AP. 2003. Integrating biological and environmental factors in crop system models [abstract]. In: Integrated Biological Systems Conference; 2003 Apr 14–16; San Antonio, TX. Beaumont (TX): Agroeconomics Research Group. p. 14–15.

Periodicals

For the basic format for an article from a periodical, see pp. 536–37. For newspaper and magazine articles, include the section designation and column number, if any, in addition to the date and the inclusive page numbers. For rules on abbreviating journal titles, consult the CSE manual, or ask an instructor to suggest other examples.

8. ARTICLE IN A JOURNAL

CITATION-SEQUENCE AND CITATION-NAME

8. Mahmud K, Vance ML. Human growth hormone and aging. New Engl J Med. 2003;348(2):2256–2257.

NAME-YEAR

Mahmud K, Vance ML. 2003. Human growth hormone and aging. New Engl J Med. 348(2):2256–2257.

9. ARTICLE IN A WEEKLY JOURNAL

CITATION-SEQUENCE AND CITATION-NAME

9. Holden C. Future brightening for depression treatments. Science. 2003 Oct 31:810–813.

NAME-YEAR

Holden C. 2003. Future brightening for depression treatments. Science. Oct 31:810–813.

10. ARTICLE IN A MAGAZINE

CITATION-SEQUENCE AND CITATION-NAME

10. Livio M. Moving right along: the accelerating universe holds secrets to dark energy, the Big Bang, and the ultimate beauty of nature. Astronomy. 2002 Jul:34–39.

NAME-YEAR

Livio M. 2002 Jul. Moving right along: the accelerating universe holds secrets to dark energy, the Big Bang, and the ultimate beauty of nature. Astronomy. 34–39.

11. ARTICLE IN A NEWSPAPER

CITATION-SEQUENCE AND CITATION-NAME

11. Kolata G. Bone diagnosis gives new data but no answers. New York Times (National Ed.). 2003 Sep 28;Sect. 1:1 (col. 1).

NAME-YEAR

Kolata G. 2003 Sep 28. Bone diagnosis gives new data but no answers. New York Times (National Ed.). Sect. 1:1 (col. 1).

Note that date placement will vary, depending on whether you are using the citation-sequence or citation-name format or the name-year format.

1 Author. List all authors' last names first, and use only initials for first and middle names. Do not place periods after or spaces between the initials. Use a period after the last initial of the last author.

2,5 Publication date. In name-year format, put the publication date after the author name(s). In citation-sequence or citation-name format, put the publication date after the periodical title. For journals, use only the year; use the year and month (and day) for publications without volume numbers.

3 Title and subtitle of article. Capitalize only the first word of the title and any proper nouns or proper adjectives.

4 Title of periodical. Capitalize all major words and end with a period. Follow the guidelines in the CSE manual for abbreviating journal titles.

6 Publication information. For articles from scholarly journals, give the volume number, the issue number if available (in parentheses), and then a colon. Give the inclusive page numbers, and end with a period.

For an article in a scholarly journal, use one of the following formats:

Citation-sequence or citation-name format

1. Last name first initial. Title of article. Journal abbreviation. Year;Volume(Issue):Pages.

Name-year format

Last name first initial. Year. Title of article. Journal abbreviation. Volume(Issue):Pages.

Citations for the article on p. 537 would look like this:

Citation-sequence or citation-name format

NOTE
NO.   AUTHOR   ARTICLE TITLE

1. Narechania A. Hearing is believing: ivory-billed sightings leave field biologists

wanting to hear more. Am Scholar. 2005;74(3):84–97.

                        JOURNAL   DATE   PUB. INFO.
                        TITLE

Name-year format

Narechania A. 2005. Hearing is believing: ivory-billed sightings leave field biologists wanting to hear more. Am Scholar. 74(3):84–97.

For more on using CSE style to cite articles in periodicals, see pp. 534–35. (For guidelines and models for using MLA style, see pp. 444–48; for APA style, see pp. 490–93; for *Chicago* style, see p. 516)

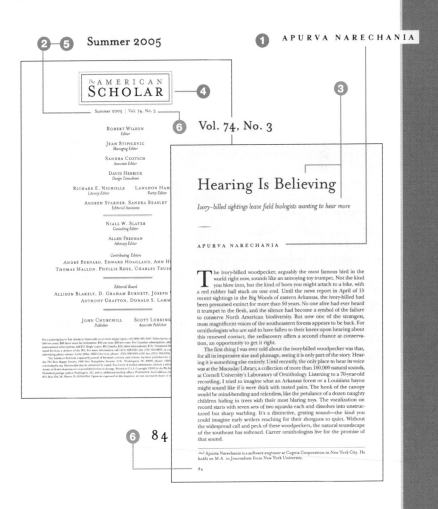

Electronic sources

These examples use the citation-sequence or citation-name system. To adapt them to the name-year system, delete the note number and place the update date immediately after the author's name.

The basic entry for most sources accessed through the Internet should include the following elements:

- *Author.* Give the author's name, if available, last name first, followed by the initial(s) and a period.

- *Title.* For book, journal, and article titles, follow the style for print materials. For all other types of electronic material, reproduce the title that appears on the screen.

- *Medium.* Indicate, in brackets, that the source is not in print format by using designations such as [Internet].

- *Place of publication.* The city usually should be followed by the two-letter abbreviation for state. No state abbreviation is necessary for well-known cities such as New York, Chicago, Boston, and London or for a publisher whose location is part of its name (for example, University of Oklahoma Press). If the city is inferred, put the city and state in brackets. It the city cannot be inferred, use the words *place unknown* in brackets.

- *Publisher.* For Web sites, pages on Web sites, and online databases, include the individual or organization that produces or sponsors the site. If no publisher can be determined, use the words *publisher unknown* in brackets. No publisher is necessary for online journals or journals accessed online.

- *Dates.* Cite three important dates if possible: the date the publication was placed on the Internet or the copyright date; the latest date of any update or revision; and the date the publication was accessed by you.

- *Page, document, volume, and issue numbers.* When citing a portion of a larger work or site, list the inclusive page numbers or document numbers of the specific item being cited. For journals or journal articles, include volume and issue numbers. If exact page numbers are not available, include in brackets the approximate length in computer screens, paragraphs, or bytes: [2 screens], [10 paragraphs], [332K bytes].

- *Address.* Include the URL or other electronic address; use the phrase *Available from:* to introduce the address. Only URLs that end with a slash are followed by a period.

12. MATERIAL FROM AN ONLINE DATABASE

For the basic format for citing an article from a database, see pp. 540–41. (Because CSE does not provide guidelines for citing an article from an online database, this model has been adapted from CSE guidelines for citing an online journal article.)

12. Shilts E. Water wanderers. Can Geographic [Internet]. 2002 [cited 2004 Jan 27]; 122(3):72–77. Expanded Academic ASAP. Farmington Hills (MI): Thomson Gale. Available from: http://web4.infotrac.galegroup.com/itw/ Document No.: A86207443.

13. ARTICLE IN AN ONLINE JOURNAL

13. Perez P, Calonge TM. Yeast protein kinase C. J Biochem [Internet]. 2002 Oct [cited 2003 Nov 3];132(4):513–517. Available from: http://edpex104.bcasj.or .jp/jb-pdf/132-4/jb132-4-513.pdf

14. ARTICLE IN AN ONLINE NEWSPAPER

14. Brody JE. Reasons, and remedies, for morning sickness. New York Times [Internet]. 2004 Apr 27 [cited 2004 Apr 30]. Available from: http://www.nytimes.com/2004/04/27/health/27BROD.html

15. ONLINE BOOK

15. Patrick TS, Allison JR, Krakow GA. Protected plants of Georgia [Internet]. Social Circle (GA): Georgia Department of Natural Resources; c1995 [cited 2003 Dec 3]. Available from: http://www.georgiawildlife.com/content/ displaycontent.asp?txtDocument=89&txtPage=9

To cite a portion of an online book, give the name of the part after the publication information: *Chapter 6, Encouraging germination.* See model 6.

16. WEB SITE

16. Geology and public policy [Internet]. Boulder (CO): Geological Society of America; c2003 [updated 2003 Apr 8; cited 2003 Apr 13]. Available from: http://www.geosociety.org/science/govpolicy.htm

17. GOVERNMENT WEB SITE

17. Health disparities: minority cancer awareness [Internet]. Atlanta (GA): Centers for Disease Control and Prevention (US); [updated 2004 Apr 27; cited 2005 May 1]. Available from: http://www.cdc.gov/cancer/minorityawareness.htm

Note that date placement will vary depending on whether you are using the citation-sequence or citation-name format or the name-year format.

1 Author. List all authors' last names first, and use only initials for first and middle names.

2, 5 Publication date. For name-year format, put the publication date after the author name(s). For citation-sequence or citation-name format, put it after the periodical title. Use the year only (for journals) or the year month day (for other periodicals).

3 Title of article. Capitalize the first word and any proper nouns/adjectives.

4 Title of periodical. Capitalize major words. Abbreviate journal titles. Follow with [*Internet*] and a period.

6 Date of access. In brackets, write *cited* and the year, month, and day. End with a semicolon.

7 Print publication information for article. Give the volume number, issue number (in parentheses), a colon, and page numbers. End with a period.

8 Name of database. End with a period.

9 Publication information for database. Include the city, the state abbreviation in parentheses, a colon, the publisher's name, and a period.

10 Web address. Write *Available from* and give the brief URL.

11 Document number. Write *Document no.* and identifying number.

(Adapted from the CSE guidelines for citing an online journal.)

For an article in a database, use the following formats:

Citation-sequence or citation-name format

1. Last name first initial(s). Title of article. Journal abbreviation [Internet]. Year [cited year month day]; Volume(Issue):Pages. Name of database. City of database publication: Database Publisher. Available from: URL Document No.: number.

Name-year format

Last name first initial(s). Year. Title of article. Journal abbreviation [Internet]. [cited year month day]; Volume(Issue):Pages. Name of database. City of database publication: Database Publisher. Available from: URL Document No.: number.

A citation for the article on p. 541 would look like this:

Citation-sequence or citation-name format

NOTE
NO. AUTHOR   ARTICLE TITLE

▼   ▼   ▼

1. Miller AL. Epidemiology, etiology, and natural treatment of seasonal affective disorder.

                PUB.   PRINT
   JOURNAL   YEAR   DATE OF ACCESS   PUB. INFO.   NAME OF DATABASE

▼   ▼   ▼   ▼   ▼

Altern Med Rev [Internet]. 2005 [cited 2006 Aug 9]; 10(1):5–13. Expanded Academic

          DATABASE PUBL. INFO.   URL

ASAP. Farmington Hills (MI): Thomson Gale. Available from: http://find.galegroup.com

   DOCUMENT NUMBER

Document No.: A131086129.

Name-year format

Miller AL. 2005. Epidemiology, etiology, and natural treatment of seasonal affective disorder. Altern Med Rev [Internet]. [cited 2006 Aug 9]; 10(1):5–13. Expanded Academic ASAP. Farmington Hills (MI): Thomson Gale. Available from: http://find.galegroup.com Document No.: A131086129.

For more on using CSE style to cite articles in a database, see pp. 538–39. (For guidelines and models for using MLA style, see pp. 449–51; for APA style, see pp. 494–97; for *Chicago* style, see p. 516.)

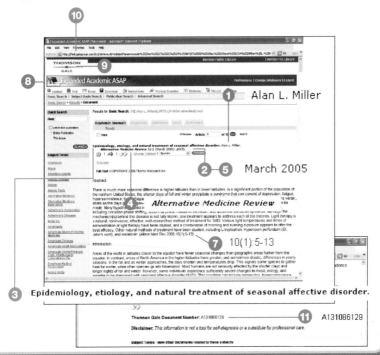

54c   An excerpt from a student research proposal, CSE style

The following excerpt from a research proposal by Tara Gupta conforms to the citation-sequence format in the CSE guidelines described in this chapter. Note that these pages have been reproduced in a narrow format to allow for annotation.

Student Writer

Tara Gupta

 bedfordstmartins.com/everydaywriter   To read the entire paper, click on **Student Writing**.

Field Measurements of
Photosynthesis and Transpiration
Rates in Dwarf Snapdragon
(*Chaenorrhinum minus* Lange):
An Investigation of Water Stress
Adaptations

Specific and informative title, name, and other relevant information centered on title page

Tara Gupta

Proposal for a
Summer Research Fellowship
Colgate University
February 25, 2004

Annotations indicate effective choices or CSE-style formatting.

Introduction

Dwarf snapdragon (*Chaenorrhinum minus*) is a weedy pioneer plant found growing in central New York during spring and summer. Interestingly, the distribution of this species has been limited almost exclusively to the cinder ballast of railroad tracks[1] and to sterile strips of land along highways[2]. In these harsh environments, characterized by intense sunlight and poor soil water retention, one would expect *C. minus* to exhibit anatomical features similar to those of xeromorphic plants (species adapted to arid habitats).

However, this is not the case. T. Gupta and R. Arnold (unpublished) have found that the leaves and stems of *C. minus* are not covered by a thick, waxy cuticle but rather with a thin cuticle that is less effective in inhibiting water loss through diffusion. The root system is not long and thick, capable of reaching deeper, moister soils; instead, it is thin and diffuse, permeating only the topmost (and driest) soil horizon. Moreover, in contrast to many xeromorphic plants, the stomata (pores regulating gas exchange) are not found in sunken crypts or cavities in the epidermis that retard water loss from transpiration.

Despite a lack of these morphological adaptations to water stress, *C. minus* continues to grow and reproduce when morning dew has been its only source of water for up to 5 weeks (2002 letter from R. Arnold to me). Such growth involves fixation of carbon by photosynthesis and requires that the stomata be open to admit sufficient carbon dioxide. Given the dry, sunny environment, the time required for adequate carbon fixation must also mean a significant loss of water through transpiration as open stomata exchange carbon dioxide with water. How does *C. minus* balance the need for carbon with the need to conserve water?

Margin annotations:

Shortened title appears next to page number

Headings throughout help organize the proposal

Introduction states scientific issue, gives background information

Documentation follows CSE citation-sequence format

Personal communication cited in parentheses within text but not included in references

Water Stress Adaptations 5

References

1. Wildrlechner MP. Historical and phenological observations of the spread of *Chaenorrhinum minus* across North America. Can J Bot. 1983;61(1):179–187.

2. Dwarf Snapdragon [Internet]. Olympia (WA): Washington State Noxious Weed Control Board; 2001 [updated 2001 Jul 7; cited 2003 Jan 25]. Available from: http://www.wa.gov/agr/weedboard/weed_info/dwarfsnapdragon.html

3. Boyer JS. Plant productivity and environment. Science. 1982 Nov 6:443–448.

4. Manhas JG, Sukumaran NP. Diurnal changes in net photosynthetic rate in potato in two environments. Potato Res. 1988;31:375–378.

5. Doley DG, Unwin GL, Yates DJ. Spatial and temporal distribution of photosynthesis and transpiration by single leaves in a rainforest tree, *Argyrodendron peralatum*. Aust J Plant Physiol. 1988;15(3):317–326.

6. Kallarackal J, Milburn JA, Baker DA. Water relations of the banana. III. Effects of controlled water stress on water potential, transpiration, photosynthesis and leaf growth. Aust J Plant Physiol. 1990;17(1):79–90.

7. Idso SB, Allen SG, Kimball BA, Choudhury BJ. Problems with porometry: measuring net photosynthesis by leaf chamber techniques. Agron. 1989;81(4):475–479.

Article for government Web site

Article in weekly journal

Article in journal

Includes all published works cited; numbers correspond to order in which sources are first mentioned

For Multilingual Writers

We're all imported.

— DEREK WALCOTT

For Multilingual Writers

Writing in U.S. Academic Genres **55**

Xiaoming Li, now a college English teacher, says that before she came to the United States as a graduate student, she had been a "good writer" in China — in both English and Chinese. Once in the United States, however, she struggled to grasp what her teachers expected of her college writing. While she could easily use grammar books and dictionaries, her instructors' unstated expectations seemed to call for her to write in a way that was new to her.

Of course, writing for college presents many challenges; such writing differs in many ways from high school writing as well as from personal writing like text messaging or postings to social networking sites. If you grew up speaking and writing in other languages, however, the transition to producing effective college writing can be even more complicated. Not only will you have to learn new information and new ways of thinking and arguing, but you also have to do it in a language that may not come naturally to you — especially in unfamiliar rhetorical situations.

55a U.S. academic writing

The expectations for college writing are often taken for granted by instructors. To complicate the matter further, there is no single "correct" style of communication in any country, including the United States. Effective oral styles differ from effective written styles, and what is considered good writing in one field of study is not necessarily appropriate in another. Even the variety of English often referred to as "standard" covers a wide range of styles (see Chapter 21). In spite of this wide variation, several features are often associated with U.S. academic English:

- conventional grammar, spelling, punctuation, and mechanics
- organization that links ideas explicitly

- readable type, conventional margins, and double spacing
- explicitly stated claims supported by evidence (Chapter 13)
- careful documentation of all sources (Chapters 48–54)
- consistent use of an appropriate level of formality (22a)
- conventional use of idioms (Chapter 59)
- conventional academic formats, such as literature reviews, research essays, lab reports, and research proposals

Most students can benefit from some instruction in how new contexts require the use of different sets of conventions, strategies, and resources. This is especially the case for multilingual writers.

55b   Genre conventions

Those who read your college writing — your teachers and peers — will hold some expectations about the features of the texts you produce. Many writers learn these expectations through practice. But if you have had limited exposure to various types, or *genres*, of academic writing in English, it may be helpful to think about these conventions explicitly.

Genres of texts

At some point in your writing process, you should consider the genre or kind of text the instructor expects you to write. In many cases, the assignment will not be explicit about what the text should look like or accomplish. If you are not sure what kind of text you are supposed to write, ask your instructor for clarification. (Examples may also be available at your school's writing center.) You may want to find multiple examples so that you can develop a sense of how different writers approach the same writing task.

55c   Adapting structures and phrases from a genre

If English is not your strongest language, you may find it useful to borrow and adapt transitional devices and pieces of sentence structure from other people's writing in the genre you are working in. You should not copy the whole structure, however, or your borrowed sentences may seem plagiarized (Chapter 17). Find sample sentence structures from similar genres but on different topics so that you borrow a typical structure (which does not belong to anyone) rather than the idea or the particular phrasing. Write your own sentences first, and look at other people's sentences only to guide your revision.

Features of Genres

Study the features of the kind of text you need to write.

- What does the genre look like? How is the text laid out on the page? How are any visual features incorporated into the main text?
- How long is the whole text, each section, and each paragraph?
- How does the text introduce the topic? Is the main point stated explicitly or implicitly?
- What are the major divisions of the text? Are they marked with transitions or headings?
- How does each section contribute to the main point? How is the main point of each section supported?
- How are the key terms defined? What kind of background information is provided?
- What is the level of formality? Does the text use technical terms or contractions (such as *I'm* and *isn't* instead of *I am* and *is not*)? Does the text take a personal stance (*I, we*), address the audience directly (*you*), or talk about the subject without explicitly referring to the writer or the reader?
- How many sources are used in the text? How are they introduced?

Original Abstract from a Social Science Paper	Effective Borrowing of Structures from a Genre
Using the interpersonal communications research of J. K. Brilhart and G. J. Galanes, and W. Wilmot and J. Hocker, along with T. Hartman's personality assessment, I observed and analyzed the leadership roles and group dynamics of my project collaborators in a communications course. Based on results of the Hartman personality assessment, I predicted that a single leader would emerge. However, complementary individual strengths and gender differences encouraged a distributed leadership style, in which the group experienced little confrontation and conflict. Conflict, because it was handled positively, was crucial to the group's progress.	Drawing on the research of Deborah Tannen on men's and women's conversational styles, I analyzed the conversational styles of six first-year students at DePaul University. Based on Tannen's research, I expected that the three men I observed would use features typical of male conversational style and the three women would use features typical of female conversational style. In general, these predictions were accurate; however, some exceptions were also apparent.

The example on p. 551 illustrates effective borrowing. The student writer borrows phrases that are commonly used in academic writing in the social sciences to perform particular functions. Notice how the student also modifies these phrases to suit the needs of the writing.

55d Checking usage with search engines

To multilingual writers, search engines such as Google can provide a useful way of checking sentence structure and word usage. For example, if you are not sure whether you should use an infinitive form (*to* + verb) or a gerund (*-ing*) for the verb *confirm* after the main verb *expect* (56d), you can search for both *"expected confirming"* and *"expected to confirm"* in quotation marks to see which search term yields more results. A Google search for *"expected confirming"* yields many entries with a comma between the two words, indicating that one phrase ends with *expected* and another begins with *confirming*.

On the other hand, a search for *"expected to confirm"* yields many more hits than a search for *"expected confirming."* These results indicate that *expected to confirm* is the more commonly used expression. Be sure to click through a few pages of the search engine's results to make sure that most results come from ordinary sentences rather than from headlines or phrases that may be constructed differently from standard English.

56 Clauses and Sentences

Short phrases, or sound bites, are everywhere — from the Dairy Council's "Got Milk?" to Volkswagen's "Drivers Wanted." These short, simple slogans may be memorable, but they don't say very much. In writing, you usually need more complex sentences to convey meaning. The requirements for forming sentences can differ across languages, and English has its own sets of rules.

56a Explicit subjects and objects

English sentences consist of a subject and a predicate. While many languages can omit a sentence subject, English very rarely allows this. Though you might write *Responsible for analyzing data* on a résumé, in most varieties of spoken and written English, you must explicitly state the subject. In fact, with only a few exceptions, all clauses in English must have an explicit subject.

▶ They took the Acela Express to Boston because ~~was~~ fast.
                                                       it

English even requires a kind of "dummy" subject to fill the subject position in certain kinds of sentences.

▶ *It* is raining.
▶ *There* is a strong wind.

Transitive verbs (30k) typically require that objects — and sometimes other information — also be explicitly stated. For example, it is not enough to tell someone *Give!* even if it is clear what is to be given to whom. You must say *Give it to me* or *Give her the passport* or some other such sentence. Similarly, saying *Put!* or *Put it!* is insufficient when you mean *Put it on the table* or *Put it down!*

Many dictionaries identify whether a verb is transitive (requiring an object) or intransitive (not followed by an object).

56b Word order

In general, subjects, verbs, and objects (30k and p. 298) must be placed in specific positions within a sentence.

    SUBJECT VERB OBJECT   ADVERB
▶ Mario left Venice reluctantly.

The only word in this sentence that can be moved to different locations is the adverb *reluctantly* (*Mario reluctantly left Venice* or *Reluctantly, Mario left Venice*). The three key elements of subject, verb, and object are moved out of their normal order only to create special effects.

56c Noun clauses

Examine the following sentence:

> In my last year in high school, my adviser urged that I apply to several colleges.

This complex sentence is built out of two sentences, one of them (B) embedded in the other (A):

    A. In my last year in high school, my adviser urged B.
    B. I (should) apply to several colleges.

When these are combined as in the original sentence, sentence B becomes a noun clause introduced by *that* and becomes the object of the verb *urged* in sentence A. Now look at the following sentence:

> It made a big difference that she wrote a strong letter of recommendation.

Here the two component sentences are C and D:

C. D made a big difference.
D. She wrote a strong letter of recommendation.

In this case, the noun clause formed from sentence D functions as the subject of sentence C so that the combination reads as follows:

> That she wrote a strong letter of recommendation made a big difference.

This sentence is gramatically acceptable but not typical. When a lengthy noun clause is the subject, it is usually moved to the end of the sentence. The result is *It made a big difference that she wrote a strong letter of recommendation*, which inserts the dummy subject *It* to fill the slot of the subject.

56d Infinitives (*to* forms) and gerunds (*-ing* forms)

Infinitives are verbs in the *to* + verb form (*to write, to read, to go*); gerunds are verbs that end in *-ing* and act as subjects or objects within a sentence. In general, infinitives tend to state intentions, desires, or expectations, and gerunds tend to state facts. Knowing whether to use a *to* form or an *-ing* form in a particular sentence can be a challenge. Though no simple explanation will make it an easy task, some hints might be helpful (see 55d for another strategy).

▶ My adviser urged me *to apply* to several colleges.
▶ *Applying* took a great deal of time.

In the first sentence, *to apply* conveys the message that the act of applying was something desired, not an accomplished fact. In the second sentence, *applying* calls attention to the fact that the application process was actually carried out.

Using infinitives (to forms) to state intentions

▶ Kumar *expected to get* a good job after graduation.
▶ Last year, Fatima *decided to become* a math major.
▶ The strikers have *agreed to go* back to work.

At the moment indicated by the verbs *expect, decide,* and *agree* in these sentences, those actions or events were merely intentions. These three verbs, as well as many others that specify intentions (or negative intentions, such as *refuse*), must always be followed by an infinitive, never by a gerund. Many learner dictionaries provide information about verbs that must be followed by an infinitive instead of a gerund.

Using gerunds (-ing *forms) to state facts*

▶ Jerzy enjoys *going* to the theater.

▶ We resumed *working* after our coffee break.

▶ Kim appreciated *getting* candy from Sean.

In all of these cases, the gerund indicates that the action or event that it expresses has actually occurred. Verbs like *enjoy, resume,* and *appreciate* can be followed only by gerunds, not by infinitives. In fact, even when these verbs do not convey clear facts, the verb form that follows must still be a gerund. Again, many dictionaries provide this information.

▶ Kim would appreciate *getting* candy from Sean, but he hardly knows her.

Understanding other rules and guidelines

A few verbs can be followed by either an infinitive or a gerund. With some, such as *begin* and *continue,* the choice makes little difference in meaning. With others, however, the difference in meaning is striking.

▶ Carlos was working as a medical technician, but he *stopped to study* English.

The infinitive *to study* indicates that Carlos intended to study English when he left his job. We are not told whether he actually did study English.

▶ Carlos *stopped studying* English when he left the United States.

The gerund *studying* indicates that Carlos actually did study English but then stopped doing so when he left.

The distinction between fact and intention is not a rule but only a tendency, and it can be outweighed by other rules. For example, use a gerund — never an infinitive — right after a preposition.

eating.
▶ This fruit is safe for ~~to eat.~~
⌃

▶ This fruit is safe ~~for~~ to eat.

us
▶ This fruit is safe for to eat.
⌃

For a full list of verbs that can be followed by an infinitive and verbs that can be followed by a gerund, see *Grammar Troublespots*, Third Edition, by Ann Raimes (Cambridge UP, 2004), or *Cambridge International Dictionary of English* (Cambridge UP, 1999).

56e Adjective clauses

An adjective clause provides more information about a preceding noun.

▶ **The company** *Yossi's uncle invested in* **went bankrupt.**

The subject is a noun phrase in which the noun *company* is modified by the article *the* and the adjective clause *Yossi's uncle invested in*. The sentence as a whole says that a certain company went bankrupt, and the adjective clause identifies the company more specifically by saying that Yossi's uncle had invested in it.

One way of seeing how the adjective clause fits into the sentence is to rewrite it like this: *The company (Yossi's uncle had invested in it) went bankrupt.* This is not a normal English sentence, but it helps demonstrate a process that leads to the sentence we started with. Note the following steps:

1. Change the personal pronoun *it* to the relative pronoun *which*: *The company (Yossi's uncle had invested in which) went bankrupt.*
2. Move either the whole prepositional phrase *in which* to the beginning of the adjective clause, or move just the relative pronoun: *The company in which Yossi's uncle had invested went bankrupt* or *The company which Yossi's uncle had invested in went bankrupt.* While both of these are correct English sentences, the first version is somewhat more formal than the second.
3. If no preposition precedes the relative pronoun, substitute *that* for *which*, or omit the relative pronoun entirely: *The company that Yossi's uncle had invested in went bankrupt* or *The company Yossi's uncle had invested in went bankrupt.* Both of these are correct English sentences. While they are less formal than the forms in step 2, they are still acceptable in much formal writing.

56f Conditional sentences

English distinguishes among many different types of conditional sentences — that is, sentences that focus on questions of truth and that are introduced by *if* or its equivalent. The following examples illustrate a range of different conditional sentences. Each of these sentences makes different assumptions about the likelihood that what is stated in the *if* clause is true.

▶ **If you *practice* (or *have practiced*) writing frequently, you *know* (or *have learned*) what your chief problems are.**

This sentence assumes that what is stated in the *if* clause may be true; as the alternatives in parentheses indicate, any tense that is appropriate in a simple sentence may be used in both the *if* clause and the main clause.

▶ **If you *practice* writing for the rest of this term, you *will* (or *may*) *understand* the process better.**

This sentence makes a prediction about the future and again assumes that what is stated may very well turn out to be true. Only the main clause uses the future tense (*will understand*) or some other modal (58a) that can indicate future time (*may understand*). The *if* clause must use the present tense.

▶ **If you *practiced* (or *were to practice*) writing every single day, it *would* eventually *seem* much easier to you.**

This sentence casts doubt on the likelihood that what is stated will happen. In the *if* clause, the verb is either past tense — actually, past subjunctive (31h) — or *were to* + the base form, even though it refers to future time. The main clause contains *would* + the base form of the main verb.

▶ **If you *practiced* writing on Mars, you *would find* no one to read your work.**

This sentence imagines a situation that is impossible now. As with the preceding sentence, the past subjunctive is used in the *if* clause, although past time is not being referred to, and *would* + the base form is used in the main clause.

▶ **If you *had practiced* writing in ancient Egypt, you *would have used* hieroglyphics.**

This sentence shifts the impossibility back to the past; obviously, you are not going to find yourself in ancient Egypt. But a past impossibility demands a form that is "more past": the past perfect in the *if* clause and *would* + the perfect form of the main verb in the main clause.

EXERCISE 56.1

Revise the following sentences as necessary. Not all sentences contain an error.

1. The scholar who deciphered finally hieroglyphics was Jean François Champollion.
2. Champollion enjoyed to study the languages of the Middle East.
3. By comparing the Greek and Egyptian inscriptions on the Rosetta Stone, he made progress in understanding hieroglyphics.
4. Was of great importance that he knew Coptic, a later form of the Egyptian language.

5. In 1822 Champollion wrote a paper which he presented his solution to the puzzle of hieroglyphics in it.

6. If the Rosetta Stone was not discovered, it would have been much more difficult to decipher hieroglyphics.

> **bedfordstmartins.com/everydaywriter** For exercises on clauses and sentences, go to **Exercise Central** and click on **For Multilingual Writers**.

57 Nouns and Noun Phrases

Although all languages have nouns, English nouns differ from those in some other languages in various ways, such as their division into count and noncount nouns and the use of plural forms, articles, and other modifiers.

57a Count and noncount nouns

Look at the following sentences:

▶ *Research* shows that this chemical can be dangerous.

▶ *Studies* show that this chemical can be dangerous.

Studies is a count noun, and *research* is a noncount noun. Count nouns (also called countable nouns) refer to separate individuals or things that you can count: *a study, a doctor, a book, a tree; studies, doctors,* three *books,* ten *trees.* Noncount nouns (also called mass nouns or uncountable nouns) refer to masses or collections without distinctly separate parts: *research, milk, ice, blood, grass.* You cannot count noncount nouns unless you use a quantifier: *one blade of grass, two glasses of milk, three pints of blood.*

Count and noncount nouns also differ in their use of plural forms. Count nouns generally have singular and plural forms: *study, studies.* Noncount nouns generally have only a singular form: *research.*

COUNT	NONCOUNT
facts	information
suggestions	advice
people (plural of *person*)	humanity
tables, chairs, beds	furniture
letters	mail
pebbles	gravel
beans	rice

Some nouns can be either count or noncount, depending on the meaning.

COUNT   Before there were video games, children played with *marbles*.

NONCOUNT   The floor of the palace was made of *marble*.

When you learn a noun in English, it is useful to know whether it is count, noncount, or both. Many dictionaries provide this information.

57b   Plural forms

Look at these sentences from a traffic report:

▶ **All four *bridges* into the *city* are jammed with *cars* right now. The *traffic* is terrible.**

The first sentence has three count nouns: *bridges*, *city*, and *cars*. *Bridges* is plural because there are four bridges. *City* is singular because the sentence is referring to only one city. *Cars* is plural because multiple cars crowd the bridges. The second sentence has one noncount noun, *traffic*. Although this noun means "vehicles moving along a route," it is singular.

Since noncount nouns generally have no plural forms, they can be counted or quantified only with a preceding phrase: *one quart of milk*, *three pounds of rice*, *several pieces of information*. In these cases, the noncount nouns remain singular. Count nouns, however, require you to use explicit plural forms when you refer to more than one of an item.

57c   Proper nouns

In addition to count and noncount nouns, English has proper nouns. These nouns include names of people, places, objects, and institutions — for example, *California*, *Yolanda*, *IBM*, and *First National Bank*. Proper nouns are always capitalized and generally cannot vary in number, so they are either singular (*John*, *the New York Times*) or plural (*the Netherlands*, *the Rocky Mountains*).

57d   Determiners

Determiners are words that identify or quantify a noun, such as *this study*, *all people*, *his suggestions*.

COMMON DETERMINERS

- the articles *a/an*, *the*
- *this, these, that, those*

- *my, our, your, his, her, its, their*
- possessive nouns and noun phrases (*Sheila's* paper, *my friend's* book)
- *whose, which, what*
- *all, both, each, every, some, any, either, no, neither, many, much, (a) few, (a) little, several, enough*
- the numerals *one, two,* etc.

Some determiners, such as *a, an, this, that, one,* and *each,* can only be used with singular nouns; others, such as *these, those, all, both, many, several,* and *two,* can only be used with plural nouns. Still other determiners — *my, the,* and *which,* for example — can be used with singular or plural nouns. See the chart on p. 561 for additional examples.

Determiners with singular count nouns

Every singular count noun must be preceded by a determiner. Place any adjectives between the determiner and the noun.

> *my*
> ▶ **sister**
>   ∧

> *the*
> ▶ **growing population**
>   ∧

> *that*
> ▶ **old neighborhood**
>   ∧

Determiners with plural count nouns or with noncount nouns

Noncount and plural count nouns sometimes have determiners and sometimes do not. For example, *This research is important* and *Research is important* are both acceptable but have different meanings.

Remembering which determiners go with which types of noun

The chart on p. 561 describes which determiners can be used with which types of nouns.

57e Articles

Articles (*a, an,* and *the*) are a type of determiner. In English, choosing which article to use — or whether to use an article at all — can be challenging. Although there are exceptions, the following general guidelines can help.

These determiners ...	... can precede these noun types	Examples
a, an, every, each	singular count nouns some proper nouns	*a* book, *an* American *each* word *every* Buddhist
this, that	singular count nouns noncount nouns	*this* book *that* milk
(*a*) *little, much*	noncount nouns	*a little* milk *much* affection
some, enough	noncount nouns plural count nouns	*some* milk, *enough* trouble *some* books *enough* problems
the	singular count nouns plural count nouns noncount nouns	*the* doctor *the* doctors *the* information
these, those, (*a*) *few, many, both, several*	plural count nouns	*these* books, *those* plans *a few* ideas *many* students *both* hands, *several* trees

Using a *or* an

Use *a* and *an*, indefinite articles, with singular count nouns. Use *a* before a consonant sound (*a car*) and *an* before a vowel sound (*an uncle*). Consider sound rather than spelling: *a house, an hour.* Do not use indefinite articles with plural count nouns or with noncount nouns.

A or *an* tells readers they do not have enough information to identify specifically what the noun refers to (in other words, it's an unspecified, or indefinite, noun). The writer may or may not have a particular thing in mind but in either case will use *a* or *an* if the reader lacks the information necessary for identification. Compare these sentences:

▶ I need *a* new coat for the winter.

▶ I saw *a coat* that I liked at Dayton's, but it wasn't heavy enough.

The coat in the first sentence is hypothetical rather than actual. Since it is indefinite to the writer and the reader, it is used with *a*, not *the*. The second sentence refers to an actual coat, but since the writer cannot expect the reader to know which one, it is used with *a* rather than *the*.

If you want to speak of an indefinite quantity rather than just one indefinite thing, use *some* or *any* with a noncount noun or a plural count noun. Note that *any* is used in negative sentences.

▶ This stew needs *some* more *salt*.

▶ I saw *some plates* that I liked at Gump's.

▶ This stew doesn't need *any* more salt.

▶ I didn't see *any* plates that I liked at Gump's.

Using the

The definite article *the* is used with both count and noncount nouns whose identity is already known or is about to be made known to readers. The necessary information for identification can come from the noun phrase itself, from elsewhere in the text, from context, from general knowledge, or from a superlative.

the
▶ Let's meet at fountain in front of Dwinelle Hall.
        ^

The phrase *in front of Dwinelle Hall* identifies the specific fountain. We know from the use of *the* that there is only one fountain in front of Dwinelle Hall.

▶ Last Saturday, a fire that started in a restaurant spread to a

The store
nearby clothing store. ~~Store~~ was saved, although it suffered
                            ^

water damage.

The word *store* is preceded by *the*, which directs our attention to the information in the previous sentence, where the store is first identified.

the
▶ She asked him to shut door when he left her office.
                      ^

She expects him to understand that she is referring to the door in her office.

The Pope
▶ ~~Pope~~ is expected to visit Africa in October.
  ^

There is only one living pope, and *the* before *pope* signals that this sentence refers to him. Similar examples include *the president* (*of the United States*), *the earth*, and *the moon*.

the
▶ Bill is now best singer in the choir.
              ^

The superlative *best* identifies the noun *singer*.

Using the zero article

If a noun appears without *the*, *a* or *an*, or any other determiner (even if it is preceded by other adjectives), it is said to have a zero article. The zero article can be used with plural count nouns (*plans*, *assignments*), noncount nouns (*homework*, *information*), and proper nouns (*Carmen*, *New York*). With plural count nouns and noncount nouns, the zero article is used to make generalizations.

▶ **In this world nothing is certain but death and taxes.**
— BENJAMIN FRANKLIN

> The zero article indicates that Franklin refers not to a particular death or specific taxes but to death and taxes in general.

Here English differs from many other languages that would use the definite article to make generalizations. In English, a sentence like *The snakes are dangerous* can refer only to particular, identifiable snakes, not to snakes in general.

It is sometimes possible to make general statements with *the* or *a/an* and singular count nouns.

▶ *First-year college students* **are confronted with many new experiences.**

▶ *A first-year student* **is confronted with many new experiences.**

▶ *The first-year student* **is confronted with many new experiences.**

These sentences all make the same general statement, but the emphasis of each sentence is different. The first sentence refers to first-year college students as a group, the second focuses on a hypothetical student taken at random, and the third sentence, which is characteristic of formal written style, projects the image of a typical student as representative of the whole class.

57f Modifiers

Modifiers are words that give more information about a noun; that is, they *modify* the meaning of the noun in some way. Some modifiers precede the noun, and others follow it, as indicated in the chart on p. 564.

If there are two or more adjectives, their order is variable, but English has strong preferences, described below.

- Subjective adjectives (those that show the writer's opinion) go before objective adjectives (those that merely describe): *these beautiful old-fashioned kitchen tiles.*
- Adjectives of size generally come early: *these beautiful large old-fashioned kitchen tiles.*
- Adjectives of color generally come late: *these beautiful large old-fashioned blue kitchen tiles.*

Modifier Type	Arrangement	Example
determiners	at the beginning of the noun phrase	*these old-fashioned tiles*
all or *both*	before any other determiners	*all these tiles*
numbers	after any other determiners	*these six tiles*
noun modifiers	directly before the noun	*these kitchen tiles*
adjectives	between determiners and noun modifiers	*these old-fashioned kitchen tiles*
phrases or clauses	after the noun	*the tiles on the wall* *the tiles that we bought*

- Adjectives derived from proper nouns or from nouns that refer to materials generally come after color terms and right before noun modifiers: *these beautiful large old-fashioned blue Portuguese ceramic kitchen tiles.*
- All other objective adjectives go in the middle, and adjectives for which no order is preferred are separated by commas: *these beautiful large decorative, heat-resistant, old-fashioned blue Portuguese ceramic kitchen tiles.*

Of course, the very long noun phrases presented above would be out of place in most kinds of writing. Academic and professional writing tend to avoid long strings of adjectives.

EXERCISE 57.1

Each of the following sentences contains an error. Rewrite each sentence correctly.

1. Before a middle of the nineteenth century, surgery was usually a terrifying, painful ordeal.

2. Because anesthesia did not exist yet, only painkiller available for surgical patients was whiskey.

3. The pain of surgical procedures could be so severe that much people were willing to die rather than have surgery.

4. In 1846, one of the hospital in Boston gave ether to a patient before he had surgery.

5. The patient, who had a large on his neck tumor, slept peacefully as doctors removed it.

EXERCISE 57.2

Insert articles as necessary in the following passage from *The Silent Language*, by Edward T. Hall. Some blanks may not need an article.

Hollywood is famous for hiring _____ various experts to teach _____ people technically what most of us learn informally. _____ case in point is _____ story about _____ children of one movie couple who noticed _____ new child in _____ neighborhood climbing _____ tree. _____ children immediately wanted to be given _____ name of his instructor in _____ tree climbing.

 bedfordstmartins.com/everydaywriter For exercises on nouns and noun phrases, go to **Exercise Central** and click on **For Multilingual Writers**.

Verbs and Verb Phrases **58**

Verbs can be called the heartbeat of every language, but in English the metaphor is especially meaningful. With a few stylistic exceptions, all written English sentences must include a verb. Some of the distinctive features of English verbs include modals, perfect tenses, and progressive forms.

58a Forming verb phrases

Verb phrases can be built up out of a main verb and one or more auxiliaries (31b).

▶ **Immigration figures *rise* every year.**
▶ **Immigration figures *are rising* every year.**
▶ **Immigration figures *have risen* every year.**
▶ **Immigration figures *have been rising* every year.**

Verb phrases have strict rules of order. If you try to rearrange the words in any of these sentences, you will find that most alternatives are impossible. You cannot say *Immigration figures rising are every year* or *Immigration figures been have rising every year*. The only permissible change to word order is to form a question, moving the first auxiliary to the beginning of the sentence: *Have immigration figures been rising every year?*

Putting auxiliary verbs in order

In the sentence *Immigration figures <u>may have been rising</u>*, the main verb *rising* follows three auxiliaries: *may, <u>have</u>,* and *been*. Together these auxiliaries and main verb make up a verb phrase.

- *May* is a modal (58b) that indicates possibility; it is followed by the base form of a verb.
- *Have* is an auxiliary verb (31b) that in this case indicates the perfect tense (31e); it must be followed by a past participle (*been*).
- Any form of *be*, when it is followed by a present participle ending in *-ing* (such as *rising*), indicates the progressive tense (31e).
- *Be* followed by a past participle, as in *New immigration policies have <u>been passed</u> in recent years*, indicates the passive voice (31g).

As shown in the chart on p. 567, when two or more auxiliaries appear in a verb phrase, they must follow a particular order based on the type of auxiliary: (1) modal, (2) a form of *have* used to indicate a perfect tense, (3) a form of *be* used to indicate a progressive tense, and (4) a form of *be* used to indicate the passive voice. (Very few sentences include all four kinds of auxiliaries.)

Only one modal is permitted in a verb phrase.

> *be able to*
▶ She will ~~can~~ speak Czech much better soon.
>   ^

Forming auxiliary verbs

Whenever you use an auxiliary, check the form of the word that follows. The guidelines that follow describe the appropriate forms.

MODAL + BASE FORM

Use the base form of a verb after *can, could, will, would, shall, should, may, might,* and *must.*

▶ Alice *can read* Latin.

▶ Sanjay *should have* studied for the test.

▶ They *must be* going to a fine school.

In many other languages, modals such as *can* and *must* are followed by an infinitive (*to* + base form). In English, only the base form follows a modal.

▶ Alice can to read Latin.

Notice that a modal auxiliary can express tense (for example, *can* or *could*), but it never changes form to agree with the subject.

	Modal	Perfect Have	Progressive Be	Passive Be	Main Verb	
Sonia	—	has	—	been	invited	to visit a family in Prague.
She	should	—	—	be	finished	with school soon.
The invitation	must	have	—	been	sent	in the spring.
She	—	has	been	—	studying	Czech.
She	may	—	be	—	feeling	nervous.
She	might	have	been	—	expecting	to travel elsewhere.
The trip	will	have	been	being	planned	for a month by the time she leaves.

PERFECT *HAVE* + PAST PARTICIPLE

To form the perfect tenses, use *have, has,* or *had* with a past participle.

▶ **Everyone *has gone* home.**

▶ **They *have been* working all day.**

PROGRESSIVE *BE* + PRESENT PARTICIPLE

A progressive form of a verb is signaled by two elements, a form of the auxiliary *be* (*am, is, are, was, were, be,* or *been*) and the *-ing* form of the next word: *The children are studying.*

        are
▶ **The children studying in school.**
        ^

           studying
▶ **The children are ~~study~~ in school.**
           ^

Some verbs are rarely used in progressive forms. These verbs express unchanging conditions or mental states rather than deliberate actions: *believe, belong, hate, know, like, love, need, own, resemble, understand.*

PASSIVE *BE* + PAST PARTICIPLE

Use *am, is, are, was, were, being, be,* or *been* with a past participle to form the passive voice.

▶ **Tagalog *is spoken* in the Philippines.**

Notice that with the progressive *be* the following word (the present participle) ends in *-ing*, but with the passive *be* the following word (the past participle) never ends in *-ing*.

▶ Takeo *is studying* music.

▶ Natasha *was taught* by a famous violinist.

If the first auxiliary in a verb phrase is *be* or *have*, it must show either present or past tense, and it must agree with the subject: *Meredith has played in an orchestra* or *Meredith had played in an orchestra before she joined the band.*

58b Modals

The nine basic modal auxiliaries are *can, could, will, would, shall, should, may, might,* and *must.* There are a few others as well, in particular *ought to,* which is close in meaning to *should.* Occasionally *need* can be a modal rather than a main verb.

The nine basic modals fall into the pairs *can/could, will/would, shall/should, may/might,* and the loner *must.* In earlier English, the second member of each pair was the past tense of the first. The second form still functions occasionally as a past tense, especially in the case of *could.*

▶ Ingrid *can* ski.

▶ Ingrid *could* ski when she was five.

But, for the most part, in present-day English, all nine modals typically refer to present or future time. When you want to use a modal to refer to the past, you follow the modal with a perfect auxiliary.

▶ If you have a fever, you *should see* a doctor.

▶ If you had a fever, you *should have seen* a doctor.

In the case of *must,* refer to the past by using *had to.*

▶ You *must* renew your visa by the end of this week.

▶ You *had to* renew your visa last week.

Using modals to make requests or to give instructions

Modals are often used in requests and instructions. Imagine making the following request of a flight attendant:

▶ *Will* you bring me a pillow?

This request may appear demanding or rude. Using a modal makes the request more polite by acknowledging that fulfilling the request may not be possible.

▶ *Can* you bring me a pillow?

Another way of softening the request is to use the past form of *will*, and the most discreet choice is the past form of *can*.

▶ **Would you bring me a pillow?**
▶ **Could you bring me a pillow?**

Using the past tense of modals seems more polite than using their present forms because it makes any statement or question less assertive.
Consider the meanings of each of the following instructions:

1. You *can* submit your report electronically.
2. You *may* submit your report electronically.
3. You *should* submit your report electronically.
4. You *must* submit your report electronically.
5. You *will* submit your report electronically.

Instructions 1 and 2 give permission to submit the report electronically but do not require it; 2 is more formal. Instruction 3 makes a strong recommendation; 4 allows no alternative; and 5 implies, "Don't even think of doing otherwise."

Using modals to indicate doubt or certainty

Modals can also indicate how confident the writer is about his or her claims. Look at the following set of examples, which starts with a tentative suggestion and ends with an indication of complete confidence:

▶ **The study *might* help explain the findings of previous research.**
▶ **The study *may* help explain the findings of previous research.**
▶ **The study *will* help explain the findings of previous research.**

58c Present and past tenses

Every English sentence must have at least one verb or verb phrase that is not an infinitive (*to write*), a gerund (*writing*), or a participle (*written*) without any auxiliaries. Furthermore, every such verb or verb phrase must have a tense (31e).

In some languages, such as Chinese and Vietnamese, the verb form never changes regardless of when the action takes place. In English, the time of the action must be clearly indicated by the tense form of every verb, even if the time is obvious or it is indicated elsewhere in the sentence.

could not
▶ **During the Cultural Revolution, millions of young people ~~cannot~~ go**
                                                                      ^

   were
to school and ~~are~~ sent to the countryside.
                ^

> *called* *lives*
> ▶ Last night I ~~call~~ my aunt who ~~live~~ in Santo Domingo.
>   ∧ ∧

Direct and indirect quotations

Changing direct quotations to indirect quotations can sometimes lead to tense shifts.

DIRECT	She said, "My work *is* now complete."
INDIRECT	She *told* me that her work *was* now complete.
INDIRECT	She *tells* me that her work *is* now complete.

In general, the verb introducing the indirect quotation (sometimes called the reporting verb) will agree in tense with the verb in the indirect quotation; there are, however, some exceptions. For example, if the reporting verb is in the past tense but the information that follows holds true in the present, shifting to a present-tense verb is acceptable.

▶ She *told* me that her work *is* as exciting as ever.

In academic writing, reporting verbs are used regularly to refer to ideas from other texts or authors. Depending on the documentation style you use, you will probably use the present tense, the present perfect tense, or the simple past for these verbs.

Lee *claims* that . . .
Lee *writes* . . .
Lee *has argued* that . . .
Lee *found* that . . .

58d Perfect and progressive verb phrases

The perfect and progressive auxiliaries combine with the present or past tense, or with modals, to form complex verb phrases with special meanings (31f).

Distinguishing the simple present and the present perfect

▶ My sister *drives* a bus.

The simple present (*drives*) tells us about the sister's current job. But if you were to add the phrase *for three years*, it would be incorrect to say *My sister <u>drives</u> a bus for three years*. Instead, you need a time frame that goes from the past up to the present. The present perfect or present perfect progressive expresses this time frame.

▶ My sister *has driven* a bus for three years.
▶ My sister *has been driving* a bus for three years.

Distinguishing the simple past and the present perfect

▶ Since she started working, she *has bought* a new car and a DVD player.

The clause introduced by *since* sets up a time frame that runs from past to present and requires the present perfect (*has bought*) in the subsequent clause. Furthermore, the sentence does not say exactly when she bought the car or the DVD player, and that indefiniteness also calls for the perfect. It would be less correct to say *Since she started working, she bought a new car and a DVD player.* But if you say when she bought the car, you should use the simple past tense.

▶ She *bought* the car two years ago.

It would be incorrect to say *She has bought the car two years ago* because the perfect cannot be used with definite expressions of time. In this case, use the simple past (*bought*).

Distinguishing the simple present and the present progressive

Use the present progressive tense when an action is in progress right now. In contrast, use the simple present for actions that frequently occur during a period of time that might include the present moment (though the simple present does not necessarily indicate that the action is taking place now).

▶ My sister *drives* a bus, but she *is taking* a vacation now.
▶ My sister *drives* a bus, but she *takes* a vacation every year.

Many languages use the simple present (*drives, takes*) for both types of sentences. In English, however, the first sentence would be incorrect if it said *but she takes a vacation now*.

Distinguishing the simple past and the past progressive

▶ Sally *spent* the summer in Italy.

The simple past tense is used in this case because the action occurred in the past and is now finished.

The past progressive tense is used relatively infrequently in English. It is used to focus on duration or continuousness and especially to call attention to past action that went on at the same time as something else.

▶ Sally *was spending* the summer in Italy when she *met* her future husband.

58e Participial adjectives

Many verbs refer to feelings — for example, *bore, confuse, excite, fascinate, frighten, interest*. The present and past participles of such verbs can be used as ordinary adjectives (see 30l). Use the past participle (which usually ends with *-ed*) to describe a person having the feeling.

▶ The *frightened* boy started to cry.

Use the present participle (which usually ends with *-ing*) to describe the thing (or person) causing the feeling.

▶ The *frightening* dinosaur display gave him nightmares.

Be careful not to confuse the two types of adjectives.

       interested
▶ I am ~~interesting~~ in African literature.
    ^

                 interesting.
▶ African literature seems ~~interested~~.
                 ^

EXERCISE 58.1

Each of the following sentences contains an error. Rewrite each sentence correctly.

1. Over the past forty years, average temperatures in the Arctic increase by several degrees.
2. A few years ago, a robin was observe in Inuit territory in northern Canada.
3. Inuit people in previous generations will never have seen a robin near their homes.
4. The Inuit language, which called *Inuktitut*, has no word for *robin*.
5. Many Inuits are concerning that warmer temperatures may change their way of life.

EXERCISE 58.2

Rewrite the following passage, adapted from "Cold Comfort" by Atul Gawande (*New Yorker*, March 11, 2002), adding appropriate auxiliaries and verb endings where necessary. The total number of words required in each case is indicated in parentheses.

    The notion that a chill _____ *(put—1)* you at risk of catching a cold is nearly universal. Yet science _____ *(find—2)* no evidence for it. One of the first studies on the matter _____ *(lead—2)* by Sir

Christopher Andrewes. He ⎯⎯⎯⎯⎯⎯ (take—1) a group of volunteers and ⎯⎯⎯⎯⎯⎯⎯⎯ (inoculate—1) them with a cold virus; previously, half of the group ⎯⎯⎯⎯⎯⎯⎯ (keep—3) warm, and the other half ⎯⎯⎯⎯⎯⎯⎯⎯ (make—1) to take a bath and then to stand for half an hour without a towel while the wind ⎯⎯⎯⎯⎯⎯⎯ (get—1) on them. The chilled group ⎯⎯⎯⎯⎯⎯⎯⎯ (blow—2) no more colds than the warm group.

> ➜ **bedfordstmartins.com/everydaywriter** For exercises on verbs and verb phrases, go to **Exercise Central** and click on **For Multilingual Writers.**

59 Prepositions and Prepositional Phrases

Words such as *to, from, over,* and *under* show the relations between other words; these words are prepositions, and they are one of the more challenging elements of English writing. You will need to decide which preposition to use for your intended meaning and understand how to use verbs that include prepositions, such as *take off, pick up,* and *put up with.*

59a Using prepositions idiomatically

Even if you know where to use a preposition, it can be difficult to determine which preposition to use. Each of the most common prepositions has a wide range of applications, and this range never coincides exactly from one language to another. See, for example, how *in* and *on* are used in English.

▶ The peaches are *in* the refrigerator.

▶ The peaches are *on* the table.

▶ Is that a diamond ring *on* your finger?

The Spanish translations of these sentences all use the same preposition (*en*), a fact that might lead you astray in English.

       on
▶ Is that a ruby ring ~~in~~ your finger?
         ^

There is no easy solution to the challenge of using English prepositions idiomatically, but the strategies on p. 575 can help.

EXERCISE 59.1

Insert prepositions as necessary in the following paragraph.

Haivan skated _____ the pond, looking _____ her new engagement ring. As she skated, she thought about the plans for her wedding. Should it be _____ September or October? Could the caterer _____ her neighborhood do a good job? Would her sister manage to be _____ time?

59b Using two-word verbs idiomatically

Some words that look like prepositions do not always function as prepositions. Consider the following two sentences:

- ▶ The balloon rose *off* the ground.
- ▶ The plane took *off* without difficulty.

In the first sentence, *off* is a preposition that introduces the prepositional phrase *off the ground*. In the second sentence, *off* does not function as a preposition. Instead, it combines with *took* to form a two-word verb with its own meaning. Such a verb is called a phrasal verb, and the word *off*, when used in this way, is called an adverbial particle. Many prepositions can function as particles to form phrasal verbs.

The verb + particle combination that makes up a phrasal verb is a single entity that usually cannot be torn apart.

         off
- ▶ The plane took ˄ without difficulty. ˄ ~~off.~~

The exceptions are the many phrasal verbs that are transitive, meaning that they take a direct object (30k). Some transitive phrasal verbs have particles that may be separated from the verb by the object.

- ▶ I *picked up my baggage* at the terminal.
- ▶ I *picked my baggage up* at the terminal.

If a personal pronoun (such as *it*, *her*, or *him*) is used as the direct object, it must separate the verb from its particle.

- ▶ I *picked it up* at the terminal.

Some idiomatic two-word verbs, however, are not phrasal verbs.

- ▶ We *ran into* our neighbor on the train.

In such verbs, the second word is a preposition, which cannot be separated from the verb. For example, it is not correct to say *We ran our*

AT A GLANCE

Using Prepositions Idiomatically

1. **Keep in mind typical examples of each preposition.**

   IN   The peaches are *in* the refrigerator.
         There are still some pickles *in* the jar.
         The book you are looking for is *in* the bookcase.

   Here the object of the preposition *in* is a container that encloses something.

   ON   The peaches are *on* the table.
         There are still some pickles *on* the plate.
         The book you are looking for is *on* the top shelf.

   Here the object of the preposition *on* is a horizontal surface with which something is in direct contact.

2. **Learn other examples that show some similarities and some differences in meaning.**

   IN   You shouldn't drive *in* a snowstorm.

   Here there is no container, but like a container, the falling snow surrounds the driver. The preposition *in* is used for other weather-related expressions as well: *in a tornado, in the sun, in the rain.*

   ON   Is that a diamond ring *on* your finger?

   The preposition *on* is used to describe things we wear: *the hat on his head, the shoes on her feet, the tattoo on his back.*

3. **Use your imagination to create mental images that can help you remember figurative uses of prepositions.**

   IN   Michael is *in* love.

   The preposition *in* is often used to describe a state of being: *in love, in pain, in a panic.* As a way to remember this, you might imagine the person immersed *in* this state of being.

4. **Try to learn prepositions not in isolation but as part of a system.** For example, in identifying the location of a place or an event, you can use the three prepositions *at, in,* and *on.*

   At specifies the exact point in space or time.

   AT   There will be a meeting tomorrow *at* 9:30 AM *at* 160 Main Street.

   Expanses of space or time within which a place is located or an event takes place might be seen as containers and so require *in.*

   IN   I arrived *in* the United States *in* January.

   On must be used in two cases: with the names of streets (but not the exact address) and with days of the week or month.

   ON   The airline's office is *on* Fifth Avenue.
         I'll be moving to my new apartment *on* September 30.

neighbor into on the train. Verbs like *run into* are called prepositional verbs, which are another kind of two-word verb.

In the preceding sample sentence, *ran into* consists of the verb *ran* followed by the preposition *into*, which introduces the prepositional phrase *into our neighbor*. Yet *to run into our neighbor* is different from a normal verb + prepositional phrase, such as *to run into the room*. If you know the typical meanings of *run* and *into*, you can interpret *to run into the room*. Not so with *to run into our neighbor*; the combination *run + into* has a special meaning ("find by chance") that could not be determined from the typical meanings of *run* and *into*.

Prepositional verbs include such idiomatic two-word verbs as *take after*, meaning "resemble" (usually a parent or other older relative); *get over*, meaning "recover from"; and *count on*, meaning "trust." They also include verb + preposition combinations in which the meaning is predictable, but the specific preposition that is required is less predictable and must be learned together with the verb (for example, *depend on, look at, listen to, approve of*). There are also phrasal-prepositional verbs, which are verb + adverbial particle + preposition sequences (for example, *put up with, look forward to, give up on, get away with*).

EXERCISE 59.2

Each of the following sentences contains a two-word verb. In some sentences, the verb is used correctly; in others, it is used incorrectly. Identify each two-word verb, indicate whether it is a phrasal or prepositional verb, and rewrite any incorrect sentences correctly.

1. Soon after I was hired for my last job, I learned that the company might lay off me.

2. I was counting on the job to pay my way through school, so I was upset.

3. I decided to pick up a newspaper and see what other jobs were available.

4. As I looked the newspaper at, I was surprised to see that I was qualified for a job that paid much better than mine.

5. I gave my old job up and took the new one, which made attending school much easier.

 bedfordstmartins.com/everydaywriter For exercises on prepositions and prepositional phrases, go to **Exercise Central** and click on **For Multilingual Writers**.

Writing in the Disciplines

Don't underestimate your readers' intelligence,
but don't overestimate their knowledge
of a particular field.

— JULIE ANN MILLER

Writing in the Disciplines

Academic Work in Any Discipline $\boxed{\textbf{60}}$

A recent survey confirmed that good writing plays an important role in almost every profession. One MBA wrote, "Those who advance quickly in my company are those who write and speak well — it's as simple as that." But while writing is always a valuable skill, writing well means different things in different disciplines. As you prepare written assignments for various courses, then, you will need to become familiar with the expectations, vocabularies, styles, methods of proof, and conventional formats used in each field.

60a Reading and writing for every discipline

Writing is central to learning regardless of the discipline. So whether you are explaining the results of a telephone survey you conducted for a psychology class, preparing a lab report for chemistry, conducting a case study for anthropology, or working on a proposal for material sciences and engineering, writing helps you get the job done.

One good way to learn to write well in a discipline is to read the texts others write. So read a lot, and pay attention to the texts you are reading. To get started, choose an article in an important journal in the field you plan to major in and then answer the following questions:

- How does a journal article in this discipline begin?
- How is the article organized? Does it have specific sections with subheads?
- What sources are cited, and how are they used — as backup support, as counter-examples, or as an argument to refute?
- How does the article conclude?
- What audience does the text seem to address? Is it a narrow technical or disciplinary audience, or is it aimed at a broader reading public? Is it addressed to readers of a specific journal? Is it published in print or online?

Finally, make sure you know whether the articles you are reading are from juried or nonjuried journals (15a). Juried journals use panels of expert readers to analyze proposed articles, so articles in juried journals have been recommended for publication by experts in the field. Nonjuried journals can also offer valuable information, but they may bear the stamp of the editor's biases more strongly than a juried journal would. To find out whether a journal is juried or nonjuried, check the submissions guidelines for information about whether submitted articles are sent to reviewers before publication.

For additional guidelines on reading critically, see Chapter 11.

60b Academic assignments and expectations

When you receive an assignment, your first job is to be sure you understand what that assignment is asking you to do. Some assignments may be as vague as "Write a five-page essay on one aspect of the Civil War" or "Write an analysis of the group dynamics at play in your recent collaborative project for this course" (see 52d for one student's response to the latter assignment). Others may be fairly specific: "Collect, summarize, and

---

AT A GLANCE

Analyzing an Assignment

- *What is the purpose of the assignment?* Are you expected to join a discussion, demonstrate your mastery of the topic in writing, or something else?

- *Who is the audience?* The instructor will be one audience, but are there others? If so, who are they?

- *What does the assignment ask of you?* Look for key terms such as *summarize, explain, evaluate, interpret, illustrate,* and *define.*

- *Do you need clarification of any terms?* If so, ask your instructor.

- *What do you need to know or find out to complete the assignment?* You may need to do background reading, develop a procedure for analyzing or categorizing information, or carry out some other kind of preparation.

- *What does the instructor expect in a written response?* How will you use sources? What kinds of sources should you use? How should you organize and develop the assignment? What is the expected format and length?

- *Can you find a model of an effective response to a similar assignment?*

- *What do other students think the assignment requires?* Talking over an assignment with classmates is one good way to test your understanding.

interpret data drawn from a sample of letters to the editor published in two newspapers, one in a small rural community and one in an urban community, over a period of three months." Whatever the assignment, use the questions in the box on p. 580 (and the information in Chapter 5) to analyze it.

EXERCISE 60.1

Analyze the following assignment from a communications course using the questions on p. 580.

Assignment: Distribute a questionnaire to twenty people (ten male, ten female), asking these four questions: (1) What do you expect to say and do when you meet a stranger? (2) What don't you expect to say and do when you meet a stranger? (3) What do you expect to say and do when you meet a very close friend? (4) What don't you expect to say and do when you meet a very close friend?

When you have collected your twenty questionnaires, read them over and answer the following questions:

- What, if any, descriptions were common to all respondents' answers?
- How do male and female responses compare?
- What similarities and differences did you find between the responses to the stranger and to the very close friend?
- What factors (environment, time, status, gender, and so on) do you think had an impact on these responses?

Discuss your findings, using concepts and theories explained in your text.

60c Disciplinary vocabulary

Entering into an academic discipline or a profession is like going to a party where you do not know anyone. At first you feel like an outsider, and you may not understand much of what you hear or see. Before you enter the conversation, you have to listen and observe carefully. Eventually, however, you will be able to join in — and if you stay long enough, participating in the conversation becomes easy and natural.

To learn the routines, practices, and ways of knowing in a new field, you must also make an effort to enter into the conversation. A good way to get started is to study the vocabulary of the field you are most interested in.

Highlight the key terms in your reading or notes to learn how much specialized or technical vocabulary you will be expected to know. If you find only a small amount of specialized vocabulary, try to master the new terms quickly by reading your textbook carefully, looking up key words or phrases, and asking questions. If you find a great deal of specialized vocabulary, however, you may want to familiarize yourself with it methodically. Any of the following procedures may help:

- Keep a log of unfamiliar words used in context. Check definitions in your textbook's glossary or index, or consult a specialized dictionary.

- See if your textbook has a glossary of terms or sets off definitions. Study pertinent sections to master the terms.

- Work with key concepts. Even if they are not yet entirely clear to you, using them will help you understand them. For example, in a statistics class, try to work out (in words) how to do an analysis of *covariance*, step by step, even if you are not sure of the precise definition of the term. Or try to plot the narrative progression in a story even if you are still not entirely sure of the definition of *narrative progression*.

- Take special note of the ways technical language or disciplinary vocabulary are used in online information related to a particular field.

60d Disciplinary style

Another important way to learn about a discipline is to identify its stylistic features. Study pieces of writing in the field with the following in mind:

- *Overall tone.* How would you describe it? (See 5f.)
- *Title.* Are titles generally descriptive ("Findings from a Double-Blind Study of the Effect of Antioxidants"), persuasive ("Antioxidants Proven Effective"), or something else? How does the title shape your expectations?
- *Stance.* To what extent do writers in the field strive for distance and objectivity? What strategies help them to achieve this stance? (See 5e.)
- *Sentence length.* Are sentences long and complex? Simple and direct?
- *Voice.* Are verbs generally active or passive? Why? (See 31g.)
- *Person.* Do writers use the first-person *I* or third-person terms such as *the investigator*? What is the effect of this choice? (See the box below.)
- *Visuals.* Do writers typically use elements such as graphs, tables, maps, or photographs? How are visuals integrated into the text? What role, if any, do headings and other formatting elements play in the writing? (See Chapter 4.)
- *Documentation style.* Do writers use MLA, APA, *Chicago*, or CSE style? (See Chapters 48–54.)

Of course, writings within a single discipline may have different purposes and different styles. A chemist may write a grant proposal, a lab notebook, a literature review, a research report, and a lab report, each with a different purpose and style.

The First Person

"Is it true that I should never use *I* in college writing?" In much writing in college, using the first-person *I* is perfectly acceptable to most instructors. As always, think about the context — if your own experience is relevant to the topic, you are better off saying *I* than trying too hard not to. But don't overdo it, especially if the writing isn't just autobiographical. And check with your instructor if you aren't sure: in certain academic disciplines, using *I* may be seen as inappropriate.

60e Use of evidence

As you grow familiar with an area of study, you will develop a sense of what it takes to prove a point in that field. You can speed up this process, however, by investigating and questioning. The following questions will help you think about the use of evidence in materials you read:

- How do writers in the field use precedent and authority? What or who counts as an authority in this field? How are the credentials of an authority established? (See 13e.)
- What kinds of quantitative data (countable or measurable items) are used, and for what purposes? How are the data gathered and presented?
- How are qualitative data (systematically observed items) used?
- How are statistics used and presented? Are tables, charts, graphs, or other visuals important, and why?
- How is logical reasoning used? How are definition, cause and effect, analogy, and example used?
- How does the field use primary materials — the firsthand sources of information — and secondary sources that are reported by others? (See 15a.) How is each type of source presented?
- What kinds of textual evidence are cited?
- How are quotations and other references to sources used and integrated into the text? (See Chapter 17.)

EXERCISE 60.2

Read a few journals associated with your prospective major or a discipline of particular interest to you, using the questions on p. 582 to study the use of evidence in that discipline. If you are keeping a writing log, make an entry summarizing what you have learned.

60f   Conventional patterns and formats

To produce effective writing in a discipline, you need to know the field's generally accepted formats for organizing and presenting evidence. Although these formats can vary widely from discipline to discipline and even from instructor to instructor, common patterns do emerge. A typical laboratory report, for instance, follows a fairly standard organizational framework and usually has a certain look (see 63c for an example). A case study in sociology or education or anthropology likewise follows a typical organizational plan. Ask your instructor to recommend good examples of the kind of writing you will do in the course; then analyze these examples in terms of format, design, and organization. You might also look at major scholarly journals in the field to see what types of formats seem most common and how each is organized.

60g   Ethical issues

Writers in all disciplines face ethical questions. Those who plan and carry out research on living people, for example, must be careful to avoid harming their subjects. Researchers in all fields must be scrupulous in presenting data to make sure that others can replicate research and test claims. And although writers in any discipline should take into consideration their own interests, those of their collaborators, and those of their employers, they must also responsibly safeguard the interests of the general public.

Fortunately, a growing number of disciplines have adopted guidelines for ethics. The American Psychological Association has been a pioneer in this area, and many other professional organizations and companies have their own codes or standards of ethics. These guidelines can help you make decisions about day-to-day writing. Even so, you will no doubt encounter situations where the right or ethical decision is murky at best. In such situations, consult your own conscience first and then talk your choices over with colleagues you respect before coming to a decision on how to proceed.

EXERCISE 60.3: THINKING CRITICALLY

Reading with an Eye for Disciplinary Discourse

The following abstract introduces an article titled "Development of the Appearance-Reality Distinction." This article appeared in *Cognitive Psychology*, a specialized academic journal for researchers in the subfield of psychology that focuses on human cognition. Read this abstract carefully to see what you can infer about the discourse of cognitive psychology — about its characteristic vocabulary, style, use of evidence, and so on.

Young children can express conceptual difficulties with the appearance-reality distinction in two different ways: (1) by incorrectly reporting appearance when asked to report reality ("phenomenism"); (2) by incorrectly reporting reality when asked to report appearance ("intellectual realism"). Although both phenomenism errors and intellectual realism errors have been observed in previous studies of young children's cognition, the two have not been seen as conceptually related and only the former errors have been taken as a symptom of difficulties with the appearance-reality distinction. Three experiments investigated 3- to 5-year-old children's ability to distinguish between and correctly identify real versus apparent object properties (color, size, and shape), object identities, object presence-absence, and action identities. Even the 3-year-olds appeared to have some ability to make correct appearance-reality discriminations and this ability increased with age. Errors were frequent, however, and almost all children who erred made both kinds. Phenomenism errors predominated on tasks where the appearance versus reality of the three object properties was in question; intellectual realism errors predominated on the other three types of tasks. Possible reasons for this curious error pattern were advanced. It was also suggested that young children's problems with the appearance-reality distinction may be partly due to a specific metacognitive limitation, namely, a difficulty in analyzing the nature and source of their own mental representations.

— JOHN H. FLAVELL, ELEANOR R. FLAVELL, and FRANCES L. GREEN,
Cognitive Psychology

Thinking about Your Own Writing in a Discipline

Choose a piece of writing you have produced for a particular discipline — a hypertext essay, a laboratory report, a review of the literature, or any other written assignment. Examine your writing closely for its use of that discipline's vocabulary, style, methods of proof, and conventional formats. How comfortable are you writing a piece of this kind? In what ways are you using the conventions of the discipline easily and well? What conventions give you difficulty, and why? You might talk to an instructor in this field about the conventions and requirements for writing in the discipline. Make notes about what you learn about being a better writer in the field.

Writing for the Humanities **61**

Disciplines in the humanities are concerned with what it means to be human: historians reconstruct the past; literary critics analyze and interpret texts portraying the human condition; philosophers raise questions about truth, knowledge, beauty, and justice; scholars of languages learn to inhabit other cultures. In these and other ways, those in the humanities strive to explore, interpret, and reconstruct the human experience.

61a   Reading texts in the humanities

The interpretation of texts is central to humanities disciplines. A reader in the humanities needs the tools to analyze a text — whether a primary or secondary source, ancient or modern, literary or historical, verbal or visual — and carefully consider the arguments it makes.

To read critically in the humanities (2c and 11a), you will need to pose questions and construct hypotheses as you read. You may ask, for instance, why a writer makes some points or develops some examples but omits others. Rather than finding meaning only in the surface information that texts or artifacts convey, use your own questions and hypotheses to create fuller meanings — to construct the significance of what you read.

AT A GLANCE

Guidelines for Reading Texts in the Humanities

1. *Be clear about the purpose of the text.* The two most common purposes for works in the humanities are to provide information and to argue for a particular interpretation. Pay attention to whether the text presents opinions or facts, to what is included and omitted, and to how facts are presented to the audience. (16c)

2. *Get an overall impression.* What does the work make you think about — and why? What is most remarkable or memorable? What confuses you?

3. *Annotate the text.* Be prepared to "talk back," ask questions, note emerging patterns or themes, and point out anything out of place or ineffective. (See Chapter 11.)

4. *Look at the context.* Consider the time and place represented in the work as well as when and where the writer lived. You may also consider social, political, or personal forces that may have affected the writer.

5. *Think about the audience.* Who are the readers or viewers the writer seems to address? Do they include you?

6. *Pay attention to genre.* What category does the work fall into (graphic novel, diary, political cartoon, sermon, argumentative essay, Hollywood western)? What is noteworthy about the form? How does it conform to or subvert your expectations about the genre? (5f)

7. *Note the point of view.* Whose point of view is represented? How does it affect your response?

8. *Notice the major themes.* Are specific claims being advanced? How are these claims supported?

9. *Understand the difference between primary and secondary sources.* Primary sources provide firsthand knowledge, while secondary sources report on or analyze the research of others. (15a)

To successfully engage texts, you must recognize that you are not a neutral observer, not an empty cup into which meaning is poured. If such were the case, writing would have exactly the same meanings for all of us, and reading would be a fairly boring affair. If you have ever gone to a movie with a friend and each come away with a completely different response, you already understand that a text never has just one meaning. Most humanities courses will expect you to exercise your interpretive powers; the following guidelines will help you build your strengths as a close reader of humanities texts.

61b Writing texts in the humanities

Strong writers in the humanities use the findings from their close examination of a text or artifact to develop an argument or to construct an analysis.

Assignments

Common assignments that make use of these skills of close reading, analysis, and argument include summaries, response pieces, position papers, critical analyses of primary and secondary sources, and research-based projects. A philosophy student, for example, might need to summarize an argument, critique a text's logic and effectiveness, or discuss a

---

COMMON ASSIGNMENTS

Summary

Summaries are commonly assigned in the humanities when instructors want you to demonstrate your understanding of texts you read. A summary assignment expects you to present the major points of a text accurately and completely in much shorter form than the original.

SPECIAL CONSIDERATIONS OF A SUMMARY ASSIGNMENT

- Include the thesis along with the most important supporting points; cover these in the same order as in the original, and show the relationship among them.
- Write as concisely and clearly as you can. Omit details.
- Leave out your own opinions or responses to the text.
- Use your own words; borrowing the words or structures of the original may be considered plagiarism. (17g)
- If you need to include a passage from the original, put it in quotation marks.

moral issue from a particular philosophical perspective. A literature assignment may ask a reader to look very closely at a particular text ("Examine the role of chocolate in Toni Morrison's *Tar Baby*") or to go well beyond a primary text ("Discuss the impact of agribusiness on modernist novels"). History students often write books or articles ("Write a critical review of Jane Addams's *Twenty Years at Hull-House*, paying special attention to the writer's purpose and goals and relating these to the larger settlement house movement in America") along with primary source analyses or research papers.

For papers in literature, modern languages, and philosophy, writers often use the documentation style of the Modern Language Association; see Chapters 48–51 for advice on using MLA style. For papers in history and other areas of the humanities, writers often use the documentation style of the University of Chicago Press; see Chapter 53 for advice on using *Chicago* style.

Analysis and critical stance

To analyze a text, you need to develop a critical stance — the approach you will take to the work — that can help you develop a thesis or major claim (see 5e and 7b). To evaluate the text and present a critical response to it, you should look closely at the text itself, including its style; at the context in which it was produced; and at the audience the text aims to reach, which may or may not include yourself.

A close look at the text itself includes considering its genre, form, point of view, and themes, and looking at the stylistic features, such as word choice, use of imagery, visuals, and design. Considering context means asking why the text was created — thinking about the original (and current) context and about how attitudes and ideas of its era may have influenced it. Considering audience means thinking about who the intended audience might be, and about how people outside this intended group might respond. Think about your personal response to the text as well. (See also p. 120 and Chapters 11 and 12.)

Carrying out these steps should provide you with plenty of material to work with as you begin to shape a critical thesis and write your analysis. You can begin by grounding your analysis in one or more important questions you have about the work.

 bedfordstmartins.com/everydaywriter For more on writing in the humanities, go to **Writing Resources / Links** and click on **Writing in the Disciplines.**

Writing a literary analysis

When you analyze or interpret a literary work, think of your thesis as answering a question about some aspect of the work. The guiding question you bring to the literary work will help you decide on a critical stance toward the work. For example, a student writing about Shake-speare's *Macbeth* might find her curiosity piqued by the many comic moments that appear in this tragedy. She could build on her curiosity by turning the question of why Shakespeare uses so much comedy in *Macbeth* into the following thesis statement, which proposes an answer to the question: "The many unexpected comic moments in *Macbeth* emphasize how disordered the world becomes for murderers like Macbeth and his wife."

 bedfordstmartins.com/everydaywriter For a glossary of literary terms, go to **Writing Resources** and click on **Writing about Literature**.

EXERCISE 61.1: THINKING CRITICALLY

Choose at least two projects or assignments you have written for different disciplines in the humanities — say, history and film. Reread these papers with an eye to their similarities. What features do they have in common? Do they use similar methods of analysis and value similar kinds of evidence, for instance? In what ways do they differ? Based on your analysis, what conclusions can you draw about these two disciplines?

61c A student's close reading of poetry

The following paper, a close reading of two poems by E. E. Cummings, was written by Bonnie Sillay, a student at the University of Georgia. This essay follows MLA style (see Chapters 48–51). Bonnie is creating her own interpretation, so the only works she cites are the poems she analyzes. Note that this essay has been reproduced in a narrow format to allow for annotation. (For sample research papers in MLA style, see 13k and Chapter 51.)

Student Writer

Bonnie Sillay

 bedfordstmartins.com/everydaywriter For additional student writing samples in the humanities, click on **Student Writing**.

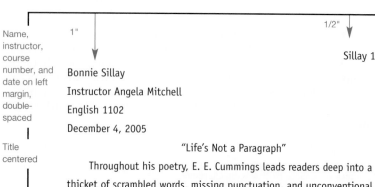

Name, instructor, course number, and date on left margin, double-spaced

Title centered

Present tense used to discuss poetry

Foreshadows discussion of work to come

Introductory paragraph ends with thesis statement

Quotation cited parenthetically

1"

1/2"

Sillay 1

Bonnie Sillay

Instructor Angela Mitchell

English 1102

December 4, 2005

"Life's Not a Paragraph"

Throughout his poetry, E. E. Cummings leads readers deep into a thicket of scrambled words, missing punctuation, and unconventional structure. Within Cummings's poetic bramble, ambiguity leads the reader through what seems at first a confusing and winding maze. However, this confusion actually transforms into a path that leads the reader to the center of the thicket where Cummings's message lies: readers should not allow their experience to be limited by reason and rationality. In order to communicate his belief that emotional experience should triumph over reason, Cummings employs odd juxtapositions, outlandish metaphors, and inversions of traditional grammatical structures that reveal the illogic of reason. Indeed, by breaking down such formal boundaries, Cummings's poems "since feeling is first" and "as freedom is a breakfastfood" suggest that emotion, which provides the compositional fabric for our experience of life, should never be defined or controlled.

In "since feeling is first," Cummings urges his reader to reject attempts to control emotion, using English grammar as one example of the restrictive conventions present in society. Stating that "since feeling is first / who pays any attention / to the syntax of things" (lines 1-3), Cummings suggests that emotion should not be forced to fit into some preconceived framework or mold. He carries this message throughout the poem by juxtaposing images of the abstract and the concrete--images of emotion and of English grammar. Cummings's word choice enhances his intentionally

Annotations indicate effective choices or MLA-style formatting.

Sillay 2

strange juxtapositions, with the poet using grammatical terms that suggest regulation or confinement. For example, in the line "And death i think is no parenthesis" (16), Cummings uses the idea that parentheses confine the words they surround in order to warn the reader not to let death confine life or emotions.

The structure of the poem also rejects traditional conventions. Instead of the final stanzas making the main point, Cummings opens his poem with his primary message, that "feeling is first" (1). Again, Cummings shows that emotion rejects order and structure. How can emotion be bottled in sentences and interrupted by commas, colons, and spaces? To Cummings, emotion is a never-ending run-on sentence that should not be diagramed or dissected.

In the third stanza of "since feeling is first," Cummings states his point outright, noting "my blood approves, / and kisses are a better fate / than wisdom" (7-9). Here, Cummings argues for reveling in the feeling during a fleeting moment such as a kiss. He continues, "the best gesture of my brain is less than / your eyelids' flutter" (11-12). Cummings wants the reader to focus on a pure emotive response (the flutter of an eyelash)--on the emotional, not the logical--on the meanings of words instead of punctuation and grammar.

Cummings's use of words such as *kisses* and *blood* (8, 7) adds to the focus on the emotional. The ideas behind these words are difficult to confine or restrict to a single definition: kisses mean different things to different people, blood flows through the body freely and continually. The words are not expansive or free enough to encompass all that they suggest. Cummings ultimately paints language as more restrictive than the flowing, powerful force of emotion.

Paper header on each page includes last name and page number

Transition sentence connects the previous paragraph to this one

Quotation introduced effectively

Writer uses a metaphor that captures the spirit of Cummings's point

Quotation integrated into writer's sentence

Sillay 3

The poet's use of two grammatical terms in the last lines, "for life's not a paragraph / And death i think is no parenthesis," warns against attempts to format lives and feelings into

Paragraph reiterates Cummings's claim and sums up his argument

conventional and rule-bound segments (15-16). Attempts to control, rather than feel, are rejected throughout "since feeling is first." Emotion should be limitless, free from any restrictions or rules.

Clear and explicit transition from discussion of first poem

While "since feeling is first" argues that emotions should not be controlled, ordered, or analyzed, "as freedom is a breakfastfood" suggests the difficulty of defining emotion. In this poem, Cummings uses deliberately far-fetched metaphors such as "freedom is a breakfastfood" and "time is a tree" (1, 26). These metaphors seem arbitrary: Cummings is not attempting to make profound statements on time or freedom. Instead, he suggests that freedom and time are subjective, and attempts at narrow definition are ridiculous. Inversions of nature, such as "robins never welcome spring" and "water most encourage flame" (16, 7), underscore emotion's ability to defy reason. These inversions suggest the arbitrariness of what "since feeling is first" calls "the syntax of things" (3).

Although most of "as freedom is a breakfastfood" defies logic, Cummings shifts the tone at the end to deliver one last metaphor: "but love is the sky" (27). The word *but* separates this definition from the rest of the poem and subtly implies that, unlike the metaphors that have come before it, "love is the sky" is an accurate comparison. In order to reach this final conclusion, however, Cummings has taken his readers on a long and often ambiguous journey.

Nevertheless, the confusion has been deliberate. Cummings wants his readers to follow him through the winding path through

Sillay 4

the thicket because he believes the path of the straight and narrow
limits the possibilities of experience. Through the unconventionality
of his poetic structures, Cummings urges his readers to question order
and tradition. He wants his readers to realize that reason and
rationality are always secondary to emotion and that emotional
experience is a free-flowing force that should not be constrained.
Cummings's poetry suggests that in order to get at the true essence
of something, one must look past the commonsensical definition and
not be limited by "the syntax of things."

Writer re-
turns to the
image of the
thicket from
the introduc-
tion to create
a closing that
resonates
with the
opening

Sillay 5

Works Cited

Cummings, E. E. "as freedom is a breakfastfood." *E. E. Cummings:*
    Complete Poems 1904-1962. Ed. George J. Firmage. New York:
    Liveright, 1991. 511. Print.

---. "since feeling is first." *E. E. Cummings: Complete Poems*
    1904-1962. Ed. George J. Firmage. New York: Liveright, 1991.
    291. Print.

Second work
by same
author uses
three hyphens
in place of
name

Writing for the Social Sciences   **62**

When do most workers begin to save toward retirement? What role do television ads play in a voter's decision-making process? How do children learn to read? The social sciences — psychology, anthropology, political science, speech, communication, sociology, economics, and education — try to answer such questions. The social sciences share with the humanities an interest in what it means to be human, and they share with the natural and applied sciences the goal of engaging in systematic, observable study. All the social sciences aim to identify, understand, and explain patterns of human behavior.

62a   Reading texts in the social sciences

Strong readers in the social sciences — as in any subject — ask questions, analyze, and interpret as they read, whether they are reading an academic paper that sets forth a theoretical premise or overall theory and defends it, a case study that describes a particular case and draws out inferences and implications from it, or a research report that presents the results of an investigation into an important question in the field. Most of what students read in the social sciences is trying to prove a point, and readers need to evaluate whether that point is supported.

The social sciences, like other disciplines, often use specialized vocabulary as shorthand for complex ideas that otherwise would take paragraphs to explain.

Qualitative and quantitative studies

Different texts in the social and natural sciences may call for different methods and strategies. Texts that report the results of *quantitative* studies collect data represented with numerical measurements drawn from surveys, polls, experiments, and tests. For example, a study of voting patterns in southern states might rely on quantitative data such as statistics. Texts that report the results of *qualitative* studies rely on non-numerical methods such as interviews and observations to reveal social patterns. A study of the way children in one kindergarten class develop rules of play, for instance, would draw on qualitative data — observations of social interaction, interviews with students and teachers, and so on. Of course, some work in the social and behavioral sciences combines quantitative and qualitative data and methods: an educational report might begin with statistical data related to a problem and then move to a qualitative case study to exemplify what the statistics reveal.

In the social sciences, both quantitative and qualitative researchers must determine what they are examining and measuring in order to get answers to research questions. A researcher who studies childhood aggression must first define and measure *aggression*. If the research is qualitative, a researcher may describe types of behavior that indicate aggression and then discuss observations of children and interviews with teachers and peers about those behaviors. A quantitative researcher, on the other hand, might design an experiment that notes how often children hit a punching bag or that asks children to rate their peers' aggression on a scale of one to ten.

It's important to recognize that both quantitative and qualitative studies have points of view, and that researchers' opinions influence everything from the hypothesis and the design of the research study to the interpretation of findings. Readers must consider whether the researchers' views are sensible and solidly supported by evidence, and they must pay close attention to the kind of data the writer is using and what those data can — and cannot — prove. For example, if researchers of childhood aggression define *aggression* in a way that readers find unpersuasive, or if they observe behaviors that readers consider playful rather than aggressive, then the readers will likely not accept their interpretation of the findings.

Conventional formats

Make use of conventional disciplinary formats to help guide your reading in the social sciences. Many such texts conform to the format and documentation style of the American Psychological Association (APA). In addition, articles often include standard features — an abstract that gives an overview of the findings, followed by the introduction, review of literature, methods, results, discussion, and references. Readers who become familiar with such a format can easily find the information they need. (For more on APA style, see Chapter 52.)

62b Writing texts in the social sciences

Perhaps because the social sciences share concerns with both the humanities and the sciences, the forms of writing within the social sciences are particularly varied, including summaries, abstracts, literature reviews, reaction pieces, position papers, radio scripts, briefing notes, book reviews, briefs, research proposals, research papers, quantitative research reports, case studies, ethnographic analyses, and meta-analyses. Such an array of writing assignments could seem overwhelming, but in fact these assignments can be organized under five main categories:

Writing that encourages student learning — reaction pieces, position papers

Writing that demonstrates student learning — summaries, abstracts, research papers

Writing that reflects common on-the-job communication tasks undertaken by members of a discipline — radio scripts, briefing notes, informational reports

Writing that requires students to analyze and evaluate the writings of others — literature reviews, book reviews, briefs

Writing that asks students to replicate the work of others or to engage in original research — quantitative research reports, case studies, ethnographic analyses

Many forms of writing in the social sciences call either explicitly or implicitly for argument (see Chapter 12). If you write an essay reporting on the results of a survey you developed about attitudes toward physician-assisted suicide among students on your campus, you will make an explicit argument about the significance of your data. But even in other forms of writing, such as summaries and book reports, you will implicitly argue that your description and analysis provide a clear, thorough overview of the text(s) you have read.

The literature review

Students of the social sciences carry out literature reviews to find out the most current thinking about a topic, to learn what research has already been carried out on that topic, to evaluate the work that has been done, and to set any research they will do in context. The following guidelines are designed to help you explore and question sources, looking for flaws or gaps. Such a critical review could then lead to a discussion of how your own research will avoid such flaws and advance knowledge.

- What is your topic of interest? What is the dependent variable (the item or characteristic being studied)?
- What is already known about this topic? What characteristics does the topic or dependent variable have? How have other researchers measured the item or characteristic being studied? What other factors are involved, and how are they related to each other and to your topic or variable? What theories are used to explain the way things are now?
- How has research been done so far? Who or what has been studied? How have measurements been taken?

- Has there been change over time? What has caused any changes?
- What problems do you identify in the current research? What questions have not been answered yet? What conclusions have researchers drawn that might not be warranted?
- What gaps will your research fill? What new information or ideas does it contribute? What problems do you want to correct?

EXERCISE 62.1

Identify a literature review in a social-science field you are interested in (ask your instructor or a librarian for help in finding one), and read it carefully, noting how it addresses the questions on pp. 597–98. Bring your notes to class for discussion.

COMMON ASSIGNMENTS

Report

Sometime in your college career, you will probably be asked to report on or explain a topic to an audience. Although reports most often present information, facts, or findings, the report still has a persuasive element; the writer makes choices about what information to present and how to present it most convincingly. Reports sometimes also make direct recommendations.

SPECIAL CONSIDERATIONS OF A REPORT ASSIGNMENT

- Think carefully about what information the audience needs most. What is the purpose of the report?
- Conduct any research necessary — including field research, which might involve conducting surveys or interviewing experts.
- Choose clear and precise language, and define any technical terms.
- Unless otherwise instructed, take as neutral a stance as possible.

EXERCISE 62.2: THINKING CRITICALLY

Reading with an Eye for Writing in the Social Sciences

Choose two readings from a social-science discipline, and read them with an eye toward issues of style. Does the use of disciplinary terms and concepts seem appropriate? In what ways do the texts attempt to engage readers? If the texts are not clear and understandable, how might they be improved?

Thinking about Your Own Writing in the Social Sciences

Choose a text you like that you have written for a social-science discipline. Then examine your style in this paper to see how well you have engaged your readers. Note variation in sentence length and type (do you, for example, use any questions?), number of active and passive verbs, use of concrete examples and everyday language, and so on. How would you rate your writing as a social scientist?

62c A student's brief psychology report

Following is an example of effective writing in the social sciences, a brief report by Katie Paarlberg requiring a series of short responses to questions about a telephone survey that she and her classmates at Hope College conducted among fellow students. (For a sample research paper in APA style, see 52d.)

Student Writer

Katie Paarlberg

 bedfordstmartins.com/everydaywriter For more student writing samples in the social sciences, click on **Student Writing**.

K. Paarlberg

Psych 100-01

February 24, 2006

Centered ti-
tle identifies
the assign-
ment clearly

Report #2—Response to Questions about Attitude Survey

**1. How could the construction of the survey and the ways in
which the questions were phrased have influenced the students'
responses?**

Passive
voice (*were
asked*) used
appropriately
to put the
emphasis on
the respon-
dent rather
than the per-
son conduct-
ing the
survey

One way in which the construction of the survey could have
influenced the results is that many of the statements that
respondents were asked to agree or disagree with centered not just
on *gender* issues but on *women's* issues as well. For example, one
statement read, "Women are just as capable as men when it comes to
holding positions of responsibility and authority" instead of "Women
and men are *equally* capable. . . ." Spotlighting women as the gender
in question may have suggested to certain respondents that a
particular answer was expected. This may well have been the point
of the survey, but the wording of certain statements could have
influenced the results.

Cautious
tone and
qualifiers
such as *may*
and *could
have* used
for reporting
more tenta-
tive results

Another factor that may have had an effect on people's
answers was the fact that demographic questions appeared in
the survey. For example, students were asked whether they were
male or female and whether their mothers worked while they
were growing up. Some may have felt that they were in some
way expected to represent their groups. For example, a survey
responder who felt that his answers had to represent the
"male/mother did not work" column might alter responses to fit
this perception.

Annotations indicate effective choices or APA-style formatting.

Attitude Survey 2

The topic of the survey was somewhat controversial; this also may have influenced students' responses. If the survey had asked about favorite colors instead of about gender attitudes, the respondents might not have felt the need to avoid offending the surveyor. If students had been asked to give their names on this survey, which they were not asked to do, their answers might have been even less truthful.

2. What effect could the identity of the surveyor have had on the students' responses? Would the survey results have been different if the surveyor had been a faculty member?

The results of the survey were most likely somewhat influenced by the fact that students were reporting their attitudes to their peers and classmates, not to their instructors. If they had been surveyed by the faculty, respondents might have been more likely to search their minds for the "right" answers on which they were being "tested" rather than expressing genuine opinions.

Writer acknowledges effect of her participation on the responses elicited

3. How did you select the respondents for your survey? Was your sample population representative of the larger college community? Why or why not? What about the national population of college students? Was your sample population representative of that larger group?

In order to obtain a representative sample of Hope students, we selected numbers at random from the Hope telephone directory. We used a random number chart to choose page and listing numbers, and then switched numbers with others in order to avoid knowing subjects' names.

Explains methods clearly

Our sample might not be representative of the Hope community because many Hope students do not have on-campus numbers in the directory. Many commute from surrounding areas, and we did not ask those students to participate. Juniors and seniors are also more likely to live off-campus; their views as a group on this topic might differ from those of freshmen and sophomores.

These survey results probably do not represent the views of the American college population as a whole. Attitudes of students vary widely. Students from a school in western Michigan, the majority of whose students come from western Michigan, cannot be used as a representative sample of all American college students.

4. Did anything about the results of your survey surprise you? Why?

The results I found most unexpected were that 64% of all students, and 58% of men, said that they would sacrifice their careers to raise a family. I was surprised that so many students—who are presumably preparing for a career—were willing to put family obligations first. The fact that men and women were closely aligned on this issue was also surprising; men are traditionally less likely to devote time to family over careers. Perhaps students felt obligated to give politically correct responses, or perhaps attitudes really are changing more than I had known.

Avoids making sweeping or unjustified claims

5. What about the results did you find most interesting? Why do you think students responded the way they did?

I was interested to see that the population was split almost evenly among students whose mothers did not work when they were

Attitude Survey   4

growing up, students whose mothers worked part-time, and students whose mothers worked full-time. Many students grew up during the 1980s, a time of developing economic freedom for women, when more mothers were entering the workforce. It was also interesting to note that while no women disagreed with the statement that women are as capable as men when it comes to holding positions of authority and responsibility, 13% of the men did disagree. Women are more likely to defend the ability of their sex and take such a statement personally, while men need not defend personal ability by agreeing with this statement. The men who disagreed may also have taken the fact that women do hold fewer powerful positions in the United States than men as evidence that women are less capable.

Maintains a neutral, objective tone throughout

Writing for the Natural and Applied Sciences

Whether they are studying geological faults or developing a stronger support structure for suspension bridges, scientists and engineers in the natural and applied sciences want to understand how the physical and natural worlds work. Natural sciences such as biology, chemistry, and physics study the natural world and its phenomena; applied sciences such as nanotechnology and mechanical engineering apply knowledge from the natural sciences to practical problems. More than many other scholars, scientists and engineers are likely to leave the privacy of their office or lab to engage in fieldwork and experimentation. Whether done in the lab or the field, however, writing — from the first grant proposal to the final report or scientific paper — plays a key role in the natural and applied sciences.

63a Reading texts in the natural and applied sciences

Scientists and engineers work with evidence that can be observed, verified, and controlled. Though they cannot avoid interpretation, they strive for objectivity by using the scientific method — observing or studying phenomena, formulating a hypothesis about the phenomena, and testing that hypothesis through controlled experiments and observations. Scientists and engineers aim to generate precise, replicable data; they develop experiments to account for extraneous factors. In this careful, precise way, scientists and engineers identify, test, and write persuasively about theoretical and real-world problems.

Identifying argument

As you read in the sciences, try to become familiar with disciplinary terms, concepts, and formats as soon as possible, and practice reading — and listening — for detail. If you are reading a first-year biology textbook, you can draw upon general critical-reading strategies. In addition, charts, graphs, illustrations, models, and other visuals often play an important role in scientific writing, so your ability to read and comprehend these visual displays of knowledge is particularly important. (See Chapter 11.)

When you read a science or engineering textbook, you can assume that the information presented there is authoritative and as objective as possible. When you read specialized materials, however, recognize that although scholarly reports undergo significant peer review, they nevertheless represent arguments (see Chapter 12). The connection between facts and claims in the sciences, as in all subject areas, is created by the author rather than simply revealed by the data. So read both facts and claims with a questioning eye: Did the scientist choose the best method to test the hypothesis? Are there other reasonable interpretations of the experiment's results? Do other studies contradict the conclusions of this experiment? When you read specialized texts in the sciences with questions like these in mind, you are reading — and thinking — like a scientist. (For additional information on assessing a source's credibility, see 16c.)

Conventional formats

As you advance in your course work, you will need to develop reading strategies for increasingly specialized texts. Many scientific texts conform to the format and documentation style of the Council of Science Editors (CSE); for more on CSE style, see Chapter 54. (However, you should be prepared to follow an instructor's guidelines for citation and references if another style is used in your discipline or in a particular course.) In addition, articles often include standard features — an abstract that gives an overview of the findings, followed by an introduction, literature review, materials and methods, results, discussion, and references.

You might expect to read a journal article for a science or engineering course from start to finish, giving equal weight to each section. However, an experienced reader in sciences and engineering might skim an abstract to see if an article warrants further reading. If it does — and this judgment is based on the reader's own research interest — he or she might then read the introduction to understand the rationale for the experiment and then skip to the results. A reader with a specific interest in the methods will read that section with particular care.

EXERCISE 63.1

Choose a respected journal in a discipline in the natural or applied sciences that interests you. (Ask your instructor or a reference librarian if you need help identifying a journal.) Then read quickly through two articles, taking notes on the author's use of any headings and subheadings, specialized vocabulary, visuals, and evidence. Bring the results of your investigation to class for discussion.

63b Writing texts in the natural and applied sciences

Students in the sciences and engineering must be able to respond to a diverse range of writing and speaking tasks. Often, they must maintain lab or engineering notebooks that include careful records of experiments. They also write memos, papers, project proposals and reports, literature reviews, and progress reports; in addition, they may develop print and Web-based presentations for both technical and lay audiences (see 3b and 3c). Particularly common writing assignments in the sciences are the literature review, research proposal, and research report.

Scientists undertake *literature reviews* to keep up with and evaluate developments in their field. Literature reviews are an essential first step in any research effort, for they enable scientists to discover what research has already been completed and how they might build on earlier efforts. Successful literature reviews demonstrate a student's ability to identify relevant research on a topic and to summarize and in some instances evaluate that research.

Most scientists spend a great deal of time writing research or *grant proposals* aimed at securing funds to support their research. Undergraduate writers often have an opportunity to make similar proposals — to an office of undergraduate research or to a science-based firm that supports student research, for instance. (See 54c for an example.) Funding agencies often have guidelines for preparing a proposal. Proposals for research funding generally include the following sections: title page, introduction, purpose(s) and significance of the study, methods, timeline, budget, and references. You may also need to submit an abstract.

Research reports, another common writing form in the sciences, may include both literature reviews and discussions of primary research, most often experiments. Like journal articles, research reports generally follow this form: title, author(s), abstract, introduction, literature review, materials and methods, results, discussion, and references. Many instructors ask students to write lab reports (63c), which are briefer versions of research reports and may not include a literature review.

Today, a great deal of scientific writing is collaborative. As students move from introductory to advanced courses and then to the workplace, they increasingly find themselves working as part of teams or groups. Indeed, in such areas as engineering, collaborative projects (6g) are often the norm.

Style in the natural and applied sciences

In general, use the present tense for most writing you do in the natural and applied sciences. Use the past tense, however, when you are describing research already carried out (by you or others) or published in the past (31e).

Writers in the sciences need to produce complex figures, tables, images, and models and use software designed to analyze data or run computer simulations. In addition, they need to present data carefully. If you

---

COMMON ASSIGNMENTS
Lab Notebook

Lab notebooks for science courses reflect your understanding of objectives and procedures. Unlike most college writing assignments, a lab notebook generally requires you not to revise or correct your writing; notebooks from real-world experiments may even be considered legal documents.

SPECIAL CONSIDERATIONS OF A LAB NOTEBOOK ASSIGNMENT

- Follow your instructor's particular guidelines for structuring your lab notebook.
- Study objectives and safety considerations before the lab, and include them in the notebook if instructed to do so.
- Record procedures and measurements meticulously.
- Note observations as they occur in the lab. Be careful not to omit or distort anything you observe.
- If you must make corrections, delete your original text with a single line so that the writing is still legible.

---

create a graph, you should provide headings for columns, label axes with numbers or units, and identify data points. Caption figures and tables with a number and descriptive title. And avoid orphan data — data that you present in a figure or table but don't comment on in your text.

Finally, make sure that any writing you do is as clear, concise, and grammatically correct as possible to ensure that readers see you as capable and credible.

EXERCISE 63.2

Team up with a classmate who is interested in the same scientific field or major. Find an article in that field that is clearly argued and well written. Read the article individually, and then go through it again together, taking notes on how it is organized, on its tone and style, and on its use of evidence and sources. Determine how effective this article is in presenting its information, and bring the results of your analysis to class for discussion.

EXERCISE 63.3: THINKING CRITICALLY

Reading with an Eye for Writing in the Sciences

Identify one or more features of scientific texts, and consider their usefulness. Why, for instance, does an abstract precede the actual article? How do scientific nomenclatures, classification systems, and other features of scientific writing aid the work of scientists? Try to identify the functions that textual elements such as these play in the ongoing work of science. Finally, research the scientific method to see how it is served by the features of scientific writing discussed in this chapter.

Thinking about Your Own Writing in the Sciences

Choose a piece of writing you did for a natural or applied science class — a lab report, a research report, a proposal — and read it carefully. Note the format and headings you used, how you presented visual data, what kinds of evidence you used, and what citation system you used. Compare your piece of writing with a similar piece of writing published in a journal in the field. How well does your writing compare? What differences are most noticeable between your writing and that of the published piece?

63c A student's chemistry lab report (excerpt)

The following piece of student writing is excerpted from a lab report on a chemistry experiment by Allyson Goldberg, a student at Yale University. Note that these sample pages have been reproduced in a narrow format to allow for annotation.

Student Writer

Allyson Goldberg

bedfordstmartins.com/everydaywriter For more student writing samples in the natural and applied sciences, click on **Student Writing**.

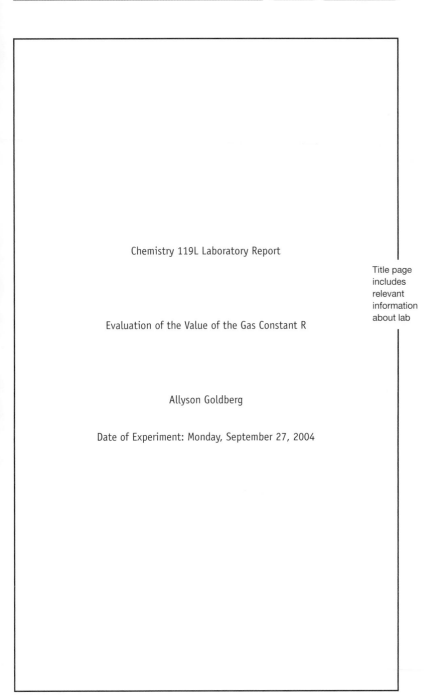

Chemistry 119L Laboratory Report

Title page
includes
relevant
information
about lab

Evaluation of the Value of the Gas Constant R

Allyson Goldberg

Date of Experiment: Monday, September 27, 2004

Goldberg 2

Introduction
explains pur-
pose of lab
and gives
overview of
results

Introduction

The purpose of this investigation was to experimentally determine
the value of the universal gas constant, R. To accomplish this goal, a
measured sample of magnesium (Mg) was allowed to react with an
excess of hydrochloric acid (HCl) at room temperature and pressure so
that the precise amount and volume of the product hydrogen gas
(H_2) could be determined and the value of R could be calculated
using the ideal gas equation, $PV=nRT$.

Materials
and methods
section ex-
plains lab
setup and
procedure

Materials & Methods

Two samples of room temperature water, one about 250mL and the
other about 400mL, were measured into a smaller and larger beaker
respectively. 15.0mL of HCl was then transferred into a side arm flask
that was connected to the top of a buret (clamped to a ringstand)
through a 5/16" diameter flexible tube. (This "gas buret" was
connected to an adjacent "open buret," clamped to the other side of
the ringstand and left open to the atmosphere of the laboratory at its
wide end, by a 1/4" diameter flexible tube. These two burets were
adjusted on the ringstand so that they were vertically parallel and
close together.) The HCl sample was transferred to the flask such that
none came in contact with the inner surface of the neck of the flask.
The flask was then allowed to rest, in an almost horizontal position,
in the smaller beaker.

Passive
voice
throughout
typical of
writing in
natural
sciences

The open buret was adjusted on the ringstand such that its
20mL mark was horizontally aligned with the 35mL mark on the gas
buret. Room temperature water was added to the open buret until the
water level of the gas buret was at about 34.00mL.

A piece of magnesium ribbon was obtained, weighed on an
analytical balance, and placed in the neck of the horizontal side arm

Goldberg 3

flask. Next, a screw cap was used to cap the flask and form an airtight seal. This setup was then allowed to sit for 5 minutes in order to reach thermal equilibrium.

After 5 minutes, the open buret was adjusted so that the menisci on both burets were level with each other; the side arm flask was then tilted vertically to let the magnesium ribbon react with the HCl. After the brisk reaction, the flask was placed into the larger beaker and allowed to sit for another 5 minutes.

Next, the flask was placed back into the smaller beaker, and the open buret was adjusted on the ringstand such that its meniscus was level with that of the gas buret. After the system sat for an additional 30 minutes, the open buret was again adjusted so that the menisci on both burets were level.

This procedure was repeated two more times, with the exception that HCl was not again added to the side arm flask, as it was already present in enough excess for all reactions from the first trial.

			Results and Calculations		
Trial #	Lab Temp. (°C)	Lab Pressure (mbar)	Mass of Mg Ribbon Used (g)	Initial Buret Reading (mL)	Final Buret Reading (mL)
1	24.4	1013	0.0147	32.66	19.60
2	24.3	1013	0.0155	33.59	N/A*
3	25.0	1013	0.0153	34.35	19.80

*See note in Discussion section.

Results and calculations show measurements and calculations of final value of R

Goldberg 8

References

Ganapathi N. Chemistry 119L laboratory manual. New Haven (CT):
    Yale University Press; 2004.

Oxtoby DW, Gillis HP, Nachtrieb NH. Principles of modern chemistry.
    5th ed. Farmington Hills (MI): Thompson Learning; 2002.

Writing for Business **64**

Written communication is essential in identifying and solving the complex problems of today's companies. To succeed in business, you need to know how to manage many kinds of writing — from negotiating an ever-increasing number of email messages to communicating effectively with readers from Manhattan, Montgomery, Mexico City, and Mumbai.

64a Reading texts for business

Readers in business face a dizzying array of demands. A team of businesspeople today has almost unlimited access to information and to people, such as economists and scientists, whose expertise can be of use in the business world. Somehow, the members of this team need to negotiate a huge stream of information and to evaluate that information.

To meet these demands, you can draw on general strategies for effective reading (11a). One such strategy — keeping a clear purpose in mind when you read — is particularly important when you are engaged in work-related reading. Are you reading to solve a problem? to gather and synthesize information? to make a recommendation? Knowing why you are reading will increase your productivity. Time constraints and deadline pressures will also affect your decisions about what and how to read; the ability to identify important information quickly is a skill you will cultivate as a business reader.

64b Writing texts for business

Writing assignments in business classes serve two related functions. While their immediate goal is to help you master the theory and practice of business, these assignments also prepare you for the kinds of writing you will face in the world of work. For this reason, students in *every* discipline need to know how to write effective business memos, emails, letters, résumés, and reports.

Memo

Memos are a common form of print or electronic correspondence sent within and between organizations. Memos tend to be brief, internal documents, often dealing with only one subject.

AT A GLANCE

Guidelines for Writing Effective Memos

- Write the name of the recipient, your name, the subject, and the date on separate lines at the top.
- Begin with the most important information: depending on the memo's purpose, you may have to provide background information, define the task or problem, or clarify the memo's goal.
- Use your opening paragraph to focus on how the information you convey affects your readers.
- Focus each subsequent paragraph on one idea pertaining to the subject.
- Present information concisely and from the readers' perspective.
- Emphasize exactly what you want readers to do and when.
- Use attachments for detailed supporting information.
- For print memos, initial your memo next to your name.
- Adjust your style and tone to fit your audience.
- Attempt to build goodwill in your conclusion.

Following is a memo, written by two student writers, Michelle Abbott and Carina Abernathy, that presents an analysis and recommendation to help an employer make a decision.

Student Writer

Michelle Abbott

Student Writer

Carina Abernathy

 bedfordstmartins.com/everydaywriter For more student samples of business writing, click on **Student Writing**.

MEMO

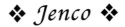

❖ *Jenco* ❖

INTEROFFICE MEMORANDUM

TO: ROSA DONAHUE, SALES MANAGER

FROM: MICHELLE ABBOTT & CARINA ABERNATHY   *MA CA*

SUBJECT: TAYLOR NURSERY BID

DATE: 1/30/2007

CC:

As you know, Taylor Nursery has requested bids on a 25,000-pound order of private-label fertilizer. Taylor Nursery is one of the largest distributors of our Fertikil product. The following is our analysis of Jenco's costs to fill this special order and a recommendation for the bidding price.

The total cost for manufacturing 25,000 pounds of the private-label brand for Taylor Nursery is $44,075. This cost includes direct material, direct labor, and variable manufacturing overhead. Although our current equipment and facilities provide adequate capacity for processing this special order, the job will involve an excess in labor hours. The overtime labor rate has been factored into our costs.

The absolute minimum price that Jenco could bid for this product without losing money is $44,075 (our cost). Applying our standard markup of 40% results in a price of $61,705. Thus, you could reasonably establish a price anywhere within that range.

In making the final assessment, we advise you to consider factors relevant to this decision. Taylor Nursery has stated that this is a one-time order. Therefore, the effort to free this special order will not bring long-term benefits.

Finally, Taylor Nursery has requested bids from several competitors. One rival, Eclipse Fertilizers, is submitting a bid of $60,000 on this order. Therefore, our recommendation is to slightly underbid Eclipse with a price of $58,000, representing a markup of approximately 32%.

Please let us know if we can be of further assistance in your decision on the Taylor Nursery bid.

Initials of senders added in ink

Paragraphs not indented

Opening paragraph provides background and states purpose

Most important information emphasized

Double-spaced between paragraphs

Options presented

Relevant factors explained

Final recommendation

Closing builds goodwill by offering further help

Email

Business email can be formatted much like a print memo but is easier to create and store and faster to distribute. Remember, however, that email is essentially public and that employers have easy access to email written by employees. As always, it's best to use discretion and caution in email, especially on the job.

Letter

When you send a business or professional letter, you are writing either as an individual or as a representative of an organization. In either case, and regardless of your purpose, a business letter should follow certain conventions.

The letter of application or cover letter (p. 617) often accompanies a résumé. The purpose of a letter of application is to demonstrate how the experiences and skills you outline in your résumé have prepared you for a particular job; it is important to focus on how you can benefit the company, not how the company can help you. If you are responding to a particular advertisement, mention it in the opening paragraph. Finally, be sure to indicate how you can be reached for an interview.

The following application letter for a summer internship was written by Nastassia Lopez, a student at Stanford University. Note that the letter has been reproduced in a narrow format to allow for annotation.

Student Writer

Nastassia Lopez

 bedfordstmartins.com/everydaywriter For more student samples of business writing, click on **Student Writing**.

LETTER OF APPLICATION

Nastassia Rose Lopez

523 Brown Avenue

Stanford, CA 94305

650-326-6790 / nrl87@hotmail.com

February 1, 2007

Mr. Price Hicks
Director of Educational Programs and Services
Academy of Arts and Sciences
5220 Lankersheim Blvd.
North Hollywood, CA 91601

Dear Mr. Hicks:

I am an enthusiastic Stanford student who believes that a Development Internship at the Academy of Arts and Sciences would greatly benefit both the Academy and me. A Los Angeles native in my first year at Stanford, I'm a serious student who is a hard worker. My current goal is to comprehend the full scope of the entertainment industry and to learn the ropes of the craft.

As an experienced writer, I am attracted to the Development Department because I am curious to learn the process of television production from paper to screen. In high school, I was enrolled in Advanced Placement Writing, and I voluntarily took a creative writing class. At Stanford, I received High Honors for maintaining an excellent grade-point average across all my classes, including several writing-intensive courses.

My passion for writing, producing, directing, and learning is real. If my application is accepted, I will bring my strong work ethic, proficiency, and creativity to the Academy.

Thank you very much for your time and consideration. My résumé is enclosed, and I look forward to hearing from you.

Sincerely yours,

Nastassia Rose Lopez

Nastassia Rose Lopez

Annotations (right margin):

- 1"
- Letterhead provides contact information
- Inside address with full name, title, and address
- Salutation addresses a specific person
- Opening provides information and lists major goals
- Background information illustrates skills and strength of interest
- Four line spaces for signature

AT A GLANCE

Guidelines for Writing Effective Letters

- Use a conventional format. (See p. 617.)
- Whenever possible, write to a specific person (*Dear Tom Robinson* or *Dear Ms. Otuteye*) rather than to a general *Dear Sir or Madam*.
- Open cordially and be polite — even if you have a complaint.
- State the reason for your letter clearly. Include whatever details will help your reader see your point and respond.
- If appropriate, make clear what you hope your reader will do.
- Express appreciation for your reader's attention.
- Make it easy for your reader to respond by including contact information and, if appropriate, a self-addressed, stamped envelope.

Résumé

While a letter of application usually emphasizes specific parts of the résumé, telling how your background is suited to a particular job, a résumé summarizes your experience and qualifications and provides support for your letter. An effective résumé is brief, usually one or two pages.

Research shows that employers generally spend less than a minute reading a résumé. Remember that they are interested not in what they can do for you but what you can do for them. They expect a résumé to be formatted neatly, and your aim is to use clear headings and adequate spacing that will make it easy to read. Although you may be tempted to use colored paper or unusual type styles, avoid such temptations. A well-written résumé with a standard format and typeface is the best way to distinguish yourself.

Your résumé may be arranged chronologically (from most to least recent) or functionally (based on skills or expertise). Include the following information:

1. *Name, address, phone and fax numbers, and email address.*
2. *Career objective(s).* List immediate or short-term goals and specific jobs for which you realistically qualify.
3. *Educational background.* Include degrees, diplomas, majors, and special programs or courses that pertain to your field of interest. List honors and scholarships and your grade-point average if it is high.
4. *Work experience.* Identify each job — whether a paying job, an internship, or military experience — with dates and names of organizations. Describe your duties by carefully selecting strong action verbs.
5. *Skills, personal interests, activities, awards, and honors.*

6. *References*. List two or three people who know your work well, first asking their permission. Give their titles, addresses, and phone or fax numbers. Or simply say that your references are available on request.

7. *Keywords* (for a scannable résumé). In general, nouns function as keywords for résumés that are scanned by search engines. Look for places where you can convert verbs (*performed laboratory tests*) to nouns (*laboratory technologist*). Place the most important keywords toward the beginning of the résumé.

Increasingly, job seekers are composing online résumés as hypertext screen documents, which make keywords more visible to search engines and thus tend to produce more hits. In addition, some businesses ask applicants to fill out résumé forms on company Web sites. In such cases, take special care to make sure that you have caught any error or typo before submitting the form.

The following pages show student Dennis Tyler's résumé in two formats, one in conventional print style, the other formatted for scanning.

Student Writer

Dennis Tyler Jr.

bedfordstmartins.com/everydaywriter For more student samples of business writing, click on **Student Writing**.

RÉSUMÉ

Name in boldface and larger type size

DENNIS TYLER JR.

CURRENT ADDRESS	PERMANENT ADDRESS
P.O. Box 12345	506 Chanelle Court
Stanford, CA 94309	Baton Rouge, LA 70128
Phone: (650) 498-4731	Phone: (504) 246-9847
Email: dtyler@yahoo.com	

Position being sought

CAREER OBJECTIVE   Position on editorial staff of a major newspaper

EDUCATION

Educational background

9/00–6/04	**Stanford University**, Stanford, CA
	BA, ENGLISH AND AMERICAN STUDIES, June 2004
9/02–12/02	**Morehouse College**, Atlanta, GA
	STANFORD STUDY EXCHANGE PROGRAM

EXPERIENCE

Work experience relevant to position being sought

6/03–9/03   **Business Scholar Intern**, Finance, AOL Time Warner, New York, NY
Responsible for analyzing data for strategic marketing plans. Researched the mergers and acquisitions of companies to which Time Inc. sells advertising space.

1/02–6/03   **Editor-in-Chief**, *Enigma* (a literary journal), Stanford University, CA
Oversaw the entire process of *Enigma*. Edited numerous creative works: short stories, poems, essays, and interviews. Selected appropriate material for the journal. Responsible for designing cover and for publicity to the greater community.

8/02–12/02   **Community Development Intern**, University Center Development Corporation (UCDC), Atlanta, GA
Facilitated workshops and meetings on the importance of home buying and neighborhood preservation. Created UCDC brochure and assisted in the publication of the center's newsletter.

6/02–8/02   **News Editor**, *Stanford Daily*, Stanford University, CA
Responsible for editing stories and creating story ideas for the newspaper. Assisted with the layout for the newspaper and designs for the cover.

SKILLS AND HONORS

Talents and honors not listed above

- Computer Skills: MS Word, Excel, PageMaker, Microsoft Publisher; Internet research
- Language: Proficient in Spanish
- Trained in making presentations, conducting research, acting, and singing
- Mellon Fellow, Gates Millennium Scholar, Public Service Scholar, National Collegiate Scholar
- Black Community Service Arts Award, 2003–2004

REFERENCES   Available upon request

SCANNABLE RÉSUMÉ

Dennis Tyler Jr.

Current Address
P.O. Box 12345
Stanford, CA 94309
Phone: (650) 498-4731
Email: dtyler@yahoo.com

Permanent Address
506 Chanelle Court
Baton Rouge, LA 70128
Phone: (504) 246-9847

Keywords: journalist; journal editor; literary publishing; finance; community development; design; leadership; newspaper writer; PageMaker; Spanish; editor-in-chief

Education
BA in English and American Studies, June 2004, Stanford University, Stanford, CA
Morehouse College Study Exchange, fall 2002, Atlanta, GA

Experience
Business Scholar Intern, fall 2003
Finance, AOL Time Warner, New York, NY
Data analyst for strategic marketing plans. Researcher for the mergers and acquisitions of companies to which Time Inc. sells advertising.

Editor-in-Chief, 2002–2003, Enigma (a literary journal), Stanford University, CA
Oversaw the entire process of Enigma. Editor for numerous works: short stories, poems, essays, and interviews. Content selection for the journal. Cover design and publicity to the greater community.

Community Development Intern, fall 2002
University Center Development Corporation (UCDC), Atlanta, GA
Workshops on the importance of home buying and neighborhood preservation. Publication responsibility for UCDC brochure and the center's newsletter.

News Editor, summer 2002, Stanford Daily, Stanford University, CA
Story editor for the newspaper. Layout and cover design for the newspaper.

Skills and Honors
Computer skills: MS Word, Excel, PageMaker, Microsoft Publisher; Internet research
Language: Proficient in Spanish
Trained presenter, researcher, actor, singer
Mellon Fellow, Gates Millennium Scholar, Public Service Scholar, National Collegiate Scholar
Black Community Service Arts Award, 2003–2004

References
Available upon request

Annotations (right margin):

Each phone number or email address on a separate line

Standard typeface (Times Roman) and type size

Keywords to aid in computer searches

White space separates sections

No underlining, italics, boxes, borders, or columns

Verbs converted to nouns wherever possible

Keywords used in body of résumé wherever possible

EXERCISE 64.1

Take a close look at the two versions of Dennis Tyler's résumé on pp. 620–21, and note the differences in presentation and content. What purposes might these differences serve? Can you identify differences in the audience — and audience expectations — for these résumés?

64c Special considerations in business writing

In the contemporary work environment, collaboration, or the ability to work with team members, is a highly valued skill. Such collaboration happens when a salesperson drafts a letter to a potential client and emails it to a manager, asking her for editorial advice. It happens when an important document such as a company brochure is reviewed online for its accuracy and effectiveness. And it happens when members of a team handle different responsibilities for a document and communicate with each other via email to complete the work. (For more on collaboration, see 6g.)

Cross-cultural communication

Precisely because people throughout the world now have the ability to work and write together, people in business must be able to communicate effectively within and across cultures. Even email conventions can vary from culture to culture or from one form of English to another. What is considered polite in one culture may be considered rude in another, so those who communicate globally must take care to avoid giving — and taking — offense where none was intended. The more knowledge you have about different cultural norms, the more effectively you can communicate with someone from a culture other than your own, whether that person is in another part of the United States or another part of the world. (For more on writing across cultures, see Chapter 19.)

EXERCISE 64.2: THINKING CRITICALLY

Reading with an Eye for Writing in Business

Monitor your mail and email for a few days, saving everything that tries to sell a product, provide a service, or solicit information or money. Then go through these pieces of business writing and advertising, and choose the one you find most effective. What about the writing appeals to you or gets and holds your attention? What might lead you to buy the product, choose the service, or make a contribution? What might make the piece of writing even more effective? Bring the results of your investigation to class for discussion.

Thinking about Your Own Business Writing

Chances are, you have written a letter of application for a job, completed a résumé, or sent some business-related letters or email messages. Choose a piece of business-related writing that is important to you or that represents your best work, and then analyze it carefully. How clear is the writing? How well do you represent yourself in the writing? Do you follow the conventions for business letters, résumés, memos, and so on? Make notes on what you could do to improve this piece of writing.

Acknowledgments

Index

Game Plans

Directory of Student Writing

IN THE BOOK

ON THE WEB SITE

Go to **bedfordstmartins.com/everydaywriter** and click on **Student Writing**. (Most student writing in the book is also available unabridged on the Web site.)

RESEARCHED WRITING

Lesk, "Red, White, and Everywhere" (First and final drafts—MLA)

Montgomery, "Do College and Religion Mix?" (MLA)

Ricker, "Video Games: Buyers Beware!" (MLA)

Clendening, "A Content Analysis of Letters to the Editor" (APA)

Palma, "Hollywood and the Hero: Solving a Case of Mistaken Identity" (MLA)

WRITING IN THE DISCIPLINES

Biology: Rao, "3D Photography for Calculating Pre- and Post-Operative Volume in Breast Surgery" (CSE)

Biology: Hays, "Niemann-Pick Disease: A Synopsis of the Genetic Variation among Various Types" (CSE)

Economics: Adamson, "Malleability, Misrepresentation, Manipulation: The Rhetoric of Images in Economic Forecasting" (APA)

History: MacKintosh-Sims, "Reflections of an Empire: The British Celts as Indicators of Roman Self-Perception" (*Chicago*)

History: Baird, "A Love 'Too Thick': Slave Mothers and Infanticide" (*Chicago*)

Literature: Schraeder, "'He Wants to Put His Story Next to Hers': Gender in Toni Morrison's *Beloved*" (MLA)

Psychology: Bredin and Rodney, "Birth Order: A Factor in Determining Parental Attention and Academic Achievement" (APA)

BUSINESS WRITING

Essay: Abbott, "McKinsey and Company: Managing Knowledge and Learning"

Proposal: Kea

ORAL AND MULTIMEDIA PRESENTATIONS

PowerPoint slides: Hornbeak, "Human Genome Project"

PowerPoint slides and script: Cabello, "Art for Your Kids"

PowerPoint presentation: Husbands and Brown, "Project W.R.I.T.E."

PowerPoint presentation video: Canning, "Health Is Golden"

Radio essay: Thrower, "Dr. Seuss and the Path to Advocating Human Equality"

Tips on Common Assignments

For Multilingual Writers

IF YOU SPEAK . . .

Advice for Considering Disabilities

Revision Symbols

Some instructors use these symbols as a kind of shorthand to guide you in revision. The numbers refer to a chapter number or a section of a chapter.

abb	abbreviation 45*a–g*		*//*	faulty parallelism 8*e*, 26
ad	adjective/adverb 34		*para*	paraphrase 16*d*, 17
agr	agreement 32, 33*f*		*pass*	inappropriate passive 27*c*, 31*g*
awk	awkward			
cap	capitalization 44		*ref*	unclear pronoun reference 33*g*
case	case 33*a*			
cliché	cliché 10*a*, 22*d*		*run-on*	run-on (fused) sentence 36
co	coordination 24*a*		*sexist*	sexist language 33*f*, 20*b*
coh	coherence 8*e*		*shift*	shift 27
com	incomplete comparison 25*e*		*slang*	slang 22*a*
			sp	spelling 22*e–f*
concl	weak conclusion 8*f*, 18*b*		*sub*	subordination 24*b*
cs	comma splice 36		*sum*	summarize 16*d*, 17, 61*b*
d	diction (word choice) 22		*t*	tone 9*d*, 16*c*, 22*a*, 22*d*
def	define 8*c*		*trans*	transition 8*e*, 29*b*
dm	dangling modifier 35*c*		*u*	unity 8*a*
doc	documentation 48–54		*vague*	vague statement
emph	emphasis unclear 24		*verb*	verb form 31*a–d*
ex	example needed 8*b–c*		*vt*	verb tense 31*e–h*
frag	sentence fragment 37		*wv*	weak verb 31
fs	fused sentence 36		*wrdy*	wordy 28
hyph	hyphen 47		*ww*	wrong word 1, 10*a*, 22*a–b*
inc	incomplete construction 25		*,*	comma 38
intro	weak introduction 8*f*, 18*b*		*;*	semicolon 39
it	italics (or underlining) 46		*. ? !*	period, question mark, exclamation point 40
jarg	jargon 22*a*		*'*	apostrophe 41
lc	lowercase letter 44		*" "*	quotation marks 42
lv	language variety 21		*() [] —*	parentheses, brackets, dash 43*a–c*
mix	mixed construction 25*a*		*: / ...*	colon, slash, ellipsis 43*d–f*
mm	misplaced modifier 35		*^*	insert
ms	manuscript form 4		*∿*	transpose
no ,	no comma 38*j*		*◡*	close up
num	number 45*h–j*		*X*	obvious error
¶	paragraph 8			

CONTENTS